The Knitting Book

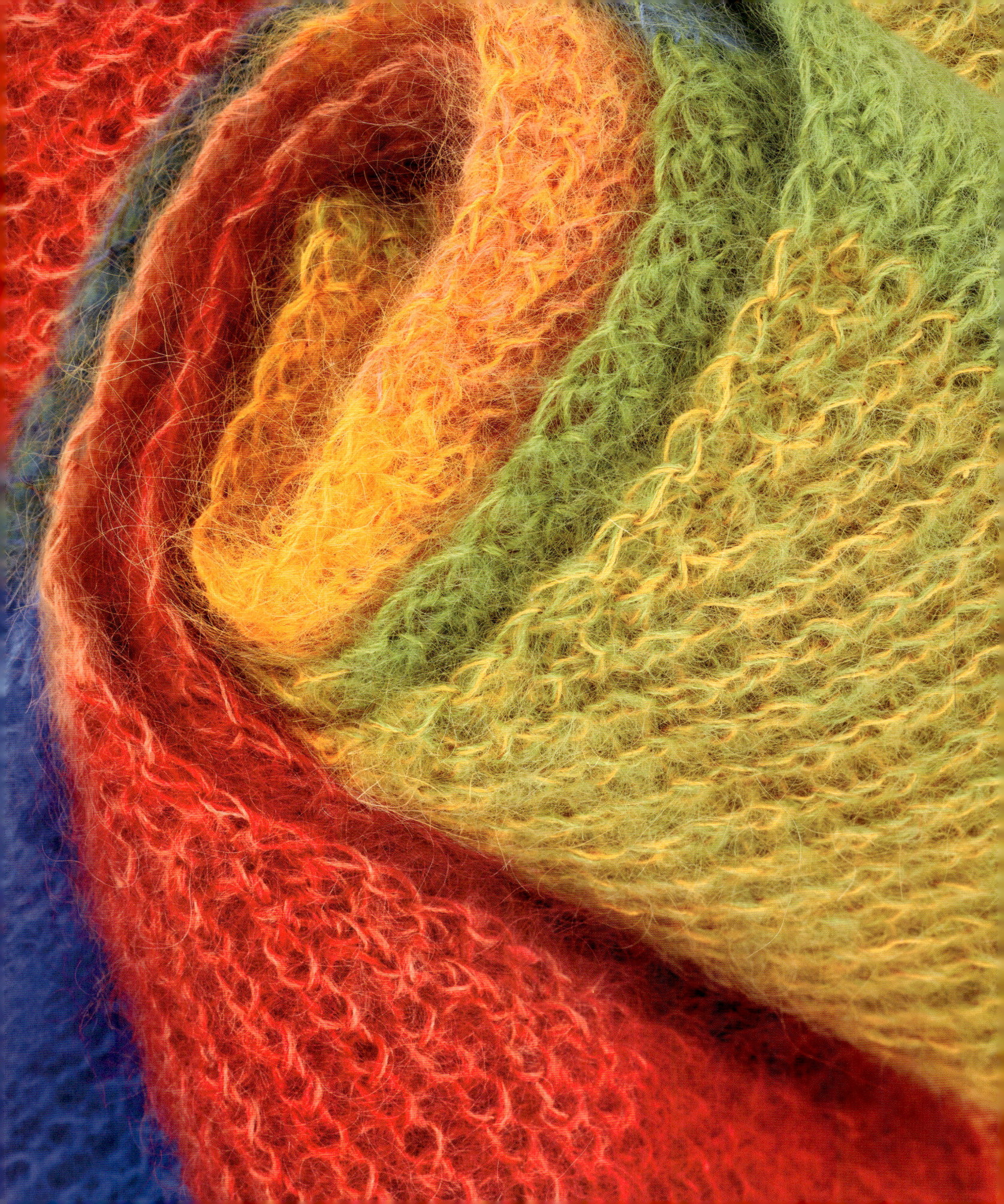

The Knitting Book

A step-by-step guide to creating imaginative projects for the home and to wear

Frederica Patmore
Dr Vikki Haffenden

Contents

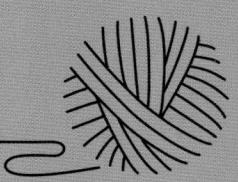

6	Introduction	116	Lace knitting	244	Striped jumper
		118	Colourwork	248	Baby cardigan
8	**MATERIALS**	129	Textural and colour effects	252	Baby blanket
10	Yarns	144	Structural effects	254	Teddy bear
32	Embellishments	150	Short rows	258	Child's Fair Isle bobble hat
		158	Circular knitting	260	Mesh tote bag
34	**TOOLS**	166	Reverse, twice knit, and tunisian	262	Beaded headband
36	Knitting needles	168	Finishing details	264	Entrelac cushion
40	Other equipment	198	Embellishments	268	Checked cushion
46	Garment care			270	Checked blanket
		216	**PROJECTS**	272	Intarsia blanket
48	**TECHNIQUES**	218	Harlequin scarf		
50	Key techniques	220	Delicate lace shawl	276	**STITCH PATTERNS**
80	Preparing and repairing	224	Cabled armwarmers	278	Stitch pattern gallery
86	Following stitch patterns	226	Fingerless gloves with mitts	328	Glossary
90	Following a pattern	230	Cosy double-sided scarf	330	Index
92	Increases and decreases	232	Fair Isle socks	335	About the authors
110	Twists and cables	236	Toe-up ankle socks	335	Acknowledgments
112	I-cord	238	Slouchy cardigan		
		242	Cable hat		

Introduction

The joy of knitting is the power to create anything from cosy scarves to intricate sweaters, from baby blankets to eye-catching statement pieces with just some needles and a ball of yarn.

Whether you're a complete beginner or an experienced knitter looking to tackle intimidating techniques, this book is here to help. It covers everything from your initial cast-ons to advanced techniques such as intarsia, cables, stranded colourwork, lace work, and beyond. You'll also find mosaic knitting, brioche techniques, double knitting, plus so much more!

The beauty of knitting is that it's both wonderfully simple and endlessly complex. Master knit and purl, and you can make scarves. Add some shaping, and you can create jumpers and toys. Throw in some colourwork or cables, and you're on your way to interesting

textiles. This book walks you through all of the fundamentals, letting you build your skills at your own pace.

I've been designing and teaching knitting for decades, and I still get excited when I see someone's face light up as they understand a new technique or finish their first project. That's why you'll find a variety of different patterns in this book – real projects that put these techniques into practice and show you just how versatile your knitting can be. That's what this book is really about – not just the technical know-how, but putting it all together; bringing you the joy of creating something beautiful with your own two hands. So grab your needles, choose your yarns, and let's get knitting!

Frederica Patmore

MATERIALS

Yarns

A yarn is the long, spun fibre that we knit with. There are many types of yarns, allowing knitters to enjoy a variety of sensory experiences as they express themselves through the medium. Yarns may be made of different fibres (see pp.10–17) and have a range of textures (see pp.18–23). Their possibilities are exciting: you can, in theory, knit with anything – from a skein of supple silk sock yarn to the plastic bag that you brought it home in. Choose from a colour palette that sweeps from subtle, muted tones to eye-popping brights.

FIBRES

Yarns, like fabrics, are made from fibres. A fibre may be the hair from an animal, man-made (synthetic), or derived from a plant. The fibres are processed and spun to make a yarn. A yarn may be made from a single fibre, such as wool, or mixed with other fibres to enhance its attributes (for example to affect its durability or softness). Different blends are also created for aesthetic reasons, such as mixing luxurious silk with wool to add a lustrous sheen. As a result, all yarns have different properties, so it is important to choose an appropriate blend for your project.

NATURAL FIBRES

Wool ▶
The wool fleece of a variety of breeds of sheep, such as the Shetland and Bluefaced Leicester, is made into pure wool yarns or blended with other fibres. It is very warm and hard-wearing, and ideal for winter wear such as jackets, cardigans, hats, and gloves. Rough-feeling wool contains short, coarse fibres that may irritate, so clothing worn next to the skin is best knitted with softer types. Unless labelled "superwash", wool should always be carefully hand-washed.

FIBRES **11**

◀ **Merino wool**
This special wool is from the merino sheep, which has one of the finest wools of any sheep breed. The long, lustrous fibres produce a soft yarn that is a fantastic choice for items that will be worn next to the skin, such as scarves, armwarmers, and children's garments. It is commonly blended with other fibres and is often treated to make it machine washable.

◀ **Mohair**
This fibre is the hair of the angora goat, and it produces a unique natural "halo" when knitted up. Working with it is quite challenging, as its frizzy appearance makes it difficult to see the structure of the knitting and any mistakes made. Mohair makes particularly interesting oversized jumpers or accessories. It is not advisable to use it for babywear as it may shed hair when newly made, which could be dangerous if inhaled.

◀ **Alpaca**
This fibre has a cosy, luxurious feel and is one of the warmest natural fibres you can knit with. Even a fine, 4-ply garment will provide ample insulation in bitterly cold weather. The alpaca is related to the llama. Alpaca yarn is perfect for ski hats, thick, cosy jumpers, and socks. You will also find baby alpaca yarn available, which is softer still.

Cashmere ▶
This fibre is the soft under-hair from a goat, which makes an ultra-luxurious, velvety-soft yarn. It is light but strong, and usually offers more meterage per gram than equivalent yarns in other fibres. Cashmere is an expensive fibre to produce and is often blended with other fibres to add softness and a touch of luxury. It should be enjoyed close to the skin in scarves, snoods, and jumpers. Only ever hand-wash this fibre.

Angora ▶
The lush coat of the angora rabbit produces a fibre that is soft and long. It is usually blended with other fibres, and resulting yarns have a furry "halo" effect similar to mohair. Each individual hair is very silky and the resulting spun yarns, although soft, are inclined to shed fibres. Angora makes delightful knits but is very delicate so is not recommended for bags or homeware. As with other delicate fibres, check the ballband for care instructions.

Matt cotton ▶
Cotton is the fluffy mass that grows around the seeds of the cotton plant. It is spun into a breathable, summery fibre. Most cotton yarns are easy to wash, and when cared for correctly, can be incredibly robust and last for decades. It is therefore a good fibre for homewares, knitted pouches, and shoulder bags. Pure, untreated cotton is ideal for hand-dyeing.

FIBRES **13**

◀ **Mercerized cotton**
Cotton yarn can be mercerized, a treatment during which it undergoes mechanical and chemical processing to compress it and transform it into an ultra-strong yarn with a reflective sheen and that does not shed lint. Mercerized cotton is usually a more expensive choice but is perfect for a project that needs to be strong and hold its shape, such as a shiny evening bag, a long summer cardigan, or a throw that requires regular washing.

◀ **Silk**
The silkworm is a caterpillar that eats mulberry leaves and makes a cocoon in which it develops into a moth. To make the cocoon, the caterpillar extrudes a fine silk filament; these filaments are twisted together to make silk yarn. Mulberry silk is very fine, lustrous, and sleek while that from the tussah silk moth is a little thicker and less lustrous; both are extremely strong. Owing to its extraordinary source, silk fibre has always been expensive. Its luxurious texture makes it ideal for wedding and christening gifts, and indulgent, luxury knitwear.

◀ **Linen**
This fibre is commonly derived from the flax plant. It is rather wiry, with an oily, waxy surface, but blossoms into a sleek, soft, breathable yarn that is ideal for knitting into lightweight cardigans and tops to wear in warm weather.

Hemp ▶
The hemp plant is particularly versatile, and the use of its fibres for knitting yarn is one of its less common applications. Hemp has an earthy roughness that will soften with age and wear. It is usually produced in an environmentally friendly way, and the strong fibre is good for knitting openwork shopping bags and homewares such as placemats and coasters.

Ramie ▶
A plant from the nettle family yields the fibre called ramie. The inner bark of the plant is processed into fibres that have a lustre but are a little brittle, so are usually blended with other fibres before being spun into yarn. As with other vegetable fibres, ramie does not insulate well but produces breathable, durable fabric.

BIO-SYNTHETIC FIBRES

Soya and milk protein ▶
Proteins derived from soya and milk (casein) can be used to make fibres, which are often seen in blended yarns. The stringy, sleek fibres add a soft, draping quality to fibres such as linen or wool. Yarns containing soya protein are less likely to be machine-washable and do not retain heat particularly well. They are more suitable for lightweight shrugs, flowing cardigans, and summer wear.

FIBRES 15

◀ **Bamboo**
Bamboo fibres used in handknitting yarns are produced by crushing the stems to produce a linen-like fibre or by chemically processing the pulped plants, in which case it is termed "bamboo viscose". The fibre has a sheen and handle that resembles silk, and it knits best when blended with other fibres. Bamboo improves the breathability and elasticity of pure cotton and is ideal for summer clothes and shawls.

◀ **Viscose**
Viscose, otherwise known as rayon, is a man-made fibre that is processed from wood or bamboo pulp. Often made from trees such as pine, beech, or eucalyptus, viscose has both a lovely drape and an airy feel. It has a similar feel to that of cotton, and it also offers very high moisture absorption and breathability qualities.

SYNTHETIC FIBRES

◀ **Microfibre**
With its velvety softness, microfibre is increasingly common in blended fibre yarns. Not considered a fibre type as such, being more of a man-made blend that creates sleek softness, it is often included in a yarn blend to reduce density and increase wearability, or to prevent excess fibre from migrating and pilling on the surface of knitted fabrics. As with all synthetic fibres, there are ongoing concerns that polymer and plastic microfibres are being released into the environment during laundering.

Metallics ▷
Although not a fibre, metallics are part of the library of yarns/fibres that is available to knitters. Lurex and other metallic yarns make highly effective trims and decorations. They may be uncomfortable to wear if used on their own, but if blended with other yarns, they create very interesting mixes and are fun to experiment with.

Acrylic ▷
This low-cost man-made fibre is a polymer, similar to plastic. Acrylic manufacturing processes have come a long way in recent years – fibres are manipulated into all sorts of textures so many acrylic yarns are extremely soft. This is often one of the cheapest fibres on the market. Somewhat frowned upon by yarn purists of old, acrylic yarns are excellent for machine washing, which makes them ideal for knitted toys and items for babies and young children.

Nylon ▷
Polyamide, or nylon, is an incredibly strong and lightweight fibre. Its elasticity makes it perfect for use in knitted fabrics, and it is often used to reinforce yarn blends for items that may be subjected to heavy wear, such as sock and darning yarns. Like other man-made fibres, nylon improves the washability of the fibres it is blended with by preventing shrinkage and felting.

YARN BLENDS

◀ **Wool and cotton mixes**
The strength and softness of cotton adds smoothness, breathability, and washability to wool's very warm (and sometimes scratchy) qualities. The blend is great for those with sensitive skin and for babies. Cotton and wool absorb dye differently, which may lead to a stranded colour appearance in such blends. Wool sheds fewer hairs when mixed with a stabilizing plant fibre.

◀ **Natural and synthetic mixes**
Man-made fibres are often blended with natural fibres to bring structure, strength, and washability; but it can be for aesthetic reasons, too, such as to add a sheen. They help bind other yarns, such as mohair and wool, together and prevent shedding; they also prevent animal fibres shrinking. The strength of such blends makes them perfect for socks or gloves.

◀ **Synthetic-only mixes**
Manufacturers can mix man-made fibres to create a variety of textures such as furry eyelash yarns, soft and smooth babywear yarns, or to add strength to yarns used for socks. Although they do not hold much warmth in comparison with animal fibres, most synthetic-only blends can be washed frequently and some can even be tumble-dried.

SPECIALITY YARNS FOR TEXTURAL EFFECTS

For knitters who love something a bit different, speciality yarns make life very exciting. From velvety chenille to yarns with different textures, there is lots to experiment with. Each creates a different effect when knitted into a fabric, perhaps even looking like a fabric that has not been knitted at all! Read this section to bring out your inner textile artist, and let the yarns inspire you to create something fresh and edgy.

Chenille yarn ▶
This yarn is often composed of cotton and synthetics, and is made up of short fibres emerging from a strong core. A fabric knitted in it will have a luxurious, velvety feel. Chenille is ideal for a plain stocking stitch, but less so for intricate patterns and for work such as lace and cables, as it can hide the detail. It is a delicate yarn, which is likely to deteriorate with heavy wear and tear. It is therefore most suitable for plain-knitted garments for adults, and hats and scarves.

Plied yarn ▶
A "ply" is a single strand. Held together with other strands, this is the traditional method by which most yarns are constructed – so with two, three or more plies twisted together. You will sometimes find yarn where each ply is a different colour, which creates wonderful colour effects as you knit.

SPECIALITY YARNS FOR TEXTURAL EFFECTS 19

◀ **Eyelash yarn**
This type of yarn has a single core with threads or strands protruding outwards to create a furry texture. Faux fur yarns, tinsel and fleece are all types of eyelash yarn – which may come in quite arty and eclectic textures. Some come with metallic or curled strands for added detail. You may find it quite tricky to count stitches when working with this yarn, so be sure to use stitch markers (see p.88) to help you keep track.

◀ **Slub yarn**
Slub yarn is characterized by varying thickness along its length. This effect resembles some hand-spun yarn, and the thick and thin areas create a unique, somewhat uneven surfaced fabric when knitted. The texture produced by slubby yarn makes for unusual accessories and outerwear such as jackets.

◀ **Braided yarn**
Also called "cord" yarn, this often has yarn made from a soft fibre, such as wool or cotton, as the core, which is then wrapped in a finer yarn, such as metallic thread or nylon. Stretch yarns are often spun in this manner, with a core of elastane. The covering yarn is generally wrapped quite densely, and this smooth surface highlights individual stitches, improving overall stitch definition.

20 MATERIALS

Soft-spun yarn ▶
This type of yarn is usually more aerated and less dense than a regular yarn; it's made from multiple strands of softly twisted fibres loosely plied together. It can be made from cotton, wool, or a blend of fibres and when knitted, it is light, bouncy, and very soft. Very thick yarns are often spun in this way to prevent knitted garments from being too heavy, or subsequently losing their shape. These thick yarns are good for chunky, quick-to-knit accessories, such as snoods and legwarmers.

Tape yarn ▶
The main characteristic of tape yarn is its flat profile. It may have been knitted as a tubular "chainette" yarn and flattened when wound into a ball. A fabric knitted in it varies depending on whether you twist the yarn when knitting or lay it flat over the needle when working each individual stitch. Twisting it will produce a nubby fabric; laying it flat will produce a smooth surface on the finished item.

Ribbon yarn ▶
The shape of ribbon yarn is similar to that of tape yarn, but it's usually a bit wider. Both yarns are often comprised of synthetic or plant-fibre blends, to give them strength and sheen. Ribbon yarn lends itself especially well to making pretty accessories such as unique evening bags, scarves, and belts. It is also suitable for summer tops. Many ribbon and tape yarns are slippery, and special attention must be paid to tension and handling.

SPECIALITY YARNS FOR TEXTURAL EFFECTS 21

◀ **Bouclé yarn**
This yarn has a unique curled or looped construction, creating rich textures when you knit with it. Most often made with natural fibres that are sometimes blended with others, you will often find that the richer texture sits on the purl side of the work, which means this yarn is ideal for reverse stocking stitch or garter stitch work. More complex patterns may become obscured by the curly nature of the fibre.

◀ **Tweed yarn**
The term "tweed" describes a classic woven cloth composed of wool, usually with flecks of contrasting colour present in the cloth. Original tweed was made of undyed fleeces from different coloured sheep, but nowadays it comes in a variety of colours with an assortment of bright to subtle flecks. Tweed yarn may have a "heathery" or a marl base and the signature flecks are added as it is spun so they sit on the surface, adding texture and colour interest.

◀ **Stretch yarn**
These yarns contain a small percentage of stretchy elastane fibre, which enhances the natural spring-back of the resulting fabric. The main fibre may be natural, such as cotton, but can also be blended or totally synthetic. Stretch yarns are more common in fine to medium weights, and are ideal for summer beachwear and active clothing.

Raffia ▶
This is a flat, ribbon-like yarn that looks and feels like natural straw. Lightweight and crisp, it is often used for crafting summer accessories, such as hats and bags, or home decor items. Although it lacks elasticity, its firm structure makes it ideal for shaping. Some versions are made from paper or wood pulp, making them biodegradable. Be careful not to overwork raffia yarn, because it can easily split or tear with repeated unravelling.

Reflective yarn ▶
This yarn is made by plying a thin strand of synthetic fibre yarn that reflects light with strands of more traditional knitting fibres, such as wool, acrylic, or nylon. Reflective yarn is fun for decorative items or partywear, but it is also perfect for scarves, hats, and gloves to provide additional but snuggly safety for night-time walkers and cyclists. It would also make an extra-safe and cosy dog coat for late-night walks. It is available in different weights across a range of colours.

RECYCLED YARNS

As our awareness of the impact of the textiles industry on the environment continues to grow, more eco-friendly options are emerging. From smaller independent spinners re-spinning floor scraps, to fabric offcuts being repurposed into knitting yarns, there is a huge variety of recycled yarns available. The nature of their production does mean that colours or styles may not be restocked, so buy enough for your project at the start.

◀ **Recycled wool**
This is often spun from leftover wool fibres reclaimed from the production process. The result is most often a rustic, lofty yarn that can have attractive tonal variations. It's an eco-friendly option that gives new life to fibres that would otherwise go to waste. Expect a bit more texture than with "virgin" wool – working with recycled wool creates really cosy and woolly knits with a conscience.

◀ **Recycled cottons**
T-shirt yarn, and other recycled cottons, are often made from fabric offcuts from the fashion industry that's cut into long strips to form a bulky, stretchy yarn. Often sold in chunky cone-type "rolls", it can vary in colour and texture depending on the fabric batch from which it was reclaimed – making each project unique. It's perfect for bold accessories and homewares but its thickness can be uneven, so it's better used for projects that don't require precise stitch definition and tension.

UNDERSTANDING YARN FORMATS

Yarns are packaged for sale in specific quantities or "put-ups". The most common ones for knitting are balls, hanks, and skeins, which usually come in quantities of 25g, 50g, or 100g. You can also buy bigger put-ups – such as cones designed for machine knitting, and giant balls of very thick yarn designed to be knitted with enormous needles.

◀ **Ball**
The stock in a yarn shop will consist mostly of balls of yarn. These are ready to use: just pull the yarn from the centre to start knitting.

Skein ▶
The oblong-shaped skein of yarn is also ready to use without any special preparation. Pulling the yarn from the middle will allow you to keep the label in place as you work to ensure that the skein doesn't totally unravel.

◀ **Cone**
This is often too heavy to carry around in a knitting bag and the yarn is best wound into balls before you start knitting. Very fine yarns designed for machine knitting are sold in cones. If you plan to use this type of yarn, it is best to wind two or more strands together into a ball before you knit with it.

Hank ▶
A twisted ring of yarn, which needs to be wound into a ball before it can be used. You can do this by hand, or by using a swift and a ball-winder (see pp.44–45). This gives you the opportunity to check that there are no knots or faults in the yarn as you wind it. Some yarns available as hanks consist of soft, delicate fibres, and these are unsuitable for certain industrial ball-winding machines.

YARN LABELS

Everything you need to know about a yarn is on its label. It will include symbols that tell you how to knit with it and how to clean it. Here is just a selection of the most common symbols. Always keep the labels: they are vital for identifying the yarn if you run short and need more. New yarn needs to have the same dye lot number as the original purchase in order to avoid a slight difference in colour in the finished item.

▲ Ballband
A yarn label is also known as a ballband. It features information on the yarn's weight and thickness, as well as washing guidelines. Tie a short length of the yarn onto the ballband and keep this with your records for future reference.

Symbols
Yarn manufacturers may use a system of symbols to give details of a yarn. These include descriptions of suitable needles and the required tension.

Yarn weight and thickness

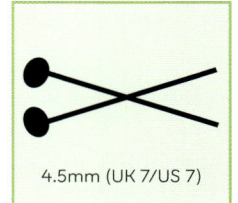
Recommended needle size

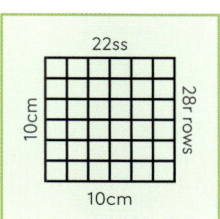
Tension over a 10cm (4in) test square

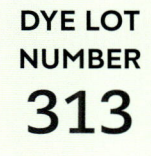
Shade/colour number

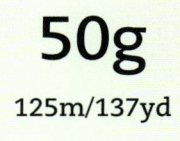
Dye lot number

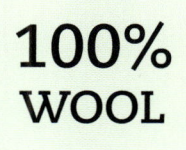
Weight and length of yarn in ball

Fibre content

Machine-wash cold

Machine-wash cold, gentle cycle

Hand-wash cold

Hand-wash warm

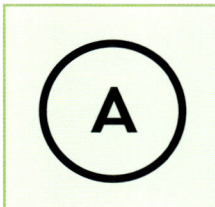
Do not bleach

Dry-cleanable in any solvent

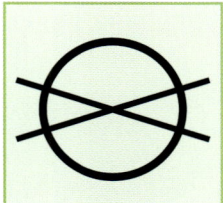
Dry-cleanable in certain solvents

Do not dry-clean

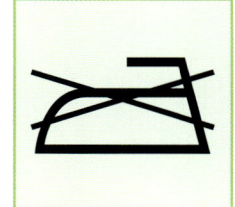
Do not tumble-dry

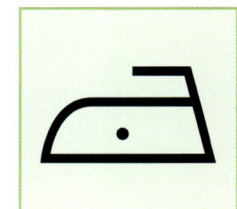
Do not iron

Iron on a low heat

Iron on a medium heat

CHOOSING YARN COLOURS

When embarking on a new knitting project, the choice of colour is a very important decision. The colour wheel is a useful tool, which will introduce you to colour theory. Each segment shows the hue, shade, tone, and tint of a colour. A hue is the pure, bright colour; a shade is the colour mixed with black; a tone is the colour mixed with grey; and a tint is the colour mixed with white (pastels). The use of colour can affect the appearance of a project dramatically. When picking colours for Fair Isle, use a mixture of dark, mid-tone, and pale shades to optimize the contrasts in the pattern.

USING A COLOUR WHEEL

Artists use this to see how colours work together. Blue, red, and yellow are primary colours; green, orange, and purple are secondary colours; and the colours in between these are tertiary colours. Colours that lie side by side harmonize with each other. Colours that are directly opposite, such as purple and yellow, complement each other and provide a bold contrast in a design.

WARM SHADES

The warm end of the colour spectrum consists mainly of red and yellow tones; browns, oranges, and purple are part of this group. Use these colours to bring richness and depth. A blend of warm shades can be a very flattering mixture to use, depending on your colouring: hold yarn against your face to see what suits you.

COOL SHADES

Blue, green, and violet are at the cool end of the spectrum, and these can be very effective when used together. Cool colours are generally darker in tone than warm ones. If used with warm shades, their impact is lessened: if you need to balance a warm mixture in a project, you will need a higher proportion of cool than warm colours to do it.

Using a colour wheel

Cool shades

Warm shades

CHOOSING YARN COLOURS **27**

PASTELS

These very pale, often cool variations of deeper, darker colours are very popular for babies' and small children's garments; consequently, a variety of suitable synthetic yarns and blends are available in these colours. Pastels also feature strongly in spring/summer knitting patterns for adults: look for ice-cream colours in lightweight yarns, and enjoy using a delicate colour palette.

BRIGHT

Vivid and fluorescent shades are fun to use in a project, and often make particularly eye-catching accessories or intarsia motifs. A great way to liven up a colourwork project that consists of muted shades is to add a bright edging or set of buttons. This burst of colour can change the project's overall impact completely.

SEASONAL MIXTURES

Nature can be a great source of inspiration, particularly when planning garments knitted in Fair Isle, intarsia, or stripes, where many colours will be used simultaneously. Think about sunsets, autumn leaves, frosted winter berries, or vibrant spring flowers. Keep a record in a sketchbook or in photographs, and notice the proportion of each colour in view. Most good yarn stockists change their range of colours according to season: in spring, for example, more pastels and brights will be available.

Pastels

Brights

Seasonal mixtures

BLACK AND WHITE

You won't see black and white on the colour wheel as they are not classified as colours. Black is an absence of all colour and white is a combination of all colours in the spectrum. In yarns this is the opposite; black will have been heavily dyed and bright white yarn will have been bleached of all colour. Bear in mind that when using black, your work will be more difficult to see, but also that complex textures will not be seen to best effect in the final garment. White, however, guarantees that every stitch and detail will be clear.

YARN WEIGHTS

Yarns come in different weights and thicknesses, and in combination with needle size, this will affect the appearance of a finished item and the number of stitches required to knit a 10cm (4in) tension square. Find the most suitable weight of yarn and needle size, according to project, below. The samples opposite show what the yarns look like when knitted in stocking stitch. The yarn weight names give the common UK term(s) first, followed by the US term(s).

YARN WEIGHT CHART

WHAT DO YOU WANT TO KNIT?	YARN WEIGHT	YARN SYMBOL	RECOMMENDED NEEDLE SIZES		
			METRIC	OLD UK	US
Lace	Lace, thread, cobweb, light fingering, 1–3-ply	0 Lace	1.5mm 2mm 2.25mm	17 14 13	000 0 1
Fine-knit socks, shawls, babywear	Sock weight, baby, superfine, fingering, 4-ply	1 Superfine	2.25mm 2.75mm 3mm 3.25mm	13 12 11 10	1 2 2.5 3
Light jumpers, babywear, socks, accessories	Sport, fine, baby, 5–6-ply	2 Fine	3.25mm 3.5mm 3.75mm	10 N/A 9	3 4 5
Jumpers, lightweight scarves, blankets, toys	Double-knit (DK), light worsted, 8-ply	3 Light	3.75mm 4mm 4.5mm	9 8 7	5 6 7
Jumpers, cabled menswear, blankets, hats, scarves, mittens	Aran, medium, worsted, Afghan, 10–12-ply	4 Medium	4.5mm 5mm 5.5mm	7 6 5	7 8 9
Rugs, jackets, blankets, hats, legwarmers, winter accessories	Chunky, bulky, craft, rug, 12–14-ply	5 Bulky	5.5mm 6mm 6.5mm 7mm 8mm	5 4 3 2 0	9 10 10½ N/A 11
Heavy blankets, rugs, thick scarves	Super chunky, super bulky, roving, 16-ply and upwards	6 Super bulky	8mm 9mm 10mm 12.75mm	0 00 000 N/A	11 13 15 17
Accessories, blankets, throws, rugs	Roving, jumbo, giant	7 Roving	12.75–25mm and larger	N/A	17–50 and larger

KNITTING WITH DIFFERENT WEIGHTS OF YARN

Lace/2-ply
This yarn is extremely light, so 50g of yarn will have plentiful meterage (yardage) and go a long way. If worked on needles of the recommended size, the yarn produces a very fine-knit, delicate result.

Aran/Worsted/ 10–12-ply
This thick, warm yarn commonly uses 5mm (UK6/US8) needles. It is good for men's garments with thick cabled detail, and the result is not too heavy. Good for functional items; many yarns in this thickness employ a large variety of fibres to make them machine-washable.

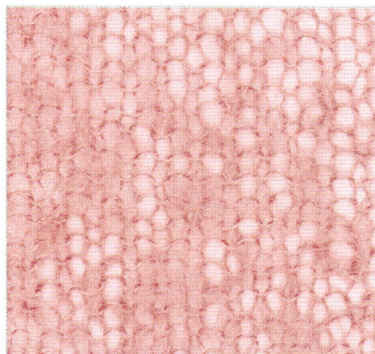

4-ply/Superfine
An ideal choice for lightweight lacework, it goes a long way per ball and requires fine needles. A mohair mix yarn such as the one shown can be worked on slightly larger needles and will produce a pretty gossamer-light, open fabric. Intricate lacework looks stunning in this yarn.

Chunky/Bulky/ 14-ply
Although bulky, the yarn mainly consists of lightweight fibres to prevent garments from drooping out of shape over time. Commonly worked on 7mm (UK2/US n/a) needles to create a chunky fabric for outerwear, hats, and legwarmers. Quick to knit; perfect for gifts.

Sport/Baby
Many knitters prefer a sport weight to a 4-ply, as it uses a more comfortable needle size yet still produces a very fine knit. This yarn is good for socks and baby clothes; the small stitches and neat appearance also suit both stitch textures and colourwork.

Super chunky/ Super bulky/ 16-ply+
The yarn thickness varies, but it is commonly used with very large needles from 10mm (UK000/ US15) upwards. A great choice for beginners, as stitches are so large that mistakes are easily visible. Knits up very quickly; good for rugged scarves.

Double-knit (DK)/ Light worsted/8-ply
Double-knit yarn is used for anything from blankets and toys to jumpers and cardigans. It is mostly associated with 4mm (UK8/US6) needles. This slightly thicker alternative, with the same attributes as 4-ply, knits up more quickly and may therefore be preferable to work with.

Roving/Jumbo/Giant
These very thick, soft yarns can be used for arm knitting or for adding embellishments to other projects. Although smaller items such as snoods can be worked on exceedingly large needles, these are not generally long enough for knitting blankets and throws.

HOW TO SUBSTITUTE YARNS

It can feel a bit perplexing to use a yarn other than that specified for any given knitting pattern, but it's surprisingly simple to substitute any recommended yarn for a different one of your choosing. You cannot choose any yarn you like for any pattern, however. Using one significantly thinner, for instance, may cause sizing problems – meaning your finished item won't fit as intended. Being a bit clever about finding alternative yarns to use will open your projects up to all sorts of possibilities – offering different textures, fibres, or completely different looks to your finished item.

WHAT WEIGHT TO GO FOR

Your starting point must always be understanding the yarn specified in the pattern, to find an adequate substitute. Use our yarn weight table on p.28 as a guide to match, as closely as possible, the recommended yarn and for guidance on what to aim for in a substitute. Some more unusual yarns may fall in between traditional thicknesses, so it's vital that you pay attention at this stage, because those types of yarns may be a bit trickier to find substitutes for.

MATCH THE TENSION

Knitting patterns will always provide you with a guide to what tension you need to achieve, and over what pattern, in order for your project to come out at the correct size. Yarn labels will also give a rough tension estimate on the recommended needle size over stocking stitch to a 10cm (4in) square. You may need to adjust needle sizes with your proposed yarn substitute to achieve the tension specified in your pattern. So it's important to take the time to knit, block, and measure tension swatches (see p.91) until you are able to match that given in the pattern. The most vital tension, or gauge, to match is the width or number of stitches per cm/in. On a plain stocking stitch piece, for instance, it's very easy to add or subtract rows to achieve the desired length. On patterns with complex shaping, however, you need to match the rows per cm/in of your pattern as well – straying might mean a warped item with an incorrect finished shape.

Cobweb: 1,000m+ (1,094+yd)

Lace: 600–1,000m (656–1,094yd)

3-ply: 450–600m (492–656yd)

4-ply: 360–450m (394–492yd)

Sport: 270–360m (295–394yd)

DK: 220–270m (241–295yd)

CALCULATING HOW MUCH TO USE

A common misconception is that you would just need the same number of balls or grams that your knitting pattern specifies, whatever yarn you end up using. But yarns are all so different, and their density variances may mean that they have different weights per metre/yard. So yarns of equivalent thicknesses, but of matching weight, will each have different yarn lengths. You will therefore need to apply a little maths to calculate the correct number of balls you will need.

Example
Substituting a specified yarn at 100m (109yd) per 50g ball for a yarn of 80m (87yd) per 50g ball, where the pattern requires 8 balls.

The total number of metres (yards) for the specified yarn in the pattern is 8 balls x 100m (109yd) = 800m (874yd) total length. To calculate amounts for our chosen substitute we need to divide the total length of the original by the length of one ball of our intended substitute to determine how many balls we need. So in the example given: 800m (874yd) ÷ 80m (87yd) = 10 balls.

Skipping this step and assuming that the same number of balls would be needed may have left us 2 balls short for our project – which would be very annoying if the same dye lot number is no longer available.

DENSITY AND FIBRE

Be cautious if you find that your proposed substitute yarn has a huge difference in the length per ball, or per gram – this may mean a significant difference in the fibre's consistency and behaviour. Substituting a bouncy and light pure wool for a more dense silk or linen, for instance, may mean that the yarn will have greater weight overall, and look and feel extremely different to the original – so an item made in it will look significantly different to the photograph with the pattern. The same the other way around – an item's drape, and how it hangs, may be altered if you use a yarn very much lighter by the metre such as swapping a pure cotton for an airier mohair.

WHERE TO FIND INFORMATION

The best place tc find everything you need to know about your yarn is on its ballband (see p.25). If you can look and compare to others in your local yarn shop, it may avoid problems later. The yarn retailers' and spinners' websites should also list key information such as fibre consistency, yarn weight, and length per ball. As a very rough guide, see below for the yarn lengths you should expect for each yarn weight, per 100g.

Worsted: 180–220m (197–241yd)

Aran: 160–180m (175–197yd)

Chunky: 90–160m (100–175yd)

Super Chunky: 90m (100yd) or less

Embellishments

Add dazzle and give your knitting an edge with embellishments, from embroidery to beads, sequins, pretty trimmings, clever fastenings, and attractive notices such as handles. These can completely change the feel of a project, depending on the way that you use them. Embellishment gives you an opportunity to express your creativity: try some of the ideas here.

◀ Embroidery thread
Silky, shiny embroidery threads come in a mixture of colours and styles. Metallic threads are particularly interesting and will jazz up a solid knitted background. Use a tapestry needle to embroider knitting, remembering that most embroidery threads stipulate that they must be hand-washed.

Sewing threads and other add-ins ▶
Many different types of thread are available, including specific add-ins to be used with yarns. You could try double-stranding a metallic thread (check its meterage) with a knitting yarn for a subtle hint of sparkle. Or use a nylon-wool blend thread to reinforce sock heels. You can also buy threads that contain conductive fibres, which can be held together with yarn to make knitted gloves work with touchscreens.

Ribbon ▶
When choosing ribbon, take the project with you to colour-coordinate effectively (although you may feel able to remember a colour, this is unreliable). Among the vast choice available, you could try organza, patterned, striped, or metallic ribbons. Thread them through your work, trim an edge, or form them into bows or rosettes.

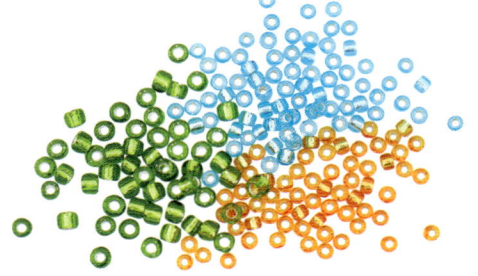

Knitting beads ▲
Most knitting beads are specially manufactured to be washable, and to not lose their colour over time, whereas other types may not withstand wear and washing. They come in sizes for a specific thickness of yarn (see p.198), such as 4-ply, for example.

EMBELLISHMENTS

◀ **Bag handles**
Knitted bags are given added strength when carried on solid bag handles. These will take the weight of the bag's contents without stretching out of shape or breaking. There are jazzy coloured plastic handles, wood, or metal versions available, which can be used to make a bag look classic, contemporary, or quirky.

▲ **Trimmings**
There is a whole world of trimmings for dressmaking: although these are less commonly used in knitting, they can impart a frilly, delicate feel to an otherwise blocky project. Trimmings come in all shapes and sizes, from the glittery to virginal broderie anglaise, fringing, and marabou feathers, to name but a few. Each can add an exciting dimension to your work.

◀ **Fastenings**
Choose fastenings with care, according to the type of project and the yarn you are using, and make sure they are not so heavy that they will pull the knitting out of shape. Buttons usually double as a feature, but other fastenings are more discreet, such as a hook and eye or a press stud. Stitch these on with knitting yarn or sewing thread. Use push-on press studs for felted work. A second, flat button or a scrap of firm fabric can be used to reinforce the back of the knitting when attaching fastenings.

◀ **Sequins**
Knit sequins into your work as you go, or embroider them on afterwards. If you're going to knit them in, look for pailettes – they have a larger hole than regular sequins, which are only suited to fine yarns. Choose flat sequins, which will sit flat against the work and each other, and are less inclined to scratch and lose surface colour. For stitch patterns using sequins, see p.327.

Safety eyes ▶
Safety eyes and noses can add character to knitted toys; choose an appropriate size for your yarn weight and project, with sturdy shanks and tight-fitting backing washers. Attach them to your projects before sewing up, positioning them symmetrically using stitch markers as guides before securing the backing washers to fix them permanently in place.

▲ **Buttons**
The choice of buttons for a garment is an important one. They are decorative as well as serving a practical purpose; make sure you select them to suit the way that the garment will be cleaned, or they may have to be removed beforehand. Coconut, shell, wooden, and metallic buttons are fairly neutral and work with many colours. Take your project with you to assess the way that button shapes, colours, and sizes work with it.

TOOLS

Knitting needles

Experienced knitters often settle on a preferred needle type according to their knitting style and tension. Needles come in assorted types and are made of different materials, and both have benefits when using particular techniques or working with certain fibres. Discover here how to choose the most suitable needles for the project you have in mind.

STRAIGHT NEEDLES

Straight needles give a great deal of support to the hand when knitting. If you are new to knitting, start with these. Short needles are recommended for small projects; long needles are more suitable for wider knits such as a jumper or a baby's blanket, and for knitters who like to work by holding the needles underneath their arms or elbows.

Metal needles ▶
When working with hairy fibres such as mohair or wool, which may stick, slippery metal needles are great. If you find that you tend to knit too tightly, the slippery surface can help as it will cause a knitter's tension to loosen. Needles of more than 8mm (UK0/US11) in diameter can be clunky to work with, so are rarely available.

Ebony/Rosewood needles ▶
These wooden needles feel luxurious to work with, and can be quite expensive. They often have a waxy surface, which becomes smooth with wear, creating a soft and tactile surface. Like bamboo needles, they help to create an even tension; they hold their shape and remain straight when used, giving them a solid feel.

STRAIGHT NEEDLES

Size
Knitting needles vary in diameter, from just 1.5mm (1/16in) thick to over 25mm (1in). There are three common needle-sizing systems: European metric, old British sizes, and American sizes. The chart opposite shows you how to convert between systems; notice that there are not always exact equivalents. Needles are also available in various lengths to suit different projects and different ways of holding needles.

▼ Carbon-fibre needles with metal tips
Needles made from carbon fibre benefit from the properties of this hi-tech material. These needles are warm to the touch and flexible like wooden needles, but are stronger and won't warp. Their sleek metal tips insert easily into stitches, and the transition between tip and shaft is smooth so stitches do not hitch as they slide along the needle. These combined materials provide a comfortable and responsive knitting experience.

◄ Plastic needles
For needles with a surface that is halfway between that of metal and that of bamboo, choose plastic. Plastic remains at a steady temperature during use, which may suit people who have arthritis. Avoid plastic needles of 4mm (UK8/US6) or smaller, as heavy projects may bend or break them.

◄ Bamboo needles
Bamboo is a lightweight, flexible material, and makes excellent knitting needles. It helps to keep stitches regularly spaced, creating an even knitted fabric with a good tension. Great for slippery fibres such as silk, mercerized cotton, and bamboo yarn. Recommended for arthritis sufferers. Thin needles will gradually warp slightly with use, to fit the curvature of your hand.

◄ Square needles
Most needles are cylindrical with a pointed tip; these unusual needles have a faceted surface and a pointed tip. Made from metal, they lie over each other better, which is particularly useful when working with double-pointed needles, and cause less strain on the hands, making them especially suitable for arthritis sufferers.

CHART
This chart gives the closest equivalents between the three needle-sizing systems. If you have some old needles and are not sure of their size, buy a knitting needle gauge (see p.40) and push the needles through the holes to establish their size.

METRIC	OLD UK	US
1.5mm	17	000 / 00
2mm	14	0
2.25mm / 2.5mm	13	1
2.75mm	12	2
3mm	11	2.5
3.25mm	10	3
3.5mm	N/A	4
3.75mm	9	5
4mm	8	6
4.5mm	7	7
5mm	6	8
5.5mm	5	9
6mm	4	10
6.5mm	3	10½
7mm	2	N/A
7.5mm	1	N/A
8mm	0	11
9mm	00	13
10mm	000	15
12mm	N/A	17
15mm	N/A	19
20mm	N/A	35
25mm	N/A	50

DOUBLE-POINTED AND CIRCULAR NEEDLES

Some projects require you to knit in the round, in order to produce a tube of knitting without a seam. You can use both double-pointed needles and circular needles to do this, but the choice of needles is usually down to length. Most circular needles are too long to knit socks or gloves on, so double-pointed needles, which can knit a very narrow tube, are used instead. Your tension and style will change according to which you use.

Bamboo and wooden double-pointed needles

Metal double-pointed needles

Plastic double-pointed needles

▲ **Double-pointed needles**
The traditional option for socks, gloves, and narrow tubes. These needles come in various lengths to accommodate different-sized projects. At first, some knitters may find that ladders form at the joins between the needles; however, this problem will disappear with practice. Double-pointed needles are less slippery when made of bamboo or wood, and most people agree that these types are more comfortable to work with.

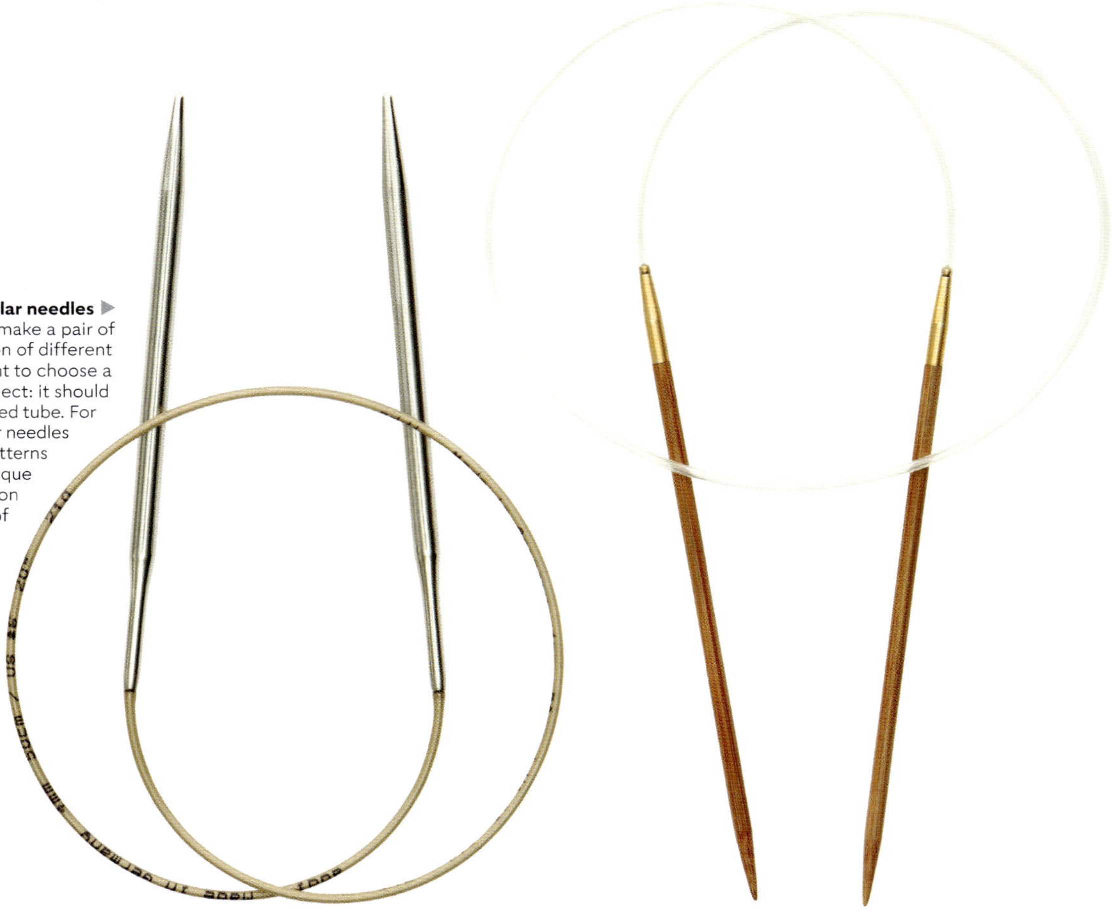

Circular needles ▶
A flexible wire joins two needle tips to make a pair of circular needles. These come in a selection of different lengths and thicknesses. It is important to choose a length that is most appropriate for your project: it should match the anticipated diameter of the knitted tube. For instance, a hat would call for shorter circular needles than a jumper knitted in this way. Knitting patterns usually specify the size required. A technique enabling the use of longer circular needles on narrower tubes is shown on p.160. A piece of flat knitting can also be worked on circular needles: just turn your needles around after each row instead of working in the round.

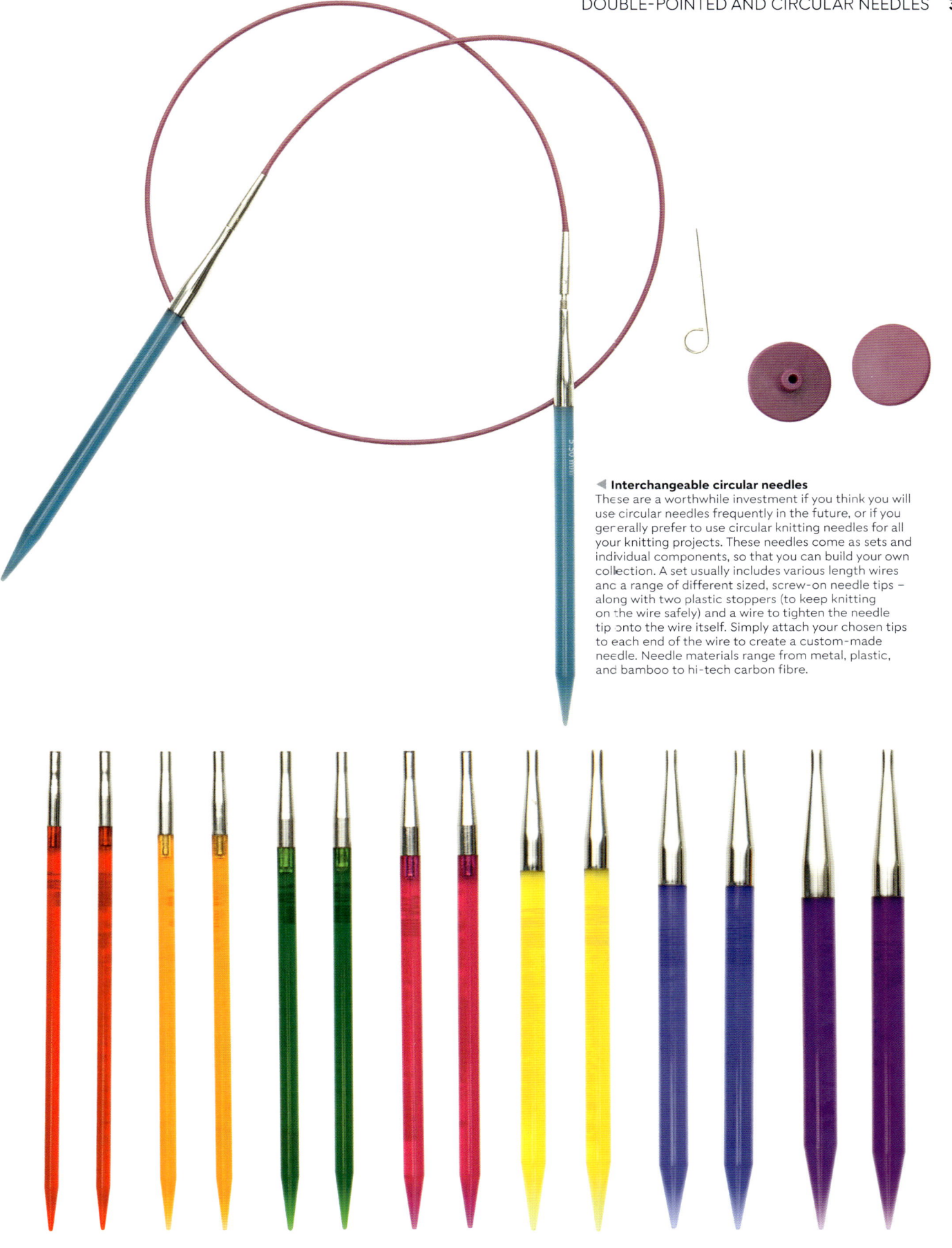

◀ **Interchangeable circular needles**
These are a worthwhile investment if you think you will use circular needles frequently in the future, or if you generally prefer to use circular knitting needles for all your knitting projects. These needles come as sets and individual components, so that you can build your own collection. A set usually includes various length wires and a range of different sized, screw-on needle tips – along with two plastic stoppers (to keep knitting on the wire safely) and a wire to tighten the needle tip onto the wire itself. Simply attach your chosen tips to each end of the wire to create a custom-made needle. Needle materials range from metal, plastic, and bamboo to hi-tech carbon fibre.

Other equipment

Hundreds of different gadgets are available to knitters. Some are merely for convenience, whereas others are absolutely vital and perform specific tasks. Here are the absolute essentials; the more advanced, specialized items are shown on pp.42–45.

THE ESSENTIALS

These basic items should always be to hand when you are working on a project. Most knitters have a portable knitting bag or case to keep them in, so that it is easy to take everything to wherever they want to sit and knit. The tools below are relatively inexpensive and can be purchased from haberdashery stores and knitting suppliers.

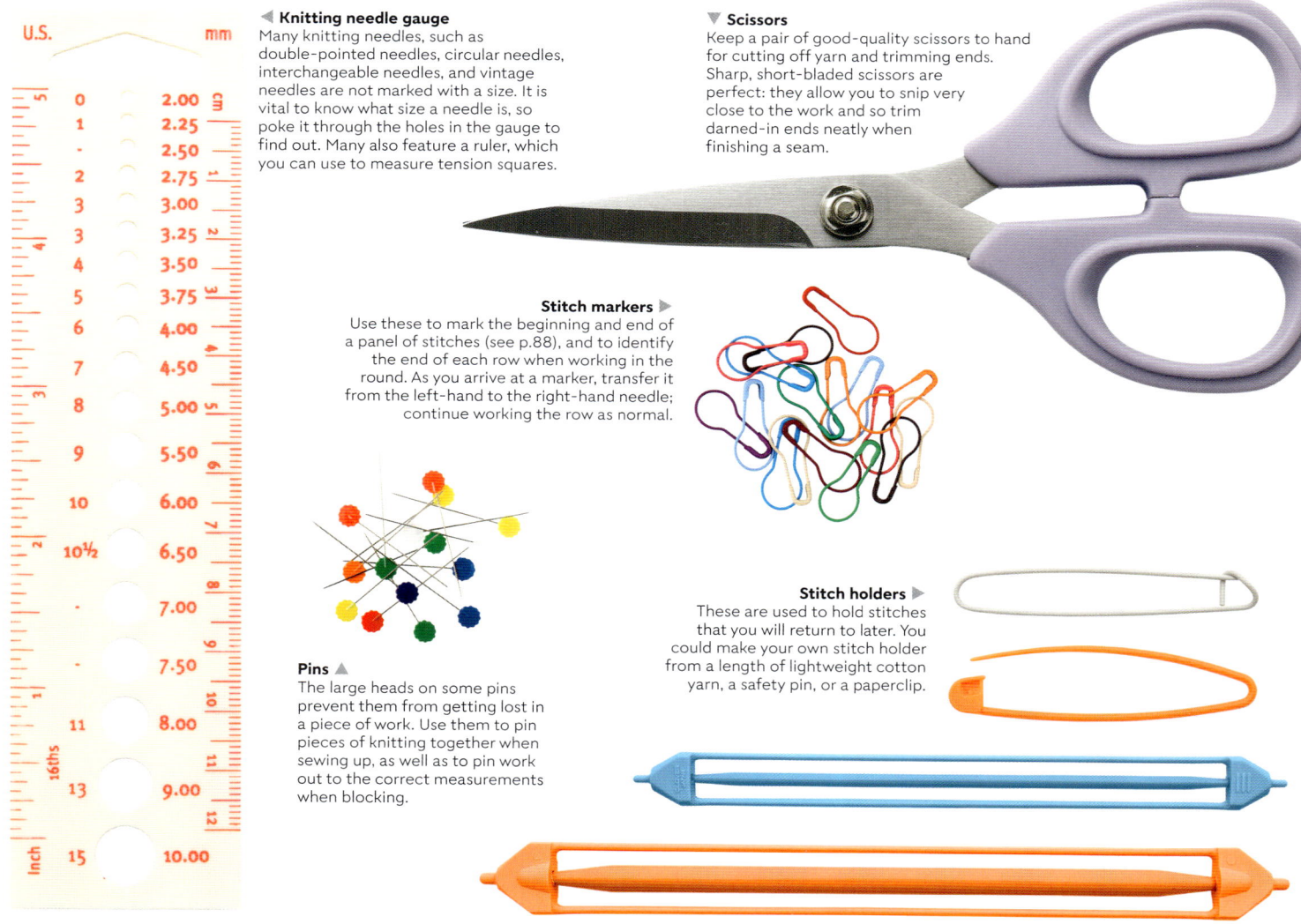

◀ Darning needles
These have a blunt tip in order to prevent damage to fibres, so are also suitable for use by knitters. Make sure that the eye is an appropriate size for the yarn: do not force yarn through an eye that is too small or it will spoil it.

◀ Knitting needle gauge
Many knitting needles, such as double-pointed needles, circular needles, interchangeable needles, and vintage needles are not marked with a size. It is vital to know what size a needle is, so poke it through the holes in the gauge to find out. Many also feature a ruler, which you can use to measure tension squares.

▼ Scissors
Keep a pair of good-quality scissors to hand for cutting off yarn and trimming ends. Sharp, short-bladed scissors are perfect: they allow you to snip very close to the work and so trim darned-in ends neatly when finishing a seam.

Stitch markers ▶
Use these to mark the beginning and end of a panel of stitches (see p.88), and to identify the end of each row when working in the round. As you arrive at a marker, transfer it from the left-hand to the right-hand needle; continue working the row as normal.

Pins ▲
The large heads on some pins prevent them from getting lost in a piece of work. Use them to pin pieces of knitting together when sewing up, as well as to pin work out to the correct measurements when blocking.

Stitch holders ▶
These are used to hold stitches that you will return to later. You could make your own stitch holder from a length of lightweight cotton yarn, a safety pin, or a paperclip.

THE ESSENTIALS 41

▲ **Tape measure**
Use this to measure the person you are knitting for, and for gauging sizing accurately. Also use it to check tension (see p.91) and measure knitting. Stick to using either metric or imperial measures, not a mixture of both.

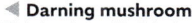

◀ **Darning mushroom**
This is placed behind a damaged area of knitted fabric to hold it steady while you repair it. This prevents any warping or puckering and preserves the original tension for the most subtle repair possible. Try it with the woven darning technique on p.85.

▲ **Needle organizer**
Use this to keep your knitting needles organized and protected against damage. Needle rolls and bags are available in a range of shapes and sizes. Thick needles are best suited to a needle bag (like a long pencil case); double-pointed needles can be stored in a short needle roll.

▼ **Knitting bag**
Bags for knitters often have many compartments, perfect for storing equipment and materials for your current project. To protect knitting from damp and moths, keep a cedar ring (see p.47) inside.

◀ **Row counter**
Available as a tube that sits at the end of a knitting needle: change the counter when you complete a row. Row counters are also available as a clicker, which you "click" each time you finish a row.

▲ **Point protectors**
Pop these over fragile needle tips to guard against damage; use them to protect your knitting bag from punctures and to stop stitches from sliding off needles and unravelling when not in use.

SPECIALIZED EQUIPMENT

As you begin to use more advanced techniques, you will find that you need specialized equipment. Each item is specific to a particular skill, such as colourwork, lace knitting, and patterning with cables. If you are a new knitter and just learning the basic stitches, do not worry about these items for now, but you will certainly need them in the future as you become more experienced and try more ambitious projects.

▶ Blunt-ended yarn needles
To sew up projects and darn in ends, you need a selection of different thicknesses of blunt, large-eyed needles. These will not damage or split delicate fibres and will slip between the stitches when sewing seams. Those with a bent tip can be more comfortable to work with. There are even needles with a latch-eye that can be opened to accommodate very thick yarns.

▲ Blocking wire and pins
These are used to block knitting, and are particularly useful for fine lace, after hand-washing or before steam blocking. Thread the wires along the edge of the wet (dry, if steam or spray blocking) fabric as if sewing a long running stitch. Measure and shape the fabric to the correct dimensions before pinning the wires down and leaving the knitting to dry naturally.

◀ Latch hook
This latch-hook tool is better than a crochet hook for picking up dropped stitches. The latch allows you to pull the stitches through each other cleanly and the solid handle and cranked shaft makes it comfortable to grip when manipulating the yarn.

▼ Blocking mats
These can be pieced together to provide the perfect surface for blocking finished knitted pieces (see Blocking, p.185). Hand-wash your finished piece and lay it flat on the mat, pinning to the desired measurements. As the item dries, it will hold its blocked shape. Blocking mats are available in interlocking foam squares for projects of any size. The waterproof surface protects the area beneath.

▲ Sharp-ended needles
Buy these with a large eye; use to secure darned-in ends after finishing with the blunt-ended needle. A sharp needle may also be required when inserting a zip or affixing trimmings to a piece of work.

◀ Crochet hook
Available in different materials such as metal, wood, and bamboo. A crochet hook makes it much easier to pick up previously dropped stitches. The slippery surface of the metal version probably makes this the most user-friendly type. You can also use a crochet hook for inserting tassels.

◀ **Chart paper**
Use this knitters' graph paper for recording a colourwork design or making a pattern chart. Knitted stitches are not square: they are wider than they are tall, so standard graph paper will not be suitable. Buy ready-printed chart paper from specialists, or download it for free from the internet.

Sock blocker ▶
This is the best way to block finished socks to a neat shape. Hand-wash the sock and pull gently to shape on the blocker. As it dries, it will take on the shape of the blocker. Sock blockers are available in a selection of sizes. If you use a wooden version, the sock can be lightly steamed to shape instead.

◀ **Yarn cutter**
A convenient alternative to scissors. Insert the yarn through the grooves in the yarn cutter in order to trim it off. You may prefer to attach it to a cord to wear around your neck while you work. When travelling by air, you can use this if you want to knit on a flight, because regulations often prohibit scissors in hand luggage.

▲ **Cable needle**
A kinked or U-shaped cable needle is used when working cables; this shape prevents cable stitches from sliding away. Choose a size that is closest to that of the needles used for the main body of the knitting.

◀ **Knit blockers**
These come in various lengths and materials; they are useful for creating crisp, even edges without placing dozens of single pins. Thread them through the edge stitches of damp knitting and shape to the correct dimensions, then pin them down and leave the item to dry naturally.

44 TOOLS

◀ **Mini knitting mill**
This mechanical, hand-wound cord-maker is suitable for 4-ply and DK-weight yarns. These usually have four latch needles and allow you to produce long lengths of i-cord much more quickly than on a knitting dolly. Use one of these to create your own "chainette" or chunky tubular yarns.

▲ **Knitting dolly/cord-maker**
An i-cord is a narrow tube of knitting; children love using this knitting dolly to produce a length of i-cord. Alternatively, a mini knitting mill, suitable for 4-ply and DK-weight yarns, allows you to make long i-cords much more quickly.

▲ **Wonder clips**
These really useful clips are an alternative to pins – they won't split yarn or catch threads. Use them to match edges securely together before seaming or when setting a neckband onto a neck edge. You can even use them to clip yarn tails to knitting.

◀ **Ball-winder**
This device allows you to speedily wind hanks of yarn into centre-pull balls, instead of doing it by hand. Alternatively, use this handy tool to wind two or more strands together before you knit them, to make a neatly wound, double-stranded yarn. Pulling one strand through the centre of the other ball will twist the yarns together at the same time.

SPECIALIZED EQUIPMENT 45

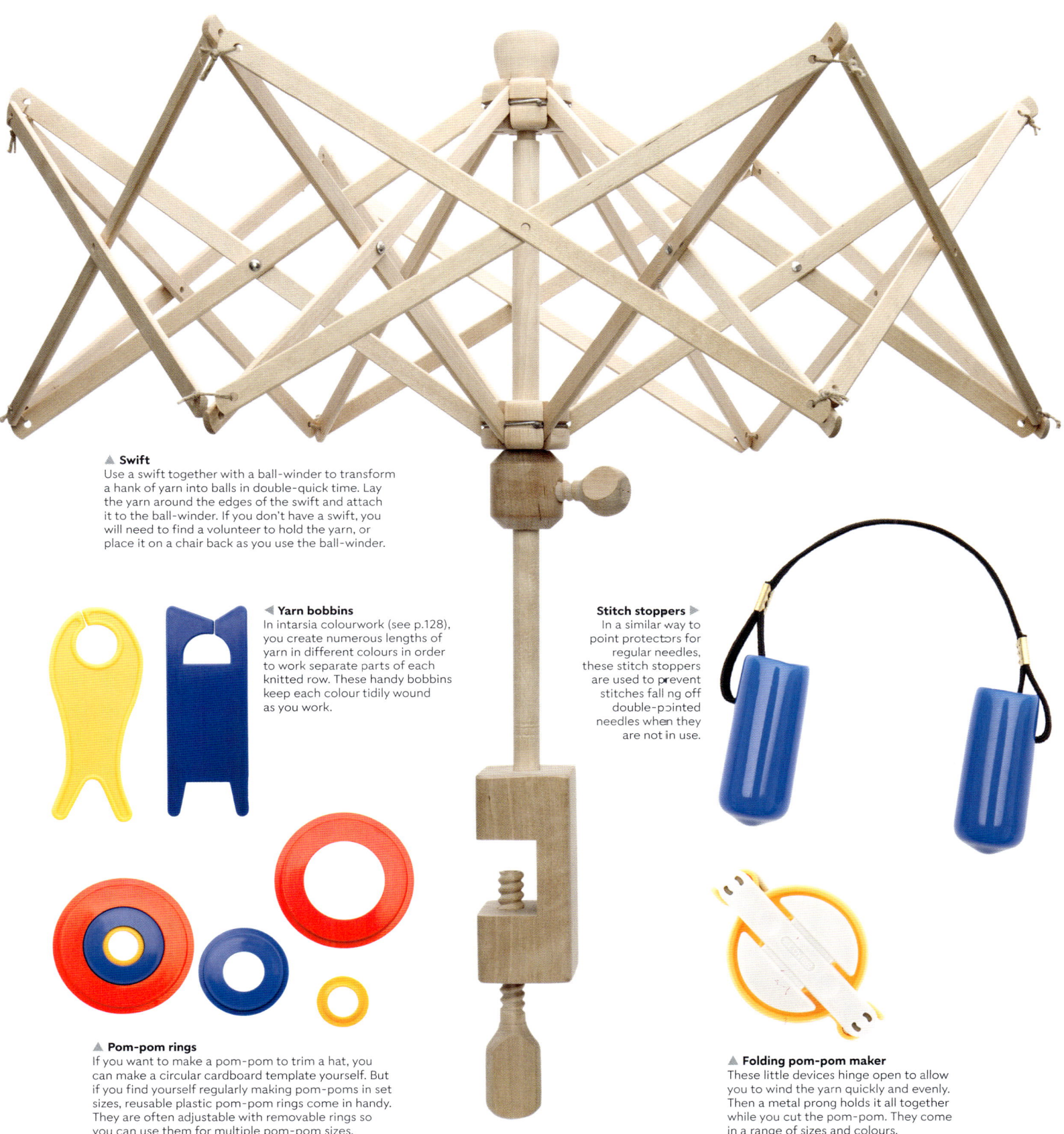

▲ **Swift**
Use a swift together with a ball-winder to transform a hank of yarn into balls in double-quick time. Lay the yarn around the edges of the swift and attach it to the ball-winder. If you don't have a swift, you will need to find a volunteer to hold the yarn, or place it on a chair back as you use the ball-winder.

◀ **Yarn bobbins**
In intarsia colourwork (see p.128), you create numerous lengths of yarn in different colours in order to work separate parts of each knitted row. These handy bobbins keep each colour tidily wound as you work.

Stitch stoppers ▶
In a similar way to point protectors for regular needles, these stitch stoppers are used to prevent stitches falling off double-pointed needles when they are not in use.

▲ **Pom-pom rings**
If you want to make a pom-pom to trim a hat, you can make a circular cardboard template yourself. But if you find yourself regularly making pom-poms in set sizes, reusable plastic pom-pom rings come in handy. They are often adjustable with removable rings so you can use them for multiple pom-pom sizes.

▲ **Folding pom-pom maker**
These little devices hinge open to allow you to wind the yarn quickly and evenly. Then a metal prong holds it all together while you cut the pom-pom. They come in a range of sizes and colours.

Garment care

After all the hard work of knitting a garment, it is important to protect it from damage and to keep it looking new. Moths are one of the biggest threats: they love to lay their eggs in natural fibres and the larvae will chew tiny holes, which are unsightly and cause knitting to fall apart. The equipment below will help you to keep your hand-knits in good condition.

Bobble remover ▶
Knitted items may pill (form bobbles on the surface). If this is severe, shave them off with a bobble-removing comb or machine. Be gentle: do not pull at your work as it may damage it. Fabric softeners may aggravate the problem.

Lavender sachets ▲
Lavender is a traditional and natural deterrent to moths. Make your own sachets from dried garden lavender, crumbled into fabric or knitted bags. Hang sachets in the wardrobe, or slip into drawers. Use also in sealed bags of yarn for storage.

Mohair brush ▶
Mohair can flatten and lose its halo-like furriness after a wash or prolonged storage. It is therefore essential to invest in a mohair brush to reinvigorate fuzzy knits with gentle brushstrokes. You can also prevent matting in areas subject to extra wear, such as the armpits of a jumper.

GARMENT CARE **47**

◀ **Garment bag**
These are a must-have and are available in a variety of styles, ranging from simple zipped bags to lavender-scented plastic bags, and bags that allow vacuum packing in order to reduce bulk and save space. Make sure that bags are sealed properly to prevent damp and insects from getting in. Although a bag may appear secure when folded over, moths are able to wriggle in and out of small spaces and make themselves comfortable.

▲ **Mothballs**
A chemical method of deterring moths and insects. Slip them into pockets or garment bags. They vary from strong-smelling to subtle; beware of the strong ones as the smell can be impossible to eradicate.

▲ **Cedarwood shapes**
Cedarwood has a subtle aroma, which some people may prefer to that of lavender and which also deters moths. Available as cubes, blocks, and rings to hang in the wardrobe, or to dot around a cupboard, or put inside bags or boxes of yarn. The aroma fades over time, but they can be sanded down to refresh the natural smell. Alternatively, apply a drop of grapefruit oil to each block, allow it to dry, and return the blocks to your yarn store for a moth deterrent with added antibacterial properties.

▲ **Wool wash**
This very gentle soap will gently cleanse fibres and remove dirt without damaging a yarn or pushing dye from it. It is now possible to buy a wool wash that does not need rinsing out, making the hand-washing of precious knitted items even more convenient.

TECHNIQUES

Key techniques

Learning to knit is a very quick process. There are only a few key techniques to pick up before you are ready to make simple shapes such as scarves, baby blankets, cushion covers, and throws. The basics include casting stitches onto the needle, the knit (p.78) and purl (p.79) stitches, and, finally, casting the stitches off the needles.

MAKING A SLIP KNOT

Before you start knitting, you must first learn how to place the first loop on the needle. This loop is called the slip knot and it is the first stitch formed when casting on stitches.

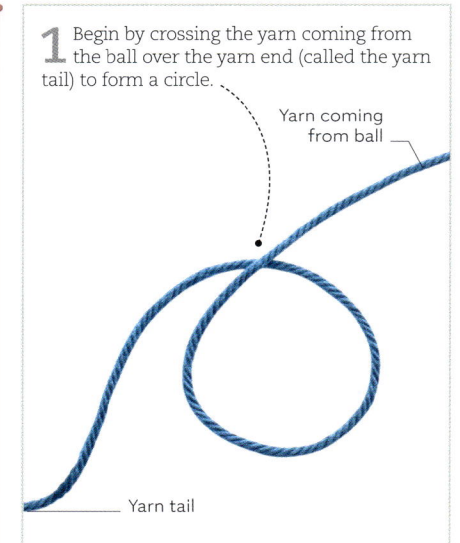

1 Begin by crossing the yarn coming from the ball over the yarn end (called the yarn tail) to form a circle.

Yarn coming from ball

Yarn tail

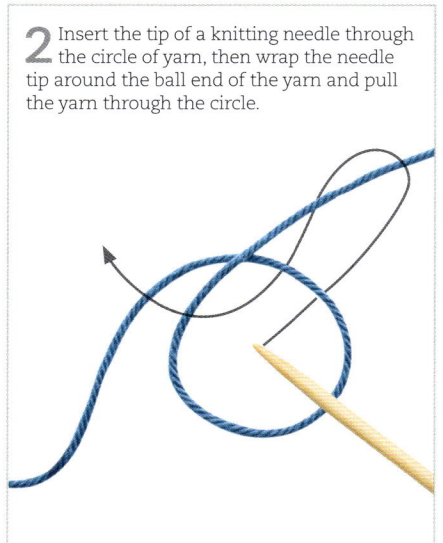

2 Insert the tip of a knitting needle through the circle of yarn, then wrap the needle tip around the ball end of the yarn and pull the yarn through the circle.

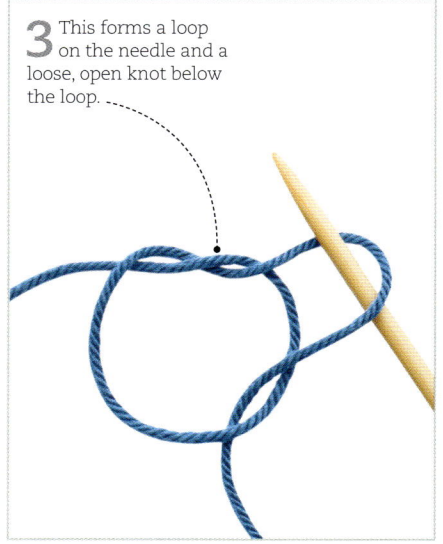

3 This forms a loop on the needle and a loose, open knot below the loop.

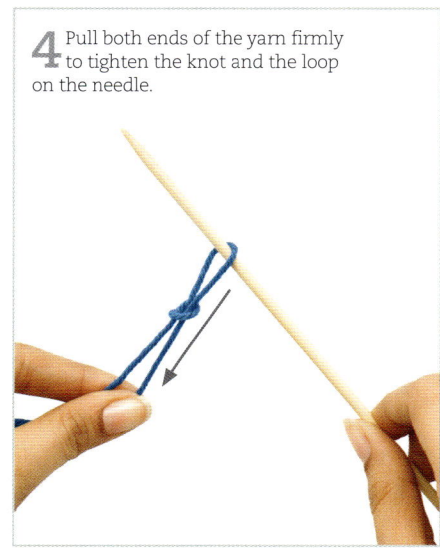

4 Pull both ends of the yarn firmly to tighten the knot and the loop on the needle.

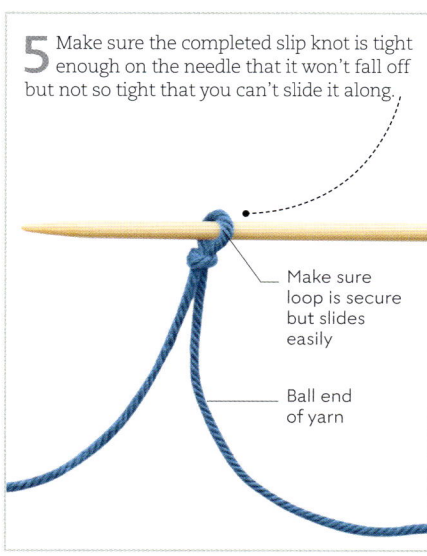

5 Make sure the completed slip knot is tight enough on the needle that it won't fall off but not so tight that you can't slide it along.

Make sure loop is secure but slides easily

Ball end of yarn

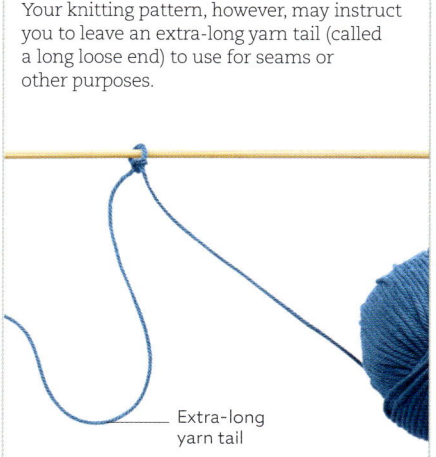

6 The yarn tail should be at least 10–15cm (4–6in) long so it can be darned in later. Your knitting pattern, however, may instruct you to leave an extra-long yarn tail (called a long loose end) to use for seams or other purposes.

Extra-long yarn tail

HOLDING YARN AND NEEDLES

Although all knitting is formed in exactly the same way, you can hold the yarn in either the right or the left hand. These two yarn-holding techniques are called the "English" and "Continental" methods. Knitting is ambidextrous, so right-handed and left-handed knitters should try both knitting styles to see which one is easier.

KNITTING "ENGLISH" STYLE

1 The yarn is laced around the fingers of the right hand. Aim to control the yarn firmly but with a relaxed hand, releasing it to flow through the fingers as the stitches are formed.

2 Try this alternative technique as well or make up your own. You need to tension the yarn just enough with your fingers to create even loops that are neither too loose nor too tight.

3 Hold the needles with the stitches about to be worked in the left hand and the other needle in the right hand. Use the right forefinger to wrap the yarn around the needle.

KNITTING "CONTINENTAL" STYLE

1 Lace the yarn through the fingers of the left hand in any way that feels comfortable. Try to both release and tension the yarn easily to create uniform loops.

2 In this alternative technique, the yarn is wrapped twice around the forefinger.

3 Hold the needle with the unworked stitches in the left hand and the other needle in the right hand. Position the yarn with the left forefinger and pull it through the loops with the tip of the right needle.

ALTERNATIVE "CONTINENTAL" STYLE KNITTING

This alternative method makes knit stitches very easy and is ideal for garter stitch (see p.76) or circular stocking stitch. As you work near the tip, short tapered needles are best for this method. When knitting Continental style you may find your tension loosens, in which case use smaller needles.

For both the knit and the purl stitches, wrap the yarn around your left little finger, but keep it over all your fingers. This makes purling easier.

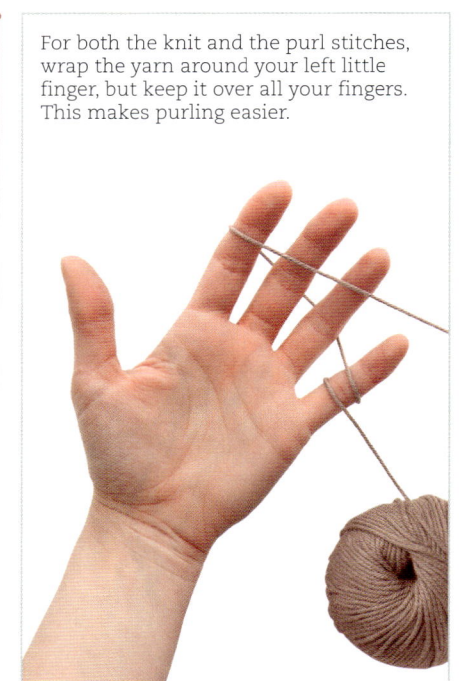

ALTERNATIVE "CONTINENTAL" KNIT STITCH

1. Hold your index finger up with the yarn over it and use the pad of your middle finger to hold the yarn against the left needle, slightly forwards of the stitch.

2. Insert the right tip into the stitch, pull and catch the yarn on your middle finger, draw it through the stitch on the left needle and off.

3. At the end of the row, keep the yarn around your left fingers. Swap the needles to start the next row.

ALTERNATIVE "CONTINENTAL" PURL STITCH

1. Hold the yarn as shown above. Bring yarn to front. With your index finger raised and your middle finger touching the left needle near the tip, insert needle as for purl (see p.79). Tilt the right tip towards you and then back in a small circular movement so that the yarn wraps over it.

2. At the same time, bring your left index finger with the yarn on it forwards, wrapping the yarn around the needle. Keep your index finger in constant contact with the left needle.

3. Immediately dip the right needle tip slightly away from you to hook the yarn and pull the old stitch open. Take the needle backwards through the old stitch and make a new purl loop. Slide the old stitch off the left needle.

- **ALTERNATIVE "CONTINENTAL" PURL STITCH – UNTWISTING AN INCORRECT STITCH**

1 If, when knitting Continental style, you wrap the yarn under, instead of over, the right-hand needle, the front "leg" of each stitch will be further from the needle-tip than the back leg. This is a twisted stitch.

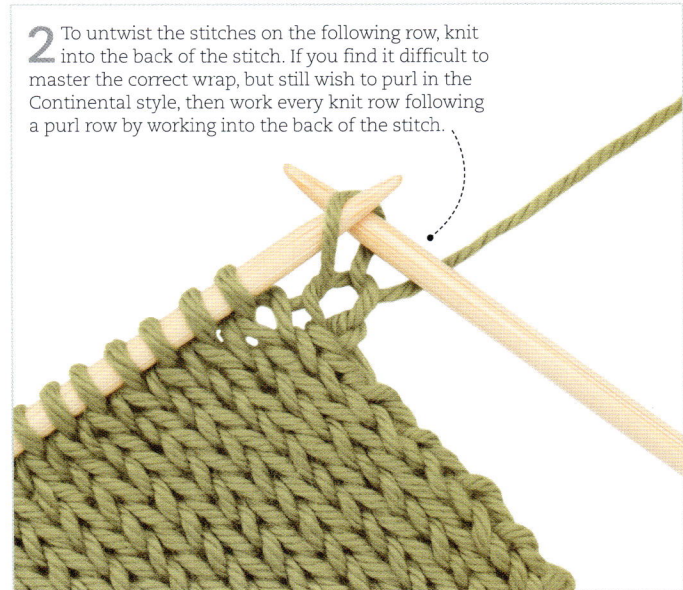

2 To untwist the stitches on the following row, knit into the back of the stitch. If you find it difficult to master the correct wrap, but still wish to purl in the Continental style, then work every knit row following a purl row by working into the back of the stitch.

SINGLE-STRAND CAST-ONS

These cast-ons are all related to the Single cast-on (below) and use one strand. They tend to be soft, but can be made firmer by twisting. Alternating loop cast-on makes a decorative edge. Casting on knitwise (see p.54) and Cable cast-on (see p.55) are useful for casting on in the middle of a piece, for example if you need to add more than one stitch when increasing. When followed by stocking stitch, casting on knitwise can curl towards the knit side. For edges where this matters, choose a two-strand Italian cast-on (see p.65).

- **SINGLE CAST-ON** (also called *Thumb cast-on*)

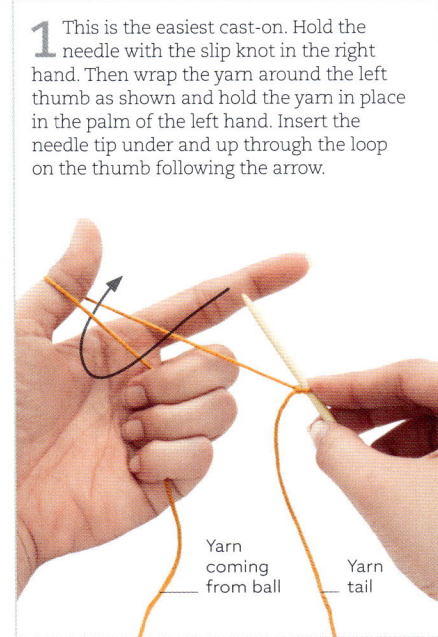

1 This is the easiest cast-on. Hold the needle with the slip knot in the right hand. Then wrap the yarn around the left thumb as shown and hold the yarn in place in the palm of the left hand. Insert the needle tip under and up through the loop on the thumb following the arrow.

Yarn coming from ball
Yarn tail

2 Release the loop from the thumb and pull the yarn to tighten the new cast-on loop on the needle, sliding it up close to the slip knot.

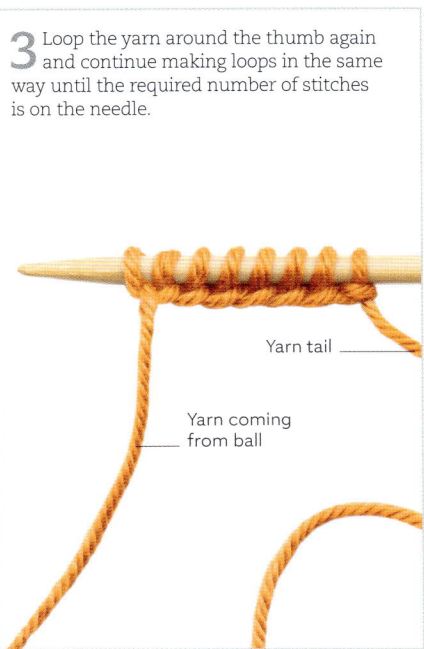

3 Loop the yarn around the thumb again and continue making loops in the same way until the required number of stitches is on the needle.

Yarn tail
Yarn coming from ball

KNIT-ON CAST-ON (also called *Knit-stitch* or *Knitted cast-on*)

1. Holding the yarn in the left or right hand as explained on p.51, place the needle with the slip knot in the left hand. Then insert the tip of the right needle from left to right through the centre of the loop on the left needle.

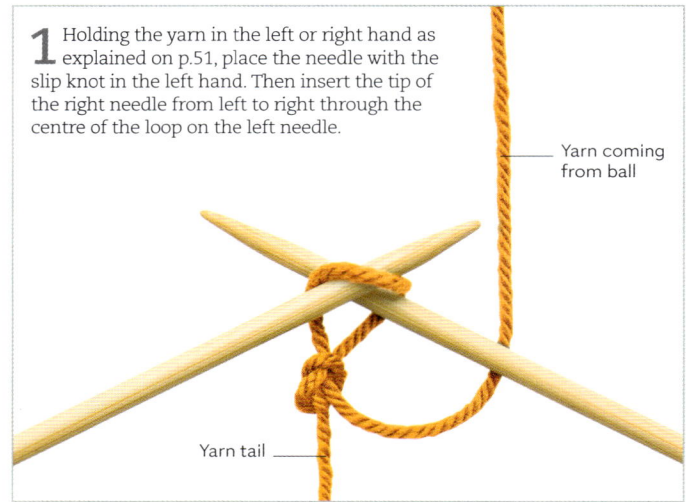

Yarn coming from ball

Yarn tail

2. With the yarn behind the needles, wrap it under and around the tip of the right needle. (While casting on, use the left forefinger or middle finger to hold the loops on the left needle in position.)

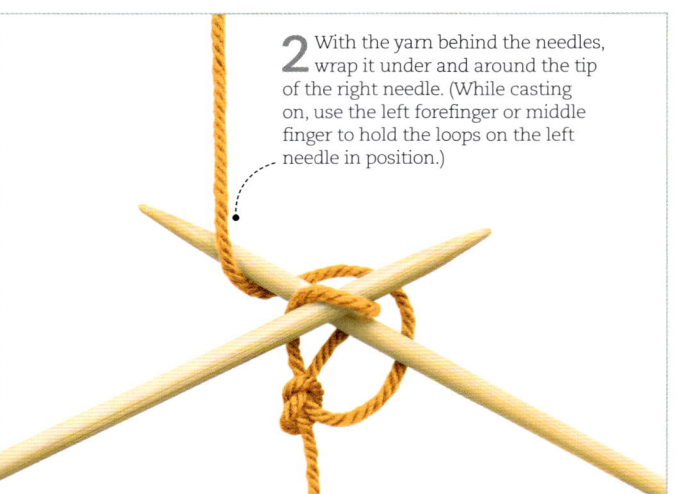

3. With the tip of the right needle, carefully draw the yarn through the loop on the left needle. (This is the same way a knit stitch is formed, hence the name of the cast-on.)

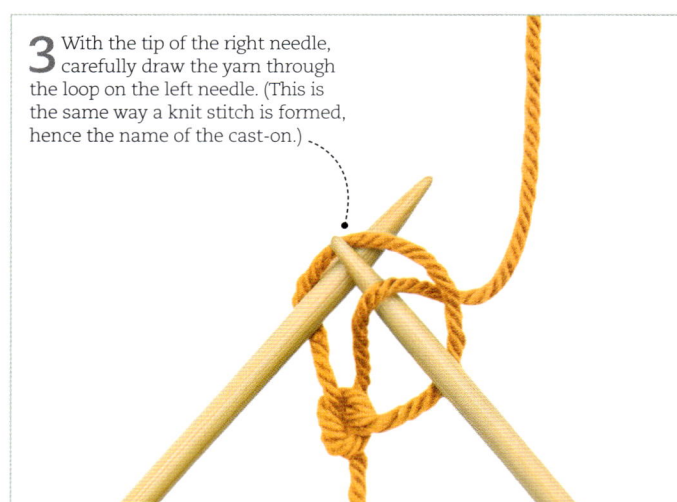

4. Insert the left needle-tip, left to right, into the loop on the right-hand needle. Slip the loop onto the left needle. For a tighter edge, insert the left needle-tip from right to left, twisting the loop as it slides across.

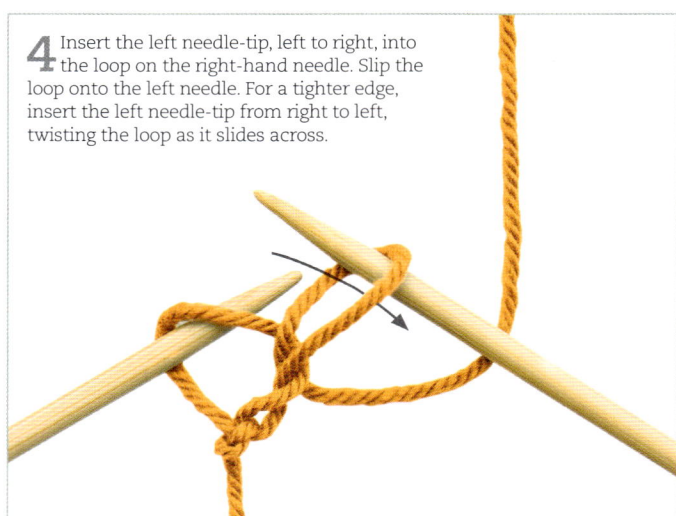

5. Pull the end of yarn attached to the ball to tighten the new cast-on loop on the needle, sliding it up close to the slip knot.

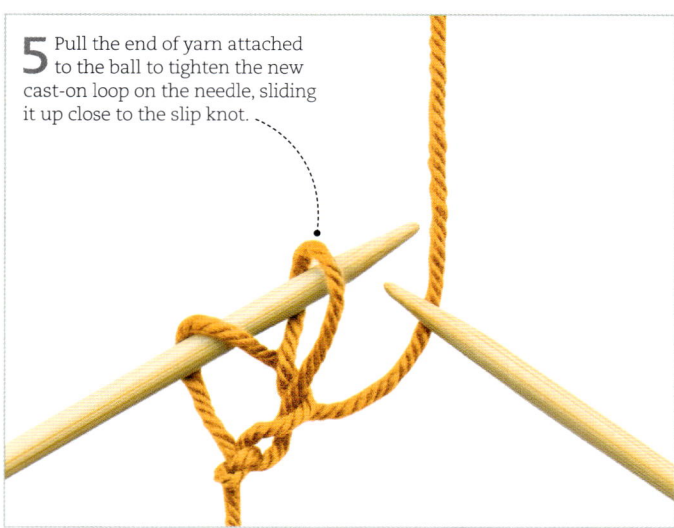

6. Continue casting on stitches in the same way until you have the required number of stitches. For a looser cast-on, hold two needles together in your left hand while casting on.

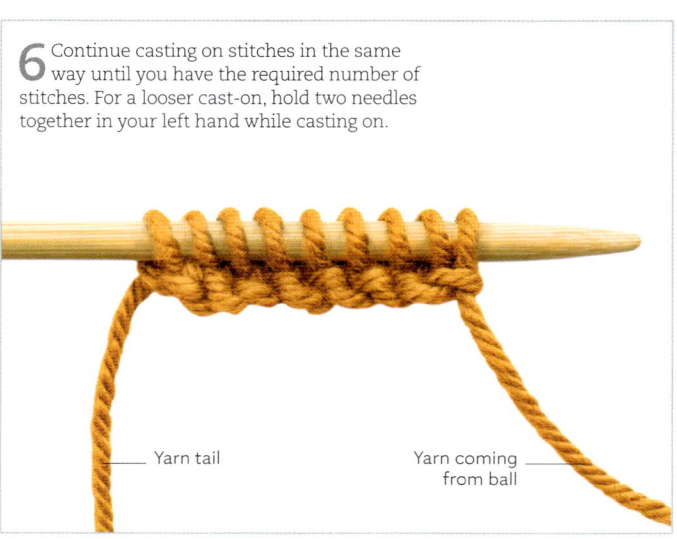

Yarn tail

Yarn coming from ball

CABLE CAST-ON

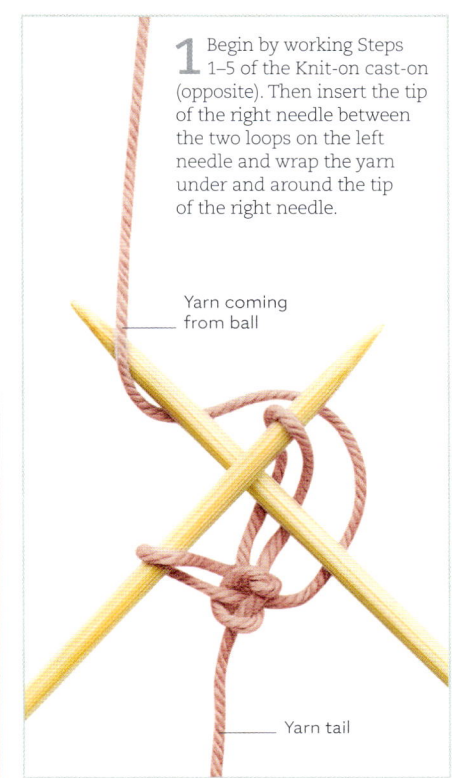

1 Begin by working Steps 1–5 of the Knit-on cast-on (opposite). Then insert the tip of the right needle between the two loops on the left needle and wrap the yarn under and around the tip of the right needle.

Yarn coming from ball

Yarn tail

2 With the tip of the right needle, draw the yarn through to form a loop on the right needle, pulling up the yarn as you go so that stitches sit neatly on the needle. When casting on before single rib, work this third and every following alternate stitch from the back, purlwise.

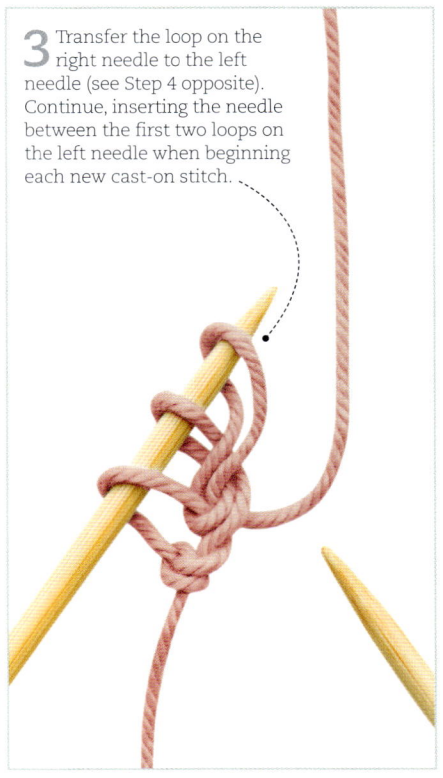

3 Transfer the loop on the right needle to the left needle (see Step 4 opposite). Continue, inserting the needle between the first two loops on the left needle when beginning each new cast-on stitch.

BACKWARDS LOOP CAST-ON

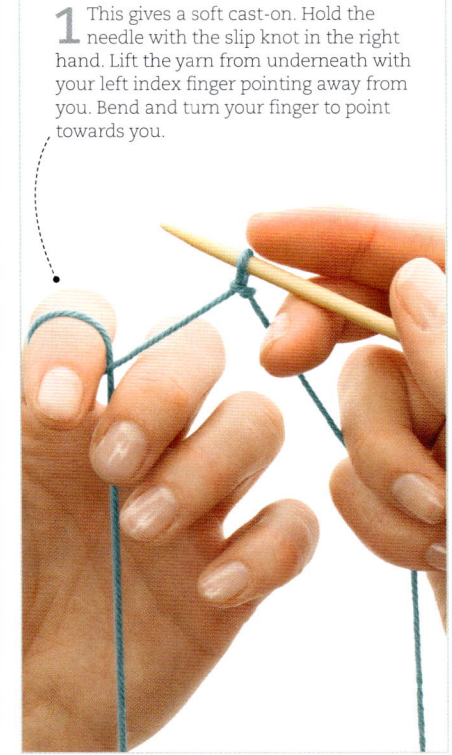

1 This gives a soft cast-on. Hold the needle with the slip knot in the right hand. Lift the yarn from underneath with your left index finger pointing away from you. Bend and turn your finger to point towards you.

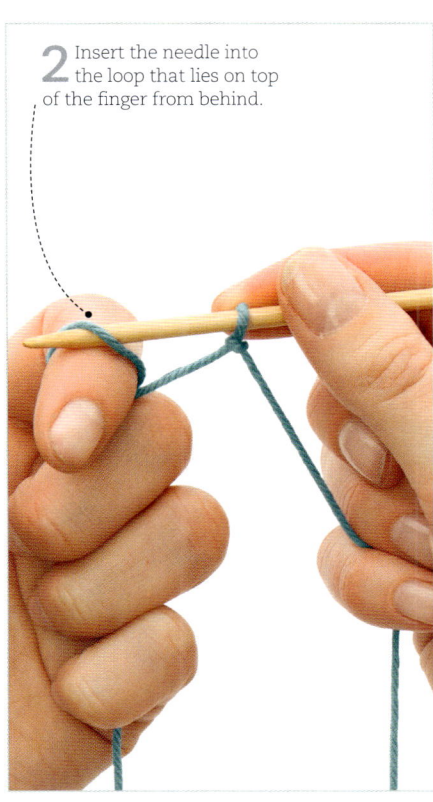

2 Insert the needle into the loop that lies on top of the finger from behind.

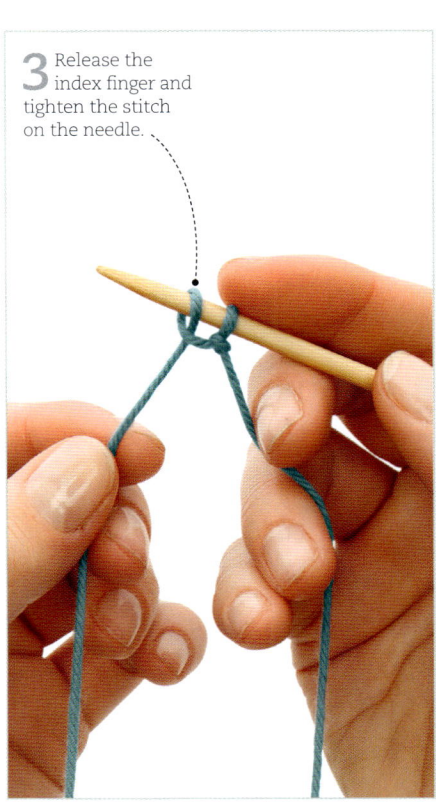

3 Release the index finger and tighten the stitch on the needle.

ALTERNATING LOOP CAST-ON

1 Work the first stitch as for Backwards loop cast-on, as shown on p.55.

2 Work the second stitch as Single cast-on (see p.53) by lifting the yarn from behind with the left thumb, winding it round the thumb and inserting the needle into the front strand.

3 Repeat Steps 1 and 2 to cast on as many stitches as you need. On the first row, work into the front of the stitches, even if they look twisted.

DOUBLE TWIST LOOP CAST-ON

This cast-on gives quite a firm edge. The additional twists make working the first row easier than in other cast-ons.

1 Hold the needle with the slip knot in your right hand. Lift the yarn from behind with your left index finger.

2 Twist the yarn by twirling your finger twice in an anticlockwise circle.

3 Place the loop from your finger on the needle and pull to tighten.

4 Repeat Steps 1–3 to cast on as many stitches as you need. The resulting decorative edge is open-textured.

TWO-STRAND CAST-ON

These cast-on techniques all use two strands, but generally only one needle, and are strong, elastic, and versatile. They are usually followed by a wrong side row, unless the reverse is the right side. As with Double cast-on (below), start all these with a slip knot made after a long tail at least three times as long as the planned knitting width.

DOUBLE CAST-ON (also called *Long-tail cast-on*)

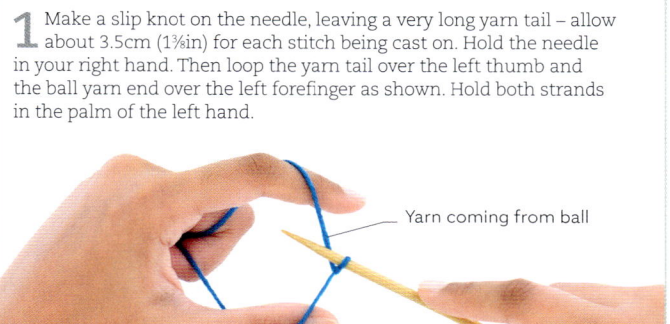

1. Make a slip knot on the needle, leaving a very long yarn tail – allow about 3.5cm (1⅜in) for each stitch being cast on. Hold the needle in your right hand. Then loop the yarn tail over the left thumb and the ball yarn end over the left forefinger as shown. Hold both strands in the palm of the left hand.

Yarn coming from ball

Long yarn tail

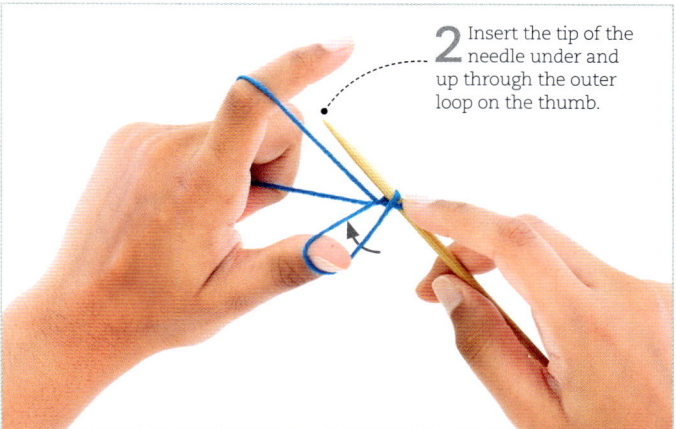

2. Insert the tip of the needle under and up through the outer loop on the thumb.

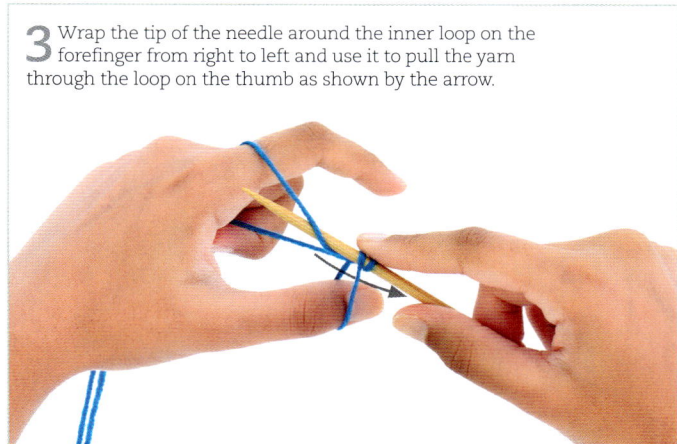

3. Wrap the tip of the needle around the inner loop on the forefinger from right to left and use it to pull the yarn through the loop on the thumb as shown by the arrow.

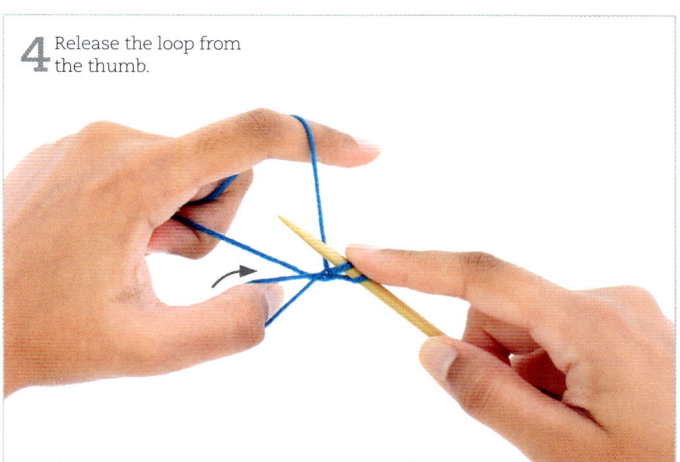

4. Release the loop from the thumb.

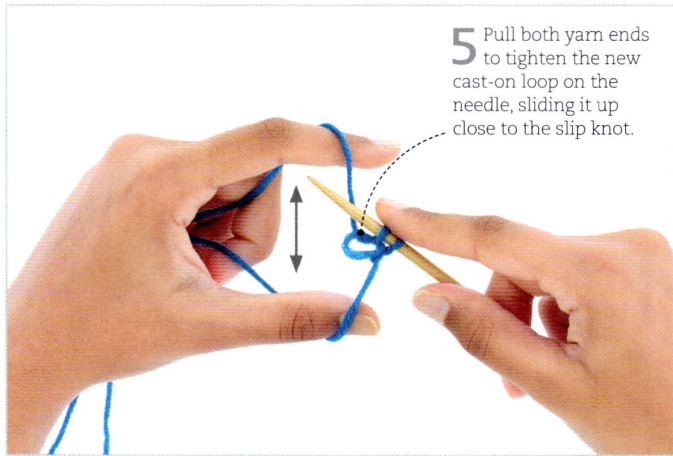

5. Pull both yarn ends to tighten the new cast-on loop on the needle, sliding it up close to the slip knot.

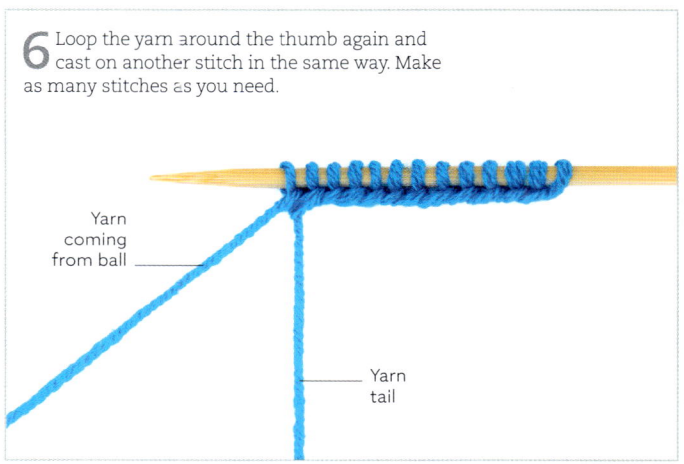

6. Loop the yarn around the thumb again and cast on another stitch in the same way. Make as many stitches as you need.

Yarn coming from ball

Yarn tail

58 TECHNIQUES

- **ALTERNATIVE DOUBLE CAST-ON** (also called *Alternative Long-tail cast-on*)

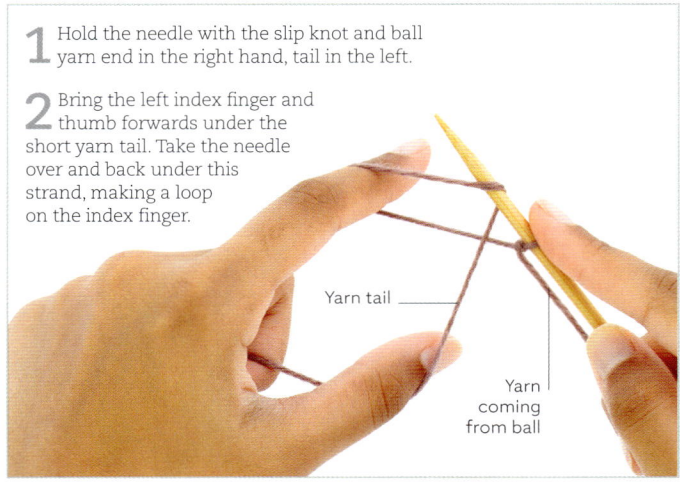

1 Hold the needle with the slip knot and ball yarn end in the right hand, tail in the left.

2 Bring the left index finger and thumb forwards under the short yarn tail. Take the needle over and back under this strand, making a loop on the index finger.

Yarn tail

Yarn coming from ball

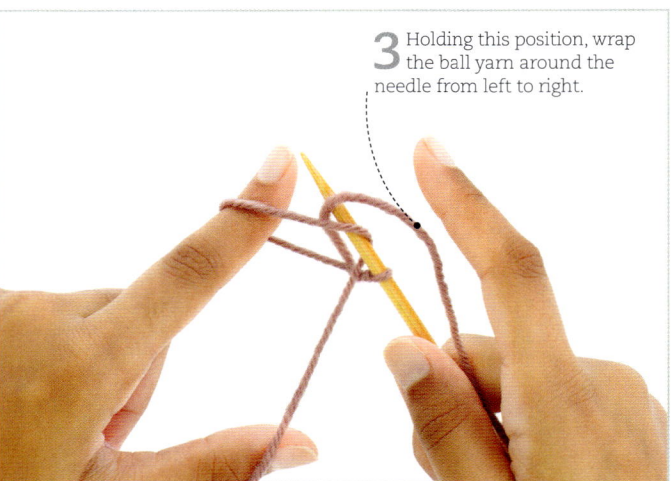

3 Holding this position, wrap the ball yarn around the needle from left to right.

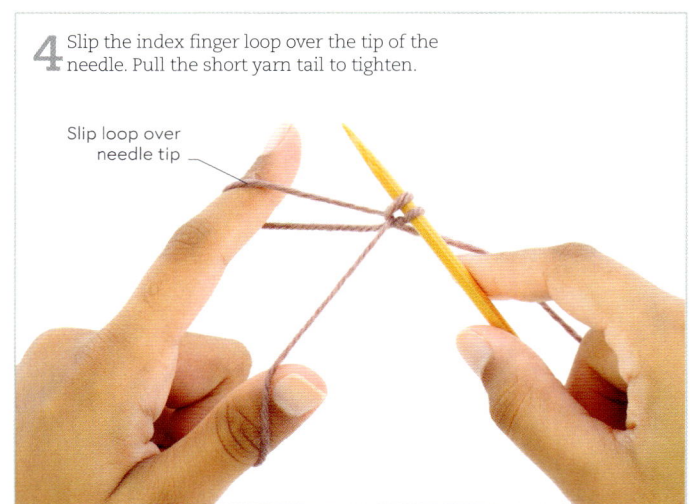

4 Slip the index finger loop over the tip of the needle. Pull the short yarn tail to tighten.

Slip loop over needle tip

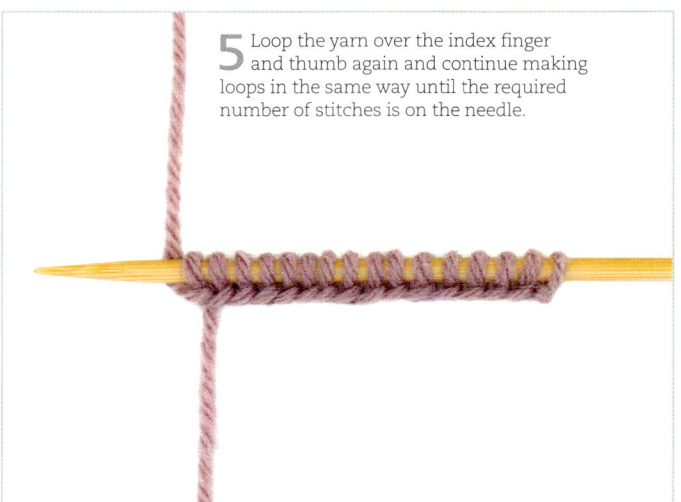

5 Loop the yarn over the index finger and thumb again and continue making loops in the same way until the required number of stitches is on the needle.

- **TWO-NEEDLE CAST-ON**

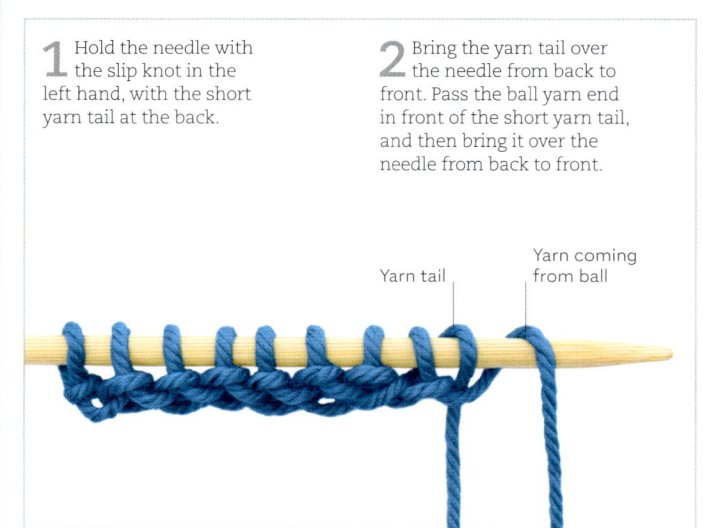

1 Hold the needle with the slip knot in the left hand, with the short yarn tail at the back.

2 Bring the yarn tail over the needle from back to front. Pass the ball yarn end in front of the short yarn tail, and then bring it over the needle from back to front.

Yarn tail

Yarn coming from ball

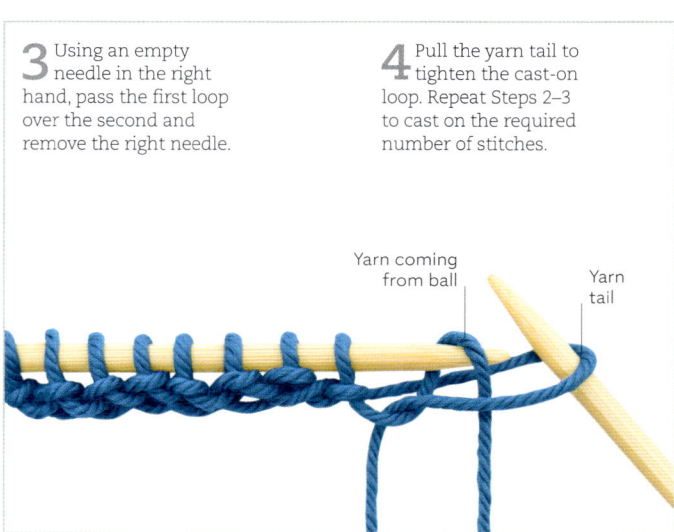

3 Using an empty needle in the right hand, pass the first loop over the second and remove the right needle.

4 Pull the yarn tail to tighten the cast-on loop. Repeat Steps 2–3 to cast on the required number of stitches.

Yarn coming from ball

Yarn tail

CONTRAST EDGE CAST-ON

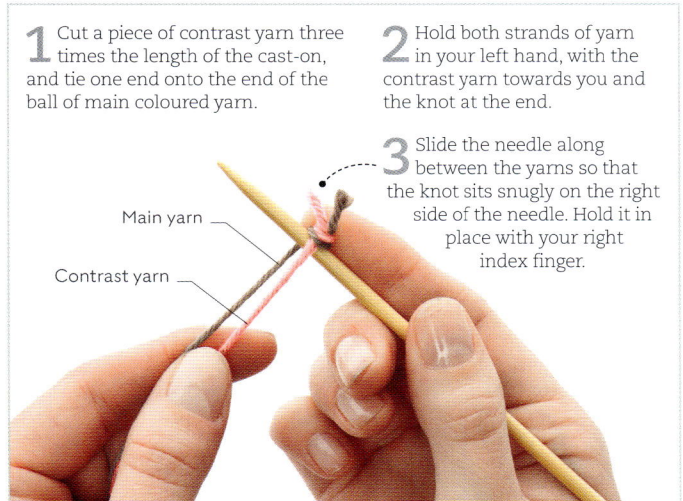

1. Cut a piece of contrast yarn three times the length of the cast-on, and tie one end onto the end of the ball of main coloured yarn.

2. Hold both strands of yarn in your left hand, with the contrast yarn towards you and the knot at the end.

3. Slide the needle along between the yarns so that the knot sits snugly on the right side of the needle. Hold it in place with your right index finger.

Main yarn

Contrast yarn

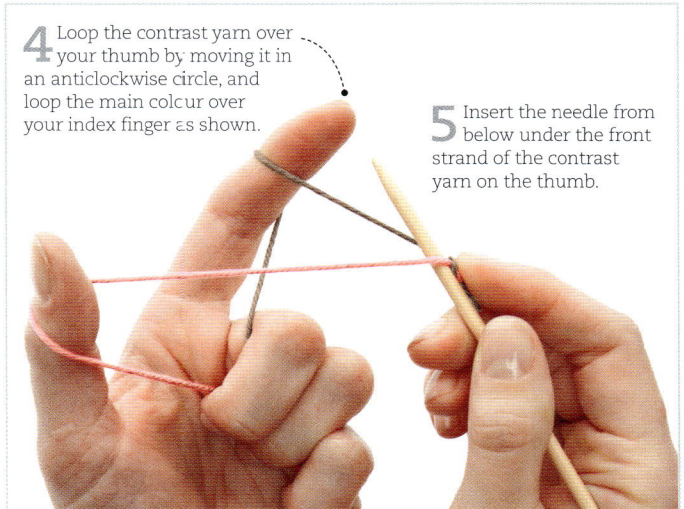

4. Loop the contrast yarn over your thumb by moving it in an anticlockwise circle, and loop the main colour over your index finger as shown.

5. Insert the needle from below under the front strand of the contrast yarn on the thumb.

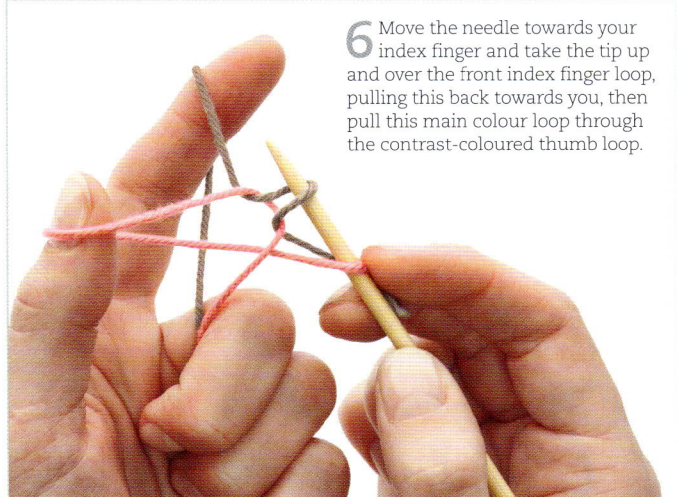

6. Move the needle towards your index finger and take the tip up and over the front index finger loop, pulling this back towards you, then pull this main colour loop through the contrast-coloured thumb loop.

7. Release the contrast yarn thumb loop. Pull both yarn ends to hold the needle snugly, and slide the cast-on stitch close to the slip knot. Repeat Steps 4–7.

8. Cast on the required stitches. Knit the next row in the main yarn and continue working in garter stitch.

TWISTED DOUBLE CAST-ON

This cast-on is stretchy, so is useful before a rib. Make it even stretchier by working it over two needles held together.

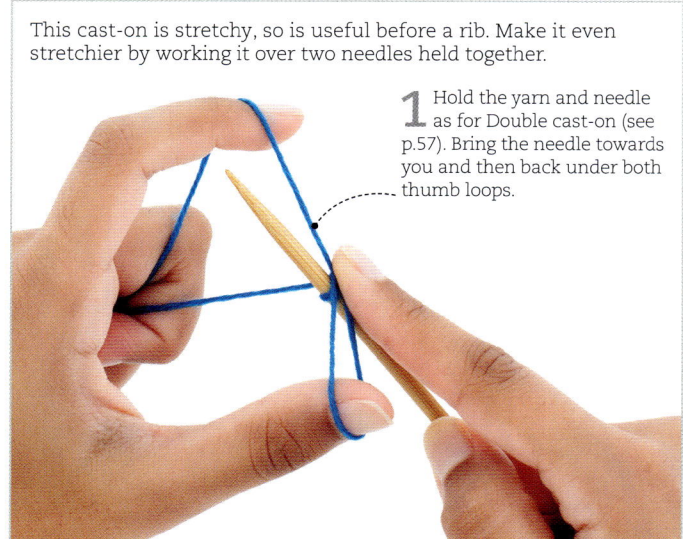

1 Hold the yarn and needle as for Double cast-on (see p.57). Bring the needle towards you and then back under both thumb loops.

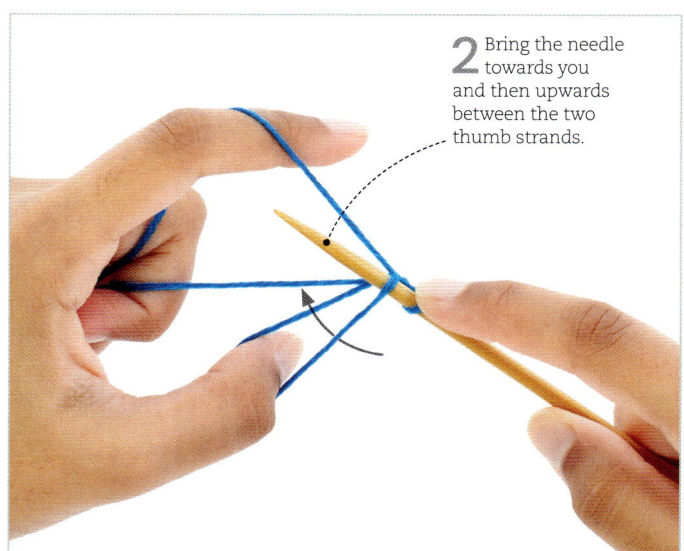

2 Bring the needle towards you and then upwards between the two thumb strands.

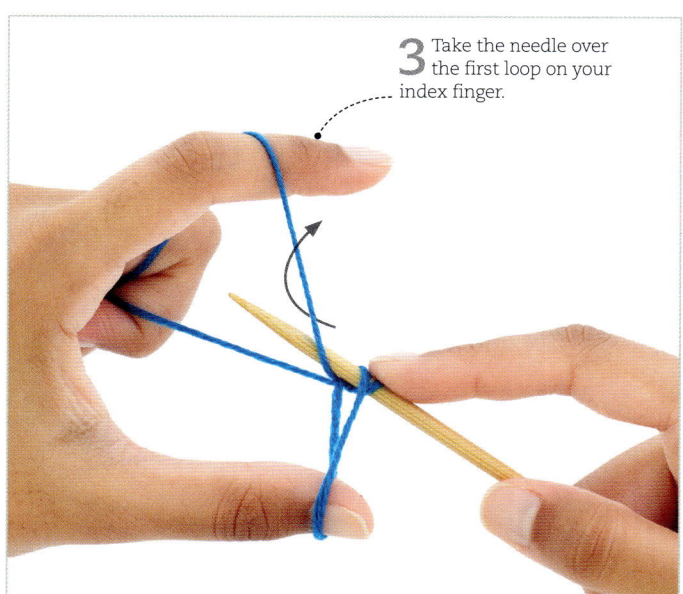

3 Take the needle over the first loop on your index finger.

4 Bring the needle towards you. Drop the end of your thumb away from you and let the loop slide down towards the end to open the thumb loop. Bring the needle down through the open thumb loop.

5 Release the thumb loop keeping the yarn around your index finger ready to start the next cast-on loop. Pull the short strand to tighten the stitch.

6 Loop the yarn around your thumb again and repeat Steps 1–4 to cast on another stitch in the same way. The stitches create a stretchy double twist effect.

COMBINED TWO-STRAND CAST-ON

Also known as Estonian cast-on, this method gives a very stretchy edge and is ideal for ribbed cuffs.

1 Make the first stitch as for Double cast-on (see p.57). The second stitch is similar, except this time you turn your thumb in the opposite direction to catch the yarn. The end of the strand is to the inside of your thumb.

2 With the needle pointing away, take it over the first thumb loop and then under the loop on the inside of the thumb. Take the needle over the nearest loop on the index finger.

3 Draw the loop through the thumb loop.

4 Drop the thumb loop. Pull the yarn tail to tighten the new loop. Repeat to cast on the required stitches.

TWO-STRAND DOUBLE CAST-ON

1 In preparation, measure the long tail length required for your cast-on. Fold the yarn so you have two strands of this length, and tie your slip knot at the free end of the yarn, catching both yarns.

2 Work as usual for Double cast-on (see p.57), or any other two-stranded cast-on, using the single ball end yarn to make the stitches and the doubled yarn for the foundation loop.

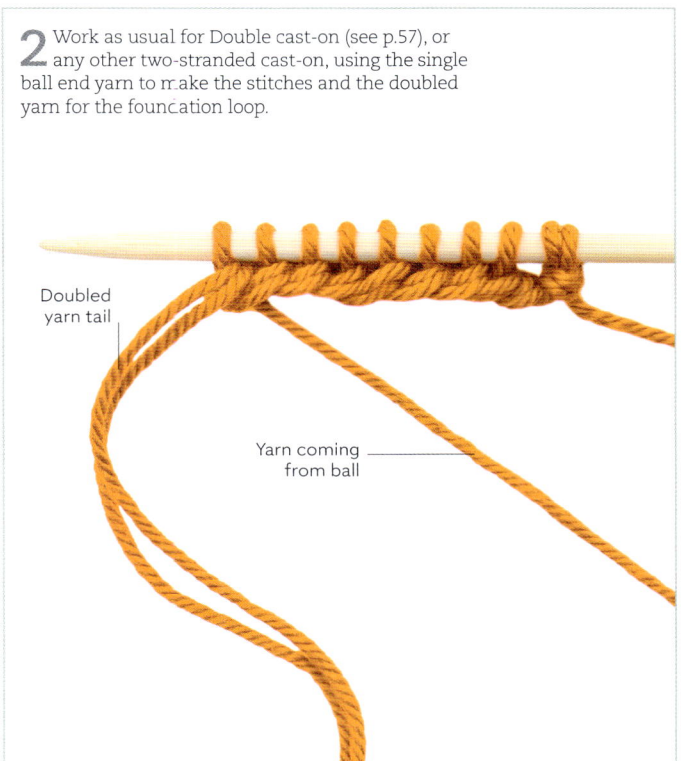

SPECIAL CAST-ONS

The following cast-ons are useful for specific purposes and may be specified in your pattern. However, many patterns simply say "cast on", in which case you should select one of these methods to add functionality or individuality to your project.

CHANNEL ISLANDS CAST-ON FOR SINGLE RIB

1 Fold the yarn tail, so that you have a doubled yarn four times the length of your cast-on edge, plus 10cm (4in).

2 Make a slip knot on the doubled strand, about 10cm (4in) from the free end. Transfer to a needle. Hold the doubled strand in the left hand, single strand and needle in the right.

3 Bring the left thumb under the doubled strand from the front, in a clockwise circle, winding the doubled yarn twice around the thumb. Insert the needle up through both loops.

4 Pass the single strand around the needle and slip the thumb loops over to make a stitch as normal.

5 Release the loop from the thumb and pull the double strand first to tighten the loop on the needle.

6 To make the next stitch, take the single yarn over the needle to the back.

7 Repeat Steps 2–4 to the required cast-on length, finishing with a thumb wrapped stitch, making an even number of stitches.

8 To work the first row, knit the first stitch (the thumb loop) and purl the next. Finally, purl into the initial double-strand slip knot.

PROVISIONAL CAST-ON

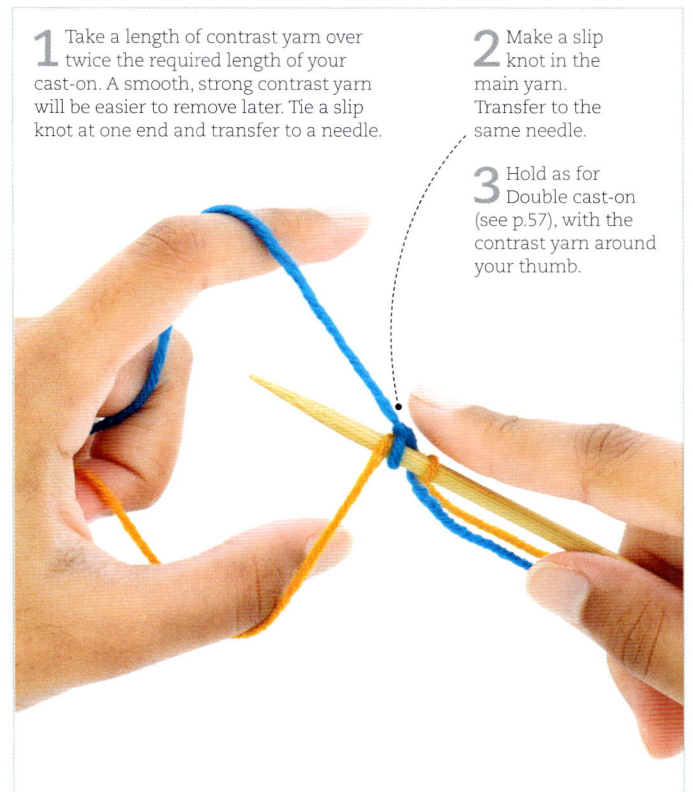

1. Take a length of contrast yarn over twice the required length of your cast-on. A smooth, strong contrast yarn will be easier to remove later. Tie a slip knot at one end and transfer to a needle.

2. Make a slip knot in the main yarn. Transfer to the same needle.

3. Hold as for Double cast-on (see p.57), with the contrast yarn around your thumb.

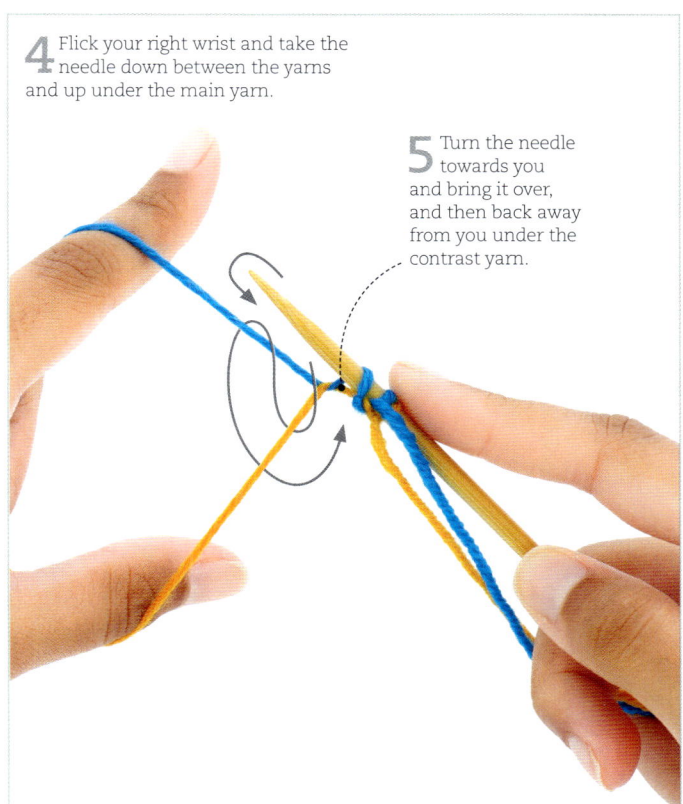

4. Flick your right wrist and take the needle down between the yarns and up under the main yarn.

5. Turn the needle towards you and bring it over, and then back away from you under the contrast yarn.

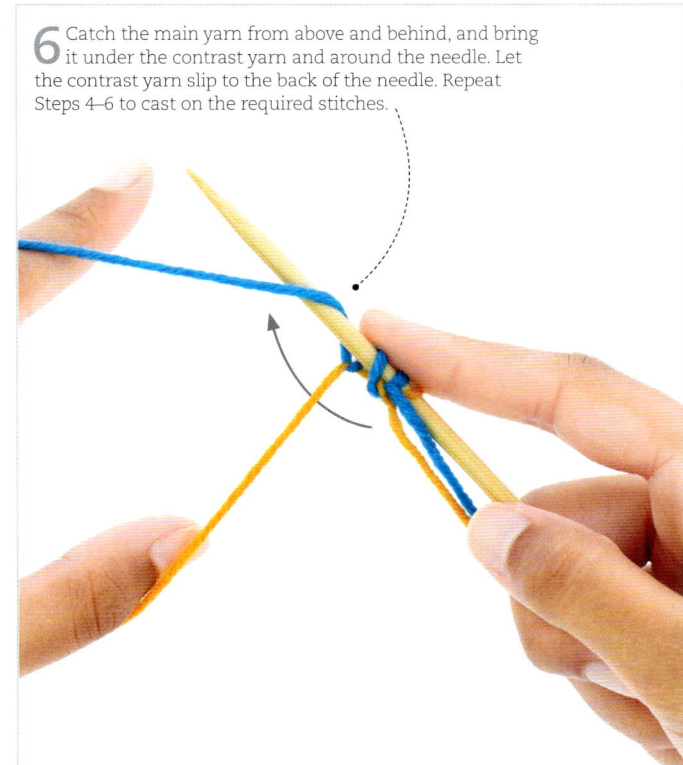

6. Catch the main yarn from above and behind, and bring it under the contrast yarn and around the needle. Let the contrast yarn slip to the back of the needle. Repeat Steps 4–6 to cast on the required stitches.

7. Drop the contrast slip knot at the end of the cast-on. Tie the contrast ends together until you want to pull the contrast yarn out and pick up the "live" open stitches. Knit into the front of the first row.

DOUBLE-SIDED CAST-ON

This cast-on is used to create two rows of stitches across opposite needles. It is ideal for working toe-up socks (see p.236) or for double knitting (see p.136). Allow a length of yarn at least three times the cast-on width. Position both needle tips pointing left.

1 Holding the yarn from the ball over your left-hand thumb, and the yarn tail with your index finger, lay the yarn over the bottom needle. This loop will later form the cast-on stitch.

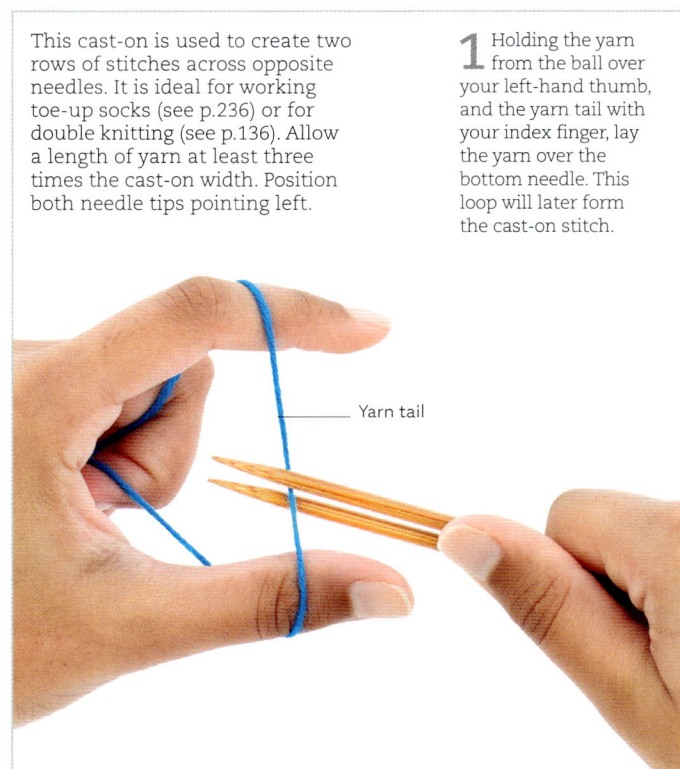

Yarn tail

2 Bring the working yarn up behind the bottom needle and in front of the top needle. Bring your left hand down behind the needles, laying the working yarn over and around the top needle. This has cast on a second stitch – there will now be one on the top needle and one on the bottom needle.

3 To cast on the next stitch to the top needle, bring the tail up between the needles. Bring the working yarn up behind the bottom needle and in front of the top needle, as in Step 1. Bring your hand down behind the needles; you will now have two stitches on each needle.

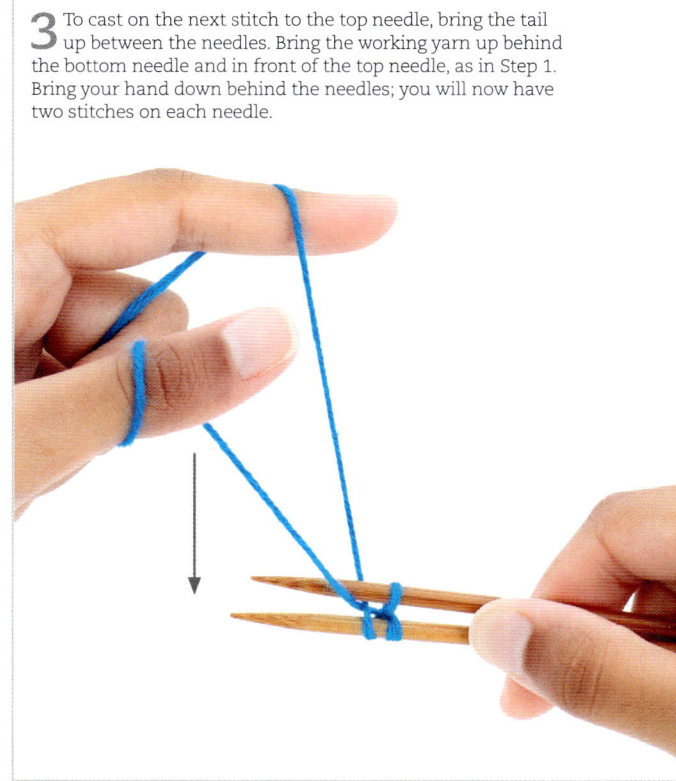

4 Repeat Steps 2 and 3 until you have the desired number of stitches, with an equal number on both needles. When ready to work on the cast-on edge, begin knitting across the lower needle using the working yarn.

CROCHET PROVISIONAL CAST-ON

1. Make a slip knot on a crochet hook with contrast yarn. Hold the yarn and needle in the left hand and hook in the right. Take the yarn behind the needle and over the left index finger. Hold the needle and hook crossed, with the hook in front. Lay the yarn in the hook with left index finger.

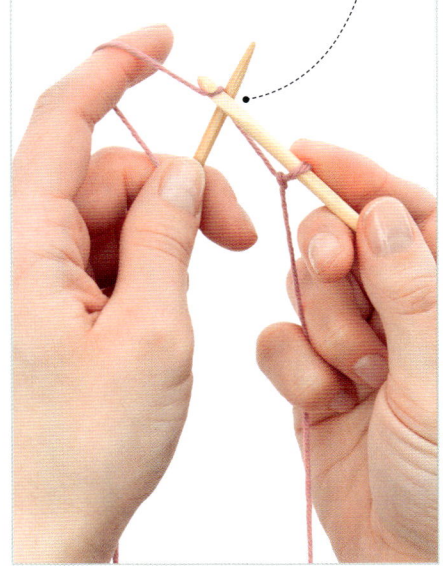

2. Pull the yarn through the slip knot – it will loop over the needle making a stitch. Take the yarn behind the needle and make another loop. Continue to cast on the required stitches. Cut the yarn and pull it through the last chain on the hook. Mark this end so it is clear which end will unravel.

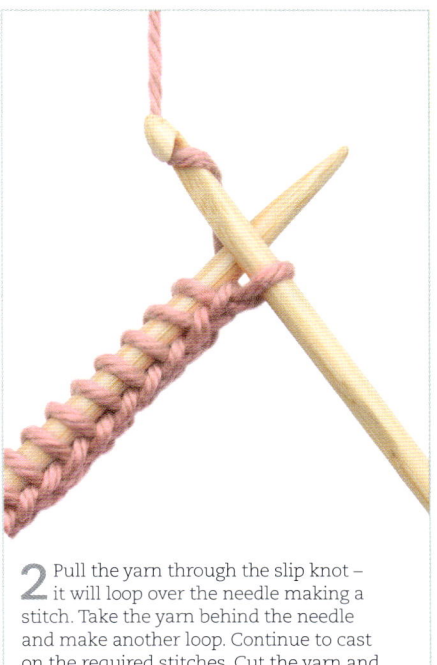

3. Work your knitting. When ready to work on the cast-on edge, pull the marked thread back out of the last chain after which the whole chain can be unravelled and the "live" open stitches picked up.

ITALIAN CAST-ON (also called *Invisible cast-on*)

This is good for single rib, but can become wavy if over-stretched. Use needles at least two sizes smaller than those used for the main fabric.

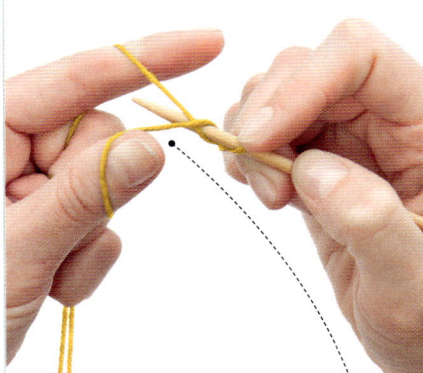

1. Hold yarn and needles as for Double cast-on (see p.57), but with the palm facing down, creating a "V" of yarn pointing to the right.

2. Bring the needle forwards, passing over and back under the inner thumb strand.

3. Catch the index-finger strand, going over and back towards you.

4. Turn your thumb away from you in a circular movement, flicking the thumb strand over the needle. Bring the left hand back to its original position, passing the yarn under the needle.

5. Make sure that the stitch goes all the way around the needle, and that it lies centrally under the needle.

6. Take the needle back over and under the index finger strand. With the needle towards you, take it over and back under the thumb strand.

7. Move your left index finger towards you in a circular movement, passing the yarn over the needle, and return your hand to its original position, making sure the stitch goes all the way around the needle. Repeat Steps 2–7 to cast on an even number of stitches.

The stitches must lie under the needle

8. At the end, wrap the two strands around each other under the needle. Knit the first row by knitting into the back of the first stitch, bring the yarn to the front and slip the next stitch purlwise. Repeat along the row. Work two or four rows of tubular knitting before starting the main fabric. Do not knit into the back of the stitches.

ALTERNATIVE ROLL-EDGE TUBULAR CAST-ON

1 Using a smooth yarn, work a Crochet provisional cast-on (see p.65) of half the required stitches plus one. In the main colour and on small-sized needles, knit three rows of stocking stitch, starting with a knit row and ending with the wrong side facing.

2 Purl one stitch and take the yarn to the back. Insert the right needle tip from top to bottom through the purl bar of the main colour bar at the colour join three rows down.

3 Insert the left needle from front to back into the picked-up stitch. Knit into the front of the stitch. Bring the yarn to the front. Repeat Steps 2 and 3 until the row is complete. Finish with a purl stitch, and no pick-up.

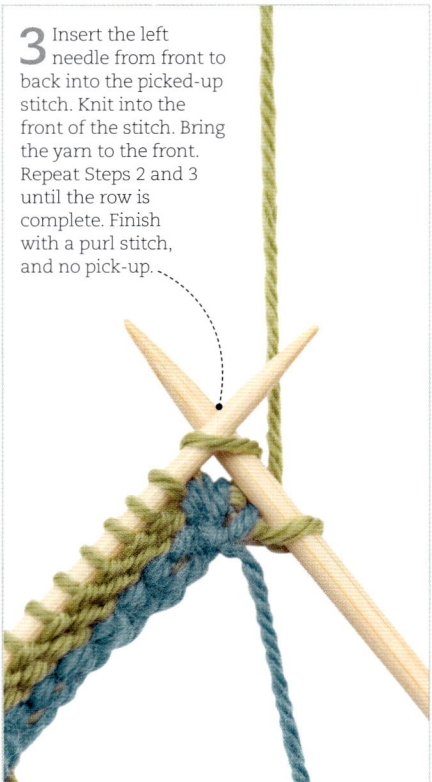

4 Change to the main needles. This cast-on makes an odd number of stitches. A single rib will have a knit stitch at each end and must be worked with rows starting as follows: knit one, purl one; then the next row purl one, knit one; and so on. Decrease one at the end of the ribbing or when convenient. Remove the Crochet provisional cast-on.

KNOTTED CAST-ON

This cast-on makes a strong, decorative edge. It can be tight, so work loosely on thick needles.

1 Make a slip knot on the needle and cast on one stitch using the Double cast-on (see p.57).

2 Hold the second needle in the left hand, insert it into the slip knot and pass this over the last stitch made and off the right needle.

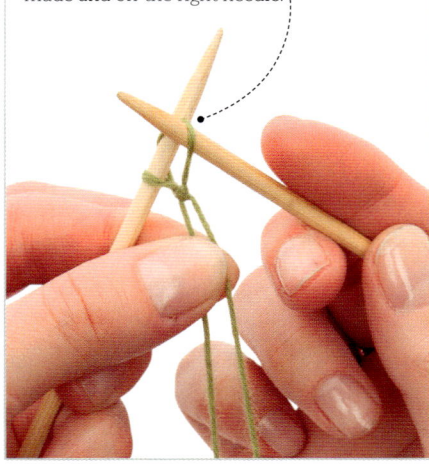

3 Repeat, casting on two stitches and passing the first over the second to the required length of cast-on. The Single cast-on (see p.53) may be substituted for a double cast-on if preferred. The first stitch of the first row should always be knitted.

TWICE-KNITTED CAST-ON

Excellent for fringed edges and before twice-knitted work. Always knit the first stitch of the first row.

1 Working loosely, make a slip knot and cast on one stitch using the Knit-on method (see p.54).

2 Insert the right needle into both loops and knit together, but do not slip stitches off. Slip the new loop from the right needle to the left. Knit the new stitch together with the preceding stitch. Repeat Step 2 to cast on the required stitches.

EDGING CAST-ON

1. Knit a piece of narrow edging to the required length of your cast-on. If you are unsure of the correct length, slip stitches onto a holder at the end (see p.69) and alter as necessary.

2. Work along the right edge, right-side facing. Hold the new yarn at the back. Insert the needle tip from front to back through the first edge stitch, wrap the yarn around the needle, and pull a loop through to the front.

3. Continue along the full length of the edge, picking up the new yarn evenly to form stitches on the needle. If necessary, miss out some rows to prevent the cast-on distorting.

4. Knit the main fabric upwards from the edge trim as required. Start with a purl row if the main fabric is stocking stitch.

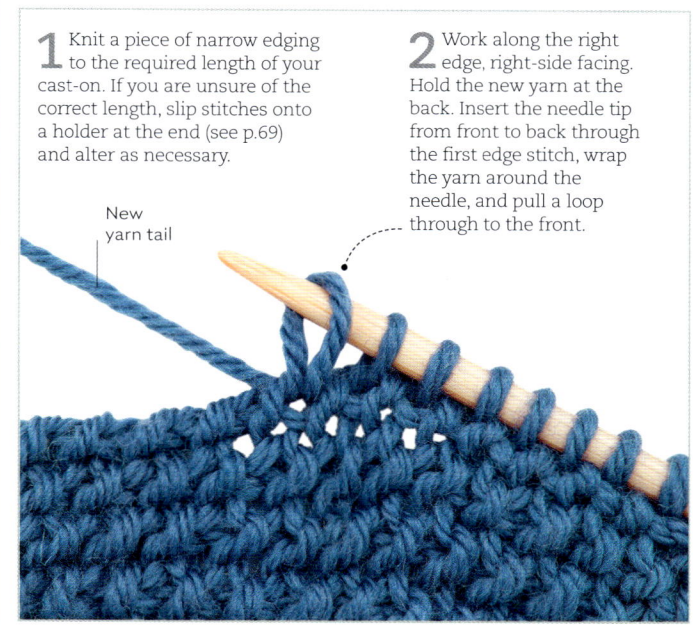

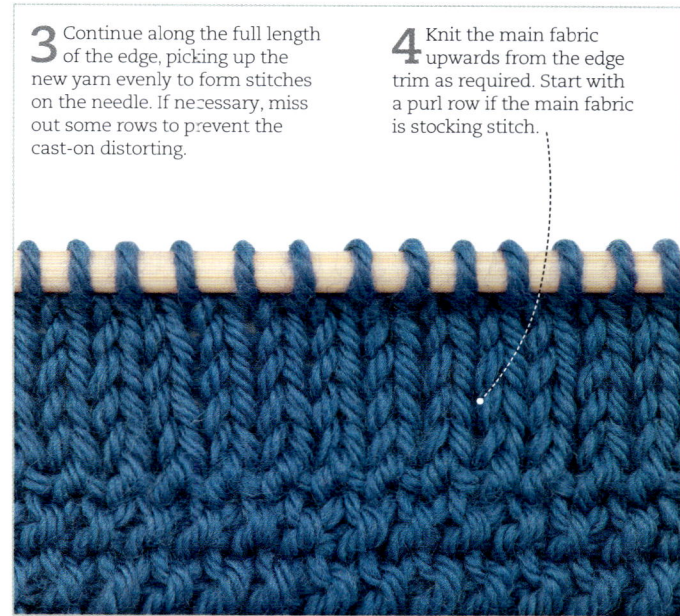

DISAPPEARING LOOP CAST-ON

This cast-on is great when you intend to work outward from a centre point, like the top of a hat.

1. Using double-pointed needles, make a small loop of yarn – with the ball end crossing over the tail end – securing where the yarns cross with your fingers.

2. Holding the needle in your right hand, insert the needle tip into the loop from front to back, wrap the yarn around the needle tip anticlockwise and bring it back through the loop.

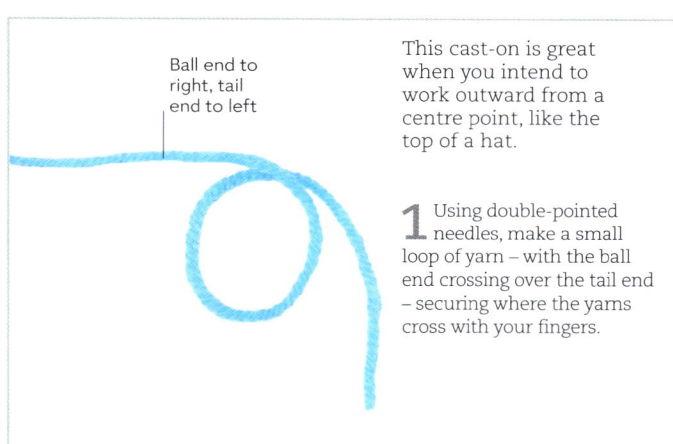
Ball end to right, tail end to left

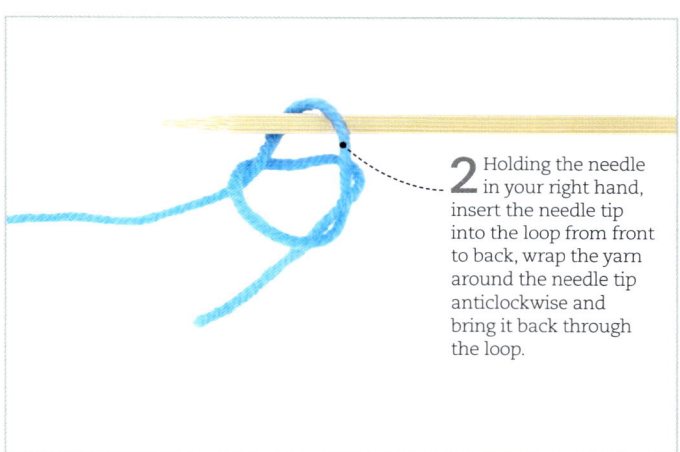

3. Without inserting the needle into the loop, wrap the yarn around the needle tip anticlockwise, pass the first loop over the second loop and then drop it off the needle using your fingers or a second needle. This is the first stitch cast on.

4. Repeat Steps 2 and 3 until you have the number of stitches needed for the pattern. Tug the end of the yarn to tighten and continue to knit in the round on the cast-on stitches.

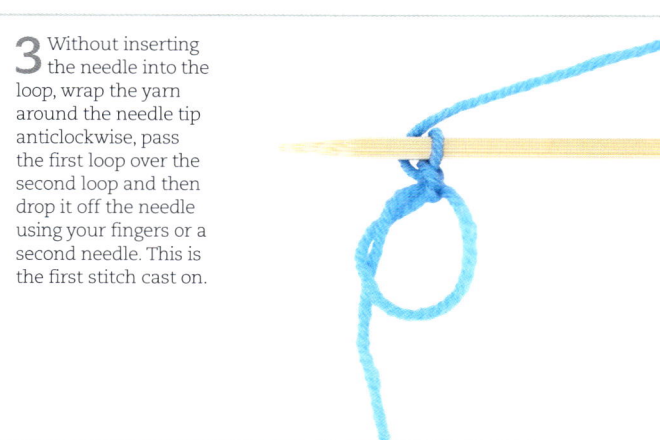

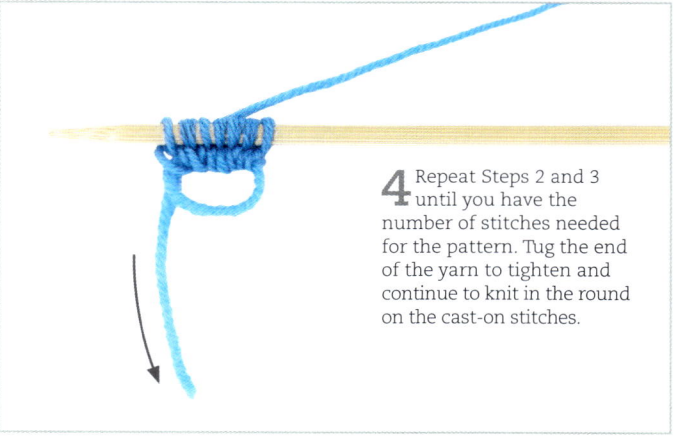

SIMPLE CAST-OFFS

When your piece of knitted fabric is complete you need to close off the loops so that they can't unravel. This is called casting off the stitches. Always take yarn to the back before casting off both knit and purl stitches. If instructed to retain stitches for future use, slip your stitches onto a spare needle or a stitch holder.

CASTING OFF KNITWISE

1 Begin by knitting the first two stitches. Then insert the tip of the left needle from left to right through the first stitch and lift this stitch up and over the second stitch and off the right needle.

2 To cast off the next stitch, knit one more stitch and repeat Step 1. Continue until only one stitch remains on the right needle. (If your pattern says "cast off in pattern", work the stitches in the specified pattern as you cast off.)

3 To stop the last stitch from unravelling, cut the yarn, leaving a yarn tail 20cm (8in) long, which is long enough to darn into the knitting later. (Alternatively, leave a much longer yarn end to use for a future seam.) Pass the yarn end through the remaining loop and pull tight to close the loop. This is called fastening off.

CASTING OFF PURLWISE

1 Purl two stitches, then take the yarn to the back. Insert the tip of the left needle into the first stitch and pass it over the second stitch and off the right needle.

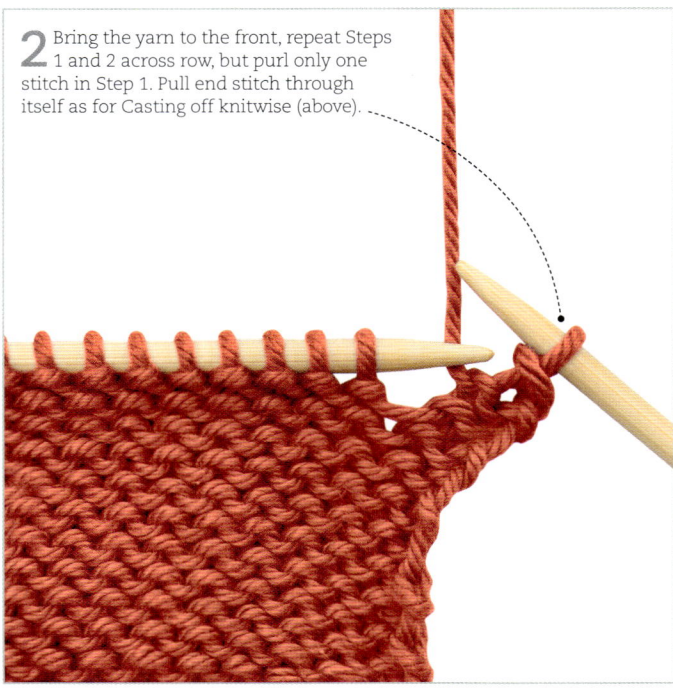

2 Bring the yarn to the front, repeat Steps 1 and 2 across row, but purl only one stitch in Step 1. Pull end stitch through itself as for Casting off knitwise (above).

ALTERNATIVE CAST-OFFS

Try using one of these casting-off techniques to complement a project. Consider using a contrast colour – in a basic cast-off or in combination with a decorative style. Cast-offs are included that give more stretch to ribs or loosen an edge, and an adaptation of the Three-needle cast-off (see p.70) may even be used to join pockets and hems.

SLIPPING STITCHES OFF THE NEEDLE

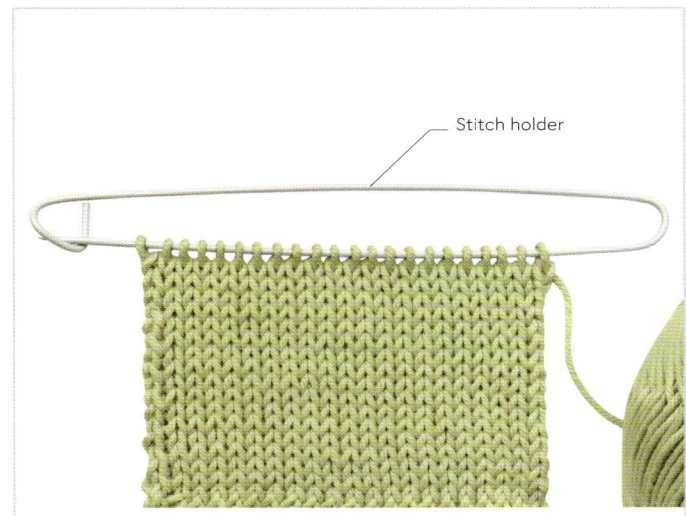

Using a stitch holder: If you are setting stitches aside to work on later, your instructions will tell you whether to cut the yarn or keep it attached to the ball. Carefully slip your stitches onto a stitch holder large enough to hold all the stitches. If you are only slipping a few stitches, use a safety pin.

Using a length of yarn: If you don't have a stitch holder or don't have one large enough, you can use a length of cotton yarn instead. Using a blunt-ended yarn needle, pass the yarn through the stitches as you slip them off the knitting needle. Knot the ends of the cotton yarn together.

CASTING OFF IN RIB EFFECT

Use after a single rib fabric to maintain the rib corrugations. This method adds a little more stretch than casting off in either all knit or all purl.

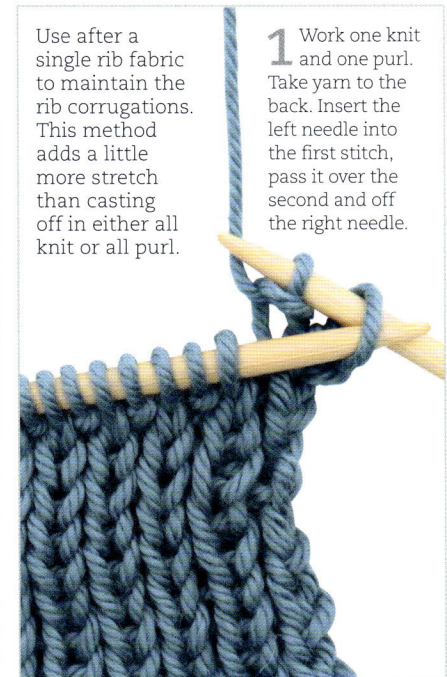

1 Work one knit and one purl. Take yarn to the back. Insert the left needle into the first stitch, pass it over the second and off the right needle.

2 Knit the next stitch then pass the first stitch over the second and off the right needle as before.

3 Bring the yarn to the front and purl next stitch, then take yarn to the back and pass the last stitch over the second. Repeat Steps 2 and 3 across the row. Pull the final stitch through itself to fasten off.

70 TECHNIQUES

SUSPENDED CAST-OFF (also called *Delayed cast-off*)

This is ideal after lace knitting.

1 Knit the first two stitches (this starts the row and is not repeated). Insert the left needle tip into the first stitch and pass it over the second and off the right tip. Do not drop it from the left tip.

2 Bring the right needle across the front of the "suspended" stitch, and knit the first stitch on the left needle.

3 Slip both loops off together as you complete the knit stitch. Continue passing and knitting stitches as in Steps 1 and 2 to the end of the cast-off.

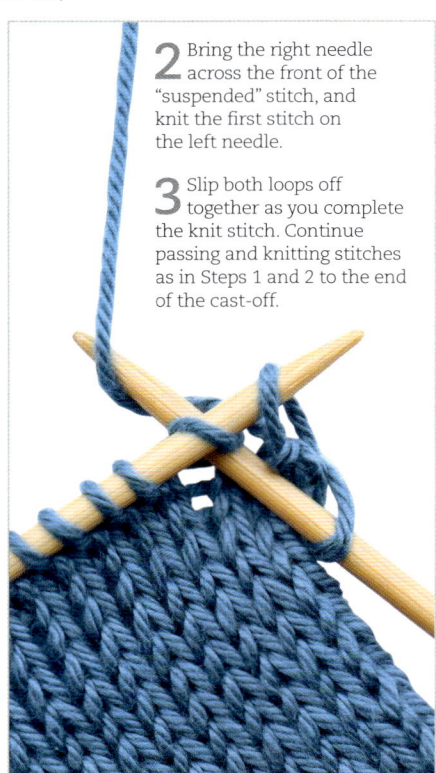

CROCHET CAST-OFF

1 Hold the yarn in your left hand and keep it at the back. Slip the first stitch purlwise onto the crochet hook.

2 Insert the hook into the next stitch and drop it from the left needle. Catch yarn with hook and pull through both stitches. Repeat across the row, pulling the end loop through itself to fasten off.

THREE-NEEDLE CAST-OFF

This technique can be worked with the right side facing as a normal seam, or with the wrong side facing (as here) to form a decorative seam.

1 Hold the needles with the stitches to be joined together with the wrong sides facing each other. Insert a third needle through the centre of the first stitch on each needle and knit these two stitches together.

2 Continue to knit together one stitch from each needle as you cast off the stitches in the usual way. (A contrasting yarn is used here to show the seam clearly.)

3 When the pieces of knitting are opened out, you will see that this technique forms a raised chain along the seam.

ALTERNATIVE CAST-OFFS 71

PICOT POINT CAST-OFF

Where there is a seam, cast off the first stitch to leave a selvedge before starting the picot edge.

1 Knit two stitches, insert the left needle into the first stitch on the right needle and pass it over the second stitch and off the right needle (Casting off knitwise, see p.68).

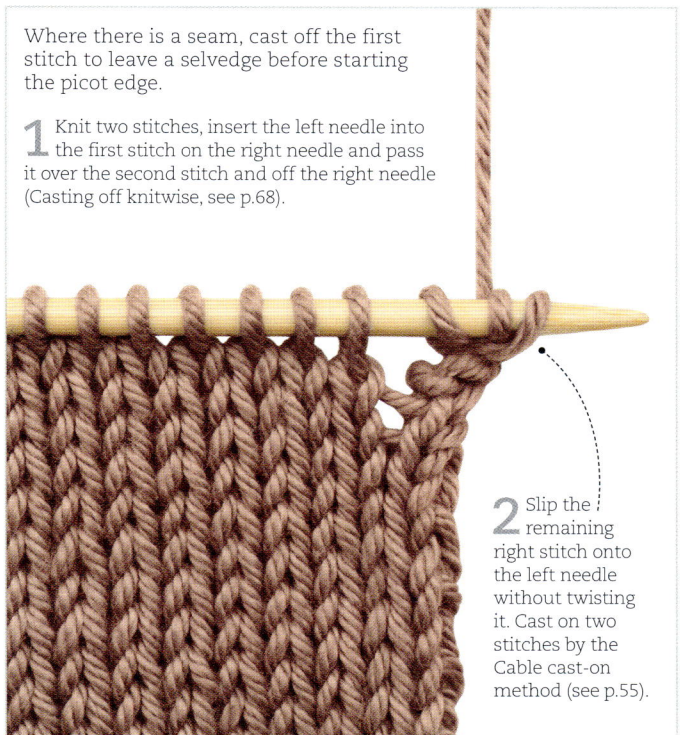

2 Slip the remaining right stitch onto the left needle without twisting it. Cast on two stitches by the Cable cast-on method (see p.55).

3 Cast off three stitches knitwise as described in Step 1. Cast off another two stitches. (These form the straight edge between the picots points.)

4 Repeat Steps 2 and 3 across the row.

Lamb's tail edge

Twisted tail

5 A lamb's tail edge can be made by casting on more stitches in Step 2 (the longer example shown has 20 stitches cast on). However many you choose, always cast off one more stitch in Step 3 than you cast on. To make the tails twist, as shown centre, cast off tighter than you cast on.

6 To use contrast colour for the picots, work the last row of the main fabric in contrast (purl row in stocking stitch). To prevent the edge rolling to the knit side, work the last two rows of the main fabric in garter stitch or moss stitch. For a clean colour join introduce contrast yarn on the knit row before you start the garter or moss stitch. A picot cast-on can also be worked using this method of casting on and casting off the extra stitches between making each group of Contrast edge cast-on stitches (see p.59).

TWO-ROW CAST-OFF

1 Work on an even number of stitches. Knit the first stitch and purl the second. With the yarn at the back, insert the left needle in the first stitch and pass it over the second stitch and off the right needle.

2 Knit and purl the next two stitches on the left needle. Take yarn to back. Pass the second (knit) stitch over the third (purl) stitch on the right needle to cast off one stitch.

3 Repeat Step 2 across the row. This leaves you with half the number of original stitches on the needle. Cut the yarn leaving a tail. Do not turn the work.

4 Slip the last stitch on the right needle onto the left needle without twisting it, slip the next stitch in the same way. Pass the second stitch along on the left needle over the last stitch.

5 Repeat across the row, slipping only one stitch each time. Sew the last stitch in with a blunt-ended darning needle and a separate piece of yarn.

DECREASE CAST-OFF

A decorative cast-off, this is stretchier than casting off knitwise and so is useful for single ribs.

Insert the tip of the right needle into the front of the first two stitches on the left needle and knit them together. Slip the new stitch on the right needle back onto the left without twisting it. Repeat across the row, pulling the thread through the last stitch to secure the end.

ALTERNATIVE CAST-OFFS **73**

TUBULAR CAST-OFF

This cast-off is almost invisible and is a perfect match to the Italian cast-on (see p.65). After completing each sewing action, pull the yarn through to draw the stitches lightly together.

1 In preparation, in single rib fabric work two rows as follows; knit one, bring the yarn forward, slip the next (purl stitch) purlwise, take the yarn back. Repeat across the row. Cut the yarn leaving four times the length to be cast off and thread onto a blunt-ended darning needle. Hold the knitting needle with yarn tail on the right.

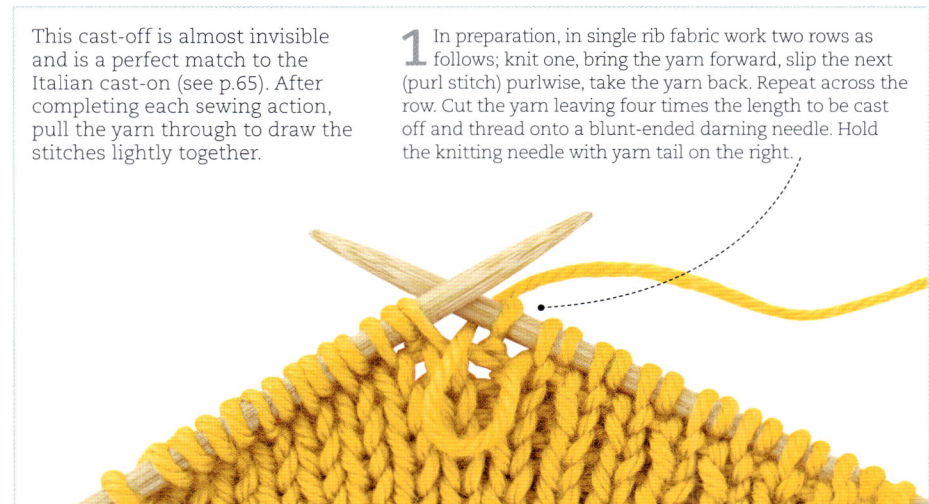

2 Insert the sewing needle into the first stitch (a knit stitch) knitwise, and drop it from the needle.

The needle goes from left to right

3 Miss the new first stitch, and insert the needle purlwise into the new second stitch (knit stitch).

The needle goes from right to left

4 Take the needle to the right and insert it purlwise into the first stitch (a purl stitch). Drop this stitch off the needle.

5 Take the sewing needle to the back and insert it from back to front between the new first and second stitches on the knitting needle.

The needle comes through from front to back

6 Insert the sewing needle knitwise through the second stitch (a purl stitch), taking it through to the back of the work. Repeat Steps 2–6 along the row. Sew in the ends.

7 The completed cast off.

VERY STRETCHY SINGLE-RIB CAST-OFF

1 On a single rib fabric, make a yarnover then work the knit stitch at the start of the row.

2 Insert the left needle in the first stitch on the right needle. Lift it over the second stitch and off.

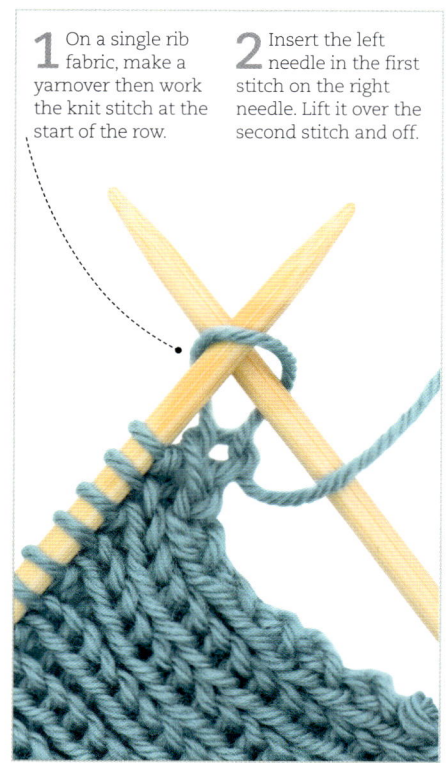

3 Bring the yarn to the front. Take it away from you over the top of the needle and back to the front. Purl the next stitch. There will be three stitches on the right needle.

4 Take yarn to back. Slip the first and second stitches on the right needle over the third and off.

5 Wrap the yarn round the needle and knit the next stitch. Slip the first and second stitches on the right needle over the third and off. Repeat Steps 3–5 along the row.

EDGING CAST-OFF

For a smooth join into a contrast edge on stocking stitch, knit the last row of the main fabric in the contrast colour. A third needle is needed for this technique.

1 Using the spare needle, cast on three stitches in contrast yarn. Work two rows of edging pattern, ending on a right-side (RS) row and stopping before the last stitch.

2 Take the needle with the stitches to be cast off in your left hand. Slip the last stitch of the edging purlwise from the right-hand needle onto the left-hand needle.

3 Knit the edging stitch and main colour stitch together through the back of both loops.

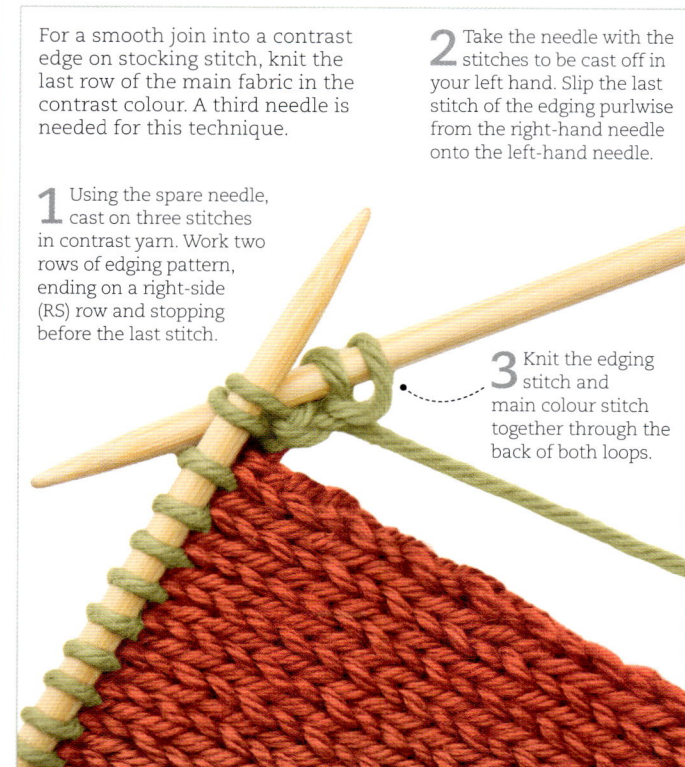

4 Turn the work. With the yarn in front, slip the first edging stitch from the left to the right needle without twisting. Work a wrong-side (WS) row along the remaining edging stitches according to the pattern.

5 Take the needle with the stitches to be cast off in your left hand. Slip the last stitch of the edging purlwise from the right-hand needle onto the left-hand needle.

CROCHET CHAIN LOOP CAST-OFF

This decorative cast-off helps prevent edges from stretching, particularly on lacy knitting.

1 The stitches should be divisible by four. Hold the stitches (right side facing you) in your left hand. Slip the first stitch onto a crochet hook.

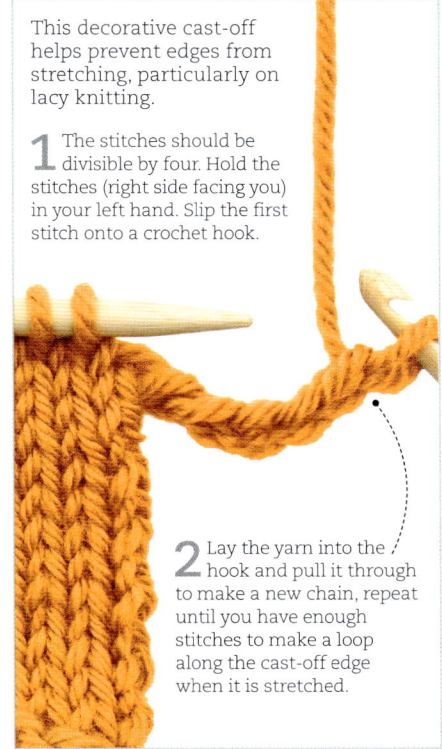

2 Lay the yarn into the hook and pull it through to make a new chain, repeat until you have enough stitches to make a loop along the cast-off edge when it is stretched.

3 Insert the hook into the first four stitches on the needle. Slip them onto the hook. Lay yarn into the hook and pull a loop through all four stitches.

4 Lay yarn into the hook and make another chain through both loops on the hook. Repeat Steps 2–4 across the edge, catching four stitches each time at Step 3.

SMOOTH DIAGONAL CAST-OFF

This example assumes you are working a pattern with a diagonal edge to cast off in groups of five (such as a shoulder seam).

1 Cast off four stitches using the Casting-off knitwise method (see p.68), leaving the last stitch of the cast-off on the right needle.

The last two stitches

2 Knit to the end of the row on the left needle, turn the work and purl until there are only two stitches remaining on the left needle.

3 Purl these two stitches together. Turn the work. Repeat Steps 2–4 until the cast-off length is completed.

BASIC KNIT AND PURL FABRICS

Simple knitting is made up of two basic stitches – knit and purl. Once you can work these with ease, you will be able to work common stitch patterns – garter stitch, stocking stitch, and single ribbing. The varied properties of these fabrics are why stocking stitch (and its reverse) are often used for garments and garter stitch and single ribs for edgings.

GARTER STITCH (Abbreviation = *g st*)

Knit right-side (RS) rows: Garter stitch is the easiest of all knitted fabrics as all rows are worked in knit stitches. When the right side of the fabric is facing you, knit all the stitches in the row.

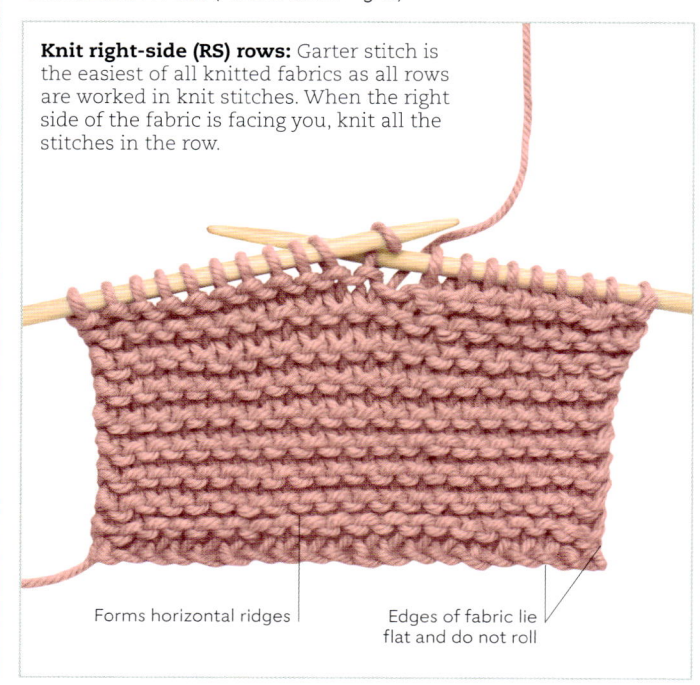

Forms horizontal ridges | Edges of fabric lie flat and do not roll

Knit wrong-side (WS) rows: When the wrong side of the fabric is facing you, knit all the stitches in the row. The resulting fabric is soft, textured, and slightly stretchy.

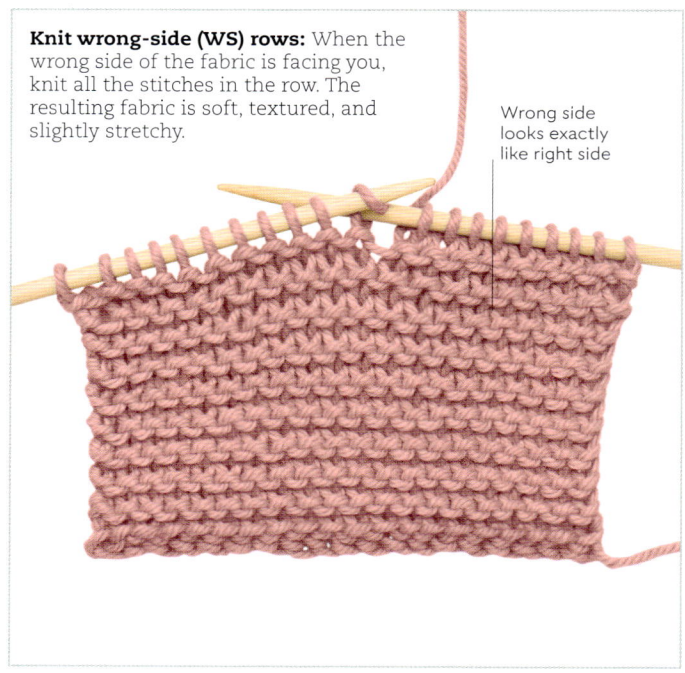

Wrong side looks exactly like right side

STOCKING STITCH (Abbreviation = *st st*)

Knit right-side (RS) rows: Stocking stitch is formed by working alternate rows of knit and purl stitches. When the right side is facing you, knit all the stitches in the row.

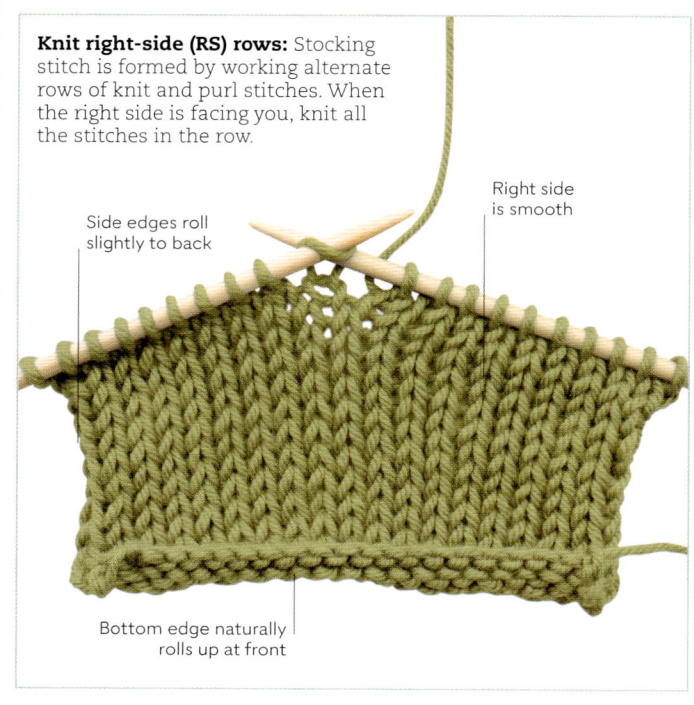

Side edges roll slightly to back | Right side is smooth | Bottom edge naturally rolls up at front

Purl wrong-side (WS) rows: When the wrong side is facing you, purl all the stitches in the row. The wrong side is often referred to as the "purl side" of the knitting.

Wrong side is knobbly

BASIC KNIT AND PURL FABRICS **77**

REVERSE STOCKING STITCH (Abbreviation = *rev st st*)

Purl right-side (RS) rows: Reverse stocking stitch is formed exactly like stocking stitch but the sides are reversed. When the right side is facing you, purl all the stitches in the row.

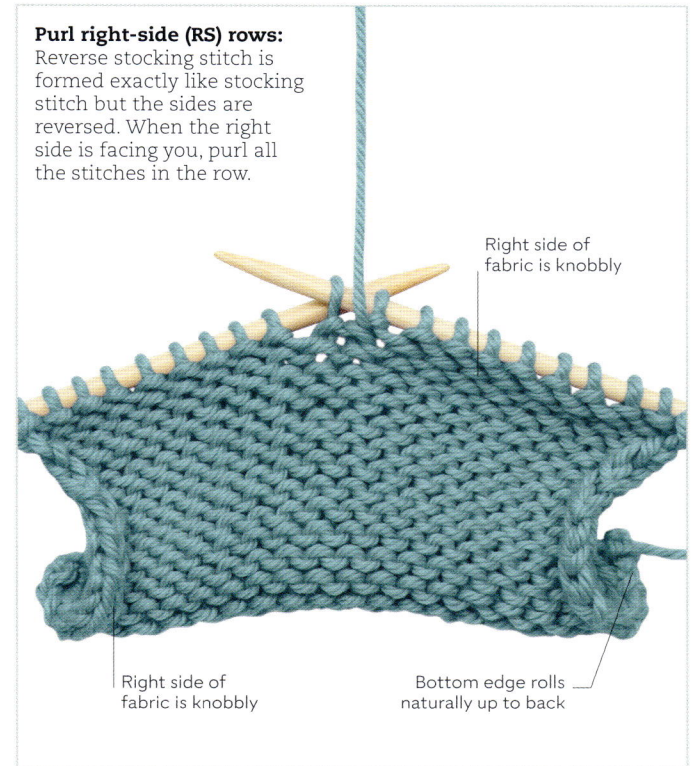

Right side of fabric is knobbly

Right side of fabric is knobbly

Bottom edge rolls naturally up to back

Knit wrong-side (WS) rows: When the wrong side is facing you, knit all the stitches in the row.

Wrong side of fabric is smooth

SINGLE RIBBING (Abbreviation = *k1, p1 rib*)

Right-side (RS) rows: Single ribbing is formed by working alternate knit and purl stitches. After a knit stitch, take the yarn to the front of the knitting between the two needles to purl the next stitch. After a purl stitch, take the yarn to the back between the two needles to knit the next stitch.

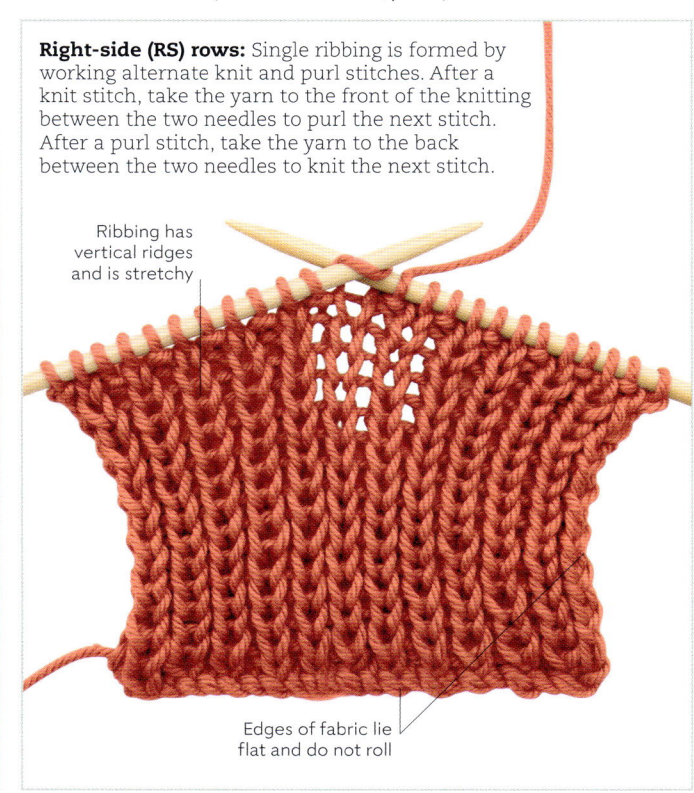

Ribbing has vertical ridges and is stretchy

Edges of fabric lie flat and do not roll

Wrong-side (WS) rows: On the wrong-side rows, knit all the knit stitches that are facing you and purl all the purl stitches. Work the following rows in the same way to form thin columns of alternating single knit and purl stitches.

Wrong side looks exactly like right side

THE FIRST BASIC STITCH – KNIT STITCH Abbreviation = k

Choose Single, Knit-on, or Cable cast-on (see pp.53–55) and start with garter stitch, which uses only knit stitch. Experiment with stripes and different yarns before you learn purl stitch (opposite). The odd dropped stitch doesn't matter, just put a safety pin through it so it does not drop further and sew it in later.

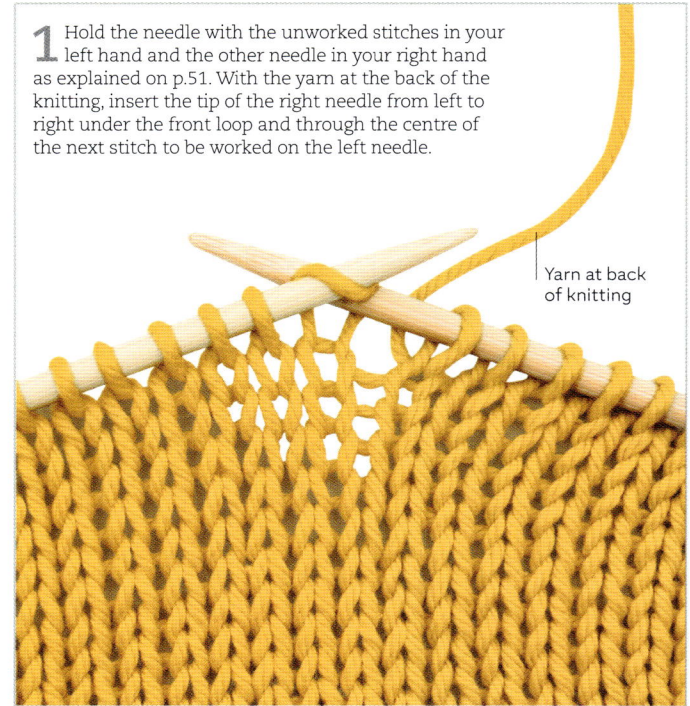

1 Hold the needle with the unworked stitches in your left hand and the other needle in your right hand as explained on p.51. With the yarn at the back of the knitting, insert the tip of the right needle from left to right under the front loop and through the centre of the next stitch to be worked on the left needle.

Yarn at back of knitting

2 Wrap the yarn under and around the tip of the right needle, keeping an even tension as the yarn slips through your fingers.

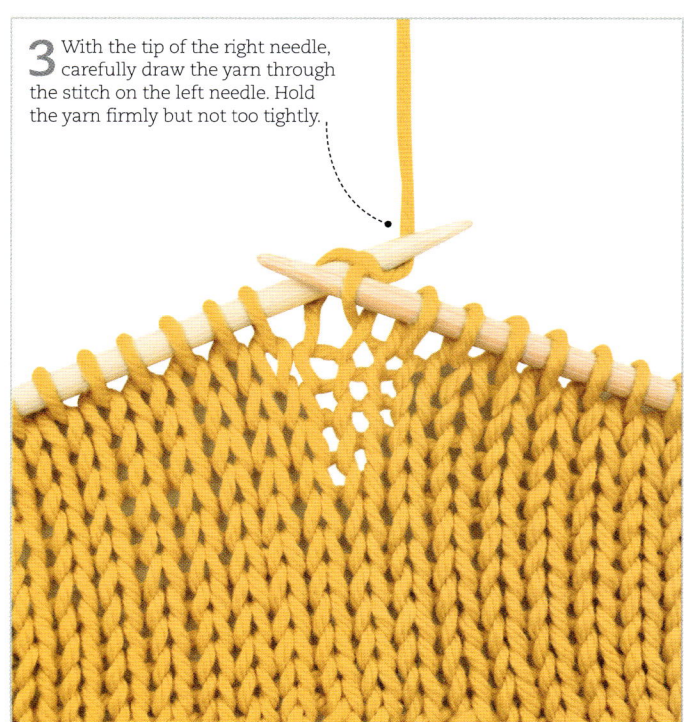

3 With the tip of the right needle, carefully draw the yarn through the stitch on the left needle. Hold the yarn firmly but not too tightly.

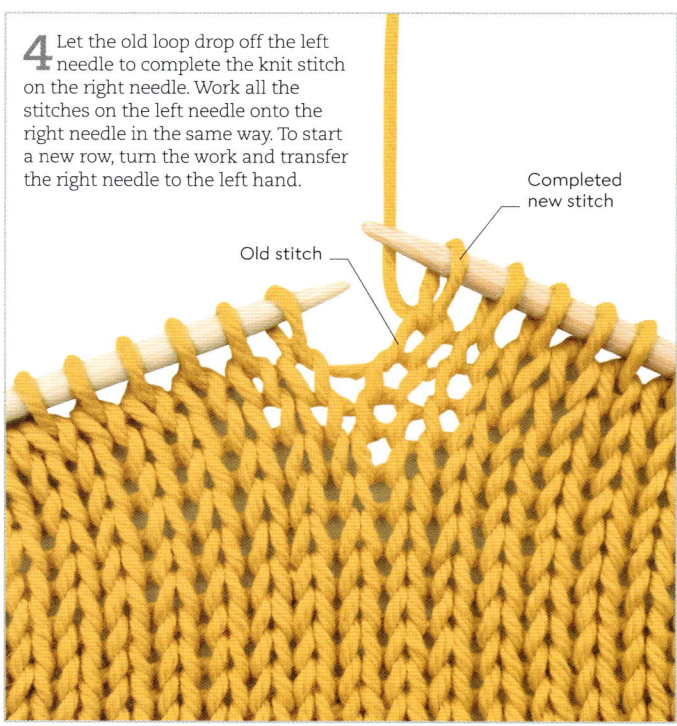

4 Let the old loop drop off the left needle to complete the knit stitch on the right needle. Work all the stitches on the left needle onto the right needle in the same way. To start a new row, turn the work and transfer the right needle to the left hand.

Completed new stitch

Old stitch

THE SECOND BASIC STITCH – PURL STITCH Abbreviation = p

The purl stitch is a little more difficult than knit stitch, but like knit stitch it becomes effortless after a little practice. Once you are a seasoned knitter, you will feel as if your hands would know how to work these basic stitches in your sleep. Work your first purl row after you have cast on and knitted a few rows of garter stitch. You may find your tension alters on purl stitches, so try holding your yarn a little tighter or looser to compensate.

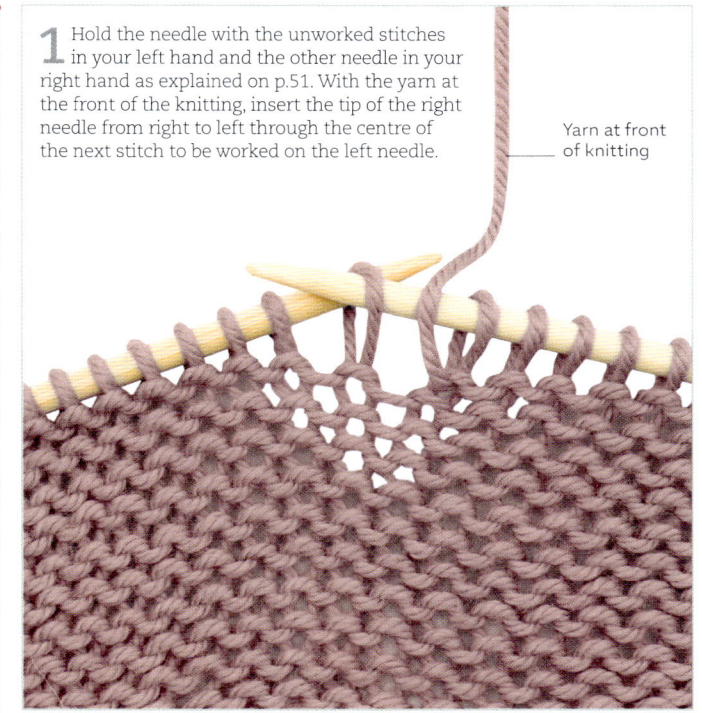

1 Hold the needle with the unworked stitches in your left hand and the other needle in your right hand as explained on p.51. With the yarn at the front of the knitting, insert the tip of the right needle from right to left through the centre of the next stitch to be worked on the left needle.

Yarn at front of knitting

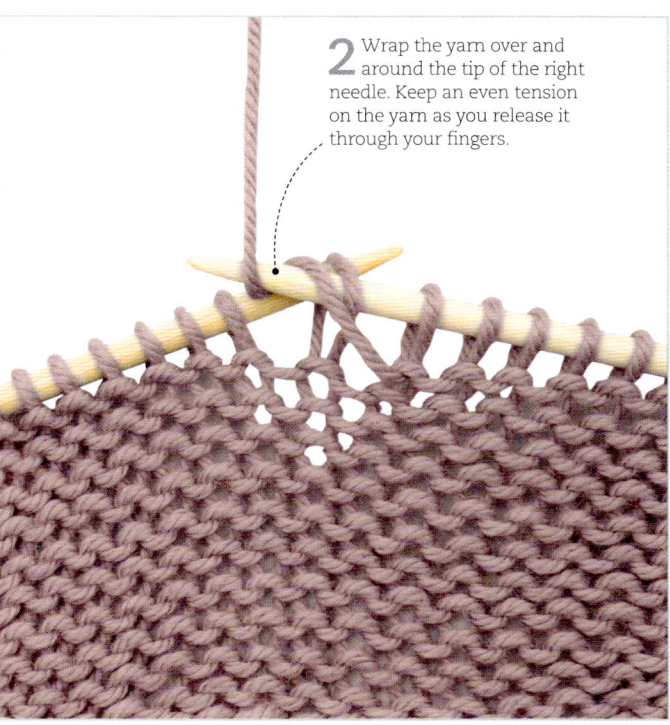

2 Wrap the yarn over and around the tip of the right needle. Keep an even tension on the yarn as you release it through your fingers.

3 With the tip of the right needle, carefully draw the yarn through the stitch on the left needle. Keep your hands relaxed and allow the yarn to slip through your fingers in a gently controlled manner.

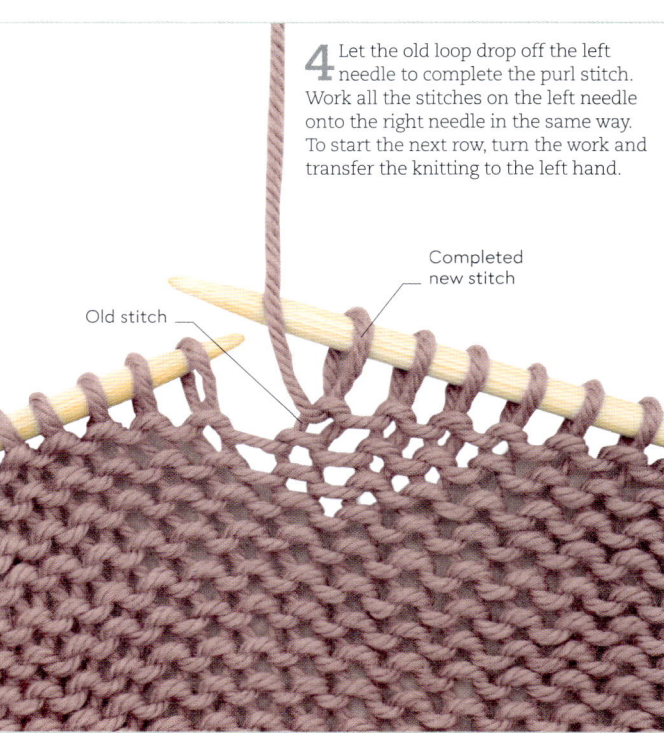

4 Let the old loop drop off the left needle to complete the purl stitch. Work all the stitches on the left needle onto the right needle in the same way. To start the next row, turn the work and transfer the knitting to the left hand.

Completed new stitch

Old stitch

Preparing and repairing

These useful tips will help both absolute beginners and more advanced knitters to prepare and complete their work with ease. Joining in a new ball of yarn can be tricky, resulting in uneven stitches, and few knitters enjoy sewing in yarn ends. However, learning to do these jobs efficiently and neatly will reward you with a professional finish.

WINDING AND JOINING YARNS

Knowing how to wind a hank into a ball is a useful skill, especially as many luxury yarns are sold as hanks. Joining a new ball of yarn when the first has run out, or a colour change is necessary, is a little daunting at first but easy to master.

WINDING A HANK INTO A BALL

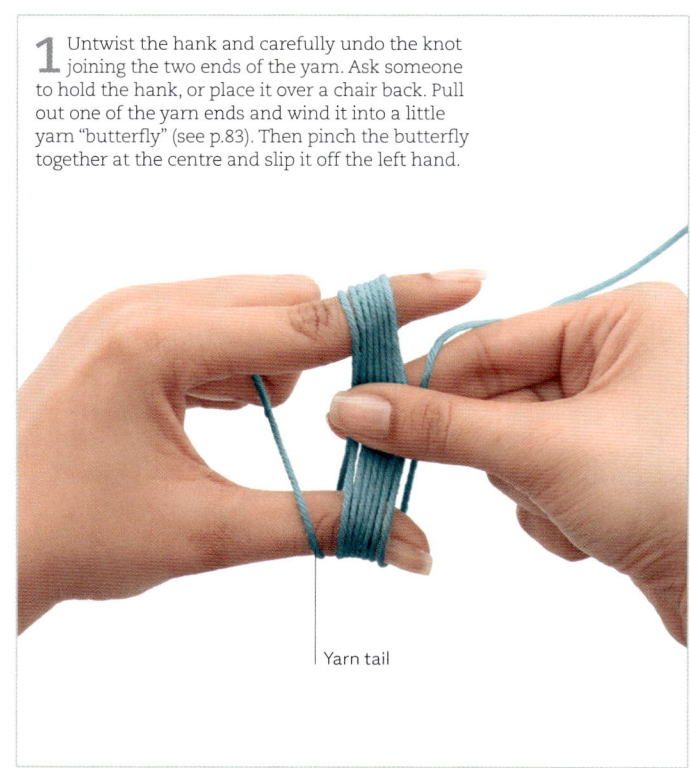

1 Untwist the hank and carefully undo the knot joining the two ends of the yarn. Ask someone to hold the hank, or place it over a chair back. Pull out one of the yarn ends and wind it into a little yarn "butterfly" (see p.83). Then pinch the butterfly together at the centre and slip it off the left hand.

Yarn tail

2 Start wrapping the yarn around the butterfly and the thumb to create a hole in the centre of the ball. Keep winding until the whole hank is used up. Be sure to change the positioning of the wraps frequently to keep the ball round. Secure the yarn end under a few of the outer wraps. When you start knitting, pull the butterfly out of the centre and use this end. Pulling the yarn from inside stops the ball rolling around.

To start using finished ball, pull butterfly from centre

▶ USING A BALL WINDER

- This is used to wind cake-shaped balls of yarn, so can be a great addition to your knitting tools. Skeins of yarn need to be wound into balls before working, which you can either do by hand (see above), or by using an automatic, or hand-wound ball winder. Place your skein over a swift (p.45) – or a willing, spare pair of hands – thread the yarn onto the winder, and just wind away. Very quickly, you will be able to create a nice tidy ball of yarn, ready to knit with. A ball winder is particularly handy if you want to split one ball of yarn into several smaller ones for colourwork techniques.

▶ WHEN TO JOIN ON A NEW YARN

- It's always good to have the new ball of yarn below you, such as on the floor in a knitting bag, so that you can spot ahead of time when the ball is running out. To calculate if there is enough yarn to complete two rows, fold the remaining yarn in half and make a slip knot at the fold. Knit the first row. If the knot comes before the end of the row you don't have enough yarn and need to join on a fresh ball. If so, just undo the slip knot and continue knitting, or use it to join in your new ball using one of the methods opposite.

WINDING AND JOINING YARNS **81**

JOINING A BALL

1. Always join on a new ball at the beginning of a row. Knot the new end of yarn onto the old yarn.

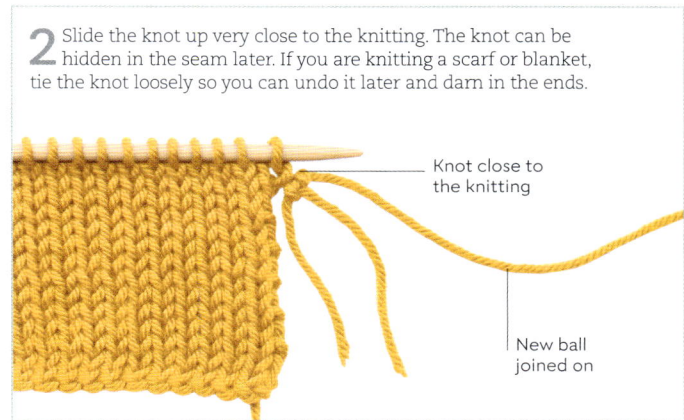

2. Slide the knot up very close to the knitting. The knot can be hidden in the seam later. If you are knitting a scarf or blanket, tie the knot loosely so you can undo it later and darn in the ends.

JOINING ON A NEW YARN – ALTERNATIVE METHOD

1. Lay the new yarn over the right needle with the old yarn tail. Knit the first stitch of the new row with both yarns. Drop the old yarn tail and continue with the new.

2. When the knitting is complete, unpick the second thread from the old yarn before darning the ends in with a blunt-ended darning needle.

CLASP WEFT JOIN

1. Fold the last 20cm (8in) or so of working yarn in half to create a loop, with the end held against the work. Knit the next few stitches with the folded yarn strand held together.

2. Interlink the new yarn through the loop and fold it back on itself a short way. Knit with the folded new yarn held together until it has been worked. Continue with a single strand of new yarn.

WEAVING AS YOU GO

1. Continue knitting with the last 20cm (8in) or so of yarn, while catching in the end of the new ball to secure it in place.

2. When only a short length of old yarn is left, begin knitting with the new ball catching in the end of the old ball. Darn in any long ends left along the reverse of the row (see p.83).

RUSSIAN JOIN

This secure join can be worked with any yarn but is easiest practised with DK and thicker yarn.

1 Close to the loop, work the needle along inside the plies of the new yarn. Once 4–5cm (1½–2in) of yarn has bunched up, push the point out of the yarn. Pull the needle so that the yarn tail emerges, and a small loop is left around the old yarn.

2 Repeat Step 1 using the old yarn. Gently pull the yarns to even out the bunched plies and smooth the join; then trim the ends.

NEEDLE JOIN

This join is smooth, strong, and almost invisible.

1 Work the needle along inside the plies of the old yarn, working away from the end, bunching plenty of yarn – at least 5cm (2in) – onto the needle. Push the needle out of the yarn and pull the yarn through. Remove the needle.

2 Thread the new yarn into the needle. Insert the needle as close as possible to where the yarns meet, and repeat Step 1. Gently pull the tails apart, then even out the bunched-up yarns with your fingers. Tails can be trimmed once the knitting is done.

FELTED YARN JOIN

1 This join can be done anywhere in the row, but only when using animal fibres such as wool or alpaca that have not been treated to become superwash, because this will prevent it felting. Begin by fraying a few cm (in) of the end on both the working yarn and the new yarn to be joined. Overlay them together, moisten the area where they overlap, and place the damp area between your palms.

2 Press the ends together firmly. Using a great deal of pressure, rub them backwards and forwards at speed until you can feel some heat being generated – it should begin to feel quite hot. Open your palms and check if the ends are firmly felted together. If not, moisten again and repeat the rubbing action until they are firmly merged with each other.

WINDING AND JOINING YARNS

WINDING UP A LONG YARN TAIL

A long loose end on your slip knot can start to get tangled when it is packed away. To keep it tidy, wind it into a yarn "butterfly" close to your knitting.

1 Starting close to the knitting, wrap the yarn around your thumb and forefinger in a figure of eight.

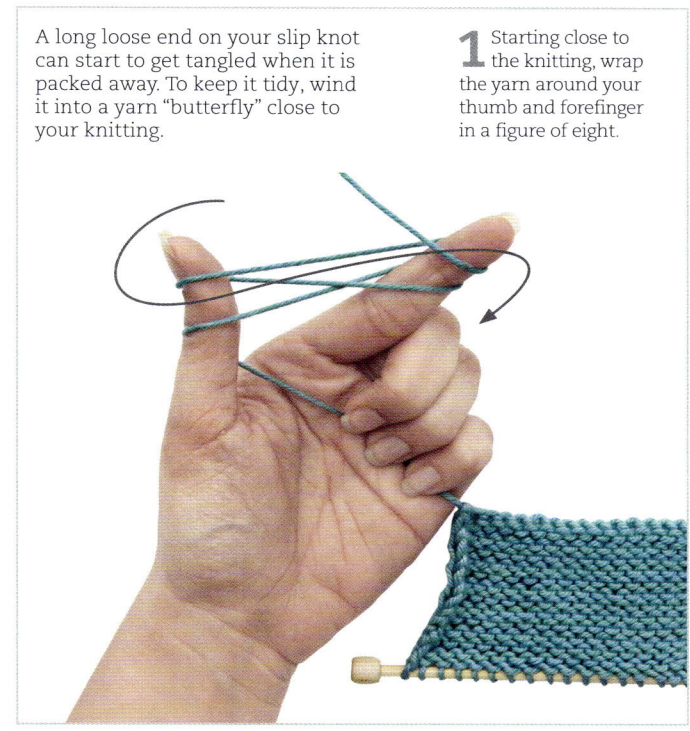

2 Remove the yarn "butterfly" from the thumb and forefinger and wrap the yarn end a few times around its centre. Tuck the end under the wrapping to secure it.

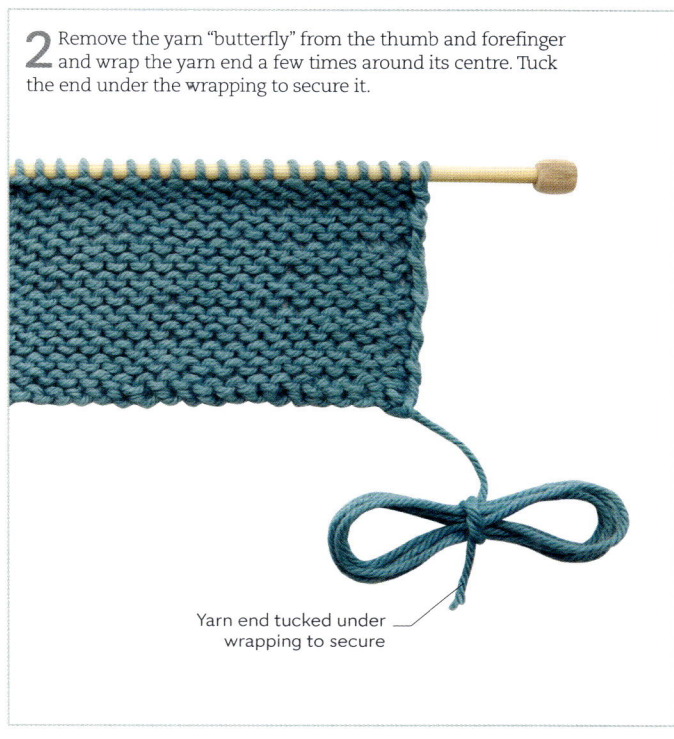

Yarn end tucked under wrapping to secure

DARNING IN AN END

1 Freshly completed knitting will have at least two yarn ends dangling from it. If you plan ahead, you can leave ends long enough to stitch pieces together on seamed items. Wait until seams are stitched before sewing in ends, because they offer a handy valley to darn ends into. Thread each end separately onto a blunt-ended darning needle and weave it vertically or horizontally through stitches on the wrong side of the work.

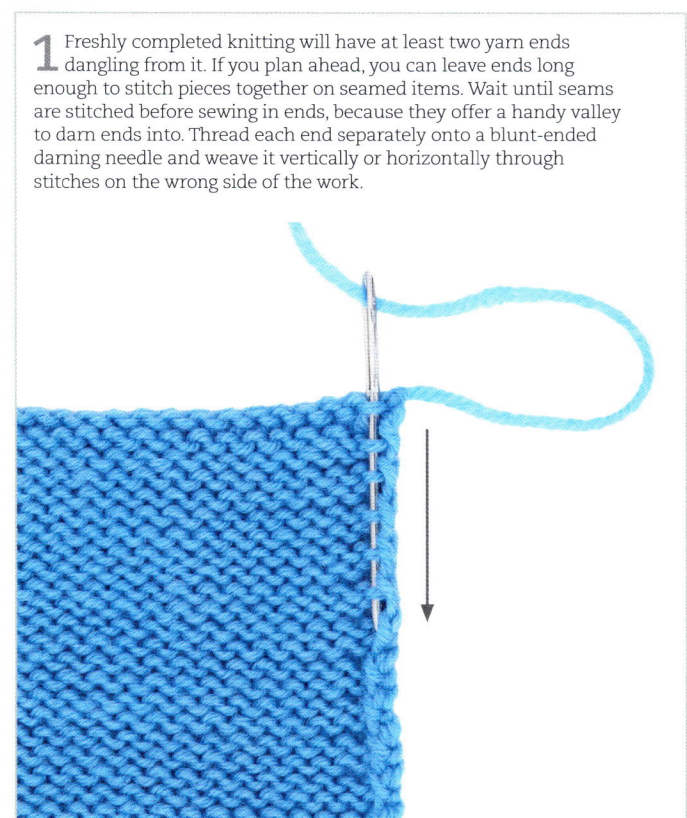

2 For an extra sturdy finish, use a sharp-ended darning needle to come back through the stitches you created on the previous step, which essentially sews down the darned-in end for extra security and longevity.

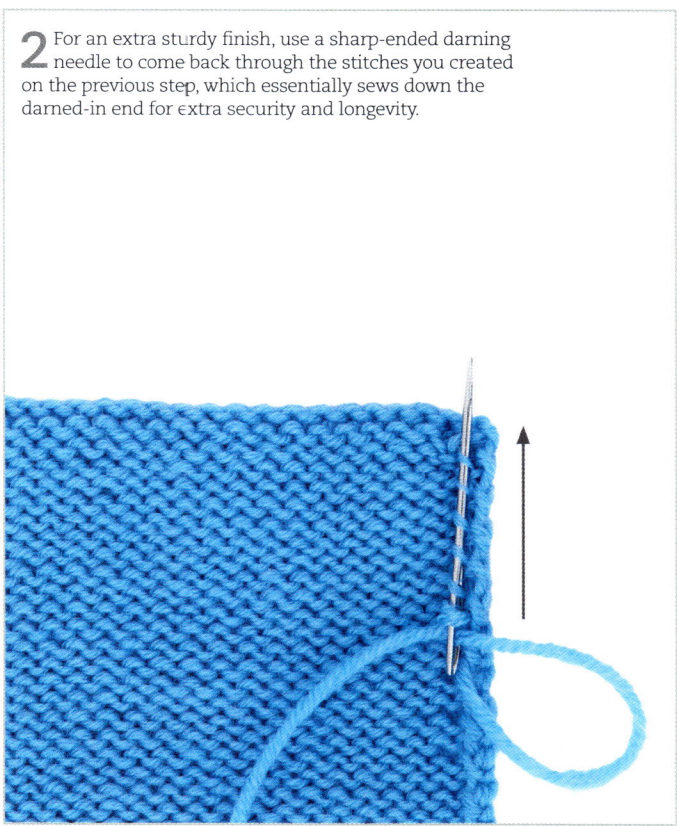

84 TECHNIQUES

CORRECTING MISTAKES

The best thing to do if you make a mistake in your knitting is to unravel it back to the mistake by unpicking the stitches one by one. If you drop a stitch, be sure to pick it up quickly before it comes undone right back to the cast-on edge.

UNPICKING A KNIT ROW

1 Hold the needle with the stitches in your right hand. To unpick each stitch individually, insert the tip of the left needle from front to back through the stitch below the first knit stitch on the right needle.

2 Transferring the stitch onto the left needle, gently pull the yarn so that the loop retracts from the stitch you are unpicking. To undo further stitches, keep the yarn at the back of the work and repeat Steps 1 and 2.

UNPICKING A PURL ROW

1 Hold the needle with the stitches in your right hand. Keeping the yarn at the front of the work, inset your needle from front to back through the loop directly beneath the stitch nearest the needle tip.

2 Transfer the stitch from the right to the left needle, pulling the yarn until the loop forming the stitch is undone. Continue to undo further stitches by repeating Steps 1 and 2.

PICKING UP A DROPPED STITCH

1 If you drop a stitch on stocking stitch, you can easily reclaim it with a crochet hook. With the right side of the knitting facing you, insert the hook through the dropped loop.

2 Grab the lowest strand between the stitches and pull a loop through the loop on the hook. Continue up the rows as if climbing a ladder, working each "rung" at a time, until you reach the top, then slip the stitch back onto the needle.

WOVEN DARNING FOR REPAIRING HOLES

Holes can appear in your knits from moths or just wear and tear. It's always a good idea to keep some leftover yarn from a project so you have matching yarn for future mends. Alternatively, try this technique in a bright contrasting yarn for a decorative effect. Creating the warp and weft takes a surprising amount of yarn, so thread a good length in the yarn needle before beginning.

1. Lightly stretch the damaged fabric over a darning mushroom and carefully trim away the fluffy edges around the hole. The darning mushroom helps to keep the hole open and stretched a little while you work, to avoid the darn puckering.

2. Work running stitch around the hole to create a rectangular frame for the darn.

3. Create a weft by taking the working yarn under the frame thread on the right side, run the yarn across with a slight tension to the other side and under the frame thread there. Work back and forth to cover the area with weft threads.

4. Create the warp threads by weaving the needle under and over the weft threads to create a woven patch of fabric. When the mend is complete, darn in the ends (see p.83) on the reverse.

Following stitch patterns

Stitch pattern instructions are written or charted directions for making all sorts of textures – knit and purl combinations, lace, and cables. Knitting stitch pattern swatches is the best possible introduction to row instructions. Beginners should try some out before attempting to follow a knitting pattern for a more ambitious project (see pp.90–91).

UNDERSTANDING WRITTEN INSTRUCTIONS

Anyone who can cast on, knit and purl, and cast off will be able to work from simple knit-and-purl-combination stitch pattern instructions with little difficulty. It is just a question of following the instructions one step at a time and getting used to the abbreviations. A list of common knitting abbreviations is given on p.89, but for simple knit and purl textures all you need to grasp is that "k1" means "knit one stitch", "k2" means "knit two stitches", and so on. And the same applies for the purl stitches – "p1" means "purl one stitch", "p2" means "purl two stitches", and so on.

To begin a stitch pattern, cast on the number of stitches that it tells you to, using your chosen yarn and the yarn manufacturer's recommended needle size. Work the stitch row by row, then repeat the rows as instructed and the stitch pattern will grow beneath the needles. When your knitting is the desired size, cast off in pattern (see p.68).

The best tips for first-timers are to follow the rows slowly; mark the right side of the fabric by knotting a coloured thread onto it; use a row counter to keep track of where you are (see p.41); and pull out your stitches and start again if you get in a muddle. Inserting a lifeline after each repeat will help if you need to unravel. Use a blunt-ended sewing needle to thread a thin, contrast-coloured yarn into each stitch along your needle. The lifeline should measure a bit longer than the full width of your knitting, so leave extra length at each end. If you love the stitch pattern you are trying out, you can make a scarf, blanket, or cushion cover with it – no need to buy a knitting pattern.

The principles for following stitch patterns are the same for cables and lace (see pp.110–111 and pp.116–117), which you will be able to work once you learn cable techniques and how to increase and decrease. Some stitch patterns will call for "slipping" stitches and knitting "through the back of the loop". These useful techniques are given next as a handy reference when you are consulting the abbreviations and terminology list.

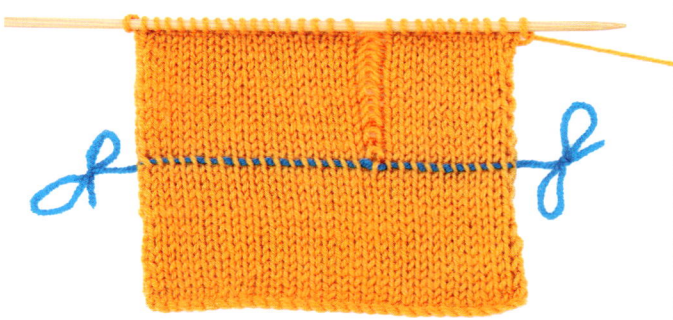

SLIPPING STITCHES PURLWISE

1 Always slip stitches purlwise, for example when slipping stitches onto a stitch holder, unless instructed otherwise. Insert the tip of the right needle from right to left through the front of the loop on the left needle.

2 Slide the stitch onto the right needle and off the left needle without working it. The slipped stitch now sits on the right needle with the right side of the loop at the front just like the worked stitches next to it.

SLIPPING STITCHES KNITWISE

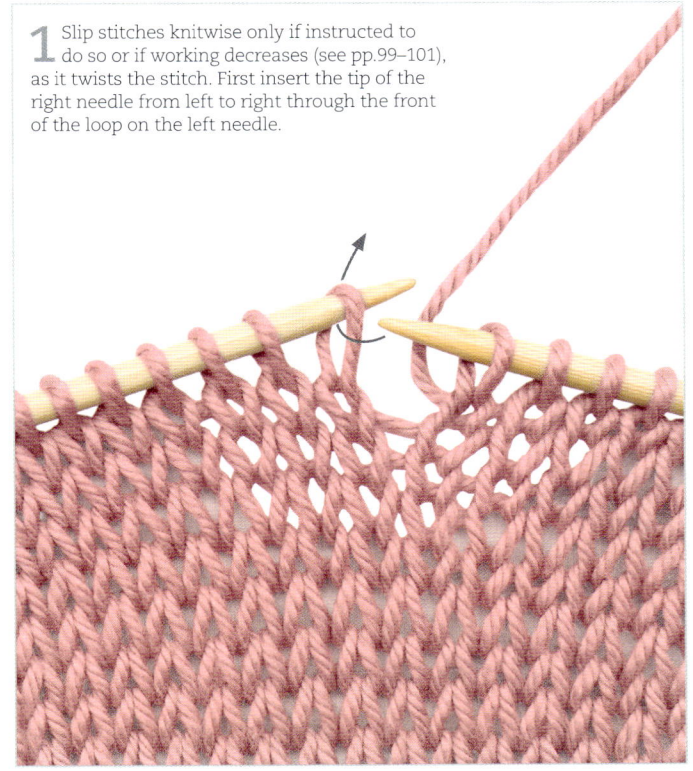

1 Slip stitches knitwise only if instructed to do so or if working decreases (see pp.99–101), as it twists the stitch. First insert the tip of the right needle from left to right through the front of the loop on the left needle.

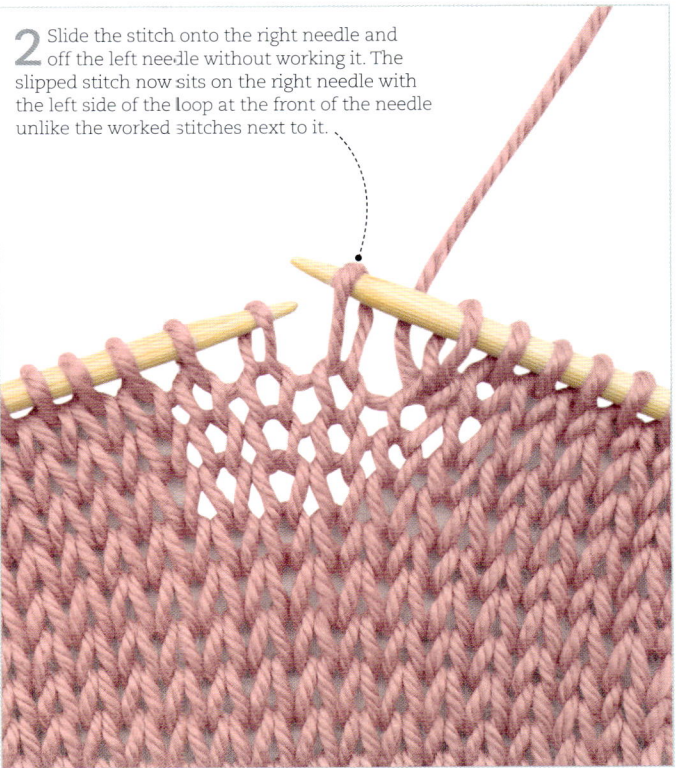

2 Slide the stitch onto the right needle and off the left needle without working it. The slipped stitch now sits on the right needle with the left side of the loop at the front of the needle unlike the worked stitches next to it.

KNITTING THROUGH BACK OF LOOP (Abbreviation = *k1 tbl*)

1 When row instructions say "k1 tbl" (knit one through the back of the loop), insert the right needle from right to left through the side of the stitch behind the left needle (called the back of the loop).

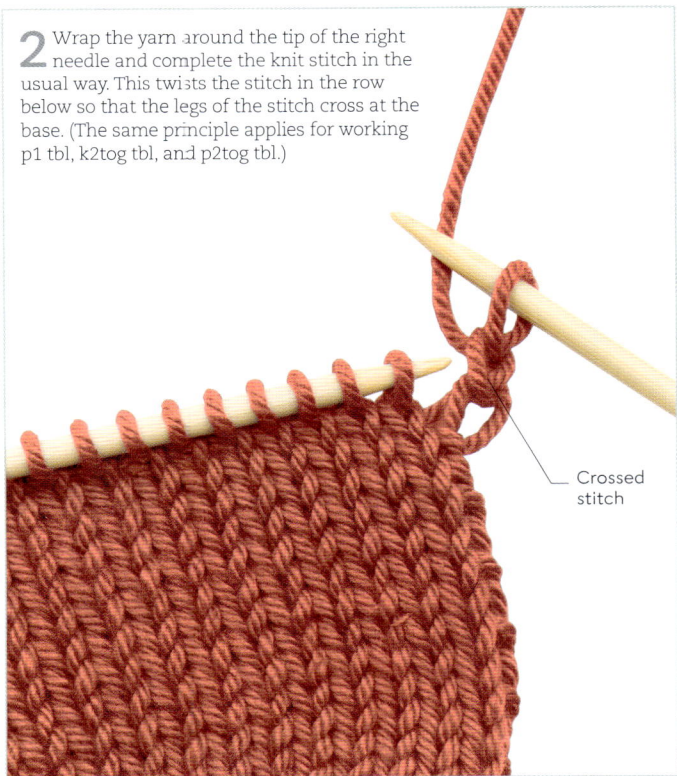

2 Wrap the yarn around the tip of the right needle and complete the knit stitch in the usual way. This twists the stitch in the row below so that the legs of the stitch cross at the base. (The same principle applies for working p1 tbl, k2tog tbl, and p2tog tbl.)

Crossed stitch

USING STITCH AND ROW MARKERS

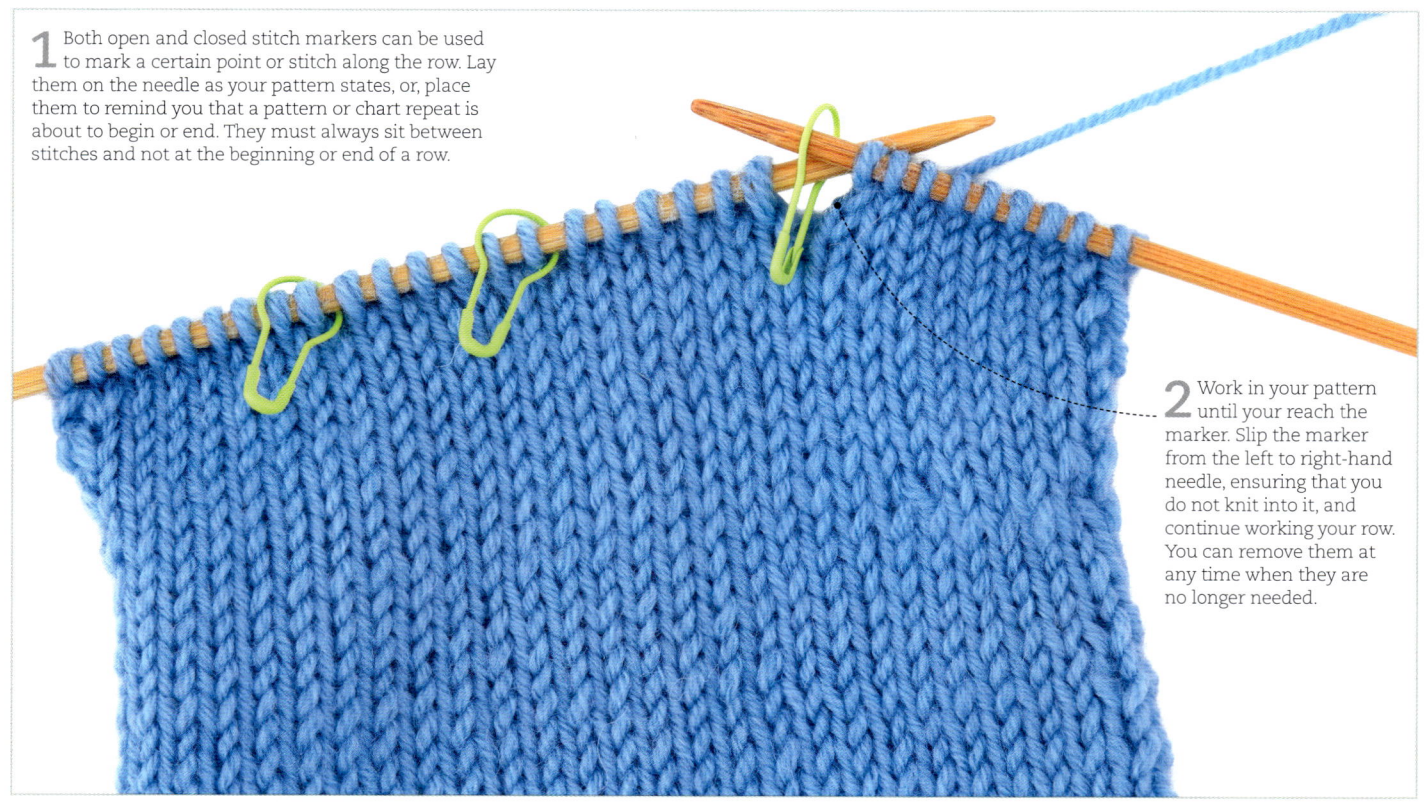

1 Both open and closed stitch markers can be used to mark a certain point or stitch along the row. Lay them on the needle as your pattern states, or, place them to remind you that a pattern or chart repeat is about to begin or end. They must always sit between stitches and not at the beginning or end of a row.

2 Work in your pattern until your reach the marker. Slip the marker from the left to right-hand needle, ensuring that you do not knit into it, and continue working your row. You can remove them at any time when they are no longer needed.

3 Locking stitch markers that open and close can be used to mark specific points in rows on your knitting, on the fabric itself. Open the marker, find the row you would like to mark and insert the stitch marker around one of the stitches.

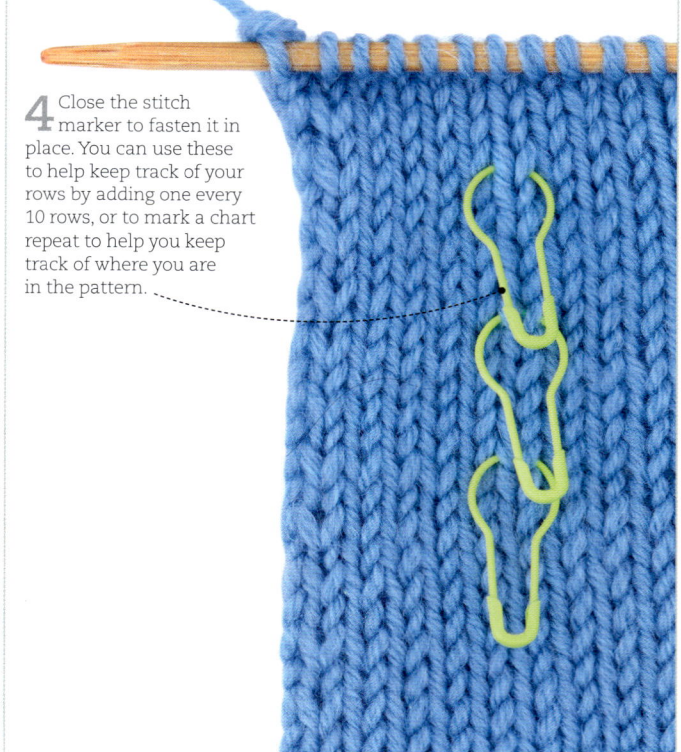

4 Close the stitch marker to fasten it in place. You can use these to help keep track of your rows by adding one every 10 rows, or to mark a chart repeat to help you keep track of where you are in the pattern.

UNDERSTANDING STITCH SYMBOL CHARTS

Knitting instructions for stitch patterns can also be given in chart form. Some knitters prefer stitch symbol charts because they build up a visual image of the stitch repeat that is quick to memorize.

Even with charted instructions, there are usually written directions for how many stitches to cast on. If not, you can calculate the cast-on from the chart, where the number of stitches in the pattern "repeat" are clearly marked. Cast on a multiple of this number, plus any edge stitches outside the repeat.

Each square represents a stitch and each horizontal line of squares represents a row. After casting on, work from the bottom of the chart upwards. Read odd-numbered rows (usually right-side rows) from right to left and even-numbered rows (usually wrong-side rows) from left to right. Work the edge stitches and then the stitches inside the repeat as many times as required. Some symbols mean one thing on a right-side row and another on a wrong-side row.

Once you have worked all the charted rows, start again at the bottom of the chart to begin the "row repeat" once more.

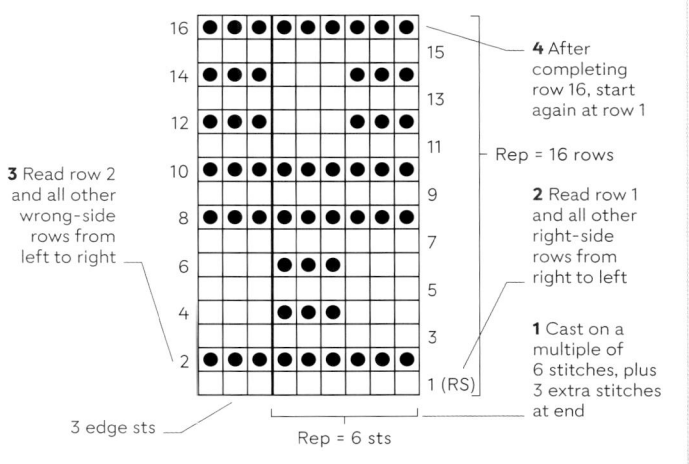

3 Read row 2 and all other wrong-side rows from left to right

4 After completing row 16, start again at row 1

Rep = 16 rows

2 Read row 1 and all other right-side rows from right to left

1 Cast on a multiple of 6 stitches, plus 3 extra stitches at end

3 edge sts   Rep = 6 sts

KNITTING ABBREVIATIONS

Below are the most often used abbreviations. Special abbreviations are always explained within the pattern.

alt	alternate	**RS**	right side (of work)
approx	approximately	**s**	slip stitch(es)
beg	begin(ning)	**s1 k1 psso**	slip one, knit one,
cm	centimetre(s)	**(or skpo)**	pass slipped st over
cont	continu(e)(ing)		(see p.100)
dec	decreas(e)(ing) by working next 2 sts together	**s2 k1 p2sso**	slip 2, knit 1, pass 2 slipped sts over (see p.101)
foll	follow(s)(ing)	**s2k**	slip 2 sts knitwise
g	gram	**ssk**	slip, slip, knit (see p.100)
g st	garter stitch		
in	inch(es)	**ssp**	slip, slip, purl (see p.101)
inc	increas(e)(ing)		
k	knit	**st(s)**	stitch(es)
k1b	knit 1 below, so knit in st below next st	**st st**	stocking stitch
		tbl	through back of loop(s)
kfb (or inc 1)	knit in front and back of next st (see p.92)	**tog**	together
		w+t	wrap and turn (see p.150)
kwise	insert right needle in st on left needle as if starting a knit st	**WS**	wrong side (of work)
		wyib	with yarn behind the work
LH	left hand	**wyif**	with yarn in front of the work
m	metre(s)		
M1 (or M1k, M1p, M1L, M1R)	make one st (see pp.93–95)	**yb**	yarn back
		yd	yard(s)
		yfrn	yarn forward round needle (US yo; see p.97)
mm	millimetre(s)		
p	purl	**yfwd**	yarn forward (US yo; see p.97)
patt	pattern or work in pattern		
prev	previous	**yo**	yarnover
psso	pass slipped st over	**yon**	yarn over needle (US yo; see p.97)
pwise	insert right needle in st on left needle as if starting a purl st		
		yrn	yarn round needle (US yo; see p.96)
rem	remain(s)(ing)	**[ ] ***	Repeat instructions in brackets, or after or between asterisks, as instructed
rep	repeat(ing)		
rev st st	reverse stocking stitch		
RH	right hand		

KNITTING TERMINOLOGY AND SYMBOLS

The following terms are commonly used in knitting patterns. Where terminology differs between the UK and US, the US equivalent is given in parentheses.

cast on Create a series of loops on a knitting needle to form the foundation for the knitting.
cast off Close off stitches and drop from knitting needle (US: bind off).
cast off knitwise/purlwise Cast off while working stitches in knit/purl.
cast off in pattern Cast off while working stitches in the pattern of the previous row.
cast off in ribbing Cast off while working stitches in the ribbing of the previous row.
decrease Decrease the number of stitches in a row (see pp.99–101).
garter stitch Knit every row. In circular knitting (see p.158), knit one round and purl one round alternately.
tension The size of the stitches in a piece of knitting (US: gauge), measured by the number of stitches and rows to 10cm (4in), or to 2.5cm (1in) on fine knitting (see p.91).
increase Increase the number of stitches in a row (see pp.92–98).
knitwise Insert the right needle into the stitch on the left needle as if starting a knit stitch.
pick up and knit Draw loops through the edge of the knitting and place them on the needle (see p.168).
purlwise Insert the right needle into the stitch on the left needle as if starting a purl stitch.
stocking stitch Knit all RS rows and purl all WS rows (US: stockinette stitch).
reverse stocking stitch Purl all RS rows and knit all WS rows (US: reverse stockinette stitch).
work straight Work in specified pattern without increasing or decreasing (US: work even).
yarnover increase Wrap yarn around right needle to make a new stitch; abbreviated yfwd, yfrn, yon, or yrn (US yo; see pp.96–98).

STITCH SYMBOLS

These are some of the commonly used knitting symbols in this book. Any unusual symbols will be explained in the pattern. Symbols can vary, so follow the explanations in your pattern.

☐ = k on RS rows, p on WS rows
● = p on RS rows, k on WS rows
O = yarnover (see p.96)
∕ = k2tog (see p.99)
∖ = ssk (see p.100)
△ = sk2p (see p.101)
△ = sk2 k1 p2sso (see p.101)

Following a pattern

Knitting patterns can look daunting to a beginner knitter, but if approached step by step they are easy to understand. This section provides an explanation of how to follow simple knitting patterns and gives tips for finishing details and seams.

SIMPLE ACCESSORY PATTERNS

The best advice for a beginner wanting to knit a first project from a knitting pattern is to start with a simple accessory. Cushion covers are especially good practice as the instructions are straightforward and usually the only finishing details are seams. This is an example of a pattern for a simple striped stocking stitch cushion cover.

[1] **At the beginning** of most patterns you will find the skill level required for the knitting. Make sure you are confident that the skill level is right for you.

[2] **Check the size** of the finished item. If it is a simple square like this cushion, you can easily adjust the size by adding or subtracting stitches and rows.

[3] **Try to use** the yarn specified, but if you are unable to obtain this yarn choose a substitute yarn as listed on pp.30–31.

[4] **Make a tension** swatch before starting to knit and change the needle size if necessary (see opposite).

[5] **Instructions for working** a piece of knitted fabric always start with how many stitches to cast on and what yarn or needle size to use. If there is only one needle size and one yarn, these may be absent here.

[6] **Consult the abbreviations list** with your pattern (or in your book) for the meanings of abbreviations (see p.89).

[7] **The back of a cushion cover** is sometimes exactly the same as the front or it has a fabric back. In this case, the stripes are reversed on the back for a more versatile cover.

[8] **After all the knitted pieces** are complete, follow the Finishing (or Making Up) section of the pattern.

STRIPED CUSHION COVER

[1] **Skill level**
Easy

[2] **Size of finished cushion**
40.5 x 40.5cm (16 x 16in)

Materials
[3] 3 x 50g (1¾oz)/125m (137yd) [9] balls in each of branded Pure Wool DK in Lavender 039 (**A**) and Avocado 019 (**B**). [10]
Pair of 4mm (US size 6) knitting needles. [11]
Cushion pad to fit finished cover. [12]

[4] **Tension**
22 sts and 30 rows to 10cm (4in) over stocking stitch using 4mm (US size 6) needles or size necessary to achieve correct tension. To save time, take time to check tension.

[5] **Front**
Using 4mm (US size 6) needles and A, cast on 88 sts.
[6] Beg with a K row, work in st st until work [13] measures 14cm (5½in) from cast-on edge, ending with RS facing for next row.
Cut off A and change to B.
Cont in st st until work measures 26.5cm (10½in) from cast-on edge, ending with RS facing for next row.
Cut off B and change to A. [14]
Cont in st st until work measures 40.5cm (16in) from cast-on edge, ending with RS facing for next row.
Cast off. [15]

[7] **Back**
Work as for Front, but use B for A, and A for B.

[8] **Finishing**
Darn in loose ends. [16]
Block and press lightly on wrong side, [17] following instructions on yarn label. With wrong sides facing, sew three sides of back and front together. Turn right-side out, insert cushion pad, and sew remaining seam. [18]

[9] **Always purchase** the same total amount in metres/yards of a substitute yarn; NOT the same amount in weight.

[10] **If desired**, select different colours to suit your décor; the colours specified are just suggestions.

[11] **Alter the needle size** if you cannot achieve the correct tension with the specified size (see left).

[12] **Extra items** needed for your project will usually be listed under Materials or Extras.

[13] **Work in the specified stitch pattern**, for the specified number of rows or cm/in.

[14] **Colours are usually changed** on a right-side row, so end with the right side facing for the changeover row.

[15] **If no stitch is specified** for the cast-off, always cast off knitwise.

[16] **See p.83 for how** to darn in loose ends.

[17] **Make sure you look** at the yarn label instructions before attempting to press any piece of knitting. The label may say that the yarn cannot be pressed or to press it only with a cool iron. (See pp.185–186 for blocking tips.)

[18] **See pp.186–193** for seaming options. Take time with seams on knitting. Practise on odd pieces of knitting before starting the main project.

GARMENT PATTERNS

Choosing the right size and knitting a tension swatch are the two most important things to get right if you want to create a successful garment. It is also quite easy to make simple alterations to patterns worked in plain garter or stocking stitch.

CHOOSING A GARMENT SIZE

Rather than looking at specific "sizes" when choosing which size to knit, select the one nearest to how you want the garment to fit. The best way to do this is to find a similar garment that fits you. Lay it flat and measure its width – choose the width on the pattern that is the closest match.

Photocopy your pattern and highlight the figures for your size throughout. Start with the number of balls of yarn, then the number of stitches to cast on, the length to knit to the armhole, and so on. The smallest size is given first and larger sizes follow in parentheses. Where only one figure is given, this applies to all sizes.

Choose your size by the width of a favourite, well-fitting jumper with the same shape and knitted fabric weight

Alter jumper length only where instructed

Check that circumference of sleeve suits your upper arm body measurement

Alter sleeve length only where specified in instructions

ALTERING PATTERNS

You can alter the length of garment patterns worked in plain garter or stocking stitch, but avoid altering armholes, necklines, or sleeve heads. As sleeves and some bodies have shaping, this must also be adjusted. Make notes at every step.
In this example, length is being added to a sleeve:
1 Copy, photocopy, or draw out the pattern diagram. Write the new required length on the diagram (for instance, 48cm).
2 Find the number of rows to 10cm in the tension note. Divide that number by 10 to calculate how many rows there are in 1cm. For example, 30 rows per 10cm. 30 ÷ 10 = 3 rows per 1cm.
3 Multiply the required new length by the number of rows in 1cm. The resulting figure is the total number in the new length. For example, 48 × 3 = 144 rows.
4 Any increasing, will also have to be recalculated. From the pattern, note the number of stitches to cast on at the cuff and how many there will be on the needle just before the start of the underarm shaping (this figure should be shown at the end of the written instruction for the increases).
5 Subtract the smallest from the largest number of stitches. The answer is the total number of stitches to be increased. Divide the answer by two (because a sleeve has two sides), to give the number of stitches to increase on each side. For example, 114 – 60 = 54 sts. 54 ÷ 2 = 27 sts.
6 To calculate the number of rows between each increase, divide the new number of rows found in Step 3 by the number of increases calculated in Step 5. If you have a fraction in this answer, round the number down. For example, 144 ÷ 27 = 4.22. Increase one stitch each side every four rows. Knit the remainder rows straight before underarm cast-offs.

MEASURING TENSION

Always knit a tension swatch from which to check your stitch size (tension) after you block it (see pp.185–186). Make sure your tension matches that recommended in the pattern, otherwise your finished piece will not have the correct measurements.

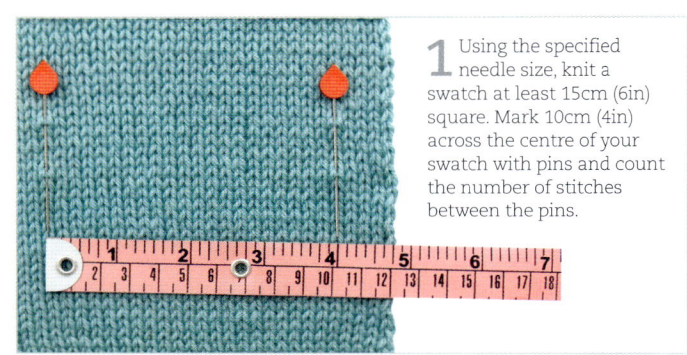

1 Using the specified needle size, knit a swatch at least 15cm (6in) square. Mark 10cm (4in) across the centre of your swatch with pins and count the number of stitches between the pins.

2 Count the number of rows to 10cm (4in) in the same way. If you have fewer stitches and rows than you should, try again with a smaller needle size; if you have more, change to a larger needle size. Use the needle size for your knitting that best matches the correct tension. (Matching stitch width is more important than matching row height.)

Increases and decreases

Knitting is shaped by adjusting the number of stitches on the needle, which changes straight row-end edges into curves and slopes. On knit and purl patterns like rib, you may need to pick which increase or decrease from this section works best. Increases and decreases can also be combined with knits and purls to form textures and lace in the knitted fabric.

SIMPLE INCREASES

The following techniques are simple increases used for shaping knitting. The first two (kfb and pfb) make two stitches out of one. The others (LL1 and M1) make a completely new stitch next to an existing stitch. Multiple increases, which add more than one stitch, are used less frequently and are always fully explained in the knitting pattern.

KNIT INTO FRONT AND BACK OF STITCH (Abbreviation = *kfb* or *inc 1*)

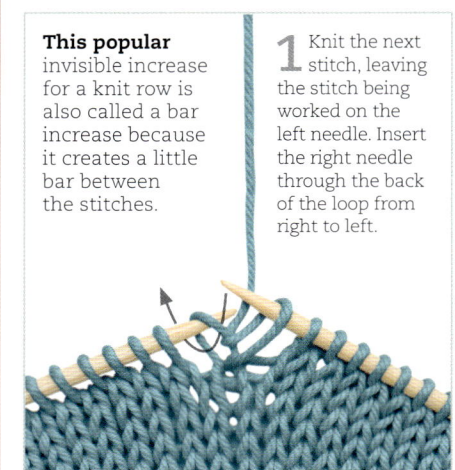

This popular invisible increase for a knit row is also called a bar increase because it creates a little bar between the stitches.

1 Knit the next stitch, leaving the stitch being worked on the left needle. Insert the right needle through the back of the loop from right to left.

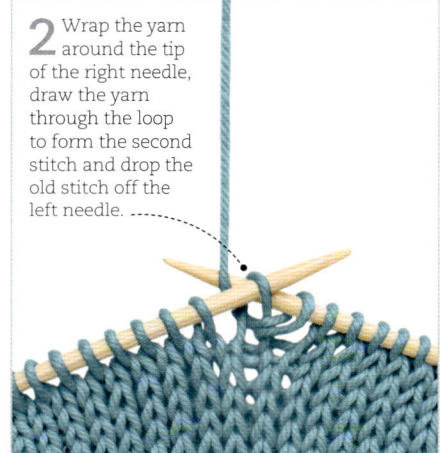

2 Wrap the yarn around the tip of the right needle, draw the yarn through the loop to form the second stitch and drop the old stitch off the left needle.

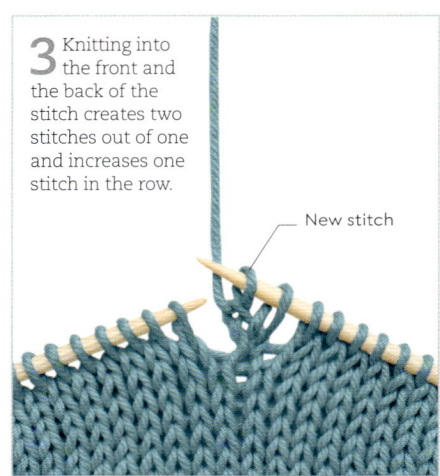

3 Knitting into the front and the back of the stitch creates two stitches out of one and increases one stitch in the row.

New stitch

PURL INTO FRONT AND BACK OF STITCH (Abbreviation = *pfb* or *inc 1*)

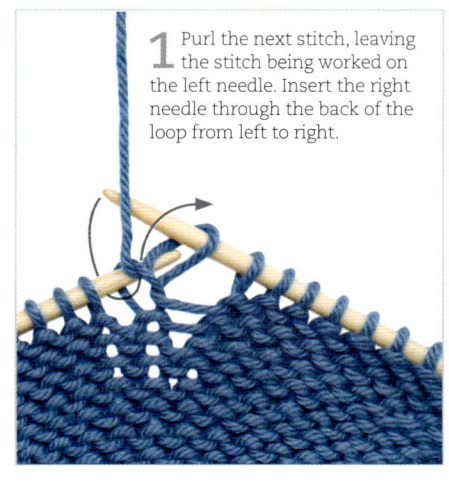

1 Purl the next stitch, leaving the stitch being worked on the left needle. Insert the right needle through the back of the loop from left to right.

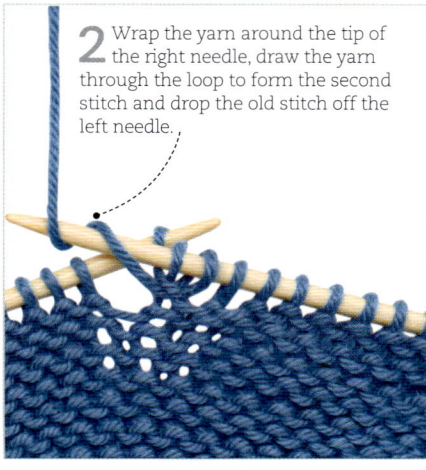

2 Wrap the yarn around the tip of the right needle, draw the yarn through the loop to form the second stitch and drop the old stitch off the left needle.

3 Purling into the front and the back of the stitch like this creates two stitches out of one and increases one stitch in the row.

New stitch

SIMPLE INCREASES **93**

LIFTED INCREASE ON KNIT ROW (Abbreviation = *RL1*, *LL1* or *inc 1*)

The easier, right Lifted increase is shown here. See p.107 for the left-lifted version.

1 Insert the tip of the right needle from front to back through the stitch below the next stitch on the left needle. Knit this lifted loop.

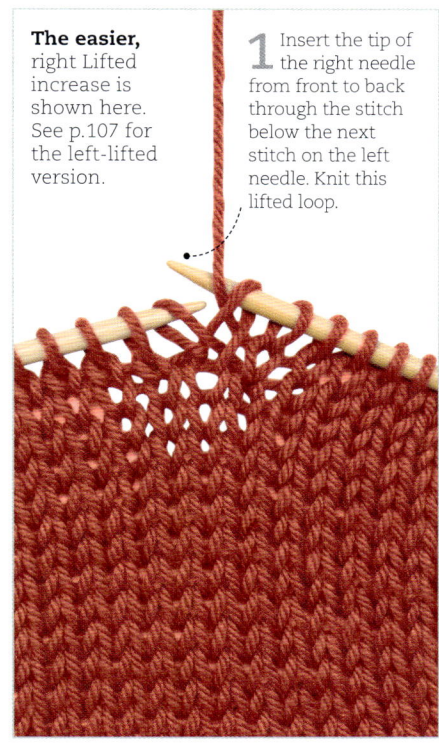

2 Knit the next stitch (the stitch above the lifted stitch on the left needle) in the usual way.

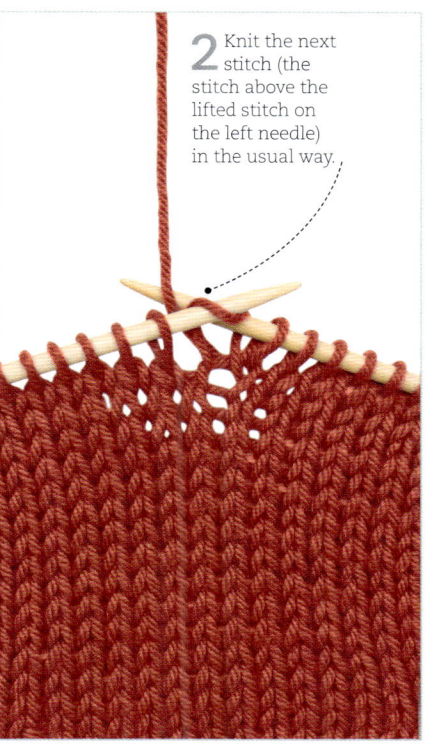

3 This creates two stitches out of one and increases one stitch in the row. (The purl version of this stitch is worked using the same principle.)

New stitch

"MAKE-ONE" LEFT CROSS INCREASE ON A KNIT ROW (Abbreviation = *M1L* or *M1k*)

1 Insert the tip of the left needle from front to back under the horizontal strand between the stitch just knitted and the next stitch. Then insert the right needle through the strand on the left needle from right to left behind the left needle.

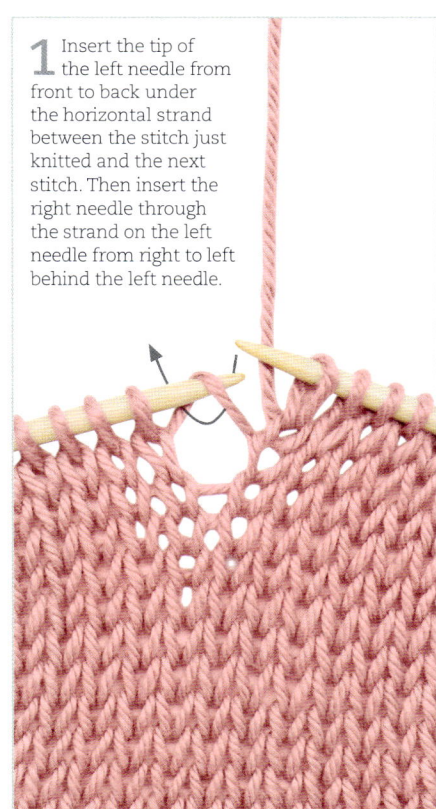

2 Wrap the yarn around the tip of the right needle and draw the yarn through the lifted loop. (This is called knitting through the back of the loop.)

3 This creates an extra stitch in the row. (Knitting through the back of the loop twists the base of the new stitch to produce a crossed stitch that closes up the hole it would have created.)

New stitch slants to the left

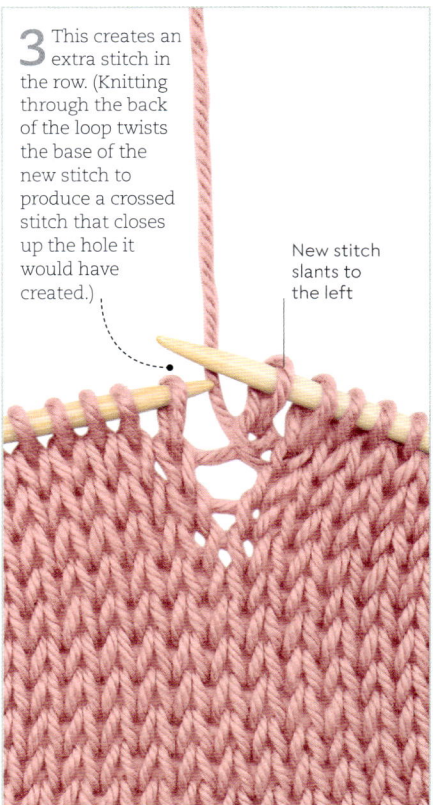

"MAKE-ONE" RIGHT CROSS INCREASE ON A KNIT ROW (Abbreviation = *M1R* or *M1k*)

Patterns do not always differentiate between left and right "make-one" increases. Choose the most suitable for your project.

1 Insert the tip of the left needle from back to front under the horizontal strand between the stitch just knitted and the next stitch. Insert the right needle from left to right into the front of this new loop, twisting the stitch.

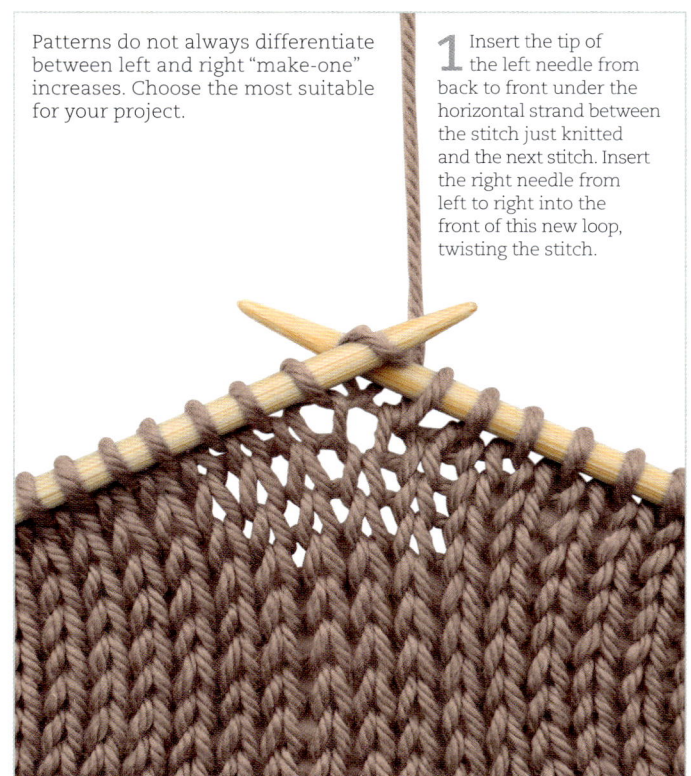

2 Wrap the yarn around the tip of the needle and draw the yarn through the lifted loop, knitting into the front of the stitch.

3 This action twists the lifted stitch, and closes the hole made by picking up the loop. The resulting increase slants to the right and is normally worked at the end of a knit row.

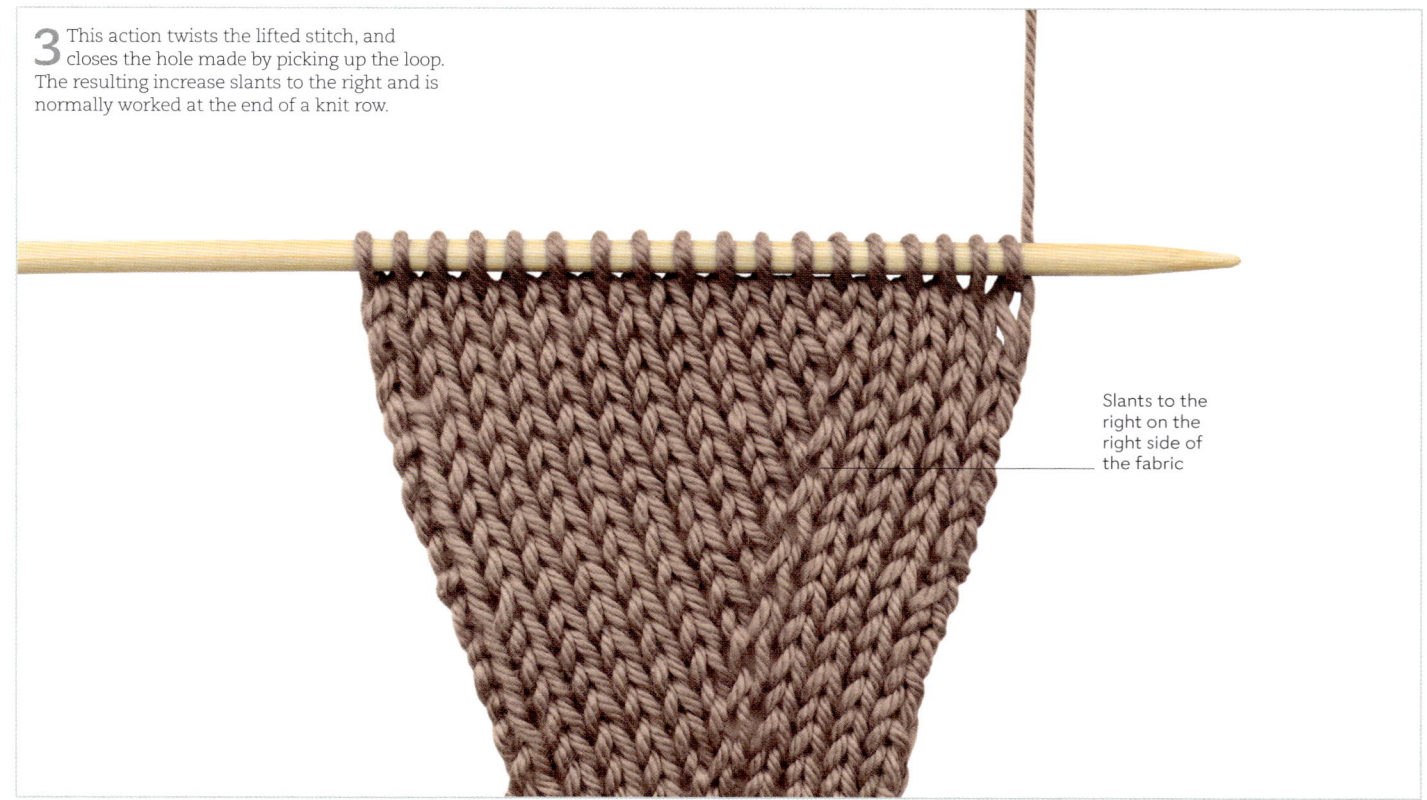

Slants to the right on the right side of the fabric

"MAKE-ONE" INCREASE ON PURL ROW (Abbreviation = M1 or M1p)

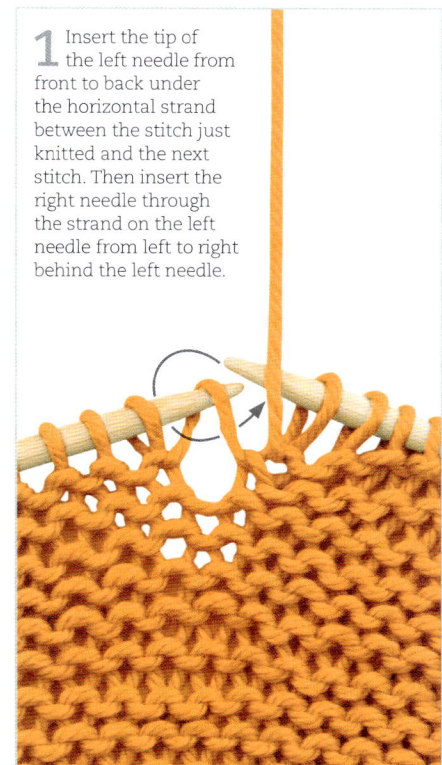

1 Insert the tip of the left needle from front to back under the horizontal strand between the stitch just knitted and the next stitch. Then insert the right needle through the strand on the left needle from left to right behind the left needle.

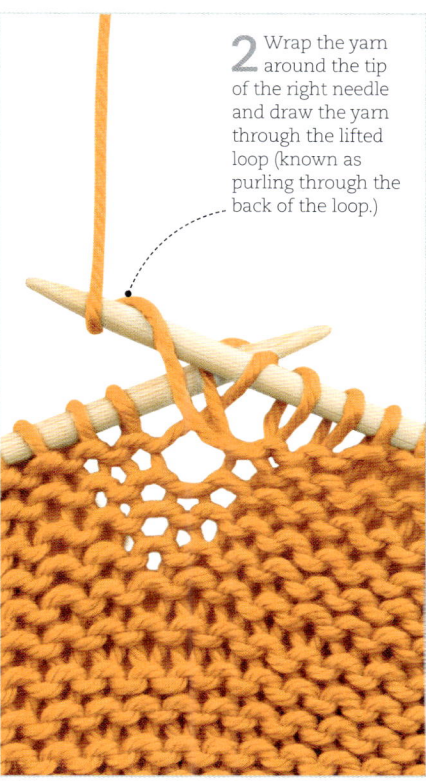

2 Wrap the yarn around the tip of the right needle and draw the yarn through the lifted loop (known as purling through the back of the loop.)

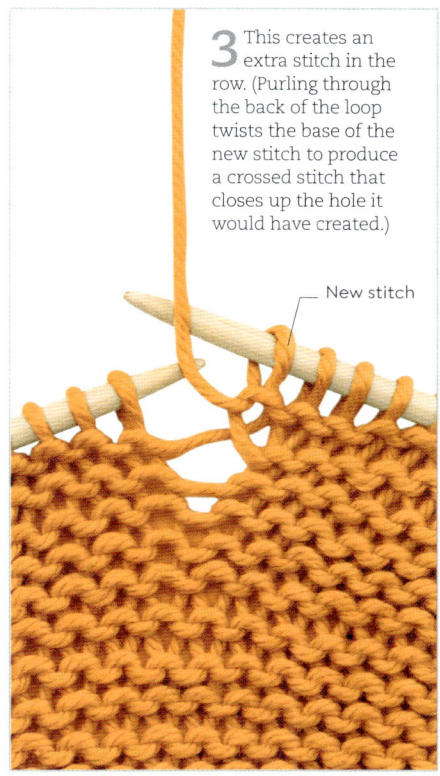

3 This creates an extra stitch in the row. (Purling through the back of the loop twists the base of the new stitch to produce a crossed stitch that closes up the hole it would have created.)

New stitch

MULTIPLE INCREASES (Abbreviation = [k1, p1, k1] into next st)

Use this very easy increase if you need to add more than one stitch to an existing stitch, but it does create a small hole under the new stitches.

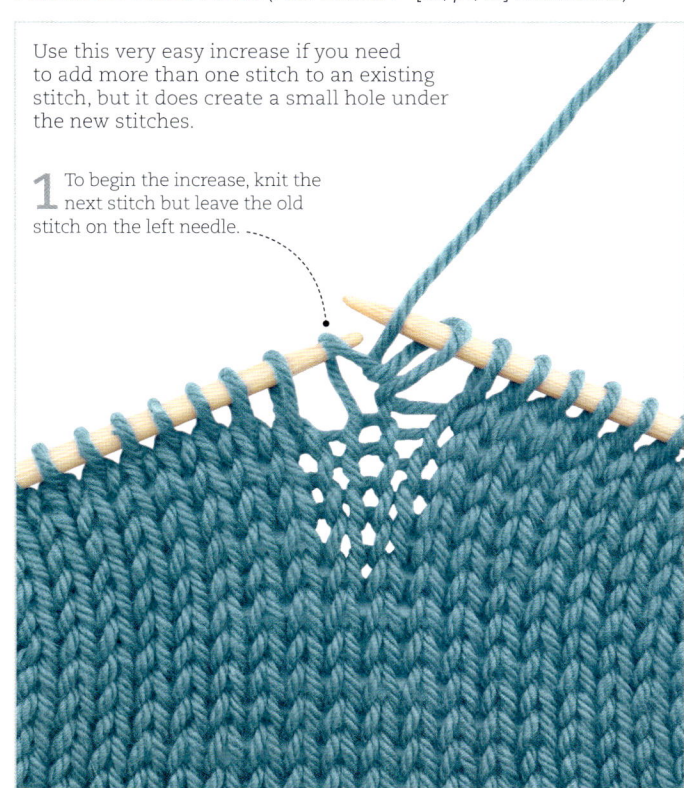

1 To begin the increase, knit the next stitch but leave the old stitch on the left needle.

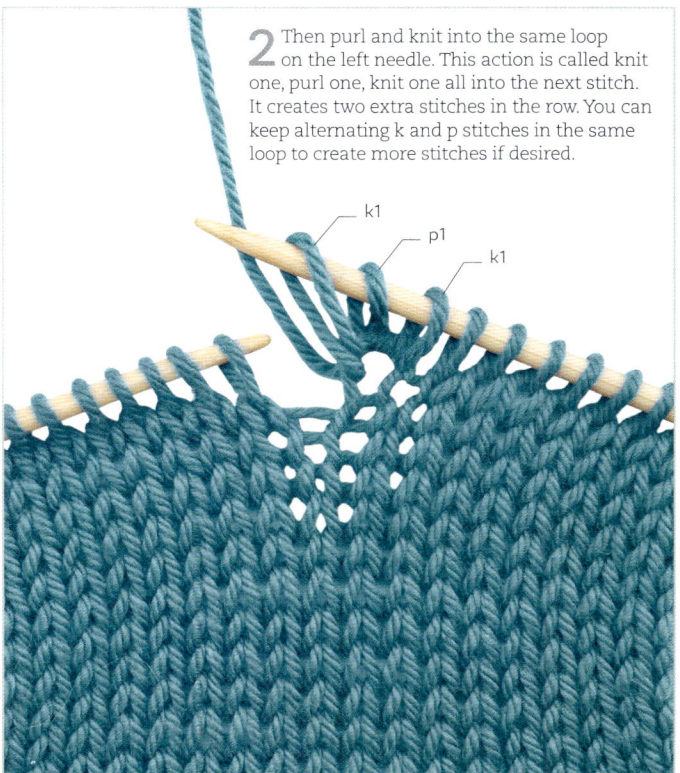

2 Then purl and knit into the same loop on the left needle. This action is called knit one, purl one, knit one all into the next stitch. It creates two extra stitches in the row. You can keep alternating k and p stitches in the same loop to create more stitches if desired.

k1 p1 k1

YARNOVER INCREASES

Yarnover increases add stitches to a row and create holes at the same time, so are often called visible increases. They are used to produce decorative mesh and lace fabrics (see pp.116–117). A yarnover is made by looping the yarn around the right needle to form an extra stitch. It is important to wrap the loop around the needle in the correct way or it will become crossed when it is worked in the next row, which closes the hole.

YARNOVER BETWEEN KNIT STITCHES (Abbreviation = UK *yfwd*; US *yo*)

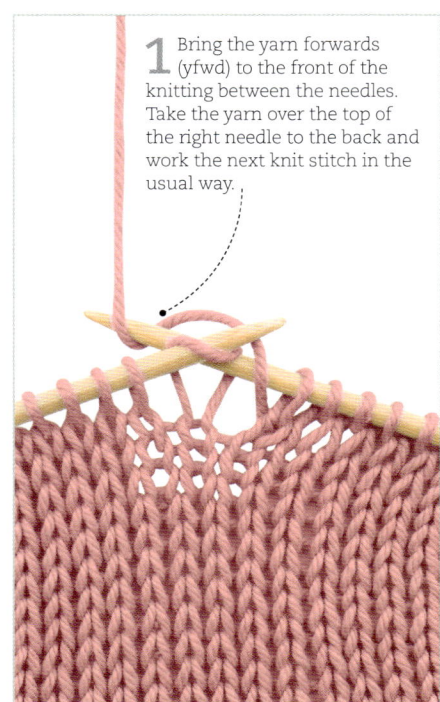

1 Bring the yarn forwards (yfwd) to the front of the knitting between the needles. Take the yarn over the top of the right needle to the back and work the next knit stitch in the usual way.

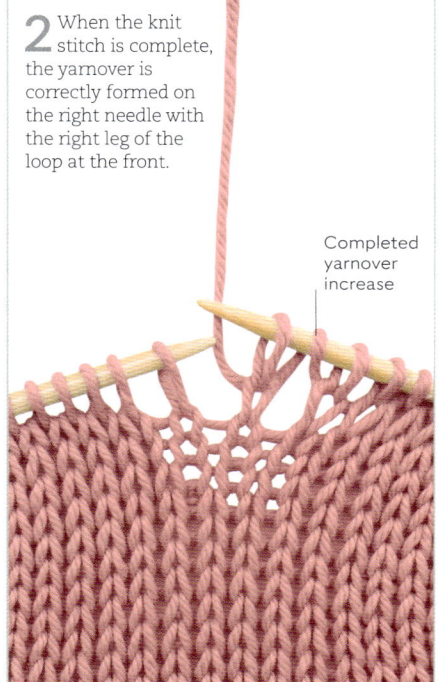

2 When the knit stitch is complete, the yarnover is correctly formed on the right needle with the right leg of the loop at the front.

Completed yarnover increase

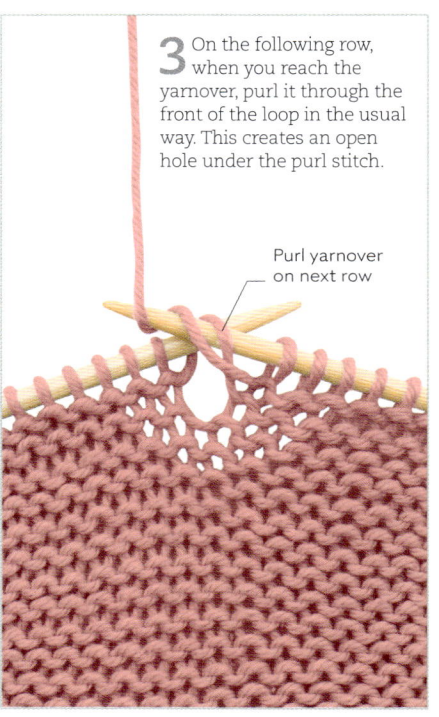

3 On the following row, when you reach the yarnover, purl it through the front of the loop in the usual way. This creates an open hole under the purl stitch.

Purl yarnover on next row

YARNOVER BETWEEN PURL STITCHES (Abbreviation = UK *yrn*; US *yo*)

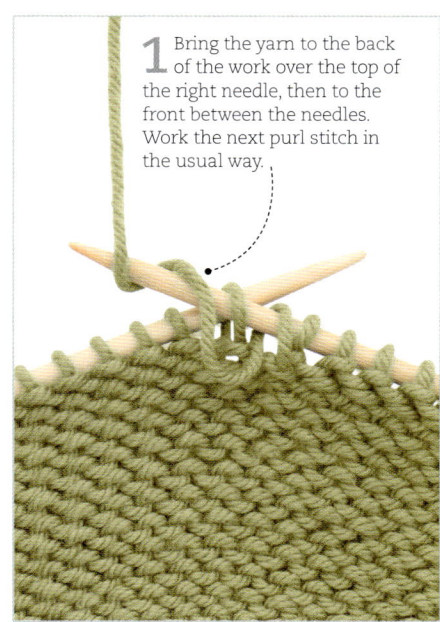

1 Bring the yarn to the back of the work over the top of the right needle, then to the front between the needles. Work the next purl stitch in the usual way.

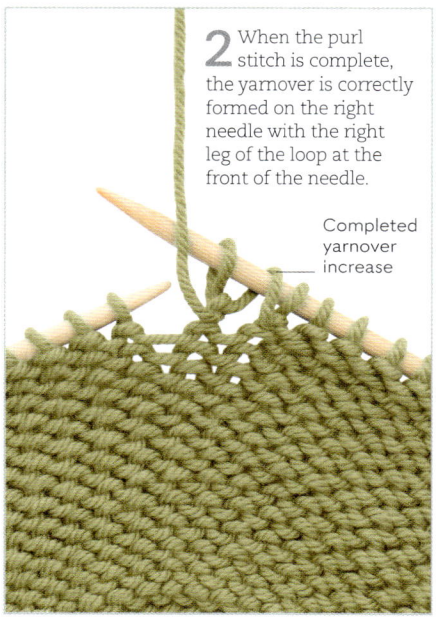

2 When the purl stitch is complete, the yarnover is correctly formed on the right needle with the right leg of the loop at the front of the needle.

Completed yarnover increase

3 On the following row, when you reach the yarnover, knit it through the front of the loop in the usual way. This creates an open hole under the knit stitch.

Knit yarnover on next row

YARNOVER BETWEEN KNIT AND PURL STITCHES (Abbreviation = UK *yfrn* and *yon*; US *yo*)

After a knit stitch and before a purl stitch (yfrn): Bring the yarn to the front between the needles, then over the top of the right needle and to the front again. Purl the next stitch. On the following row, work the yarnover through the front of the loop in the usual way to create an open hole.

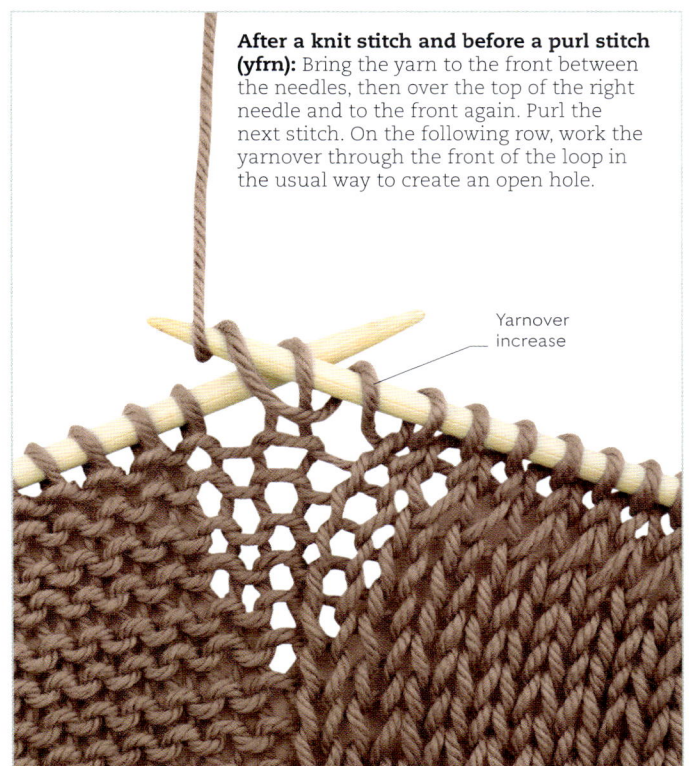

Yarnover increase

After a purl stitch and before a knit stitch (yon): Take the yarn over the top of the right needle and to the back of the work, then knit the next stitch. On the following row, work the yarnover through the front of the loop in the usual way to create an open hole.

Yarnover increase

YARNOVER AT THE BEGINNING OF A ROW (Abbreviation = UK *yfwd* and *yrn*; US *yo*)

At the beginning of a row before a knit stitch (yfwd): Insert the tip of the right needle behind the yarn and into the first stitch knitwise. Then take the yarn over the top of the right needle to the back and complete the knit stitch. On the following row, work the yarnover through the front of the loop in the usual way to create an open scallop at the edge.

Yarnover increase

At the beginning of a row before a purl stitch (yrn): Wrap the yarn from front to back over the top of the right needle and to the front again between the needles. Then purl the first stitch. On the following row, work the yarnover through the front of the loop in the usual way to create an open scallop at the edge.

Yarnover increase

DOUBLE YARNOVER (Abbreviation = UK *yfwd* twice; US *yo2*)

1 For a double yarnover between two knit stitches, take the yarn over the top of the right needle to the back of the work, between the needles to the front again, and over the top of the right needle to the back again, ready to knit the next stitch.

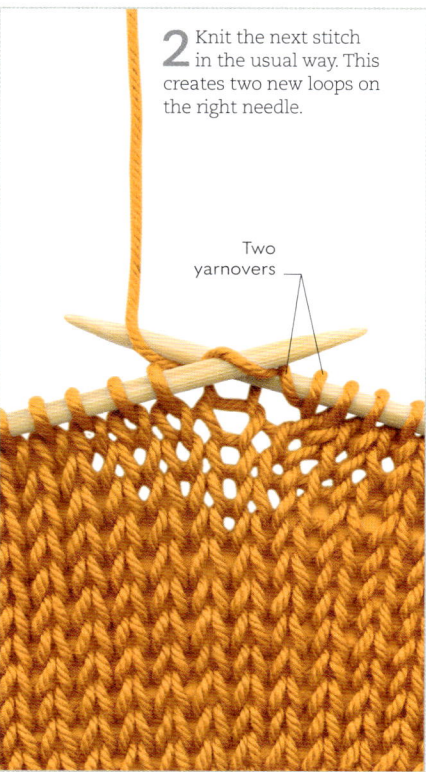

2 Knit the next stitch in the usual way. This creates two new loops on the right needle.

Two yarnovers

3 On the following row (a purl row), purl the first yarnover and knit the second. A double yarnover creates a bigger hole than a single yarnover. It is frequently used for lace knitting and buttonholes.

Knit second yarnover

Purl first yarnover

CLOSED YARNOVER ON GARTER STITCH

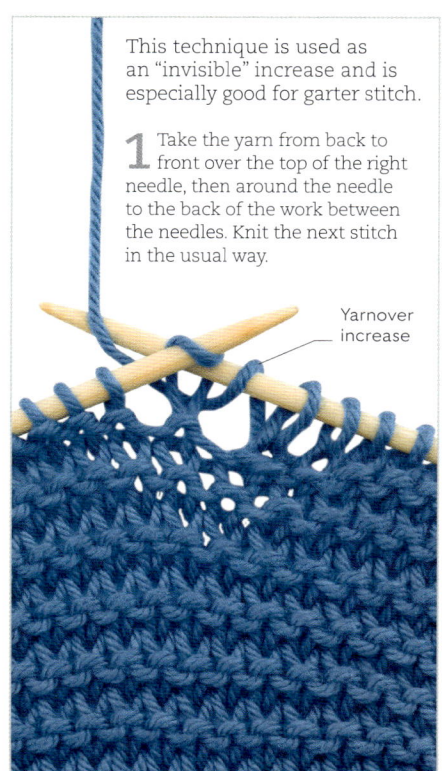

This technique is used as an "invisible" increase and is especially good for garter stitch.

1 Take the yarn from back to front over the top of the right needle, then around the needle to the back of the work between the needles. Knit the next stitch in the usual way.

Yarnover increase

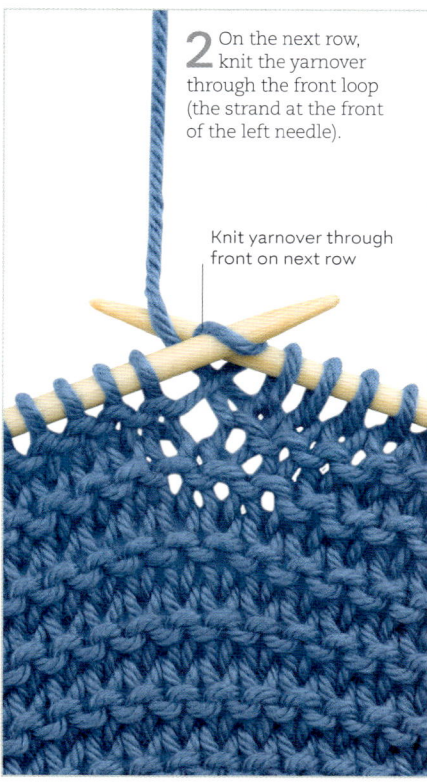

2 On the next row, knit the yarnover through the front loop (the strand at the front of the left needle).

Knit yarnover through front on next row

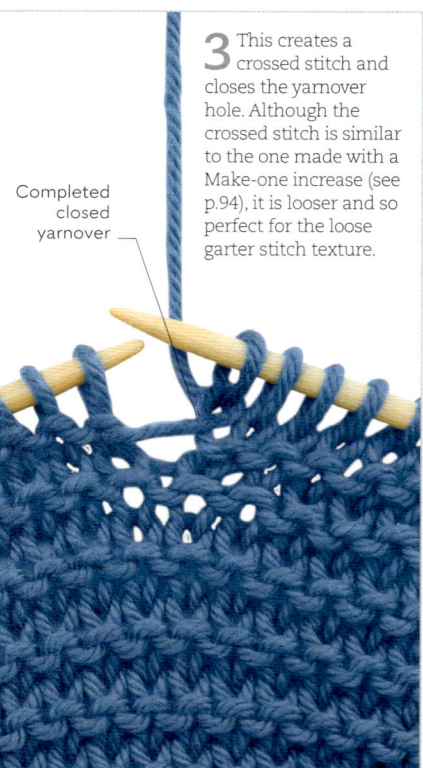

3 This creates a crossed stitch and closes the yarnover hole. Although the crossed stitch is similar to the one made with a Make-one increase (see p.94), it is looser and so perfect for the loose garter stitch texture.

Completed closed yarnover

SIMPLE DECREASES

These simple decreases are often used for shaping knitting and, paired with increases, for textured and lace stitches. More complicated decreases are always explained in knitting instructions. Most of the decreases that follow are single decreases that subtract only one stitch from the knitting, but a few double decreases are included.

KNIT TWO TOGETHER (Abbreviation = *k2tog* or *dec 1*)

1 Insert the tip of the right needle from left to right through the second stitch then the first stitch on the left needle.

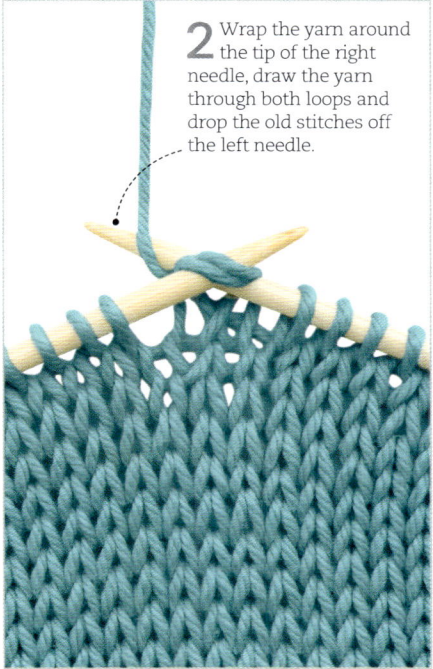

2 Wrap the yarn around the tip of the right needle, draw the yarn through both loops and drop the old stitches off the left needle.

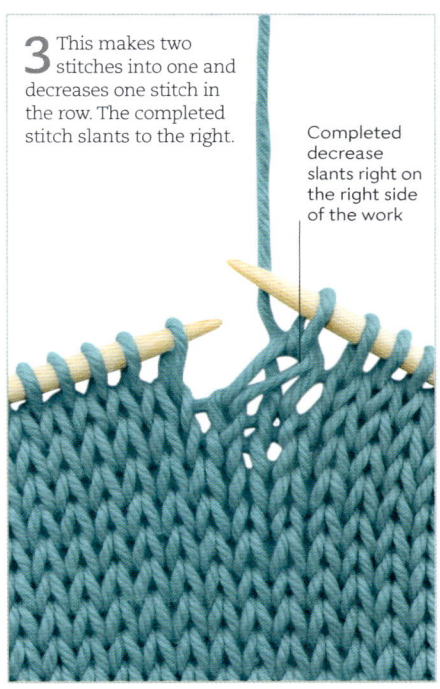

3 This makes two stitches into one and decreases one stitch in the row. The completed stitch slants to the right.

Completed decrease slants right on the right side of the work

PURL TWO TOGETHER (Abbreviation = *p2tog* or *dec 1*)

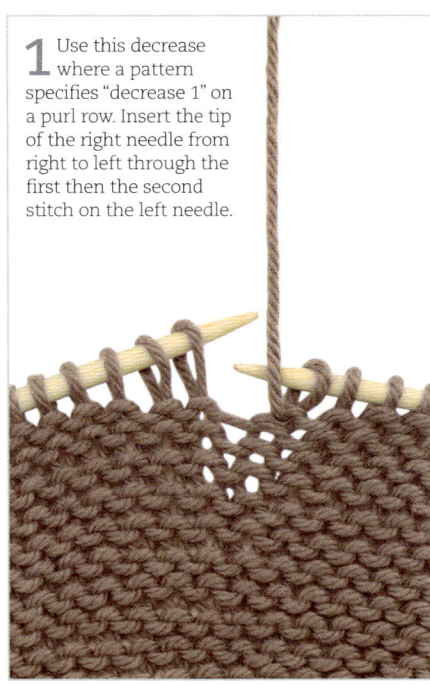

1 Use this decrease where a pattern specifies "decrease 1" on a purl row. Insert the tip of the right needle from right to left through the first then the second stitch on the left needle.

2 Wrap the yarn around the tip of the right needle, draw the yarn through both loops and drop the old stitches off the left needle.

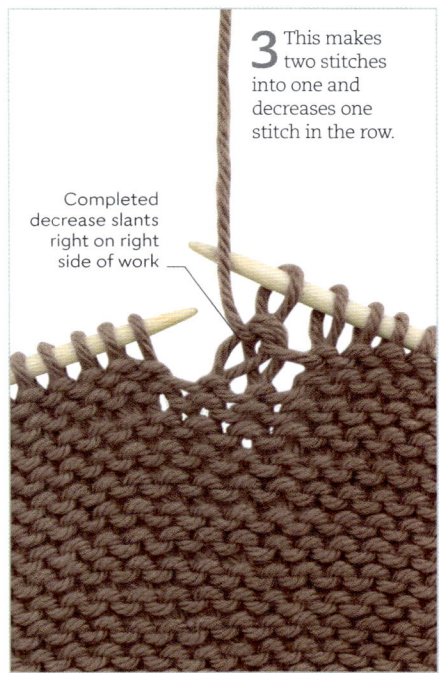

3 This makes two stitches into one and decreases one stitch in the row.

Completed decrease slants right on right side of work

SLIP ONE, KNIT ONE, PASS SLIPPED STITCH OVER (Abbreviation = *s1 k1 psso or skpo*)

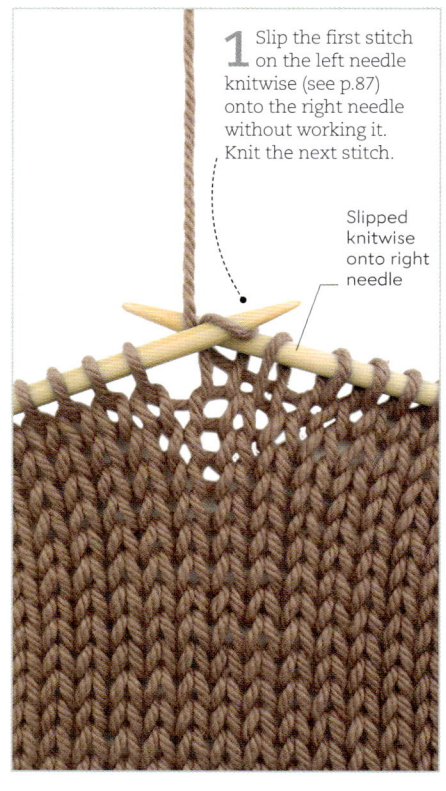

1 Slip the first stitch on the left needle knitwise (see p.87) onto the right needle without working it. Knit the next stitch.

Slipped knitwise onto right needle

2 Pick up the slipped stitch with the tip of the left needle and pass it over the knit stitch and off the right needle.

3 This makes two stitches into one and decreases one stitch in the row.

Completed decrease slants left on the right side of the fabric

SLIP, SLIP, KNIT (Abbreviation = *ssk*)

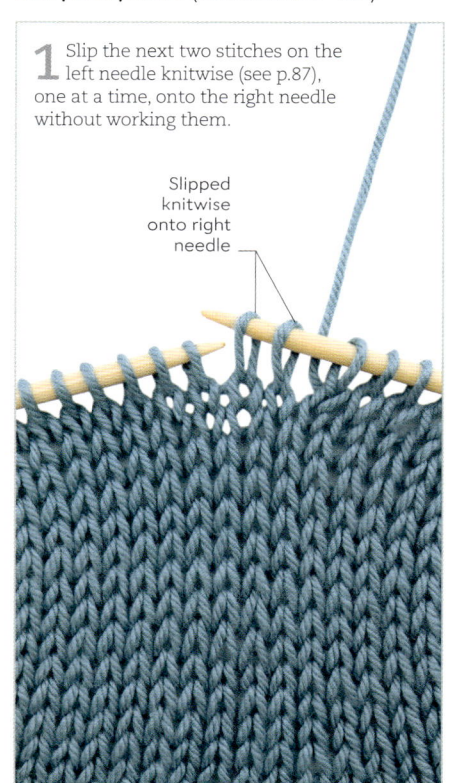

1 Slip the next two stitches on the left needle knitwise (see p.87), one at a time, onto the right needle without working them.

Slipped knitwise onto right needle

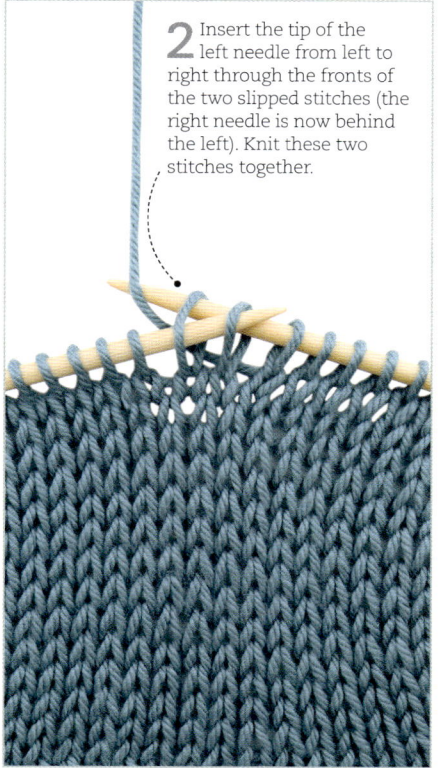

2 Insert the tip of the left needle from left to right through the fronts of the two slipped stitches (the right needle is now behind the left). Knit these two stitches together.

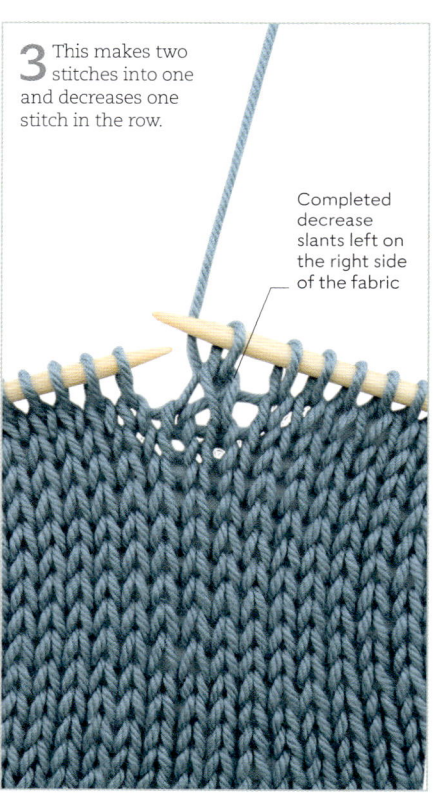

3 This makes two stitches into one and decreases one stitch in the row.

Completed decrease slants left on the right side of the fabric

SLIP, SLIP, PURL (Abbreviation = ssp)

1 Keeping the yarn at the front, slip two stitches, one at a time, knitwise (see p.87) onto the right needle without working them as for ssk decrease.

2 Holding the needles tip to tip, insert the left needle into both stitches and transfer back to the left needle without twisting them.

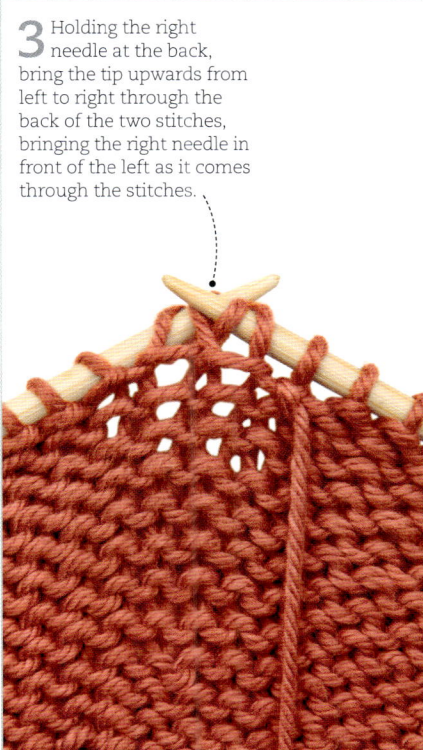

3 Holding the right needle at the back, bring the tip upwards from left to right through the back of the two stitches, bringing the right needle in front of the left as it comes through the stitches.

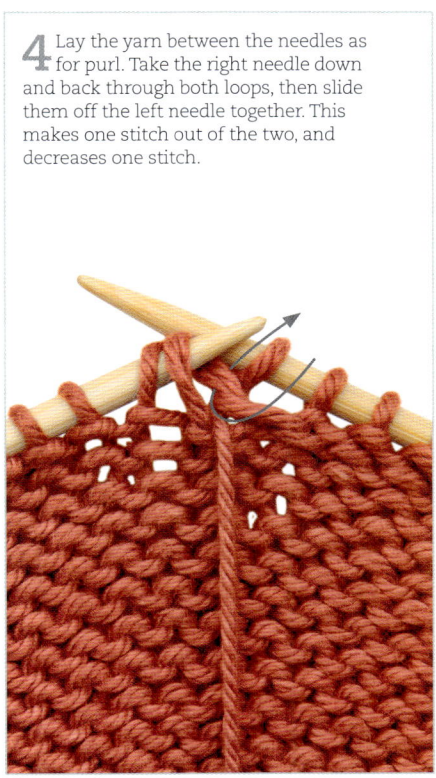

4 Lay the yarn between the needles as for purl. Take the right needle down and back through both loops, then slide them off the left needle together. This makes one stitch out of the two, and decreases one stitch.

DOUBLE DECREASES

k3tog: Insert the tip of the right needle from left to right into the third stitch on the left needle, then the second, then the first. Knit the three together. This decreases two stitches at once.

Top stitch in decrease slants right on the right side of the fabric

s1 k2tog psso: Slip one stitch knitwise onto the right needle, knit next two stitches together, then pass the slipped stitch over the k2tog and off the right needle. This decreases two stitches at once. See also p.105.

Top stitch in decrease slants left on the right side of the fabric

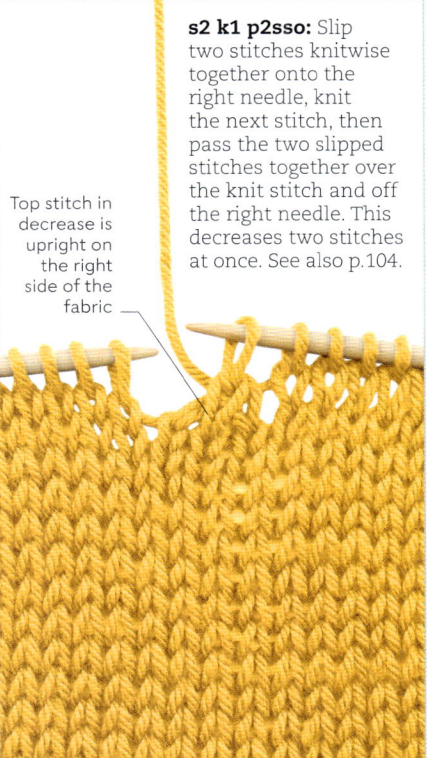

s2 k1 p2sso: Slip two stitches knitwise together onto the right needle, knit the next stitch, then pass the two slipped stitches together over the knit stitch and off the right needle. This decreases two stitches at once. See also p.104.

Top stitch in decrease is upright on the right side of the fabric

DECORATIVE CENTRAL INCREASES AND DECREASES

Although paired increases and decreases are most commonly used for edge shaping in knitting, they become highly decorative as well as functional when worked close together within the main fabric. For example, central decreases might be spaced around a flared peplum as part of the pattern while central increases could emphasize waist-to-bust darting. Decorative central decreases are sometimes combined with yarnover increases in more complex lace patterns. All increase or decrease two stitches in the row.

KNIT INTO FRONT AND BACK AS A PAIRED CENTRAL INCREASE (Abbreviation = *cdi* and *incto3*)

1 This example works a central paired increase on the knit rows of stocking stitch. It uses the Knit into front and back increase (see p.92). This forms a "bar" to the left of the stitch into which the increase is worked; therefore it must be offset when worked as a balanced, paired increase. Mark the centre stitch, moving this up as you work.

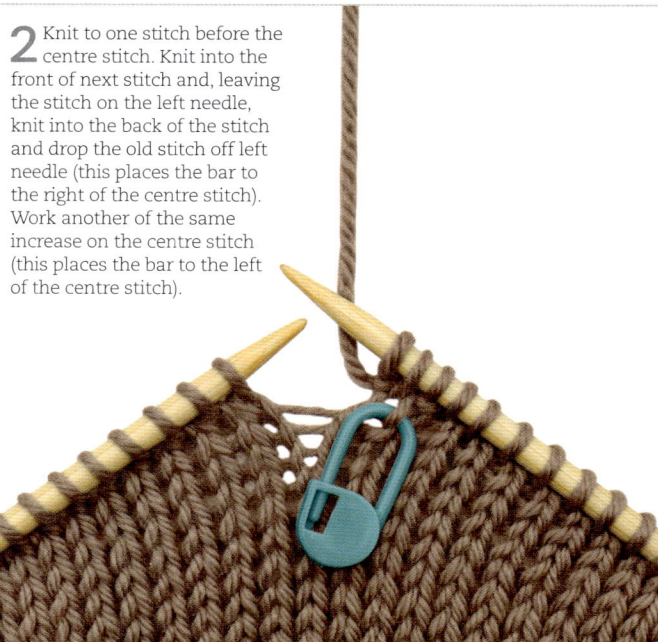

2 Knit to one stitch before the centre stitch. Knit into the front of next stitch and, leaving the stitch on the left needle, knit into the back of the stitch and drop the old stitch off left needle (this places the bar to the right of the centre stitch). Work another of the same increase on the centre stitch (this places the bar to the left of the centre stitch).

3 Knit to the end of the row. Purl one complete row, and repeat the increase sequence. This increase can be made in a similar manner into a purl stitch, in which case the bar lies to the right of the stitch.

4 This increase can be used in fully fashioned shaping (see p.109), in which case work the increase on the second stitch from the beginning of the row and the third from the end to leave two stitches symmetrically along the selvedges.

DECORATIVE CENTRAL INCREASES AND DECREASES **103**

• **OPEN CENTRAL INCREASE** (Abbreviation = *kyok*)

1 Knit to the stitch where the increase will be made. Insert the right needle into the stitch knitwise and knit, but do not drop the stitch off the left needle.

2 Bring the yarn to the front between the needles, then over the right needle to the back (creating a yarnover). Knit into the same stitch again, then drop the old stitch off the left needle.

3 This creates three stitches (knit, yarnover, knit) from one. Repeat Steps 1 and 2 in the same stitch on following alternate rows to create a decorative double increase on every other row.

• **CLOSED CENTRAL INCREASE** (Abbreviation = *cdi* and *incto3*)

1 Work the row, stopping before knitting the central stitch. Knit into the back and the front of the central stitch and slide off the left needle. Gently pull the yarn to tension the last stitch.

2 Look for the vertical strand stretching downwards immediately to the right of this stitch. Insert the tip of the left needle from the left into this strand and knit into the back of the loop.

3 Knit to the end of the row. Purl the next row. Repeat Steps 1–3, remembering that there will be one more stitch to knit on each row before working the increase.

RAISED CENTRAL DECREASE (Abbreviation = *cdd*)

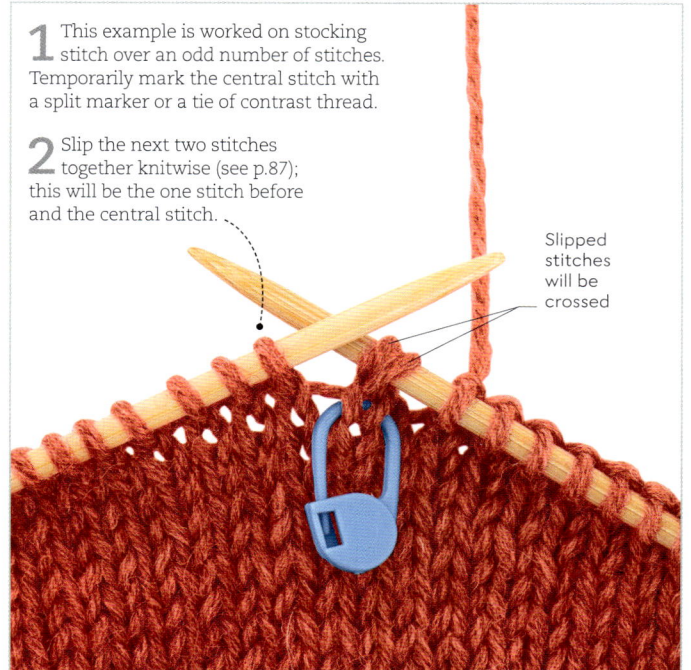

1. This example is worked on stocking stitch over an odd number of stitches. Temporarily mark the central stitch with a split marker or a tie of contrast thread.

2. Slip the next two stitches together knitwise (see p.87); this will be the one stitch before and the central stitch.

Slipped stitches will be crossed

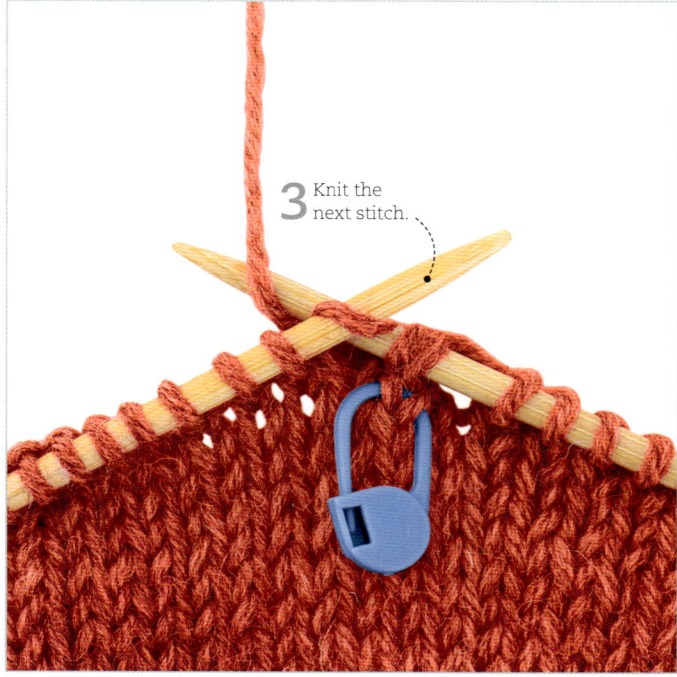

3. Knit the next stitch.

4. Insert the tip of the left needle into both slipped stitches and pass them together over the first stitch and off the right needle. This decreases two stitches. Knit to the end of the row, or to the next decrease. Purl the next row.

5. Repeat Steps 2–4 as required. To ensure that the decrease is worked in the correct place on each decreasing row, work to one stitch before the marked raised central stitch. If you find it difficult to see this, move the stitch marker upwards as you knit.

▶ TIP

- The technique of s2 k1 p2sso is also described on p.101. Worked once as shown there it's a simple decrease, but when worked in the same spot on alternate rows as described on this page, it gives the appearance of a raised central stitch travelling up the front of the work in a straight line.

FLAT CENTRAL DECREASE (Abbreviation = cdd)

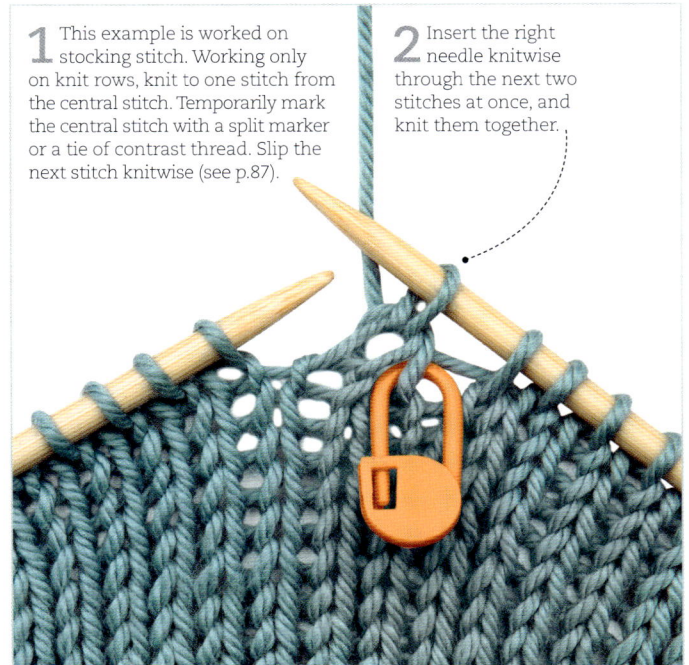

1. This example is worked on stocking stitch. Working only on knit rows, knit to one stitch from the central stitch. Temporarily mark the central stitch with a split marker or a tie of contrast thread. Slip the next stitch knitwise (see p.87).

2. Insert the right needle knitwise through the next two stitches at once, and knit them together.

3. Insert the left needle into the second stitch on the right needle and pass it over the last stitch and off the needle. Knit to the end of the row.

4. To keep the decrease central, knit to one stitch before the central stitch of the decrease below before repeating Steps 1–3. This technique decreases one stitch either side of the central stitch.

▶ TIP

- The technique of s1 k2tog psso is also described on p.101. Worked once as shown there it's a simple decrease, but when worked in the same spot on alternate rows as described on this page, it creates a subtle line of decreases, which is ideal if a stylized and visible line of shaping is not desirable in your project.

PAIRED INCREASES AND DECREASES

Increases or decreases at each end of a row can be worked to slant left or right so that the edges mirror each other. When working a pattern, one or two edge stitches can be worked plain so that the shaping does not affect the pattern. The traditional pairings below give a smooth finish, but can be reversed to create an alternative edge.

SUMMARY OF INCREASES AND DECREASES

PAIRED INCREASES			
WHEN MADE AT END OF A ROW	**ABBREVIATION**	**WHEN MADE AT BEGINNING OF A ROW**	**ABBREVIATION**
Slants left on the knit side of stocking stitch – increases the right edge		Slants right on the knit side of stocking stitch – increases the left edge	
Knit (or purl) in front and back of stitch	*kfb or inc1*	Knit (or purl) in front and back of stitch	*kfb or inc1*
Purl in front and back increases: • on a purl row seen from knit side, bar to the right of the stitch into which increase is made		Knit in front and back increases: • on a knit row seen from knit side, bar to the left of the stitch into which increase is made	
Left lifted increase	*LL1 or M1L*	Right lifted increase	*RL1 or M1R*
• virtually invisible • must have rows between or will pull • shows to right of increased stitch – slants the original stitch to the left and towards the selvedge when used for edge shaping		• virtually invisible • must have rows between or will pull • shows to left of increased stitch – slants the original stitch to the right and towards the selvedge when used for edge shaping	
Make one knit (or purl) left cross	*M1L*	Make one knit (or purl) right cross	*M1R*
• virtually invisible • must have rows between or will pull • made between stitches, so shows where placed • slants the stitch worked after it to the left		• virtually invisible • must have rows between or will pull • made between stitches, so shows where placed • slants the stitch worked before it to the right	

PAIRED DECREASES			
WHEN MADE AT END OF A ROW	**ABBREVIATION**	**WHEN MADE AT START OF A ROW**	**ABBREVIATION**
Right slant – decreases the left of the knit side of stocking stitch		Left slant – decreases the right of the knit side of stocking stitch	
Knit (or purl) two together	*k2tog (p2tog)*	Slip, slip, knit (or slip, slip, purl)	*ssk (ssp)*
		Slip one, knit one, pass slipped stitch over	*skp, s1 k1 psso, or skpo*
		Knit (or purl) two together through back of loops	*k2tog tbl (p2tog tbl) or k-b2tog (p-b2tog)*

PAIRED INCREASES AND DECREASES **107**

PAIRED LIFTED EDGE INCREASE

This example increases each side of stocking stitch using a right Lifted increase (see p.93) at the start, and its paired left Lifted increase at the end of every alternate knit row.

1 On an increase row, knit one stitch. Make a right Lifted increase by inserting the tip of the right needle from front to back into the right side of the stitch below the next stitch on the left needle (be careful not to catch more than one strand of yarn). Knit this lifted loop.

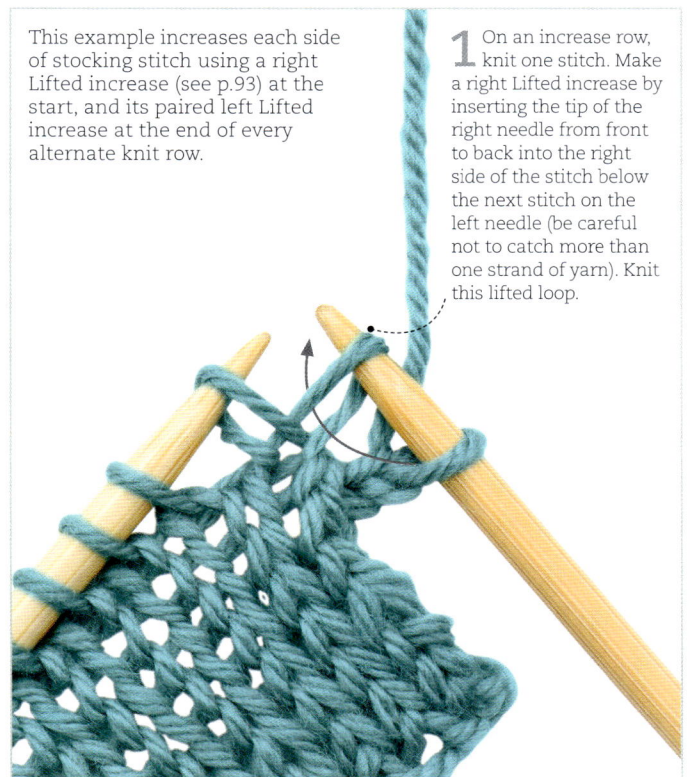

2 Knit to the last but one stitch of the row. Make a left Lifted increase by inserting the left needle tip from front to back into the left side of the stitch two rows below the new stitch on the right needle. Knit this loop, and knit the last stitch.

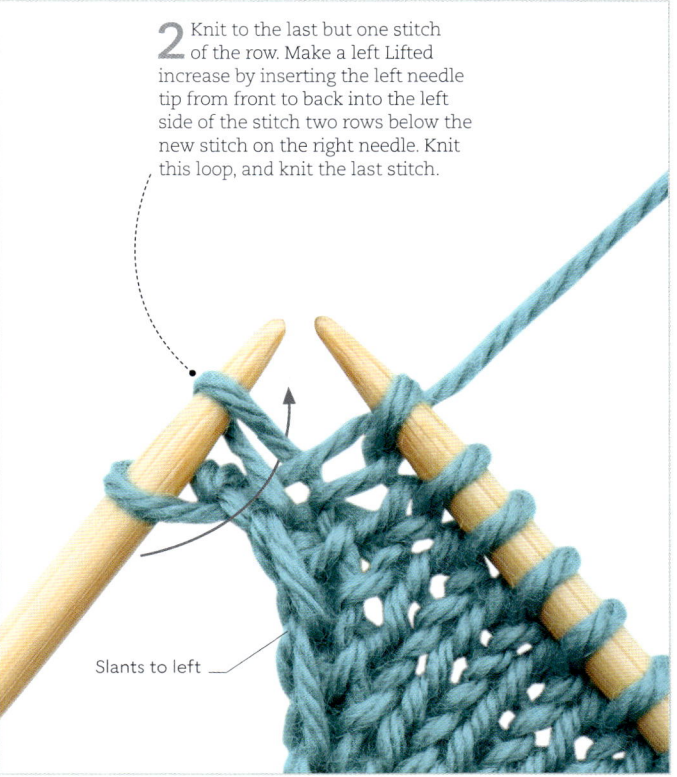

Slants to left

3 If you find the left Lifted increase awkward, pick the loop up with the left needle from back to front, slip it onto the right needle, twisting it as it is returned to the left. Knit into the front of the loop.

4 The paired increases look like this when completed over a number of rows.

PAIRED EDGE DECREASES (Abbreviation = *skp* and *k2tog*)

This example has decreases on each side of stocking stitch. It has a slip one, knit one, pass slipped stitch over (skp) at the beginning of the row, which is paired with knit two together (k2tog) at the end of the row. Slip, slip, knit (ssk) may be substituted for skp if preferred.

1 At the start of a knit row, work a slip1, knit1, psso as shown on p.100.

2 Knit to two stitches from the end of the row and knit two stitches together as shown on p.99.

"k2tog" slants to the right on left edge

"skp" slants to the left on right edge

FULLY FASHIONED SHAPING **109**

FULLY FASHIONED SHAPING

This is a method of increasing or decreasing width while preserving a line of stitches along the edge. In knit and purl textures, switching to two stitches in stocking stitch at the edge enables you to decrease over textured fabric and create an attractive seam edge that also makes sewing up easier. Use paired increases and decreases on a symmetrical piece: a left slope mirrored by a right slope on the other side.

ON A KNIT ROW (Abbreviation = *ssk* and *k2tog*)

This example decreases one stitch at each end of a knit row but leaves two plain stitches at the selvedge.

1 Knit the first two stitches. Slip the next two stitches knitwise, one by one onto the right needle. Insert the left needle from left to right through the front of both stitches and knit together. This is a left-slanting ssk decrease (see p.100).

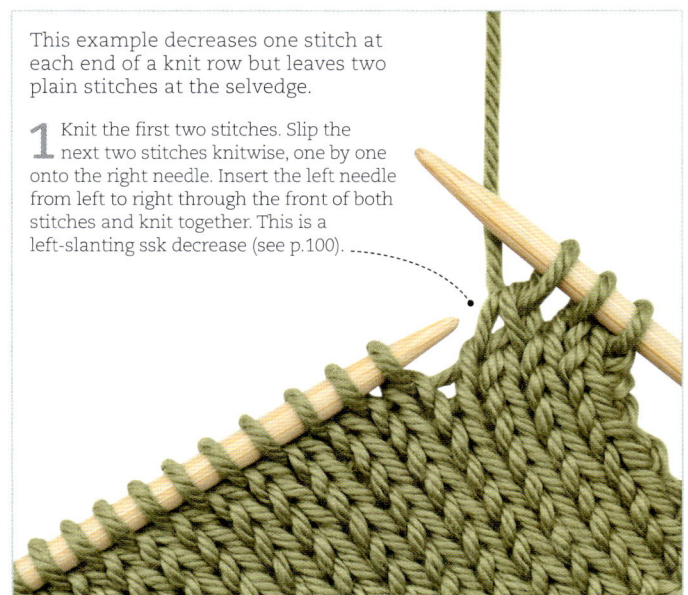

2 Knit to four stitches from the end of the row. Knit two stitches together (see p.99) and then knit the last two stitches. This slopes to the right.

"k2tog" on stitches slanting to right on left edge

"ssk" on stitches slanting to left on right edge

ON A PURL ROW (Abbreviation = *ssp* and *p2tog*)

This example decreases one stitch at each end of a purl row but leaves two plain stitches at the selvedge.

1 Purl the first two stitches. Slip the next two stitches one at a time knitwise onto the right needle. Slip them back together without twisting. Insert the right needle into the front of both stitches from the right and purl them together (ssp). This slopes to the right.

2 Work to four stitches from the end, purl two stitches together (see p.99) and purl the last two stitches. This slopes to the left. Ssk and ssp work better than other decreases when paired with k2tog or p2tog

"ssp" on stitches slanting to right on left edge

"p2tog" on stitches slanting to left on right edge

Twists and cables

Many interesting textures can be created by combining knit and purl stitches in various sequences (see pp.278–282), but if you are looking for textures with higher relief and more sculptural qualities, cables and twists are the techniques to learn. Both are made by crossing stitches over each other in different ways to form an array of intricate patterns.

SIMPLE TWISTS

A simple twist is made over only two stitches, without a cable needle. Although twists do not create such high relief as cables, their ease and subtlety makes them very popular. The following twists are worked in stocking stitch on a stocking stitch ground. They can also be worked with one knit and one purl stitch – the principle is the same.

RIGHT TWIST (Abbreviation = *t2r*)

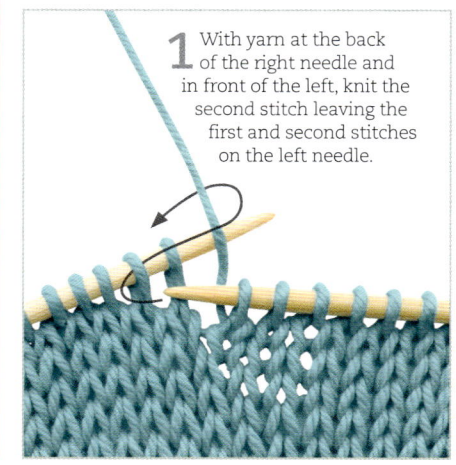

1 With yarn at the back of the right needle and in front of the left, knit the second stitch leaving the first and second stitches on the left needle.

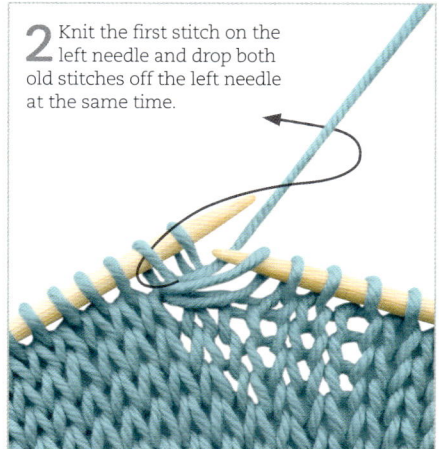

2 Knit the first stitch on the left needle and drop both old stitches off the left needle at the same time.

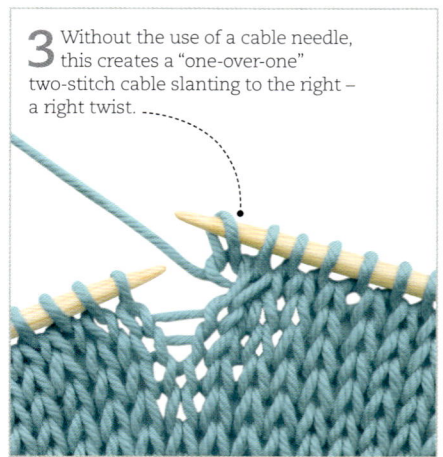

3 Without the use of a cable needle, this creates a "one-over-one" two-stitch cable slanting to the right – a right twist.

LEFT TWIST (Abbreviation = *t2l*)

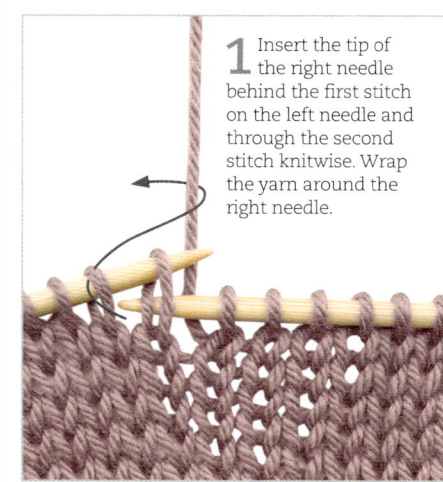

1 Insert the tip of the right needle behind the first stitch on the left needle and through the second stitch knitwise. Wrap the yarn around the right needle.

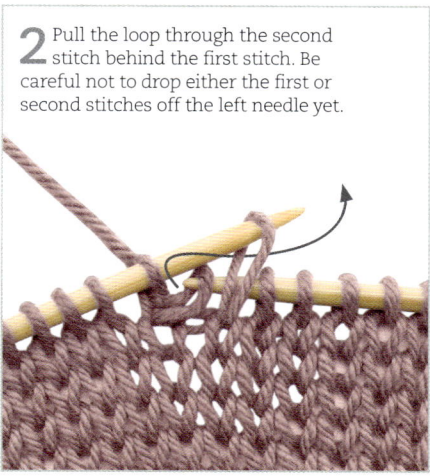

2 Pull the loop through the second stitch behind the first stitch. Be careful not to drop either the first or second stitches off the left needle yet.

3 Knit the first stitch on the left needle and drop both old stitches off the left needle. This creates a two-stitch cable slanting to the left – a left twist.

CABLES

Cables are usually worked in stocking stitch on a reverse stocking stitch (or garter stitch) ground. They are made by crossing two, three, four or more stitches over other stitches in the row. This technique is illustrated here with the cable 4 front and cable 4 back cables, which are crossed on every sixth row.

CABLE 4 FRONT (Abbreviation = c4f)

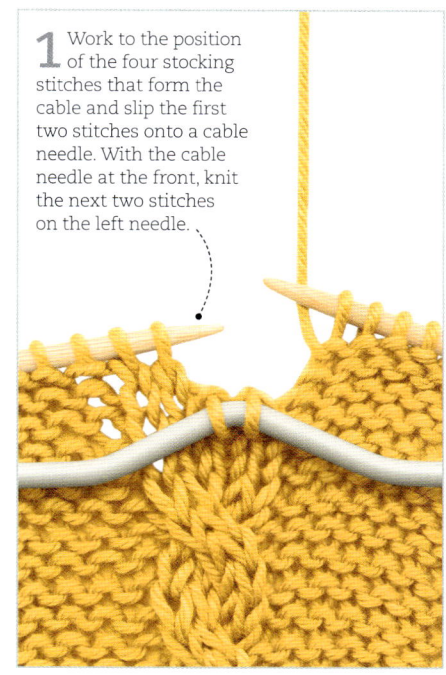

1 Work to the position of the four stocking stitches that form the cable and slip the first two stitches onto a cable needle. With the cable needle at the front, knit the next two stitches on the left needle.

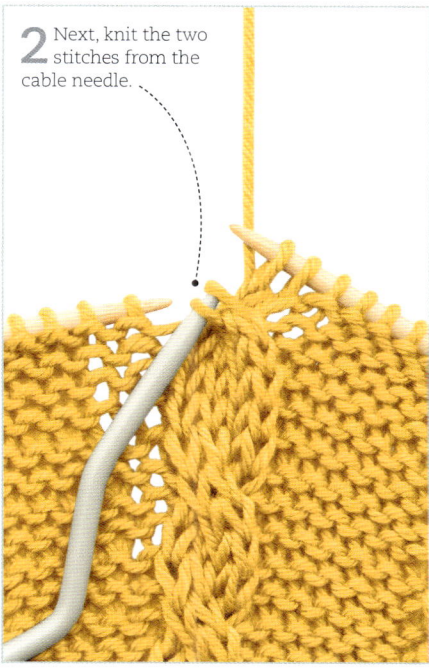

2 Next, knit the two stitches from the cable needle.

3 This creates a cable crossing that slants to the left. For this reason, a "front" cable is also called a "left" cable.

CABLE 4 BACK (Abbreviation = c4b)

1 Work as for Step 1 of Cable 4 front (above), but hold the cable needle to the back instead of the front of the knitting.

2 Knit the two stitches from the cable needle.

3 This creates a cable crossing that slants to the right. For this reason, a "back" cable is also called a "right" cable.

I-Cord

I-cord stands for "idiot" cord and is also known as slip cord. An i-cord makes a neat edging or can be used for straps and ties, or for appliqué in a contrast colour. Use smaller needles for a tighter edge and work at a firm tension. i-cords can be knitted using double-pointed needles or circular needles.

FREE FORM I-CORD

These cords can be applied to an item later, so it is possible to add extra detail as they are worked. Stripes, texture, structural effects, and even beads can be incorporated. With its simple method but multiple uses, i-cord is a very versatile technique.

SIMPLE I-CORD – FOR APPLIQUÉ, TIES, AND STRAPS

1 Cast on five stitches using the Single cast-on shown on p.53. Knit one row.

2 Transfer the needle to your left hand without turning it, and slide all the stitches to the right end of the needle, so that the yarn appears to be at the wrong end to knit another row.

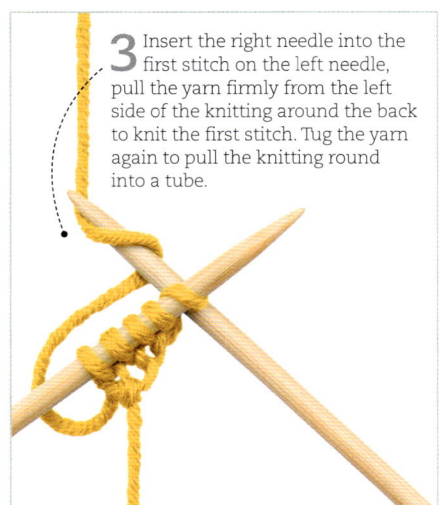

3 Insert the right needle into the first stitch on the left needle, pull the yarn firmly from the left side of the knitting around the back to knit the first stitch. Tug the yarn again to pull the knitting round into a tube.

4 Repeat Steps 2 and 3 until the cord is the required length.

SPIRAL I-CORD

This version works up shorter than stocking stitch i-cord (above), but it is stretchier.

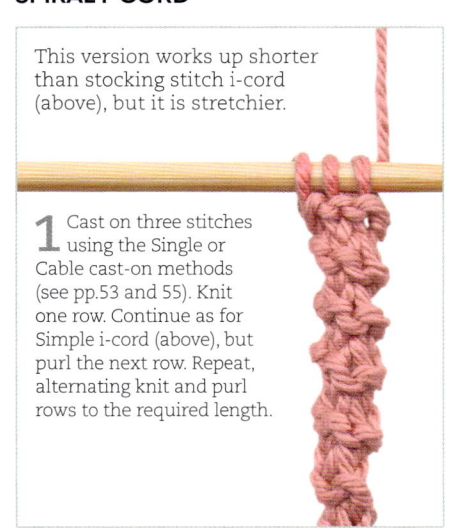

1 Cast on three stitches using the Single or Cable cast-on methods (see pp.53 and 55). Knit one row. Continue as for Simple i-cord (above), but purl the next row. Repeat, alternating knit and purl rows to the required length.

TWO-COLOURED I-CORD

1 Cast on five stitches using Single cast-on (see p.53). Knit the first stitch in the main colour.

2 Insert the right needle into the second stitch and lay the contrast yarn between the needles. Knit the second stitch.

3 Drop the contrast, pick up the main colour, and knit the third stitch. Repeat, alternating colours, ending with the main colour.

4 Slide stitches to the other end of the needle as in Simple i-cord (above). Keeping the colours in sequence, knit the next row. Repeat Steps 2–4 to required length. See techniques for holding the yarns on p.51.

ATTACHED I-CORD

Attaching i-cords as you work saves time sewing up later on. I-cords can be added to a finished piece for edging, or form part of the main project as a cast-off. Their use as button loops and soft buttons add attractive and unique finishes to garments.

I-CORD EDGING

1 Cast on between two and five stitches. Knit one row. Transfer the needle to your left hand. Slide stitches as for Simple i-cord (see opposite).

2 Pull the yarn around back of the stitches and knit all but the last stitch of the next row. Slip the remaining stitch knitwise from left to right.

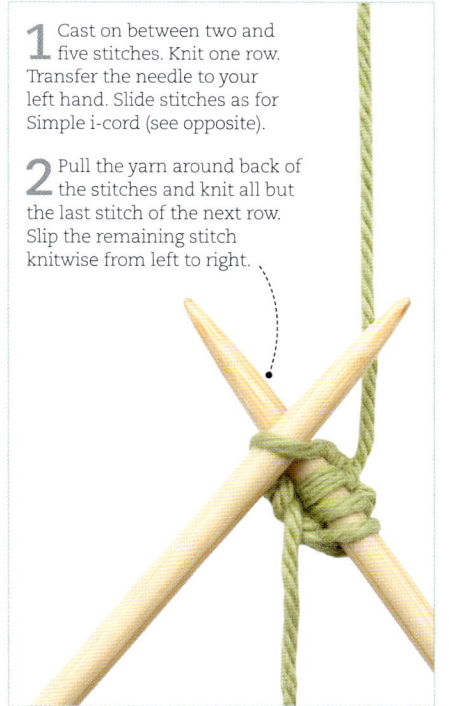

3 With an empty left needle, pick up the extreme right loop of the lowest stitch on the main fabric edge from left to right. (This ensures the stitch is correctly positioned for Step 4.)

4 Hold the needle with i-cord to the right of the edge of the main fabric. Knit the stitch on the left needle onto the right one. There will now be one extra stitch on the right needle. Insert the left needle into the second stitch on the right needle (slipped stitch) and pass it over the first stitch.

5 Repeat Steps 2–4. If the i-cord is joined, graft open stitches (see p.190) for a smooth join. When edging curves, use a larger needle in the right hand, reverting to the original size on straight sections.

I-CORD BUTTON LOOP

1 Leave a tail of yarn four times the selvedge length. Using a circular needle and the yarn tail, pick up into the selvedge (RS facing). Return to the starting end of the needle, and cast on three stitches using Cable cast-on (see p.55).

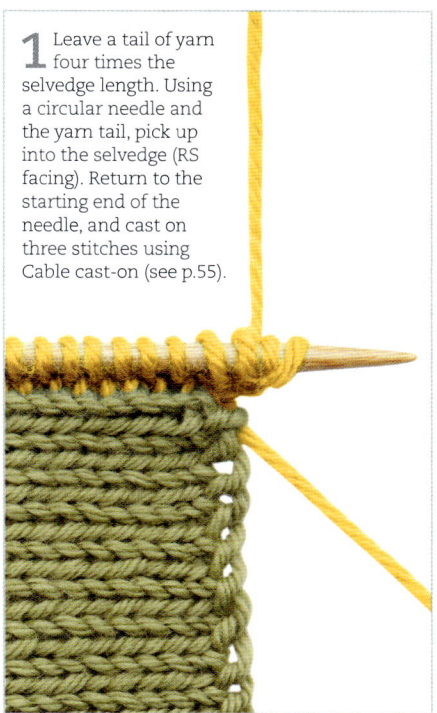

2 Using a double-pointed needle, knit two stitches. Slip the last i-cord and first edge stitch onto the right needle, knitwise, one by one. Insert a double-pointed needle from left to right into the front of both stitches and knit together (ssk). Repeat this step to the position of the button loop.

3 Continue with the unattached i-cord until the loop is the correct size for the button. Join the i-cord to the main fabric as in Step 2.

I-CORD CAST-OFF

1 If the i-cord is to be in a contrast colour, work the last row of the main piece in the contrast yarn. Holding the work to be cast off in the left hand, add three stitches to left needle using Cable cast-on (see p.55).

2 Knit two stitches. Slip the next two stitches (last of i-cord and first of edge stitches) onto the right needle one by one knitwise. Insert a double-pointed needle from left to right into the front of both stitches and knit together (ssk).

3 Slip the three stitches on the double-pointed needle to the opposite end. Repeat Steps 2 and 3 to end of cast-off. This technique is worked the same on the purl side of the work. Work loosely as i-cord can pucker the cast-off edge if worked tight.

I-CORD CAST-ON

1 Using a needle size slightly larger than that to be used for the project, make an i-cord of three stitches (see p.112), with a number of rows equivalent to the number of stitches you need to cast on.

2 After the final row, work s2 k1 p2sso (see p.101) to bring the stitch count down to one.

3 Change to the needle size for the main project, pick up and knit (see p.168) into one stitch for every row worked on your i-cord, being sure to go under both loops of the "V" in your stitches.

I-CORD ON KNITTING DOLLY

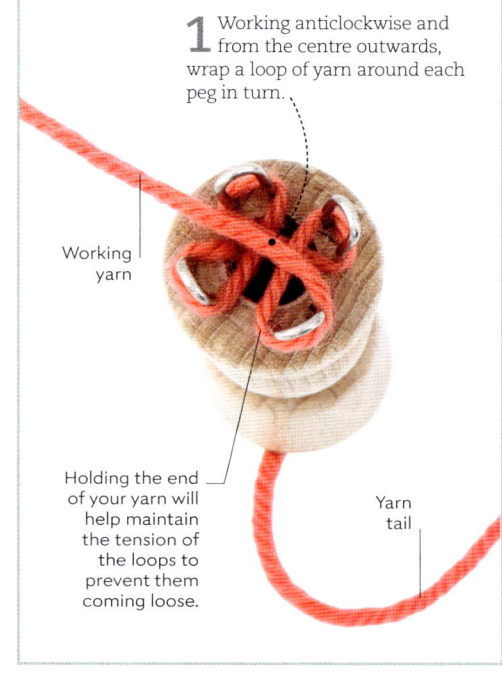

1 Working anticlockwise and from the centre outwards, wrap a loop of yarn around each peg in turn.

Working yarn

Holding the end of your yarn will help maintain the tension of the loops to prevent them coming loose.

Yarn tail

2 Repeat Step 1 so that each peg has two loops of yarn. Using the pin that came with the knitting dolly, lift the first loop over the second on each peg.

Hold your working yarn against the dolly while you work this step.

3 Continue to wrap loops around each peg, so that each has two loops, and then lift the first loop over the second. Continue in this way until the i-cord reaches the required length, remembering that part of it will be inside the knitting dolly. To finish, remove the last loops from the peg and draw up the remaining stitches using a darning needle.

Lift the i-cord upwards on finishing.

When measuring your i-cord prior to finishing, be sure to include the length of the dolly, as some of the cord will be hidden within.

▶ USING A KNITTING DOLLY

- A knitting dolly (see p.44) usually has four pegs set around the top, so this would create an i-cord four stitches wide.
- At the start you will need to tuck the yarn end down through the central hole of the knitting dolly. You can use a darning needle for this if necessary.
- You will need to hold on to the starting yarn end as you work to maintain the tension.

Lace knitting

The airy openwork texture of knitted lace is formed by combining yarnovers and decreases to create holes (or eyelets) all over the fabric. Although lace knitting looks complicated, the techniques are relatively easy. If you choose a lace stitch with a short horizontal stitch repeat, you can work the openwork fabric quickly and still produce impressive delicate textures.

CHAIN EYELET

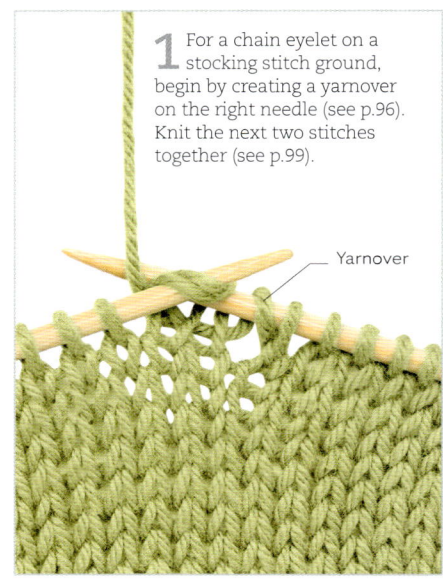

1 For a chain eyelet on a stocking stitch ground, begin by creating a yarnover on the right needle (see p.96). Knit the next two stitches together (see p.99).

Yarnover

2 The yarnover creates a hole in the knitting and the k2tog decrease compensates for the extra loop so that the knitting remains the same width.

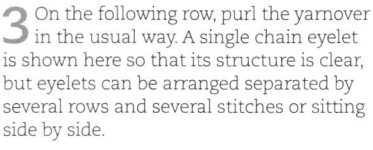

3 On the following row, purl the yarnover in the usual way. A single chain eyelet is shown here so that its structure is clear, but eyelets can be arranged separated by several rows and several stitches or sitting side by side.

OPEN EYELET

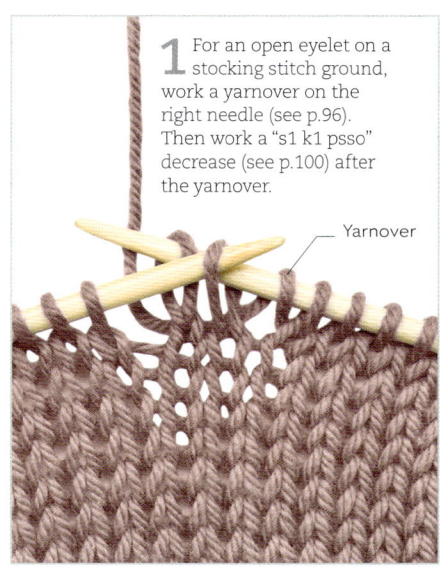

1 For an open eyelet on a stocking stitch ground, work a yarnover on the right needle (see p.96). Then work a "s1 k1 psso" decrease (see p.100) after the yarnover.

Yarnover

2 The yarnover creates a hole and the decrease compensates for the extra loop so that the knitting remains the same width.

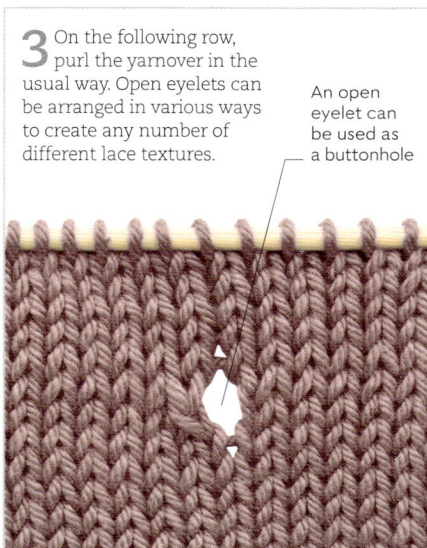

3 On the following row, purl the yarnover in the usual way. Open eyelets can be arranged in various ways to create any number of different lace textures.

An open eyelet can be used as a buttonhole

▶ **TIPS FOR LACE KNITTING**

• Eyelets arranged in various ways are the basis of all lace stitches. Eyelets are made up of yarnovers (see pp.96–98), which produce the holes in the fabric, and decreases, which frame the eyelets and compensate for these increases in the row to keep the knitting the same width. The techniques for two simple eyelets are given here, but there are other ways of producing eyelets and these methods are always explained in full in the stitch instructions.

• Cast on loosely for lace patterns. This is best achieved not by trying to make loose loops but by spacing the cast-on stitches farther apart on the knitting needle, with at least 3mm (⅛in) between the loops. If you find this difficult to do evenly, then use a needle one or two sizes larger than the size you are using for the lace and switch to the correct needle size on the first row. Depending on the yarn, long-tipped metal needles may be easier to work with than wooden ones.

• Start simply. Lace patterns can have yarnovers and decreases in the first row. These are not easy to work on cast-on loops, so you can start with a plain row then begin the lace pattern on the following row.

• Use a row counter to keep track of where you are in the pattern. Inserting a lifeline (see p.86) by using a sewing needle to thread a thin, contrast colour yarn into each stitch along the same, plain row in every repeat will enable unravelling. This is especially important for intricate lace worked over a long row-repeat. If you do get lost in your pattern, unravel back to the lifeline and start over. Use stitch markers to separate each pattern repeat until you know it by heart.

• Count your stitches frequently when knitting lace to make sure you still have the right number of stitches. If you are missing a stitch you may have left out a yarnover. There is no need to undo stitches all the way back, simply work to the position of the missing yarnover on the following row, then insert the left needle from front to back under the strand between the stitch just worked and the next stitch on the left needle (see below). Work this stitch through the front of the loop in the usual way.

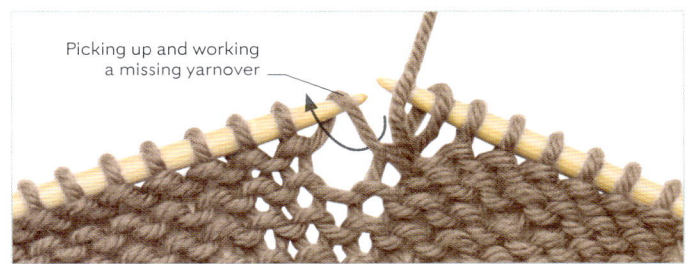

Picking up and working a missing yarnover

YARNS FOR LACE

Knitted lace was first designed to look similar to traditional needle lace, so it was worked on thin needles in white cotton thread. Lace weight and fine yarns (see pp.28–29) enhance the delicacy, but openwork knitting can look interesting in other yarns. Here are a few examples.

PSEUDO LACE

The quickest way to produce a delicate effect is to knit garter stitch using fine yarn and very large needles. You can make an attractive scarf this way in a flash, and any type of yarn, such as this metallic one, is suitable for the pseudo lace technique.

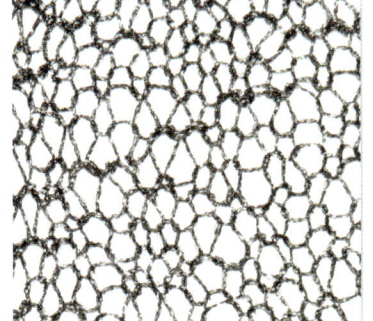

MULTICOLOURED OPENWORK

For added interest, use a double-knitting-weight yarn with variegated colours for openwork. This stitch pattern is Grand eyelet mesh stitch (see p.300), which looks the same on both sides and is extremely easy to work.

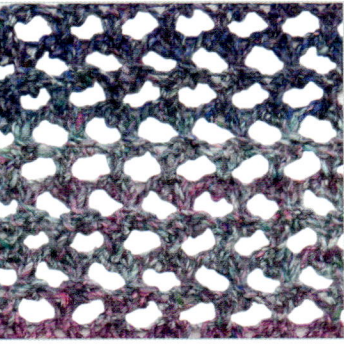

MOHAIR LACE

Fine mohair yarn highlights the delicacy of the lacy stitches. Try easy lace patterns such as this Mini-leaf pattern (see p.302) when using mohair, as it is more difficult to knit with than smooth yarn, and complicated lace doesn't show up clearly in textured yarns.

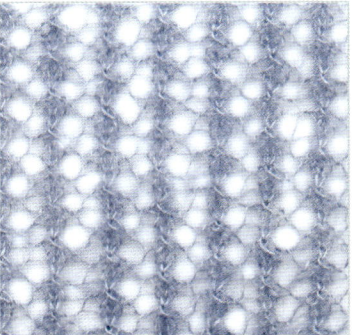

TRADITIONAL-STYLE KNITTED LACE

Fine cotton thread on very thin needles can be used to work traditional-style knitted lace. You can see how much more delicate this Domino eyelet pattern looks when knitted in lace weight yarn instead of a lightweight cotton yarn as on p.298.

Colourwork

You have many technique choices if you like adding colours to your knitting. The easiest method is to knit plain stocking stitch using a multicoloured yarn or a variegated yarn, which changes colour along the strand. To add colours into the knitting yourself, you can work simple stripes, easy colourwork stitch patterns, or charted Fair Isle or intarsia motifs.

SIMPLE STRIPES

Horizontal stripes are perfect for knitters who want to have fun with colour without learning more advanced techniques. These examples show the variety of stripe widths, colours, and textures available. You can follow any plain coloured pattern and introduce stripes in the same yarn without affecting the tension or shape of the knitting.

TWO-COLOUR GARTER STITCH STRIPE

This stripe pattern is worked in garter stitch in two colours (A and B). To work the stripe, knit 2 rows in each colour alternately, dropping the colour not in use at the side of the work and picking it up when it is needed again.

TWO-COLOUR KNIT AND PURL PINSTRIPE

Knit this stripe in two colours (A and B). Work 6 rows in stocking stitch in A. Drop A at the side and knit 2 rows in B – the second of these rows creates a purl ridge on the right side. Repeat this sequence for the pinstripe effect. To avoid loose strands of B at the edge, wrap A around B at the start of every right side row.

FIVE-COLOUR STOCKING STITCH STRIPE

To work multiple stripes and carry the colours up the side, use a circular needle. Work back and forth in rows. If a yarn you need to pick up is at the opposite end, push all the stitches back to the other end of the circular needle and work the next row with the same side of the knitting facing as the last row.

TIDYING THE EDGES

When working two-coloured, even row stripes, twist the yarns around each other every 1–2cm (½–¾in) up the side of the piece. Alternating the direction of the twist after each colour change prevents the yarns becoming tangled. Be careful not to pull them tightly or the edge will pucker. This technique may make a bulky seam if used with more than two colours.

DOMINO SQUARES

Also known as modular or mitred square knitting, in this technique small squares are worked individually and joined as you go. Each is started from the outer edge, decreasing toward the centre. This method is great for using up leftover yarns from your stash – and is perfect for blankets and scarves.

PLAIN-COLOUR DOMINO SQUARES

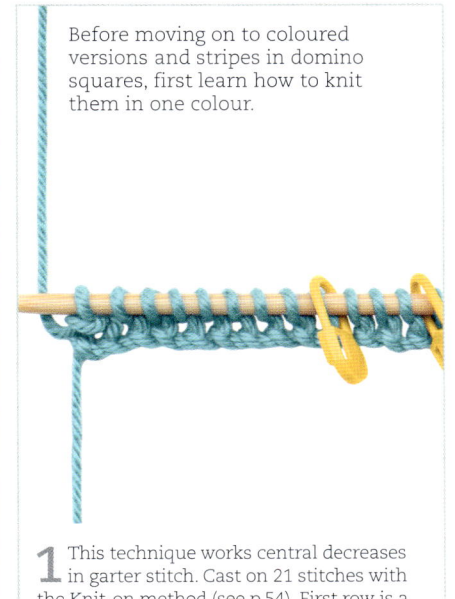

1 This technique works central decreases in garter stitch. Cast on 21 stitches with the Knit-on method (see p.54). First row is a wrong-side (WS) row. Slip first stitch knitwise, knit eight stitches. Add a marker, knit three stitches, and add another marker. Knit next eight stitches and purl the final one.

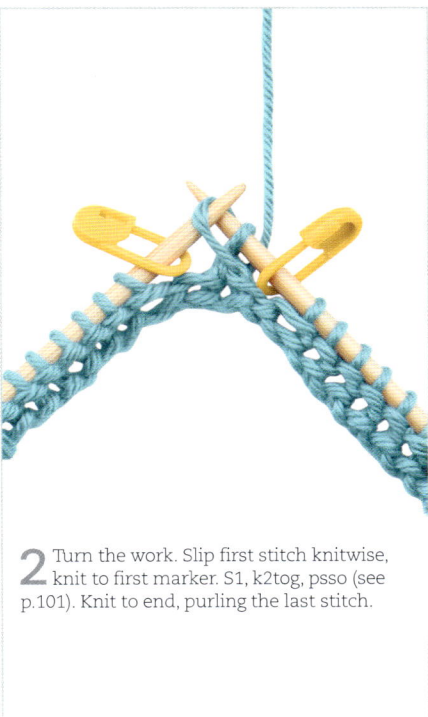

2 Turn the work. Slip first stitch knitwise, knit to first marker. S1, k2tog, psso (see p.101). Knit to end, purling the last stitch.

3 Slip the first stitch knitwise, knit to the last but one stitch, then purl the last stitch. Right side rows, on which the s1 k2tog psso is worked on the centre three stitches, are identified by the yarn tail being at the right.

4 Repeat Steps 2 and 3 until you have one stitch left. Cut the yarn and pull the end through as normal, but not tightly so that it can be re-threaded when another square is knitted on.

JOINING DOMINO SQUARES

1 With right side of original square facing and needle with remaining end stitch from last square in right hand, pick up and knit 10 stitches along the edge of the original square using the yarn for the new square (see p.168). Pick up through the centre of loops of edge stitches.

2 Cast on 10 stitches on the left needle using the Knit-on method (see p.54). Knit this square as for Plain-colour domino knitting (see above).

3 Continue to add squares, using different coloured yarns as required. When combined with the following technique, no sewing is required at all.

120 TECHNIQUES

• WEAVING IN ENDS DURING DOMINO KNITTING

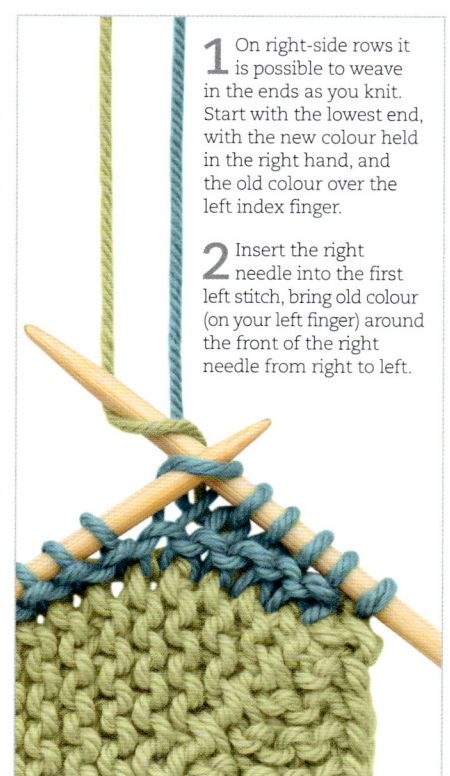

1 On right-side rows it is possible to weave in the ends as you knit. Start with the lowest end, with the new colour held in the right hand, and the old colour over the left index finger.

2 Insert the right needle into the first left stitch, bring old colour (on your left finger) around the front of the right needle from right to left.

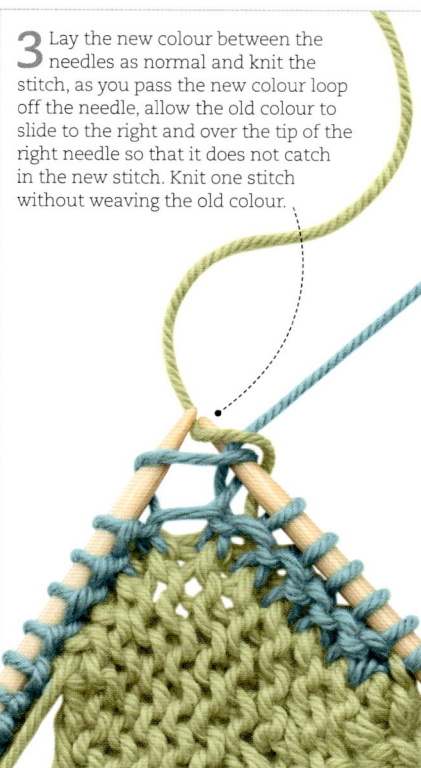

3 Lay the new colour between the needles as normal and knit the stitch, as you pass the new colour loop off the needle, allow the old colour to slide to the right and over the tip of the right needle so that it does not catch in the new stitch. Knit one stitch without weaving the old colour.

4 Repeat Steps 2 and 3 until the tail of the old colour is woven in and then drop it for trimming later and complete the square. Trim it leaving about 1cm (½in) of yarn to prevent it unravelling on the right side.

• STRIPED DOMINO SQUARES

1 Working as Plain domino square (see p.119), cast on 21 stitches. Knit the first row in the main colour.

2 Continue as plain domino square, alternating two rows of contrast and main colour as you work. To join in the contrast yarn see p.81. Carry the yarns up the side as you work.

▶ TIPS FOR DOMINO KNITTING

• Save all your yarn oddments in the same thickness and use them to make domino square projects. You can create vibrant and attractive colour mixes with surprisingly small leftover yarn amounts.

• Mix sizes of squares to create varied geometric patterns – four individual squares arranged to form a larger square can sit next to a single large square that is twice the size.

• Domino squares in garter stitch prevent curling, which is perfect for scarves and blankets.

• Try larger domino squares arranged in a strip one above the other to create a scarf in your chosen width.

• Using a self-striping yarn or variegated yarn throughout a domino knitting project can present a whole host of different coloured squares, but will help to keep the colours complementary to each other.

MULTICOLOUR SLIP-STITCH PATTERNS

Slip-stitch patterns are designed especially to use more than one colour in the overall pattern but only ever use one colour in a row. With this technique, geometric patterns are created by working some stitches in a row and slipping others. The pattern here is shown in two different colourways and is one of the easiest to work.

CHECK SLIP-STITCH PATTERN

Follow this pattern to work the stitch and use the steps below as a guide.
Use three colours for the pattern that contrast in tone: A (a medium-toned colour), B (a light-toned colour), and C (a dark-toned colour).
Note: Slip all slip stitches purlwise with the yarn on the wrong side (WS) of the work.
Using A, cast on a multiple of 4 stitches, plus 2 extra.
Row 1 (WS) Using A, p to end.
Row 2 (RS) Using B, k1, s1, *k2, s2; rep from * to last 3 sts, k2, s1, k1.
Row 3 Using B, p1, s1, *p2, s2; rep from * to last 3 sts, then p2, s1, p1.
Row 4 Using A, k to end.
Row 5 Using C, p2, *s2, p2; rep from *.
Row 6 Using C, k2, *s2, k2; rep from *.
Rep rows 1–6 to form patt.

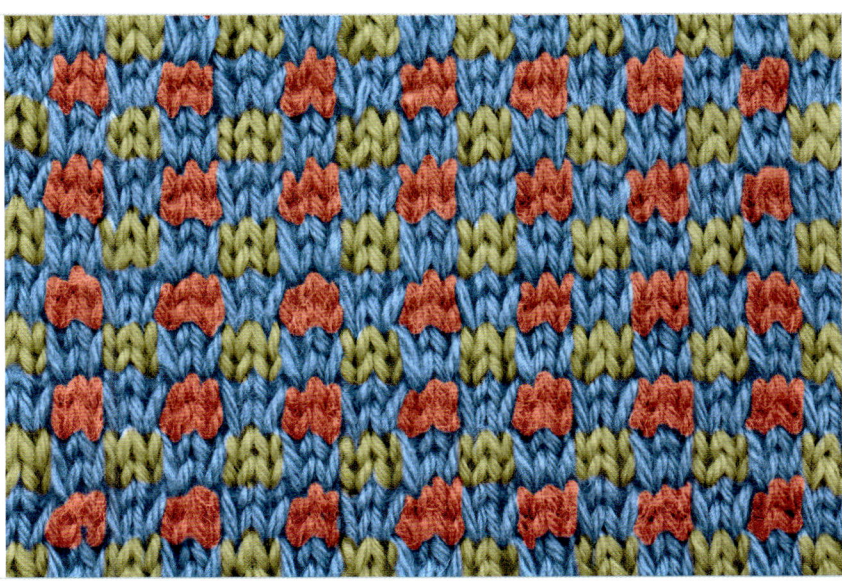

WORKING A CHECK SLIP-STITCH PATTERN

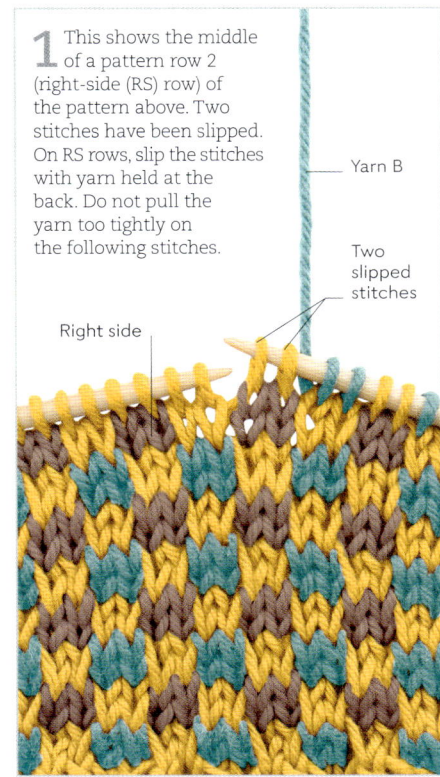

1 This shows the middle of a pattern row 2 (right-side (RS) row) of the pattern above. Two stitches have been slipped. On RS rows, slip the stitches with yarn held at the back. Do not pull the yarn too tightly on the following stitches.

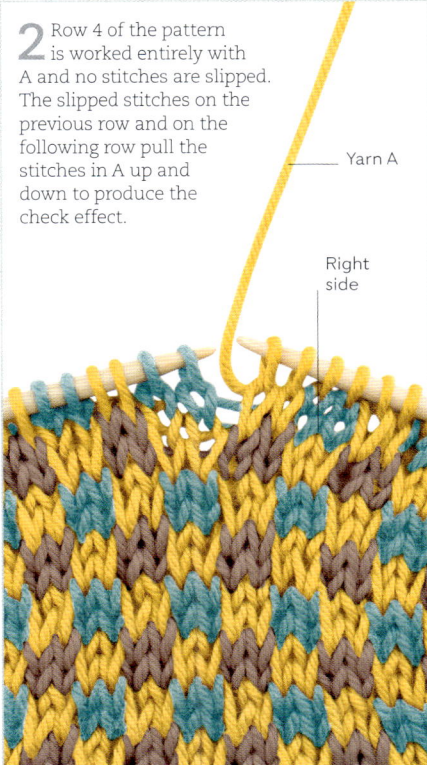

2 Row 4 of the pattern is worked entirely with A and no stitches are slipped. The slipped stitches on the previous row and on the following row pull the stitches in A up and down to produce the check effect.

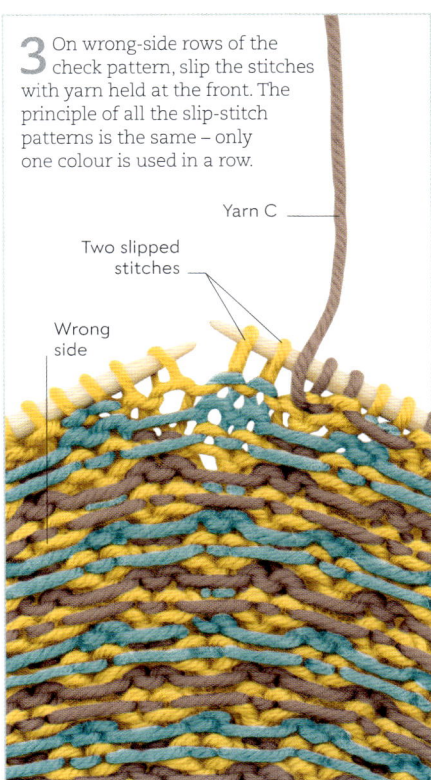

3 On wrong-side rows of the check pattern, slip the stitches with yarn held at the front. The principle of all the slip-stitch patterns is the same – only one colour is used in a row.

122 TECHNIQUES

CHARTED COLOURWORK

The techniques for charted stocking stitch colourwork – stranded colourwork and intarsia – open up a world of richly coloured designs. In stranded colourwork a yarn colour is carried across the wrong side until required. In intarsia, a separate length of yarn is used for each colour and yarns are twisted together at the colour change.

FOLLOWING A COLOURWORK CHART

The first step in understanding charted colourwork is to grasp how easy the charts are to follow. Rather than writing out how many stitches in which colours to work across a row, your knitting pattern provides a chart with the colours marked on it in symbols or in blocks of colour.

If a pattern covers the whole garment back, front, and sleeve and cannot be repeated, a large chart is provided for each of these elements with all the stitches on it for the entire piece. Where a pattern is a simple repeat, the repeat alone is charted. Each square on a stocking stitch colourwork chart represents a stitch and each horizontal row of squares represents a knitted row. You follow the chart from the bottom to the top, just as your knitting forms on the needles.

The key provided with the chart tells you which colour to use for each stitch. All odd-numbered rows on a colourwork chart are usually right-side (knit) rows and are read from right to left. All even-numbered rows on a colourwork chart are usually wrong-side (purl) rows and are read from left to right. Always read your knitting pattern instructions carefully to make sure that the chart follows these general rules.

FAIR ISLE CHART

The example below of a stranded colourwork chart illustrates very clearly how easy it is to knit simple repeating patterns. No more than two colours are used in a row, which makes it ideal for colourwork beginners. The colour not in use is stranded across the back of the knitting until it is needed again.

To identify if a colourwork chart should be worked in the stranded colourwork technique, check that both colours in a row are used across the entire row. If each colour is used after every three or four stitches (as in this chart), use the stranding technique (opposite). If the colours are not used over a span of five or more stitches, use the weaving-in technique (see pp.124–127) so that the loose strands (called floats) don't become too long.

KEY
☐ = background colour
⬛ = motif colour

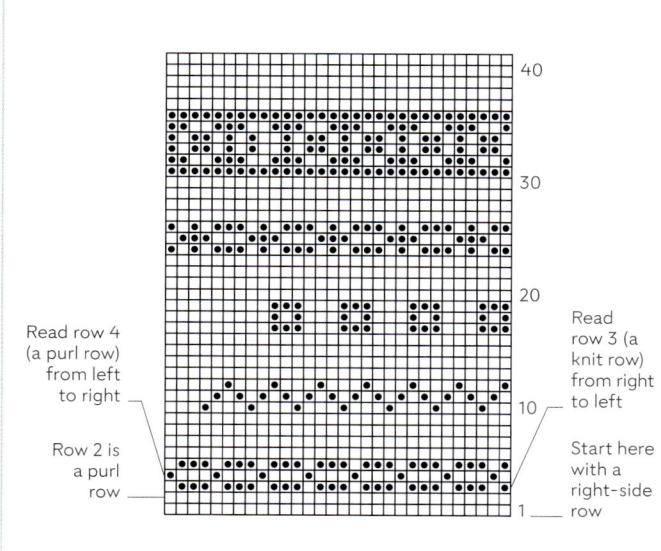

INTARSIA CHART

The heart below is an example of a simple intarsia colourwork chart. Each colour on the chart is represented by a different symbol. The blank square (the background) also represents a colour.

You can tell that a charted design should be worked in the intarsia technique if a colour appears only in a section of a row and is not needed across the entire row. Use a separate long length of yarn, or yarn on a bobbin, for each area of colour in intarsia knitting (including separated background areas). Twist the colours where they meet (see p.128).

KEY
⬛ = background colour
⬛ = motif colour

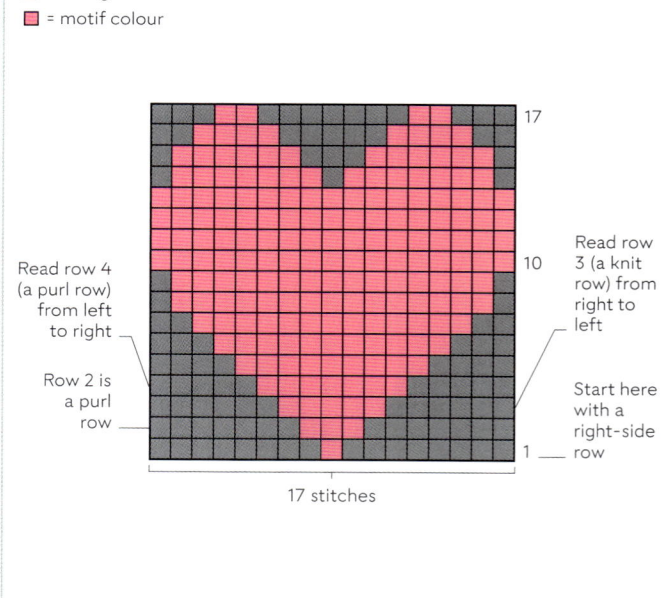

STRANDED COLOURWORK METHOD

This is where two or more colours are used in a row, with the non working colour carried at the back and brought into use when needed. Traditional Fair Isle, a type of stranded colourwork, uses only two colours per row for small repeating patterns in stocking stitch.

STRANDING TECHNIQUE

1 On the knit rows, knit the stitches in the first colour, then drop it at the back and knit the stitches in the second colour. Strand the colour not in use loosely across the back of the work until required.

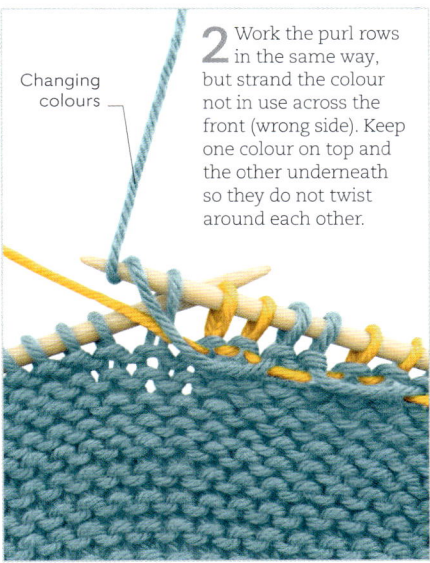

2 Work the purl rows in the same way, but strand the colour not in use across the front (wrong side). Keep one colour on top and the other underneath so they do not twist around each other.

Changing colours

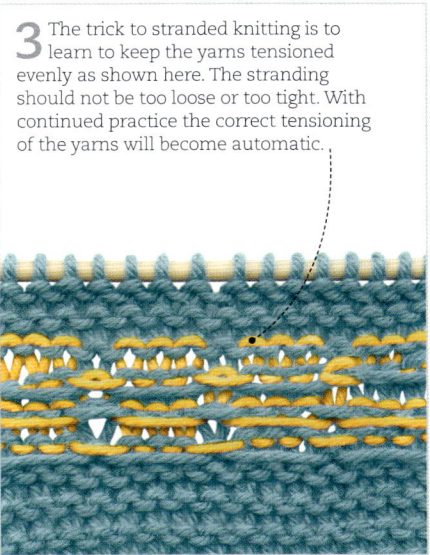

3 The trick to stranded knitting is to learn to keep the yarns tensioned evenly as shown here. The stranding should not be too loose or too tight. With continued practice the correct tensioning of the yarns will become automatic.

HOLDING THE YARNS

These techniques for holding the yarns will speed up your work and produce more even results. To maintain consistent weight fabric, always carry both yarns to the edge even if no stitch is required there, and twist them before starting the next row.

HOLDING ONE YARN IN EACH HAND

1 This method works well when there are only two colours in a row. Hold the first yarn over your right index finger as normal and the second over your left index finger, as shown in Knitting "Continental" style (see p.51).

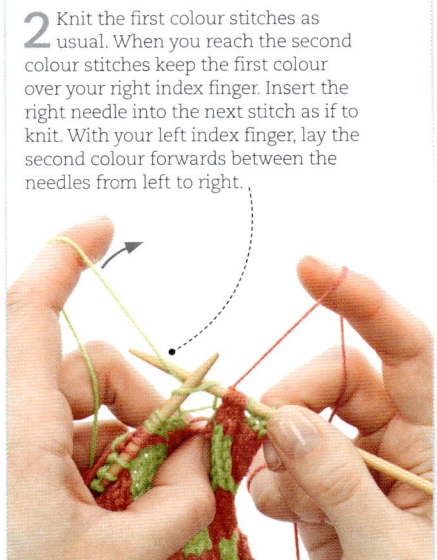

2 Knit the first colour stitches as usual. When you reach the second colour stitches keep the first colour over your right index finger. Insert the right needle into the next stitch as if to knit. With your left index finger, lay the second colour forwards between the needles from left to right.

3 Pull the new knit loop through as usual, keeping both yarns over the correct index finger. On a purl row, follow the instructions for Alternative "Continental" purl stitch (see p.52) to work the colour over your left index finger.

BOTH YARNS IN THE RIGHT HAND

Place one colour over your right index finger, and one over your middle finger. Knit as normal, throwing the second colour with your middle finger. This method allows you the flexibility of potentially adding a third colour over your ring finger.

BOTH YARNS IN THE LEFT HAND

This is ideal for those who knit Continental style. Hold the first yarn over the index finger, and the second over the middle finger of your left hand. Throw the yarns with their respective finger for knit and purl as shown on p.52.

TECHNIQUES FOR WEAVING

When strands (or floats as they are also known) are longer than five stitches, they may catch on fingers or rings. To prevent this, weave the non-working yarn into the back of the knitting by taking the weaving yarn over and under the working yarn. This can be done on every other stitch, which makes a denser fabric, or whenever a float is longer than three stitches, in which case weave into occasional stitches.

WEAVING THE LEFT YARN, KNIT OR PURL

1 Hold one yarn in each hand. Keep the left yarn and finger below and to the left of the needles when not weaving it in. Lift the weaving yarn up, put the right needle through the stitch to knit or purl, underneath weaving in the yarn. Make the stitch with the main yarn, slipping the weaving yarn over the needle without catching it.

2 Knit or purl the stitch, catching the floating yarn in the back of the fabric. Knit the next stitch without weaving in the left yarn, by dropping your left finger to the back, so the yarn lies below the needles before making the stitch. Weave in as necessary to prevent long floats.

Weaving yarn (left)
Working yarn (right)

WEAVING THE RIGHT YARN, KNIT STITCH

1 This method uses one yarn in each hand. Keep the right yarn above and to the right of the needles when not weaving it in. To weave, insert the right needle into the stitch. Wind the right yarn around the needle as to knit, throw the left yarn as usual to knit.

2 Return the right yarn back along its route to its original position and knit the stitch. Knit the next stitch without wrapping the right yarn. Weave in as necessary to prevent long floats.

Working yarn (left)
Weaving yarn (right)

WEAVING THE RIGHT YARN, PURL STITCH

1. This method uses one yarn in each hand. On a purl stitch, keeping the left index finger and yarn below the needles, wind the right yarn under the right needle. Throw left yarn as usual to purl, return right yarn back along its route to original position and purl the stitch. Work the next stitch without weaving the right yarn. Weave in as necessary to prevent long floats.

Working yarn (left)

Weaving yarn (right) – under needle

WEAVING THE INDEX FINGER YARN

1. Holding both yarns in your right hand, insert the right needle into the stitch, wind both yarns around the needle as if to knit.

2. Return index finger yarn to its original position. Knit the stitch with the remaining yarn. Keep weaving yarn above the needles when not weaving. Knit the next stitch without weaving the index finger yarn in. Weave in as necessary to prevent long floats.

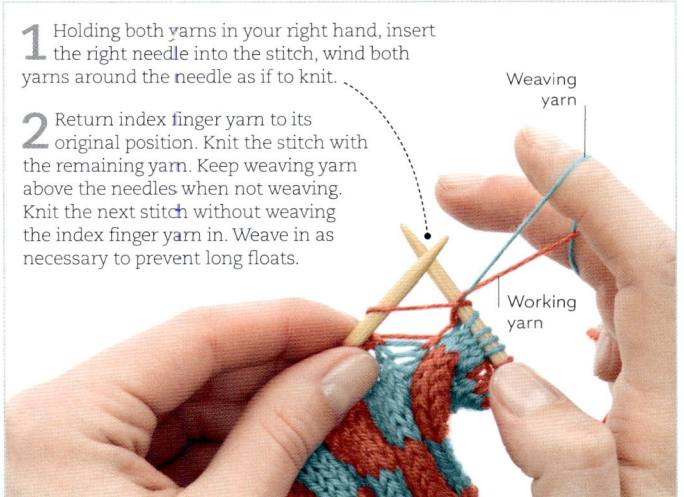

Weaving yarn

Working yarn

[RIGHT HAND] WEAVING THE MIDDLE FINGER YARN WHILE KNITTING OR PURLING A STITCH

1. Hold both yarns in your right hand. Keep the middle finger yarn above the work when not weaving in. To knit or purl, insert the right needle into the stitch. Bring the middle finger yarn above the index finger yarn, across the front of both needles to the left.

2. Holding the yarn in place to the left of the needles, take it round to the right behind the needles.

Catch middle finger yarn with left thumb and/or index finger

Hold both yarns in right hand

3. Throw the index finger yarn as if to knit or purl, then return the middle finger yarn back along its route to its original position at the right back of the work. Work the next stitch without weaving, temporarily lowering your middle finger so the index finger yarn wraps around the middle finger yarn. Weave in as necessary to prevent long floats.

Working yarn (index)

[LEFT HAND] WEAVING THE INDEX FINGER YARN WHILE KNITTING OR PURLING A STITCH

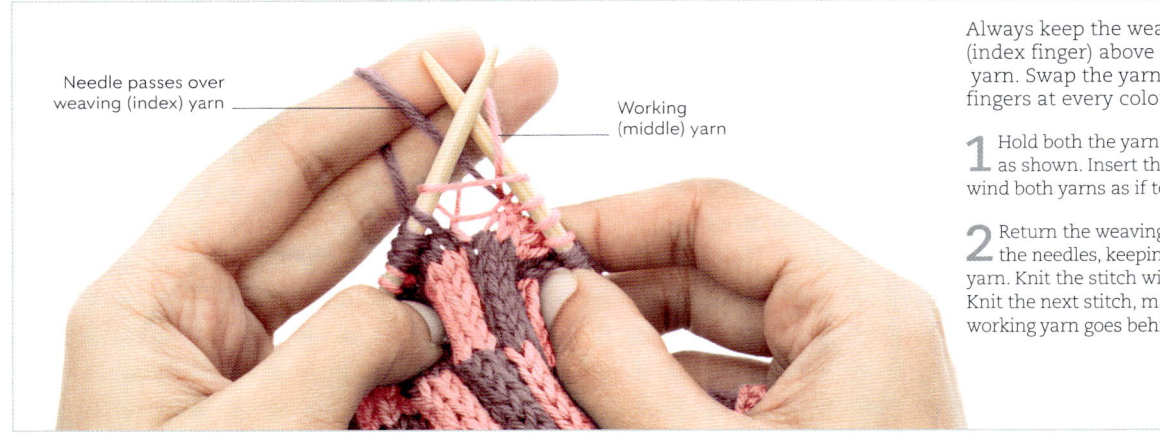

Needle passes over weaving (index) yarn

Working (middle) yarn

Always keep the weaving yarn (index finger) above the working yarn. Swap the yarns on your fingers at every colour change.

1. Hold both the yarns in your left hand as shown. Insert the right needle and wind both yarns as if to knit.

2. Return the weaving yarn back between the needles, keeping it above the working yarn. Knit the stitch with the working yarn. Knit the next stitch, making sure that the working yarn goes behind the weaving yarn.

HOLDING BOTH YARNS IN THE LEFT HAND – WEAVING THE MIDDLE FINGER YARN

1 Here, the middle finger yarn is more awkward to weave than that on the index finger. Keep your middle finger below the work when not weaving. Insert the right needle into the stitch, and ensure it passes under both yarns.

2 Bring the tip back over the middle finger (weaving) yarn and catch the index finger yarn. Draw it under the middle finger yarn to make a new stitch. Work the next stitch without weaving. Weave to prevent long floats.

STRANDED COLOURWORK WITH TEXTURE

1 At the position where a purl stitch is to be introduced, bring the working yarn to the front and purl the required number of stitches. Take the yarn to the back and continue the pattern in knit stitch. Strand the yarns at the back of the knitting.

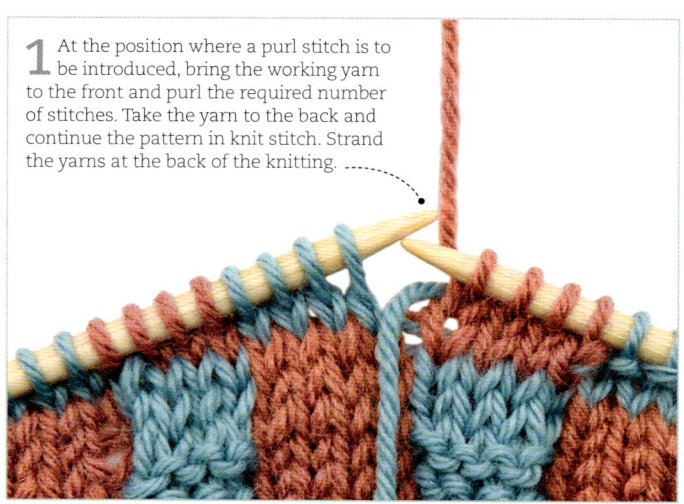

2 If you wish to maintain clear colour transitions, knit the first row of a new colour, purl the middle rows, and knit the row immediately before a colour change.

STRANDED COLOURWORK WITH GARTER STITCH

1 Knit the first row (right side), stranding on the back. Start the second wrong-side (WS) row with the non-working yarn at the front, and the working one at the back.

2 When it is time to change colour, swap the yarn positions from front to back, and continue, stranding the non-working yarn at the front (WS) of the work.

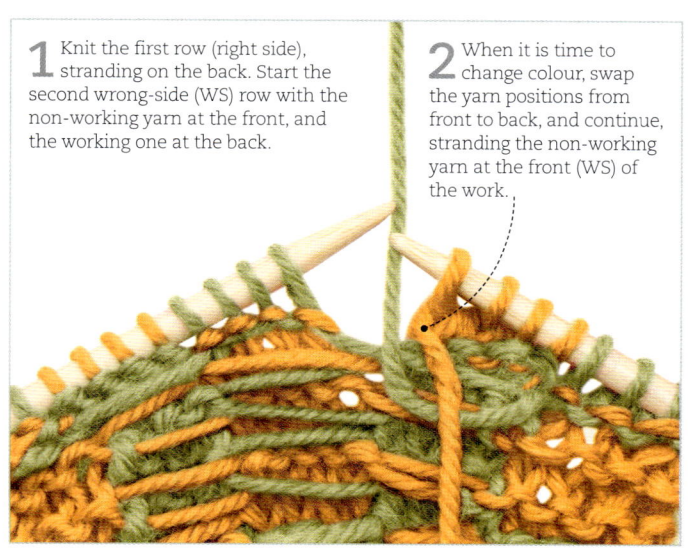

3 Work every row of pattern twice, knit all rows. At the end of every row, wrap the yarns around each other to secure them.

4 For smooth transition when changing or finishing a colour, do so on the first of the two row pattern (RS) row.

TECHNIQUES FOR WEAVING 127

TEA-COSY STITCH

1 Twist yarns at the start of each row. Pull the stranding yarn gently throughout to slightly gather the knitting. Knit eight stitches in the first colour, stranding the second yarn at the back. Swap yarns, knit eight stitches in the second colour stranding the first yarn at the back. Repeat along the row.

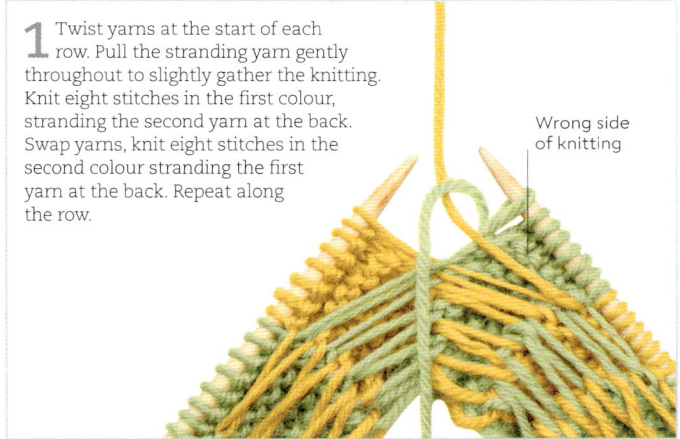

Wrong side of knitting

2 Next row. First colour to the back, second to the front, knit first eight stitches. First colour to the front, second to the back, knit eight stitches in the second colour. Repeat along the row, swapping yarns from front to back so that both yarns strand on the front. Repeat Steps 1 and 2.

TWO STRAND LAYING-IN

1 Work stocking stitch in the main yarn, with all yarns at the back. When decorative yarns are required on the knit side, bring to the front between the needles. Work the number of stitches required in the main yarn. Decorative yarns to the back. Work in the main yarn.

2 Do not twist main and decorative yarns when they are moved from front to back.

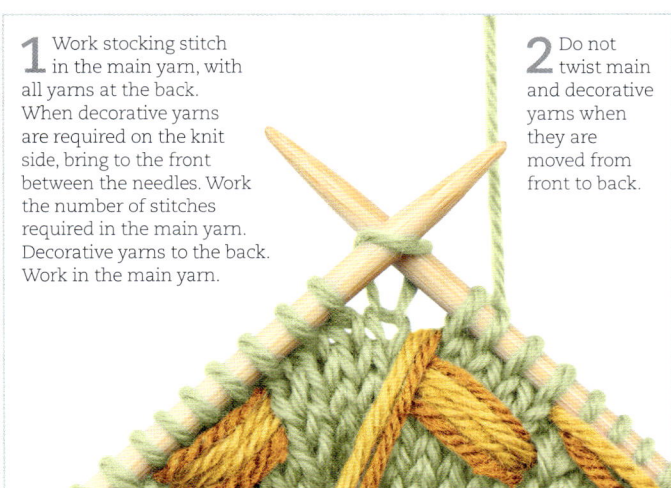

3 On a purl row, all yarns to the front. When decorative yarns are required to lie on the knit side, take back between the needles and work the number of stitches required in the main yarn. Decorative yarns to the front between the needles. Work in the main yarn.

KNIT WEAVE

Shows on reverse of stocking stitch. Always work one plain stitch between weaves. Twist the yarns at the start of every row. The weaving yarn lies alternately over and under the main yarn.

1 On a knit row. With both yarns at the back, insert the needle to knit. Lay the weaving yarn right to left between the needles. Knit with the main yarn, taking care not to catch the weaving yarn.

2 On a purl row. With both yarns at the front, the weaving yarn below the main yarn between weaves. Insert the needle to purl, lay the weaving yarn right to left between the needles. Purl with the main yarn.

128 TECHNIQUES

INTARSIA

Here each yarn is worked separately and no strands are carried along the back. Each area of colour in a row must have its own small ball of yarn. Cut short lengths from the main balls and wind onto bobbins to prevent tangles.

INTARSIA TECHNIQUE

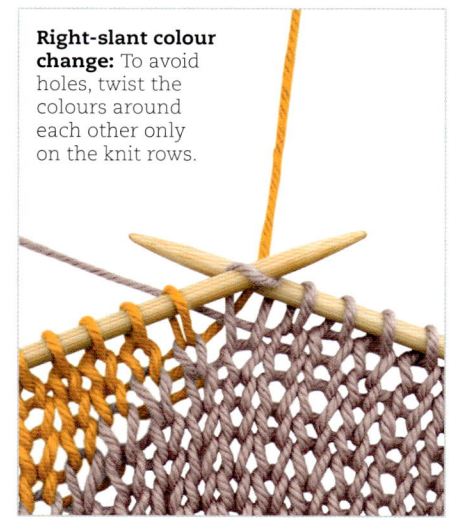

Right-slant colour change: To avoid holes, twist the colours around each other only on the knit rows.

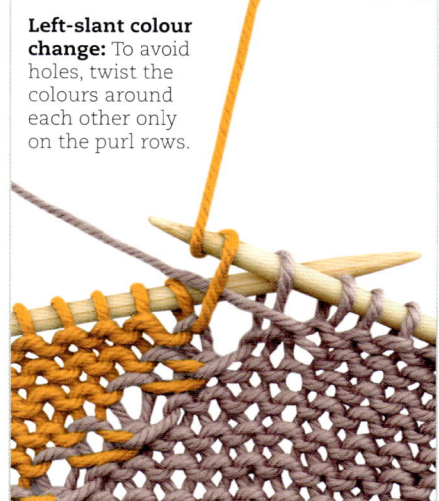

Left-slant colour change: To avoid holes, twist the colours around each other only on the purl rows.

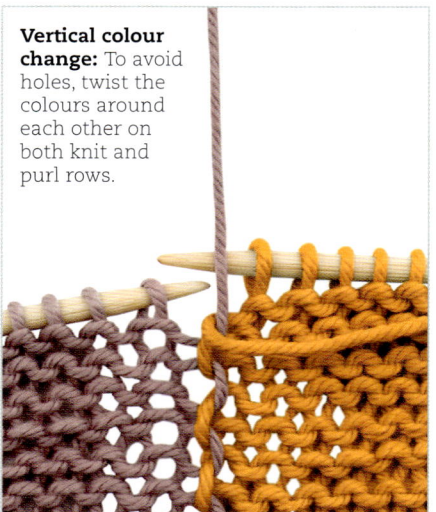

Vertical colour change: To avoid holes, twist the colours around each other on both knit and purl rows.

TWO-COLOUR CABLES

1 Wind sufficient small balls for intarsia. Work two vertical stripes of A with three-stitch vertical stripes in B and C in between (this is the six-stitch cable). Stop after the purl row before the first crossover.

2 Knit A to cable position. Slip the three C stitches off the left needle onto a cable needle and put to the back.

3 Bring B under A (this is the twist) and take behind the stitches on the cable needle. Knit the three B stitches off the left and onto the right needle.

4 With C, and without twisting the yarn, knit the three C stitches off the cable needle and onto the right needle.

5 Twist A under C and knit stitches between cables. On the next (purl) row, when twisting B and A the yarns will stretch diagonally at rear of crossover. Do not pull too tightly.

6 Work seven rows of stripes to the next crossover row. Repeat Steps 2–5 but reversing C and B.

Textural and colour effects

With a simple stocking and garter stitch base, prettily knotted, shaded, pulled, and gathered effects can be achieved. Loop stitch variations offer versatile decorative edging possibilities and careful yarn colour and type choices will also enhance these techniques.

WORKING INTO LOWER STITCHES

The following techniques add texture to the knitted surface. Combinations of textural and open lace-like knitting can be produced by dropping and unravelling stitches, while dip stitch adds colour. The pull-up stitch creates three-dimensional effects.

FISHERMAN'S RIB

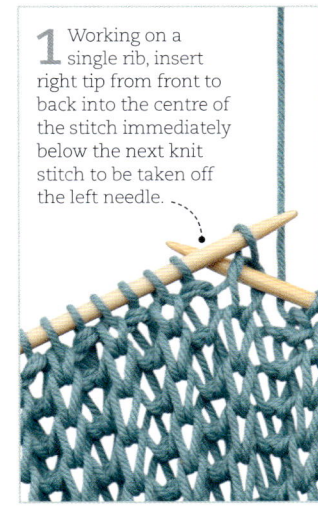

1 Working on a single rib, insert right tip from front to back into the centre of the stitch immediately below the next knit stitch to be taken off the left needle.

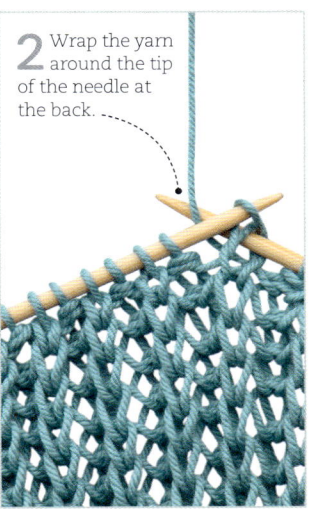

2 Wrap the yarn around the tip of the needle at the back.

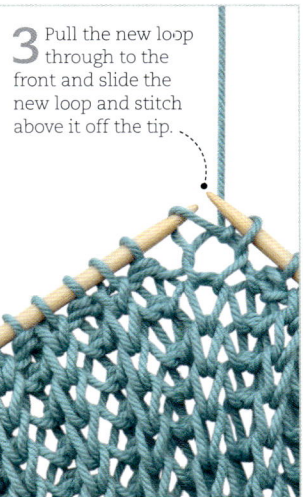

3 Pull the new loop through to the front and slide the new loop and stitch above it off the tip.

4 Purl the next stitch. Repeat Steps 1–3 for each double stitch. A plain stitch is always worked between each double.

DROPPING AND UNRAVELLING STITCHES AND ROWS

1 When you reach the desired position, drop the stitch that you wish to unravel and pull on it until it unravels to the desired position.

2 Making sure you put the needle beneath the unravelled strands, insert the right needle into the last stitch below that has not unravelled.

3 Knit the loose strands and the stitch together. Knit the next stitch before dropping another stitch.

PULL-UP STITCH

1 Work stocking stitch to the position of the pull-up stitch on a purl row. Reach the right needle down the purl side and insert the tip into the top loop of the stitch to be pulled up.

2 Slip the stitch knitwise onto the left needle and purl together with the following stitch on the needle. Space as required along the row.

3 When the piece is completed the pull-up stitch creates a tucked, raised effect.

DIP STITCH

Dip stitch can be vertical or angled across the front or the reverse of knitting, and worked in the main colour for texture or contrast for a colour effect.

1 Knit to where the effect is to occur. Reach the right needle tip down a number of rows and insert tip through a stitch (or the space between two stitches).

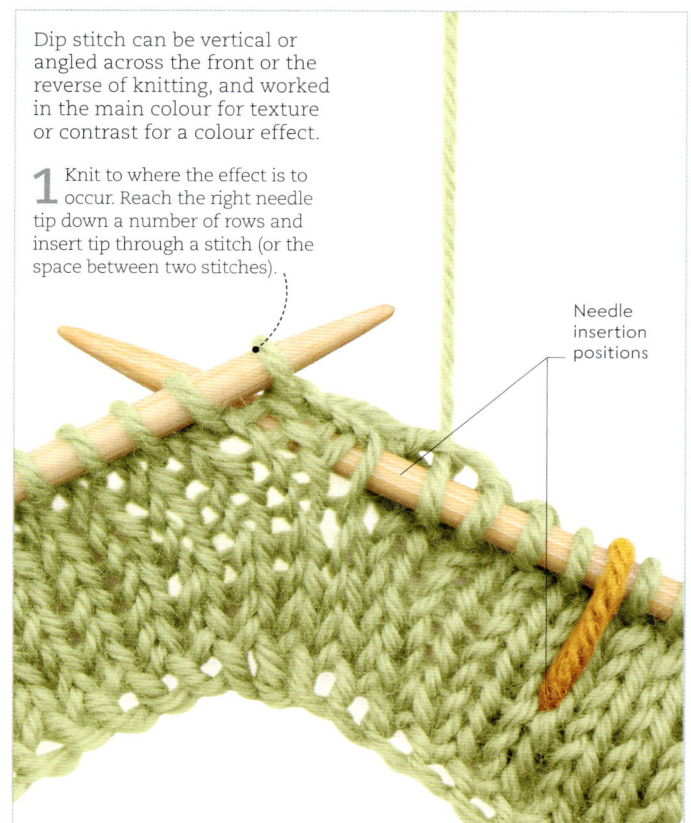

Needle insertion positions

2 Holding the second yarn at the back, catch the "dip" yarn with the needle and pull through to the front. Pull enough through, and make the rear strands loose enough so that the main fabric is not distorted. On the next row, knit or purl the "dip" stitch together with the following stitch. Repeat Steps 1 and 2 whenever a dip stitch is required.

ONE-COLOUR BRIOCHE

Single-colour brioche can be worked on straight needles and creates a ridged and airy double-sided fabric perfect for scarves, cowls and textured garments. Every row adds yarnovers around slipped stitches, which are treated as one stitch in patterns. This technique introduces the brioche knit (brk) stitch.

WORKING ONE-COLOUR BRIOCHE

1 Cast on an even number of stitches. Work a preparation row of *k1, yo, s1, repeat from * to last stitch, k1. All stitches are to be slipped purlwise. This sets up your brioche structure with alternating knit stitches and slipped stitches wrapped with yarnovers, which will be worked together later.

2 Begin the brioche pattern on row 1: S1, *brioche knit (brk) by knitting the slipped stitch together with its yarnover from the previous row, yo, s1, repeat from last st, p1.

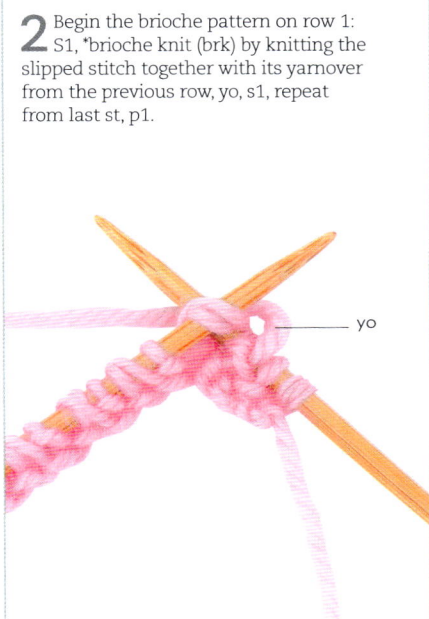

brk	Brioche knit: knit slipped st together with its yarnover
brkyobrk	2-st increase in brioche knit: brioche knit, yarnover, brioche knit in same yarn
brLsl	2-st decrease slanting left, over three sts: slip first st knitwise, brk following two sts together, pass slipped st over
brp	Brioche purl: purl slipped st together with its yarnover
brpyobrp	2-st increase in brioche purl: brioche purl, yarnover, brioche purl into same st
brRsl	2-st decrease slanting right, over three sts: slip first st knitwise, knit next st, pass slipped st over, place st on LH needle and pass following st over. Place st back on RH needle.

3 On row 2, s1, *brk, yo, s1 wyif, repeat from * to last stitch, k1 through the back loop (k1tbl). Always ensure you are working through both the slipped stitch and its yarnover to maintain the spongy brioche texture.

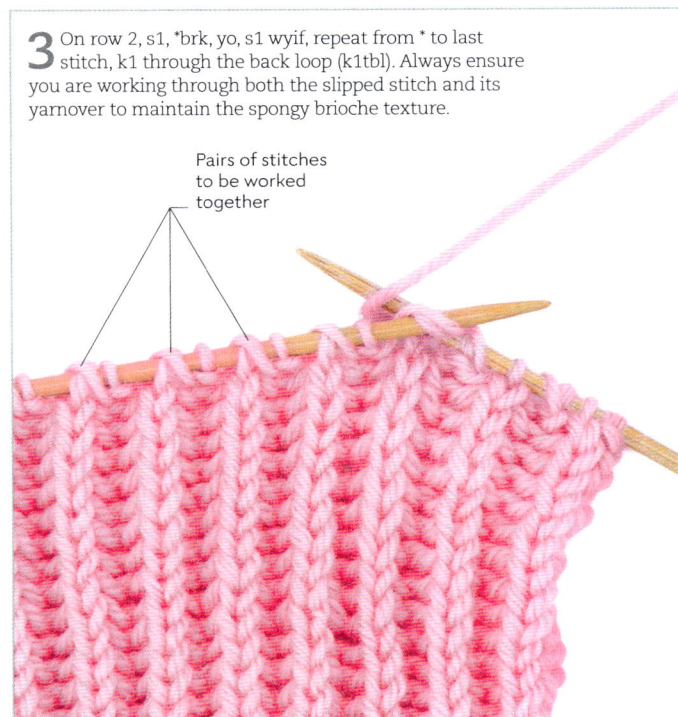

Pairs of stitches to be worked together

4 Repeat rows 1 and 2 to continue the brioche pattern. The fabric will be fully reversible because it has identical texture on each side, making it ideal for items where both sides will be visible. To finish off, on an odd-numbered row, work as follows: s1,* brk, p1, rep from * to end, so no yarnovers remain, and cast off in your chosen method.

TWO-COLOUR BRIOCHE

Two-colour brioche creates a reversible fabric with different colours dominating each side, often called "dark" and "light" rather than right and wrong sides. Bringing in the brioche purl stitch, it must be worked on circular or double-pointed needles long enough to accommodate your stitch count, as you need to slide stitches to work from both ends.

WORKING TWO-COLOUR BRIOCHE

For additional two-colour brioche stitches and variations, see pp.316–17.

1 Cast on an even number of stitches using a repeating sequence of one stitch in each colour, such as in the Italian cast-on variation on p.149. Work with the first colour (A): *k1, yo, s1, repeat from * to end. Slide stitches back to the other end of the needle to work the same row with the second colour (B).

2 Using colour B, work the same stitches from the opposite end: *brioche purl (brp) the slipped stitch together with the yarn wrapped around it, yo, s1, repeat from * to end. Turn your work. You have now completed one full row of two-colour brioche with both colours worked.

3 Turn to start the next row, this time beginning with colour B: *brioche knit (brk) the slipped stitch together with its yarnover, yo, s1, repeat from * to end. Slide stitches back to work with colour A from the opposite end: *brp the slipped stitch together with its yarnover, yo, s1, repeat from * to end. This concludes the second row, having now been worked in both colours.

4 Repeat the pattern by alternating colours every two rows. Each colour dominates one side of the fabric, the other creates subtle accents, so the fabric is completely reversible without a "wrong" side. Remember: always slip stitches purlwise so the yarn is at the front, ready to work a yarnover around the slipped stitch.

To continue: **Row 1** Using A, *brk, yo, s1, repeat from * to end. Do not turn. Slide stitches. Using B, *brp, yo, s1, repeat from * to end. Turn. **Row 2** Using B, *brk, yo, s1, repeat from * to end. Do not turn. Slide stitches. Using B, *brp, yo, s1, repeat from * to end. Turn. Repeat rows 1 and 2, then to finish work one row of 'wrapped' stitches worked together. Cast off with the tubular cast-off (p.73).

LOOP-PILE OR FUR KNITTING

Loops can be added to the front or the back, usually working a plain row between. Garter stitch or stocking stitch make good base fabrics. You can adjust the density by altering the frequency of the loops. Try embellishing the loops with beads or varying the loops' length for a surface effect.

LOOPS TO FRONT

1 At position of loop, with RS facing, knit the next stitch but do not drop from the left needle. Bring the yarn forwards between the needles. Wind a loop around your left thumb from back to front once.

2 Yarn back. Knit the original stitch again, dropping it off the left needle while withdrawing your thumb from the loop.

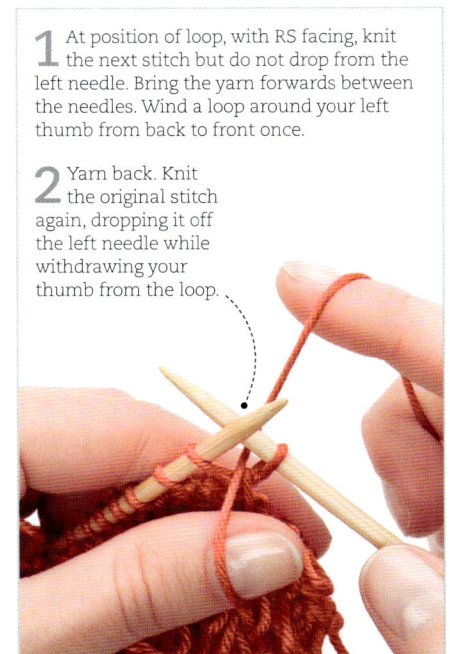

3 Insert the left needle into the last two stitches on the right needle from the front, as in ssk (see p.100) and k2tog with the main yarn.

4 Repeat Steps 1–3 at regular intervals, keeping the length of the loop consistent. Gently tug the loops to tighten the stitches.

LOOPS TO BACK

1 At the position of the loop, with RS facing, wind the yarn around two left fingers as well as the needle at the back of the work and knit the stitch. Do not drop the stitch off the left needle.

2 Slip the new stitch loop onto the left needle and k2tog through the back of the loops. Drop the loop from your finger. Gently tug the loops at the end of the row to tighten the stitches.

LONG LOOPS MADE WITH A RULER

1 Worked on a WS row. Hold a ruler at the back to the right of the needles. Insert the right needle into the next stitch knitwise. Wind the yarn clockwise around the right needle, take it around the ruler and bring the yarn back under the right needle.

2 Draw both the loops on the right needle through the stitch on the left needle and drop this off the left needle. Slide the ruler out of loops at the end of the row. On the next row, k2tog into the back of the two wraps made in the last row.

MOSAIC KNITTING

Mosaic knitting creates striking geometric patterns using two colours, worked over two rows at a time. Unlike traditional colourwork, you work with one colour at a time, slipping stitches to reveal the colour beneath. All charts in this book are worked in garter stitch, meaning both right and wrong side rows are knitted.

WORKING MOSAIC KNITTING

Mosaic knitting uses strategically placed slipped stitches to create its distinctive fabric. The frequent use of slipped stitches creates a warm and slightly dense fabric, with yarns stranded along the reverse of the work behind the slipped stitches. Stitches must always be slipped with yarn held at the reverse of the work to achieve this effect.

1 Cast on the required number of stitches using the alternate colour to the first chart row. Start by knitting two rows in your main colour.

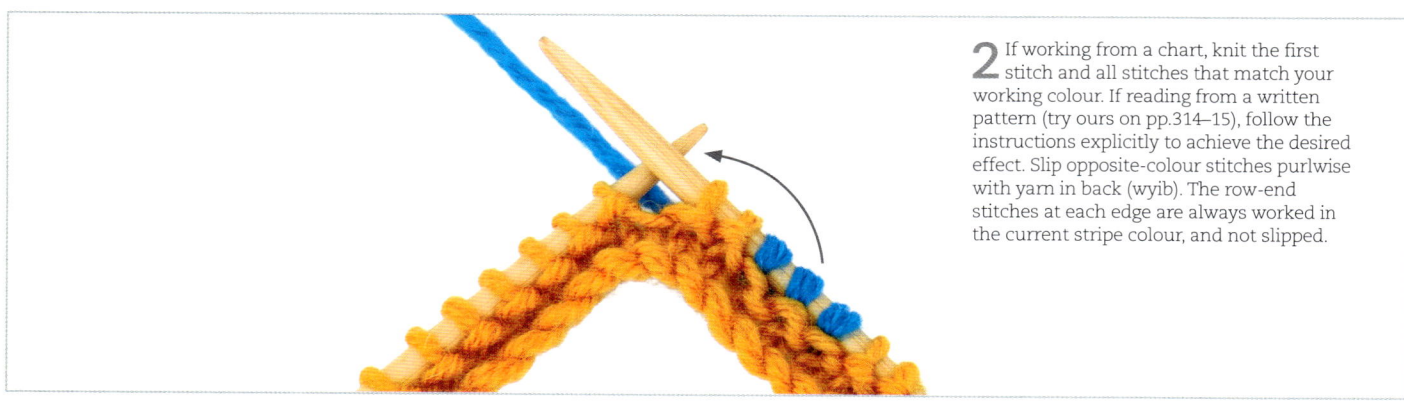

2 If working from a chart, knit the first stitch and all stitches that match your working colour. If reading from a written pattern (try ours on pp.314–15), follow the instructions explicitly to achieve the desired effect. Slip opposite-colour stitches purlwise with yarn in back (wyib). The row-end stitches at each edge are always worked in the current stripe colour, and not slipped.

3 On wrong-side rows, read the chart from left to right. Knit the stitches that were knitted on the previous row, and slip the alternate-colour stitches purlwise with yarn in front (wyif). Both sides create garter stitch texture while revealing the slipped stitches beneath.

4 Change colour every two rows, carrying the unused yarn up the right-hand row-end edge of your work. When you're finishing up and getting ready to cast off, make sure you end by working two rows worked in knit, in the same colour used for the two plain rows above the cast-on edge, for a neat finish.

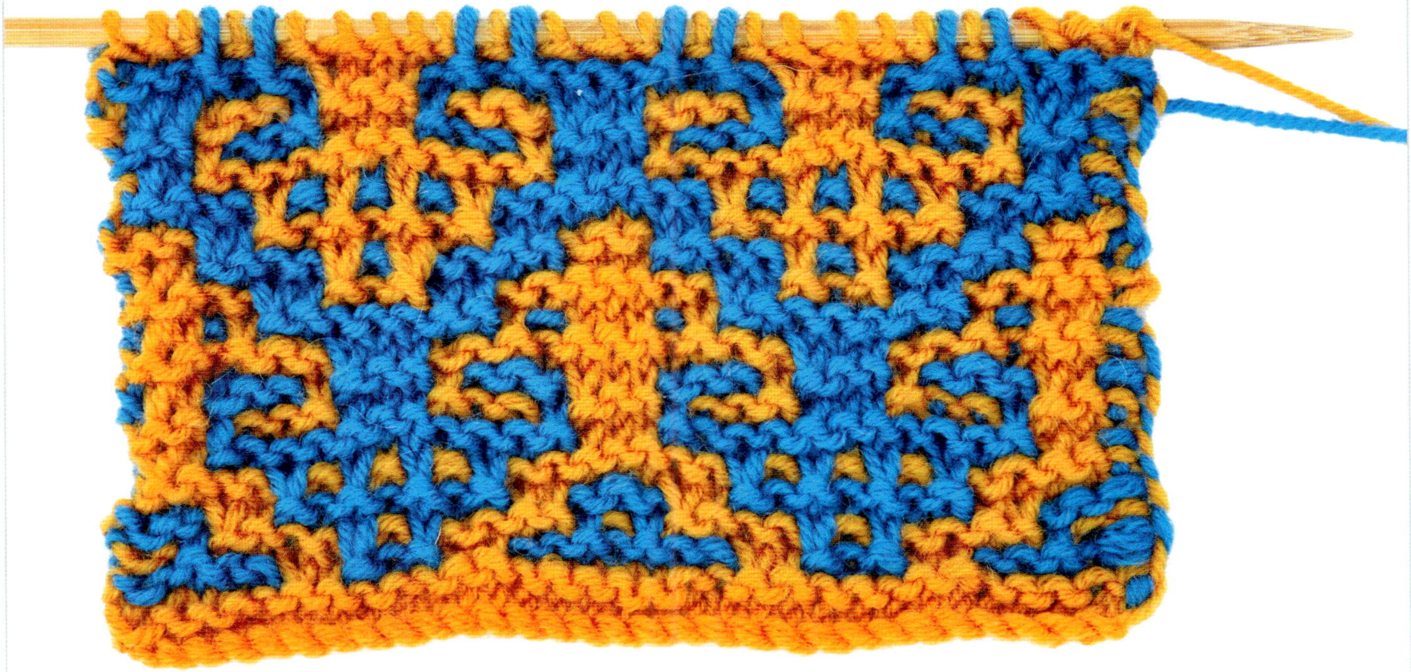

READING MOSAIC CHARTS

Each square represents one stitch, with colours indicating which yarn to use. Mosaic knitting is traditionally worked in only two colours. Knit each chart row twice in each colour, effectively working two-row stripes. Remember that slipped stitches from previous rows will pull up the colour from the row below, creating the mosaic pattern without trickier colour changes within rows.

The first stitch on your charted right-side row, so when reading the chart from right to left, is an indicator of which colour you work those two rows with. Work across the row, and when you approach a stitch in the other colour, that is where you slip a stitch.

Many mosaic knitting patterns are only available as charts – others offer both charts and a written version. Mosaic charts can be worked in all knit (garter stitch), or for a smoother fabric you can also use stocking stitch, working the second row of each colour repeat in purl instead.

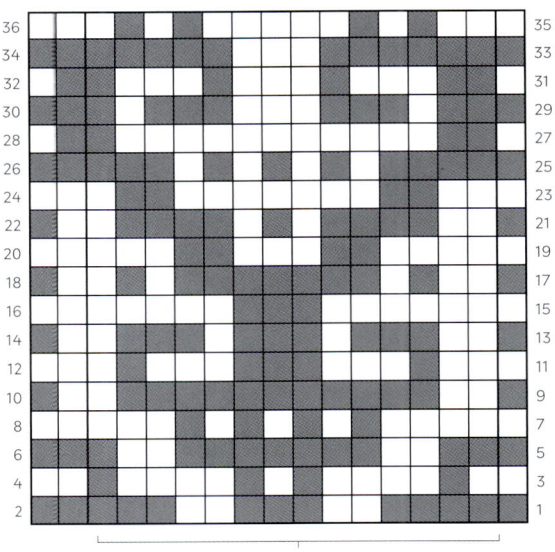

14 stitches

DOUBLE KNITTING

This creates a double-sided piece of knitting, usually stocking stitch, where wrong-sides face inwards and aren't visible. It uses lots of slipped stitches, which can loosen your tension; going down a needle size can help prevent that. Both variations of this technique use the tubular cast-off method shown on p.73.

WORKING IN ONE COLOUR

Using one ball of yarn, you will essentially be working half a row at a time – which can be a little slow going, but is absolutely worth a little patience to achieve a firm and sturdy finished fabric. This technique can be worked on straight knitting needles.

1 Cast on an even number of stitches using the Italian cast-on shown on p.65. You should aim to cast on twice the required number of stitches for the fabric width you need.

2 Knit the first stitch, and slip the second holding your yarn at the front of the work (wyif).

3 Continue along the row, alternating knit and slipped stitches until you reach the end of the row, slipping the last stitch.

4 Turn, and repeat – working [k1, s1 wyif] until you reach the end of the row. This second row works the unworked stitches left from the first, so completing one full row on both sides despite having turned your work. Continue to work rows of (k1, s1 wyif) to end until your work reaches the desired length.

WORKING IN TWO COLOURS

Using two contrasting colours, you will need a circular needle, or a set of double-pointed needles, to slide stitches to the right end of your needle after you finish each row.

1 Cast on an even number of stitches using the Italian cast-on variation shown on p.149. As with the one-colour method, you should be casting on double the width you need for the item you're making, as it will shrink inwards by half as you begin to work.

Colour A

2 Using the first colour, work as given for steps 2 and 3 of the one-colour method, ensuring you work this first step using the matching yarn colour of the first stitch cast on (colour A). Slide the stitches to the other end of the needle to be worked again in the second colour (B), and work the other side of the fabric from the reverse with (s1 wyib, p1) to end.

DOUBLE KNITTING 137

3 You will now find both yarns sit at the right-hand row-end edge with the rows you have just completed facing you. It's vital at this stage that you twist the yarns once around one another to prevent gaps from forming. Turn the work over to work the next row. Using B, work the right-side stitches facing you by working (k1, s1 wyif) to end.

Colour B

4 Without turning your knitting over, slide the stitches back to the other end of the needle ready to work with colour A. Work the wrong-side stitches by working (s1 wyib, p1) to end.

To continue, work as follows:

Row 1 Using A, [k1, s1 wyif] to end. Do not turn. Slide sts back to the other end of the needle, using B, [s1 wyib, p1] to end, turn.

Row 2 Using B, [k1, s1 wyif] to end. Do not turn. Slide sts back to the other end of the needle, using A, [s1 wyib, p1] to end, turn.

Rows 1 and 2 form 2 rows of each colour on each side. After a few rows, you notice that you are now knitting one piece with two different coloured sides. You can choose to cast off after either row 1, or row 2 has been completed.

▶ TIPS

• This technique can also be used to create more complex colourwork techniques like the chequerboard pattern on p.317.

• The two-colour method can be adapted to create reversible colourwork patterns. As you work each colour along each row, you can dip over from right-side to wrong-side stitches in sequence or use a chart to form more complex designs.

• Both double-sided knitting techniques shown here will create a hollow tubular piece of knitting, but more complex colourwork will bring yarns between the two separate pieces of fabric to join them at the point where yarns cross from front to the back and vice versa.

• When working from a chart, each square represents a stitch pair for both sides of your fabric. Start from the bottom row and work across, referring to the legend to determine which colour represents your front side. For each square, knit one stitch with your front colour, then purl one stitch with your back colour, continuing this alternating pattern across the row. At the end of each row, turn your work and repeat the process, always checking the chart for the correct colour placement.

• For an open-edged variation of this technique, see Tubular knitting on p.149.

DECORATIVE STITCHES

With a few uncomplicated moves, elaborate-looking effects are possible. Elongated stitches lighten fabric and look particularly effective in slippery ribbon yarns. In their simplest form these can be worked in stripes but may also form more elaborate effects, particularly in floral and lozenge patterns. Picot point chains can be worked into filet lace-like fabrics or make delicate trims.

THREE-INTO-THREE STITCH

1 On a knit row, work to the position of the decorative stitch. Bring the yarn to the front, and purl three stitches together, but do not take the stitches off the left needle.

2 With the yarn to the back, knit into the three stitches that are still on the left needle, but do not take the stitches off the left needle.

3 With the yarn to the front, purl into the same three stitches again, then slide the three stitches off the left needle. Take the yarn to the back and knit any intervening stitches in pattern.

4 The next row is usually a plain row, either knit or purl depending on your overall pattern.

5 The three-into-three stitch forms a raised bobble on the surface of the knitting, creating a pattern when worked regularly.

ELONGATED STITCHES (ALSO CALLED DROP STITCH)

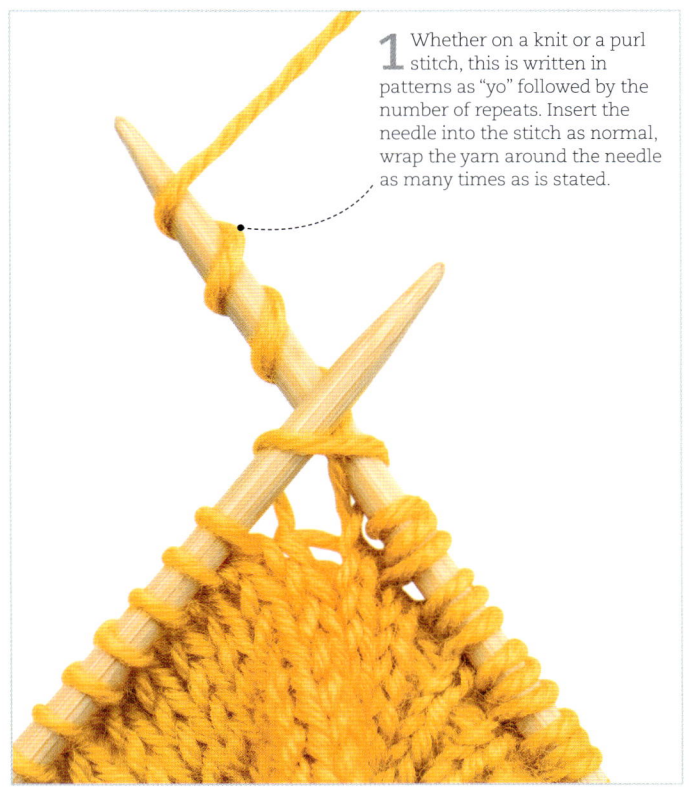

1 Whether on a knit or a purl stitch, this is written in patterns as "yo" followed by the number of repeats. Insert the needle into the stitch as normal, wrap the yarn around the needle as many times as is stated.

2 Draw all the wraps through the stitch so that you have them all on the right needle.

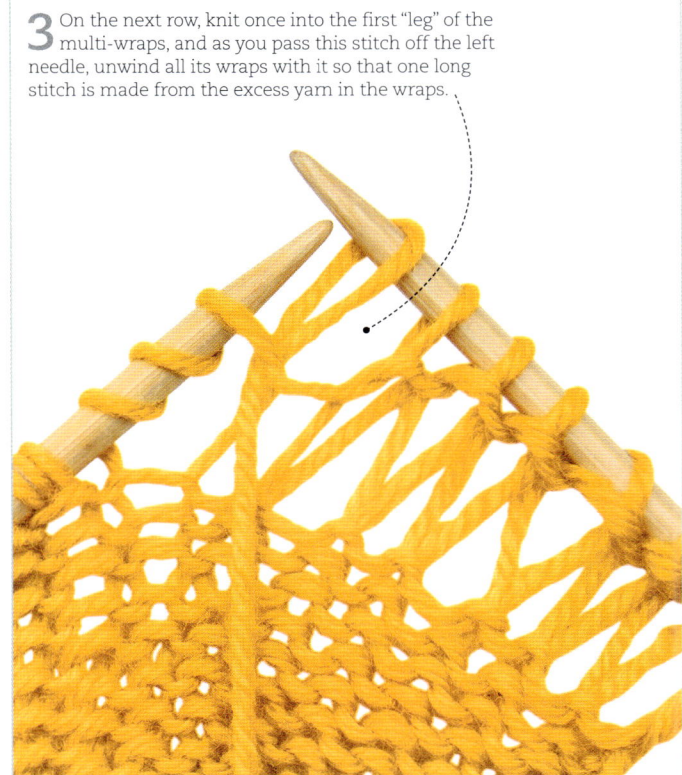

3 On the next row, knit once into the first "leg" of the multi-wraps, and as you pass this stitch off the left needle, unwind all its wraps with it so that one long stitch is made from the excess yarn in the wraps.

4 Elongated stitches can be worked all the way across a row for a lacy effect or in isolation as part of an openwork pattern.

WRAPPED CLUSTERS

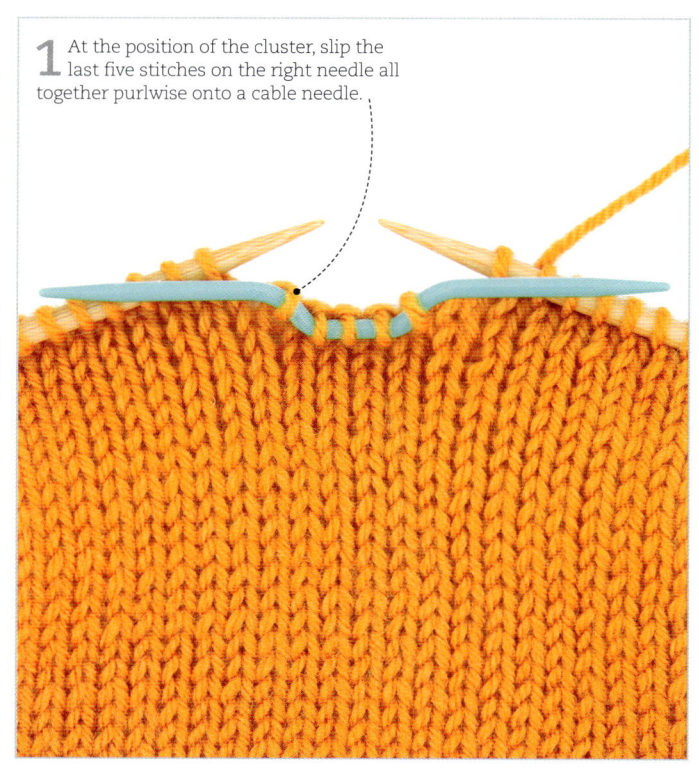

1. At the position of the cluster, slip the last five stitches on the right needle all together purlwise onto a cable needle.

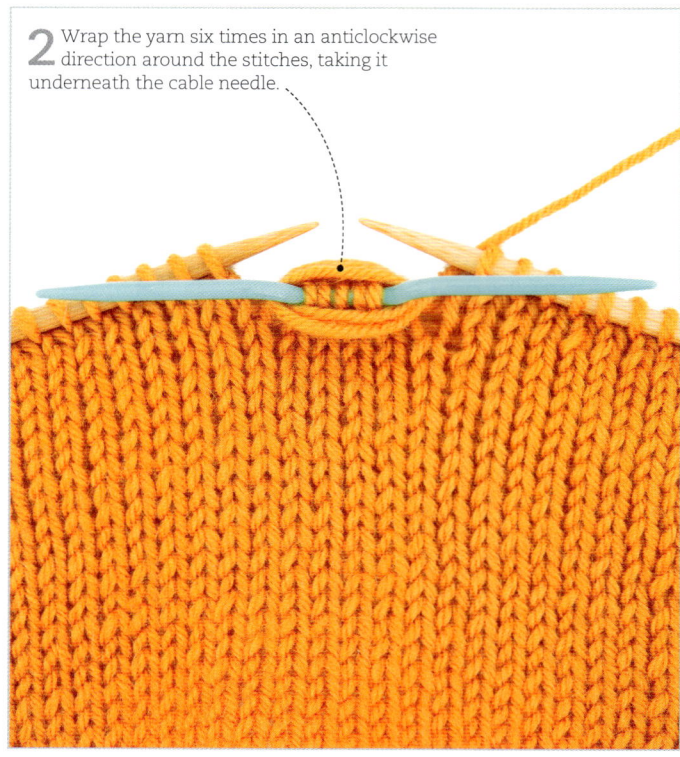

2. Wrap the yarn six times in an anticlockwise direction around the stitches, taking it underneath the cable needle.

3. Slip the cable needle stitches straight back onto the right needle, one at a time, so that they are ready to be worked.

4. Knit across the stitches for the cluster and continue to complete your row.

DECORATIVE STITCHES **141**

KNITTED-IN SMOCKING

1 Cast on a multiple of eight stitches plus three, and work a purl three, knit one rib. This is a right-side row. Knit an even number of rows in rib until the position of the first smocking is reached.

2 Work eight stitches of the rib. Slip the last five stitches on the right needle together onto a cable needle. Bring the smocking yarn from the back to the front between the right needle and the cable needle, leaving a 10cm (4in) tail at the back. Wind this yarn twice clockwise around the stitches on the cable needle, leaving it at the back of the work.

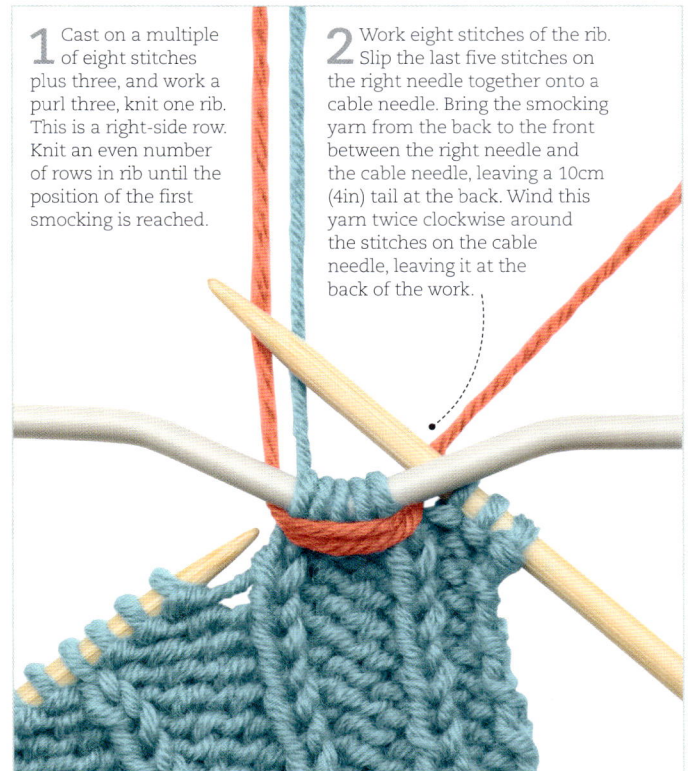

3 Slip the stitches together off the cable needle back onto the right needle. Repeat Steps 2 and 3 across the row, stranding the smocking yarn across the back of the work and cutting with a 10cm (4in) tail at the end.

4 Work three rows of rib and then repeat Steps 2 and 3 but work the first 12 stitches before introducing the smocking yarn.

5 Continue to work smocking, alternating the start of eight or 12 stitches with three rows in between. When complete, secure the ends of the smocking yarn up one edge. Gently draw up each row of smocking, easing the ribs together until finally securing the smocking yarn at the other edge.

142 TECHNIQUES

SHADOW KNITTING

1 The design chart shows the finished effect.

2 This chart has to be "exploded", and drawn on a knitting chart that is four times as long as the original.

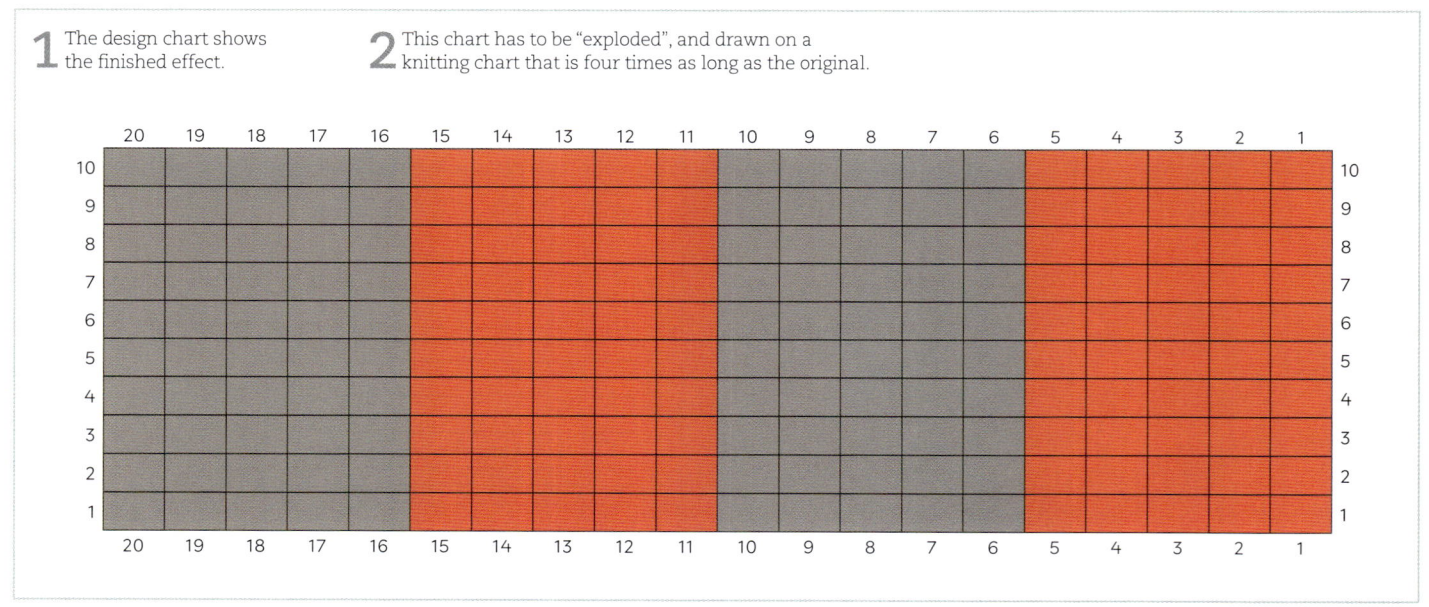

3 The first row of the exploded chart is always left blank. On the second row, draw the main (pink) stitches from row 1 of the original chart.

4 Leave three rows blank, then draw the main (pink) stitches from row 2 of the original chart; continue in this manner to the final row (row 10).

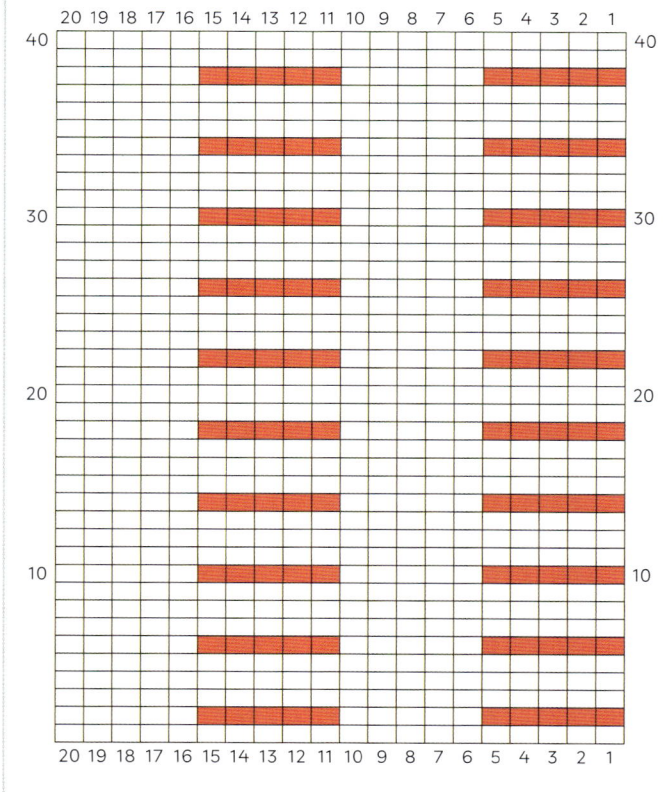

5 Go back to the beginning of the exploded chart, and on the middle row of the three blank rows, draw the contrast (grey) stitches from row 1 of the original chart. Continue up the exploded chart matching the original chart stitches to the middle of the blank rows.

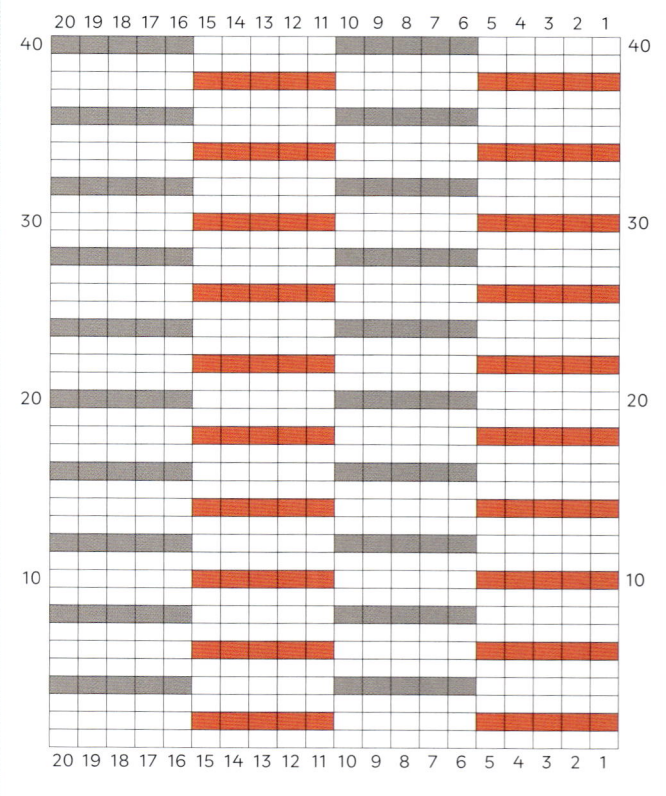

6 Annotate the chart in your own way to show the purl and knit stitches. Colour every two rows in alternating colours, starting with two rows of main colour. This example shows purl stitches as white to help read the chart, but work them in whichever colour stripe they fall in.

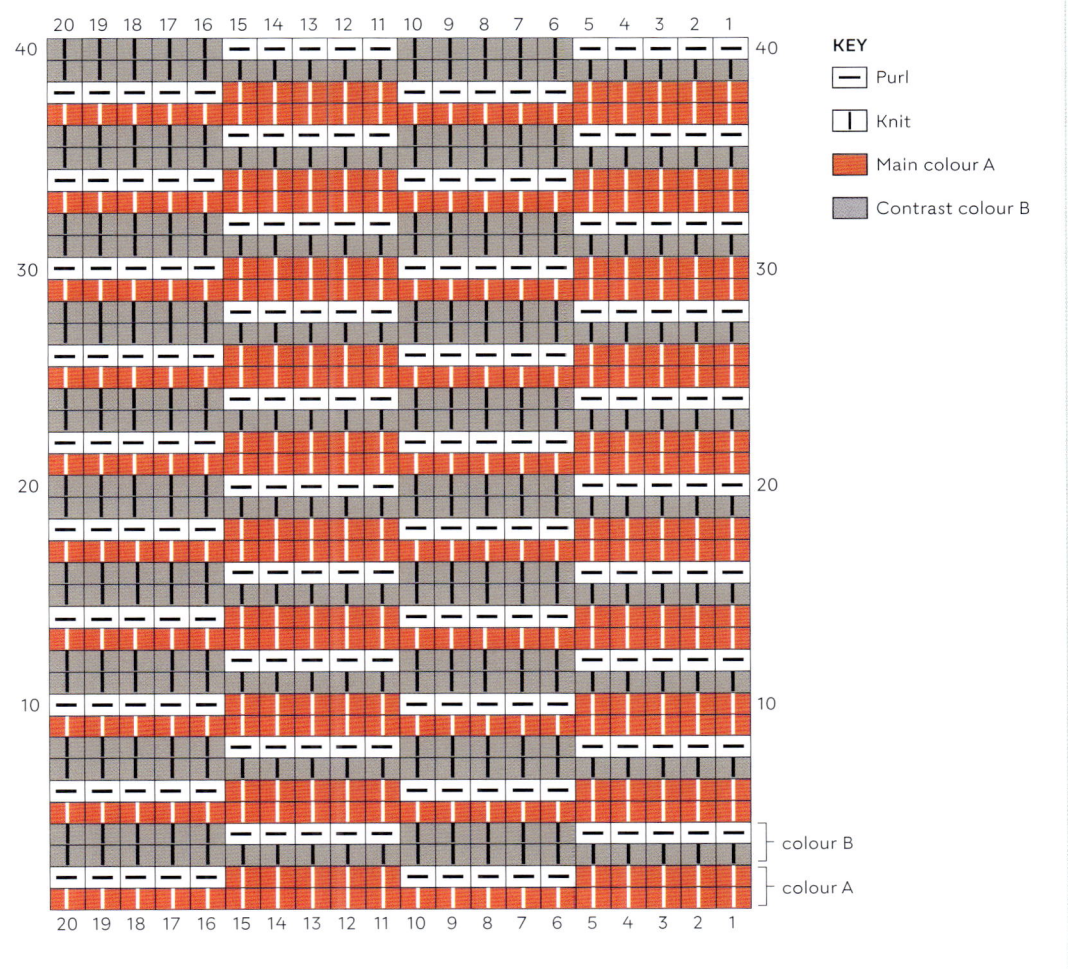

KEY
— Purl
| Knit
■ Main colour A
■ Contrast colour B

7 Cast on 20 stitches and, working from the chart, knit the first row in A. Work the second row in A, purling the white squares and knitting the coloured ones.

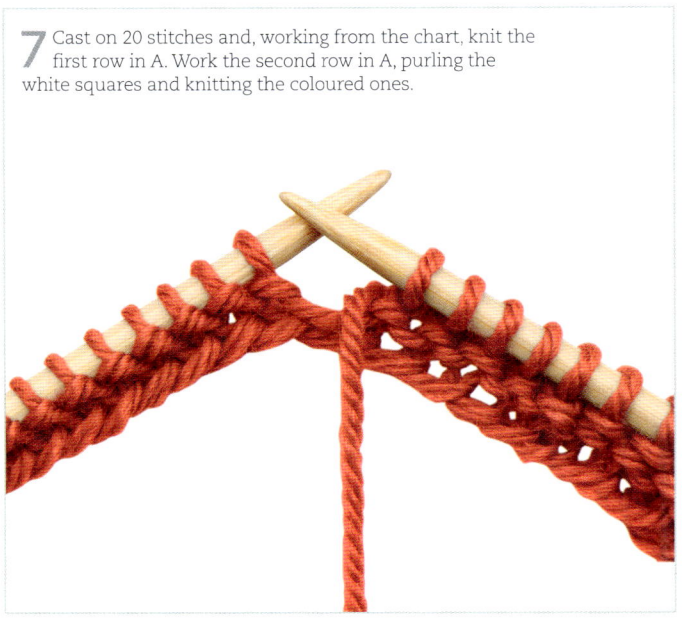

8 Change to B, knit one plain row and then work as row 4 of the chart, purling the blank squares and knitting the coloured ones. Repeat the colour sequence of two rows of each colour as you follow the chart upwards.

Structural effects

Structural knitting techniques are challenging and satisfying to work and can be used in combination with varied colours and textural yarns. Entrelac squares offer scope for colour choices whilst pleats, gathering, and doubling can add style details to garments. Tubular knitting is an interesting technique and, alongside bias knitting, may inspire new ideas.

ENTRELAC

Here squares create a diagonal basketweave effect. Squares can be worked in stocking stitch, garter stitch, cables, lace, or textural stitches. Each square has twice as many rows as stitches and alternating series of squares are worked in opposite directions. All the stitches for one series are on the needle at the same time, although squares are worked individually. A line of short row triangles at the start, finish, and each side, create straight edges. Try this technique in the cushion on p.264.

1 This example makes three eight-stitch squares. In colour A, loosely cast on 24 stitches using the Knit-on method (see p.54). Knit two stitches and turn work. Purl one stitch, slip one purlwise, turn; this slip stitch makes picking up in Step 7 easier.

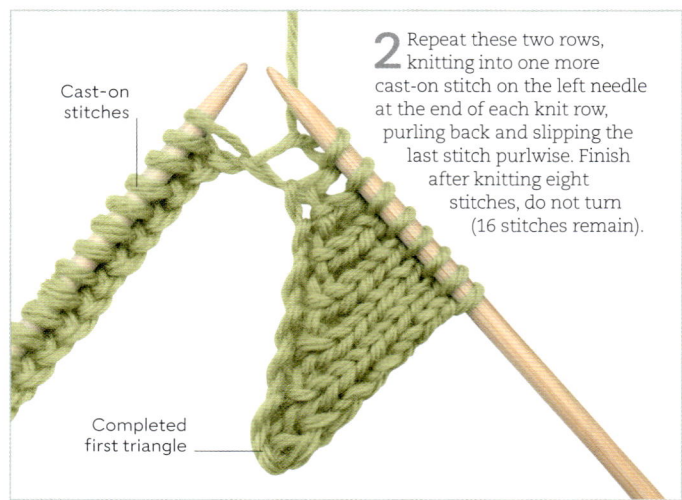

2 Repeat these two rows, knitting into one more cast-on stitch on the left needle at the end of each knit row, purling back and slipping the last stitch purlwise. Finish after knitting eight stitches, do not turn (16 stitches remain).

Cast-on stitches

Completed first triangle

3 Work the next triangle as in Steps 1 and 2 over the following eight stitches, and the third triangle over the final eight stitches. There are now three triangles on the needle.

4 Left side triangle. With the wrong side (WS) facing, join in colour B and purl two stitches, turn, knit two, turn. Purl into the front and back of the edge stitch (see p.92); this shapes the edge. Purl the last stitch in colour B together with the first stitch in colour A (p2tog, see p.99) on the right needle.

P2tog

5 Repeat Step 4, purling one more stitch for each repeat and knitting back to the edge each time. Stop after purling into the front and back, purling five and purling colour B and colour A together. Do not turn the work. Leave this completed edge triangle on the right needle.

6 With WS facing and the yarn at the front, insert the right needle from the back to the front into the edge stitches and pick up and purl eight stitches evenly along the free edge of the first triangle.

7 Turn the work and knit seven stitches, slip one purlwise, turn work. Purl seven, then purl the last stitch in colour B together with the first stitch in colour A (p2tog, see p.99) on the right needle. This joins the new square to the old triangle. Turn the work.

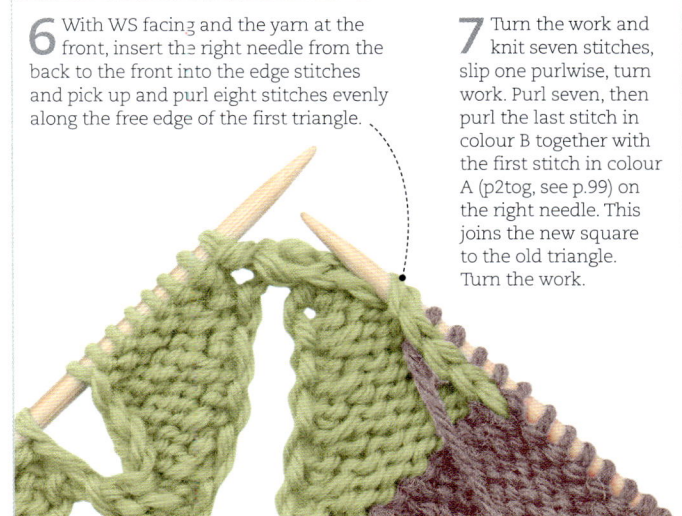

8 Repeat Step 7 seven more times, but do not turn the work after the last row; all the stitches of the first square are now on the left needle. Work the next square as Steps 6–8.

9 To work the right-edge triangle. WS facing, pick up the edge as Step 6. Work every knit row, slipping the end stitch purlwise. P2tog at the end of all but the first purl row. One stitch remains.

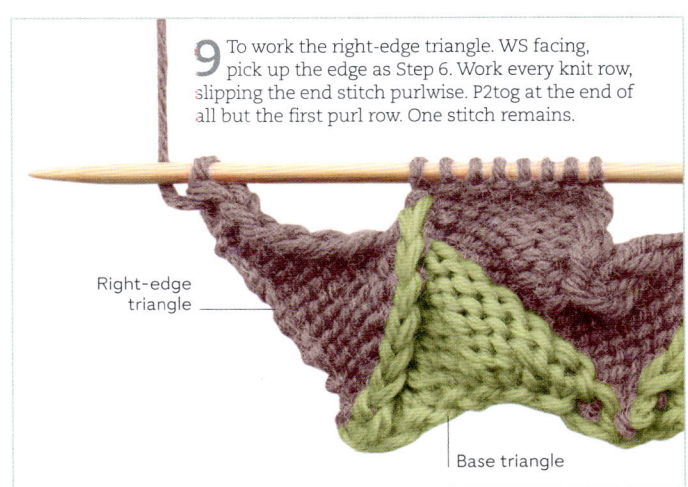

Right-edge triangle

Base triangle

10 To work the right-edge square. Join in colour A. With the right side (RS) facing, slip first stitch onto right needle. Pick up and knit seven stitches along the edge of right-hand square (eight stitches on the needle). Purl seven, slip one purlwise, turn.

11 Knit seven. Work ssk with next two stitches (one of each colour). Repeat the last two rows to the end of the join. Work Steps 10 (omit slip, pick up eight stitches instead) and 11 for all squares. Steps 4–11 make one whole pattern repeat.

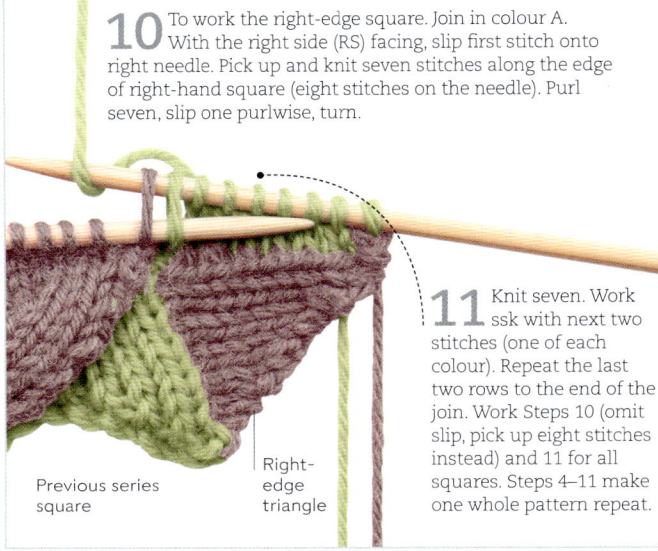

Previous series square

Right-edge triangle

12 Work the finished triangles (these follow a series with edge triangles – see Steps 4–9). In the appropriate colour, work as Step 10, purling eight in the final instruction. Turn. Knit seven, work a ssk as in Step 11. Turn, purl six, p2tog at the end to create the flat top edge. Turn, knit six and ssk as before.

13 Continue working ssk and p2tog each time until the triangle is complete. Repeat for all the triangles. Pull the final stitch through itself to finish.

PLEATS

To make a pattern for pleats, fold a sheet of squared paper alternately away from and towards you along lines at 10 and 5 square intervals. Each square represents a stitch. Use the pattern to count the stitches required to make the visible face, underside, and turn-back of each pleat. Add one stitch at each fold – slipped on the right-side rows, purled on the wrong-side rows, or purled every row. Use the same method for all folds.

KNITTING PLEATS

1 This example creates two left-facing five-stitch pleats. Cast on 44 stitches (this includes an extra four stitches for fold lines).

2 Add markers as you work. First row: k10, p1, k5, p1, k10, p1, k5, p1, k10.

3 Purl one complete row. Repeat to the required length, finishing after a purl row.

4 With pleats completed, cast off four stitches knitwise (see p.68). Slip the next five stitches purlwise (including fold stitch) onto a double-pointed needle (dpn). Slip the next six stitches purlwise (including the fold stitch) onto another dpn. Turn the needles to fold the pleat.

5 Slip one stitch from the rear dpn to the right needle. Knit the first stitch on the left needle onto the right needle and pass both stitches on the right needle over the first one and needle tip, one by one.

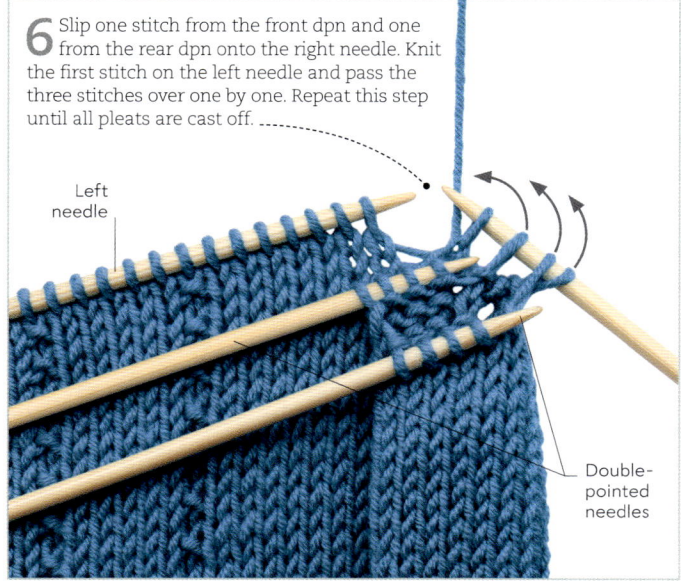

6 Slip one stitch from the front dpn and one from the rear dpn onto the right needle. Knit the first stitch on the left needle and pass the three stitches over one by one. Repeat this step until all pleats are cast off.

7 Cast off the remaining stitches as normal.

GATHERING AND DOUBLING

Gathering removes multiple stitches evenly along a row, and doubling (also called blousing) adds stitches in the same manner. Another form of gathering can be created by working multiple rows of rib on smaller needles preceded and followed by non-rib knitting. Doubling can be used after a cuff rib, giving fullness to a sleeve.

GATHERING

1. To calculate even gathering, decide how many stitches are to be removed, and divide the stitches on the needle by this number. For example if you cast on 30 stitches and wish to evenly remove 10 stitches, the sum is 30 ÷ 10 = 3. Therefore one stitch must be decreased in every three stitches. To do this, knit one stitch, then knit two stitches together (k2tog, see p.99). Repeat along the row.

2. To make a fuller gather, try k2tog all across the row, or knit three stitches together or even work two consecutive k2tog, p2tog rows. To create a gathered edge, knit two or more stitches together as you cast off.

DOUBLING

1. To calculate doubling, do the same sum as for Gathering (above) but remember that doubling adds stitches. If the answer is three, then three stitches must be made out of every one stitch. To do this, knit into the front, the back, and the front again of each stitch.

2. To use both doubling and gathering to work a horizontal ruffle, knit one row, knitting into the front and the back, and the next row purling into the front and the back of each stitch. Knit between 16 and 20 rows in stocking stitch. Knit one row of k2tog across the row, and then p2tog across the next row. Continue in stocking stitch.

148 TECHNIQUES

BIAS KNITTING

This method creates diagonal-shaped pieces, sloping left or right. Chevron knitting (see p.283) is created by working opposing bias panels in one piece. Increasing into lower rows or working increases tightly can force bias knitting to curve attractively.

BIAS KNITTING – STRAIGHT AND CURVED

Cast on 20 stitches. At the start of the first knit row, slip the first and second stitches one by one onto the right needle, insert the left needle into the front and knit them together (ssk, see p.100). Knit the row to one before the end stitch, knit into the front and the back of the edge stitch. Purl one row. Repeat the knit row. This piece of knitting will slant to the left.

Ssk

Kfb

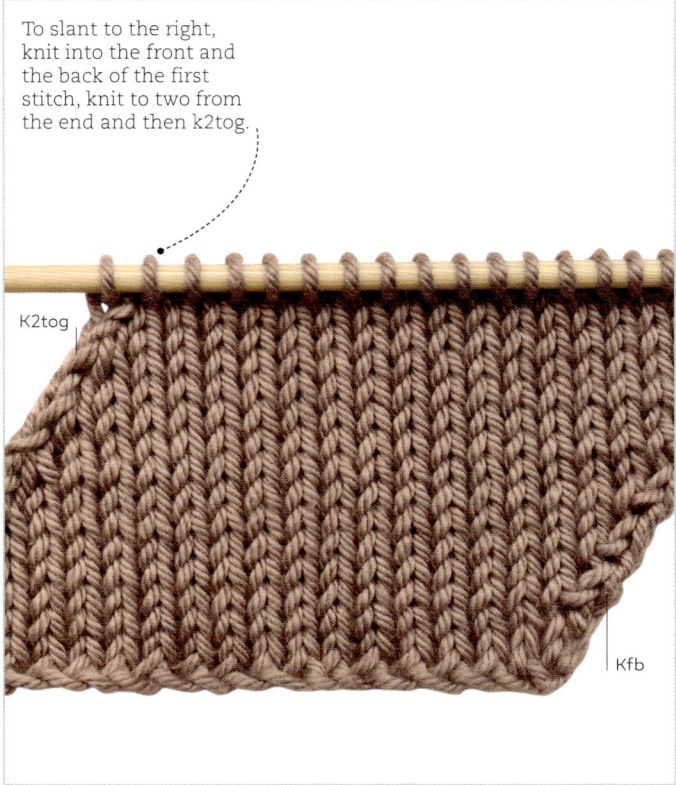

To slant to the right, knit into the front and the back of the first stitch, knit to two from the end and then k2tog.

K2tog

Kfb

LL1

Knit to three stitches from the end. Insert the left needle-tip from front to back into the left side of the stitch two rows below the just-completed stitch on the right needle. Knit this stitch. This makes a left Lifted increase (LL1; see p.107). Knit to the end. Purl the next row and repeat the ssk and LL1 on each knit row.

To add neat, decorative edges slanting to the left, knit two stitches, then work the ssk decrease.

Ssk

TUBULAR KNITTING

This term is sometimes used to refer to double or circular knitting. Unlike circular knitting (p.158), this method uses straight needles and creates a tube with the knitting travelling in a horizontal direction, ideal for snoods. Unlike closed-edge double knitting (pp.136–37), this creates an open-sided tube. You can work it in two colours as shown, or by using two balls of the same shade.

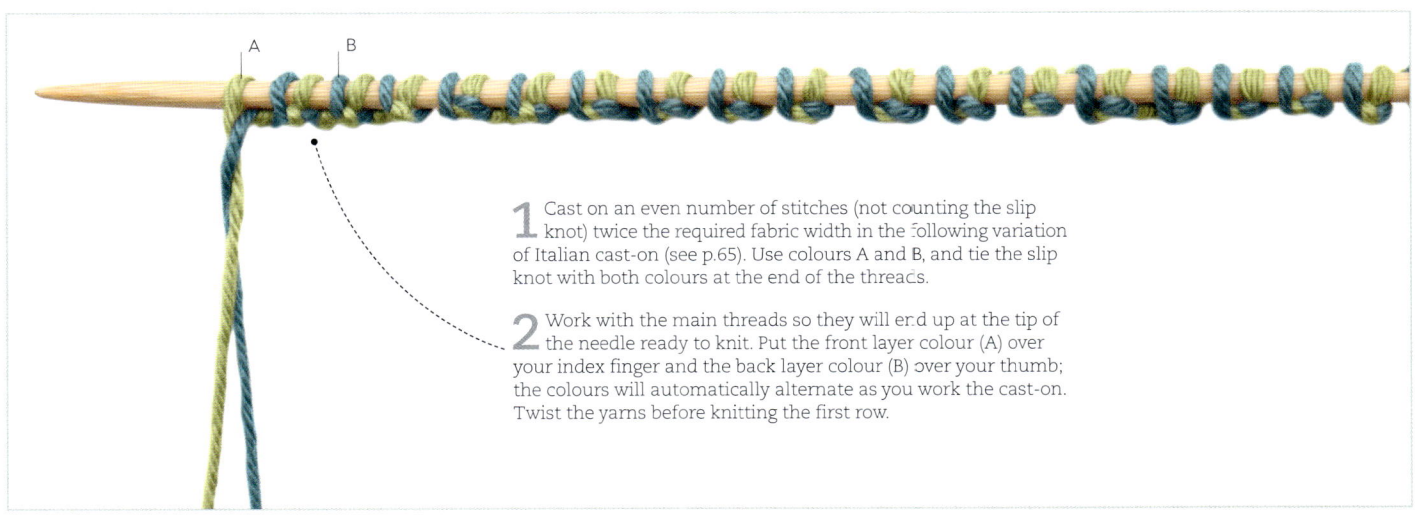

1 Cast on an even number of stitches (not counting the slip knot) twice the required fabric width in the following variation of Italian cast-on (see p.65). Use colours A and B, and tie the slip knot with both colours at the end of the threads.

2 Work with the main threads so they will end up at the tip of the needle ready to knit. Put the front layer colour (A) over your index finger and the back layer colour (B) over your thumb; the colours will automatically alternate as you work the cast-on. Twist the yarns before knitting the first row.

3 With colour B, knit a stitch, then bring the yarn to the front, and slip one stitch of colour A purlwise, take the yarn to the back, repeat along the row. Drop the slip knot and tie the ends together under the needle.

4 With colour B, purl the B stitches of the last row, taking the yarn to the back to slip the A stitches purlwise. Bring the yarn to the front and repeat along the row.

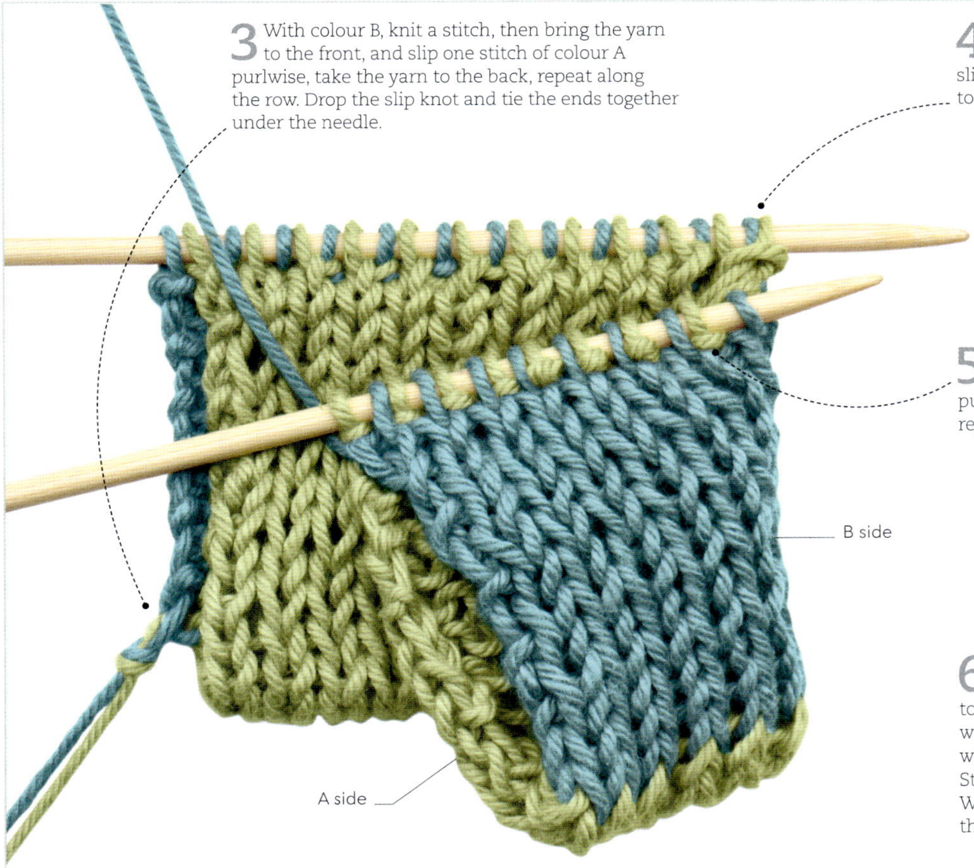

5 With colour A, purl the A stitches, take the yarn to the back and slip B stitches purlwise. Bring the yarn to the front and repeat along the row.

6 With colour A, knit the purled A stitches of the last row, bringing the yarn forwards to slip the B stitches. Using two colours in this way results in open sides. To work two colours with closed edges, use double-pointed needles. Start when both yarns are at the same end. Work Step 3, Step 5, Step 4, and Step 6 in that order, twisting the yarns every two rows.

Short rows

Rows of knitting do not necessarily have to be knitted end to end. Short rowing, or "partial knitting", involves knitting two rows across some of the stitches, thereby adding rows in only one part of the fabric. It is popular for creating smooth edges in shoulder shaping, curving hems, making darts, and turning sock heels. It is most commonly used on stocking stitch.

PREVENTING HOLES

In most shaping applications a concealed turn is required and there are at least five ways to work this: the "wrap" or "tie" (easiest and neat); the "over" (loosest); and the "catch" (neatest) are shown here. Garter stitch does not require wrapping.

WRAP OR TIE TO CLOSE HOLES

1 On a knit row: at the turn position, wrap and turn (w&t) as follows: slip the next stitch purlwise onto the right needle (see p.86), bring the yarn to the front. Return the slip stitch to the left needle, take the yarn back. Turn and purl the short row. Repeat the wrap at each mid-row turn.

2 To work a w&t on a purl row: at the turn, slip the next stitch purlwise, take the yarn to the back. Slip stitch back onto left-hand needle, bring yarn to the front. Turn and knit the short row. Repeat wrap at each turn.

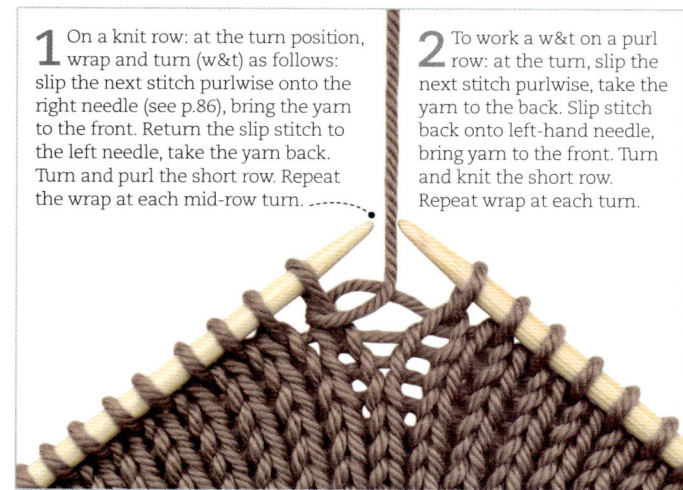

3 When working across all stitches on completion of short rowing: at the wrap, insert the right needle up through the front (knit) or the back (purl) of the wrap. Work the wrap together with the next stitch.

OVER TO CLOSE HOLES

1 Knit or purl to the turn position. Take the yarn to the other side of the work and turn the work. Bring the yarn over (not around) the needle to work the next stitch back along the short row.

2 When knitting across all stitches on completion of short rowing, knit each yarnover together with the next stitch. When purling across all stitches on completion of short rowing, slip the yarnover and next stitch knitwise, one by one, to the right needle. Return both stitches to the left needle and purl together through the back of the loops (ssp, see p.101).

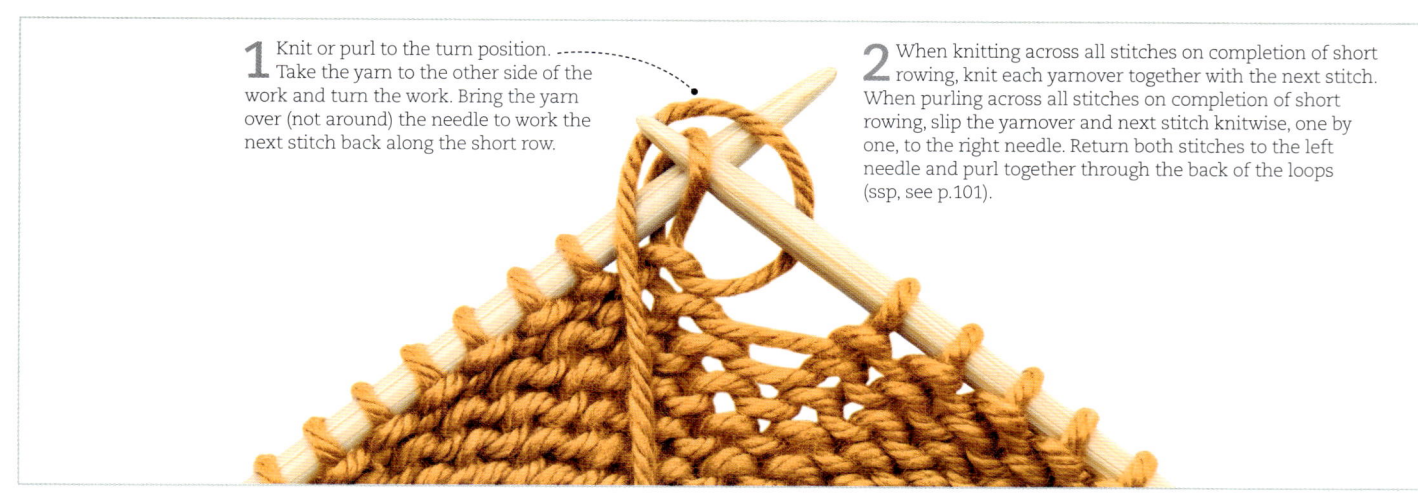

CATCH TO CLOSE HOLES

1 On either a knit or a purl row, work a short row. Turn the work, slip the first stitch purlwise (see p.86), and work back along the short row.

2 When knitting a completion row (knitting is temporarily reversed as this makes the step easier), insert the right needle down through the strand between the first and second stitches on the left needle as shown. Lift onto the left needle.

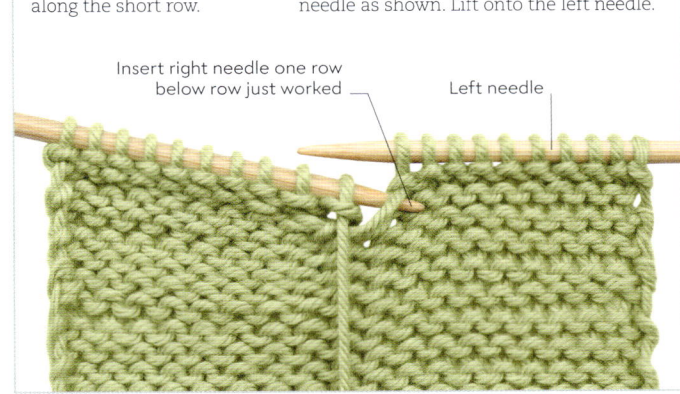

Insert right needle one row below row just worked — Left needle

3 Turn the work again and knit the picked-up loop together with the next stitch on the left needle.

4 If completion row is purl, insert the left needle upwards through the strand between the first and second stitch two rows below right needle. Stretch this loop, then drop it. Slip the next stitch from the left to the right needle. Pick up the dropped loop again with the left needle. Return the slipped stitch to the left needle. Purl these two together.

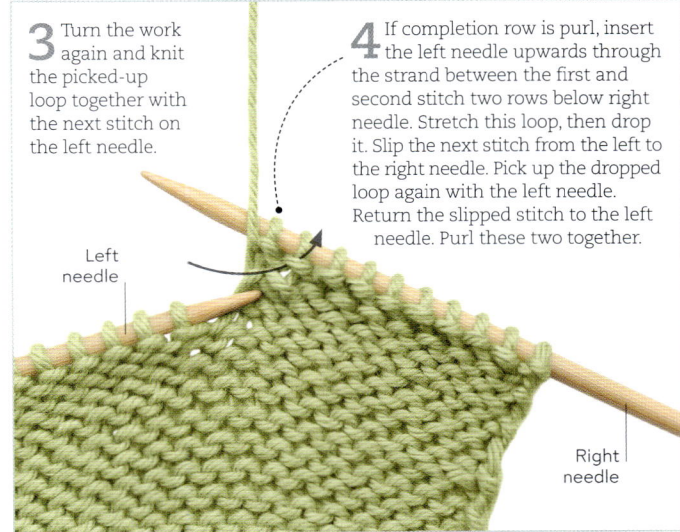

Left needle — Right needle

SHAPING: ADAPTING A CAST-OFF SHOULDER TO SHORT ROW SHAPING

1 This example adapts an existing left shoulder worked in stocking stitch. The left shoulder is 24 stitches wide and the original instruction is to cast off eight stitches every alternate row. These cast-offs can be substituted by working short rows with eight fewer stitches on alternate rows.

2 Cast on 24 stitches and work to the shoulder shaping. Ignore the cast-off instruction, and knit a row.

3 Turn the work. Purl to eight stitches from the end and work a wrap (slip next stitch purlwise, take the yarn back, return the slip stitch, bring the yarn forwards, see opposite). Turn. Knit to the end.

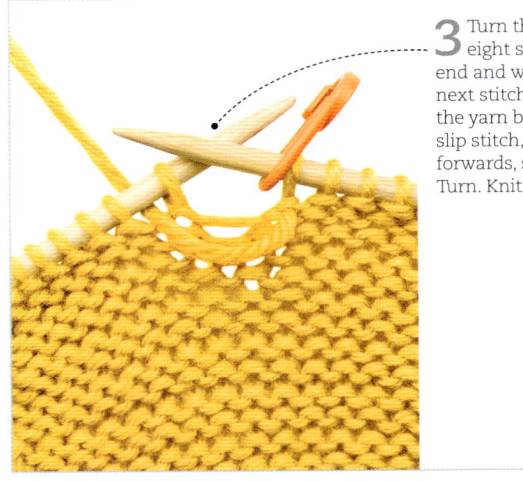

4 Purl to 16 stitches from the end, work wrap and turn. Knit to end (eight stitches remain on the needle).

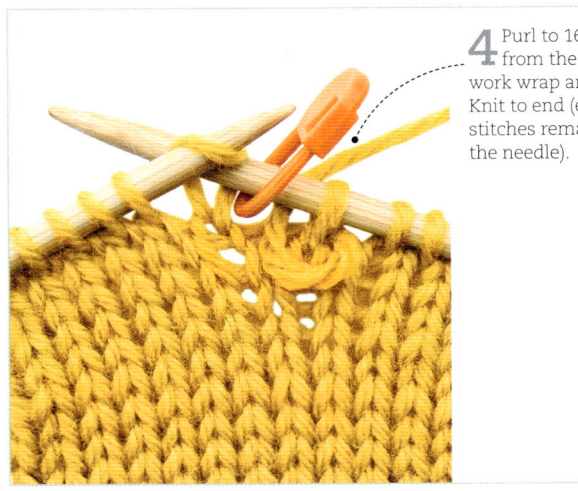

5 Purl across all the stitches, picking up the wraps by slipping them onto the left needle and purling together with the next stitch (see top opposite). Either cast off all the stitches or put them onto a stitch holder for grafting later.

GERMAN SHORT ROWS

German short rows are a simple variation on short-row shaping with less chance of creating holes. By creating double stitches at the turning point, you add extra fabric for three-dimensional shapes, such as when turning a sock heel (pp.154–155) or creating bust darts. This technique can be used in different stitches, but are shown here in stocking stitch.

ON KNIT SIDES

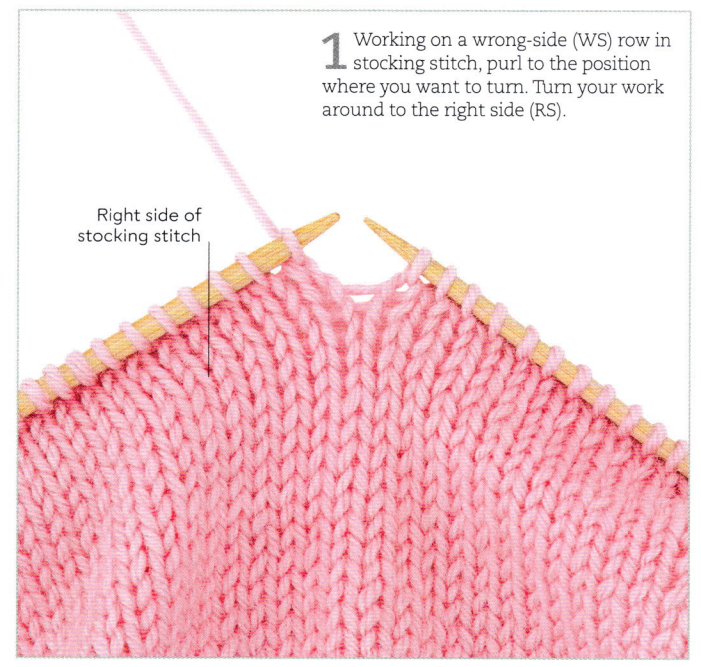

1 Working on a wrong-side (WS) row in stocking stitch, purl to the position where you want to turn. Turn your work around to the right side (RS).

Right side of stocking stitch

2 Slip the next stitch back to the right-hand needle purlwise.

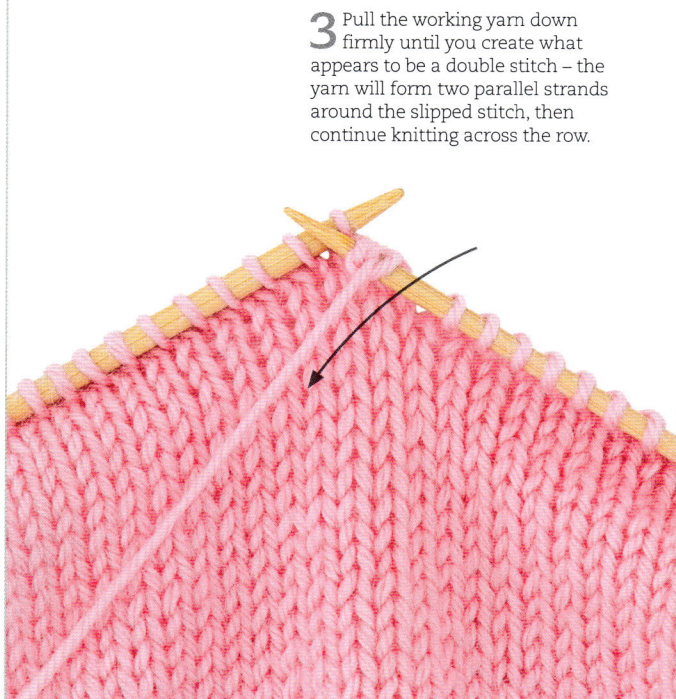

3 Pull the working yarn down firmly until you create what appears to be a double stitch – the yarn will form two parallel strands around the slipped stitch, then continue knitting across the row.

4 When working stitches, on a wrong-side (WS) row, purl them together as p2tog so that your stitch count remains correct, avoiding any accidental increases.

GERMAN SHORT ROWS **153**

ON PURL SIDES

1 Working in stocking stitch, on a right-side (RS) row, knit to the position where you want to turn. Turn your work around to the wrong-side (WS).

Wrong side of stocking stitch

2 Slip the next stitch back to the right-hand needle purlwise.

3 Pull the working yarn down firmly until you create the double stitch – the yarn from the previous row will pull up and over the right-hand needle to form two parallel strands around the slipped stitch. Continue purling across the rest of the row as normal, or until you want to turn.

4 Repeat this process as many times as needed, creating additional double stitches with each turn. When you're ready to work across the short rows, knit across without turning and work each double stitch as k2tog, knitting both strands of the pulled-down yarn together.

▶ TIPS

- For twisted double stitches that create a tighter turn, on both RS (K) or WS (P), slip the stitch knitwise instead of purlwise when creating the double stitch. Work the twisted stitches together through the back of the loop.

- Choose your slipping method based on what's best for your project – slip stitches purlwise for standard double stitches, or slip knitwise for twisted versions. The twisted technique often creates neater results for heel turns, while standard double stitches work well for colourwork and shaping.

SOCK HEELS

These examples are worked in stocking stitch but other stitches may be used. Socks are usually knitted over a multiple of 4 stitches, which can easily be divided for the heel. Maths is needed to work out stitch counts, but patterns (see pp.232–37) do it for you.

SHORT-ROW HEEL

1 To separate out your heel stitches, knit across a quarter of the total stitches, then turn and purl back across those stitches plus another quarter of the total stitches. This separates the total into half for the heel. Leave the remaining half unworked to pick up later for the top of foot.

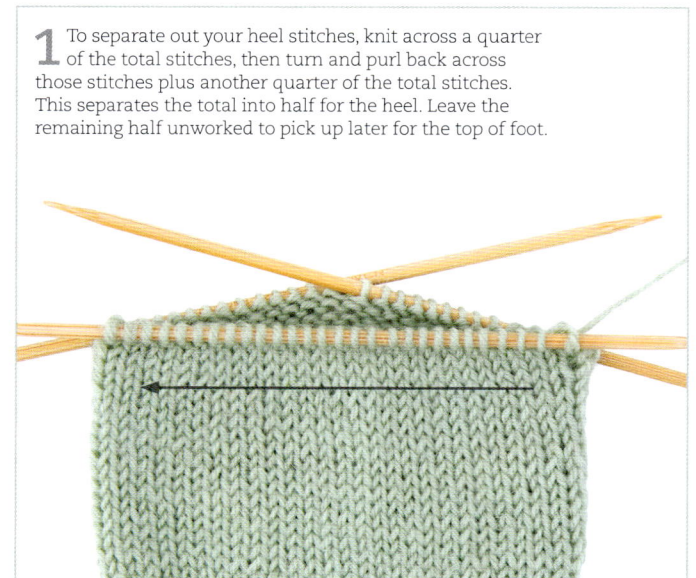

2 Work short rows (p.150) to turn the heel. Knit to the last live stitch, wrap and turn (w&t). Purl to the last live stitch, w&t. Continue creating shorter and shorter rows in this way, until you have around a third of your heel stitches still to work, ending with a right-side (knit) row.

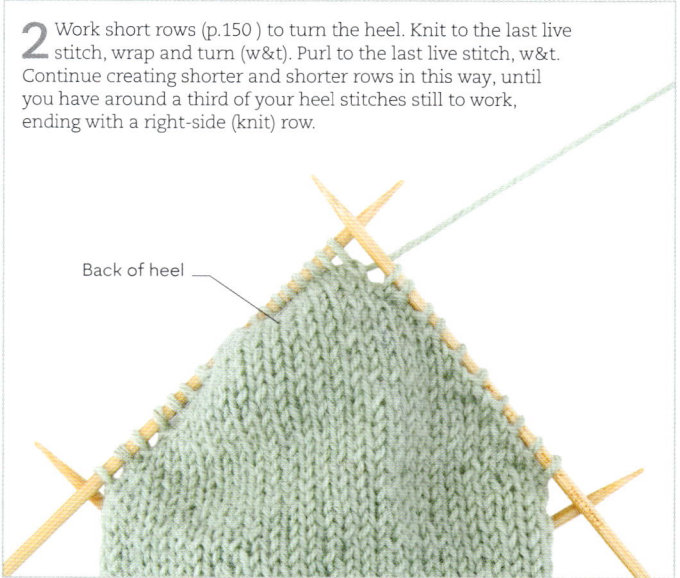

Back of heel

3 Purl to the first wrapped stitch, pick up the wrap and purl it together with the stitch. Turn. Slipping the first stitch, knit to the first wrapped stitch, and work the stitch and wrap together. Turn. Repeat until all stitches have been worked, ending with a purl row. Knit across all stitches, and those on hold, to rejoin the round.

Bottom of heel

4 This method is the perfect option to add a contrast colour for the heel. It's also the go-to choice for toe-up socks. If you find gaps start to form, try the German short-row method (p.152), or picking up an extra stitch where heel stitches meet the stitches from the top of the foot, and decrease on the following round.

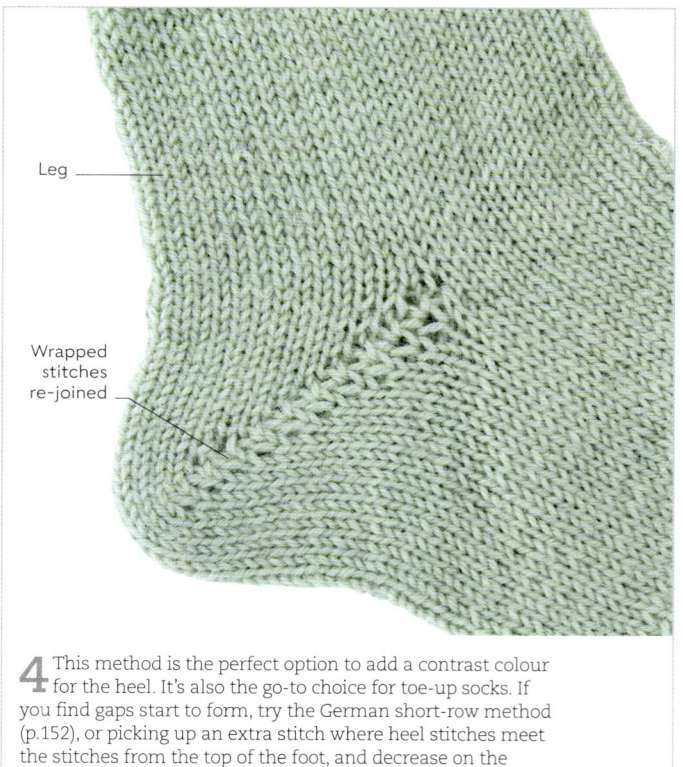

Leg

Wrapped stitches re-joined

HEEL FLAP

1 Divide the stitches in half. Put one half on hold for the top of the foot. Create the heel flap by working alternate rows across the other half set of stitches only, slipping the first stitch of each row. Your heel flap should be the same number of rows as half your total stitch count. You can adjust this for a deeper or shallower instep. End with a purl row.

2 Turn the heel. Including the slipped first stitch, knit to half the heel sts + 2 stitches, ssk, k1 and turn. On the next row s1, p5, p2tog, p1, turn. On the next row s1, k to the previous ssk worked, ssk, k1. Continue until all stitches have been worked. The last two rows should end with the decrease over the last two stitches of each row. Knit across the remaining heel stitches.

3 Pick up and knit the slipped stitches along the row-end edge of the heel flap. Knit across the top of foot stitches on hold. Pick up and knit across the remaining row-end edge of the heel flap. You have re-joined into a round, with its start at the centre of your heel stitches. Now work in rounds, decreasing 1 stitch every alternate round, just before and just after the top of foot stitches, to reach your starting number of total stitches.

4 This technique can be used on a sock worked in the round from the top (cuff edge) downwards. Heel flaps can be adjusted in length before Step 2 is worked, to give shallower or greater depth to an instep for a better fit. For a reinforced heel flap, slip every alternate stitch along the knit rows on Step 1.

SHORT ROW CIRCULAR MEDALLION

This example is in garter stitch, but medallions can be knitted in other stitches. There is no need to pick up the wraps in garter stitch.

1 Cast on 16 stitches in colour A with a Provisional cast-on (see p.63).

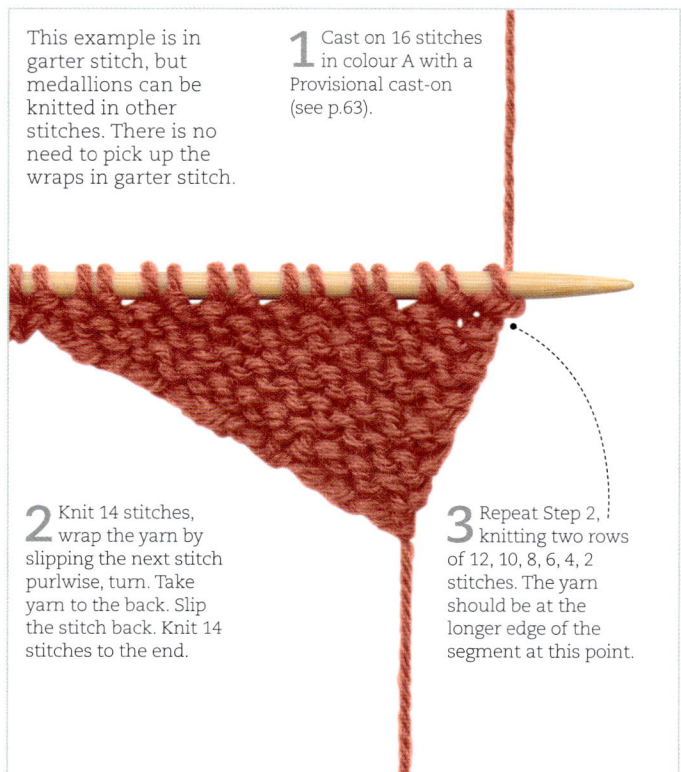

2 Knit 14 stitches, wrap the yarn by slipping the next stitch purlwise, turn. Take yarn to the back. Slip the stitch back. Knit 14 stitches to the end.

3 Repeat Step 2, knitting two rows of 12, 10, 8, 6, 4, 2 stitches. The yarn should be at the longer edge of the segment at this point.

4 Turn the work and knit 14 stitches. Bring the yarn to the front. Slip the last two stitches on the left needle purlwise onto the right needle. Cut colour A yarn with a 10cm (4in) tail (yarn is part way along a row). One segment of the circle is complete.

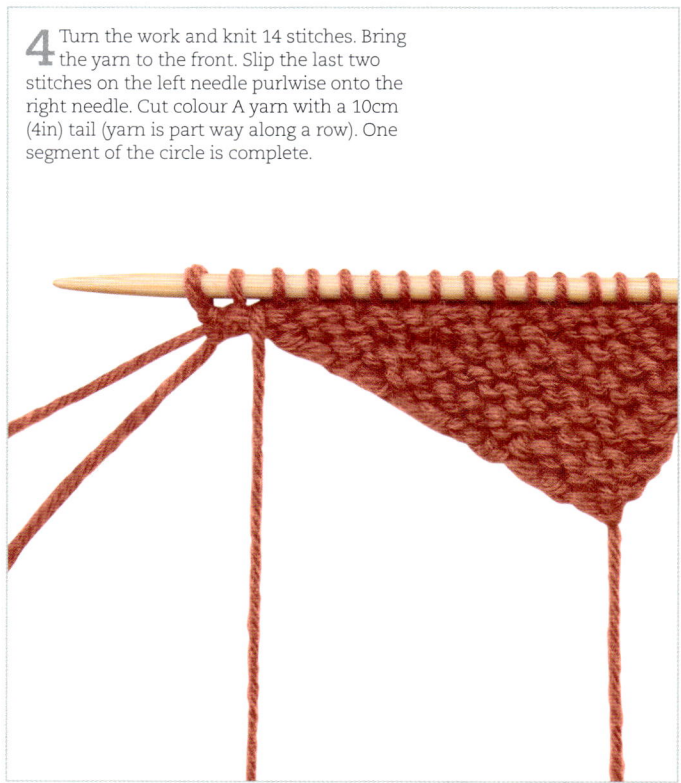

5 Hold the needle with the stitches in your left hand, change to colour B, knit 16 stitches. Then repeat Steps 2–5 in B, swapping to colour A at Step 5.

6 Work eight segments, alternating colours A and B. Finish by placing the stitches on a holder (see p.69) after Step 5 on the final segment. Graft the seam (see p.190) and sew in the yarn ends to complete.

RUFFLES

By working a straight band vertically at the same time as working short rows, ruffles can be built up. The fullness of the ruffle is dictated by the number of times the short rows are worked compared with the rows of the vertical band. Varying the stitch, as shown in edge ruffles (below), can add extra effect to the finished ruffle.

SHORT ROW EDGE RUFFLES

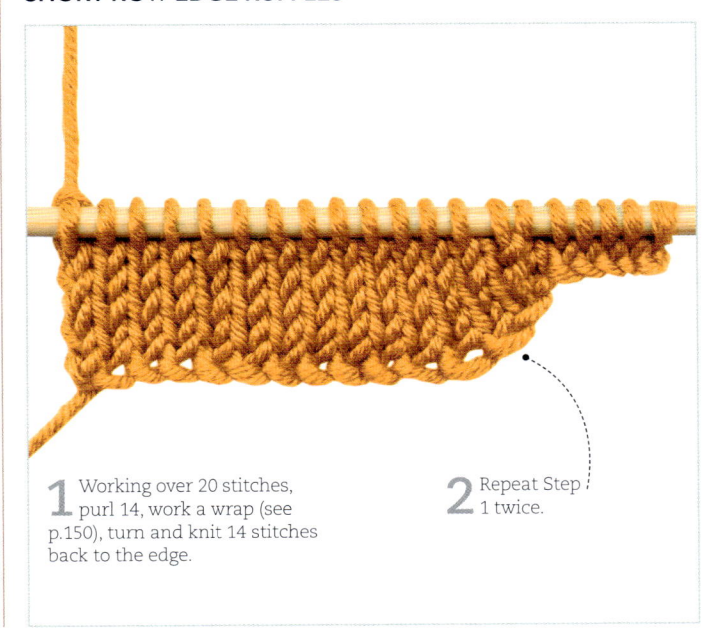

1 Working over 20 stitches, purl 14, work a wrap (see p.150), turn and knit 14 stitches back to the edge.

2 Repeat Step 1 twice.

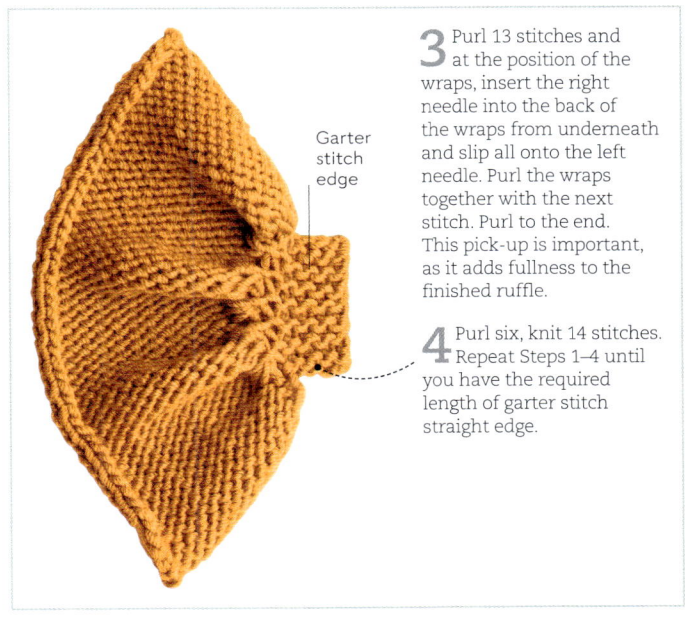

Garter stitch edge

3 Purl 13 stitches and at the position of the wraps, insert the right needle into the back of the wraps from underneath and slip all onto the left needle. Purl the wraps together with the next stitch. Purl to the end. This pick-up is important, as it adds fullness to the finished ruffle.

4 Purl six, knit 14 stitches. Repeat Steps 1–4 until you have the required length of garter stitch straight edge.

VERTICAL RUFFLES INSET INTO FABRIC

1 Working over 20 stitches, purl 14, work a wrap (see p.150), turn and knit 14 stitches back to the edge.

2 Purl eight stitches, wrap, and turn.

3 Knit eight stitches, wrap, and turn. Repeat Step 2.

4 Knit 16 stitches, picking up wraps (see p.150).

5 Purl 24 stitches, doing pick-up on the other side of the ruffle, as in Step 4. This completes two rows of the main fabric and four rows of the inset ruffle.

6 Repeat from knit instruction in Step 1 to end of Step 5 for required number of side panel rows. Group vertically for greater effect.

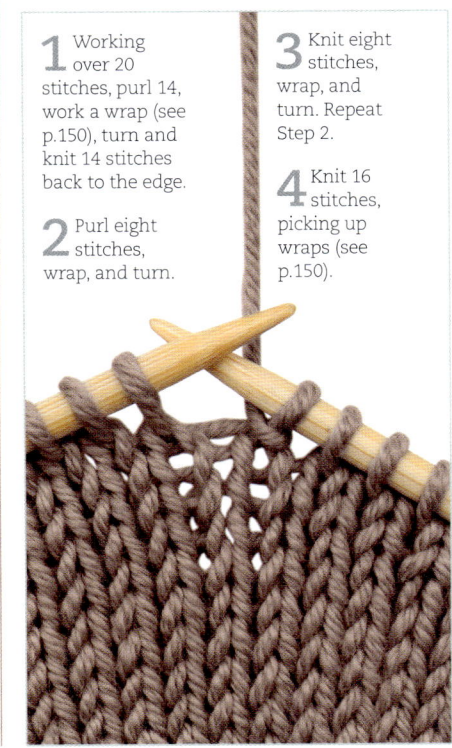

Circular knitting

Circular knitting, or knitting in the round, is worked on a circular needle or with a set of four or five double-pointed needles. With the right side always facing, the knitting is worked round and round to form a tube or a flat shape (a medallion). A circular needle is easy to master, while working with double-pointed needles is best suited to knitters with intermediate skills.

KNITTING TUBES

For those who don't enjoy stitching seams, knitting seamless tubes is a real plus. Large tubes can be worked on long circular needles, for example for the body of a jumper or a bag. Short circular needles are used for seamless neckbands, armhole bands, and hats. Double-pointed needles are used for smaller items, such as mittens and socks.

WORKING WITH A CIRCULAR KNITTING NEEDLE

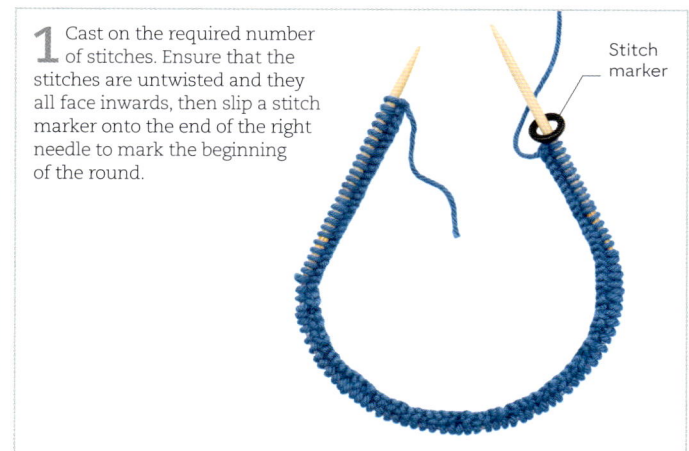

1 Cast on the required number of stitches. Ensure that the stitches are untwisted and they all face inwards, then slip a stitch marker onto the end of the right needle to mark the beginning of the round.

Stitch marker

2 Hold the needle ends in your hands and bring the right needle up to the left needle to work the first stitch. Knit round and round on the stitches. When the stitch marker is reached, slip it from the left needle to the right needle.

Knit the first stitch of the first round tightly

3 If you are working a stocking stitch tube on a circular needle, the right side of the work will always be facing you and every round will be a knit round.

JOINING A ROUND OF STITCHES

This is a neat way of closing the circle in circular knitting.

1 Cast on the required number of stitches plus one stitch.

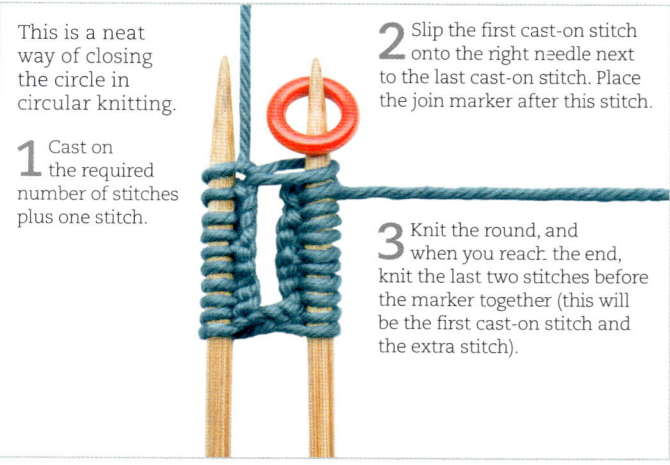

2 Slip the first cast-on stitch onto the right needle next to the last cast-on stitch. Place the join marker after this stitch.

3 Knit the round, and when you reach the end, knit the last two stitches before the marker together (this will be the first cast-on stitch and the extra stitch).

KNITTING A MÖBIUS LOOP

1 Using a Double cast-on (see p.57), cast on enough stitches to work a circle on a short circular needle. Knit the first round but stop before joining the circle.

2 Deliberately twist the stitches around the wire so that there is one clear twist visible, but the end stitches are facing each other with the loops facing inwards.

3 Join the circle, maintaining the twist, and knit the round. The first few rounds can be fiddly, but once there are a few rows and the twist is established it becomes easier.

4 Continue until the loop is as deep as required. Cast off. A deep Möbius loop makes a great hair band.

5 If using the Magic loop technique (see p.160), moving the twist to the stitches on the right end of the needle for the first few rounds makes working them easier.

160 TECHNIQUES

"MAGIC LOOP" KNITTING – WORKING A SMALL TUBE ON A LONGER CIRCULAR NEEDLE

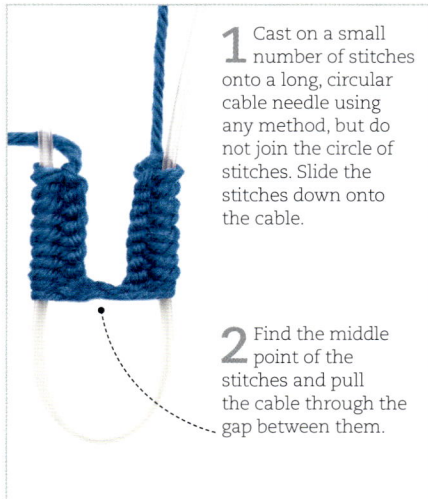

1 Cast on a small number of stitches onto a long, circular cable needle using any method, but do not join the circle of stitches. Slide the stitches down onto the cable.

2 Find the middle point of the stitches and pull the cable through the gap between them.

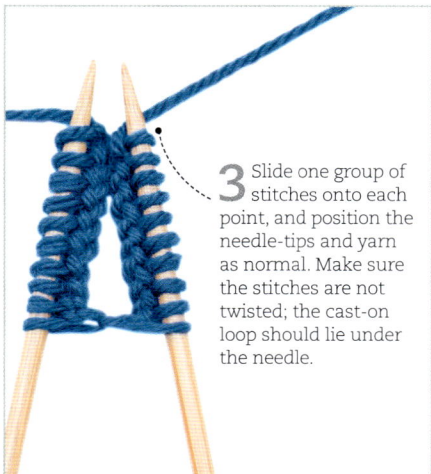

3 Slide one group of stitches onto each point, and position the needle-tips and yarn as normal. Make sure the stitches are not twisted; the cast-on loop should lie under the needle.

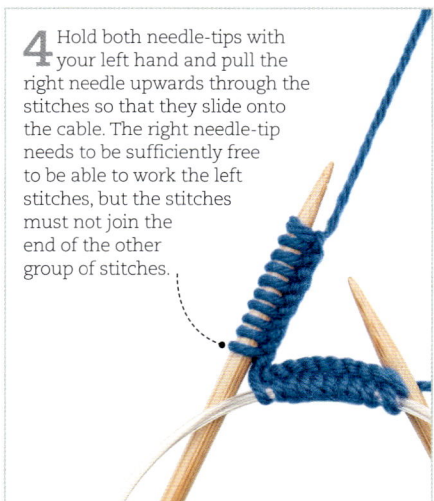

4 Hold both needle-tips with your left hand and pull the right needle upwards through the stitches so that they slide onto the cable. The right needle-tip needs to be sufficiently free to be able to work the left stitches, but the stitches must not join the end of the other group of stitches.

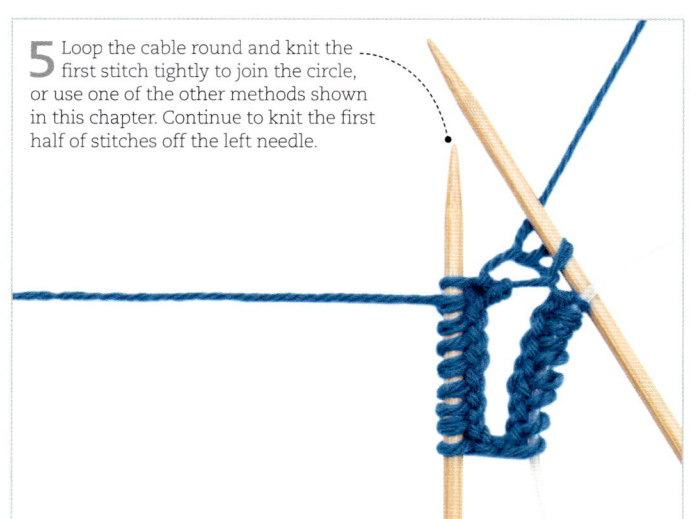

5 Loop the cable round and knit the first stitch tightly to join the circle, or use one of the other methods shown in this chapter. Continue to knit the first half of stitches off the left needle.

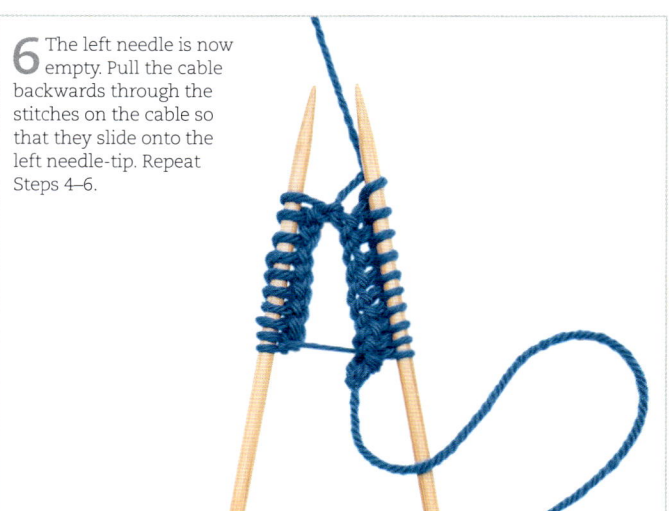

6 The left needle is now empty. Pull the cable backwards through the stitches on the cable so that they slide onto the left needle-tip. Repeat Steps 4–6.

KNITTING TWO TUBES AT ONCE ON TWO CIRCULAR NEEDLES

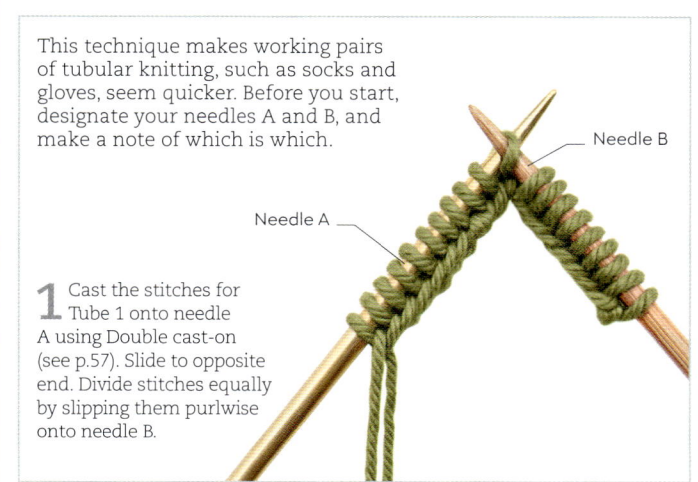

This technique makes working pairs of tubular knitting, such as socks and gloves, seem quicker. Before you start, designate your needles A and B, and make a note of which is which.

Needle B

Needle A

1 Cast the stitches for Tube 1 onto needle A using Double cast-on (see p.57). Slide to opposite end. Divide stitches equally by slipping them purlwise onto needle B.

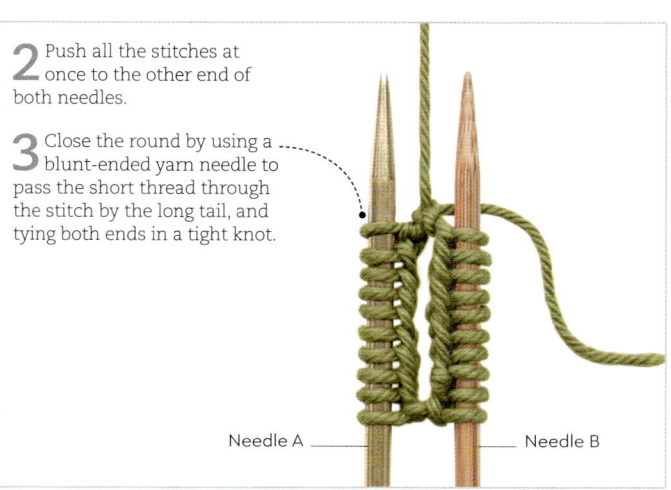

2 Push all the stitches at once to the other end of both needles.

3 Close the round by using a blunt-ended yarn needle to pass the short thread through the stitch by the long tail, and tying both ends in a tight knot.

Needle A

Needle B

KNITTING TUBES **161**

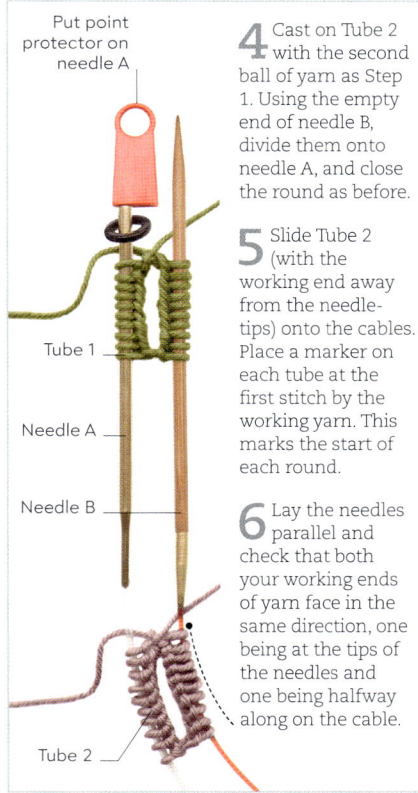

Put point protector on needle A

Tube 1

Needle A

Needle B

Tube 2

4 Cast on Tube 2 with the second ball of yarn as Step 1. Using the empty end of needle B, divide them onto needle A, and close the round as before.

5 Slide Tube 2 (with the working end away from the needle-tips) onto the cables. Place a marker on each tube at the first stitch by the working yarn. This marks the start of each round.

6 Lay the needles parallel and check that both your working ends of yarn face in the same direction, one being at the tips of the needles and one being halfway along on the cable.

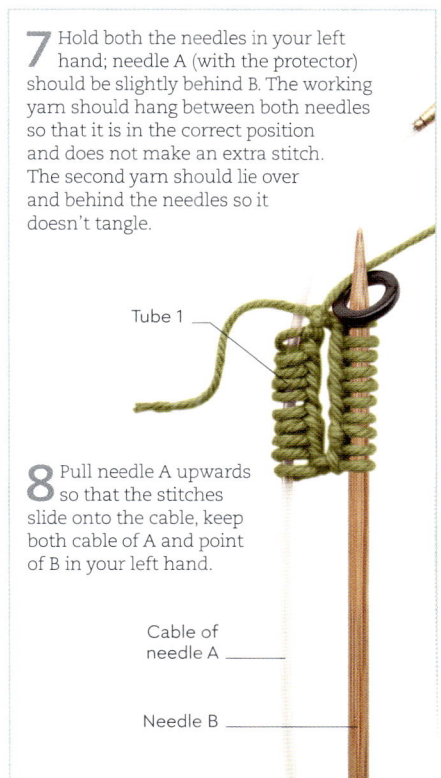

Tube 1

Cable of needle A

Needle B

7 Hold both the needles in your left hand; needle A (with the protector) should be slightly behind B. The working yarn should hang between both needles so that it is in the correct position and does not make an extra stitch. The second yarn should lie over and behind the needles so it doesn't tangle.

8 Pull needle A upwards so that the stitches slide onto the cable, keep both cable of A and point of B in your left hand.

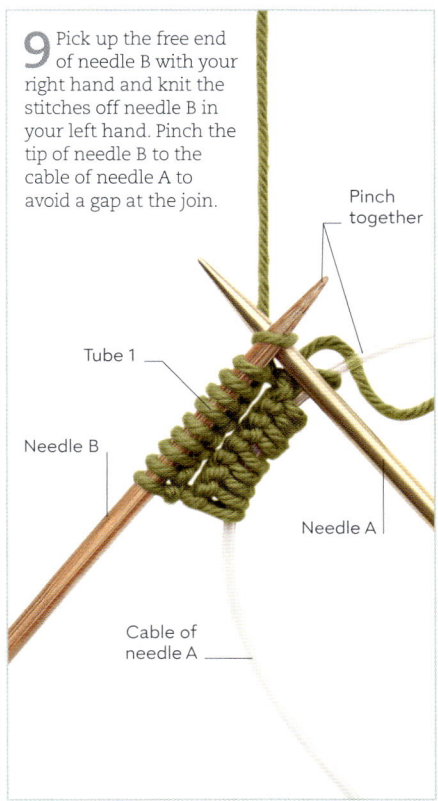

Pinch together

Tube 1

Needle B

Needle A

Cable of needle A

9 Pick up the free end of needle B with your right hand and knit the stitches off needle B in your left hand. Pinch the tip of needle B to the cable of needle A to avoid a gap at the join.

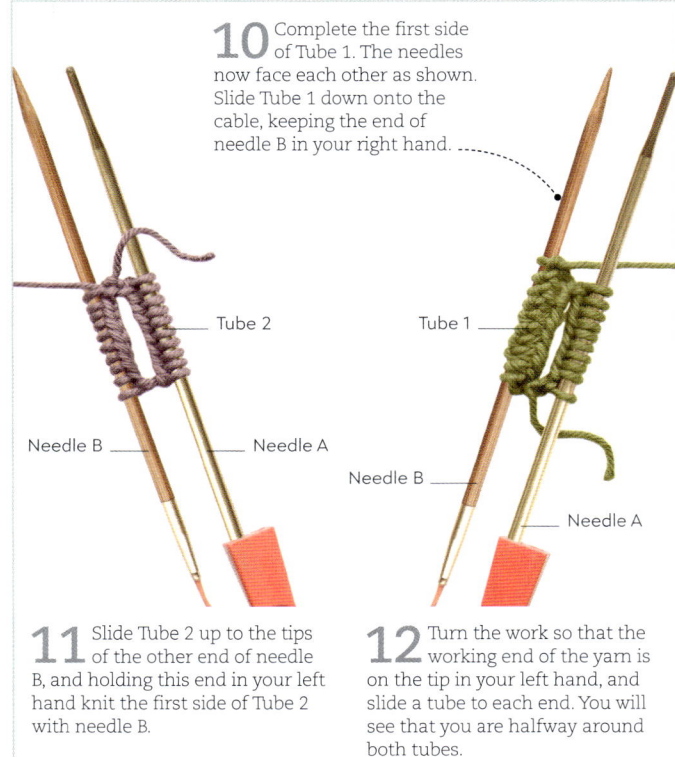

Tube 2

Needle B

Needle A

Tube 1

Needle B

Needle A

10 Complete the first side of Tube 1. The needles now face each other as shown. Slide Tube 1 down onto the cable, keeping the end of needle B in your right hand.

11 Slide Tube 2 up to the tips of the other end of needle B, and holding this end in your left hand knit the first side of Tube 2 with needle B.

12 Turn the work so that the working end of the yarn is on the tip in your left hand, and slide a tube to each end. You will see that you are halfway around both tubes.

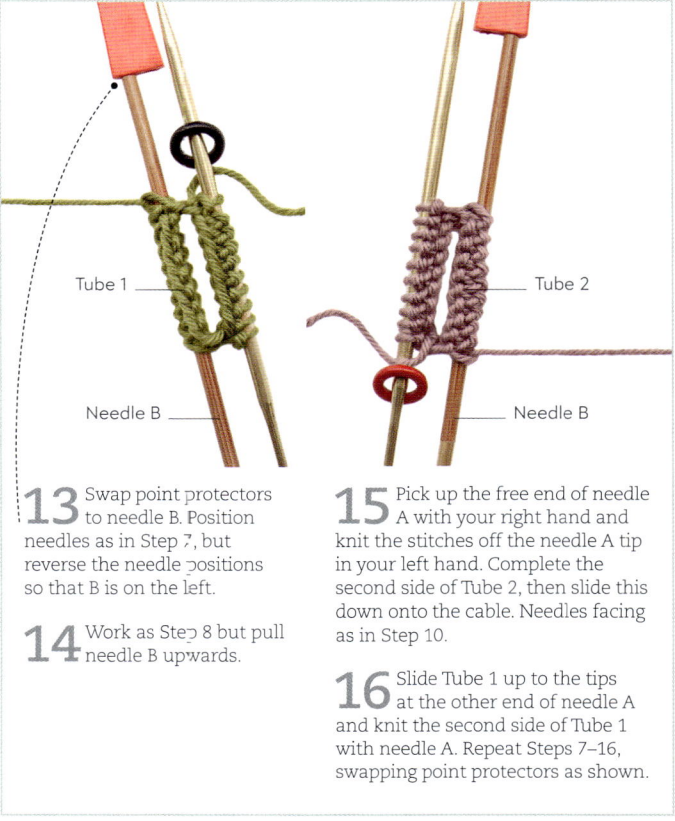

Tube 1

Needle B

Tube 2

Needle B

13 Swap point protectors to needle B. Position needles as in Step 7, but reverse the needle positions so that B is on the left.

14 Work as Step 8 but pull needle B upwards.

15 Pick up the free end of needle A with your right hand and knit the stitches off the needle A tip in your left hand. Complete the second side of Tube 2, then slide this down onto the cable. Needles facing as in Step 10.

16 Slide Tube 1 up to the tips at the other end of needle A and knit the second side of Tube 1 with needle A. Repeat Steps 7–16, swapping point protectors as shown.

HELIX KNITTING

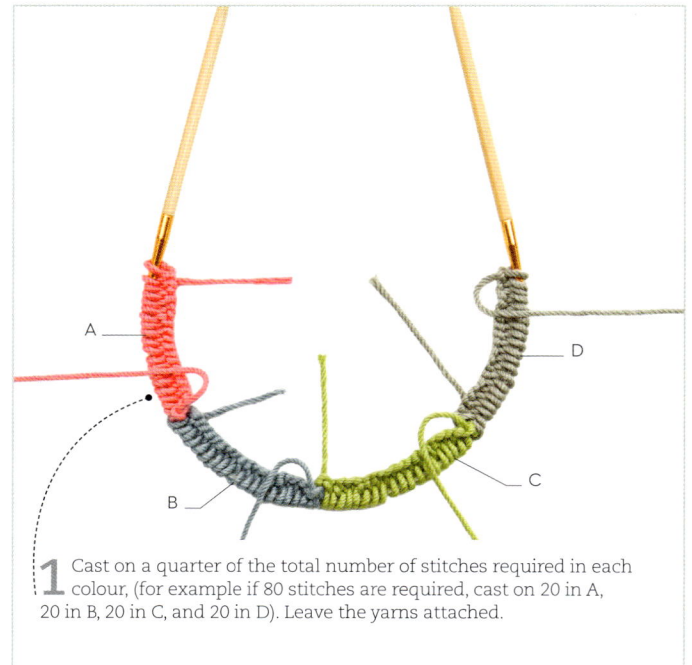

1 Cast on a quarter of the total number of stitches required in each colour, (for example if 80 stitches are required, cast on 20 in A, 20 in B, 20 in C, and 20 in D). Leave the yarns attached.

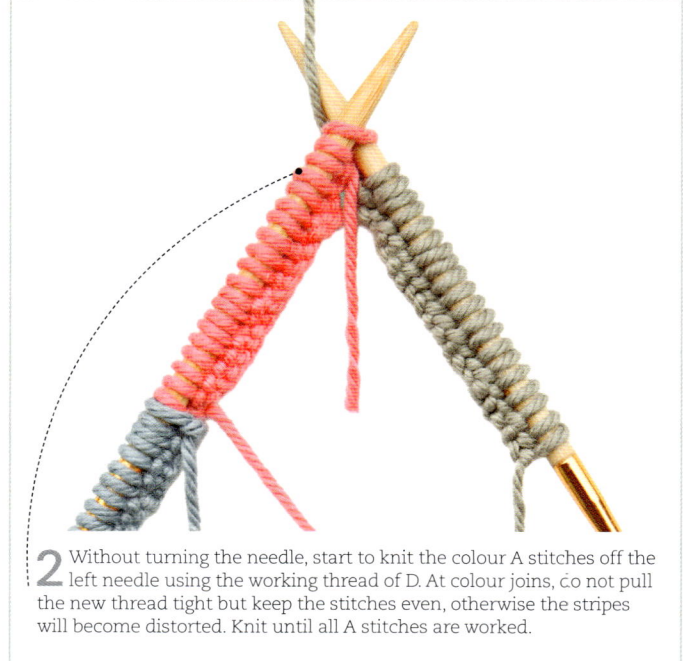

2 Without turning the needle, start to knit the colour A stitches off the left needle using the working thread of D. At colour joins, do not pull the new thread tight but keep the stitches even, otherwise the stripes will become distorted. Knit until all A stitches are worked.

3 Pick up the working thread of A and knit the next colour. Continue to the end of each colour, picking up the yarn above the next colour.

4 After one round, there will be no yarn waiting at the end of the last colour, so work to the point at which the next yarn is attached, pick it up and continue as Step 3.

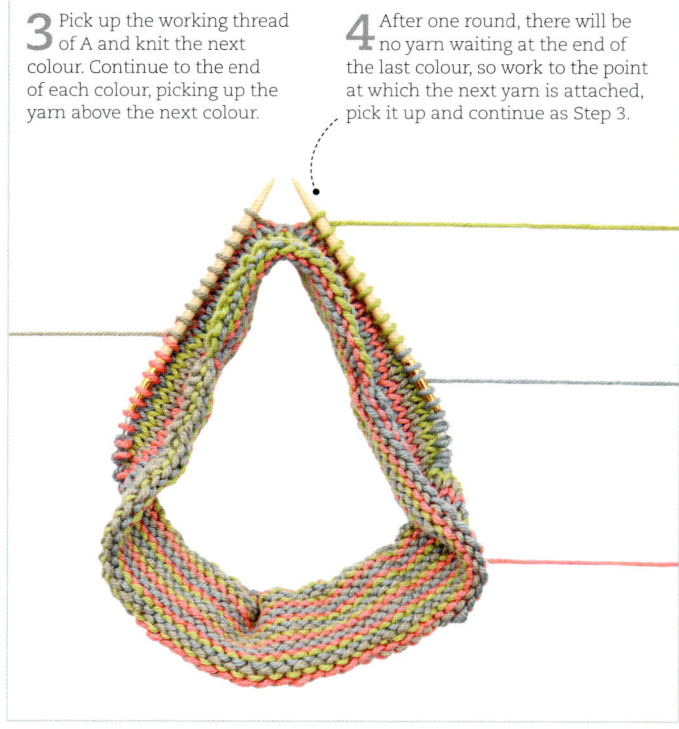

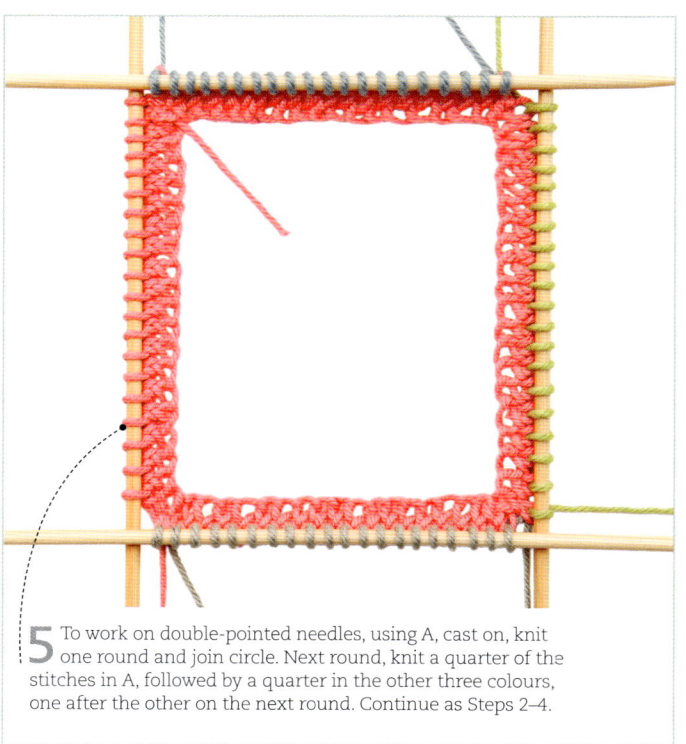

5 To work on double-pointed needles, using A, cast on, knit one round and join circle. Next round, knit a quarter of the stitches in A, followed by a quarter in the other three colours, one after the other on the next round. Continue as Steps 2–4.

▶ HELIX KNITTING WITH HAND-DYED YARNS

• Yarns that have been hand-dyed, even in batches, will naturally have slight variations in how they knit up. This can be a particular issue with multi-coloured hand-dyed yarns, leading to problems such as unintentional striping or "pooling", in which unpredictable colour changes cause big chunks of colour to sit in one place on your knitting. Using multiple balls of the same colourway in the helix knitting technique is more likely to break up or spread out the colour changes and so help them to blend together better.

WORKING WITH A SET OF FOUR DOUBLE-POINTED NEEDLES

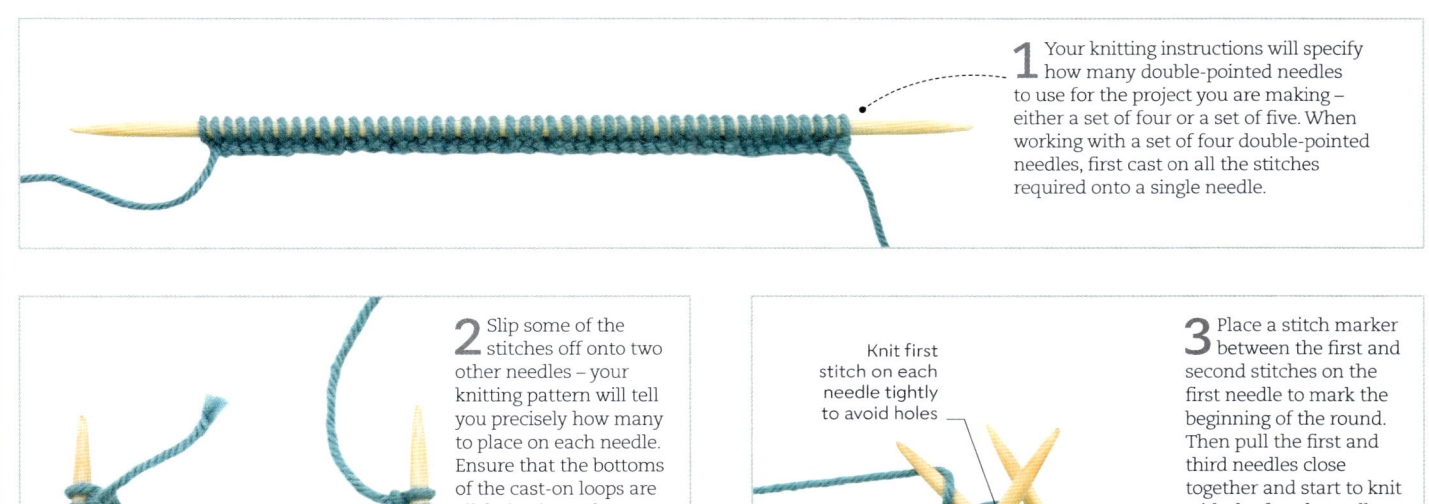

1 Your knitting instructions will specify how many double-pointed needles to use for the project you are making – either a set of four or a set of five. When working with a set of four double-pointed needles, first cast on all the stitches required onto a single needle.

2 Slip some of the stitches off onto two other needles – your knitting pattern will tell you precisely how many to place on each needle. Ensure that the bottoms of the cast-on loops are all facing inwards.

Make sure stitches are not twisted

3 Place a stitch marker between the first and second stitches on the first needle to mark the beginning of the round. Then pull the first and third needles close together and start to knit with the fourth needle. Knit round and round in this way as for knitting with a circular needle.

Knit first stitch on each needle tightly to avoid holes

Stitch marker

WORKING WITH A SET OF FIVE DOUBLE-POINTED NEEDLES

1 Cast on, distribute the stitches and position a stitch marker as for working with four needles, but distribute the stitches over four needles.

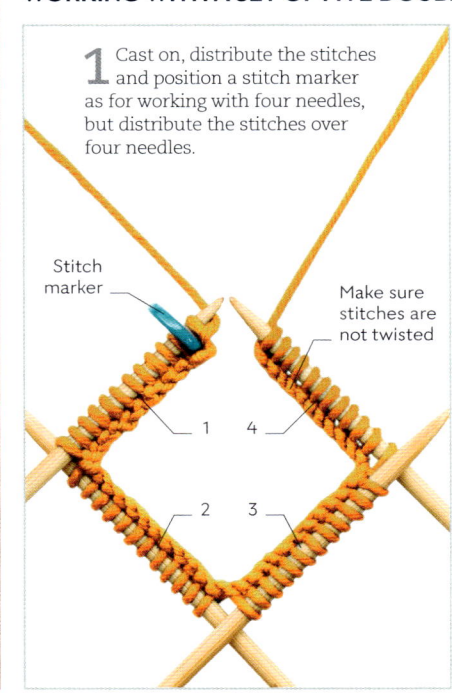

Stitch marker

Make sure stitches are not twisted

2 Use the fifth needle to knit with. Knit the first stitch tightly to close the gap between the first cast-on stitch and the last.

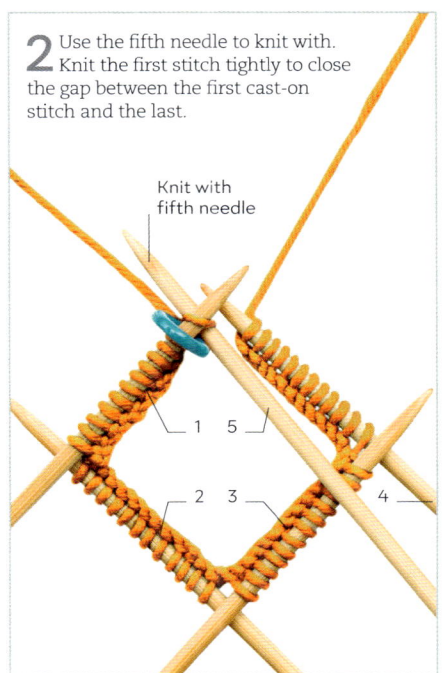

Knit with fifth needle

3 When all the stitches on the first needle have been knitted off onto the spare needle, use this empty needle to work the stitches on the second needle. Continue round and round like this, slipping the stitch marker from the left needle to the right needle when it is reached.

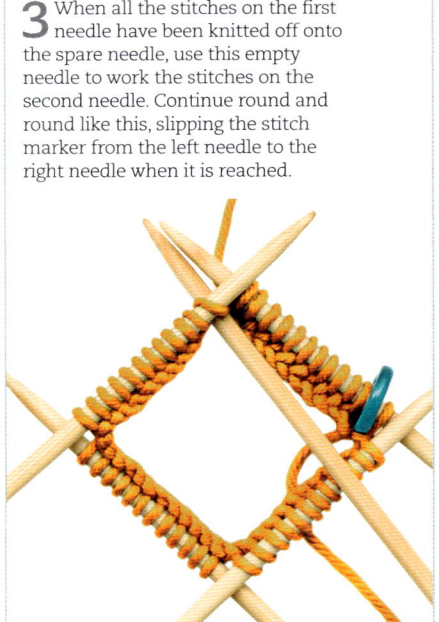

SPIRAL KNITTING

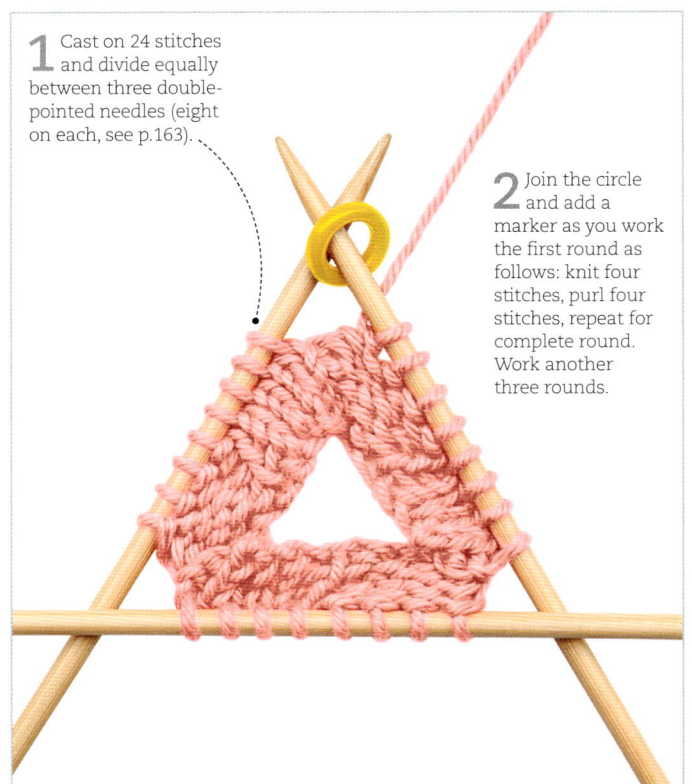

1 Cast on 24 stitches and divide equally between three double-pointed needles (eight on each, see p.163).

2 Join the circle and add a marker as you work the first round as follows: knit four stitches, purl four stitches, repeat for complete round. Work another three rounds.

3 On the next round, purl the first stitch, then knit four, purl four around the complete round, finishing with purl three to meet the first purl stitch.

4 This has moved the whole rib one stitch over. Continue moving the rib one stitch in the same direction every four rows as you work the required length.

5 This technique is particularly successful as jewellery when it incorporates fancy and sparkly yarns or beading.

KNITTING MEDALLIONS

Medallions are flat shapes knitted from the centre outwards. They are worked on a set of four or five double-pointed needles. Although the steps below show a square being worked, the technique is the same for knitting circles, hexagons, octagons, and so on.

WORKING A SIMPLE SQUARE

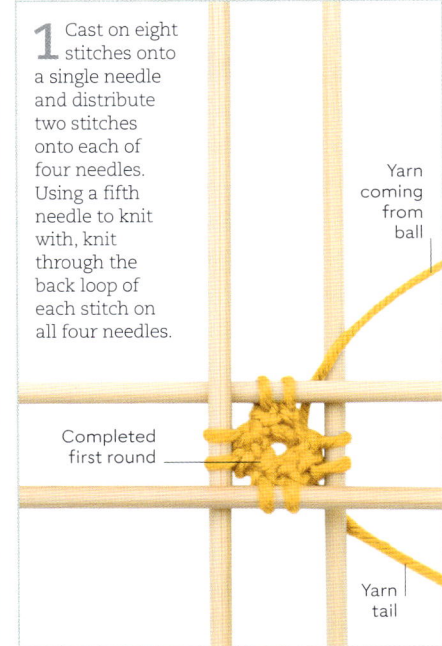

1 Cast on eight stitches onto a single needle and distribute two stitches onto each of four needles. Using a fifth needle to knit with, knit through the back loop of each stitch on all four needles.

Yarn coming from ball

Completed first round

Yarn tail

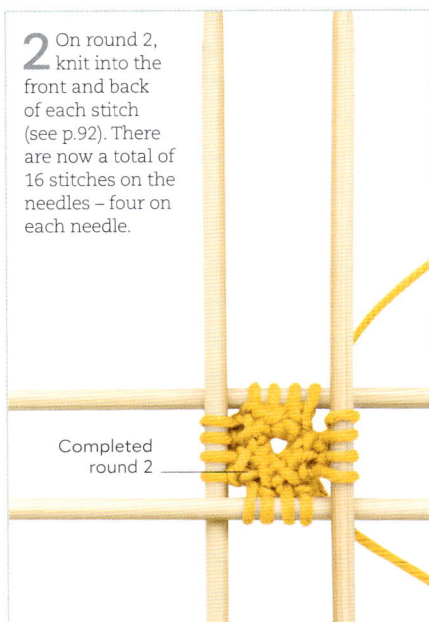

2 On round 2, knit into the front and back of each stitch (see p.92). There are now a total of 16 stitches on the needles – four on each needle.

Completed round 2

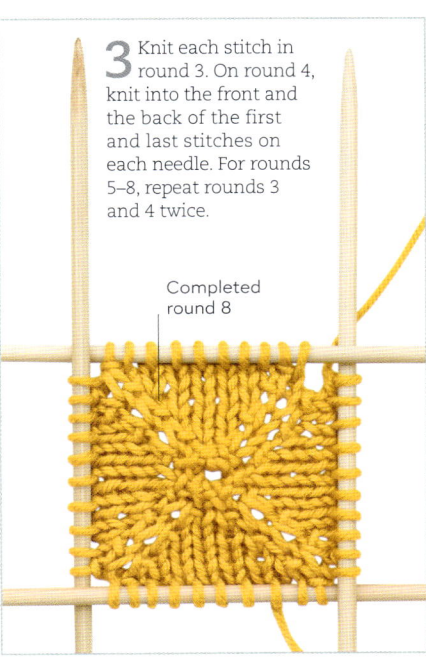

3 Knit each stitch in round 3. On round 4, knit into the front and the back of the first and last stitches on each needle. For rounds 5–8, repeat rounds 3 and 4 twice.

Completed round 8

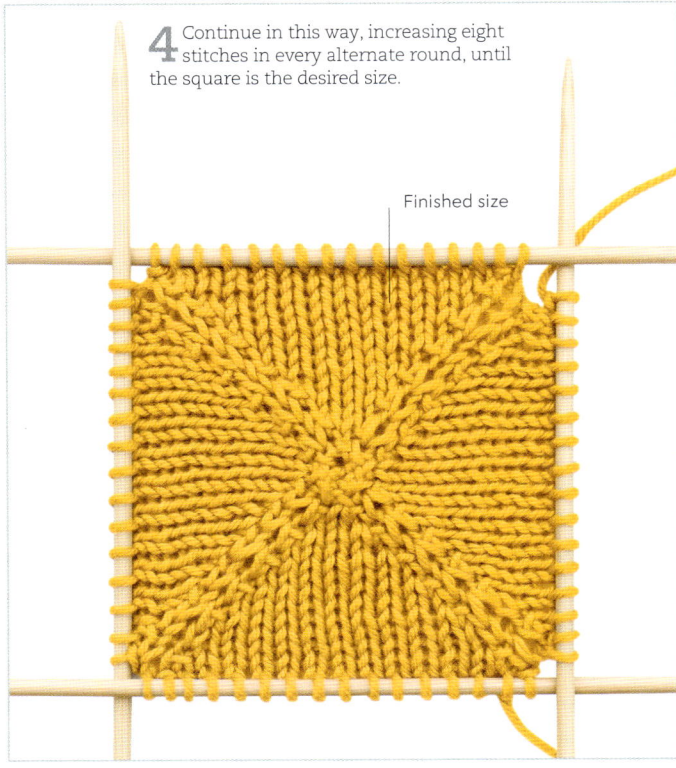

4 Continue in this way, increasing eight stitches in every alternate round, until the square is the desired size.

Finished size

5 Cast off in the usual way, leaving a long yarn tail. Using a blunt-ended yarn needle, pass the yarn tail under the top of the first cast-off stitch and back though the centre of the fastened-off stitch. Darn in the yarn ends on the wrong side of the work, using the yarn end at the centre to pull the hole together if necessary.

Reverse, twice knit, and tunisian

Reverse knitting is simply a quicker way of working. All these techniques produce a quite different, firmer, and less stretchy result than traditional knitting. In some cases the results can look more like crochet than knitting and can be used for a similar effect.

REVERSE KNITTING

Reverse, or backwards, knitting is useful for narrow areas when frequent turning is otherwise required. When working reverse knit stitches on stocking stitch, every row is worked from the right side. Reverse knitting purl stitches is more unusual.

REVERSE KNIT STITCH

1 At the end of a knit row, do not turn the work.

2 Insert the left needle into the back of the first stitch on the right needle. Bring the yarn forwards over the left-hand needle from left to right

3 Slide the right needle along the left needle and slip the loop over the left tip, then slide the right needle down out of the old stitch.

REVERSE PURL STITCH

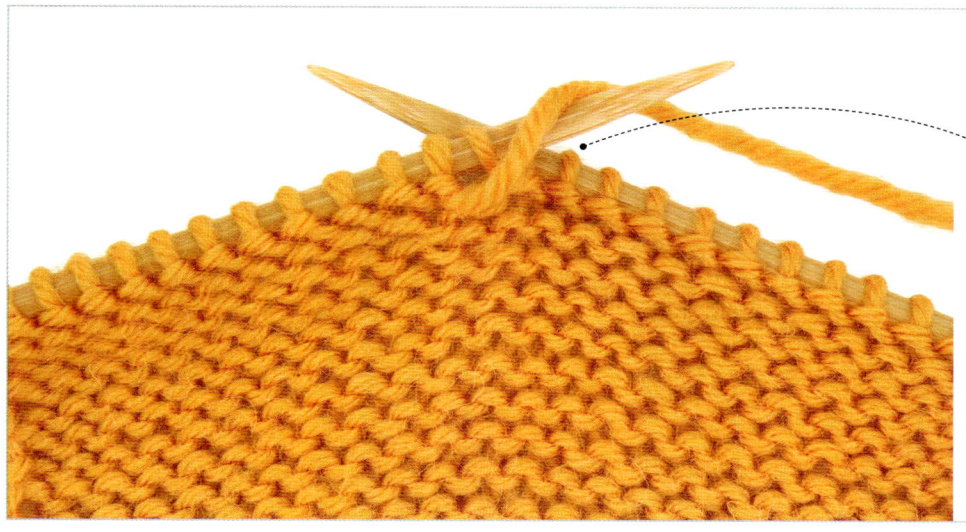

1 At the end of a purl row, do not turn the work. Keep the yarn at the front.

2 Insert the left needle from the back to the front through the left leg of the first stitch on the right needle and in front of the right needle. Take the yarn in a clockwise direction from left to right, over the top of the left-hand needle.

3 Slide the left needle through the stitch backwards under the right needle to catch the loop. Slide the left needle to the right to slip the old stitch over the right tip.

TWICE KNIT KNITTING

Twice knit is not stretchy, which makes it very dense, and should be worked on larger needles than normal for the yarn. The stitches will work out wider than the rows unless larger needles are used, and work will be very slow to grow.

1 Cast on with Twice-knitted cast-on (see p.66).

2 Knit two stitches together. Drop only the first stitch, leaving the second on the left needle.

3 Insert the right needle into both the remaining stitch and the following one on the left needle and knit them together. Repeat this step to end of row.

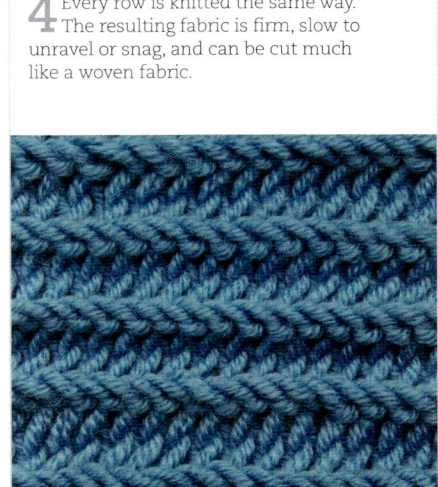

4 Every row is knitted the same way. The resulting fabric is firm, slow to unravel or snag, and can be cut much like a woven fabric.

TUNISIAN KNITTING

Tunisian knitting results in flat, dense, and thick fabric that looks a little like crochet. It can be worked on standard needles, although it is usually worked loosely or on slightly larger needles than normal for the yarn. The first row is always a wrong side row.

1 Slip one stitch knitwise, then make a yarnover from front to back, taking the yarn right round the needle and to the front. Slip the next stitch knitwise, yarnover. Repeat this slip and yarnover along the row.

Slip stitch

2 The last yarnover will be loose, so hold it at the front with your left thumb. Turn the work, keeping thumb and yarnover in place (it will now be at the back of the work).

3 Work the next row by knitting each yarnover and stitch together through the back of the loop (k2 tbl). To start the row, insert the right needle into the back of the first stitch and yarnover on the left needle, bring the yarnover thread round the right needle (see p.96) and knit the yarnover and the first stitch together. Repeat Steps 1–3.

4 It is easier to work this k2 tbl by inserting the right needle tip into the front of the stitch and yarnover, and then sliding it backwards over the left needle shaft before knitting into the back of both.

5 Cast off with a larger than usual needle, by knitting three stitches, and passing the first over the second two. Knit another stitch and repeat the pass over. Repeat along the edge.

Finishing details

Finishing, as its name suggests, is the final stage of a project. Details that will make your knitting easier to assemble and look more professional, such as adding borders, hems, pockets, and fastenings, can, with a little planning, be incorporated into the actual knitting itself.

PICKING UP STITCHES

Picking up edges is a technique that even experienced knitters can find challenging. Careful preparation and lots of practice will help. Try it out on small pieces of knitting to perfect the technique before moving on to more important projects.

ALONG A CAST-ON/OFF EDGE

With right side facing, insert the needle into the first stitch. Leaving a long tail, wrap the tail around the tip and pull it through, as if knitting a stitch. Continue, picking up and knitting through every cast-on or cast-off stitch.

ALONG ROW-ENDS

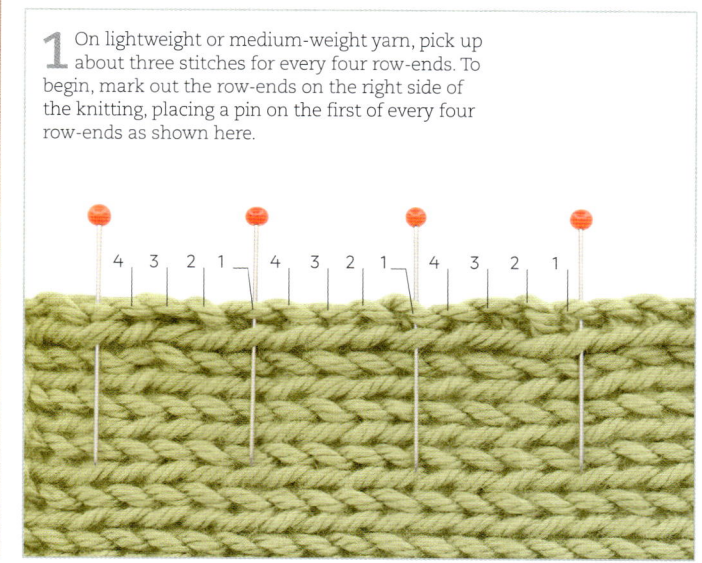

1 On lightweight or medium-weight yarn, pick up about three stitches for every four row-ends. To begin, mark out the row-ends on the right side of the knitting, placing a pin on the first of every four row-ends as shown here.

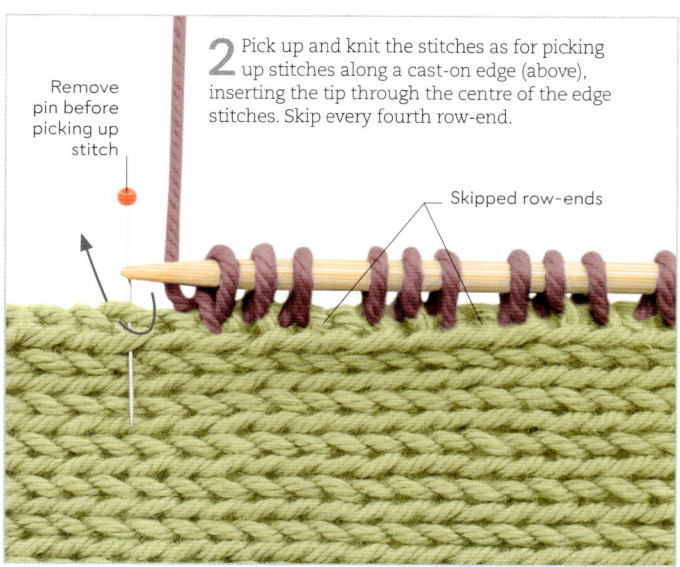

2 Pick up and knit the stitches as for picking up stitches along a cast-on edge (above), inserting the tip through the centre of the edge stitches. Skip every fourth row-end.

Remove pin before picking up stitch

Skipped row-ends

WITH A CROCHET HOOK

1 Use a hook that fits through the stitches. With right side facing, insert the hook through the first stitch, wrap the hook behind and around the yarn from left to right and pull through.

Yarn coming from ball

Yarn tail

2 Transfer the loop on the hook onto a needle. Pull the yarn to tighten. Repeat, transferring the loops to the needle.

▶ TIPS FOR PICKING UP STITCHES

• A yarn in a contrasting colour is used in the step-by-step instructions for picking up stitches to clearly illustrate the process. You can hide picking-up imperfections, however, if you use a matching yarn. For a contrasting border, switch to the new colour on the first row of the border, providing this is a plain row.

• Always pick up and knit stitches with the right side of the knitting facing you, as picking up stitches creates a ridge on the wrong side.

• Your knitting pattern will specify which needle size to use for picking up stitches – usually one size smaller than the size used for the main knitting.

• After you have picked up the required number of stitches, work the border following the directions in your pattern, whether it is ribbing, moss stitch, garter stitch, or a fold-over hem.

• If it is difficult to pick up stitches "evenly" along an edge, try casting it off again, either looser or tighter. If this doesn't work, pull out the border and try again, adjusting the number of stitches or spreading them out in a different way. Alternatively, try a smaller needle size if the border looks too stretched, or a larger needle size if it looks too tight.

ALONG A CURVED EDGE

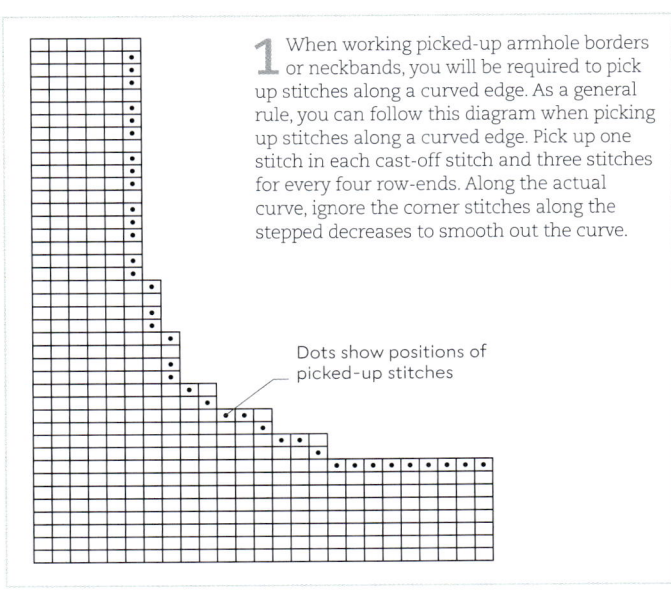

1 When working picked-up armhole borders or neckbands, you will be required to pick up stitches along a curved edge. As a general rule, you can follow this diagram when picking up stitches along a curved edge. Pick up one stitch in each cast-off stitch and three stitches for every four row-ends. Along the actual curve, ignore the corner stitches along the stepped decreases to smooth out the curve.

Dots show positions of picked-up stitches

2 Once all the stitches have been picked up, work the border as instructed in your knitting pattern.

A picked-up border with five rows of single ribbing

170 TECHNIQUES

SELVEDGES

The selvedge can make all the difference to a free edge and there are many methods that are decorative as well as functional. Loose edges can be tightened with chain or slipped garter and rolling edges controlled with a garter selvedge. Both selvedges do not have to be worked in the same way.

GARTER SELVEDGE

1 This is best for edges that will not be sewn together as it can make a bumpy seam. It encourages the edge of stocking stitch to lie flat. Each "bump" equals two rows.

2 On stocking stitch, knit the first and last stitch of every row.

SLIPPED GARTER SELVEDGE

A firmer selvedge than Garter selvedge.

1 Slip the first stitch knitwise and knit the last stitch on all rows.

2 The resulting edge is firmer than garter selvedge, and smoother. The slipped stitches can aid picking up on some projects.

SELVEDGES **171**

DOUBLE SLIPPED GARTER SELVEDGE

Good for slightly decorative free edges.

1 Work all edge stitches the same way for each row. Insert the right needle into the back of the first stitch from right to left and slip the stitch.

2 Knit the second stitch. Work as pattern to two from the end of row and knit the last two stitches.

CHAIN SELVEDGE

Best for picking up stitches into (see pp.168–169), crochet edgings, and backstitch (but not mattress stitch) seams (see p.188).

1 On stocking stitch, all right-side rows slip first stitch knitwise, and knit last stitch. On all wrong-side rows, slip first stitch purlwise, and purl last stitch.

2 On garter stitch, with yarn in front slip first stitch purlwise, yarn back and knit to end.

PICOT LOOP SELVEDGE

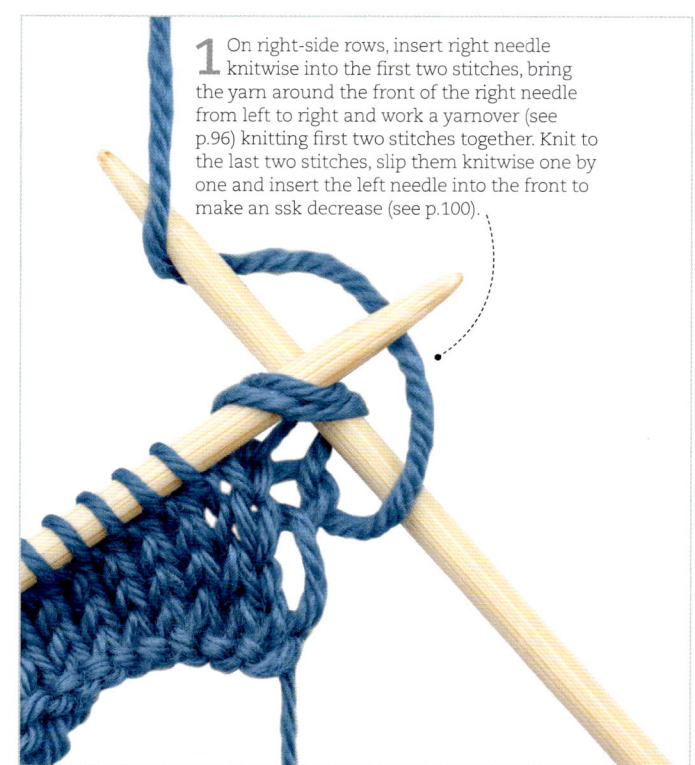

1 On right-side rows, insert right needle knitwise into the first two stitches, bring the yarn around the front of the right needle from left to right and work a yarnover (see p.96) knitting first two stitches together. Knit to the last two stitches, slip them knitwise one by one and insert the left needle into the front to make an ssk decrease (see p.100).

2 On wrong-side rows, loosely work a purl yarnover (see p.96), hold it open with your thumb if necessary), and purl the rest of the row. On garter stitch, purl the first and the last two stitches.

PICOT POINT SELVEDGE

1 On stocking stitch on a knit row, Knit-on cast-on two stitches, then cast off knitwise the same two stitches.

2 Slip the remaining stitch on the left needle without twisting onto the right needle. Knit to the end of the row.

3 On the purl row, cast on two stitches as Step 1, bring the yarn to the front and cast off both stitches purlwise (see p.68).

4 With the yarn to front, slip the remaining stitch on the left needle, without twisting, onto the right needle. Purl to the end of the row.

BUTTONHOLES

The simplest form of buttonhole is an eyelet, but there are techniques for larger, stronger ones that will take different sized buttons. Although horizontal buttonholes are the most common, vertical and diagonal variations are also included in this section.

POSITIONING BUTTONS AND BUTTONHOLES

Decide on the number of buttons before knitting buttonholes. Work holes to match button size. Top and bottom buttons are usually positioned between 1cm (½in) and 3cm (1¼in) from the neck and the hem edge. Start buttonholes at least three stitches from the edge. Count rows and stitches, as measuring may be inaccurate. For vertically worked bands, knit and attach the buttonband first. Mark the top and bottom button position with thread.

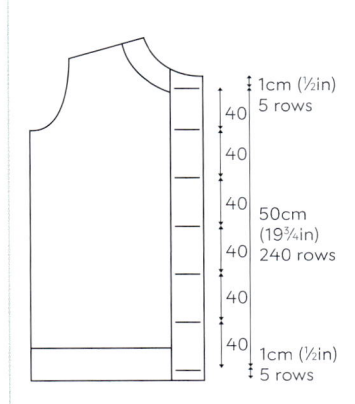

1 Knit the buttonhole band, working the calculated number of rows between buttonholes, allowing two rows for a two-row buttonhole. Work vertical buttonhole rows so that they centre on the marker.

2 For a horizontally worked picked-up buttonband, count stitches rather than rows to calculate the spacing as described in Step 1.

MAKING BUTTON LOOPS

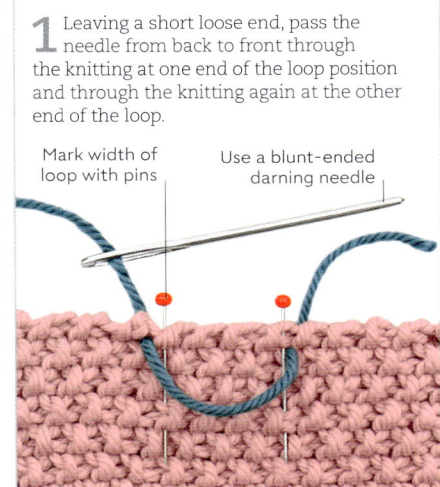

1 Leaving a short loose end, pass the needle from back to front through the knitting at one end of the loop position and through the knitting again at the other end of the loop.

Mark width of loop with pins
Use a blunt-ended darning needle

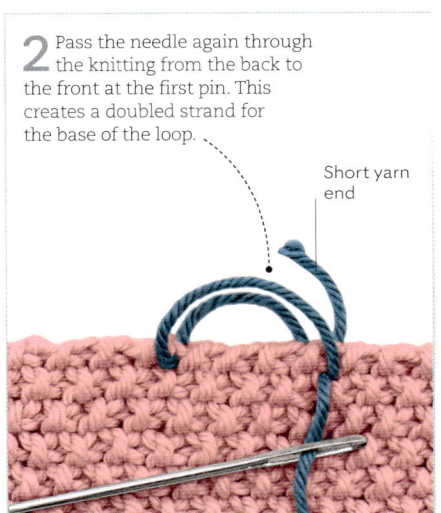

2 Pass the needle again through the knitting from the back to the front at the first pin. This creates a doubled strand for the base of the loop.

Short yarn end

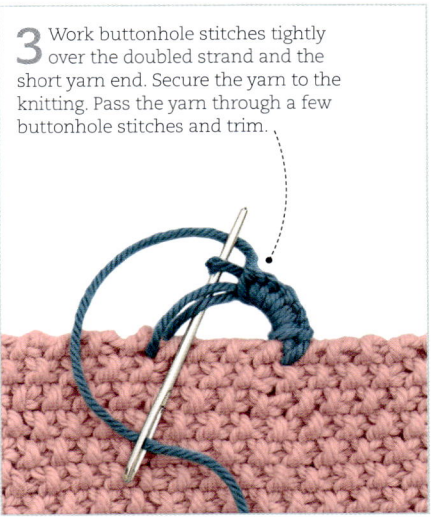

3 Work buttonhole stitches tightly over the doubled strand and the short yarn end. Secure the yarn to the knitting. Pass the yarn through a few buttonhole stitches and trim.

KNITTED BUTTON LOOP

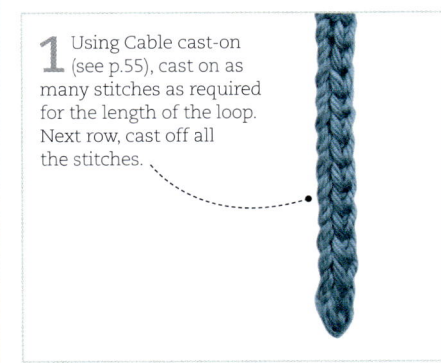

1 Using Cable cast-on (see p.55), cast on as many stitches as required for the length of the loop. Next row, cast off all the stitches.

2 Fold the loop in half. Use the ends to sew the loop neatly and firmly to the inside edge of the item.

REINFORCED EYELET BUTTONHOLE

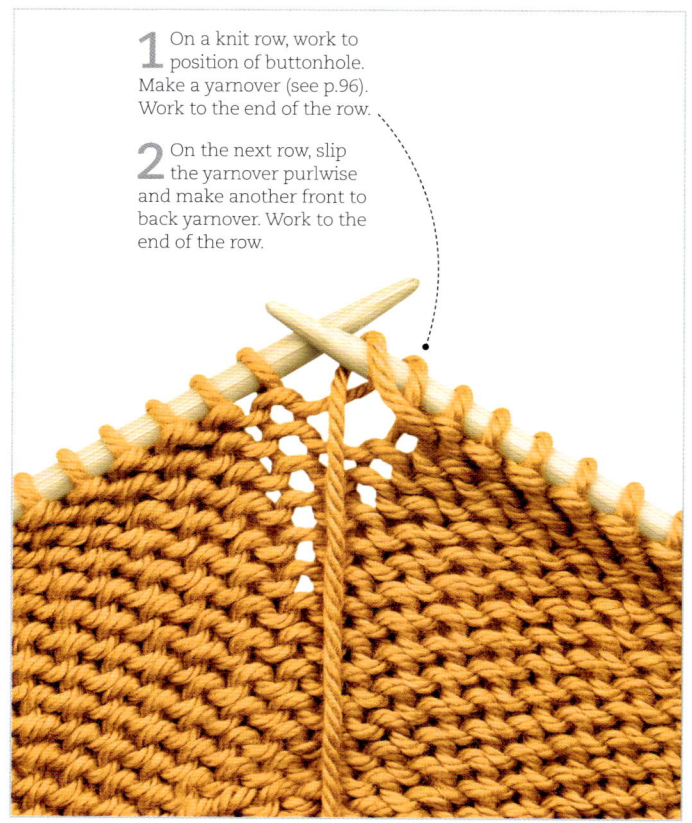

1 On a knit row, work to position of buttonhole. Make a yarnover (see p.96). Work to the end of the row.

2 On the next row, slip the yarnover purlwise and make another front to back yarnover. Work to the end of the row.

3 On the next row, slip the stitch before the yarnovers knitwise. Knit both yarnovers together but do not drop from the left needle.

4 Pass the slipped stitch over the newly made stitch. Knit three stitches together (the yarnovers and the following stitch). Work to the end of the row.

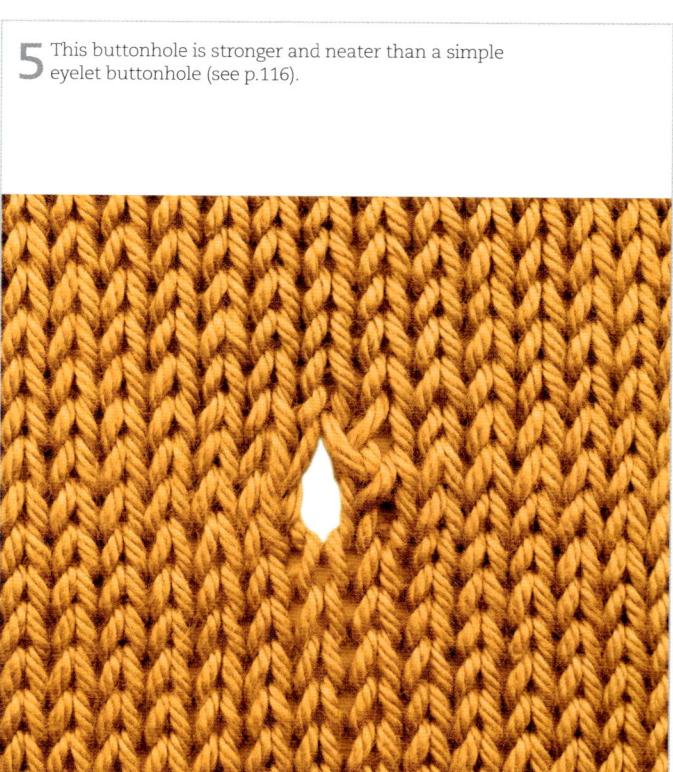

5 This buttonhole is stronger and neater than a simple eyelet buttonhole (see p.116).

ONE-ROW HORIZONTAL BUTTONHOLE

A strong buttonhole that is worked on stocking stitch in this example, but looks particularly neat on a garter stitch or reverse stocking stitch project.

1 Work to the buttonhole position (this should be a knit row on reverse stocking stitch). Bring the yarn to the front. Slip one stitch purlwise. Take the yarn back.

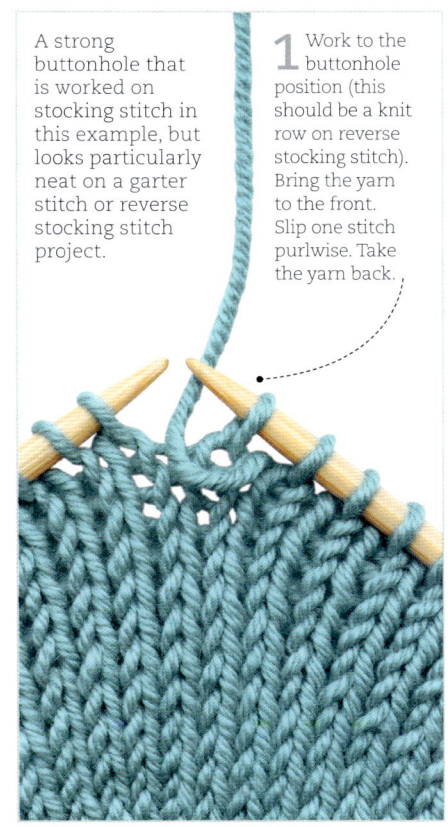

2 Slip one stitch purlwise and pass the previous stitch over. Repeat this step across the number of buttonhole stitches required.

3 Slip the last stitch on the right needle back to the left. Turn the work. Take the yarn back.

4 Cast on the number of stitches for the buttonhole using Cable cast-on (see p.55). Cast on one more stitch, bring the yarn forwards after making the stitch but before placing it on the left needle. Turn.

5 Slip one stitch knitwise and pass the last cast-on stitch over it. Work the rest of the row.

6 This buttonhole is worked the same on reverse stocking stitch.

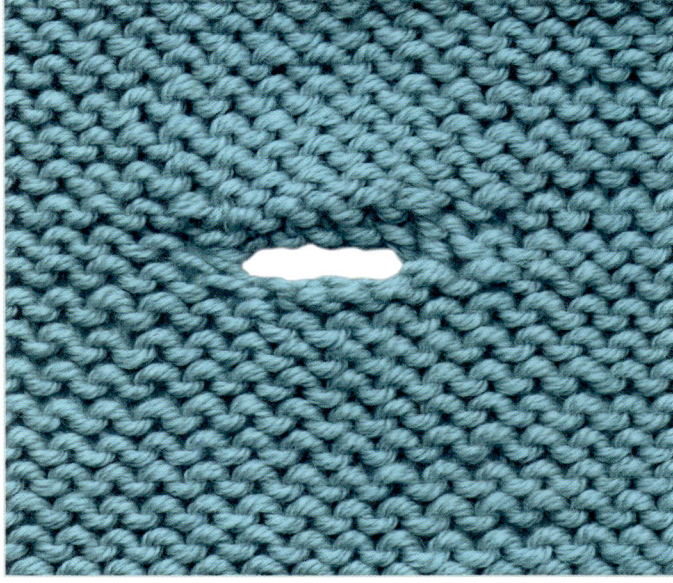

CAST-OFF HORIZONTAL BUTTONHOLE

1 On a knit row, work to the buttonhole position. Work two more stitches before passing one over the other in a Knitwise cast-off (see p.68) for the number of buttonhole stitches. When the last cast-off loop is on the right needle, slip the first stitch on the left needle onto the right needle and pass the last cast-off loop over this stitch. Pull the yarn tight. Work the next row to the buttonhole.

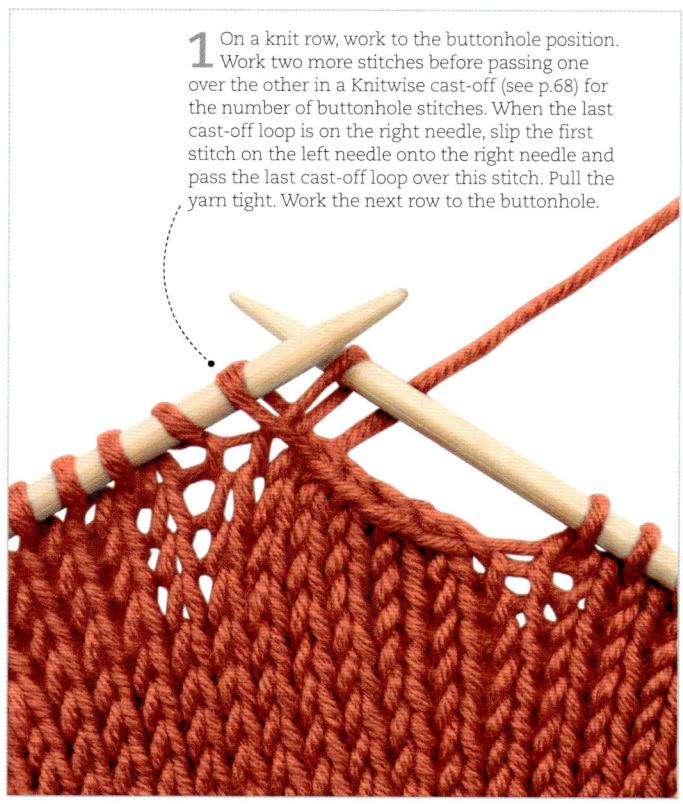

2 For advanced completion using buttonhole cast-on, miss this step and work Steps 3–5. For simple completion, turn work and use Cable cast-on (see p.55). When the last cast-on loop is still on right needle, bring the yarn to the front between the needles and transfer the stitch to the left needle. Take the yarn to the back, turn, and knit the rest of the row. Buttonhole is now completed.

3 Drop the left needle (use point protector to retain stitches if necessary) and work only with the right. Hold the yarn and the needle in your right hand. With left thumb pointing downwards, pick up the yarn from behind, and wind thumb to the right in an anticlockwise circle so the yarn crosses near the needle. Insert the right needle into the front thumb loop.

4 Bring your left index finger from beneath, catching the yarn. Take the yarn left behind the needle and then wind to the right, over the needle.

5 Slip the thumb loop over the tip of the right needle. Hold the new loop in place with your right index finger and tighten the yarn with your left hand, making sure the loop goes all round the needle. Repeat for each cast-on stitch. Knit to the end of the row.

INCREASED HORIZONTAL BUTTONHOLE

1 Work to the buttonhole position. Work two more stitches before passing one over the other in a Knitwise cast-off (see p.68) for the number of buttonhole stitches (five in this example).

2 When the last cast-off loop is on the right needle, slip it onto the left needle and pass the second stitch over the cast-off loop. Pull the yarn tight.

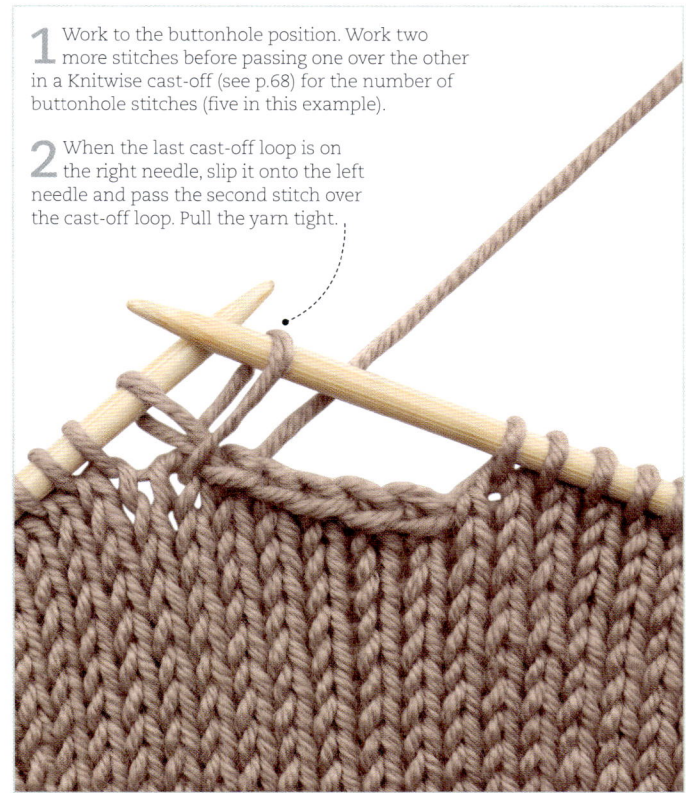

3 Yarnover twice (once for a two- to three-stitch buttonhole – dependent on tension and yarn). Knit to the end of the row.

4 Next row, work to the yarnovers. Drop the yarnovers and pull up the end stitch on the left needle so that it draws the yarn from the yarnovers and is elongated.

5 Purl into the front and back (see p.92) repeatedly the same number of times as stitches cast off plus one. Work to the end of the row.

VERTICAL BUTTONHOLE

1. This example is in stocking stitch. Work to the position of the buttonhole. Slip the stitches that will be to the left of the buttonhole onto a stitch holder. Turn the work.

2. Work the right side of the buttonhole starting with a purl row, making a Chain selvedge (see p.171) by slipping the first edge stitch purlwise on all wrong-side (WS) rows, and knitting the last edge stitch on all right-side (RS) rows.

3. Once the RS is long enough, finish on a purl side row, cut yarn with a long tail and slip RS stitches onto another holder. Slip held stitches back onto the left needle with knit side facing. Join in the new end of yarn (leaving a long tail) and make a right Lifted increase (see p.93) between the first and second stitches.

Rejoin yarn here

4. Slip the last stitch knitwise on the next and all WS rows and knit it into the back of the first stitch on all RS rows. This creates a variation of a chain selvedge on the left side of the buttonhole.

5. When both sides have equal rows, making sure you finish on a purl row, cut the yarn with a long tail and restore all the stitches to the needles in the correct order. Join the yarn in and work a complete row, working the two selvedge stitches of the buttonhole together. Sew in ends neatly.

DIAGONAL BUTTONHOLE

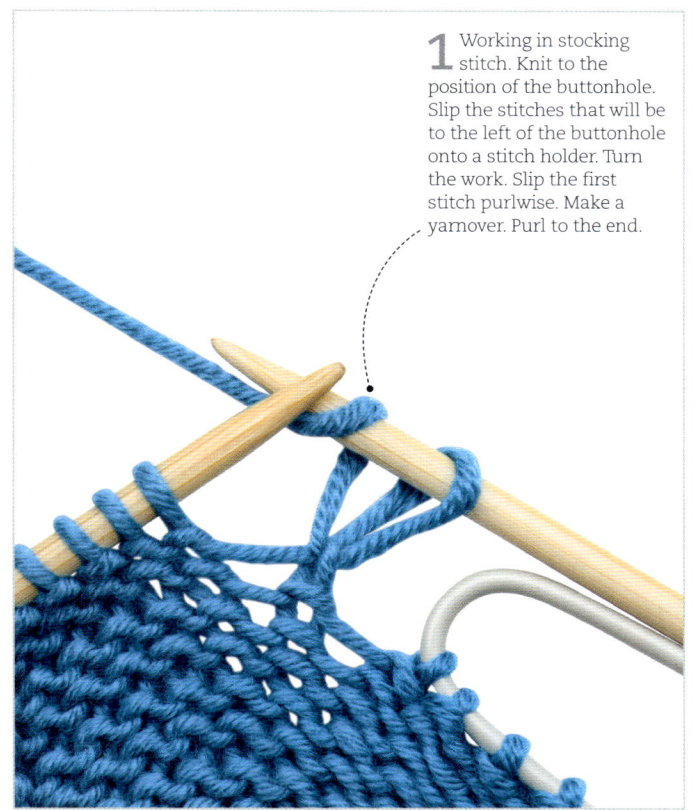

1 Working in stocking stitch. Knit to the position of the buttonhole. Slip the stitches that will be to the left of the buttonhole onto a stitch holder. Turn the work. Slip the first stitch purlwise. Make a yarnover. Purl to the end.

2 Knit the next row to the yarnover, and knit into back of yarnover, twisting it to close the hole. Knit the last stitch. Repeat for the required length of the buttonhole, ending with a purl row. Repeat knit instruction in Step 1.

3 Cut the yarn with a long tail and slip the right side stitches onto another holder. Slip the held stitches back onto the left needle with knit side facing. Join in the new end of yarn and make a right Lifted increase (see p.93) between the first and second stitches.

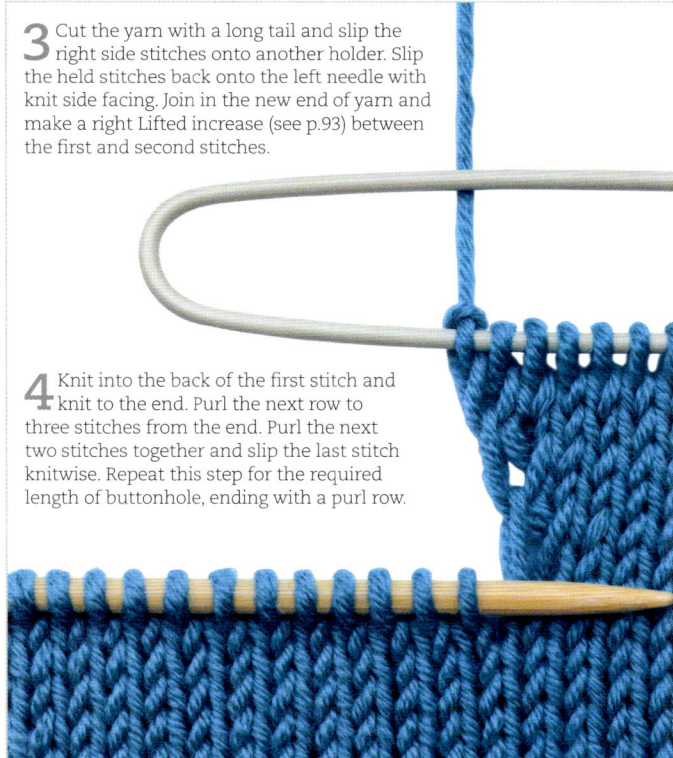

4 Knit into the back of the first stitch and knit to the end. Purl the next row to three stitches from the end. Purl the next two stitches together and slip the last stitch knitwise. Repeat this step for the required length of buttonhole, ending with a purl row.

5 Cut the yarn with a long tail and restore all stitches to the needles in the correct order. Join the yarn in and work a complete row, working the two selvedge stitches of the buttonhole together. Sew in the ends neatly. To slant the buttonhole the other way, reverse the increase and decrease.

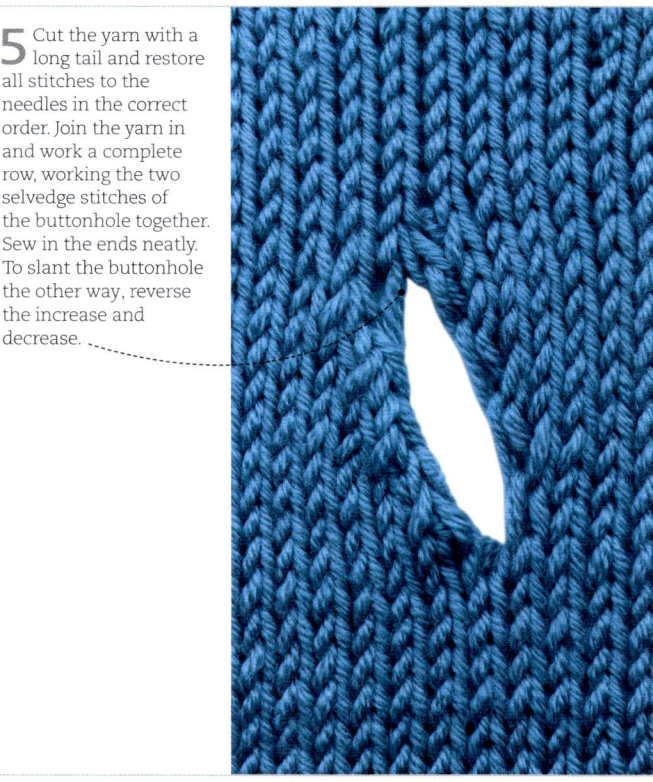

POCKETS

Patch pockets can be knitted separately and sewn on or picked up from the main knitting. Inset versions are particularly neat on garments and can be edged with textural and colour stitch details, and even knitted in lighter yarns to avoid bulk.

PICKED-UP PATCH POCKET

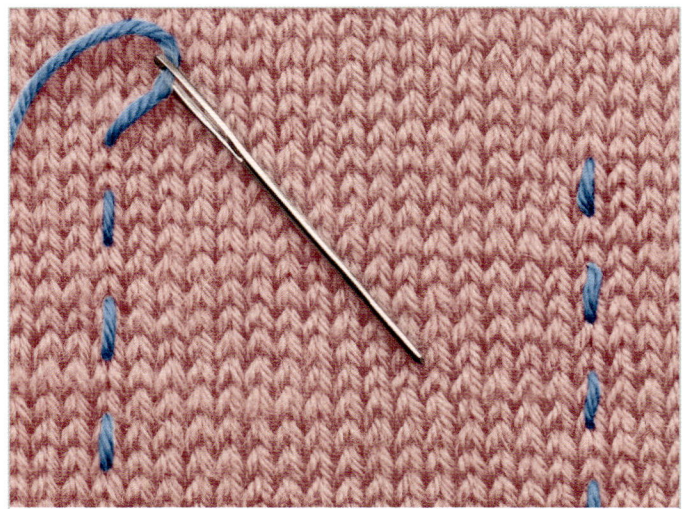

1 Work the garment piece first. Tack the side and bottom position of the pocket on the garment with thin contrast-colour yarn. To ensure a straight pocket bottom, either pick up into the row after the welt or tack through the left side of the stitches along the base row.

2 Thread the pocket yarn on a large-eyed darning needle, take the end to the wrong side and secure it, leaving a long tail. Have a knitting needle ready to receive stitches as they are made. Starting at the lower right-hand corner of the marked stitches, insert a crochet hook through the middle of the "V" of the first stitch, under the top loop and back out to the front. Lay the yarn from right to left into the hook, and draw a loop of yarn through.

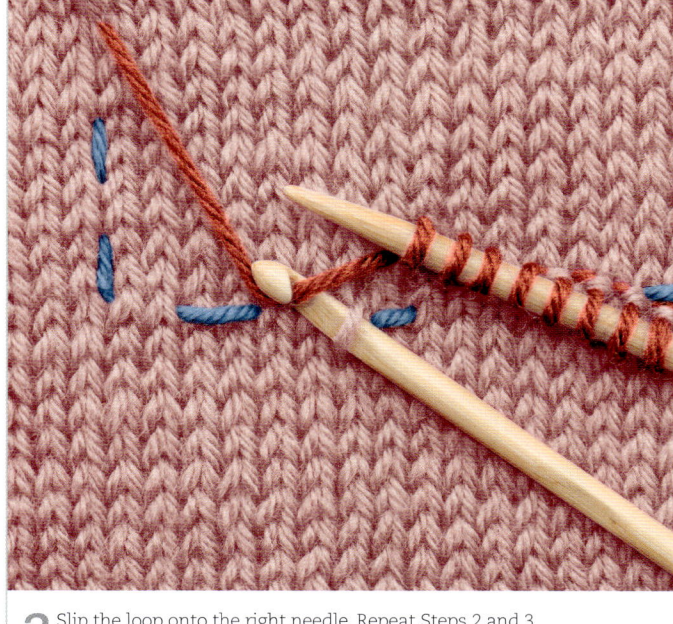

3 Slip the loop onto the right needle. Repeat Steps 2 and 3 to the left along the row for each pocket base stitch.

4 Beginning with a wrong side row, work as many rows as necessary for the pocket depth, adding a ribbed or patterned welt as desired. Cast off.

5 Sew the sides in place with mattress stitch (see p.188) using the yarn ends if possible. Remove the tacking stitches.

HORIZONTAL INSET POCKET

1 Knit the pocket lining before you knit the garment piece; this will be two stitches wider than the cast-off for the pocket. Leave on a spare needle after working the last knit row or put on a stitch holder.

2 With right side facing, work to the pocket position. Cast-off knitwise (see p.68) the stitches for the pocket opening and knit to the end of the row.

3 Turn and purl back to one stitch from the pocket position. Take the needle with lining stitches on it in your left hand, and purl the last main stitch and the first lining stitch together.

4 Purl across the lining stitches. Purl the last stitch together with the first one on the left needle. Continue. Complete garment piece.

5 An alternative to Step 2 is to place the opening stitches without casting off onto a stitch holder. This allows you to knit an edging to the pocket later on.

6 When sewing the garment together, whipstitch the lining to the garment without pulling the stitches too tight. This example has a contrast lining, but the lining would normally be made in the main yarn.

VERTICAL INSET POCKET

1. The opening is at the left of the actual pocket in this example, and the lining is worked at the same time as the pocket front. On a right-side (RS) row, work to the pocket position, then slip the remaining stitches on the left needle onto a stitch holder.

2. Work the front of the pocket: turn the work and work a garter stitch edge border by knitting the first two stitches, purling the rest of the row. On the next row, work to two from the end and then knit both edge stitches. Continue to work the rows, with border stitches included, for the depth of the pocket. Finish the pocket front by working a purl row and slip stitches onto a stitch holder. Cut a long yarn tail.

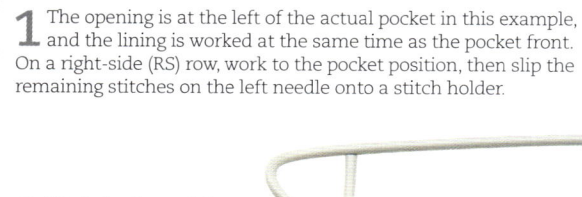

3. The right side and lining is worked in one: with RS facing, slip the stitches off the first stitch holder onto a needle, unless you use a double-pointed needle, you may need to transfer them from this needle to one that has its tip facing to the right. Join in the yarn.

4. Cable cast-on (see p.55), the number of stitches required for the width of the pocket lining. Turn and work the same number of rows for the lining and the left side as were worked for the pocket front. End with a purl row.

5. Join the top of the pocket: with RS facing, slip stitches off the second stitch holder onto a needle pointing right (stitch holder should be pointing left). Knit the next row. At the pocket position, place the lining needle behind the left needle and knit them together. Complete the row.

6. Complete the piece and sew the lining to the garment front.

HEMS

A traditional ribbed hem is often knitted at the start of a garment, whereas others may be sewn on afterwards. Hems make great cuffs and can be added vertically along front openings. Two different methods for finishing hems are shown here. Alternatively, use a Provisional cast-on (see p.63) and graft the live stitches to the main fabric.

PICKED-UP HEM

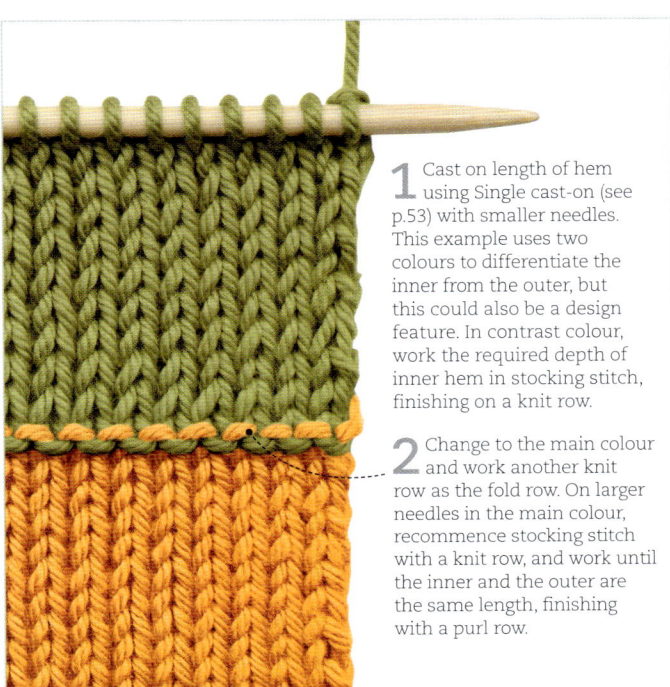

1 Cast on length of hem using Single cast-on (see p.53) with smaller needles. This example uses two colours to differentiate the inner from the outer, but this could also be a design feature. In contrast colour, work the required depth of inner hem in stocking stitch, finishing on a knit row.

2 Change to the main colour and work another knit row as the fold row. On larger needles in the main colour, recommence stocking stitch with a knit row, and work until the inner and the outer are the same length, finishing with a purl row.

3 Take a smaller needle and a spare length of main yarn. Working with the right side (RS) facing, pick up and knit through the centre of each cast-on stitch.

Inner

Main colour (front)

4 These stitches may need transferring to another needle, as the needle must point in the same direction as that of the hem stitches. Fold the hem up along the fold line with RS out. Hold the two needles together in the left hand.

5 Taking a larger needle and re-joining main yarn if necessary, knit the corresponding stitches of both needles together onto the right needle.

6 Block the hem with the garment to achieve the final effect.

PICOT HEM

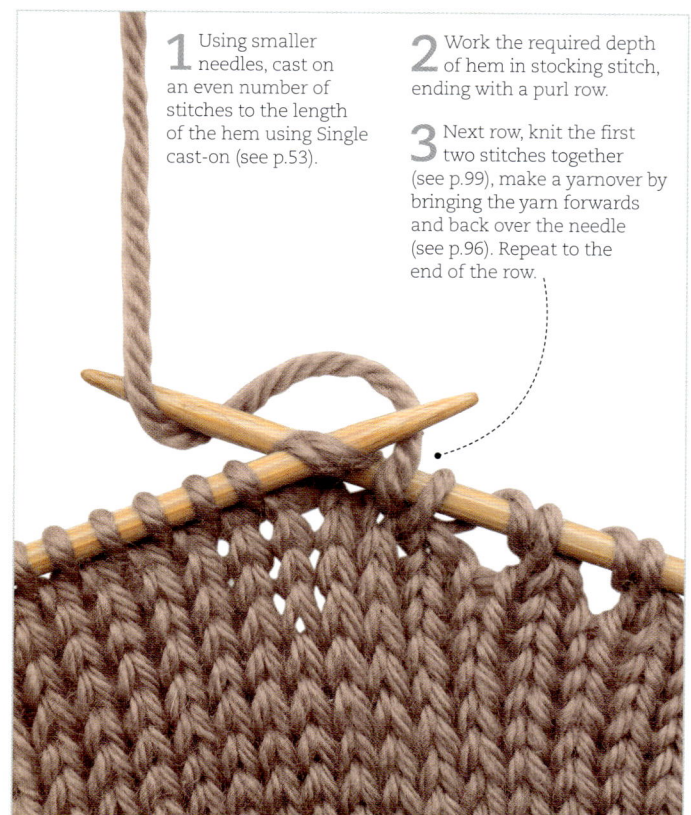

1 Using smaller needles, cast on an even number of stitches to the length of the hem using Single cast-on (see p.53).

2 Work the required depth of hem in stocking stitch, ending with a purl row.

3 Next row, knit the first two stitches together (see p.99), make a yarnover by bringing the yarn forwards and back over the needle (see p.96). Repeat to the end of the row.

Yarnover lace holes

4 Change to larger needles. Knit the stitches and yarnovers on the first row, work an equal depth of hem in stocking stitch, ending on a purl row.

5 When the piece is completed, fold the hem up at the lace holes with the wrong sides together. Pin so that the stitches are in line. Working from the wrong side, oversew in place along a row using hem yarn and a darning needle as follows: insert the needle into a reverse stitch loop and then its vertically matching cast-on loop, pull the yarn through and repeat. Do not allow the sewing to pucker the knitting.

6 Block the hem with the garment to achieve the final effect.

BLOCKING

Always refer to your yarn label before blocking. Textured stitch patterns, such as garter stitch, ribbing, and cables, are best wet blocked or steamed extremely gently so that their texture is not altered – they should not be pressed or stretched.

WET BLOCKING

If your yarn allows, wet blocking is the best way to even out your knitting. Using lukewarm water, either wash the piece or simply wet it. Squeeze and lay it flat on a towel, then roll the towel to squeeze out more moisture. Pin the piece into shape on layers of dry towels covered with a sheet. Leave to dry.

STEAM BLOCKING

Only steam block if your yarn allows. Using a steamer or iron, and having pinned your item to its desired dimensions as it lies flat, allow steam to permeate your finished item for a minute or two. Your heat source should not make direct contact with your project – it should hover slightly above the fabric, or over a cloth, with the steam pointing downwards.

SPRAY BLOCKING

Spray blocking is the gentlest of blocking methods. It involves pinning your dry, finished item to its intended dimensions or placing over a sock blocker (see p.186), and spraying with water to moisten. The item should be left to dry completely before being removed from where it has been pinned out.

▶ TIPS FOR BLOCKING

- If wet blocking extremely delicate yarns, the use of a non-rinse wool wash will save additional manipulation and potential unwanted stretching before being pinned out. For larger items, a blocking mat (see p.42) may be needed and, when placed together, this will give you a nice flat base over which to lay very large items, such as blankets or shawls.

- While it's tempting to pull and stretch your knitting at blocking stage, trust the process – any over-manipulation when your fabric is dampened, steamed or wet, may result in damage that cannot later be reversed.

- Blocking should always be done before sewing up to help give you best access to the full piece of fabric and ensure it sits at the correct dimensions before final finishing steps are completed.

- Try ionized water or specific ironing waters, which come with added fragrance, to prevent any limescale build-up in your iron or steamer.

SOCK BLOCKING

Socks benefit from blocking to give them a neat finish. A pair of sock blockers in the correct size is a must if you often make socks, especially if they're gifts.

1 If your yarn ballband allows, gently hand-wash your finished socks. Remove excess water by rolling up in a clean towel and squashing gently, or placing in a protective laundry bag for a spin-only cycle in a washing machine.

2 While still damp, place the socks over a sock blocker and pull into shape gently so the heel centre sits along the point where the socks fold flat. Lay flat to dry, ideally over an airer, and do not remove the socks from the blockers until they are completely dry.

SEAMS

The most popular seam techniques for knitting are edge-to-edge seam, mattress stitch (see p.188), backstitch, and overcast stitch (see p.189). Cast-off and grafted seams are sometimes called for and learning to graft open stitches together for a seamless join is very useful.

▶ TIPS

- Block knitted pieces before sewing together. After seams are completed, open them out and steam very lightly if the yarn allows.
- Always use a blunt-ended darning needle for all seams; a pointed needle will puncture the yarn strands and you won't be able to pull the yarn through the knitting successfully.
- Although the seams are shown here worked in a contrasting yarn for clarity, use a matching yarn for all seams.
- If the knitting is in a fancy yarn, find a smooth strong yarn of a similar colour to sew in. It is generally better, particularly with mattress stitch, to work with shorter lengths as long strands become weakened and may break.
- Before starting a seam, pin the knitting together at wide intervals. At the start of the seam, secure the yarn to the edge of one piece of knitting with two or three overcast stitches.
- Make seams firm but not too tight. They should have a little elasticity, to match the elasticity of the knitted fabric.

EDGE-TO-EDGE SEAM

This seam is suitable for most stitch patterns, but is particularly good for garter stitch or flat seams for blankets, like the chunky blanket on p.270. To start, align the pieces of knitting with the wrong sides facing you. Work each stitch of the seam through the little pips formed along the edges of knitting as shown below.

Wrong sides

FIGURE-OF-EIGHT START FOR SEAMS

A figure of eight makes a strong, secure start to a seam, and is particularly useful before mattress stitch.

1 Align the edges of the pieces to be seamed with both the right sides facing you. After working the figure of eight, turn the work as required for your chosen seaming method.

2 Thread needle with knitting yarn or substitute.

3 Bring the needle from back to front through the bottom stitch of the right piece, as close to both edges as possible.

4 Take the needle behind the left piece, and insert it from back to front through the bottom edge stitch.

5 Take the needle to the right piece and repeat Step 2. This makes a figure of eight, which is both a strong and a neat start to a seam.

▶ WHERE TO USE THIS SEAM

- Figure-of-eight starts should be used as close to the lower edge of your work as possible, for a super-smooth join along the lower seam edge.

- Be sure not to split your yarn as you work a figure-of-eight start, as this will prevent the stitches from tightening together when you continue along the seam, leaving them loose.

- Leaving a long tail before you begin will enable you to close up any gaps or add a couple of stitches to mimic the open edge of your work, such as a cast-on or cast-off edge, with a few carefully placed stitches. You can then darn it in when you're finished.

- If joining two corners of knitting together alone, you can use the figure-of eight start as a single stitch, which will give strength to your join. It simply needs to be worked before darning both ends in on the wrong side of your knitting afterwards.

BACKSTITCH SEAM

Backstitch can be used for almost any seam on knitting, but is not suitable for super-bulky yarns.

Align the pieces of knitting with the right sides together. Make one stitch forwards and one stitch back into the starting point of the previous stitch as shown. Work the stitches as close to the edge of the knitting as possible.

MATTRESS STITCH

Mattress stitch is almost invisible, and is ideal for seaming stocking stitch and ribs. It is always worked from the right side.

1 After a figure-of-eight start (see above), take the needle back under the left piece and bring it through the same place as before. This positions the first stitch in the correct place.

2 Insert the needle from the front through the centre of the first knit stitch on one piece of knitting and up through the centre of the stitch two rows above. Repeat on the other edge, working up the seam and keeping the stitches loose. After about six stitches, gently pull the thread to draw the edges together without puckering the seam.

▶ USING MATTRESS STITCH ALONG SHAPED EDGES

- You may need to adjust the precise number of stitches you skip along when joining shaped edges or when stitching a cast-on or cast-off edge to a row-end edge, as their width/height per stitch will vary.
- This is far from an exact science, and you will need to use your judgement as you go and keep an eye on both sides of the fabric you are joining to make sure no stitches are pulling or looking very stretched or puckered.
- It's a good idea to use pins or locking stitch markers along the length of your seam to make sure you're keeping everything aligned as you go along. For example, if joining a straight cast-on edge to a straight row-end edge, stitch tensions tend to fall at around a ratio of 2 stitches to every 3 rows in stocking stitch. So you would need to be moving your needle along 2 stitches on the cast-on edge, but 3 rows along the row-end edge.

OVERCAST SEAM

Right sides of knitting together

This seam is also called an oversewn seam or a whipped stitch seam.

With the right sides together, insert the needle from back to front through both layers, working through the centres of the edge stitches (not through the pips). Make each stitch in the same way.

GRAFTED SEAM

This seam can be worked along two pieces of knitting that have not been cast off or along two cast-off edges as shown here; the principle for both is the same.

1 With the right sides facing you, follow the path of a row of knitting along the seam as shown.

2 When worked in a matching yarn as here, the seam blends in completely and it looks like a continuous piece of knitting.

▶ SPECIALTY SEAMS AND WHERE TO USE THEM

- Overcast seams are a perfect choice when working with textured yarns, like eyelash yarn, where the stitches are very difficult to see.
- Overcast seams are also a good choice for garter stitch, where mattress stitch may appear misaligned with garter stitch ridges sat awkwardly. Be sure not to pull too tight as you work or dip too deeply into your fabric with the stitches, which may make your seam look messy.
- Try using an overcast seam to stitch steeks down after cutting. This method will securely wrap around the raw edge of the fabric preventing any unravelling later.
- Try a grafted seam when joining shoulders on a garment for a smooth and seamless look. Try not to pull the stitches too tight to help give the appearance and feel of a totally seamless knitted piece for added comfort on wearing, such as with the baby cardigan shoulder seams on p.245.
- Grafted seams can also be utilized for joining stocking stitch blanket squares along cast-on and cast-off edges to give the look and feel of an entirely knitted piece that appears totally seamless. Try this technique with the blanket on p.270.

GRAFTING OPEN KNIT STITCHES TOGETHER

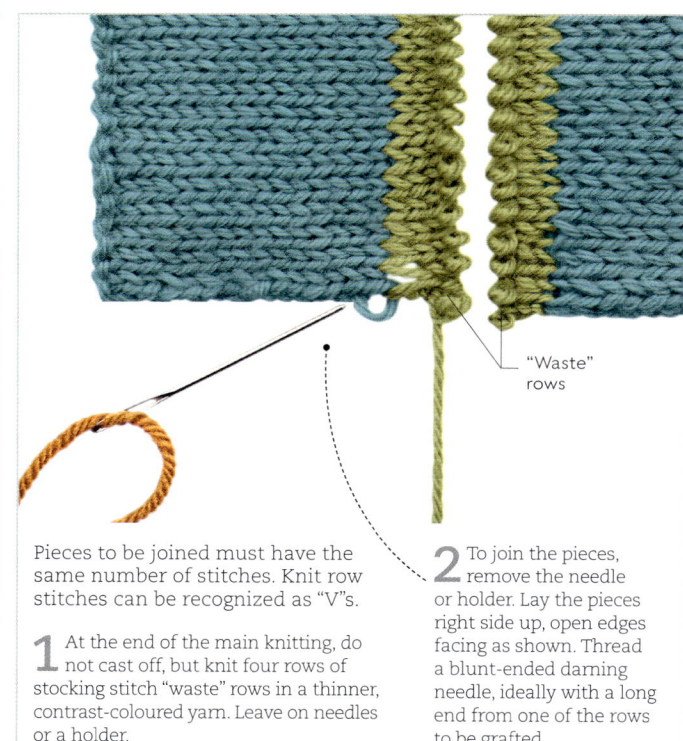

"Waste" rows

Pieces to be joined must have the same number of stitches. Knit row stitches can be recognized as "V"s.

1 At the end of the main knitting, do not cast off, but knit four rows of stocking stitch "waste" rows in a thinner, contrast-coloured yarn. Leave on needles or a holder.

2 To join the pieces, remove the needle or holder. Lay the pieces right side up, open edges facing as shown. Thread a blunt-ended darning needle, ideally with a long end from one of the rows to be grafted.

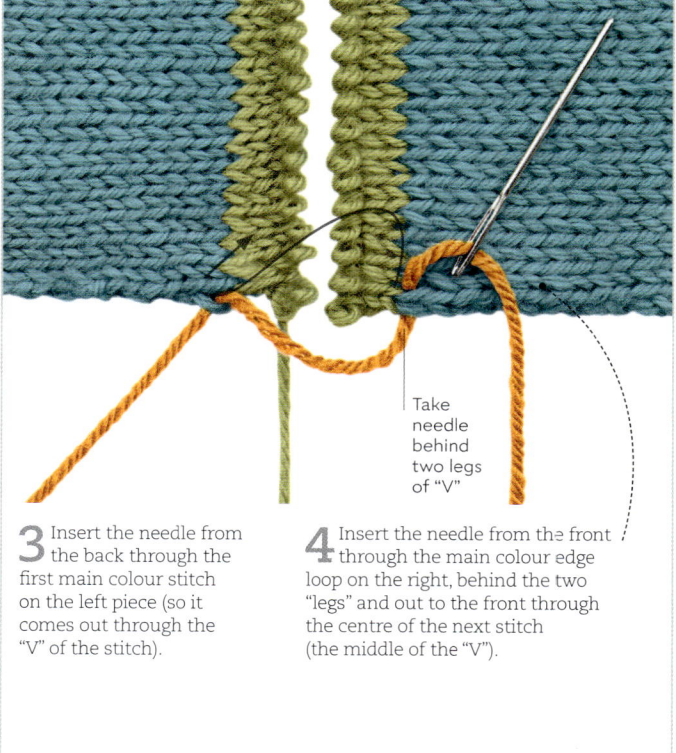

Take needle behind two legs of "V"

3 Insert the needle from the back through the first main colour stitch on the left piece (so it comes out through the "V" of the stitch).

4 Insert the needle from the front through the main colour edge loop on the right, behind the two "legs" and out to the front through the centre of the next stitch (the middle of the "V").

5 Continue, taking the needle back into the "V" of the left-hand stitch that it emerges from, behind the two "legs" and out of the next "V". Gently pull the yarn until the sewn stitch is the same size as the knit stitches. As you pull, fold the waste fabric under to close the gap.

6 Repeat, taking the needle to the right side.

7 Repeat Steps 5 and 6 along the row. Secure the ends and unravel the waste yarns. With more experience it becomes possible to graft the pieces together straight off the needles without knitting waste rows.

▶ **TIPS**
- Joining together live stitches, or grafting, can risk the stitches coming undone as you work.
- Knitting a few waste rows, for removal later, or holding your stitches on needles as you join them, will prevent them from coming undone.

KITCHENER'S STITCH

Named after Horatio Herbert Kitchener, a WW1 Army officer, this grafting technique was first popularized as a more comfortable way to finish socks worn by serving soldiers. This is because it leaves no inner seam, but joins stitches to leave a smooth reverse.

Also known as grafting, Kitchener's stitch is worked on two live sets of knitted stitches. This is not completed with any waste rows as shown on p.190. Pieces to be joined must have the same number of stitches.

1 Knit row stitches can be recognized as "V"s. As you are working with live stitches, leave them on the knitting needles as you work, otherwise they may begin to come undone. Hold both needles parallel with right sides facing you, with the working yarn emerging from the needle on the right.

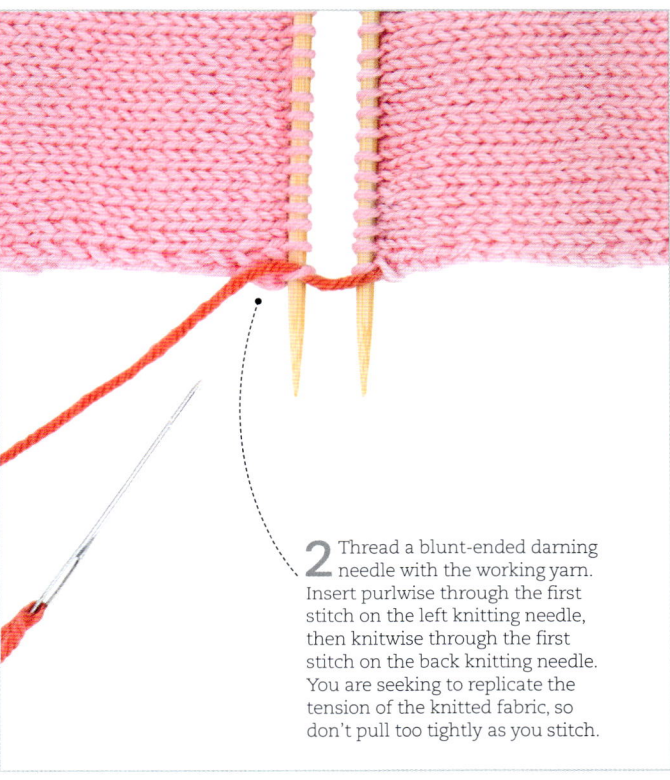

2 Thread a blunt-ended darning needle with the working yarn. Insert purlwise through the first stitch on the left knitting needle, then knitwise through the first stitch on the back knitting needle. You are seeking to replicate the tension of the knitted fabric, so don't pull too tightly as you stitch.

3 Insert the sewing needle knitwise through the right stitch and slip it off, then purlwise through the next stitch on the needle. Insert purlwise through the back stitch and slip it off, then knitwise through the next stitch on the left needle.

4 Repeat the four-step sequence across all stitches, maintaining consistent tension. At the end, only go through each remaining stitch one final time. All stitches should have been stitched into twice.

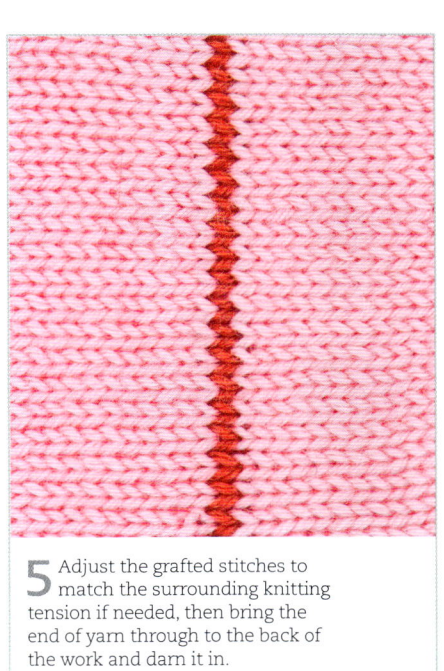

5 Adjust the grafted stitches to match the surrounding knitting tension if needed, then bring the end of yarn through to the back of the work and darn it in.

GRAFTING KNIT AND PURL STITCHES TOGETHER

Grafting open stitches that vary between knit and purl is trickier. You will need to do this if joining a ridged row – a row of purl stitches – to a smooth row – a row of knit stitches – for example; or when joining reverse stocking stitch to stocking stitch.

It is best to leave your stitches on the needles for this technique with right sides of both facing you. Thread a blunt-ended yarn needle with a matching yarn – use the working yarn end to save extra darning in later.

1 At the end of the main knitting, do not cast off. Arrange both pieces so that live stitches are facing one another on each needle, with the piece showing knit stitches on the right, and the purls on the left. Leave the stitches on needles with both points facing downwards.

2 Insert the darning needle through the first stitch on the left needle from front to back, then through the first stitch on the right needle from back to front.

3 Go back into the first stitch on the left from back to front, and into the second stitch on the left needle from front to back. Slide the first stitch from the left-hand needle. Each time you have entered a stitch twice, it can be removed from the needle.

4 Go back over to the knit stitches and insert your needle through the first stitch from front to back, before removing it from the knitting needle. Bring the yarn up through the back of the next stitch to the front.

Repeat Steps 3 and 4 along the row until each stitch has been stitched into twice. Darn in the ends.

SEWING ON AN EDGING

Edgings are often worked on slightly smaller knitting needles than the main body of knitting, most often to give the edging more density and less inclination to curl or look unsightly when in place.

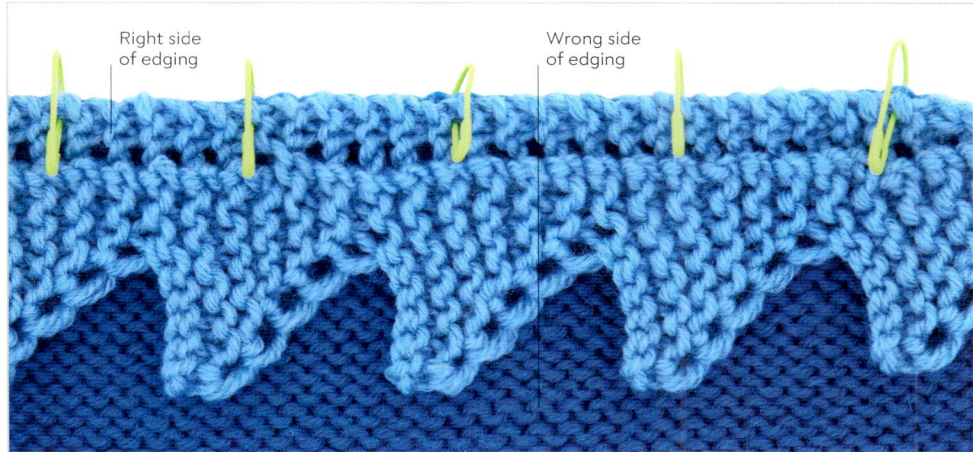

1 Align your edging with the edge of the fabric. Use pins or stitch markers at even spaces to hold the pieces together and help keep track of any uneven stitching not bringing in enough fabric as you go.

2 Join using mattress stitch, judging how many loops are needed to stitch across each edge at a time – it is likely that more will be needed along the edging than on the main piece (see the tips at the bottom of p.188). If at a marker and one piece is out of alignment, you will need to undo the stitching and rework with a slightly different stitch ratio.

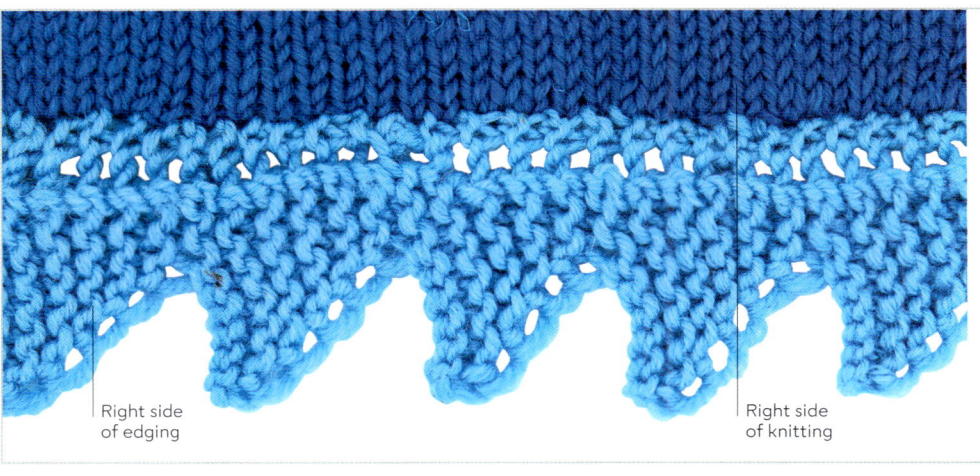

3 Block gently according to your ballband instructions (see p.185) to set in place and prevent unruly curling

CUTTING INTO YOUR KNITTING

Cutting can be a time-saving way of completing projects, particularly for circular knitted garments. Hairy wool that clings to itself and felts slightly when washed is ideal. "Steek" or "bridge" are common terms for the extra stitches knitted where openings will later be cut. You can machine sew edges prior to picking up.

STEEKS OR BRIDGES

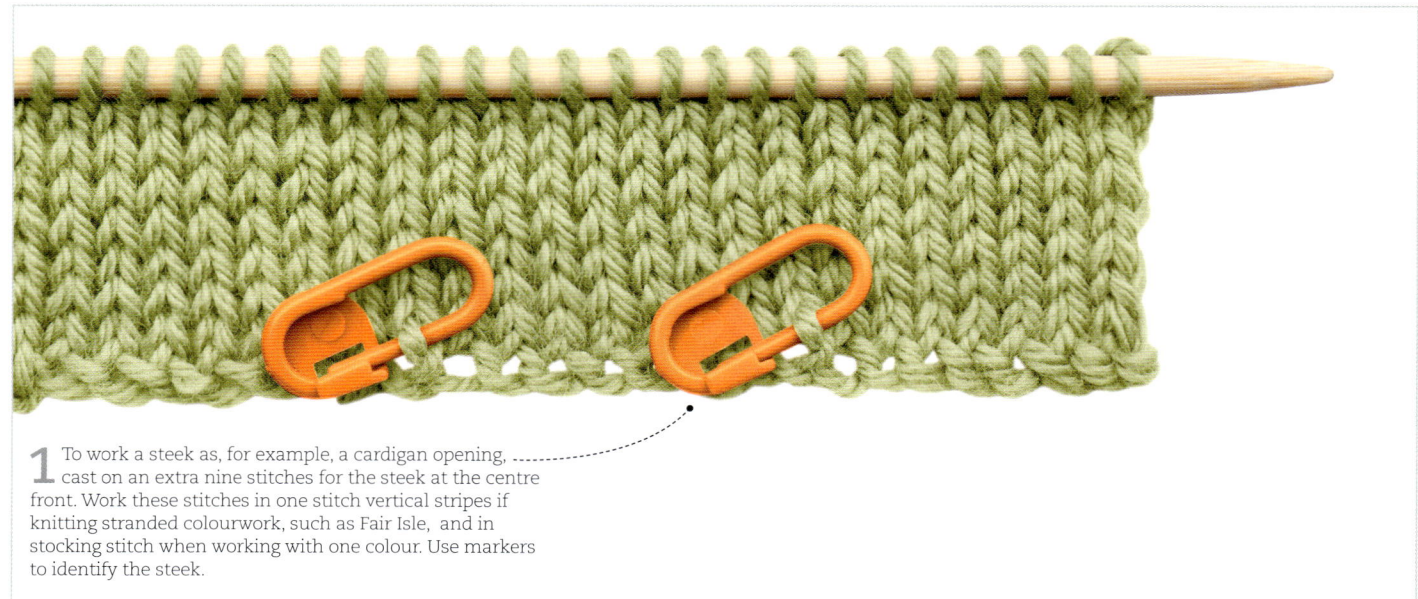

1 To work a steek as, for example, a cardigan opening, cast on an extra nine stitches for the steek at the centre front. Work these stitches in one stitch vertical stripes if knitting stranded colourwork, such as Fair Isle, and in stocking stitch when working with one colour. Use markers to identify the steek.

2 Work complete front. Block the piece and cut straight up the centre stitch of the steek. If the knitting is likely to unravel, such as with a slippier silk or cotton yarn, run a line of small machine stitches along the inside of the steek before cutting to prevent this.

3 Pick up and knit (see p.168) all along the edge, going either between the last steek stitch and the first main fabric stitch or wherever the new edge is to be positioned. Work the required edging. Cast off.

CUTTING INTO YOUR KNITTING **195**

4 Turn the work inside out, trim any unravelled ends with sharp scissors and oversew the cut edge down to the back of the main fabric using main colour yarn. Sew the back, crossing the first stitches.

5 The cut edge is neatly folded under and invisible on the right side of the completed cardigan opening.

REINFORCING STEEKS

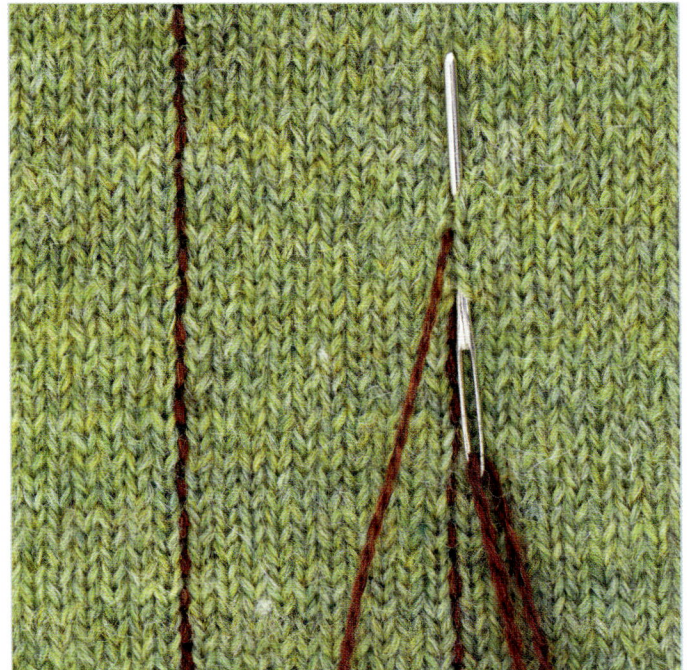

Strengthening the surrounding fabric before you cut a steek will prevent unravelling when you pick up stitches to add edgings later. This method uses backstitch (p.188) but you can also use a sewing machine or even needle-felt where you're intending to cut your steek.

1 With the right side of your work facing, work two parallel lines of small backstitches either side of your cutting line, spacing them a few stitches apart. Be careful to stitch around any yarns stranded on the wrong side – if your stitches are too shallow, any stranded yarns won't be secured.

2 Cut carefully between the stitched lines. Pick up your stitches away from the raw, freshly-cut edge as shown on Step 3 of steeks or bridges (left). Fold the cut edges to the wrong side of the work and stitch them down as shown on Steps 4 and 5 above. Your backstitch line will be hidden because it is folded to the reverse of the work.

FASTENINGS

Choose an appropriate size and material for your project. Although nylon and plastic fastenings are lighter and less obtrusive, metallic or contrast-coloured ones can make a statement. Riveted press studs can be used; insert the shank between stitches and when connecting top to bottom, make sure there are no sharp edges to cut stitches.

SEWING IN A ZIP

1 Match the colour and the weight of zip to the yarn, and knit the length of the garment to match zip lengths available. Work a Garter selvedge (see p.170) at the zip edge.

2 Close the zip. With right sides facing, pin the top and the bottom of the knitting to the zip first, making sure the teeth are covered by the knitted edge. Pin the centre, then the centres of the remaining sections, easing the rows so they are distributed evenly. Pin horizontally rather than vertically. Do one side at a time and use plenty of pins.

3 Tack the zip in place with contrast sewing thread, sewing between the same vertical lines of stitches.

4 With a sharp large-eyed needle and knitting yarn (or matching sewing thread), backstitch neatly upwards from the hem, sewing between the same vertical lines of stitches.

5 Turn the garment inside out. With knitting yarn, or matching sewing thread, slip stitch the outer edges of the zip to the knitting, sewing into the back of the same vertical lines of stitches.

ATTACHING PRESS STUDS

The protruding side of the stud goes on the inside of the outer of a garment. Decide the position of the studs. Measuring can be inaccurate; count exact stitches and rows on each piece and mark positions with contrast thread.

1 Make a knot and sew in the end of the thread at a marker, catching only half of each strand of yarn so that stitches don't go through to right side. Place the stud in position centrally over the marker and insert the needle inwards through the surface of the yarn near a stud hole just below the stud edge, then bring it up through the stud hole.

2 Repeat this three or four times through each hole, never taking the needle through to the right side. Move the needle to the next hole and repeat. To secure the thread, sew two small backstitches, then sew a loop, thread the needle back through and pull tightly to secure the thread.

SEWING ON A BUTTON

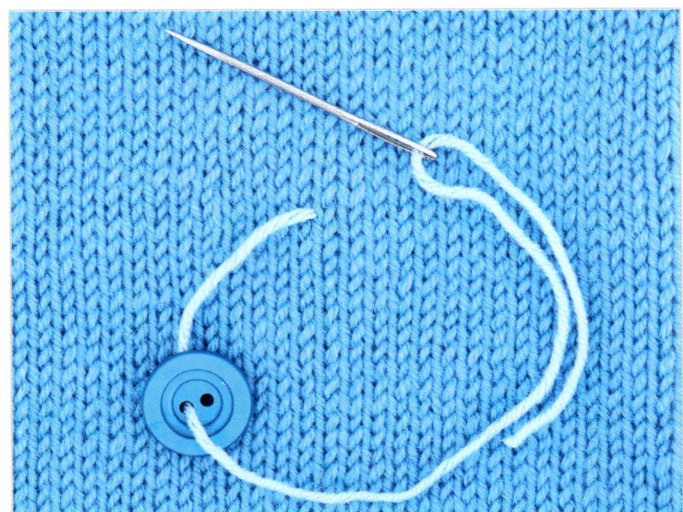

1 Use the same yarn as your knitted item to stitch on a button; if it is too thick to fit through the button, split it in half. Thread the yarn onto a blunt-ended darning needle. Fasten the yarn at the reverse of your work near to where your button is to be stitched on, then bring it through to the front.

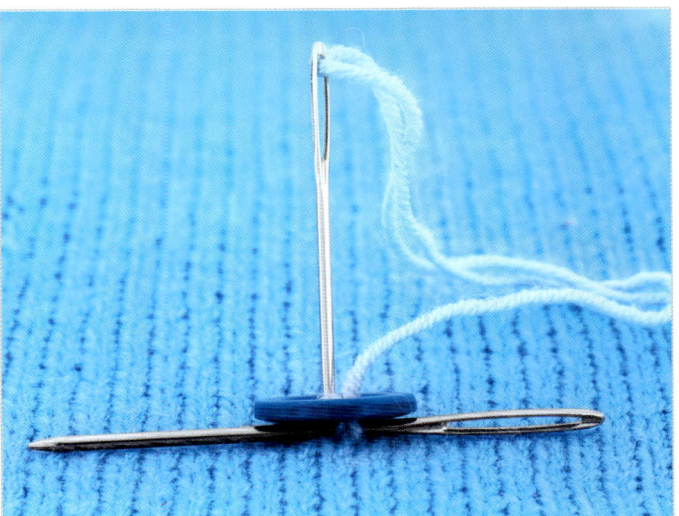

2 To allow space for thick knitted fabric to sit behind a button when fastened, place a spare large darning needle behind your button as you stitch it on. This will ensure that the stitching is not too tight, and that the button fits firmly. Work a few stitches through the button and the fabric, working over the needle, then wrap the yarn a couple of times around the strands under the button before fastening off securely on the wrong side of your work.

Embellishments

Plain knitting sometimes calls out for a little embellishment. Embroidery, a few well-placed beads, or a decorative edging are good candidates for the perfect finishing touch. Pockets, collars, hems, and cuffs are ideal positions for these.

BEAD KNITTING

Choose beads carefully – glass beads are attractive, but can weigh knitting down. Make sure that the bead hole is large enough for the yarn, or consider using a second thread, or enclosing large beads. A beaded cast-on or cast-off (p.201) makes an effective edging.

BEADS FOR DIFFERENT YARN WEIGHTS

When knitting with DK or 4-ply weight yarn, use size 8/0 or 11/0 knitting beads that will slide easily over your yarn and sit proportionally against the finer gauge fabric.

With a worsted weight yarn, choose larger beads such as size 6/0 purpose-made knitting beads, or small round beads that accommodate the thicker yarn while sitting neatly within the size of the stitches.

THREADING BEADS ONTO YARN

Make sure you have the right beads before starting to thread them onto the yarn. Consider their size and weight. If your knitting is to be entirely covered with scattered beads, large heavy beads will be unsuitable as they would weigh the knitting down too much. Adding a little weight to the knitting can, however, produce the extra drape needed for a graceful shawl, scarf, or evening knit.

Thread the beads onto the yarn before you begin knitting. The last bead to be used is threaded on first and the first bead to be used is threaded on last. Fold a short length of sewing thread in half, thread both cut ends together through the eye of an ordinary sewing needle, and pass the end of the yarn through the sewing-thread loop. Thread the beads onto the sewing needle, over the thread and onto the yarn.

SLIP STITCH BEADING

1 There is usually a chart provided for positioning the beads on slip stitch beading, unless only a few beads are to be added, in which case the bead placements will be within the written instructions. The sample chart here illustrates how slip stitch beads are staggered. This is because the slipped stitches at the bead positions pull in the knitting and alternating the bead placements evens out the fabric.

KEY
- □ = k on RS rows, p on WS rows
- ▣ = place bead and slip stitch

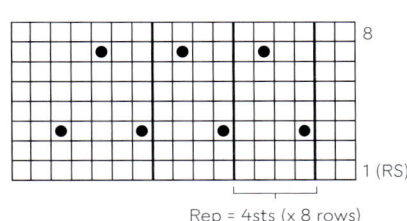

Rep = 4sts (x 8 rows)

2 The beads are placed on knit (right-side) rows. Knit to the position of the bead, then bring the yarn to the front of the work between the two needles. Slide the bead up close to the knitting and slip the next stitch purlwise from the left needle to right needle.

Slipping stitch purlwise

3 Take the yarn to the wrong side between the two needles, leaving the bead sitting on the right side in front of the stitch just slipped. Knit the next stitch firmly to tighten the strand holding the bead at the front.

Slipped stitch

SIMPLE GARTER STITCH BEADING

1 This method can be used to create bands of beads along borders or at intervals for beaded stripes. Start with a right-side row and work at least three rows of plain garter stitch before adding any beads. On the next row (a wrong-side row), knit two edge stitches before adding a bead. Then push a bead up close to the knitting before working each stitch. At the end of the row, add the last bead when two stitches remain on the left needle, then knit the last two stitches.

Wrong side of knitting

2 Knit the next row with no beads. Alternate a bead row and a plain row to form a band of beads of the desired depth. This technique could be used to create a piece entirely covered with beads for a small bag, but would create a fabric too heavy for a large garment.

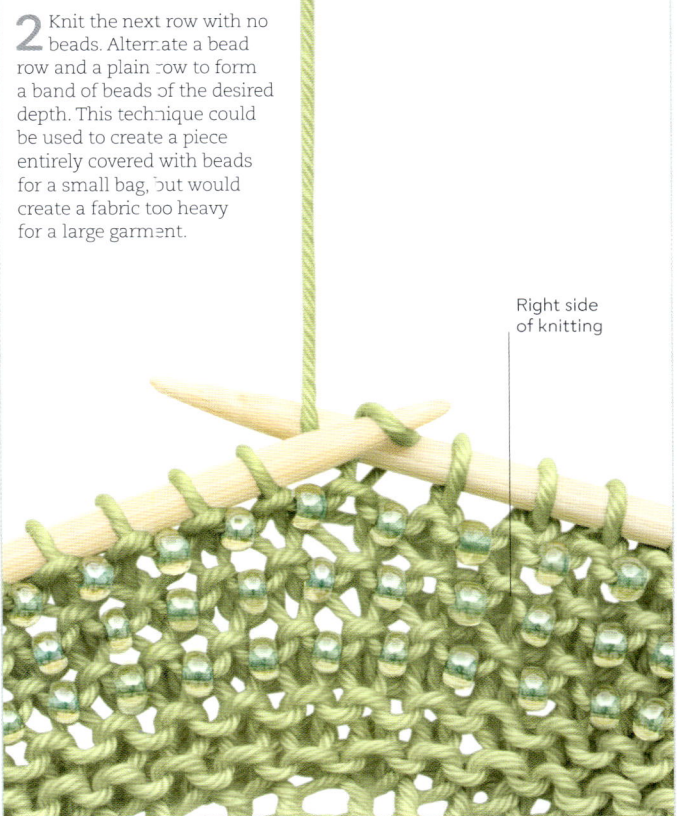

Right side of knitting

CLOSE BEADING

1 Work at a tight tension so the beads stay at the front. Thread the beads on the yarn. Slide the bead along close to the needle.

2 On a knit row: knit into the back of the stitch, draw the loop and a bead through the stitch, with a bead behind the right needle. Tighten the stitch with a bead at the front.

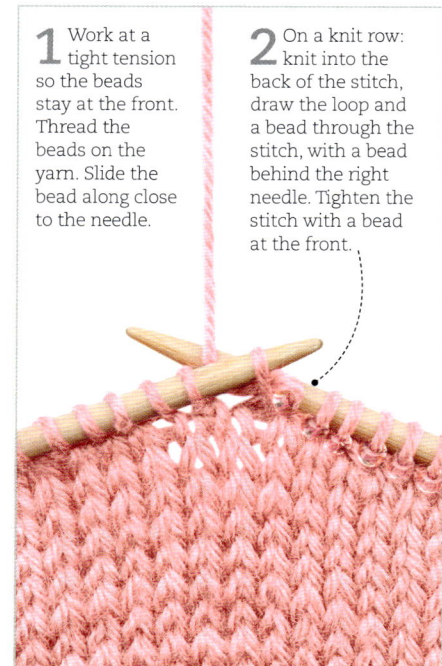

3 On a purl row: slide a bead along close to the needle. Purl into the back of the stitch, positioning the right needle above the bead from the previous row.

4 Draw both loop and bead through the stitch, with the bead behind the right needle. Tighten to ensure the bead stays on the right side.

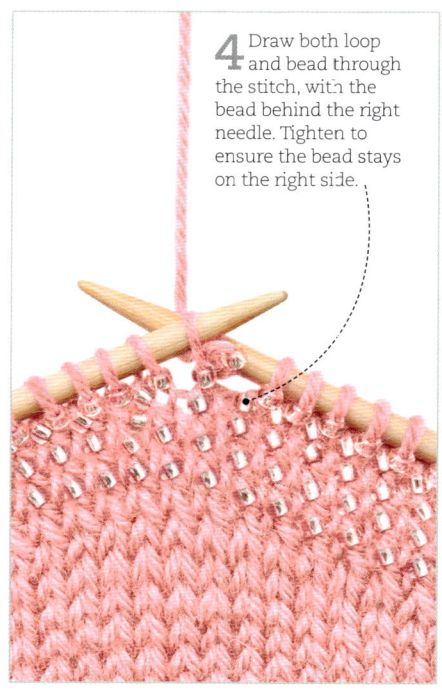

REVERSE STITCH BEADING

1 Thread beads onto the knitting yarn. Working in stocking stitch, knit to one stitch before the bead position. Bring the yarn to the front.

2 Purl one. The bead must sit tight against the right needle, so slide it along the yarn to this position and hold it there. Purl the next stitch. Take the yarn to the back and work to the next bead position.

Hold bead in position

INSET BEAD WITH A HOOK

1 With this technique the bead shows from both sides and is inset into the knitting. Knit to the bead position.

2 Place the bead on a fine crochet hook. Pick the next stitch off the left needle with a hook. Slide the bead onto the stitch and return it to the left needle. Knit or purl the stitch as required. A needle and thread can be used instead of a crochet hook, in which case, make a loop of thread through the stitch and slide the bead down the thread.

USING A SECOND YARN

1 Thread beads onto a fine yarn that matches the main yarn colour. Bigger, heavier beads may "dangle" rather than lie on the fabric, so choose beads carefully. Bugle and tiny glass beads work well.

2 Work all stitches with both yarns.

3 When the bead position is reached, leave the main yarn at the back. Bring the bead thread and bead to the front and slip the bead along the thread until close to the front of the knitting.

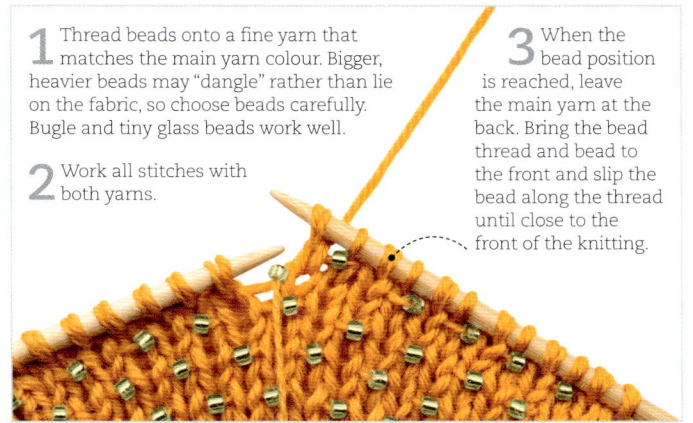

4 Leave the bead and thread at the front and knit a stitch with the main yarn. Take the fine thread to the back and knit the next stitch with both yarns. Work to the next bead position.

BEADED CAST-ON

1 Thread beads onto knitting yarn. Make a slip knot at the end of the yarn leaving a 10cm (4in) tail, and place on the needle. Hold the needle in your right hand, and the yarn in your left. Push a bead along the yarn between your left hand and the needle. Hold the yarn and wrap it around your thumb as shown, then insert the right needle to work a Single cast-on (see p.53). Make sure that the bead remains under the needle.

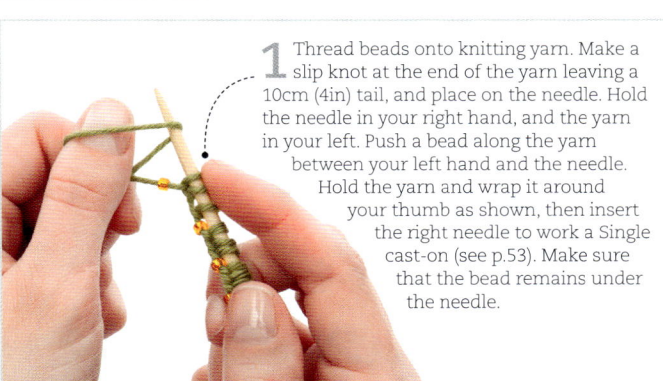

2 Repeat for each cast-on stitch, or space the beads as required along the edge; this example has three stitches between each bead.

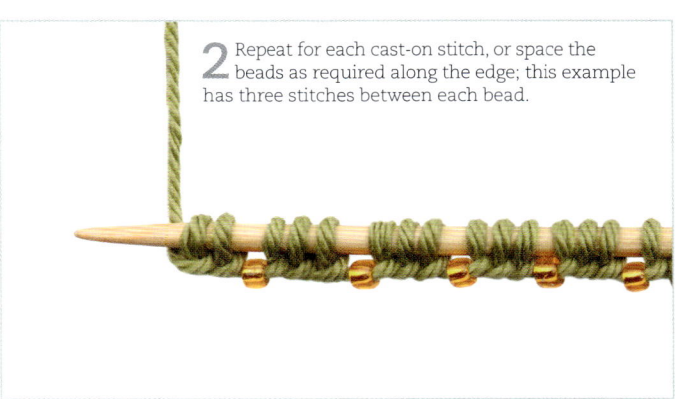

BEADED CAST-OFF

1 Cut a piece of the main colour yarn five times the width of the knitting. Thread one bead for each stitch to be beaded, less one, onto the yarn. Tie the last bead (which will not be worked) to the end of the yarn to prevent the beads sliding off.

2 With the beaded yarn, knit the first two stitches of cast-off. Pass the second over the first as normal. This leaves a selvedge stitch for seaming.

3 Push a bead close to the back of the fabric. For a firm edge (as shown here), knit a stitch drawing both bead and yarn through the stitch. To alter the lie of the bead, change which side of the bead the stitch is passed over in Step 4. For a dangling bead, knit the next stitch leaving the bead at the back as the new loop is formed.

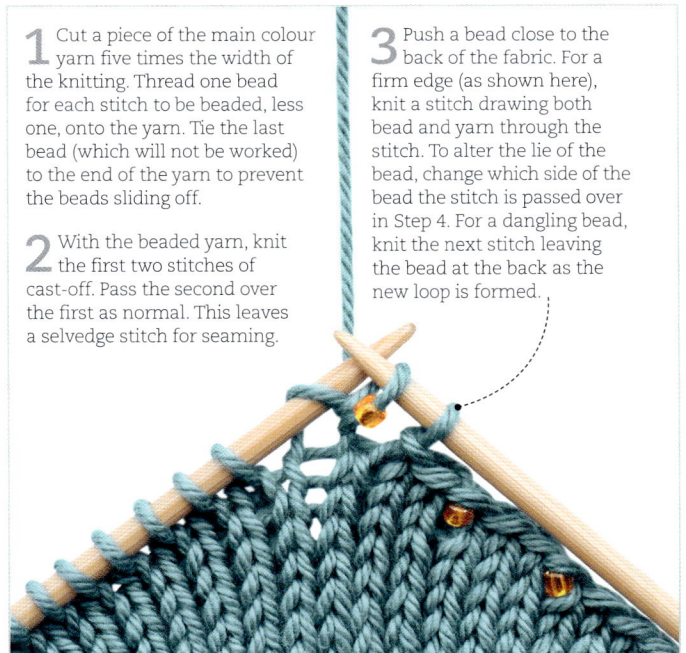

4 For either method, pass the second stitch on the right needle over the first and off the tip of the needle.

5 Repeat Steps 3 and 4 along the cast-off, either working one bead per stitch or some plain cast-offs in between, depending on the size of the bead and effect required.

6 The last stitch should not be beaded if it will be seamed, so remove the end bead. Then work this last stitch plain and pull the end through as normal.

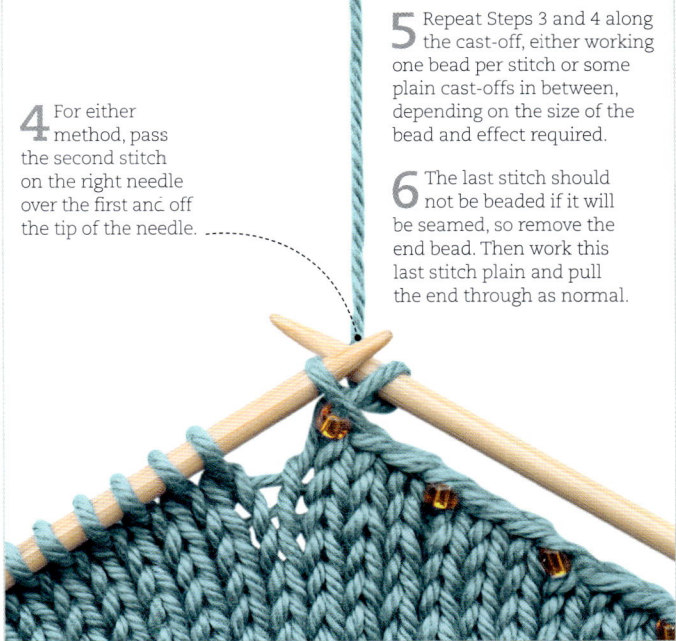

BOBBLES AND EMBOSSING

Popcorns and bobbles look similar but are worked differently. Bells are larger variations of tulip clusters but become partially detached from the knitting. Flaps are worked separately and integrated as the work progresses, while curls combine short rows with tubular knitting. Try using Reverse knitting (see p.166) to avoid turning the work.

POPCORNS

1 This example is worked on a knit row on stocking stitch fabric. Knit to the popcorn position.

2 Insert the right needle as if to knit into the next stitch, then knit into the front, back, front, back of the stitch. Slip the stitch off the needle. Four stitches are made from one. Knit to next popcorn position.

3 On the next row, purl to the popcorn position. Insert the tip of the left needle into the second stitch on the right needle and pass it over the first stitch and over the tip. Repeat with the third and fourth stitches.

4 Purl to the next popcorn position. On the next row, knit to the next popcorn position and repeat Steps 2–4 as required.

DETACHED BOBBLES

1 This example is worked on a knit row on stocking stitch fabric, making a reverse stocking stitch bobble. Knit to the bobble position. Insert the right needle knitwise into the next stitch. Knit it without removing from the left needle. Bring the yarn to the front between the needles and purl into the same stitch. Take the yarn to the back and knit it again; bring the yarn to the front, purl it again; take the yarn to the back and knit it again.

2 Slide the stitch off the left needle. Five stitches are made from one.

3 Turn the work. Knit across the five stitches and loops just made.

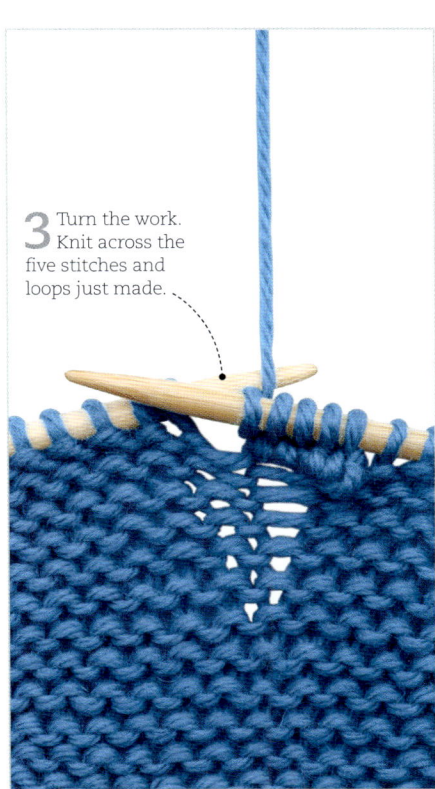

4 Turn and purl across the five stitches just worked. Take the yarn to the back.

5 Insert the tip of the left needle into the second stitch on the right needle and pass it over the first stitch and over the tip of needle. Repeat with the third and fourth stitches. One bobble stitch left. Knit to the next bobble position.

6 Repeat Steps 1–5 to make the next bobble. Bobbles can be purely decorative or be used as a functional fastener on garments or accessories.

TULIP CLUSTER BOBBLE

1 Makes a stocking stitch cluster on a reverse stocking stitch fabric. On a right-side row, purl to the bobble position. Make five stitches out of one as described in Step 2 of Detached bobbles (see p.203). Purl to the next bobble or the end of the row.

2 Work three rows, working the background as stocking stitch and the bobble as reverse stocking stitch. (When the background is knit, purl bobbles and vice versa).

Wrong side

3 On the next row, with right side facing, purl to the bobble position. Slip the first bobble stitch to the right needle, knit one and pass the slipped stitch over it. Knit one, k2tog; three stitches remain of the bobble.

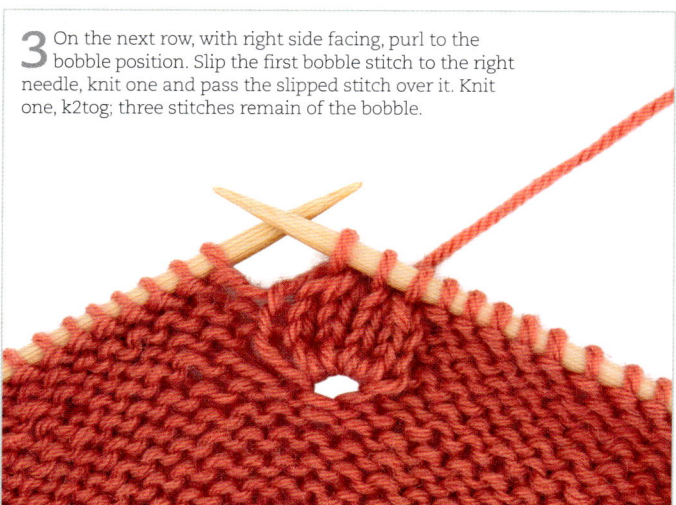

4 On the next row, knit to the bobble position and purl the three bobble stitches.

5 On the next row, purl to the bobble position, slip the first stitch, k2tog and pass the first stitch over and off the right needle. Purl to the next bobble.

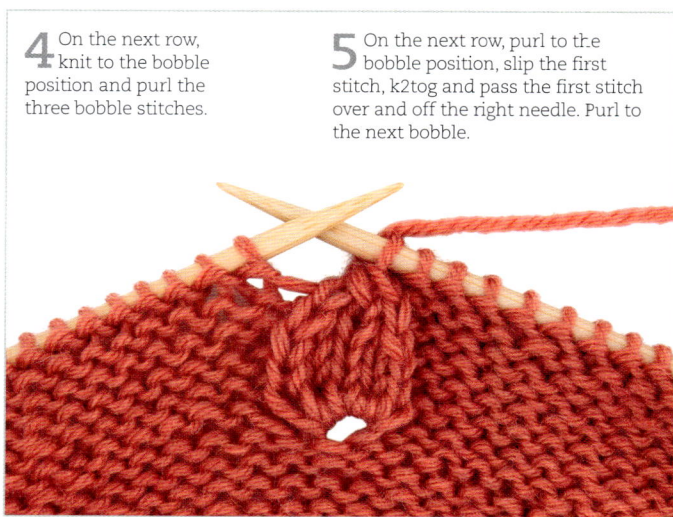

6 Bobbles can be made larger by working more rows. For a more prominent version, try working Bells (opposite).

BELLS

1 This example works a stocking stitch bell on a reverse stocking stitch background. With the right side (RS) facing, purl to the position of the bell. Turn the work and Cable cast-on (see p.55) eight stitches onto what is temporarily the left needle. Turn the work and work to the next bell or the end of the row.

Wrong side

2 Work five more complete rows working the background as reverse stocking stitch and the bell stitches as stocking stitch.

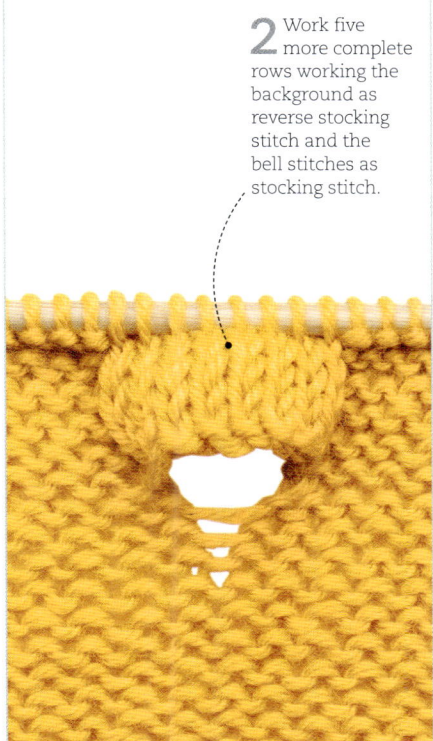

3 RS facing, continue as Step 2, but slip the first two stitches of the bell knitwise, one by one, knit together with the left needle through the front (ssk, see p.100). Knit to two stitches from the end of the bell, k2tog (see p.99).

4 Repeat Step 3 on every RS row, until only two stitches are left of the bell. Knit these together on the next knit row, and then knit the last remaining stitch of the bell together with the following one to complete the bell.

FLAPS

1 Working on separate needles, knit a garter stitch triangle by casting on one stitch. Knit into the front, back, and front of this stitch. Kfb each end stitch on alternate rows until nine stitches wide. Place stitches on a spare needle. Work to the position of the flap. Place the needle with the flap stitches in front of the main needle. Insert the right needle into the first stitch of both left-hand needles. Knit together.

2 For the purl version, see Step 3 of Horizontal inset pocket (see p.181). Flaps can be made from any shape knitted in a stitch that lies flat; try moss-stitch rectangles or diamonds.

CURLS

1 Work in stocking stitch and colour A. With the wrong side facing, purl to the position of the curl.

2 Work a purl right Lifted increase using colour B by picking up and purling into the right side of the stitch below the next stitch (this is picked up the same as a right Lifted increase on a knit row, see p.93).

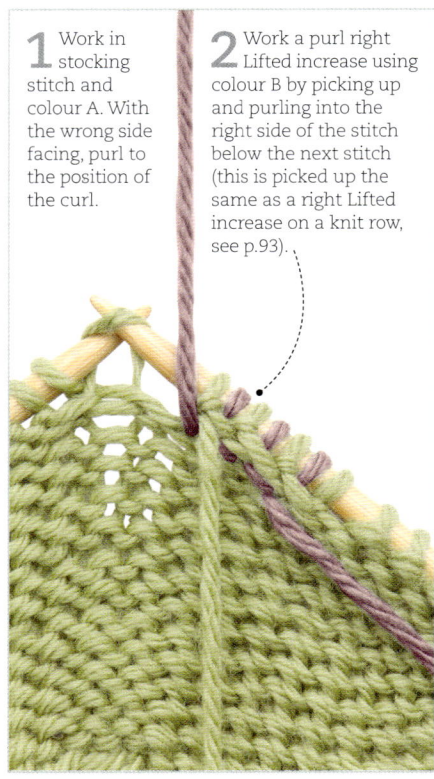

3 Purl one stitch in colour A. Repeat this increase, purl one sequence across the width of the curl (six for this example, so the curl will be 12 stitches wide). Purl to the end of the row.

4 Knit to the curl in colour A. With colour A and B at back, knit all the colour B stitches in colour B, taking the yarn forwards and back to slip each colour A stitch purlwise in between. Turn at the end of the curl.

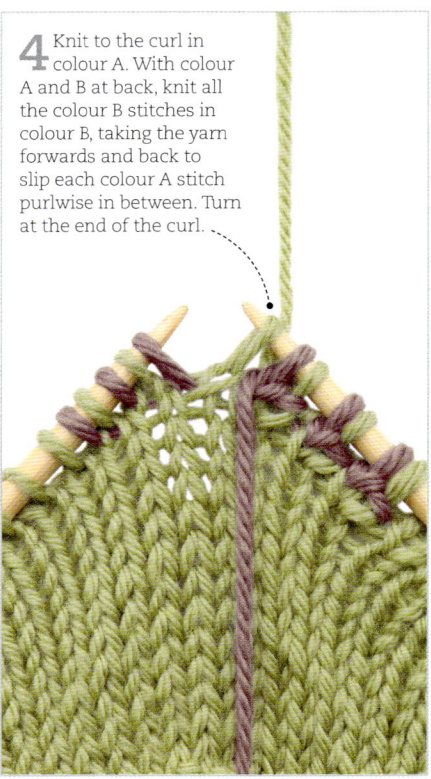

5 Keep colour A at the front. In colour B, purl all colour B stitches, taking the yarn back and forwards to slip each colour A stitch in between. Turn at the end of the curl.

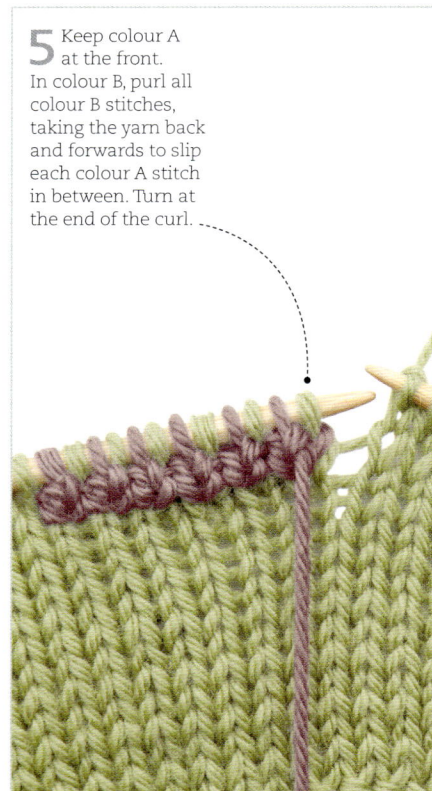

6 Repeat Steps 4 and 5 two or more times, working only over the curl stitches.

7 Colour A and B to back. With colour A work to the end of the row and then work a complete row, knitting each colour B stitch together with the following colour A stitch. Trim the ends of colour B and sew in on the reverse.

EMBROIDERY ON KNITTING

Swiss darning, bullion stitch, lazy daisies, and chain stitch are most commonly used on knitting, although running and satin stitch can also be very attractive. Use a smooth yarn that is the same weight as that used for the knitting, or slightly thicker, together with a blunt-ended darning needle to avoid splitting the knitting yarn.

SWISS DARNING CHART

As Swiss darning embroidery imitates and covers the knit stitches on the right side of the stocking stitch, you can work any charted colourwork motif using the technique. (Cross-stitch books are also good sources of motifs for Swiss darning.) The completed embroidered motif will look as if it has been knitted into the fabric.

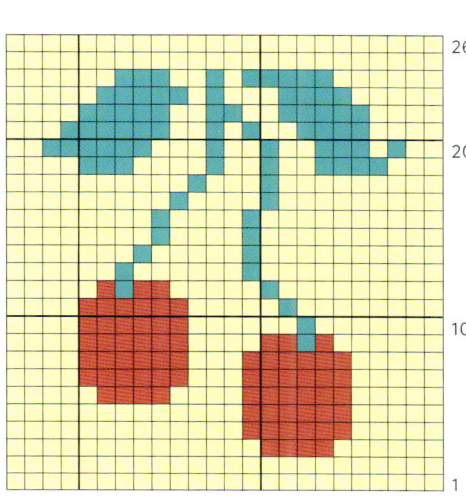

SWISS DARNING WORKED HORIZONTALLY

1 Secure the embroidery yarn to the wrong side of the stocking stitch, then pass the needle from back to front through the centre of a knit stitch, and pull the yarn through. Next, insert the needle from right to left behind the knit stitch above, as shown, and pull the yarn through gently so it "mirrors" the knit stitch size.

2 Insert the needle from right to left into the knit stitch below and out at the centre of the next knit stitch to the left to complete the stitch, as shown. Continue in this way, tracing the path of the knitting horizontally.

SWISS DARNING WORKED VERTICALLY

1 Secure the embroidery yarn on the wrong side of the stocking stitch, then pass the needle from back to front through the centre of a knit stitch and pull the yarn through. Next, insert the needle from right to left behind the knit stitch above, as shown, and pull the yarn through.

2 Insert the needle from front to back and to front again under the top of the stitch below so it comes out in the centre of the stitch just covered, as shown. Continue in this way, tracing the path of the knitting vertically.

SATIN STITCH

1 Secure the yarn on the wrong side. Bring the needle through to the front between two stitches, at one side of the shape to be worked.

2 Take the needle to the back between two stitches at the opposite side of the shape.

3 Bring the needle to the front again at the original side, but spacing it a yarn's width away by angling the needle very slightly while at back of work. The stitches should lie flat and parallel to each other.

4 Continue to work the shape in long smooth stitches that do not pucker the fabric.

RUNNING STITCH

1 Secure the yarn on the wrong side of the work. Bring the needle through to the front between two stitches, at the end of the line to be worked.

2 Take the needle to the back between two stitches a measured number of stitches or rows to the right (or the left).

3 Repeat, spacing the stitches in an even pattern, as required, being careful not to pucker the fabric.

BULLION STITCH

1 Secure the yarn on the wrong side. Take the needle to the back at one end of the stitch, then bring it back to the front a short distance away without pulling through. Wrap the yarn at least six times around the needle close to the knitting.

2 Holding the wraps in place with a finger, pull the needle carefully through the wraps. Re-insert the needle through the knitting at the starting point as shown by the arrow. Bullion stitches can be arranged to form a star or simple flower, or in spirals to form a rose.

LAZY DAISY STITCH

1 Secure the yarn on the wrong side, then bring the needle through at the base of the chain. Re-insert the needle in the same place and bring it through to the front again a short distance away.

2 Wrap the yarn around the tip of the needle once to form the chain loop. Pull through, and then take the needle through to the back on the other side of the chain loop to secure it. The individual chain stitches are traditionally worked in a circle to form simple flower shapes.

CHAIN STITCH ON STRIPES

Knitted stripes can be turned into a plaid or check pattern with lines of chain stitch worked vertically between stitches. Bring a blunt-ended darning needle out in position for the first stitch. Re-insert the needle where it emerged and bring the tip out a short distance below with the yarn looped under it. Pull the yarn through. To continue, insert the needle back into the hole from which it has just emerged and bring it out a short distance below.

EMBROIDERED SMOCKING

Smocking draws the knitting in, so knit the fabric one and half times the required width.

1 Cast on a multiple of eight plus three extra stitches (35 in this example). Work a wide rib fabric starting with three purl stitches and one knit stitch that repeats across the row, ending with three purl stitches. This is the right side. Work 30 rows and cast off.

2 Mark the second rib stitch from the right four rows up the work from the cast-on. Thread a needle with contrast yarn, secure the yarn to the wrong side of the work and bring the needle from the back to the front just between last purl stitch and the knit stitch of the marked rib stitch.

3 Working to the left, re-insert the needle to the back after the third rib knit stitch. Re-thread yarn in the same direction once more, making sure not to catch the yarn with the needle and ending with the needle at the back. Gently pull the yarn to gather the two ribs. Continue along the row, working into each pair of rib stitches, as shown. Gather each wound stitch as it is completed. Fasten and cut the yarn at the other end.

4 Move four rows up and work the next gathers. Re-fasten the yarn to the right edge, bring the needle from back to front just before the first rib knit stitch, re-insert just after the second rib knit stitch, thread the yarn around and gather as in Step 3. Repeat along the row, starting by bringing the yarn to the front after the next three purl stitches as in Step 3. Continue as Steps 3 and 4, spacing each repeat four rows apart up the fabric.

3D EMBELLISHMENTS

Surface embellishments and edge decorations can be attached to knitting once it is completed. These are easy, fun to make, and extremely effective, but remember to buy extra yarn. Simple tools are required to make pom-poms and tassels while a specially worked cast-on, cast-off, or selvedge will make adding a fringe easier.

TWIZZELS

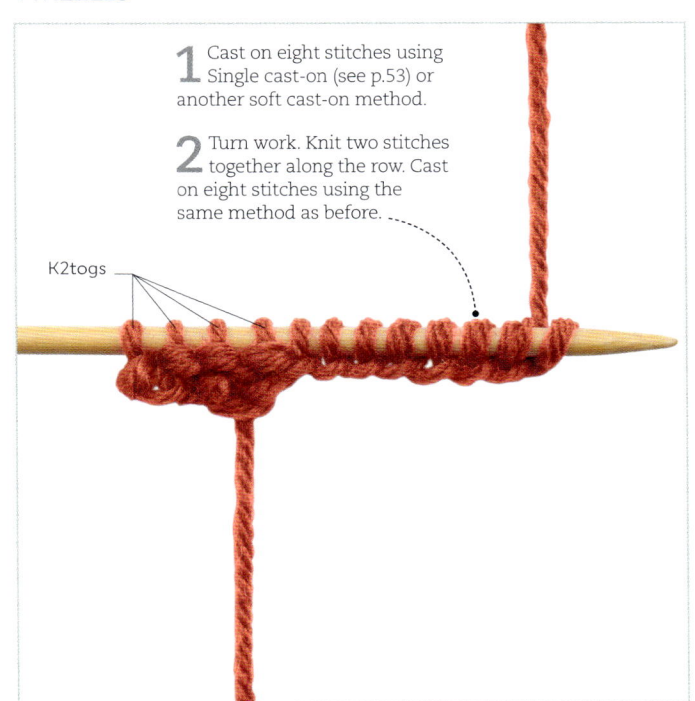

1 Cast on eight stitches using Single cast-on (see p.53) or another soft cast-on method.

2 Turn work. Knit two stitches together along the row. Cast on eight stitches using the same method as before.

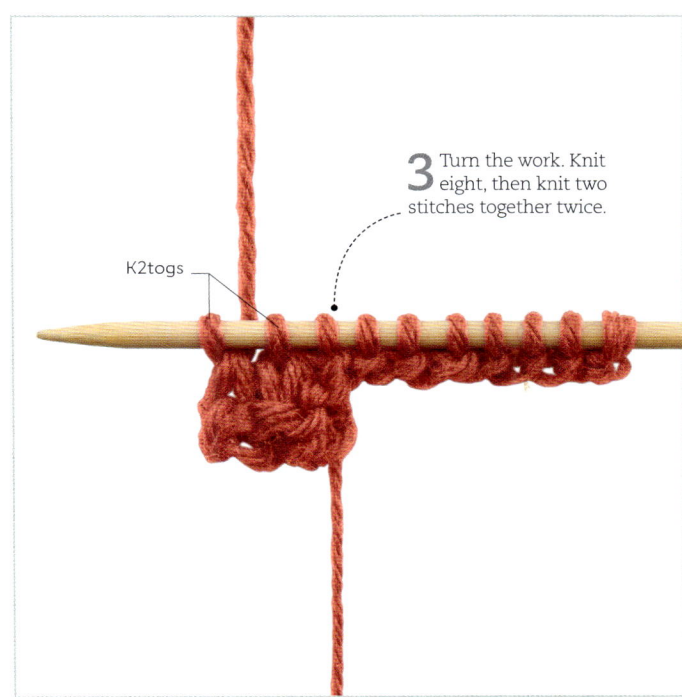

3 Turn the work. Knit eight, then knit two stitches together twice.

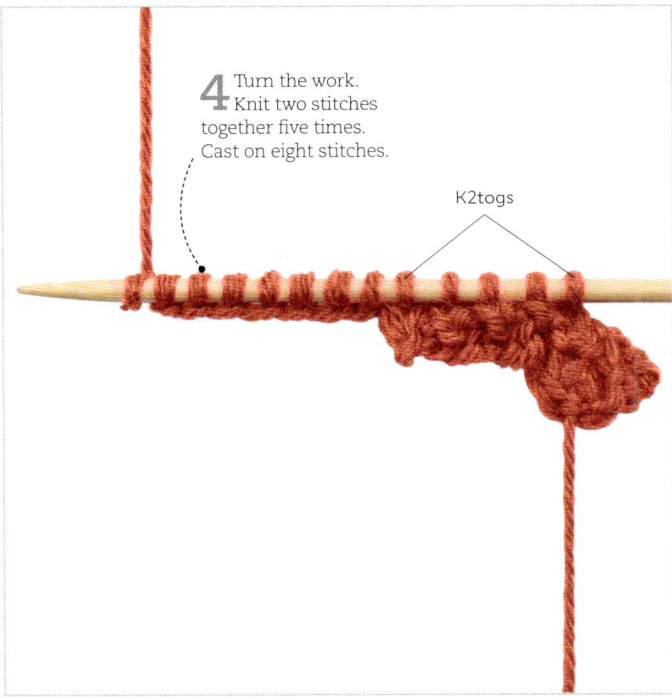

4 Turn the work. Knit two stitches together five times. Cast on eight stitches.

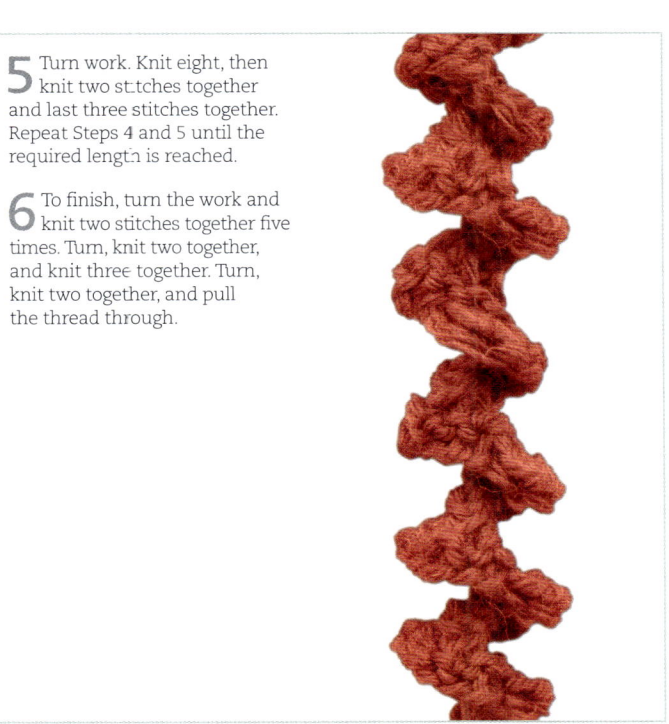

5 Turn work. Knit eight, then knit two stitches together and last three stitches together. Repeat Steps 4 and 5 until the required length is reached.

6 To finish, turn the work and knit two stitches together five times. Turn, knit two together, and knit three together. Turn, knit two together, and pull the thread through.

POM-POMS

1 Draw two 8cm (3¼in) diameter circles on firm card. Draw another 2.5cm (1in) diameter circle in the centre. The diameter of the outer circle minus that of the inner will be the approximate size of the pom-pom. A smaller centre circle makes a denser pom-pom. Cut out the circles and the centres so they look like doughnuts.

2 Cut a few 1m (1yd) lengths of yarn and wind together into a small ball. Put the circles together. Hold the yarn ends at the edge of the circle, and insert the ball into centre, winding yarn through the circles. Continue winding.

3 When the first ball runs out make another. If the centre becomes too tight, thread as many strands of yarn as possible onto a large-eyed needle, and use this to complete the winding. Next, insert the point of scissors into the outside of the circle and cut through the wraps.

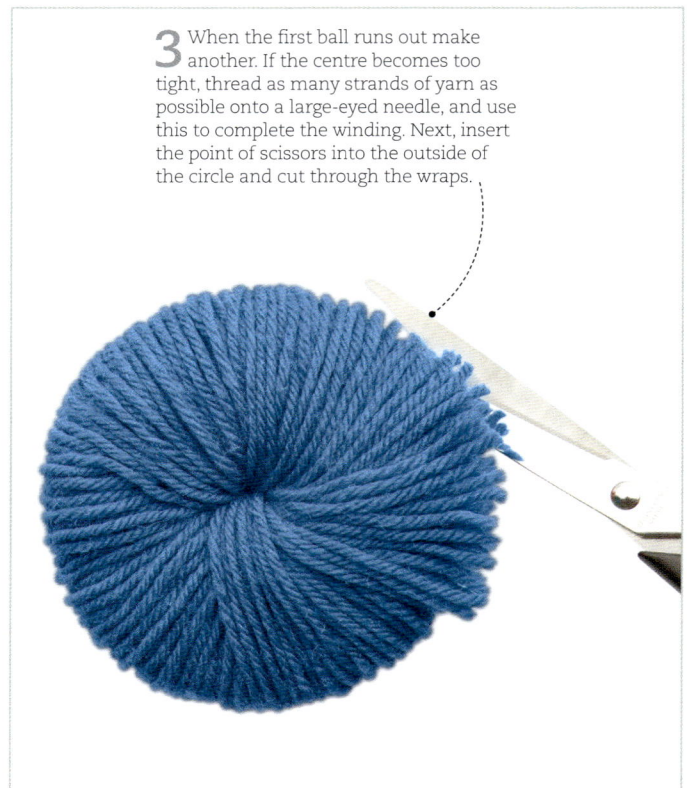

4 Slide a long, doubled strand of yarn between the circles, wrap and knot it tightly around the core.

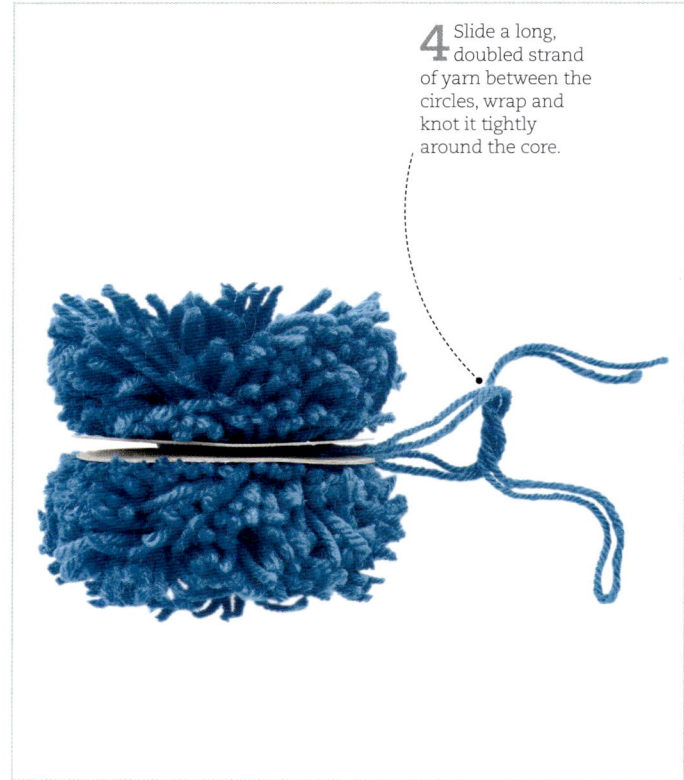

5 Thread the yarn onto a needle and make a few stitches through the knot. Gently remove the circles. Shake and trim the pom-pom, but do not cut the tie strands. Suspending a wool pom-pom in steam will make it even fuller (hang it at the end of a long needle for safety).

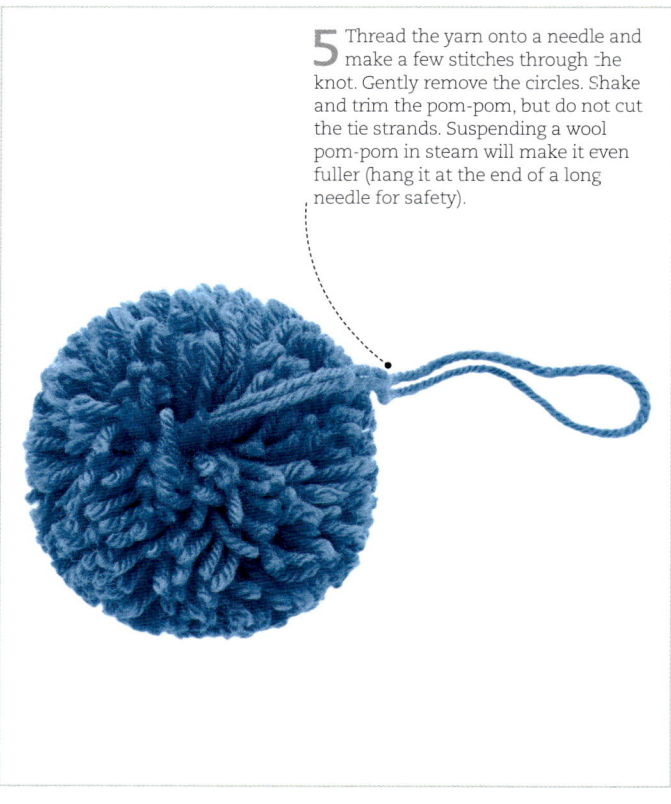

TASSELS

1 Select a template approximately the length of the finished tassel; this can be cut card, but a book is often ideal. Holding the end with your thumb, wrap the yarn repeatedly around the template using single or varied colours. Fifty wraps is average, more wraps make a thicker tassel. With a threaded needle, pull a long doubled strand of yarn between the yarn and the template, and slide it up to end. Tie tightly around the strands, leaving long ends.

2 Insert scissors at the base of the wraps and cut across all the strands. Remove the template.

3 Wrap another strand of yarn tightly around the top a short distance below the head, then tie securely and sew the ends through the wraps and into the tassel head a few times.

4 Trim the ends of the tassel and sew to the project with the remaining long strand at the head. Light pressing or steaming at the end of Step 2 will make the tassel sleeker.

214 TECHNIQUES

FRINGE

1 Cut a card template a little wider than the fringe length. Wind yarn repeatedly around the card. Cut along one side of the card, making lengths of yarn double the width of the card.

2 Take several lengths (more make a thicker fringe), fold in half and hold the folded loop in front of the fabric edge. Insert a crochet hook through the back of the fabric close to the edge or through purpose-made selvedge holes. Catch the folded loop and pull it through to back.

3 Catch the strands in the hook again and pull through the first loop. Repeat along the edge, spacing as required. Trim ends evenly. Fringes can be beaded, knotted, or worked in silky or contrast coloured yarns.

DRAWTHREAD BOBBLE

1 Using smaller needles than normal for the yarn, cast on five stitches using Single cast-on (see p.53). Work a number of rows in garter or stocking stitch as desired. Finish with the wrong side facing, and slip all the stitches, one by one, over the first one.

2 Cut the yarn leaving a 20cm (8in) tail and pull through the remaining stitch. Sew a running stitch with the yarn tail around the edge, and pull tightly. (Contrast yarn has been used here for clarity.)

3 Sew together to secure and use the same thread to attach to the project.

COVERED BUTTONS

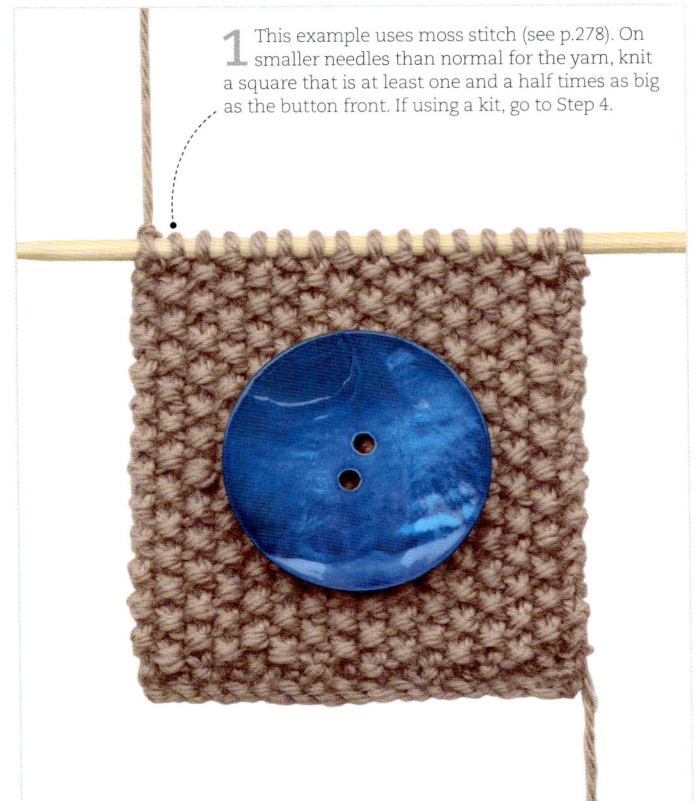

1 This example uses moss stitch (see p.278). On smaller needles than normal for the yarn, knit a square that is at least one and a half times as big as the button front. If using a kit, go to Step 4.

2 Cut the yarn with a 20cm (8in) tail, thread a large-eyed needle with the tail and thread back through the stitches as they are removed from the needle. Sew small running stitches around the three edges of the knitting, leave the thread end loose. (A contrast thread has been used here for clarity.)

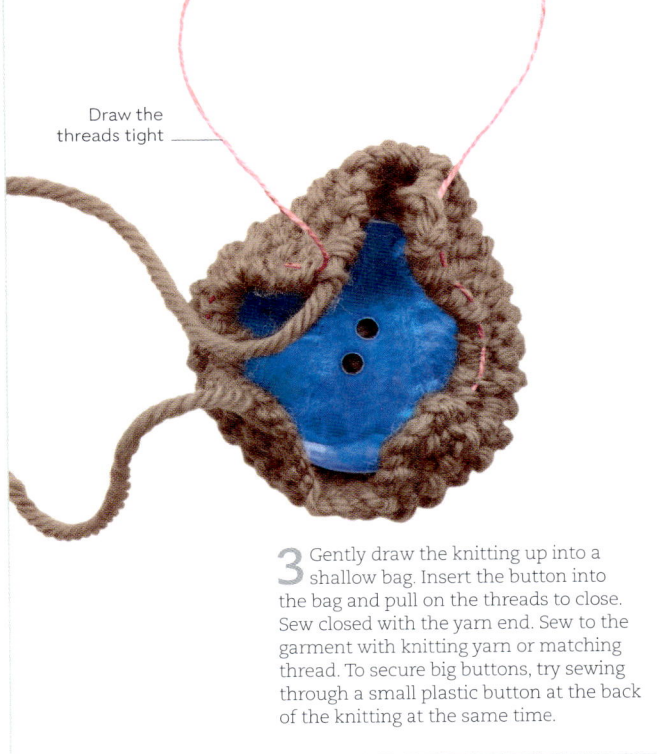

Draw the threads tight

3 Gently draw the knitting up into a shallow bag. Insert the button into the bag and pull on the threads to close. Sew closed with the yarn end. Sew to the garment with knitting yarn or matching thread. To secure big buttons, try sewing through a small plastic button at the back of the knitting at the same time.

4 If using a kit, cast off the square, and follow the manufacturer's instructions to complete the button in either method. A layer of fine woven fabric can be inserted under the knitting to prevent the button showing through the stretched stitches.

PROJECTS

Harlequin scarf

Experiment with blending colour in this super-warm scarf. By holding two strands of this soft mohair together as you knit, the combined colours will create a mélange yarn effect. The scarf is worked as a bias knit with increases and decreases on the edge.

FINISHED SIZE 14cm (5½in) wide x 212m (7ft) long approx.
TECHNIQUES USED Twisted double cast-on **p.60**, Single ribbing **p.77**, Bias knitting **p.148**, Casting off in rib effect **p.69**

MATERIALS REQUIRED

- **Yarn:** Rowan Kidsilk Haze (70% mohair, 30% silk) 25g (210m/230yd)
  A: 715 Scarlett x 2
  B: 680 Burnt Caramel x 2
  C: 696 Mineral x 2
  D: 597 Jelly x 2
  E: 704 Bluebell x 2
  F: 709 Rose x 1

- **Needles:** 1 pair of 4mm (UK8/US6) needles

- **Tension:** 26 sts and 31 rows to 10cm (4in) over single rib with yarn held double

- **Abbreviations:** See p.89

PATTERN

Note: The whole scarf is made by holding two strands of yarn together. For example, the first stripe uses two strands of A, therefore referred to as AA. AB is one strand of A and one of B, and so on.
Using AA cast on 50 sts using a stretchy method suitable for single rib.
Row 1 (WS) [K1, p1] to end.
Row 2 S1, p1, psso, [k1, p1] to last 2 sts, k1, [p1, k1] into next st. (50 sts)
Row 3 [P1, k1] to last 2 sts, p2.
Row 4 S1 k1 psso, [p1, k1] to last 2 sts, p1 [k1, p1] into next st. (50 sts)
Last 4 rows set diagonal patt. Work a further 20 rows as set.
Working in diagonal patt as set, break off one strand of yarn and join in one of B. Commence stripe pattern as set, working 24 rows in each colour pattern:
AB, BB, BC, CC, CD, DD, DE, EE, EF, FF, EF, EE, DE, DD, DC, CC, CB, BB, BA, AA.
21 stripes worked in total.
Cast off in rib effect. Darn in all ends.

Fine mohair really lends itself to the darning-in process (see p.83). The ends are well hidden beneath the furry surface fibres.

COLOUR MIXING

See how a gradient of colour is created from the use of two of the six yarn colours – A, B, C, D, E and F – at the same time.

Delicate lace shawl

Knitting a luxurious, lace-weight shawl can be a little tricky, but the result is truly rewarding. The gossamer shawl will add an elegant touch to any outfit, and the cotton blend feels light and airy against the skin. Knits and purls add texture to this pretty lace pattern.

FINISHED SIZE 50 x 130cm (19½ x 51in) approx.
TECHNIQUES USED Knit-on cast-on **p.54**, Yarnover increases **p.96**, Simple decreases **p.99**, Casting off knitwise **p.68**

MATERIALS REQUIRED
- **Yarn:** Scheepjes Whirl (60% cotton, 40% acrylic) 100g (1000m/1093yd) 553 Indigo Plane x 1

- **Needles**: 1 pair of 3.75mm (UK9/US5) needles
1 pair of 4.5mm (UK7/US7) needles
1 pair of 6mm (UK4/US10) needles

- **Tension:** 19 sts and 28 rows to 10cm (4in) over patt

- **Abbreviations:** See p.89

PATTERN
Using 6mm (UK4/US10) needles, cast on 190 sts using a knit-on cast-on. Change to 4.5mm (UK7/US7) needles and cont as follows:
Work edging
Row 1 (WS) K.
Row 2 [Knit but wrap yarn twice around needle, bringing both loops through] to end.
Row 3 [Purl into one of two loops in next st, knock off other loop] to end. Change to 3.75mm (UK9/US5) needles.
Row 4 [K2tog] to end. (95 sts)
Commence pattern
Row 1 K3, *[p2, k1] twice, yo, k2tog, yo, k1, yo, s1 k1 psso, yo, [k1, p2] twice, k1; rep from * to last 2 sts, k2. (105 sts)
Row 2 K2, [p1, k2] twice, p9, *k2, [p1, k2] three times, p9; rep from * to last 8 sts, k2, [p1, k2] twice.
Row 3 K3, *[p2, k1] twice, yo, k2tog, yo, k3, yo, s1 k1 psso, yo [k1, p2] twice, k1; rep from * to last 2 sts, k2. (115 sts)
Row 4 K2, [p1, k2] twice, p11, *k2, [p1, k2] three times, p11; rep from * to last 8 sts, k2, [p1, k2] twice.
Row 5 K3, *[p2tog, k1] twice, yo, k2tog, yo, s1 k1 psso, k1, k2tog, yo, s1 k1 psso, yo, [k1, p2tog] twice, k1; rep from * to last 2 sts, k2. (95 sts)

Row 6 K2, [p1, k1] twice, p11, *k1, [p1, k1] three times, p11; rep from * to last 6 sts, [k1, p1] twice, k2.
Row 7 K3, *[p1, k1] twice, yo, k2tog, yo, k1 tbl, yo, s1 k2tog psso, yo, k1 tbl, yo, s1 k1 psso, yo, [k1, p1] twice, k1; rep from * to last 2 sts, k2. (105 sts)
Row 8 K2, [p1, k1] twice, p13, *k1, [p1, k1] three times, p13; rep from * to last 6 sts, [k1, p1] twice, k2.
Row 9 K3, *[k2tog] twice, yo, k2tog, yo, k3, yo, k1, yo, k3, yo, s1 k1 psso, yo, [s1, k1, psso] twice, k1; rep from * to last 2 sts, k2.
Row 10 K2, p to last 2 sts, k2.
Row 11 K3, *[k2tog, yo] twice, s1 k1 psso, k1, k2tog, yo, k1, yo, s1 k1 psso, k1, k2tog, [yo, s1, k1, psso] twice, k1; rep from * to last 2 sts, k2. (95 sts)
Row 12 Rep row 10.
Row 13 K2, [k2tog, yo] twice, k1 tbl, yo, s1 k2tog psso, yo, k3, yo, s1 k2tog psso, yo, k1 tbl, yo, s1 k1 psso, *yo, s1 k2tog psso, yo, k2tog, yo, k1 tbl, yo, s1 k2tog psso, yo, k3, yo, s1 k2tog psso, yo, k1 tbl, yo, s1, k1, psso; rep from * to last 4 sts, yo, s1 k1 psso, k2.
Row 14 Rep row 10.
Row 15 K3, *yo, s1 k1 psso, yo, [k1, p2] four times, k1, yo, k2tog, yo, k1; rep from * to last 2 sts, k2. (105 sts)
Row 16 K2, p5, [k2, p1] three times, k2, *p9, [k2, p1] three times, k2; rep from * to last 7 sts, p5, k2.

Row 17 K4, yo, s1 k1 psso, yo, [k1, p2] four times, k1, yo, k2tog, *yo, k3, yo, s1 k1 psso, yo, [k1, p2] four times, k1, yo, k2tog; rep from * to last 4 sts, yo, k4. (115 sts)
Row 18 K2, p6, [k2, p1] three times, k2, *p11, [k2, p1] three times, k2; rep from * to last 8 sts, p6, k2.
Row 19 K3, *k2tog, yo, s1 k1 psso, yo, [k1, p2tog] four times, k1, yo, k2tog, yo, s1 k1 psso, k1; rep from * to last 2 sts, k2. (95 sts)
Row 20 K2, p6, [k1, p1] three times, k1, *p11, [k1, p1] three times, k1; rep from * to last 8 sts, p6, k2.
Row 21 K2, k2tog, yo, k1 tbl, yo, s1 k1 psso, yo, [k1, p1] four times, k1, yo, k2tog, yo, k1 tbl, *yo, s1 k2tog psso, yo, k1 tbl, yo, s1 k1 psso, yo, [k1, p1] four times, k1, yo, k2tog, yo, k1 tbl, rep from * to last 4 sts, yo, s1 k1 psso, k2. (105 sts)
Row 22 K2, p7, [k1, p1] three times, k1, *p13, [k1, p1] three times, k1; rep from * to last 9 sts, p7, k2.

Row 23 K3, *yo, k3, yo, s1 k1 psso, yo, [s1 k1, psso] twice, k1, [k2tog] twice, yo, k2tog, yo, k3, yo, k1; rep from * to last 2 sts, k2.
Row 24 Rep row 10.
Row 25 K3, *yo, s1 k1 psso, k1, k2tog, [yo, s1 k1 psso] twice, k1, [k2tog, yo] twice, s1 k1 psso, k1, k2tog, yo, k1; repeat from * to last 2 sts, k2. (95 sts)
Row 26 Rep row 10.
Row 27 K4, yo, s1 k2tog psso, yo, k1 tbl, yo, s1 k1 psso, yo, s1 k2tog psso, yo, k2tog, yo, k1 tbl, yo, s1 k2tog psso, *yo, k3, yo, s1 k2tog psso, yo, k1 tbl, yo, s1 k1 psso, yo, s1 k2tog psso, yo, k2tog, yo, k1 tbl, yo, s1 k2tog psso; rep from * to last 4 sts, yo, k4.
Row 28 Rep row 10.
These 28 rows set lace patt. Rep rows 1–28 twelve times more, ending with a WS row.
Work top edging
Row 1 [(K1, p1) into next st] to end. (190 sts)

Casting on with larger needles creates a soft edge, and working a row of dropped stitches, followed by knitting stitches together, produces the frilled edge.

Change to 4.5mm (UK7/US7) needles and work as follows:
Row 2 [Purl but wrap yarn twice around needle, bringing both loops through] to end.
Row 3 [Knit into one of two loops in next st, knock off other loop] to end.
Cast off using a 6mm (UK4/US10) needle.

FINISHING
Hand-wash and wet block (see p.185), making sure to stretch lace pattern out until visible and keep edges of scarf straight. Blocking wires (see p.42) would be useful for keeping the edges straight.

DELICATE LACE SHAWL **223**

Blocking is essential for lace to showcase the intricate pattern – it won't reveal its full detail until blocking (see p.185) allows the yarn to relax into the intended drape.

Working with larger needles creates a soft edge, and working a row of increases, followed by dropped double stitches, produces the frilled upper edge.

This yarn changes colour very slowly over a longer length of knitting. More vibrant and quicker-changing coloured yarns may interfere with the lace pattern, making it harder to see the finer detail.

Cabled armwarmers

When you want to keep cosy but need your fingers to remain free, reach for these practical and stylish armwarmers. The cable is easy to follow, and they have a simple, buttonhole-style thumb opening. You could also knit these on a circular needle using a Magic Loop (see p.160).

FINISHED SIZE To fit an average adult woman.
TECHNIQUES USED Cable cast-on **p.55**, Working with a set of four double-pointed needles **p.163**, Cables **p.111**, Single cast-on **p.53**, Casting off in rib effect **p.69**

MATERIALS REQUIRED

- **Yarn:** Debbie Bliss Donegal Luxury Tweed Aran (100% wool) 50g (88m/96yd) 36 Gold x 2

- **Needles:** Four 4mm (UK8/US6) double-pointed needles (dpns) Cable needle

- **Tension:** 20 sts and 28 rows to 10cm (4in) over 2 x 2 rib using 4mm (UK8/US6) needles

- **Abbreviations:** See p.89

- **Special abbreviations:**
  C6F (cable 6 front) S3 to cable needle, hold in front, k3, k3 from cable needle
  C6B (cable 6 back) S3 to cable needle, hold in back, k3, k3 from cable needle

PATTERN

LEFT ARMWARMER

Cast on 40 sts onto one needle using cable cast-on. Divide sts between three dpns: 13 sts on needles 1 and 3, and 14 sts on needle 2.
Working 8 circular rounds of 2 x 2 rib as foll:
*K1, p2, k1; rep from * to end of round, joining after first round (see p.158).
Inc round Rib 14, M1p, [rib 4, M1p] three times, rib to end of round. (44 sts)
You should now have 13 sts on needles 1 and 3, and 18 sts on needle 2.
Set cable panel
Rib 13, work next 18 sts from chart, rib 13.
Rep last round until work measures 22cm (9in).**
Shape thumb
Round 1 Rib 3, cast off 6 sts, patt to end. (38 sts)
Round 2 Rib 3, cast on 4 sts using single cast-on method, patt to end. (42 sts)
Round 3 K1, p1, k2, p1, k2, patt to end.
Rep round 3 until work measures 3cm (1¼in) from thumb opening, ending at least 2 rounds after last cable row.
Dec round Patt 3, k2tog tbl, patt 8, k2tog tbl, k2, k2tog, p2, k2tog tbl, k2, k2tog patt to last 2 sts, p2tog. (36 sts)
Change to 2 x 2 rib:
Next 5 rounds K1, [p2, k2] to last 3 sts, p2, k1.
Cast off in rib. Darn in ends.

RIGHT ARMWARMER

Work as for Left armwarmer to **.
Shape thumb
Round 1 Work in patt as set to last 9 sts, cast off 6 sts, rib to end. (38 sts)
Round 2 Work in patt as set to last 3 sts, cast on 4 sts, patt to end. (42 sts)
Round 3 Patt to last 7 sts, k2, p1, k2, p1, k1.
Rep round 3 until work measures 3cm (1¼in) from thumb opening, ending at least 2 rounds after last cable row.
Dec round P2tog, patt 13, k2tog tbl, k2, k2tog, p2, k2tog tbl, k2, k2tog, p2, k1, p1, k1, p1, k2, k2tog tbl, k1, p1, k1. (36 sts)
Next 5 rounds K1, [p2, k2] to last 3 sts, p2, k1.
Cast off in rib.

FINISHING

Darn in ends. Hand-wash, pin out to shape and dry flat.

CABLE CHART

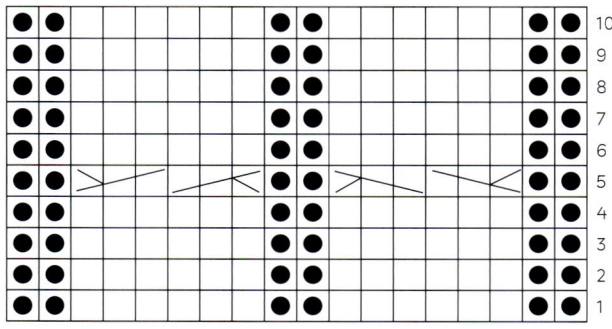

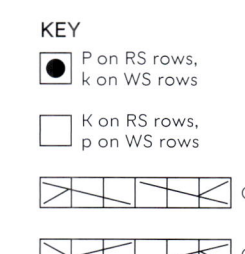

KEY
● P on RS rows, k on WS rows
☐ K on RS rows, p on WS rows
C6F
C6B

Fingerless gloves with mitts

Fingertips are needed to work digital devices, so gloves with fingers are less popular – but fingerless gloves can be chilly. This pattern has a handy mitt top that can be buttoned back when you need your fingers free.

FINISHED SIZE To fit 4–7 years(8–12 years:Small adult:Large adult)
Actual width above thumb: 14.5(15.5:17.5:19.5)cm/5¾(6¼:7:7¾)in
TECHNIQUES USED Twisted double cast-on **p.60**, Backwards loop cast-on **p.55**, Mattress stitch **p.188**, Knitted button loop **p.173**

MATERIALS REQUIRED

- **Yarn**: King Cole Homespun Prism DK (22% Merino wool, 22% alpaca, 23% acrylic, 23% polyamide, 10% viscose) 50g (175m/191yd))
  5187 Jade Lagoon x 1

- **Needles:** 1 pair of 3.75mm (UK9/US5) needles
  1 pair of 3mm (UK11/US2.5) needles

- **Notions:** 2 x buttons
  Stitch markers (optional)

- **Tension:** 24 sts and 30 rows to 10cm (4in), over st st using 3.75mm (UK9/US5) needles

- **Abbreviations:** See p.89

- **Special abbreviations:**
  pm – place marker
  sm – slip marker

PATTERN

RIGHT FINGERLESS GLOVE

Using 3mm (UK11/US2.5) needles, cast on 34(38:42:46) sts using twisted double cast-on.
Row 1 (RS) K2, [p2, k2] to end.
Row 2 P2, [k2, p2] to end.
Last 2 rows set 2 x 2 rib patt. Cont in patt until work measures 5(6:7:8)cm/2(2¼:2¾:3¼)in, ending with a RS row.
Next row Rib 7, M1, [rib 5(6:7:8), M1] 4 times, rib to end. (39(43:47:51) sts)
Change to 3.75mm (UK9/US5) needles.
Row 1 (RS) K.
Row 2 P.
Last 2 rows set st st. Cont in st st for a further 4 rows, ending with a WS row.
Shape thumb gusset
Row 7 (RS) K19(21:23:25), pm, M1R, k3, M1L, pm, k to end. (41(45:49:53) sts)
Starting with a p row, work 3 rows in st st.
Row 11 K to marker, M1R, k to marker, M1L, k to end. (43(47:51:55) sts)
Row 12 and all foll alt rows P.
Rep last 2 rows 3(3:4:5) times. (49(53:59:65) sts)
Divide for thumb
Next row (RS) K32(34:38:42), turn.
Next row P13(13:15:17), turn. Remove markers.
Working only on these 13(13:15:17) sts work 2(2:2:4) rows in st st.

Next row K1, [p1, k1] to end.
Next row P1, [k1, p1] to end.
Rep last 2 rows once more. Cast off in rib.
With RS facing, rejoin yarn at base of thumb and knit to end. (36(40:44:48) sts)
Working across the gap created by the thumb, and starting with a P row, work 7(9:11:13) rows in st st without shaping, ending with a WS row.
You will now divide for fingers.
Index finger
Next row (RS) K23(25:28:30), turn.
Next row P11(11:13:13), turn.
Cast on 2 sts using backwards loop cast-on. (13(13:15:15) sts)
Working only on these 13(13:15:15) sts for the index finger, and leaving rem sts unworked, cont as folls:
**Next row K1, [p1, k1] to end.
Next row K1, [p1, k1] to end.
Rep last 2 rows 0(0:1:1) more times. Cast off in rib.**
Middle finger
With RS facing, rejoin yarn and pick up and k 2 sts from cast-on sts at base of index finger, k5(6:6:7), turn.
Next row P11(13:13:15), turn and cast on 2 sts using backwards loop cast-on. (13(15:15:17) sts)
Working only on these 13(13:15:15) sts for the middle finger, and leaving rem sts unworked, complete as given from ** to ** of index finger.

The button loop is knitted independently and then hand-sewn in position, creating a very neat finish.

Ensuring your button is not sewn on too tightly will allow the button loop to have the space it needs to sit neatly and securely when fastened.

Third finger
With RS facing, rejoin yarn and pick up and k 2 sts from cast-on sts at base of middle finger, k4(5:5:6), turn.
Next row P10(12:12:14), turn and cast on 2 sts using backwards loop cast-on. (12(14:14:16) sts)
Working only on these 12(14:14:16) sts for the third finger, and leaving rem sts unworked, cont as folls:
***Next row** [K1, p1] to end.
Next row [P1, k1] to end.
Rep last 2 rows 0(0:1:1) times more.
Cast off in rib.***
Little finger
With RS facing, rejoin yarn and pick up and k 2 sts from cast-on sts at base of third finger, k4(4:5:5), turn.

Next row P to end. (10(10:12:12) sts)
Working only on these 10(10:12:12) sts for the little finger, and leaving rem sts unworked, complete as given for third finger from *** to ***.

LEFT FINGERLESS GLOVE

Work as Right fingerless glove to Shape thumb gusset.
Row 7 (RS) K17(19:21:23), pm, M1R, k3, M1L, pm, k to end. (41(45:49:53) sts)
Starting with a p row, work 3 rows in st st.
Row 11 K to marker, M1R, k to marker, M1L, k to end. (43(47:51:55) sts)
Row 12 and all foll alt rows P.
Rep last 2 rows 3(3:4:5) times. (49(53:59:65) sts)

Divide for thumb
Next row K30(32:36:40), turn.
Next row K13(13:15:17), turn. Remove markers.
Working only these 13(13:15:17) sts work 2(2:2:4) rows in st st.
Next row K1, [p1, k1] to end.
Next row P1, [k1, p1] to end.
Rep last 2 rows once more.
Cast off in rib. With RS facing, rejoin yarn at base of thumb and knit to end. (36(40:44:48) sts)
Working across gap created by thumb, and starting with a p row, work 7(9:11:13) rows in st st without shaping, ending with a WS row.
Complete as given from Divide for fingers on Right fingerless glove.

FINGERLESS GLOVES WITH MITTS **229**

A stretchy cast-on ensures an elasticated cuff that springs back to sit snugly around the wrist when worn. Looser cast-on techniques may start to look untidy and loose after prolonged wear.

If you find you cast off too tightly, try using a slightly larger needle for that step alone. This will ensure that the fingers of your gloves aren't too tight at the top edge.

DETACHABLE MITTS (MAKE 2)
Using 3mm needles (UK11/US2.5) cast on 35(39:43:47) sts using Twisted double cast-on.
Row 1 (RS) K1, [p1, k1] to end.
Row 2 P1, [k1, p1] to end.
Rep last 2 rows once more.
Change to 3.75mm (UK9/US5) needles.
Row 5 K.
Row 6 P.
Last 2 rows set st st.
Cont in st st for a further 10(10:12:12) rows, ending with a WS row.
Shape top
Next row (RS) K1, ssk, k12(14:16:18), k2tog, pm, k1, ssk, k12(14:16:18), k2tog, pm, k1. (31(35:39:43) sts)
Next row P.

Next row K1, ssk, k to 2 sts before marker, k2tog, sm, k to 2 sts before marker, k2tog, sm, k1. (27(31:35:39) sts)
Rep last 2 rows 2(4:4:6) times more. (19(15:19:15) sts)
Next row P.
Cast off.

FINISHING
Join all finger seams, and outer row-end edge seam, using mattress stitch. Join mitt row-end edge and fold in half to join cast-off edge, leaving cast-on edge open. Sew half of cast on edge of mitt to back of glove 1cm (½in) below division for fingers. Make a 10-st button loop using knitted button loop technique (p.173), and join at top of mitt. Sew button to back of glove to align with loop when mitt is folded back. Block as given on yarn ballband instructions. See ballband for washing and further care instructions.

Cosy double-sided scarf

This duo-toned and ultra-warm scarf may be a labour of love to knit, but tuck it into your coat and you'll never be cold. While this project enlists the use of circular needles, it's also workable on double-pointed needles, if you prefer.

FINISHED SIZE 17cm (6¾in) x 215cm (84¾in) approx.
TECHNIQUES USED Italian cast-on **p.65**, Double knitting **p.136**, Tubular cast-off **p.73**

MATERIALS REQUIRED

- **Yarn:** King Cole Luxury Merino DK (100% merino wool) 50g (140m/153yd)
  A: 2625 Mustard x 5
  B: 3327 Pebble x 5

- **Needle:** 3.75mm (UK9/US5) circular needle, 40cm (15¾in) long

- **Tension:** 21 sts and 27 rows to 10cm (4in) over st st using 3.75mm (UK9/US5) circular needle

- **Abbreviations:** See p.89

PATTERN

Using A, cast on 70 sts using Italian cast-on.
Row 1 (WS) Using A, *k1, s1 wyif, rep from * to end. Without turning your work, push sts up to tip of circular needle in your left hand, to be reworked. This will be where you worked the beginning of the last row.
Row 2 Using B, *s1 wyib, p1; rep from * to end of row.
Turn work over, to now go in the opposite direction. Twist yarns together once to prevent holes from forming.
Row 3 Using B, work as given for row 1.
Row 4 Using A, work as given for Row 2. Turn work over, to now go in the opposite direction. Twist yarns together once.
These last 4 rows form patt.
Cont rep last 4 rows until work measures 215cm (84¾in), ending with patt row 4. Cast off, using B and a Tubular cast-off. Fasten off.

FINISHING

Darn in ends. Block lightly with a warm iron under a damp cloth.

The Italian cast-on creates a totally invisible edge, which sets up your project perfectly for a double-sided project. To mirror this neat finish at your cast-off edge, at the end you will also need to work a tubular cast-off to graft your stitches together using a darning needle, while they're still on your knitting needle. Other cast-on or cast-off techniques may result in bulkier and untidy edges.

Fair Isle socks

This pattern is great to use up oddments or mini-skeins from your stash, and the stranded colourwork makes them thick and cosy. Be sure to weave in any long floats at the back of your work (p.124) to prevent toes getting caught.

FINISHED SIZE To fit shoe size UK 3–5(6–7:8–9:10–12:13–14)/US 5.5–7.5(8–9:9.5–10.5:11–13:14–15)/EU 35.5–38 (39–41:42–43:44–46.5:46–48.5)
Actual foot circumference: 19.5(22:24:26.5:29)cm/7¾(8¾:9¾:10¾:11¾)in
TECHNIQUES USED Twisted double cast-on **p.60**, Turning a heel **p.154**, Stranded colourwork **p.123**, Kitchener's stitch **p.191**, Working with a set of four double-pointed needles **p.163**

MATERIALS REQUIRED

- **Yarn**: West Yorkshire Spinners Signature 4-ply (75% wool, 25% nylon) 100g (400m/437yd)
  A: Butterscotch 240 x 1
  B: Amber 1004 x 1
  C: Juniper 157 x 1
  D: Cayenne Pepper 510 x 1
  E: Milk Bottle 010 x 1

- **Needles**: Four 2.25mm (UK13/US1) double-pointed needles (dpns)
  Four 2.75mm (UK12/US2) double-pointed needles (dpns)

- **Notions**: Stitch marker (optional)
  Blunt-ended darning needle

- **Tension**: 33 sts x 32 rounds to 10cm (4in) over charted patt in the round on 2.75mm (UK12/US2) needles

- **Abbreviations**: See p.89

PATTERN

SOCK (MAKE 2)

Using 2.25mm (UK13/US1) dpns and A, cast on 64(72:80:88:96) sts using twisted double cast-on. Divide evenly over 3 dpns and join to form a round.
Cont working in rounds as folls:
Round 1 (RS) [K1, p2, k1] to end.
Last round sets 2 x 2 rib. Cont in rib as set, work 1 more round.
Break off A and join in B. Work a further 30(32:34:36:38) rounds in rib.
Break off B.
Change to 2.75mm (UK12/US2) dpns and working in st st from chart, cont until work measures approx. 24(24.5:25:25.5:26)cm/9½(9¾:10:10:10¼)in or desired length, ending after 2 rows of plain st st at end of a patt section on chart. Keep working colour attached.

Divide for heel

Next row (RS) K16(18:20:22:24) sts and turn, leaving rem sts unworked. If not working in A, break off yarn and join in A.
Next row (WS) Using A, s1, p31(35:39:43:47).
Cont working across these 32(36:40:44:48) sts only to form heel flap. Leave rem 32(36:40:44:48) sts divided between 2 dpns. You will return to these later. Join in D.
Next row (RS) S1, [k1D, k1A] to last st, k1D.
Next row S1, [p1D, p1A] to last st, p1D.
Rep last 2 rows 15(17:19:21:23) times more. 32(36:40:44:48) rows worked. Break off A.

Turn the heel

Next row (RS) Using D, s1, k18(20:22:26:28), ssk, k1, turn.
Next row S1, p7(7:7:11:11), p2tog, p1, turn.
Next row S1, k to 1 st before gap, ssk, k1.
Next row S1, p to 1 st before gap, p2tog, k1.
Rep last 2 rows until all sts have been worked. You should have 20(22:24:28:30) sts rem.

Note: If you have one or two extra stitches or are missing a stitch or two, simply work the appropriate increase or decrease in the following row to adjust your count. You may find it useful at this stage to place a marker at the centre of these stitches to mark the beg of round.

Rejoin to form a round

Next row will rearrange sts to sit on specific double-pointed needles, henceforth referred to as needles 1, 2 and 3, which will be worked in that order on future rounds. Working from chart and picking up where you left off, with colour needed for next 2 rows, using needle 1, k across heel sts, and pick up and k 16(18:20:22:24) sts along heel flap edge.

CHART

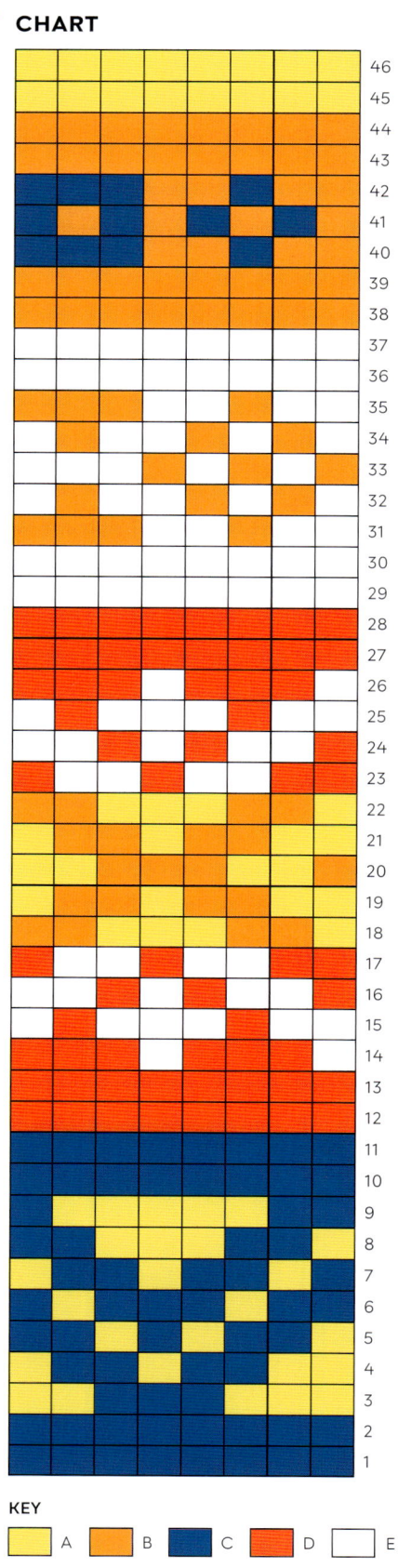

KEY: A, B, C, D, E

Using needle 2, k across instep sts. Using needle 3, pick up and k 16(18:20:22:24) sts and k to marker. You should have 26(29:32:35:38) sts on each of needles 1 and 3, 32(36:40:44:48) sts on needle 2, a total of 84(94:104:114:124) sts.

Note: On the following round you need to lay the charted pattern over specific stitches to ensure they realign when you complete decreasing for the gusset. Use stitch markers to plot out where each chart repeat begins to help you keep track. This may mean that needle 2 pattern repeats do not, at first, match up with the pattern on needles 1 and 3. Following these instructions, they will come together again after the decrease rounds have been worked.

Decrease for instep
Next round Starting at first st of chart, patt across needle 1 to last 3 sts, k2tog, k1. On needle 2, starting with 1st (3rd:5th:7th:1st) st of chart, patt to end. On needle 3, starting with 1st(5th:2nd :6th:3rd) st of chart, patt to end. You should end having finished the 8th st of the charted pattern at the end of the round and will need to keep the patt correct as you decrease on following rounds.
Next round Patt to end.
Rep last 2 rounds 9(10: 11: 12: 13) times more. (64(72:80:88:96) sts)
Cont in patt as set by chart until work measures 17.5(19:21.5:23:25)cm/7(7½:8½: 9:10)in from start of heel turning rows, or your desired length minus 4(4:4.5:5:5) cm/1½(1½:1¾:2:2)in ending after 2 plain rows of st st at end of a patt section, from chart.

Shape toe
You should have 16(18:20:22:24) sts on needles 1 and 3, and 32(36:40:44:48) sts on needle 2.
Change to A or your chosen colour for the toe. Change to 2.25mm (UK13/ US1) needles.

Round 1 K.
Round 2 K to last 3 sts of needle 1, k2tog, k1. On needle 2, k1, ssk, k to last 3 sts, k2tog, k1. On needle 3, k1, ssk, k to end. (60(68:76:84:92) sts)
Rep last 2 rounds until 44(48:52:60:64) sts rem.
Rep row 2 only until 20(24:28:28:32) sts rem. K across needle 1. Move sts from needle 3 to sit on needle 1, so that needles 3 and 1 each hold 10(12:14:14: 16) sts.

FINISHING
Break yarn leaving a long tail. Using Kitchener's stitch, close live toe sts. Darn in all ends. Block as given on yarn ballband instructions. See ballband for washing and further care instructions.

Top left
Kitchener's Stitch, otherwise known as grafting, creates a totally seamless join at the tip of the toe. While a 3-needle cast-off (see p.70) is an alternative option for closing the toe stitches, this will leave a ridge on the inside of the work, which may cause a bit of rubbing when the socks are worn.

Top right
Alternating single stitches in each colour over the heel reinforces the fabric with stranded yarn behind each stitch across each row.

Bottom left
On rejoining your stitches after the heel to form a round, your charted pattern will not match up across the needles. By lining them up correctly at this stage, after the gusset increases have been worked, the pattern will realign at the foot when decreases are completed.

Bottom right
A stretchy cast-on for top-down socks is vital for ensuring a comfortable fit. If you find you cast on stitches too tightly, try casting on using bigger needles or over two needles held together.

Toe-up ankle socks

Working socks from toe to ankle allows you to easily extend the leg to make them longer. It's helpful to place a marker on the beginning half of the round to remind you which side is the start as you work the magic loop method.

FINISHED SIZE To fit shoe size UK 3–5(6–7:8–9:10–12:13)/US 5.5–7.5(8–9:9.5–10.5:11–13:14–15)/EU 35.5–38 (39–41:42–43:44–46.5:46–48.5)
TECHNIQUES USED Double-sided cast-on **p.64**, Magic loop method **p.160**, German short rows **p.152**, Short-row heel **p.154**, Very stretchy single-rib cast-off **p.74**

MATERIALS REQUIRED

- **Yarn**: Stylecraft Life DK (75% premium acrylic, 25% wool) 100g (298m/326yd) 1029 Copper 1029 x 1

- **Needle:** 3.5mm (UK9/US4) circular needle, 80–100cm (32–40in) long

- **Notions:** Stitch marker (optional)

- **Tension:** 26 sts x 34 rows to 10cm (4in) over st st in the round using 3.5mm (UK9/US4) needles

- **Abbreviations:** See p.89

- **Special abbreviations:**
  w&t – wrap and turn (see p.150)

PATTERN

SOCK (MAKE 2)
Toe
Cast on 12(12:12:14:14) sts using double-sided cast-on, divided so you have 6(6:6:7:7) sts on each needle.
Use magic loop method, keeping sts divided by half across each needle.
Round 1 (RS) K.
Round 2 [K1, M1R, k to last st on needle, M1L, k1] twice. (16(16:16:18:18) sts)
Rep last round 2(3:4:5:6) times. (24(28:32:38:42) sts)
Next round K.
Next round Rep round 2. (28(32:36:42:46) sts)
Rep last 2 rounds 2(3:4:4:5) times more. (36(44:52:58:66) sts)
Next 2 rounds K.
Next round Rep round 2. (40(48:56:62:70) sts)
Foot
Next round K.
Prev round sets st st. Cont in st st without shaping until work measures 15(15.5:16:18:19.5)cm/6(6:6½:7:8)in, or 4(4.5:5:5.5:5.5)cm/1½(1¾:2:2:2¼)in shorter than desired length from cast-on.
Shape heel
Working in short rows and on front needle only, and leaving 2nd needle sts unworked, cont to reduce sts by 1 on each row.
Row 1 (RS) K19(23:27:30:34), w&t.
Row 2 (WS) P18(22:26:29:33), w&t.
Row 3 K17(21:25:28:32), w&t.
Row 4 P16(20:24:27:31), w&t.
Row 5 K15(19:23:26:30), w&t.
Cont working in this way, taking in 1 extra st until you reach the row where you work k9(11:13:14:16), w&t.
Beg picking up wraps as you work and knitting them tog with st over which they were wrapped:
Next row (RS) P10(12:14:15:17), turn.
Next row S1 wyif, k10(12:14:15:17), turn.
Next row S1 wyib, p11(13:15:16:18), turn.
Next row S1 wyib, k12(14:16:17:19), turn.
Cont working in this way, taking in 1 extra st until you reach row where you work S1 wyif, k18(22:26:29:33), turn.
Leg
Rejoin completed short-row heel to rem sts, cont k to end of round.
Next round K.
Last row sets st st, cont in st st for a further three rounds.
Cuff
Next round [K1tbl, p1] to end.
Last row sets twisted rib. Cont in twisted rib for a further 8 rounds.
Cast off using very stretchy single-rib cast-off method.

FINISHING
Darn in ends. Block as given on yarn ballband instructions.

Slouchy cardigan

This is made in five pieces and sewn together. Hold live stitches on holders at the top of pieces for the rib border later. Track shaping at the front and armhole edges, using row counters or notes to count decreases at each edge.

FINISHED SIZE To fit an adult: Extra small (Small-Medium:Large:Extra large:Extra extra large:Extra extra extra large)
To fit chest 76 (91.5:101.5:111.5:122:142)cm/30(36:40:44:48:56)in
Actual chest 91(105:116:126:137:158)cm/36(41½:45½:50:54:62)in
TECHNIQUES USED Fully fashioned shaping **p.109**, Slipping stitches off the needle **p.69**, Picking up stitches **p.168**, Purl two together **p.99**, Slip, slip, knit **p.100**

MATERIALS REQUIRED

- **Yarn**: Wool and The Gang Alpachino Merino 100g (100m/109yd), (60% merino, 40% baby alpaca)
  Lime Sorbet x 7(8:9:10:12:14)

- **Needles**: 1 pair of 6mm (UK4/US10) needles
  1 pair of 7mm (UK2/US10½–11) needles
  7mm (UK2/10½–11) circular needle, 100cm (40in) long

- **Notions**: 3(3:3:4:4:5) buttons
  Stitch holders
  Stitch markers

- **Tension**: 11.5 sts and 16.5 rows to 10cm (4in) in st st using 7mm (UK2/US10½–11) needles

- **Abbreviations**: See p.89

PATTERN

BACK

Using 6mm (UK4/US10) needles, cast on 57(65:71:77:83:95) sts.
Row 1 (RS) K1, [p1, k1] to end.
Row 2 P1, [k1, p1] to end.
Last 2 rows set 1 x 1 rib, cont in rib for a further 8 rows, dec 4 sts evenly over last row. (53(61:67:73:79:91) sts)
Change to 7mm (UK2/US10½–11) needles.
Row 11 K.
Row 12 P.
Last 2 rows set st st. Cont in st st until work measures 40.5(40.5:40.5:43:43:45.5)cm/16(16:16:17:17:18)in ending with a p row.
Shape armholes
Cont in st st, cast off 4(4:5:5:6:8) sts at beg of next 2 rows. (45(53:57:63:67:75) sts)
Row 1 K2, k2tog, k to last 4 sts, ssk, k2. (43(51:55:61:65:73) sts)
Row 2 P2, p2tog, p to last 4 sts, ssp, p2. (41(49:53:59:63:71) sts)
Cont shaping as set by prev 2 rows, dec at each end of next 1(1:2:2:2:2) rows and foll 3rd(3rd:4th:4th:4th:4th) row. (37(45:47:53:57:65) sts)
Cont in st st and work a further 18(12:11:7:7:3) rows without shaping, ending with a p row.
Next row K2, ssk, k to last 4 sts, k2tog, k2. (35(43:45:51:55:63) sts)
Next and all foll alt rows P.
Cont in fully fashioned shaping as set, dec at each end of foll 3rd, and 5(9:9:12:13:16) foll alt rows. (23(23:25:25:27:29) sts)
Break off yarn. Place rem 23(23:25:25:27:29) sts on st holder.

LEFT FRONT

Using 6mm (UK4/US10) needles, cast on 29(33:37:39:43:49) sts.
Row 1 (RS) K1, [p1, k1] to end.
Row 2 P1, [k1, p1] to end.
Last 2 rows set 1 x 1 rib, cont in rib for a further 7 rows ending with a RS row.
Row 10 (WS) P1, [k1, p1] to last 2 sts, p2tog. (28(32:36:38:42:48) sts)
Change to 7mm (UK2/US10½–11) needles.
Row 1 K.
Row 2 P.
Last 2 rows set st st. Cont in st st until work measures 33cm (13in) to cast-on edge, ending with a p row. **
Shape front edge
Next row K to last 4 sts, k2tog, k2. (27(31:35:37:41:47) sts)
Cont in fully fashioned shaping as set by prev row, dec at front edge of 5(6:5:6:6:6) foll 6th rows. These extend beyond beg of armhole shaping which is worked at same time. Cont until work measures 40.5(40.5:40.5:43:43:45.5)cm/16(16:16:17:17:18)in, ending with a p row.

Shape armhole
Next row (RS): Cast off 4(4:4:5:5:6:8) sts, patt to end.
Next row P to last 4 sts, ssp, p2.
Next row K2, ssk, patt to end.
Cont in fully fashioned shaping as set, dec at armhole edge of next 1(1:2:2:2:2) rows and foll 3rd(3rd:4th:4th:4th:4th) row.
Work 11(7:4:4:4:0) rows without shaping at armhole edge.
Maintaining front edge shaping, dec as set at armhole edge on next row, foll 4th row, and 8(11:12:13:14:15) foll alt rows.
P 1 row.
Break off yarn. Place rem 5[5:7:7:8:12] sts on a stitch holder and set aside.

RIGHT FRONT
Work as given for left front to **.
Shape front edge
Place marker to mark beg of row edge to be used as reference point for placing buttonholes, leave until edging is worked.
Next row K2, ssk, k to end.
(28(32:36:38:42:48) sts)

Cont in fully fashioned shaping as set, dec at front edge of 5(6:5:6:6:6) foll 6th rows. These will extend beyond beg of armhole shaping, which will be worked at same time as foll:
Cont until work measures 40.5(40.5:40.5:43:43:45.5cm/ 16(16:16:17:17:18)in, ending with a k row.
Shape armhole
Next row (WS) Cast off 4(4:4:5:5:6:8) sts, patt to end.
Next row Patt to last 4 sts, k2tog, k2.
Next row P2, p2tog, p to end.
Cont in fully fashioned shaping as set, dec at armhole edge of next 1(1:2:2:2:2) rows and foll 3rd(3rd:4th:4th:4th:4th) row.
Work 12(8:5:5:5:1) rows without shaping at armhole edge.
Maintaining front edge shaping, dec as set at armhole edge on next row, foll 4th row, and 8(11:12:13:14:15) foll alt rows.
P 1 row.
Break off yarn. Place rem 5[5:7:7:8:12] sts on a stitch holder and set aside.

SLEEVES
Using 6mm (UK4/US10) needles, cast on 29(29:33:33:35:35) sts.
Row 1 (RS) K1, [p1, k1] to end.
Row 2 P1, [k1, p1] to end.
Last 2 rows set 1 x 1 rib, cont in rib for a further 8 rows ending with a WS row.
Change to 7mm (UK3/US10½–11) needles.
Row 1 K.
Row 2 P.
Last 2 rows set st st. Cont in st st for a further 2 rows.
Row 5 K1, M1R, k to last st, M1L, k1. (31(31:35:35:37:37) sts)
Cont inc as set by prev row and working in st st, inc at each end of foll 4th row 6(7:7:8:8:9) times and foll 6th row 2 times. (47(49:53:55:57:59) sts)
Cont working in st st without shaping until sleeve measures 40.5cm (16in), ending with a p row.
Shape head of sleeve
Cast off 4(4:4:5:6:7) sts at beg of next 2 rows. (39(41:45:45:45:45) sts)

Shaping at the armhole creates the relaxed, slouchy silhouette while maintaining a flattering and comfortable drape.

The neat rib button band is cast off in all-knit stitches from the right side for a particularly straight and smooth edge.

The ribbed hem offers stretch and recovery, lying flat against the body for a polished, comfortable fit.

Next row K2, ssk, k to last 4 sts, k2tog, k2. (37(39:43:43:43:43) sts)
Next row P2, ssp, p to last 4 sts, p2tog, p2. (35(37:41:41:41:41) sts)
Cont in fully fashioned shaping as set, dec at each end of next 0(0:0:0:3:3) rows. (35(37:41:41:35:35) sts)
Cont in st st and work a further 12(12:8:12:17:19) rows without shaping, ending with a p row.
Next row K2, ssk, k to last 4 sts, k2tog, k2. (33(35:39:39:33:33) sts)
Next and all foll alt rows P.
Cont in fully fashioned shaping as set, dec at each end of next 12(13:15:14:11:11) rows. (9(9:9:11:11:11) sts)
P 1 row.
Break off yarn. Place rem 9(9:9:11:11:11) sts on a stitch holder and set aside.

EDGING
With RS facing, using 6mm (UK4/US10) circular needles and starting at right side cast-on edge, pick up and k 84(88:88:92:93:98) sts evenly along, k 3[4:4:5:6:7] sts from top of first sleeve, k23(23:25:25:27:29) sts from back of neck, k 3[4:4:5:6:7] sts from top of second sleeve, pick up and k 84(88:88:92:93:98) sts evenly along left side front edge. (197[207:209:219:225:239] sts)
Row 1 (WS) P1, [k1, p1] to end.
Row 2 K1, [p1, k1] to end.
Last 2 rows set 1 x 1 rib.
Row 3 Rep Row 1.
Place 3(3:3:4:4:5) markers evenly spaced along edging thus far, between marker and right front cast-on edge to denote where buttonholes will be placed.
Remove original marker from right front, so only buttonhole markers rem.
Row 4 [Rib to marker, yo, ssk] 3(3:3:4:4:5) times, rib to end.
Work 2 more rows in rib.
Cast off kwise.

FINISHING
Block as given on yarn ballband instructions. Sew on buttons to match with the placement of buttonholes. Join sleeve and side seams and darn in ends.

Cable hat

This cabled hat knits up in next to no time, in a cosy aran-weight yarn. The pattern covers a variety of sizes, and you can also make it a little longer above the brim if you prefer more of a slouchy finish at the top.

FINISHED SIZE To fit 8–11 years (12–14 years:Small adult:Large adult)
To fit head circumference: 48(53:57:61)cm /19(21:22½:24]in
Actual head circumference: 41(45.5:50:54.5)cm/16½(18:20:22)in
TECHNIQUES USED Cable cast-on **p.55**, Increasing **p.92**, Slip, slip, knit **p.100**, Decreases **p.99**, Cable 4 back, **p.111**

MATERIALS REQUIRED

- **Yarn:** Lion Brand Wool Ease (80% acrylic, 20% wool) 85g (180m/197yd)
  115 Blue Mist x 1 (2:2:2)

- **Needles:** 1 pair of 4mm (UK8/US6) needles
  1 pair of 4.5mm (UK7/US7) needles

- **Tension:** 22 sts and 26 rows to 10cm (4in) square over C8B cable patt using 4.5mm (UK7/US7) needles

- **Abbreviations:** See p.89

- **Special abbreviations:**
  C8B – slip next 4 sts to cable needle and hold at back of work, k4, then k4 from cable needle
  C4B – slip next 2 sts to cable needle and hold at back of work, k2, then k2 from cable needle
  Tw2B – knit into back of 2nd st on left needle, then knit into front of first st, then slip both sts off left needle together

PATTERN

Using 4mm (UK8/US6) needles, cast on 74(82:90:98) sts using cable cast-on.
Row 1 (RS) P2, [k2, p2] to end.
Row 2 (WS) K2, [p2, k2] to end.
Last 2 rows set rib. Cont in rib until work measures 11.5(11.5:13:14)cm/4½(4½:5: 5½)in, ending with a RS row.
Next row *K2, p2, [inc] twice, p2, rep from * to last 2 sts, k2. (92(102:112:122) sts)
Change to 4.5mm (UK7/US7) needles.
Row 1 (RS) P2, [work as chart] to end.
Row 2 K2, [work as chart] to end.
Rep last 2 rows until work measures 20.5(22:26:30)cm/8(8¾:10¼:11¾)in, ending after chart row 6.
Shape top
Row 1 (RS) P2, *k2, [k2tog] twice, k2, p2, rep from * to end. (74(82:90:98) sts)
Rows 2 and 4 K2, [p6, k2] to end.
Row 3 P2, [k6, p2] to end.
Row 5 P2tog, [k6, p2tog] to end. (64(71:78:85) sts)
Rows 6 and 8 K1, [p6, k1] to end.
Row 7 P1, [C6B, p1] to end.
Row 9 P1, *k1, [k2tog] twice, k1, p1, rep from * to end. (46(51:56:61) sts)
Rows 10, 12 and 14 K1, [p4, k1] to end.
Row 13 P1, [C4B, p1] to end.
Row 15 P1, *[k2tog] twice, p1, rep from * to end. (28(31:34:37) sts)
Rows 16 and 18 K1, [p2, k1] to end.
Row 17 P1, [Tw2B, p1] to end.
Row 19 P1, [s2 kwise, k1, p2sso] to end. (10(11:12:13) sts)

FINISHING

Cut yarn leaving a long end. Thread into a darning needle and draw through rem sts. Use this end to join row-end edge seams with RS facing, using mattress stitch. Block as given on yarn ballband instructions.

CHART

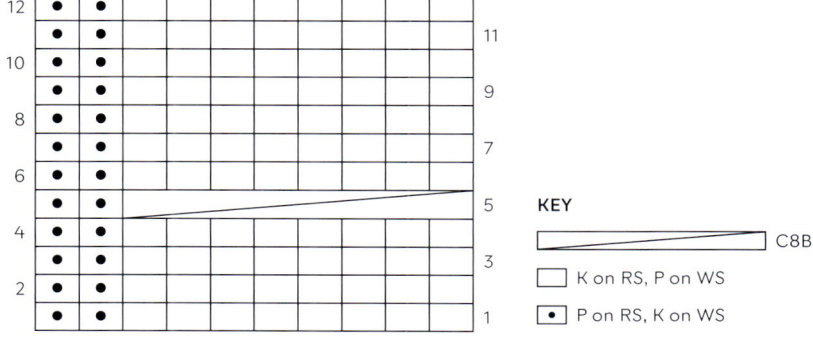

Striped jumper

Stripes are never out of fashion and are a great way to explore working with colour. This design features stripes that highlight the raglan sleeves and tie in with the bands at the hem. With a relaxed, unisex fit, it's easy to pull on and enjoy as a warm, woolly classic for adults.

FINISHED SIZE To fit an adult: Medium (Extra large:Extra extra extra large), Garment chest size M (XL:XXXL): 107cm (42in) (120cm (47¼in):133.5cm (52½in)), Length to shoulder M (XL:XXXL): 76cm (30in) (78cm (30¾in):80cm (31½in)), Sleeve length (from cuff to underarm), M (XL:XXXL): 54cm (21¼in) (55cm (21¾in): 56cm (22in))
TECHNIQUES USED Knit-on cast-on **p.54**, Stocking stitch **p.76**, Paired decreases **p.106**, Simple increases **p.92**, Mattress stitch **p.188**

MATERIALS REQUIRED

- **Yarn:** West Yorkshire Spinners The Croft Aran (100% Shetland Islands wool) 100g (166m/182yd)
  A: Melby x 8(9:9)
  B: Tirvister x 1

- **Needles:** 1 pair of 4.5mm (UK7/US7) needles
  1 pair of 5mm (UK6/US8) needles

- **Tension:** 18 sts and 24 rows to 10cm (4in) over st st using 5mm (UK6/US8) needles

- **Abbreviations:** See p.89

PATTERN

BACK
Using 4.5mm (UK7/US7) needles and A, cast on 98(110:122) sts.
Rib row 1 (RS) K2, [p2, k2] to end.
Rib row 2 P2, [k2, p2] to end.
Rep these 2 rows 4 more times.
Change to 5mm (UK6/US8) needles.
Beg with a k row cont in st st and stripes of [8 rows A, 4 rows B] 3 times, then cont in A only until back measures 45(46:47)cm (17¾(18:18½)in) from cast-on edge, ending with a WS row.
Shape raglan armholes as foll:
Cast off 6(7:8) sts at beg of next 2 rows. (86:96:106) sts)
1st and 2nd sizes only
Next row (RS) K2, s1 k1 psso, k to last 4 sts, k2tog, k2.
Next row P to end.
Next row K to end.
Next row P to end.
Rep last 4 rows 3(1:–) more times. (78(92:106) sts)
All sizes
Next row (RS) K2, s1 k1, psso, k to last 4 sts, k2tog.
Next row P to end ******.
Rep last 2 rows 23(28:33) more times.
Leave rem 30(34:38) sts on a holder.

FRONT
Work as given for back to ******.
Rep last 2 rows 14(19:24) more times. (48(52:56) sts)
Shape front neck
Next row (RS) K2, s1 k1, psso, k13, s1 k1, psso, turn and work on these sts for first side of front neck. (17 sts)
Next row P to end.
Next row K2, s1 k1 psso, k to last 2 sts, s1 k1, psso.
Rep last 2 rows 5 more times. (5 sts)
Next row P to end.
Next row K2, s1 k1 psso, k1. (4 sts)
Next row P to end.
Next row K2, s1 k1 psso. (3 sts)
Next row P3, leave these sts on a holder. With RS facing place centre 10(14:18) sts on a holder, rejoin yarn to rem sts, k2tog, k to last 4 sts, k2tog, k2. (17 sts)
Next row P to end.
Next row K2tog, k to last 4 sts, k2tog, k2.
Rep last 2 rows 5 more times. (5 sts)
Next row P to end.
Next row K1, k2tog, k2. (4 sts)
Next row P to end.
Next row K1, k2tog. (3 sts)
Next row P3, leave these sts on a holder.

SLEEVES

With 4.5mm (UK7/US7) needles and A, cast on 46(50:54) sts.
Rib row 1 (RS) K2, [p2, k2] to end.
Rib row 2 P2, [k2, p2] to end.
Rep these 2 rows 4 more times.
Change to 5mm (UK6/US8) needles.
Beg with a k row work in st st.
Work 4 rows.
Inc row (RS) K4, m1, k to last 4 sts, m1, k4.
Work 9 rows.
Rep last 10 rows 9 more times and the inc row again. (68(72:76) sts)
Cont straight until sleeve measures 54(55:56)cm/21¼(21¾:22)in) from cast-on edge, ending with a WS row.
Shape raglan top
Cast off 6(7:8) sts at beg of next 2 rows. 56(58:60) sts.
Work foll in stripes of [8 rows A, 4 rows B] 3 times, then cont in A only; at the same time, work the shaping as foll:
Next row (RS) K2, s1 k1 psso, k to last 4 sts, k2tog, k2.
Next row P to end.
Next row K to end.
Next row P to end.
Rep last 4 rows 10 more times. (34(36:38) sts)
Next row K2, s1 k1 psso, k to last 4 sts, k2tog, k2.
Next row P to end.
Rep last 2 rows 9(10:11) more times.
Leave rem 14 sts on a holder.

NECKBAND

Block the pieces, then join raglan seams using mattress stitch.
With RS facing, using 4.5mm (UK7/US7) needles and A work across left sleeve, front, right sleeve, and back as foll:
Row 1 K12, s1 k1 psso across sts of left sleeve, k2tog, k1, from left front holder, pick up and k 13 sts down left side of front neck, k10(14:18) sts from front centre neck holder, pick up and k 13 sts up right side of front neck, s1 k1 psso, k1, from right front holder, k2tog, k10, s1 k1 psso across sts of right sleeve, k2tog, k28(32:36) sts from back neck holder. (94(102:110) sts)
Rib row 1 (WS) P2, [k2, p2] to end.
Rib row 2 K2, [p2, k2] to end.
These 2 rows form the rib.
Work a further 5 rows in rib.
Cast off in rib.

FINISHING

Join side and sleeve seams. Darn in all ends. Lightly re-block, paying close attention to seams.

The neckband is knitted last after picking up the stitches on the various stitch holders. Its ribbing is stretchy so it's comfortable to get over heads but springs back, making a close fit at the neck.

The neat stripe pattern creates visual interest while maintaining clean, even lines across the fabric. The ribbed cuff creates a tidy, professional finish.

A well-constructed shoulder seam lies flat and maintains the garment's shape and drape.

Baby cardigan

This simple pattern uses basic knit and purl stitches with light shaping. Traditionally cardigan buttons sit on the left for girls, right for boys, but you can choose either. The moss stitch edge is a neat finish and prevents curling.

FINISHED SIZE Premature, (Newborn:0–3 months:3–6 months:6–9 months:9–12 months)
To fit chest: 30½(38:44½:48:52:54½)cm/12¼(15¼:17¾:19¼:20¾:21¾)in
Actual chest: 30.5(38:44.5:48:52:54.5)cm/12(15:17½:19:20½:21½)in
TECHNIQUES USED Long-tail cast-on **p.57**, Single cast-on **p.53**, Purl two together **p.99**, Slip, slip, knit **p.100**, Picking up sts **p.168**

MATERIALS REQUIRED

- **Yarn**: Drops Baby Merino Uni Colour (100% Merino wool) 50g (175m/191yd) 43 Light Sea Green x 2(2:3:3:3:4)

- **Needles:** 1 pair of 3.25mm (UK9/US3) needles
1 pair of 2.75mm (UK12/US2) needles

- **Notions:** 4(4:4:5:5:5) buttons
1 stitch holder

- **Tension:** 32 sts x 40 rows to 10cm (4in) over st st using 3.25mm (UK9/US3) needles

- **Abbreviations:** See p.89

PATTERN

BACK
Using 2.75mm (UK12/US2) needles, cast on 51(63:73:79:85:89) sts using double cast-on.
**Row 1 (RS) K1, [p1, k1] to end.
Row 2 Rep row 1.
Last 2 rows set moss st. Cont in moss st for a further 8 rows, ending with a WS row. Change to 3.25mm (UK9/US3) needles.
Row 11 (RS) K.
Row 12 P.
Last 2 rows set st st. Cont in st st until work measures 11(13:13:15:17:19)cm/ 4½(5:5:6:6¾:7½)in, ending with a WS row.**
Shape armholes
Next row (RS) K2, ssk, k to last 4 sts, k2tog, k2. (49(61:71:77:83:87) sts)
Next row (WS) P2, p2togtbl, p to last 4 sts, ssp, p2. (47(59:69:75:81:85) sts)
Cont dec in patt as set for a further 1(2:2:3:3:3) rows. (45(55:65:69:75:79) sts)
Cont in st st without shaping until armholes measure 7(8:11:11:12:12)cm/ 2¾(3:4½:4½:4¾:4¾)in, ending with a WS row.
Shape shoulders
Next row (RS) Cast off 5(7:9:9:10:10) sts kwise, k to end. (40(48:56:60:65:69) sts)
Next row Cast off 5(7:9:9:10:10) sts pwise, p to end. (35(41:47:51:55:59) sts)
Next row Cast off 5(8:10:10:10:11) sts kwise, k to end. (30(33:37:41:45:48) sts)
Next row Cast off 5(8:10:10:10:11) sts pwise, p to end. (25(25:27:31:35:37) sts)
Place rem 25(25:27:31:35:37) sts on a stitch holder.

LEFT FRONT
Using 2.75mm (UK12/US2) needles, cast on 23(29:35:37:41:43) sts using double cast-on.
Work as given for back from ** to **.
Shape armhole
Next row (RS) K2, ssk, k to end. (22(28:34:36:40:42) sts)
Next row P to last 4 sts, p2togtbl, p2. (21(27:33:35:39:41) sts)
Cont dec in patt as set at armhole edge only for a further 1(2:2:3:3:3) rows. (20(25:31:32:36:38) sts)
Cont in st st without shaping until armhole measures 4(5:7:7:7:7)cm/ 1½(2:2¾:2¾:2¾:2¾)in, ending with a RS row.
Shape neck
Next row (WS) Cast off 5(5:5:6:7:8) sts pwise, p to end. (15(20:26:26:29:30) sts)
Next row K to last 4 sts, k2tog, k2. (14(19:25:25:28:29) sts)
Next row P2, p2tog, p to end. (13(18:24:24:27:28) sts).
Cont dec in patt as set by prev 2 rows for a further 4(4:4:4:4:4) rows. (9(14:20:20:23:24) sts)
Cont in st st and dec in patt at neck edge as set, dec on next row 0(0:1:1:1:1) times and every foll alt row 0(0:0:0:2:2) times. (9(14:19:19:20:21) sts)
Cont in st st without shaping until

armhole measures 7(8:11:11:12:12)cm/ 2¾(3:4½:4½:4¾:4¾)in, ending with a WS row.
Shape shoulder
Next row (RS) Cast off 5(7:9:9:10:10) sts kwise, k to end. (4(7:10:10:10:11) sts)
Next row P.
Cast off rem sts kwise.

RIGHT FRONT
Using 2.75mm (UK12/US2) needles, cast on 23(29:35:37:41:43) sts using double cast-on.
Work as given for back from ** to **.
Shape armhole
Next row (RS) K to last 4 sts, k2tog, k2. (22(28:34:36:40:42) sts)
Next row P2, p2tog, p to end. (21(27:33:35:39:41) sts)
Cont dec in patt as set at armhole edge only for a further 1(2:2:3:3:3) rows. (20(25:31:32:36:38) sts)
Cont in st st without shaping until armholes measure 4(5:7:7:7:7)cm/ 1½(2:2¾:2¾:2¾:2¾)in, ending with a WS row.
Shape neck
Next row (RS) Cast off 5(5:5:6:7:8) sts kwise, k to end. (15(20:26:26:29:30) sts)
Next row P to last 4 sts, p2tog, p2. (14(19:25:25:28:29) sts)
Next row K2, k2tog, k to end. (13(18:24:24:27:28) sts)
Cont dec in patt as set by prev 2 rows for a further 4(4:4:4:4:4) rows. (9(14:20:20:23:24) sts)
Cont in st st and dec in patt at neck edge as set, dec on next row 0(0:1:1:1:1) times and every foll alt row 0(0:0:0:2:2) times. (9(14:19:19:20:21) sts)
Cont in st st without shaping until armhole measures 7(8:11:11:12:12)cm/ 2¾(3:4½:4½:4¾:4¾)in, ending with a RS row.
Shape shoulder
Next row (WS) Cast off 5(7:9:9:10:10) sts pwise, p to end. (4(7:10:10:10:11) sts)
Next row K.
Cast off rem sts pwise.

SLEEVES
Using 2.75mm (UK12/US2) needles, cast on 37(43:47:47:47:51) sts using double cast-on.
Row 1 (RS) K1, [p1, k1] to end.
Row 2 Rep row 1.
Last 2 rows set moss st. Cont in moss st for a further 8 rows, ending with a WS row.
Change to 3.25mm (UK9/US3) needles.
Row 11 (RS) K.
Row 12 P.
Last 2 rows set st st. Cont in st st for a further 2 rows.
Row 15 K2, M1R, k to last 2 sts, M1L, k2. (39(45:49:49:49:53) sts)
Cont in st st and inc as set by prev row, inc at each end of 1(4:5:6:5:6) foll alt(6th:8th:6th:4th:6th) rows and then 3(0:0:1:4:3) foll 4th(0:0:8th:6th:8th) rows. (47(53:59:63:67:71) sts)
Cont in st st without shaping until sleeve measures 9(12:16:17:18:20)cm/ 3½(4¾:6¼:6¾:7:8)in, ending with a WS row.
Shape head of sleeve
Next row (RS) K2, ssk, k to last 4 sts, k2tog, k2. (45(51:57:61:65:69) sts)
Next row P2, p2tog, p to last 4 sts, ssp, p2. (43(49:55:59:63:67) sts)
Cont shaping as set by prev 2 rows for a further 1(2:2:3:3:3) rows. (41(45:51:53:57:61) sts)
P 1(0:0:1:1:1) row.
Next row (RS) Cast off 4(2:3:2:3:3) sts kwise, k to end. (37(43:48:51:54:58) sts)
Next row Cast off 4(2:3:2:3:3) sts pwise, p to end. (33 41:45:49:51:55) sts)
Rep last 2 rows 3(0:3:0:5:4) times, ending with a WS row. (9(41:27:49:21:31) sts)

Use mattress stitch to join armhole seams, creating an invisible seam that lies flat and maintains the garment's shape.

When picking up stitches around a neckline, adjust your pickup ratio as you work around curves – pick up fewer stitches on tighter curves and more on straight edges to create a smooth, well-fitting neckband.

It's essential that buttons are not sewn on too tightly (see Sewing on a button, p.197), so they sit neatly when fastened.

1st size only
Cast off.
2nd, 3rd, 4th and 5th sizes only
Next row (RS) Cast off –(3:4:3:4:4) sts kwise, k to end. (38:23:46:17:27) sts
Next row Cast off –(3:4:3:4:4] sts pwise, p to end. (35:19:43:13:23) sts)
Rep last 2 rows –(4:1:5:0:1) times, ending with a WS row. (11:11:13:13:15) sts)
Cast off rem sts kwise.

NECKBAND
Join shoulder seams. With RS facing and using 2.75mm (UK12/US2) needles, pick up and k 21(21:23:23:29:31) sts along right front neck, k across 25(25:27:31:35:37) sts from stitch holder on back, pick up and k 21(21:23:23:29:31) sts along left front neck. (67(67:73:77:93:99) sts)
**Row 1 (WS) S1, [p1, k1] to last 2 sts, p2.
Row 2 Rep row 1.
Last 2 rows set moss st. Cont in moss st for a further 5 rows.
Cast off.**

LEFT FRONT BORDER
With RS facing and using 2.75mm (UK12/US2) needles, pick up and k 4 sts along neckband, 39(45:51:57:61:67) sts along front edge, 6 sts along moss st edging. (47(55:61:67:71:77) sts)
For a girl
Work as given for Neckband from ** to **.
For a boy
Row 1 (WS) S1, [p1, k1] to last 2 sts, p2
Rows 2 and 3 Rep row 1.
Rows 1 and 2 set moss st. Cont in moss st patt as set, work buttonholes as foll:
Row 4 (WS) Patt 3(3:2:2:2:3), yfwd, ssk, [patt 11(14:16:13:15:16), yfwd, ssk] 3(3:3:4:4:4) times, patt to end.
Work 3 more rows in moss st.
Cast off kwise.

RIGHT FRONT BORDER
With RS facing and using 2.75mm (UK12/US2) needles, pick up and k 4 sts along neckband, 39(45:51:57:61:67) sts along front edge, 6 sts along moss st edging. (49(55:61:67:71:77) sts)

For a boy
Work as given for Neckband from ** to **.
For a girl
Row 1 (WS) S1, [p1, k1] to last 2 sts, p2.
Rows 2 and 3 Rep row 1.
Rows 1 and 2 set moss st. Cont in moss st patt as set, work buttonholes as foll:
Row 4 (WS) Patt 2(2:2:3:2:3), yfwd, ssk, [patt 11(14:16:13:15:16), yfwd, ssk] 3(3:3:4:4:4) times, patt to end.
Work 2 more rows in moss st.
Cast off kwise.

FINISHING
Block as given on yarn ballband instructions. Sew on buttons to match buttonholes. Join seams and sew in ends.

Baby blanket

A super-soft, fabric-backed blanket for a new baby is always a welcome gift. A garter-stitch edging frames this ridge-stitch blanket and also serves as a way of securing the fabric neatly on one side. Enjoy choosing the yarn colour and fabric combinations for this cute baby knit.

FINISHED SIZE 70 x 90cm (27½ x 35½in) approx.
TECHNIQUES USED Cable cast-on **p.55**, Garter stitch **p.76**, Blocking **p.185**

MATERIALS REQUIRED

- **Yarn**: Sirdar Snuggly Cashmere Merino (33% acrylic, 27% wool, 10% cashmere) 50g (130m/142yd)
  472 Corn x 8

- **Needle**: 4mm (UK8/US6) circular needle 70cm (27½in) long

- **Notions**: Backing fabric 68 x 88cm (26¾ x 34½in)
  Sharp needle and sewing thread

- **Tension**: 21 sts and 28 rows to 10cm (4in) over st st using 4mm (UK8/US6) needles
  21 sts and 38 rows to 10cm (4in) over ridge stitch using 4mm (UK8/US6) needles

- **Abbreviations**: See p.89

PATTERN

Using 4mm (UK8/US6) circular needle cast on 147 sts using cable cast-on.

EDGING

Work 8 rows (4 ridges) of g st with chain edging.
Row 1 S1 pwise wyif, k to last st, k1 tbl.

MAIN BLANKET

Ridge stitch with g st border and chain edging.
Row 1 (RS) S1 pwise wyif, k4, p1, k to last 6 sts, p1, k4, k1 tbl.
Row 2 S1 pwise wyif, k5, p to last 6 sts, k5, k1 tbl.
Row 3 S1 pwise wyif, k4, p1, (k1, yo, s1) to last 7 sts, k1, p1, k4, k1 tbl.
Row 4 S1 pwise wyif, k5, (p1, k2tog) to last 7 sts, p1, k5, k1 tbl.
These 4 rows set ridge patt. Cont rep rows 1–4 until work measures 87.5cm (34½in), ending with patt row 1.
Work 8 rows (4 ridges) of g st with chain edging as before.
Cast off. Darn in loose ends.
Pin out and block to size using a hot iron over a damp cloth.

FABRIC BACKING

Turn under 1.5cm (¾in) around all edges of backing fabric and press along edges. With WS together, pin then tack backing fabric to knitted blanket, leaving garter border uncovered. Slip stitch in place.

The blanket fabric backing's edge neatly fits with the garter stitch border, so there are no holes for little fingers to get caught up in.

Teddy bear

Knitted in an eyelash yarn (see p.19) to create an all-over fur effect, teddy is super cuddly and machine washable – although the furry fibre can make it tricky to see your stitches. Tension does not need to be precise, providing your stitches are tight enough that stuffing doesn't poke through them later.

FINISHED SIZE 34cm (13½in) from top of head to soles of feet, approx 16.5cm (6½in) wide at waist
TECHNIQUES USED Knit-on cast-on **p.54**, Simple decreases **p.99**, Knit into front and back of stitch **p.92**, Mattress stitch **p.188**

MATERIALS REQUIRED

- **Yarn**: King Cole Cuddles Chunky (100% polyester) 50g (125m/137yd) 300 Teddy brown x 2

- **Needles**: 1 pair of 3.5mm (UK9–10/US4) needles

- **Notions**: Pair of 12mm safety toy eyes
  12mm safety toy nose
  Washable toy stuffing
  Locking stitch markers (optional)

- **Tension**: 17.5 sts and 27 rows to 10cm (4in) over st st using 3.5mm (UK9–10/US4) needles

- **Abbreviations**: See p.89

PATTERN

BODY
Worked from bottom to neck edge.
Using 3.5mm (UK9–10/US4) needles, cast on 12 sts using knit-on cast-on.
Row 1 (WS) [Kfb] to end. (24 sts)
Row 2 and all foll alt rows P.
Row 3 [K1, kfb] to end. (36 sts)
Row 5 K.
Row 7 [K2, kfb] to end. (48 sts)
Row 9 K.
Row 11 [K3, kfb] to end. (60 sts)
Row 13 K.
Last 2 rows set reverse st st. Cont in reverse st st for a further 21 rows.
Row 35 [K4, k2tog] to end. (50 sts)
Row 37 K.
Row 39 [K3, k2tog] to end. (40 sts)
Work a further 19 rows in st st without shaping.
Row 59 [K2, k2tog] to end. (30 sts)
Row 61 [K1, k2tog] to end. (20 sts)
Row 63 [K2tog] to end. 10 sts.
Cut yarn leaving a long tail, and thread through rem sts using a blunt-ended darning needle. Fasten off.

ARM (MAKE 2)
Worked from paw to shoulder edge.
Using 3.5mm (UK9–10/US4) needles, cast on 9 sts using knit-on cast-on.
Row 1 (WS) [Kfb] to end. (18 sts)
Row 2 and all foll alt rows P.
Row 3 [K2, kfb] to end. (24 sts)

Row 5 K.
Last 2 rows set reverse st st. Cont in reverse st st for a further 5 rows.
Row 11 K2tog, k to last 2 sts, k2tog. (22 sts)
Rows 13 and 15 K.
Rep last 6 rows once more. (20 sts)
Shape shoulder
Row 23 (WS) Cast off 4 sts, k to end. (16 sts)
Row 24 Cast off 4 sts, p to end. (12 sts)

The arm is cast on at the paw edge and decreased at a slow rate to create a taper towards the shoulder. Stitch the arm on at the cast-on edge, adding a little more stuffing as you bring your stitching to a close.

Row 25 Ssk, k to last 2 sts, k2tog. (10 sts)
Row 26 Ssp, p to past 2 sts, p2tog. (8 sts)
Rep last 2 rows once more. (4 sts)
Cast off.

LEG (MAKE 2)
Worked from sole to hip edge.
Using 3.5mm (UK9–10/US4) needles, cast on 14 sts using knit-on cast-on. Place a marker between 7th and 8th st on cast-on edge.
Row 1 (WS) [Kfb] to end. (28 sts)
Row 2 and all foll alt rows P.
Row 3 K8, [kfb, k1] 5 times, k to end. (33 sts)
Row 5 K8, [kfb, k2] 5 times, k to end. (38 sts)
Row 7 K.
Last 2 rows set reverse st st. Cont in reverse st st for a further 3 rows.
Row 11 K8, [k2tog, k2] 5 times, k to end. (33 sts)
Row 13 K8, [k2tog, k1] 5 times, k to end. (28 sts)
Starting with a p row, work 15 rows in reverse st st.
Cast off, placing markers between 7th and 8th and between 21st and 22nd sts.

HEAD
Worked from back of head to tip of nose.
Using 3.5mm (UK9–10/US4) needles, cast on 8 sts using knit-on cast-on.
Row 1 (WS) [Kfb] to end. (16 sts)
Row 2 and all foll alt rows P.
Row 3 [K1, kfb] to end. (24 sts)
Row 5 [K2, kfb] to end. (32 sts)
Row 7 [K3, kfb] to end. (40 sts)
Row 9 K.
Row 11 [K4, kfb] to end. (48 sts)
Row 13 K.
Row 15 [K5, kfb] to end. (56 sts)
Row 17 K.
Last 2 rows set reverse st st. Cont in reverse st st for a further 13 rows.
Row 31 [K5, k2tog] to end. (48 sts)
Row 33 [K4, k2tog] to end. (40 sts)
Place marker between 20th and 21st st.
Starting with a p row, work 7 rows in reverse st st.
Row 41 [K3, k2tog] to end. (32 sts)
Row 43 K.
Row 45 [K2, k2tog] to end. (24 sts)
Row 47 [K1, k2tog] to end. (16 sts)
Row 49 [K2tog] to end. (8 sts)
Cut yarn leaving a long tail and draw through rem sts to fasten off.

EAR (MAKE 2)
Worked from top of ear downwards.
Using 3.5mm (UK9–10/US4) needles, cast on 16 sts using knit-on cast-on.
Row 1 (RS) K.
Rows 2 and 3 Rep row 1.
Row 4 [K2tog] to end. (8 sts).
Cut yarn leaving a long tail. Draw yarn through rem sts and pull tight.

FINISHING
Join row-end edge seam on body using mattress stitch and stuff firmly. Gather cast-on edge and pull tight. Fasten off.

Safety eyes and nose have a secure washer fastening that prevents them coming loose, but if knitting for babies and toddlers use embroidery for embellishment instead.

While leg seam will sit at the back, the leg needs to be folded across the top edge and stitched flat before joining to the underside of the body so Teddy can sit upright.

For arm seam, first gather up cast-on sts and pull tight. Cont stitching up row-end edge seam to first set of cast-off rows, leaving shoulder edge open. Stuff, then stitch arms to body, positioning row-end edge of arm seam against body.

Fold leg at marker on cast-on edge and stitch cast-on edges together. Join row-end edge seam. Stuff foot firmly and leg lightly. Folding at markers on cast-off edge, stitch edge closed and stitch legs to underside of body with row-end edge seam facing downwards. Join row-end edge seam on head to cast-on edge, stuff lightly and place toy eyes equidistant from marker. Place nose at cast-off sts. Stuff firmly and gather up cast-on edge sts to close. Work a row of running stitch around muzzle to accentuate shaping. Stitch head to body.

Stitch row-end edge of each ear to head.

Sewing on the ears with a slight curve to the joining seam will ensure that they stand prominently tall in a pleasing cup shape.

Teddy will be well-loved; to keep knitted toys looking their best, stuff firmly to prevent them looking a little deflated as they get older.

Child's Fair Isle bobble hat

Make a colourful statement with this vibrant bobble hat. Use the stranded colourwork technique to create a striking, patterned child's hat. You can make the pom-pom from a cardboard cut-out (see p.212)

FINISHED SIZE To fit a child's head (approx. 43cm/17in) in circumference), suitable for ages 5–9.
TECHNIQUES USED Twisted double cast-on **p.60**, Stocking stitch **p.76**, Charted colourwork **p.122**, Stranded colourwork **p.123**, Pom-poms **p.212**

MATERIALS REQUIRED
- **Yarn:** King Cole Merino Blend DK (100% wool) 50g (112m/123yd)
  A: 1985 Adriatic x 2
  B: 1988 Redwood x 1
  C: 855 Mustard x 1

- **Needles:** 1 pair of 3.25mm (UK10/US3) needles
  1 pair of 4mm (UK8/US6) needles

- **Notions:** Pom-pom maker (optional)

- **Tension:** 22 sts and 28 rows to 10cm (4in) square over st st using 4mm (UK8/US6) needles

- **Abbreviations:** See p.89

PATTERN
Using A and 3.25mm (UK10/US3) needles, cast on 111 sts using twisted double cast-on.
Row 1 (RS) K1, [p1, k1] to end.
Row 2 P1, [k1, p1] to end.
Rep last 2 rows 11 more times. Change to 4mm (UK8/US6) needles. Beginning on a k row, work in st st for 4 rows.
Cont in st st and work in patt, stranding yarn not in use loosely across WS of work, reading chart from right to left on RS (k) rows and from left to right on WS (p) rows, thus:
Row 1 (RS) K1 st from A to B, rep 6 sts from B to C to last 2 sts, k2 sts from C to D.
Row 2 P2 sts from D to C, rep 6 sts from C to B to last st, p1 st from B to A.
Cont until all 19 patt rows have been worked.
Cont with B only, st st 7 rows beg p row.
Shape crown
Row 1 K3, [ssk, k4] to end. (93 sts)
P 1 row.
Row 3 K3, [ssk, k3] to end. (75 sts)
P 1 row.
Row 5 K3, [ssk, k2] to end. (57 sts)
P 1 row.
Row 7 K3, [ssk, k1] to end. (39 sts)
P 1 row.
Row 9 K3, [ssk] to end. (21 sts)
P 1 row.
Break yarn, thread through remaining sts and fasten off securely.

FINISHING
Join the back seam and darn in loose ends. Make a pom-pom about 8cm (3¼in) diameter and attach securely to the top of the hat.

CHART

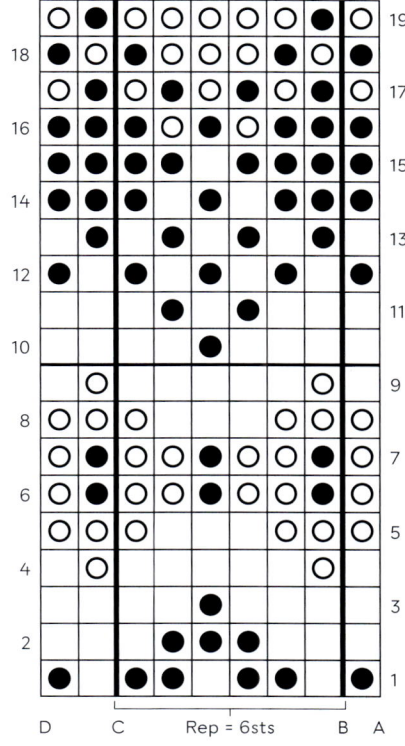

Mesh tote bag

This stylish reusable shopper is made in a sturdy mercerized cotton for strength and durability, so it's perfect for all kinds of goodies when you hit the shops. Knitted in a flexible mesh lace stitch, it's very stretchy and has a knitted-in handle for less hassle at sewing-up stage.

FINISHED SIZE Approx. 46.5 x 38cm (18 x 15in) not including handles
TECHNIQUES USED Knit-on cast-on **p.54**, Single cast-on **p.53**, Backwards loop cast-on **p.55**, Purl two together **p.99**, Slip, slip, knit **p.100**, Yarnover increases **p.96**

MATERIALS REQUIRED

- **Yarn**: Sirdar Cotton DK (100% cotton) 100g (212m/232yd)
  543 Sunshine x 2 ball

- **Needles**: 1 pair of 3.5mm (UK9/US4) needles
  1 pair of 2.75mm (UK12/US2) needles

- **Tension**: 15 sts x 25 rows to 10 cm (4in) over lace patt using 3.5mm (UK9/US4) needles

- **Abbreviations**: See p.89

PATTERN

SIDE PIECE (MAKE 2)
Using 3.5mm (UK9/US4) needles, cast on 70 sts using knit-on cast-on.
Row 1 (WS) K2, *yo, ssk; rep from * last 2 sts, k2.
Row 2 P4, *yrn, p2tog; rep from * to last 2 sts, p2.
Last 2 rows set lace patt. Cont in patt as set until work measures 38cm (15in), ending with a WS row.
Next row [Ssk] to end. (35 sts)
Cast off pwise.

UPPER EDGING
Using 2.75mm (UK12/US2) needles, and with RS facing, pick up and k 70 sts along cast-on edge.

Row 1 (WS) K.
Row 2 K.
Last 2 rows set g st. Cont in g st for a further 9 rows, ending with a WS row.
Row 12 (RS) K17, cast off 36 sts, k to end. (34 sts)
Row 13 K17, cast on 96 sts using backwards loop cast-on, k to end. (130 sts)
Cont in g st for a further 9 rows.
Cast off kwise.

FINISHING
Darn in ends. With right sides facing, join row-end and cast-on edge using mattress stitch. Block lightly as given by yarn ballband instructions.

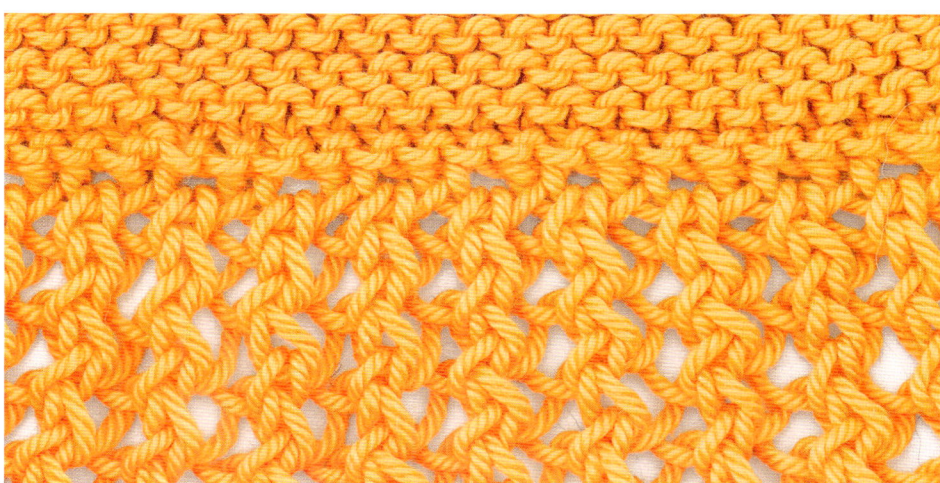

Picking up stitches for the edging means you change direction to knit upwards from the bottom. This creates an attractive join between the main body and the edging.

Beaded headband

This stylish headband features purpose-made washable knitting beads incorporated in stretchy rib fabric. The standout feature is a dramatic cable twist positioned at centre front, creating an eye-catching focal point. The ribbing ensures a secure fit and the beading adds some elegant detailing.

FINISHED SIZE To fit 8–11 years(12–14 years:Small adult:Large adult)
To fit head circumference: 48(53:58½:62)cm /19(21:23:24½)in
Actual head circumference: 40.5(45.5:51:55)cm/16(18:20:21¾)in
TECHNIQUES USED Knit cast-on **p.54**, Chain selvedge **p.171**, Slip stitch beading **p.199**, Knit into front and back of stitch **p.92**, Cables, **p.111**

MATERIALS REQUIRED

- **Yarn**: West Yorkshire Spinners Elements (60% Lyocell, 40% Falkland Islands wool) 50g (112m/122yd)
  1100 Seashell x 1(1:1:2)

- **Needles:** 1 pair of 3.25mm (UK10/US3) needles
  Cable needle

- **Notions:** 250(282:316:332) size 6 Debbie Abrahams knitting beads in colour 40 (Mink)
  Sewing needle and thread
  Blunt-ended darning needle

- **Tension:** 34 sts and 30 rows to 10cm (4in) over beaded rib patt on 3.25mm (UK10/US3) needles.

- **Abbreviations:** See p.89

- **Special abbreviations:**
  pb – place bead: Slide bead up yarn to needle, then slip next st pwise wyif, ensuring bead sits in front of work

PATTERN

Using a fine needle threaded with a loop of sewing cotton, thread 250(282:316:332) beads onto your yarn before casting on. Using 3.25mm (UK10/US3) needles, cast on 34 sts using knit cast-on.
Row 1 and all foll alt rows (WS) S1 wyif, p1, [k2, p2] to end.
Row 2 (RS) S1 wyib, k1, [p2, k2, pb, s1 wyif, k2] to end.
Row 4 S1 wyib, k1, [pb, s1 wyif, k2, p2, k2] to end.
Last 4 rows set beaded rib patt. Cont in beaded rib patt until work measures 19[21.5.24:26]cm/7½[8½:9½:10¼]in, ending after row 3.
Next row (RS) S1 wyib, k1, pb, s1 wyif, k2, p2, k2, pb, s1 wyif, k2, p2, [kfb] twice, [pb, s1 wyif, k2, p2, k2] twice. (36 sts)

Next row (WS) Slip next 18 sts onto a cable needle and hold at front of work. P2, [k2, p2] 4 times, then (p2, [k2, p2] 4 times) from cable needle.
Next row S1 wyib, k1, p2, k2, pb, s1 wyif, k2, p2, k2, pb, s1 wyif, [k2tog] twice, [p2, k2, pb, s1 wyif, k2] twice. (34 sts)
Next row Rep row 1.
Starting with row 4, work in patt until work measures 40.5[45.5:51:55]cm/16(18:20:21¾)in.
Cast off.

FINISHING

With RS facing, join cast-on and cast-off edges using mattress stitch. Block as given for yarn ballband instructions.

The beads are placed such that they sit nestled in the ridges of an all-over 2 x 2 rib pattern.

Entrelac cushion

Entrelac, from French 'entrelacer' meaning 'interlace', uses pick-up stitches and strategic shaping to create the illusion of woven fabric. This cushion's front panel is worked in one piece, starting with triangles then overlaying with triangles and rectangles in sections for this richly-textured pattern.

FINISHED SIZE Approx. 42 x 42cm (16½ x 16½in)
TECHNIQUES USED Knit-on cast-on **p.54**, Picking up stitches **p.168**, Simple decreases **p.99**, Knit into front and back of stitch **p.92**, Entrelac **p.144**

MATERIALS REQUIRED

- **Yarn**: Rowan Pure Wool Superwash Worsted (100% wool) 100g (200m/219yd)
  A: 133 Gold x 2
  B: 189 Windsor x 2

- **Needles**: 1 pair of 4.5mm (UK7/US7) needles
  Two 4mm (UK8/US6) double-pointed needles (DPNs)

- **Notions**:
  40cm (16in) zip
  40 x 40cm (16 x 16in) cushion pad or polyester stuffing

- **Tension**: 18 sts and 24 rows to 10cm (4in) over st st using 4.5mm (UK9/US4) needles

- **Abbreviations**: See p.89

- **Design note**: One pattern repeat measured diagonally over 16 sts on 4.5mm (UK7/US7) needles = 14cm (5.5in). To be worked over 3 pattern repeats, equivalent to 42cm (16.5in).

PATTERN

FRONT

Foundation triangles section
Using A and 4.5mm (UK7/US7) needles, cast on 48 st using knit-on cast-on. Work a row of base triangles as foll:
Rows 1 (RS) and 2 (WS) **K1, turn, p1, turn. (1 st worked)
Rows 3 and 4 S1 wyib, k1, turn. P2, turn. (2 sts worked)
Rows 5 and 6 S1 wyib, k2, turn. K1, p2, turn. (3 sts worked)
Rows 7 and 8 S1 wyib, k1, p1, k1, turn. K1, p3, turn. (4 sts worked)
Rows 9 and 10 S1 wyib, k2, p1, k1, turn. [K1, p1] twice, p1, turn. (5 sts worked)
Rows 11 and 12 S1 wyib, [k1, p1] twice, k1, turn. [K1, p1] twice, p2, turn. (6 sts worked)
Rows 13 and 14 S1 wyib, k2, [p1, k1] twice, turn. [K1, p1] 3 times, p1, turn. (7 sts worked)
Rows 15 and 16 S1 wyib, [k1, p1] 3 times, k1, turn. [K1, p1] 3 times, p2, turn. (8 sts worked)
Rows 17 and 18 S1 wyib, k2, [p1, k1] 3 times, turn. [K1, p1] 4 times, p1, turn. (9 sts worked)
Rows 19 and 20 S1 wyib, [k1, p1] 4 times, k1, turn. [K1, p1] 4 times, p2, turn. (10 sts worked)
Rows 21 and 22 S1 wyib, k2, [p1, k1] 4 times, turn. [K1, p1] 5 times, p1, turn. (11 sts worked)

Picking up stitches and decreasing to join rectangles creates the effective entrelac technique. Pick high-contrast colours for a bold finish.

Rows 23 and 24 S1 wyib, [k1, p1] 5 times, k1, turn. [K1, p1] 5 times, p2, turn. (12 sts worked)
Rows 25 and 26 S1 wyib, k2, [p1, k1] 5 times, turn. [K1, p1] 6 times, p1, turn. (13 sts worked)
Rows 27 and 28 S1 wyib, [k1, p1] 6 times, k1, turn. [K1, p1] 6 times, p2, turn. (14 sts worked)

Rows 29 and 30 S1 wyib, k2, [p1, k1] 6 times, turn. [K1, p1] 7 times, p1, turn. (15 sts worked)
Row 31 S1 wyib, [k1, p1] 7 times, k1. Do not turn.
Rep from ** twice more.
Break off A and join in B.
Section 1 (WS)
This row starts and ends with an edge triangle. In between, work two full rectangles using B.
(WS facing, starting with edge triangle)
Rows 1 (WS) and 2 (RS) P1, turn, kfb, turn. (2 sts, 1 st increased)
Rows 3 and 4 P1, p2tog, turn, s1 wyib, kfb, turn. (3 sts)
Rows 5 and 6 P2, p2tog, turn, s1 wyib, kfb, k1, turn. (4 sts)
Rows 7 and 8 P3, p2tog, turn, s1 wyib, k1, kfb, k1, turn. (5 sts)
Rows 9 and 10 P4, p2tog, turn, s1 wyib, k2, kfb, k1, turn. (6 sts)
Rows 11 and 12 P5, p2tog, turn, s1 wyib, k3, kfb, k1, turn. (7 sts)
Rows 13 and 14 P6, p2tog, turn, s1 wyib, k4, kfb, k1, turn. (8 sts)
Rows 15 and 16 P7, p2tog, turn, s1 wyib, k5, kfb, k1, turn. (9 sts)
Rows 17 and 18 P8, p2tog, turn, s1 wyib, k6, kfb, k1, turn. (10 sts)
Rows 19 and 20 P9, p2tog, turn, s1 wyib, k7, kfb, k1, turn. (11 sts)
Rows 21 and 22 P10, p2tog, turn, s1 wyib, k8, kfb, k1, turn. (12 sts)
Rows 23 and 24 P11, p2tog, turn, s1 wyib, k9, kfb, k1, turn. (13 sts)
Rows 25 and 26 P12, p2tog, turn, s1 wyib, k10, kfb, k1, turn. (14 sts)
Rows 27 and 28 P13, p2tog, turn, s1 wyib, k11, kfb, k1, turn. (15 sts)
Rows 29 and 30 P14, p2tog, turn, s1 wyib, k12, kfb, k1, turn. (16 sts)
Row 31 P15, p2tog, do not turn.
Pick up 15 sts pwise along edge of rectangle/triangle worked directly beneath and cont as foll to complete full rectangle, purling sts tog with triangle/rectangle from prev row on each alt row:
***Row 1 (RS)** S1 wyib, k15, turn.
Row 2 (WS) S1 wyif, p14, p2tog, turn.
Rep these 2 rows 15 times more, but do not turn after last p row. Rep from *** once more to work another rectangle.
Work end triangle
Pick up and k 15 sts pwise along edge of rectangle/triangle worked directly beneath and cont as foll:
Row 1 (RS) S1 wyib, k15, turn.
Rows 2 (WS) and 3 (RS) S1 wyif, p13, p2tog, turn, k15, turn. (15 sts)
Rows 4 and 5 S1 wyif, p12, p2tog, turn, k14, turn. (14 sts)
Rows 6 and 7 S1 wyif, p11, p2tog, turn, k13, turn. (13 sts)
Rows 8 and 9 S1 wyif, p10, p2tog, turn, k12, turn. (12 sts)
Rows 10 and 11 S1 wyif, p9, p2tog, turn, k11, turn. (11 sts)
Rows 12 and 13 S1 wyif, p8, p2tog, turn, k10, turn. (10 sts)
Rows 14 and 15 S1 wyif, p7, p2tog, turn, k9, turn. (9 sts)
Rows 16 and 17 S1 wyif, p6, p2tog, turn, k8, turn. (8 sts)
Rows 18 and 19 S1 wyif, p5, p2tog, turn, k7, turn. (7 sts)
Rows 20 and 21 S1 wyif, p4, p2tog, turn, k6, turn. (6 sts)
Rows 22 and 23 S1 wyif, p3, p2tog, turn, k5, turn. (5 sts)
Rows 24 and 25 S1 wyif, p2, p2tog, turn, k4, turn. (4 sts)
Rows 26 and 27 S1 wyif, p1, p2tog, turn, k3, turn. (3 sts)
Rows 28 and 29 P1, p2tog, turn, k2, turn. (2 sts)
Row 30 P2tog, turn. (1 st)
Break off B and join in A.
Section 2 (full row of rectangles, RS)
This row is worked as a full row of rectangles to fill spaces between each of triangles/rectangles directly below. Every alt row, work ssk tog with live sts you are working, and sts from row below. As you work through each new rectangle/triangle on this row, you will absorb sts from adjacent triangle/rectangle worked on prev row, before moving to next one.
Using A and with RS facing, k1, pick up and k 15 sts along row-end edge of triangle from end of prev row. (16 sts)
****Row 1 (WS)** S1 wyif, [k1, p1] 6 times, k1, p2.
Row 2 S1 wyib, [k1, p1) 7 times, ssk.
Row 3 S1 wyif, [p1, k1] 6 times, p3.
Row 4 S1 wyib, k1, [k1, p1] 6 times, k1, ssk.
Rep last 4 rows 7 times more. Do not turn on last rep.****
Pick up and k 16 sts along next triangle/rectangle row-end edge from prev row. Rep from **** to **** twice more.

Inserting a zip (see p.196) means your cushion cover can be removed easily for washing. Alternatively, you can fill the cover with polyester toy stuffing and stitch it closed.

Break off A and join in B.
Rep sections 1 and 2 once more, then rep section 1 again.

Finishing off row
This row completes top triangles to create a straight top edge. No full rectangles are worked on this section. Use ssk to absorb sts from triangles/rectangles worked on prev row below. When each top triangle is completed, all sts from shape on row below should have been used, leaving you free to work along next one.

Using A, with RS facing, k1, pick up and k 16 sts along row-end edge of triangle from end of prev row. (17 sts)

*****Row 1 (WS)** S1 wyif, [k1, p1] to end, turn.

Rows 2 (RS) and 3 (WS) S1 wyib, [p1, k1] 7 times, p1, ssk, turn. S1 wyif, [p1, k1] 7 times, p2tog, turn. (16 sts)

Rows 4 and 5 S1 wyib, [p1, k1] 7 times, ssk, turn. S1 wyif, [k1, p1] 6 times, k1, p2tog, turn. (15 sts)

Rows 6 and 7 S1 wyib, [p1, k1] 6 times, p1, ssk, turn. S1 wyif, [p1, k1] 6 times, p2tog, turn. (14 sts)

Rows 8 and 9 S1 wyib, [p1, k1] 6 times, ssk, turn. S1 wyif, [k1, p1] 5 times, k1, p2tog, turn. (13 sts)

Rows 10 and 11 S1 wyib, [p1, k1] 5 times, p1, ssk, turn. S1 wyif, [p1, k1] 5 times, p2tog, turn. (12 sts)

Rows 12 and 13 S1 wyib, [p1, k1] 5 times, ssk, turn. S1 wyif, [k1, p1] 4 times, k1, p2tog, turn. (11 sts)

Rows 14 and 15 S1 wyib, [p1, k1] 4 times, p1, ssk, turn. S1 wyif, [p1, k1] 4 times, p2tog, turn. (10 sts)

Rows 16 and 17 S1 wyib, [p1, k1] 4 times, ssk, turn. S1 wyif, [k1, p1] 3 times, k1, p2tog, turn. (9 sts)

Rows 18 and 19 S1 wyib, [p1, k1] 3 times, p1, ssk, turn. S1 wyif, [p1, k1] 3 times, p2tog, turn. (8 sts)

Rows 20 and 21 S1 wyib, [p1, k1] 3 times, ssk, turn. S1 wyif, [k1, p1] twice, k1, p2tog, turn. (7 sts)

Rows 22 and 23 S1 wyib, [p1, k1] twice, p1, ssk, turn. S1 wyif, [p1, k1] twice, p2tog, turn. (6 sts)

The i-cord replicates the look of traditional piping around the edge of a cushion. Leave it on the needle as you reach the finished length, so you can adjust it to fit.

Rows 24 and 25 S1 wyib, [p1, k1] twice, ssk, turn. S1 wyif, k1, p1, k1, p2tog, turn. (5 sts)

Rows 26 and 27 S1 wyib, p1, k1, p1, ssk, turn. S1 wyif, p1, k1, p2tog, turn. (4 sts)

Rows 28 and 29 S1 wyib, p1, k1, ssk, turn. S1 wyif, k1, p2tog, turn. (3 sts)

Rows 30 and 31 S1 wyib, k1, ssk, turn. S1 wyif, p2tog, turn. (2 sts)

Rows 32 and 33 S1 wyib, ssk, turn. P2tog, turn. (1 st)

Row 34 Ssk, do not turn.

With RS facing, pick up and k 16 sts along row-end edge of next rectangle from row below. Rep from ***** twice more. Break yarn and thread through rem st.

BACK
Using B, 4.5mm (UK7/US7) needles, cast on 74 sts using knit-on cast-on.
Row 1 (RS) K.
Row 2 (WS) P.
Last 2 rows set st st. Cont in st st until work measures 42cm (16½in), cast off.

EDGING
Using 4mm (UK8/US6) double-pointed needles, cast on 5 sts.
Row 1 (RS) K.
Sliding sts to other end of needle, and keeping RS facing, rep as given for row 1 until cord measures 160cm (63in). Cast off.

FINISHING
Darn in ends and block both pieces lightly. Do not flatten the texture formed by the pattern by being too heavy-handed with blocking on the front piece. Join along row-end and cast-off/finished-off edges, leaving the cast-on/starting edges open.
Insert zip along cast-on edge. Affix i-cord along front open edge and along seam, all around the cushion cover.

Checked cushion

Liven up any chair or sofa with this colourful and cuddly cushion. It is an ideal first project as it requires no shaping. All you need to know is how to do garter stitch and how to join in a new colour. It is a good idea to insert a zip into a seam to make the cover easier to remove for washing.

FINISHED SIZE 50 x 50cm (20 x 20in) approx.
TECHNIQUES USED Knit-on cast-on **p.54**, Garter stitch **p.76**, Casting off knitwise **p.68**, Overcast seam **p.189**, Sewing in a zip **p.196**

MATERIALS REQUIRED
- **Yarn**: Rowan Big Wool (100% wool) 100g (80m/87yd)
  A: 89 Cerise x 2
  B: 95 Nougat x 2
  C: 94 Melon x 2
  D: 01 White x 2

- **Needles**: 1 pair of 10mm (UK000/US15) needles

- **Notions**: 50 x 50cm (20 x 20in) cushion pad or polyester stuffing 50cm (20in) zip (optional)

- **Tension**: 10 sts and 19 rows to 10cm (4in) over g st using 10mm (UK000/US15) needles

- **Abbreviations**: See p.89

USE OF COLOUR

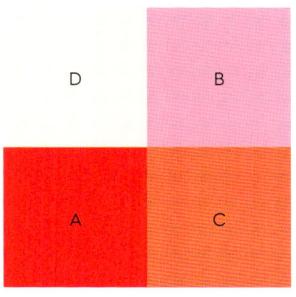

PATTERN
Slip the first stitch on every row. This gives a neat, firm edge and enables an easier sewing up if choosing to use mattress stitch to seam rather than an overcast seam. Cushion cover is constructed of four strips, worked bottom to top and from left to right, as follows:

STRIP 1 (MAKE 2)
Using A, and 10mm (UK000/US15) needles, cast on 25 sts.
Knit 46 rows.
Change to D, knit 46 rows.
Cast off.

STRIP 2 (MAKE 2)
Using C, and 10mm (UK000/US15) needles, cast on 25 sts.
Knit 46 rows.
Change to B, knit 46 rows.
Cast off.

FINISHING
When sewing up, use short lengths of yarn and a blunt-ended, large-eyed needle. The yarn will split quite easily so take care pulling the yarn through the fabric.
  Lay the strips alongside each other and match cast-on and cast-off edges. Sew up, with WS facing, using overcast seam. (It is best to oversew garter stitch strips as this blends with the ridged texture of the knitted fabric.) Insert zip, if using. Darn in all ends and block.

An overcast seam creates a strong, flat join perfect for chunky knitting. Place pieces with right sides together and work small, evenly spaced diagonal stitches over the edge, catching both fabric layers. This seam type prevents thick yarns from creating bulk and lies completely flat when opened.

Checked blanket

This luxuriously thick and warm blanket knits up fast. The garter stitch is easy to do and the knitted fabric is identical on both sides, which prevents it from curling, so little blocking is required. Why not knit the coordinated cushion, too (see pp.268–269)?

FINISHED SIZE 100 x 125cm (40 x 49in) approx.
TECHNIQUES USED Knit-on cast-on **p.54**, Garter stitch **p.76**, Casting off knitwise **p.68**, Overcast seam **p.189**

MATERIALS REQUIRED

- **Yarn:** Rowan Big Wool (100% wool) 100g (80m/87yd)
  A: 89 Cerise x 4
  B: 95 Nougat x 4
  C: 94 Melon x 3
  D: 01 White x 3

- **Needles:** 1 pair of 10mm (UK000/US15) needles

- **Tension:** 10 sts and 19 rows to 10cm (4in) over g st using 10mm (UK000/US15) needles

- **Abbreviations:** See p.89

USE OF COLOUR

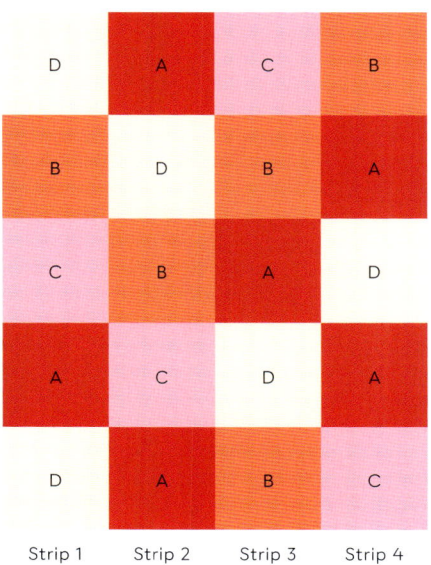

Strip 1   Strip 2   Strip 3   Strip 4

PATTERN

The blanket is constructed of four strips, worked bottom to top and from left to right, as follows (see also below left):

STRIP 1
Using D and 10mm (UK000/US15) needles, cast on 25 sts.
Knit 46 rows.
Change to A, k 46 rows.
Change to C, k 46 rows.
Change to B, k 46 rows.
Change to D, k 46 rows.
Strip should measure 125cm (49in).
Cast off.

STRIP 2
Using A and 10mm (UK000/US15) needles, cast on 25 sts.
Knit 46 rows.
Change to C, k 46 rows.
Change to B, k 46 rows.
Change to D, k 46 rows.
Change to A, k 46 rows.
Strip should measure 125cm (49in).
Cast off.

STRIP 3
Using B and 10mm (UK000/US15) needles, cast on 25 sts.
Knit 46 rows.
Change to D, k 46 rows.
Change to A, k 46 rows.
Change to B, k 46 rows.
Change to C, k 46 rows.
Strip should measure 125cm (49in).
Cast off.

STRIP 4
Using C and 10mm (UK000/US15) needles, cast on 25 sts.
Knit 46 rows.
Change to A, k 46 rows.
Change to D, k 46 rows.
Change to A, k 46 rows.
Change to B, k 46 rows.
Strip should measure 125cm (49in).
Cast off.

FINISHING

When sewing up use short lengths of yarn and a blunt-ended, large-eyed needle. The yarn will split quite easily so take care pulling the yarn through the fabric.

Lay the strips alongside each other and match cast-on and cast-off edges. Sew up, with WS facing, using an overcast seam. (It is best to oversew garter stitch strips as this blends with the ridged texture of the knitted fabric.) Darn in all ends and block.

Intarsia blanket

This striking blanket showcases bold geometric circle motifs created using intarsia colourwork. Each circle is carefully crafted with separate yarns, creating clean lines and vibrant colour blocks without floats on the back. The edging is worked after all the squares have been stitched together.

FINISHED SIZE Approx. 109 x 129cm (43 x 50¾in)
TECHNIQUES USED Stocking stitch **p.76**, Moss stitch **p.278**, Following a colourwork chart **p.122**, Intarsia **p.128**, Picking up stitches **p.168**

MATERIALS REQUIRED

- **Yarn:** Stylecraft Special Aran (100% acrylic) 100g (196m/214yd)
  A: 1822 Pistachio x 2
  B: 1065 Meadow x 1
  C: 1081 Saffron x 1
  D: 1218 Parchment x 1
  E: 1820 Duck Egg x 1
  F: 1841 Cornish Blue x 1
  G: 1839 Watermelon x 1

- **Needles:** 1 pair of 5mm (UK6/US8) needles
  4.5mm (UK7/US7) circular needle, 100cm (40in) long

- **Notions:** Yarn bobbins (optional)

- **Tension:** 16 sts and 23 rows to 10cm (4in) over st st using 5mm (UK6/US8) needles

- **Abbreviations:** See p.89

- **Design note:** This pattern consists of 30 squares, each worked in a different combination of colours for the background and the circle in the middle. See chart on p.274 for the colour combinations for each square.

PATTERN

SQUARE (MAKE 30)
Using background colour yarn and 5mm (UK6/US8) needles, cast on 34 sts. Working in st st and using Intarsia method, complete as given for circle chart. Cast off.

MAKING UP
Darn in all ends and join squares using mattress stitch according to Use of Colour chart on p.274.

BOTTOM AND TOP BORDERS
Using A and 4.5mm (UK7/US7) circular needles, and with RS facing, pick up and k 161 sts across bottom edge of blanket (cast-on edge of squares).
Row 1 (WS) K1, [p1, k1] to end.
Row 2 Rep row 1.
Last 2 rows set moss st. Cont in moss st for a further 8 rows.
Cast off.
Rep for top edge of blanket.

SIDE BORDERS
Using A and 4.5mm (UK7/US7) circular needle, pick up and k 5 sts from right bottom border edge, 193 sts along blanket squares, and 5 sts from top border edge. (203 sts)
Work 10 rows in moss st as given for bottom and top borders.
Cast off.
Rep for left border.

FINISHING
Darn in ends. Hand-wash, reshape and lay to dry flat, or block as given on yarn ballband instructions.

CIRCLE CHART

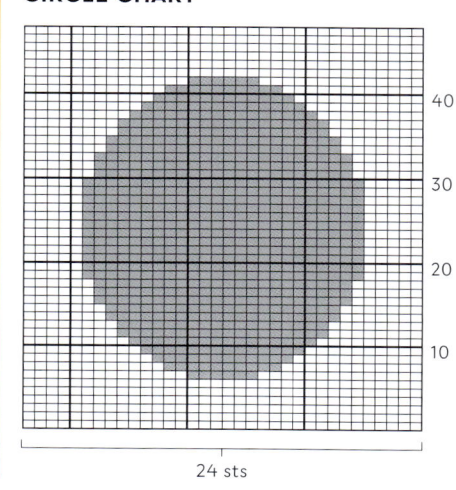

24 sts

USE OF COLOUR

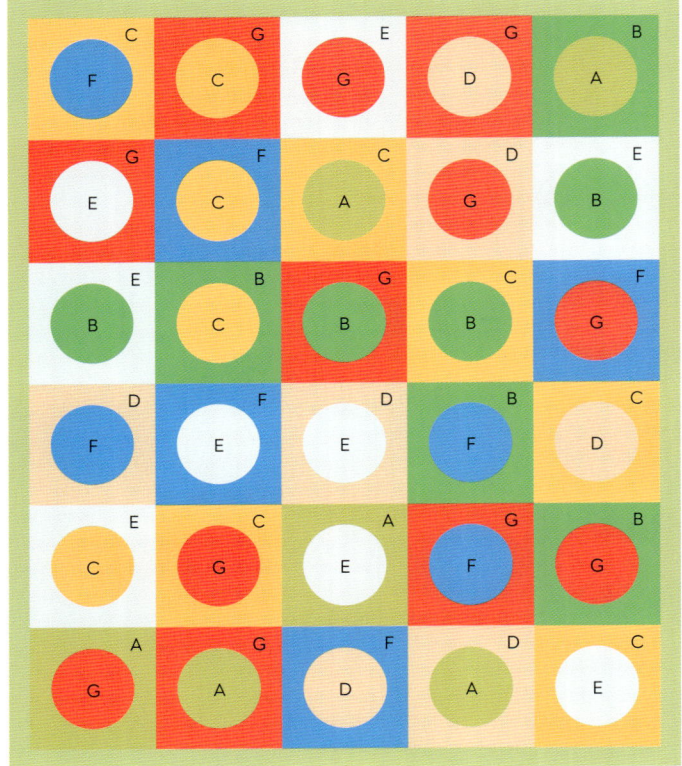

The edging is worked by picking up stitches along each edge. Using a smaller needle and a double-sided stitch such as moss stitch, will prevent unsightly curling.

Intarsia uses separate balls of yarn for each colour section, with yarns twisted together only at colour changes. This eliminates the floats of unused yarn carried across the back that make stranded colourwork fabrics thicker and in need of greater yarn quantities.

You can go as big or as small with this blanket as you like, making a grid of more – or fewer squares – to change the size. Just be sure that, when working the border, you adjust the number of stitches that you pick up around the edge to allow for a different number of squares.

While the charted pattern is identical for each circle, using different combinations of colours creates the bold geometric patterns in simple shapes.

STITCH PATTERNS

Stitch pattern gallery

These swatches demonstrate how the techniques on pp.50–215 can be turned into interesting and original knitted fabrics. Even if you are new to knitting, you have probably already heard of some of the well-known stitches, such as stocking stitch and moss stitch, but what you might not know is that there are many, many alternatives, creating any number of attractive effects, from striking cables and colourwork to delicate lace patterns and beading. Take a look through this chapter to establish the kinds of effects that appeal to you. Each swatch includes the pattern to make it, and also any chart that might be needed.

KNIT AND PURL STITCH PATTERNS

Here are a few of the vast array of stitch patterns created by combining knit and purl stitches. Each one produces a flat, reversible knitted fabric and is simple to work. Those that have no specific right side look exactly the same on both the front and the back, and the few with a marked right side have an attractive texture on the wrong side as well. Because the edges of these stitches do not curl, they are ideal for making simple scarves, baby blankets, and throws. See pp.78–79 for step-by-step guidance on knit and purl stitches.

MOSS STITCH (SEED STITCH)

For an even number of sts:
Row 1 *K1, p1, rep from * to end.
Row 2 *P1, k1, rep from * to end.
Rep rows 1 and 2 to form patt.

For an odd number of sts:
Row 1 *K1, p1, rep from * to last st, k1.
Rep row 1 to form patt.

SINGLE RIB

For an even number of sts:
Row 1 *K1, p1, rep from * to end.
Rep row 1 to form patt.

For an odd number of sts:
Row 1 *K1, p1, rep from * to last st, k1.
Row 2 *P1, k1, rep from * to last st, p1.
Rep rows 1 and 2 to form patt.

KNIT AND PURL STITCH PATTERNS **279**

DOUBLE RIB

Cast on a multiple of 4 sts.
Row 1 *K2, p2, rep from * to end.
Rep row 1 to form patt.

BASKETWEAVE STITCH

Cast on a multiple of 8 sts.
Rows 1–5 *K4, p4, rep from * to end.
Rows 6–10 *P4, k4, rep from * to end.
Rep rows 1–10 to form patt.

TEXTURED CHECK STITCH

Cast on a multiple of 4 sts plus 3 extra sts.
Row 1 K3, *p1, k3, rep from * to end.
Row 2 K1, *p1, k3, rep from * to last 2 sts, p1, k1.
Rows 3–6 [Rep rows 1 and 2] twice.
Row 7 K1, *p1, k3, rep from * to last 2 sts, p1, k1.
Row 8 K3, *p1, k3, rep from * to end.
Rows 9–12 [Rep rows 7 and 8] twice.
Rep rows 1–12 to form patt.

STRIPED CHECK STITCH

Cast on a multiple of 6 sts plus 3 extra sts.
Row 1 and all foll alt rows (RS) K.
Row 2 K.
Rows 4 and 6 P3, *k3, p3, rep from * to end.
Rows 8 and 10 K.
Rows 12 and 14 K3, *p3, k3, rep from * to end.
Row 16 K.
Rep rows 1–16 to form patt.

DIAMOND STITCH

Cast on a multiple of 9 sts.
Row 1 (RS) K2, *p5, k4, rep from * to last 7 sts, p5, k2.
Row 2 P1, *k7, p2, rep from * to last 8 sts, k7, p1.
Row 3 P.
Row 4 Rep row 2.
Row 5 Rep row 1.
Row 6 P3, *k3, p6, rep from * to last 6 sts, k3, p3.
Row 7 K4, *p1, k8, rep from * to last 5 sts, p1, k4.
Row 8 Rep row 6.
Rep rows 1–8 to form patt.

LITTLE CHECK STITCH

Cast on a multiple of 10 sts plus 5 extra sts.
Row 1 *K5, p5, rep from * to last 5 sts, k5.
Row 2 P.
Rep last 2 rows twice more, then row 1 again.
Row 8 K5, *p5, k5, rep from * to end.
Row 9 K.
Rep last 2 rows twice more, then row 8 again.

GARTER RIB

Cast on a multiple of 8 sts plus 4 extra sts.
Row 1 (RS) K4, *p4, k4, rep from * to end.
Row 2 P.
Rep rows 1 and 2 to form patt.

ENGLISH RIB (see Working into lower stitches, p.129)

Cast on an odd number of sts.
Row 1 S1, *p1, k1, rep from * to end.
Row 2 S1, *k1b, p1, rep from * to end.
Rep rows 1 and 2 to form patt.

FISHERMAN'S RIB (see Working into lower stitches, p.129)

Cast on an odd number of sts and knit 1 row.
Row 1 (RS) S1, *k1b, p1, rep from * to end.
Row 2 S1, *p1, k1b, rep from * to last 2 sts, p1, k1.
Rep rows 1 and 2 to form patt.

DOUBLE MOSS STITCH

Cast on an odd number of sts.
Row 1 (RS) *K1, p1, rep from * to last st, k1.
Row 2 *P1, k1, rep from * to last st, p1.
Row 3 Rep row 2
Row 4 Rep row 1.
Rep rows 1–4 to form patt.

HALF MOSS STITCH

Cast on an odd number of sts.
Row 1 (RS) *P1, k1, rep from * to last st, k1.
Row 2 K.
Rep rows 1 and 2 to form patt.

TRAVELLING RIB

Cast on a multiple of 4 sts.
Row 1 (RS) *K2, p2, rep from * to end.
Row 2 Rep row 1.
Row 3 *K1, p2, k1, rep from * to end.
Row 4 *P1, k2, p1, rep from * to end.
Row 5 *P2, k2, rep from * to end.
Row 6 Rep row 5.
Row 7 Rep row 4.
Row 8 Rep row 3.
Rep rows 1–8 to form patt.

BROKEN RIB

Cast on a multiple of 4 sts plus 2 extra sts.
Row 1 (RS) *K3, p1, rep from * to last 2 sts, k2.
Row 2 P1, *k3, p1, rep from * to last st, k1.
Rep rows 1 and 2 to form patt.

BROKEN MOSS STITCH

Cast on an odd number of sts.
Row 1 (RS) K.
Row 2 *P1, k1, rep from * to last st, k1.
Rep rows 1 and 2 to form patt.

MOSS STITCH COLUMNS

Cast on a multiple of 6 sts plus 4 extra sts.
Row 1 (RS) K4, *k1, p1, k4, rep from * to end.
Row 2 *P5, k1, rep from * to last 4 sts, p4.
Rep rows 1 and 2 to form patt.

HONEYCOMB STITCH

Cast on a multiple of 6 sts plus 2 extra sts.
Row 1 (RS) K.
Row 2 K2, *p4, k2, rep from * to end.
Row 3 Rep row 1.
Row 4 P2, *p1, k2, p3, rep from * to end.
Rep rows 1–4 to form patt.

INCREASING AND DECREASING

Knitted increases and decreases add shape and texture to a knitted piece. A huge variety of shapes and patterns can be achieved by increasing or decreasing the number of stitches on the needle. As your knitted structure changes shape the cast-on edge will not always remain straight, adding an attractive wavy edge in most cases. This selection of all-over patterns are worked by repeating a sequence, with each pattern repeat combining increases and decreases to cancel each other out so that the overall number of stitches remains the same. These stitches will produce particularly interesting scarves, shawls, and blankets. See pp.92–105 for step-by-step guidance on increases and decreases.

BASIC CHEVRON

Cast on a multiple of 12 sts.
Row 1 (RS) *K2tog, k3, [inc in next st] twice, k3, s1 k1 psso, rep from * to end.
Row 2 P.
Rep rows 1 and 2 to form patt.

GARTER CHEVRON

Cast on a multiple of 11 sts.
Row 1 (WS) K.
Rows 2, 3, 4, and 5 [Rep row 1] four times.
Row 6 *K2tog, k2, [inc in next st] twice, k3, s1 k1 psso, rep from * to end.
Row 7 P.
Rep last 2 rows twice more, then row 6 again.
Rep rows 1–12 to form patt.

FEATHER AND FAN STITCH

Cast on a multiple of 18 sts plus 2 extra sts.
Row 1 (RS) K.
Row 2 P.
Row 3 K1, *[k2tog] three times, [yo, k1] six times, [k2tog] three times, rep from * to last st, k1.
Row 4 K.
Rep rows 1–4 to form patt.

DIAGONAL RIB

Cast on a multiple of 2 sts.

Row 1 (WS) *K1, p1, rep from * to end.

Row 2 S1 p1 psso, *k1, p1, rep from * to last 2 sts, k1, [p1, k1] into next st.

Row 3 *P1, k1, rep from * to last 2 sts, p2.

Row 4 S1 k1 psso, *p1, k1, rep from * to last 2 sts, p1, (k1, p1) into next st.

Rep rows 1–4 to form patt.

BLACKBERRY STITCH

Cast on a multiple of 4 sts plus 2 extra sts.

Row 1 (RS) P.

Row 2 K1, *(k1, p1, k1) into next st, p3tog, rep from * to last st, k1.

Row 3 P.

Row 4 K1, *p3tog, (k1, p1, k1) into next st, rep from * to last st, k1.

Rep rows 1–4 to form patt.

PUFF STITCH

Cast on a multiple of 4 sts plus 1 extra st.

Row 1 (RS) K.

Row 2 P.

Row 3 K1, *p3tog without removing these sts from needle, yrn, re-insert RH needle into 3 previously worked sts and p3tog, this time removing them from LH needle, k1, rep from * to end.

Row 4 P.

Rep rows 1–4 to form patt.

BOBBLE STITCH

Cast on an odd number of sts.

Row 1 (RS) K.

Row 2 K1, *[p1, k1] twice into next st, pass 2nd, 3rd, and 4th sts over first st on RH needle, k1, rep from * to end.

Row 3 Rep row 1.

Row 4 K2, *[p1, k1] twice into next st, pass 2nd, 3rd, and 4th sts over first st on RH needle, k1, rep from * to last st, k1.

Rep rows 1–4 to form patt.

INCREASING AND DECREASING: FLOWER PATTERNS

These flowers have all been designed to be simple to make using easy increasing and decreasing techniques, paired with some casting-on and casting-off to create ornate shaping. Each flower is worked as one piece, with little or no sewing-up required. As a bonus, there is no need to darn in ends because you can use the yarn tails to plait a simple stem or to attach a brooch back. The finished flowers are perfect for use as corsages, appliqué on blankets, cushion covers, bags, scarves, and jumpers, or to decorate greeting cards. See pp.92–105 for step-by-step guidance on increases and decreases.

TWELVE-PETAL FLOWER

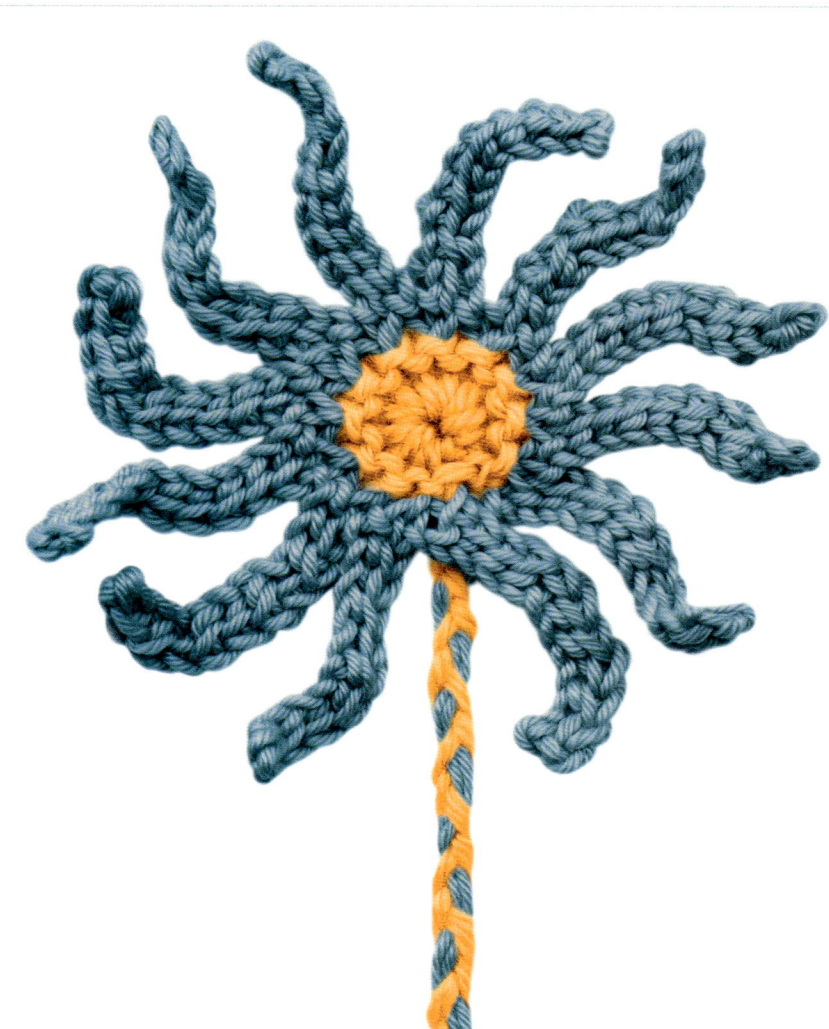

Worked in A (petals) and B (flower centre).

Using Knit-on cast-on method (see p.54) and A, cast on 12 sts, leaving a yarn tail at least 25cm (10in) long.

Row 1 (RS) Cast off 10 sts knitwise and slip st on RH needle back on to LH needle. (2 sts)

Note: Do not turn work when working petals, but keep RS always facing.

Row 2 (RS) Cast on 12 sts on LH needle using knit-on cast-on method, then cast off 10 sts knitwise and slip st on RH needle back on LH needle. (4 sts)

Rows 3–12 [Rep row 2] 10 times more to make a total of 12 petals. (24 sts – 2 sts at base of each petal)

Cut off A.

Using B and working across all 24 sts, cont in usual rows for flower centre as foll:

Row 13 (RS) [K2tog] 12 times. (12 sts)

Row 14 (WS) K.

Row 15 (RS) K.

Slip all sts back on LH needle. Then cut off yarn, leaving a yarn tail at least 25cm (10in) long. Thread yarn tail through a blunt-ended darning needle. With RS facing, thread yarn through rem sts, slipping them off knitting needle as you proceed. Pull yarn tightly to gather sts firmly. With WS facing and still using threaded yarn needle, oversew row ends of flower centre together, working from centre to beginning of petal yarn. Knot ends of matching yarn together, close to work on WS, then knot all yarn ends together close to WS. To form stem, plait together yarn ends, holding two ends of A together and using B strands singly for three strands of plait. Knot end of stem and trim yarn ends.****

Do not press.

SPINNING-PETAL FLOWER

Worked in A (petals) and B (flower centre).

Using Knit-on cast-on method (see p.54) and A, cast on 10 sts, leaving a yarn tail at least 25cm (10in) long.

Row 1 (RS) K8 and turn, leaving rem sts unworked.

Row 2 (WS) K to end.

Rows 3 and 4 Rep rows 1 and 2.

Row 5 (RS) Cast off 8 sts loosely knitwise, slip st on RH needle back on to LH needle. (2 sts)

Note: Do not turn work after last row of each petal (cast-off row), but keep RS facing for next row.

Row 6 (RS) Cast on 10 sts on LH needle using knit-on cast-on method, k8 and turn.

Rows 7, 8, 9, and 10 [Rep rows 2–5 of first petal] four times. (4 sts)

[Rep rows 6–10] five times more to make a total of 7 petals. (14 sts – 2 sts at base of each petal)

Cut off A.

Using B and working across all 14 sts, cont in usual rows for flower centre as foll:

K 3 rows.

P 1 row.

K 1 row, so ending with a RS row.

Finish as for Twelve-Petal Flower (see p.285) from ** to **.

Do not press.

Decorate centre with small button if desired.

ANEMONE

Note: Slip all slip sts purlwise with yarn at WS of work.

Worked in A (petals) and B and C (flower centre).

Using Double cast-on method (see p.57) and A, cast on 41 sts, leaving a yarn tail at least 25cm (10in) long.

Row 1 (RS) *S1, k7, rep from * to last st, p1.

Row 2 *S1, k to end.

Row 3 Rep row 1.

Row 4 S1, p7, *s1, take yarn to back of work between two needles then around knitting over cast-on edge, over top of knitting between two needles and around cast-on edge again, so ending at front of work, pull yarn to gather knitting tightly, p7, rep from * to last st, k1.

Cut off A and change to B.

Row 5 *K2tog, rep from * to last 3 sts, s1 k2tog psso. (20 sts)

Row 6 K.

Cut off B and change to C.

Row 7 [K2tog] ten times. (10 sts)

Finish as for Twelve-Petal Flower (see p.285) from ** to **, but also using A to sew short petal seam (leaving part of seam unworked to create indent between petals as between other petals) and making plait with two strands each of A, B, and C.

Do not press.

FLOWER WITH SMALL CENTRE

Worked in A (outer petal), B (inner petal), and C (flower centre).

Using Double cast-on method (see p.57) and A, cast on 90 sts, leaving a yarn tail at least 25cm (10in) long.

Row 1 (WS) K6, s1 k2tog psso, *k12, s1 k2tog psso, rep from * to last 6 sts, k6.

Cut off A and change to B.

Row 2 (RS) *K1, cast off next 11 sts knitwise, rep from * to end. (12 sts)

Cut off B and change to C.

Row 3 P.

Row 4 *K2tog, k1, rep from * to end. (8 sts)

Finish as for Twelve-Petal Flower (see p.285) from ** to **, but also using A to sew beginning and end of cast-on sts together and making plait with two strands each of A, B, and C.

Do not press.

FLOWER WITH LARGE CENTRE

Worked in A (outer petal), B (inner petal), and C (flower centre).

Using Double cast-on method (see p.57) and A, cast on 72 sts, leaving a yarn tail at least 25cm (10in) long.

Cut off A and change to B.

Row 1 (RS) K.

Row 2 *Kfb, cast off next 10 sts knitwise, rep from * to end. (18 sts)

Cut off B and change to C.

Row 3 K.

Row 4 *K4, k2tog, rep from * to end. (15 sts)

Row 5 K.

Row 6 P.

Row 7 *K1, k2tog, rep from * to end. (10 sts)

Finish as for Twelve-Petal Flower (see p.285) from ** to **, but also using A to sew beginning and end of cast-on sts together and making plait with two strands each of A, B, and C. Do not press. Decorate centre with small button if desired.

PUFFBALL FLOWER

Cast on 7 sts.

Row 1 (RS) *K1, yo, rep from * to last st, k1. (13 sts)

Row 2 and all foll alt rows (WS) P.

Row 3 *K2, yo, rep from * to last st, k1. (19 sts)

Row 5 *K3, yo, rep from * to last st, k1. (25 sts)

Row 7 *K4, yo, rep from * to last st, k1. (31 sts)

Row 9 *K5, yo, rep from * to last st, k1. (37 sts)

Row 11 *K6, yo, rep from * to last st, k1. (43 sts)

Row 13 *K7, yo, rep from * to last st, k1. (49 sts)

Row 15 K.

Row 17 *K6, k2tog, rep from * to last st, k1. (43 sts)

Row 19 *K5, k2tog, rep from * to last st, k1. (37 sts)

Row 21 *K4, k2tog, rep from * to last st, k1. (31 sts)

Row 23 *K3, k2tog, rep from * to last st, k1. (25 sts)

Row 25 *K2, k2tog, rep from * to last st, k1. (19 sts)

Row 27 *K1, k2tog, rep from * to last st, k1. (13 sts)

Row 29 *K2tog, rep from * to last st, k1. (7 sts)

Cut yarn, leaving a long tail, and draw through remaining 7 sts. Using the tail of yarn, continue to join row ends using mattress stitch with RS facing, draw through cast-on edge, and pull tight. Align cast-on edge centre with cast-off edge, and squash flower flat so that these two edges meet. Join with a few stitches through the centre, and embellish with beads or buttons at centre if desired.

LARGE LEAF

Cast on 3 sts on double-pointed needle and k 1 row (RS).

Cord row (RS) With RS still facing, slide sts to opposite end of needle, take yarn across WS of work, pull tightly and k to end.

Rep cord row until stem is desired length.

Row 1 (RS) With RS of work still facing, slide sts to opposite end of needle, across WS of work, pull tightly and work k1, [yfwd, k1] twice. (5 sts)

Change to ordinary needles, cont in rows, turning work in usual way.

Row 2 K2, p1, k2.

Row 3 K2, yfwd, k1, yfwd, k2. (7 sts)

Row 4 Cast on 1 st on LH needle (using Knit-on cast-on method p.54), cast off 1 st (knitwise), k to centre st, p centre st, k to end. (7 sts)

Row 5 Cast on 1 st on LH needle, cast off 1 st, k to centre st, yfwd, k centre st, yfwd, k to end. (9 sts)

Row 6–9 [Rep rows 4 and 5] twice. (13 sts)

Row 10 Rep row 4. (13 sts)

Row 11 Cast on one st on LH needle, cast off one st, k to end. (13 sts)

Row 12 Rep row 4. (13 sts)

Row 13 Cast on 1 st on LH needle, cast off 1 st, k to 2 sts before centre st, k2tog, k centre st, ssk, k to end. (11 sts)

Row 14–19 [Rep rows 4 and 13] three times. (5 sts)

Row 20 K2, p1, k2.

Row 21 K2tog, k1, ssk. (3 sts)

Row 22 K1, p1, k1.

Row 23 S1 k2tog psso and fasten off.

Darn in yarn ends. Do not press.

CABLE AND TWIST STITCH PATTERNS

These patterns for cables and twists are all easy to work and are a good introduction to such textures for beginners. To knit these, try working the patterns from the written instructions for the first repeat; then follow the chart for the next repeat to see how much easier it is to use a chart for cables and twists. The twist patterns add a more subtle texture and, with no cable needle necessary, are quick to work, too. Cables and twists add texture and thickness to a project, and are therefore ideal for plain garments and accessories, such as a cushion cover. Cables will inevitably shrink your project widthways, so remember to cast on more stitches than you would normally need. See pp.110–111 for step-by-step guidance on cables and twists.

CHART KEY

- K on RS rows, P on WS rows
- P on RS rows, K on WS rows
- C4B
- C4F
- MB = make bobble
- yfwd
- C8B
- C8F
- CR4L
- CR4R
- T2L
- T2R
- C6B
- C6F
- k2tog
- ssk
- s1 k2tog psso
- s2 K1 p2sso
- CR2R
- CR2L

DIAMOND CABLE

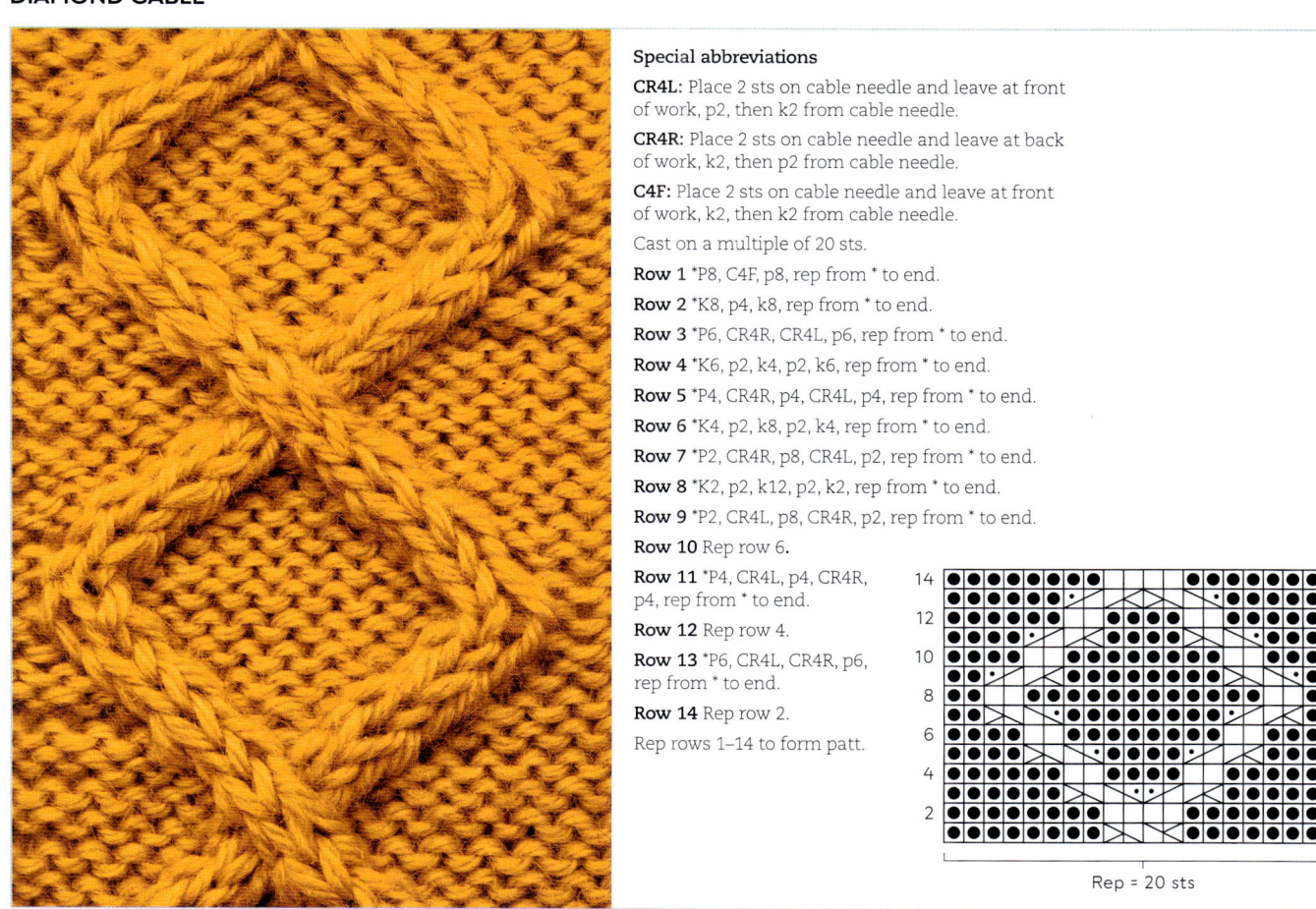

Special abbreviations

CR4L: Place 2 sts on cable needle and leave at front of work, p2, then k2 from cable needle.

CR4R: Place 2 sts on cable needle and leave at back of work, k2, then p2 from cable needle.

C4F: Place 2 sts on cable needle and leave at front of work, k2, then k2 from cable needle.

Cast on a multiple of 20 sts.

Row 1 *P8, C4F, p8, rep from * to end.
Row 2 *K8, p4, k8, rep from * to end.
Row 3 *P6, CR4R, CR4L, p6, rep from * to end.
Row 4 *K6, p2, k4, p2, k6, rep from * to end.
Row 5 *P4, CR4R, p4, CR4L, p4, rep from * to end.
Row 6 *K4, p2, k8, p2, k4, rep from * to end.
Row 7 *P2, CR4R, p8, CR4L, p2, rep from * to end.
Row 8 *K2, p2, k12, p2, k2, rep from * to end.
Row 9 *P2, CR4L, p8, CR4R, p2, rep from * to end.
Row 10 Rep row 6.
Row 11 *P4, CR4L, p4, CR4R, p4, rep from * to end.
Row 12 Rep row 4.
Row 13 *P6, CR4L, CR4R, p6, rep from * to end.
Row 14 Rep row 2.
Rep rows 1–14 to form patt.

Rep = 20 sts

FOUR-STITCH CABLE PATTERN

Special abbreviations

C4F: Slip next 2 sts on to cable needle and hold at front of work, k2 from LH needle, then k2 from cable needle.

C4B: Slip next 2 sts on to cable needle and hold at back of work, k2 from LH needle, then k2 from cable needle.

Cast on a multiple of 14 sts plus 3 extra sts.

Row 1 (RS) P3, *k4, p3, rep from * to end.
Row 2 K3, *p4, k3, rep from * to end.
Row 3 P3, *k4, p3, C4F, p3, rep from * to end.
Row 4 Rep row 2.
Row 5 P3, *C4B, p3, k4, p3, rep from * to end.
Rep rows 2–5 to form patt.

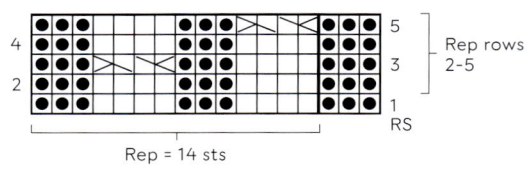

SIX-STITCH CABLE PATTERN

Special abbreviations

C6F: Slip next 3 sts on to cable needle and hold at front of work, k3 from LH needle, then k3 from cable needle.

C6B: Slip next 3 sts on to cable needle and hold at back of work, k3 from LH needle, then k3 from cable needle.

Cast on a multiple of 18 sts plus 3 extra sts.

Row 1 (RS) P3, *k6, p3, rep from * to end.
Row 2 and all foll alt rows (WS) K3, *p6, k3, rep from * to end.
Row 3 P3, *k6, p3, C6F, p3, rep from * to end.
Row 5 Rep row 1.
Row 7 P3, *C6B, p3, k6, p3, rep from * to end.
Row 9 Rep row 1.
Rep rows 2–9 to form patt.

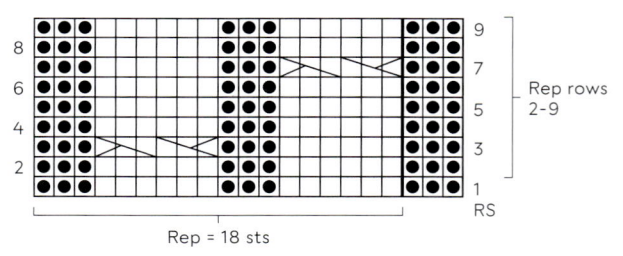

CHAIN CABLE PATTERN

Special abbreviations

C4F: Slip next 2 sts on to cable needle and hold at front of work, k2 from LH needle, then k2 from cable needle.

C4B: Slip next 2 sts on to cable needle and hold at back of work, k2 from LH needle, then k2 from cable needle.

Cast on a multiple of 22 sts plus 3 extra sts.

Row 1 (RS) P3, *k8, p3, rep from * to end.
Row 2 and all foll alt rows (WS) K3, *p8, k3, rep from * to end.
Row 3 P3, *k8, p3, C4B, C4F, p3, rep from * to end.
Row 5 P3, *C4B, C4F, p3, k8, p3, rep from * to end.
Row 7 P3, *k8, p3, C4F, C4B, p3, rep from * to end.
Row 9 P3, *C4F, C4B, p3, k8, p3, rep from * to end.
Rep rows 2–9 to form patt.

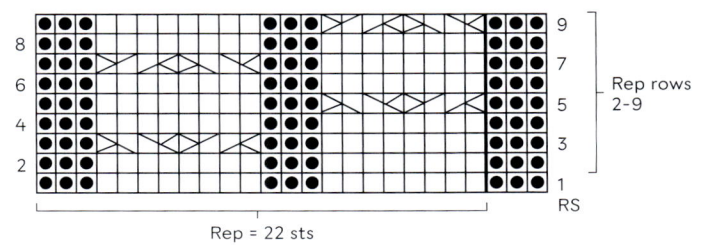

HORSESHOE CABLE PATTERN

Special abbreviations

C4F: Slip next 2 sts on to cable needle and hold at front of work, k2 from LH needle, then k2 from cable needle.

C4B: Slip next 2 sts on to cable needle and hold at back of work, k2 from LH needle, then k2 from cable needle.

Cast on a multiple of 22 sts plus 3 extra sts.

Row 1 (RS) P3, *k8, p3, rep from * to end.
Row 2 and all foll alt rows (WS) K3, *p8, k3, rep from * to end.
Row 3 P3, *k8, p3, C4B, C4F, p3, rep from * to end.
Row 5 Rep row 1.
Row 7 P3, *C4B, C4F, p3, k8, p3, rep from * to end.
Row 9 Rep row 1.
Rep rows 2–9 to form patt.

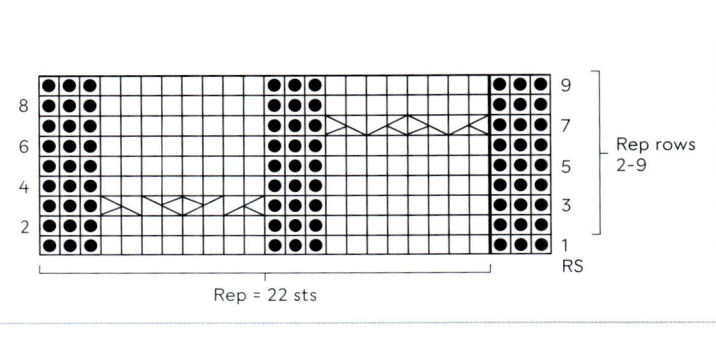

PLAIT CABLE

Special abbreviations

C8F: Place 4 sts on cable needle and leave at front of work, k4, then k4 from cable needle.

C8B: Place 4 sts on cable needle and leave at back of work, k4, then k4 from cable needle.

Cast on a multiple of 20 sts.

Row 1 *P4, k12, p4, rep from * to end.

Row 2 and all foll alt rows (WS) *K4, p12, k4, rep from * to end.

Row 3 *P4, C8F, k4, p4, rep from * to end.

Rows 5 and 7 [Rep row 1] twice.

Row 9 *P4, k4, C8B, rep from * to end.

Row 11 Rep row 1.

Row 12 Rep row 2.

Rep rows 1–12 to form patt.

Rep = 20 sts

CABLE-EFFECT STITCH

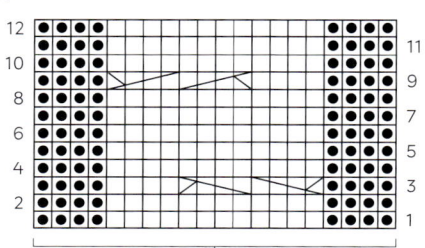

Cast on a multiple of 5 sts plus 2 extra sts.

Note: The stitch count varies from row to row.

Row 1 (RS) P2, *yarn to back of work between 2 needles, s1p k2 psso, p2, rep from * to end.

Row 2 K2, *p1, yrn, p1, k2, rep from * to end.

Row 3 P2, *k3, p2, rep from * to end.

Row 4 K2, *p3, k2, rep from * to end.

Rep rows 1–4 to form patt.

GARTER STITCH CABLE

Special abbreviations

C8F: Place 4 sts on cable needle and leave at front of work, k4, then k4 from cable needle.

Cast on a multiple of 18 sts.

Row 1 (RS) *P5, k8, p5, rep from * to end.

Row 2 *K9, p4, k5, rep from * to end.

Rep last 2 rows twice more.

Row 7 P5, *C8F, p5, rep from * to end.

Row 8 *K5, p4, k9, rep from * to end.

Row 9 Rep row 1.

Rep last 2 rows four times more, then row 8 again.

Row 19 Rep row 7.

Row 20 Rep row 2.

Row 21 Rep row 1.

Row 22 Rep row 2.

Row 23 Rep row 1.

Row 24 Rep row 2.

Rep rows 1–24 to form patt.

Rep = 18 sts

GARTER ZIGZAG TWIST

Special abbreviations

T2R (twist 2 right): Skip first st on LH needle and k 2nd st through front of loop (do not drop st off LH needle), then k first st on LH needle and drop both sts off LH needle at same time.

T2L (twist 2 left): Skip first st on LH needle and k 2nd st by taking RH needle behind first st to do so (do not drop st off LH needle), then k first st on LH needle and drop both sts off LH needle at same time.

Cast on a multiple of 6 sts plus 1 extra st.

Row 1 (RS) K.
Row 2 *K5, p1, rep from * to last st, k1.
Row 3 K1, *T2L, k4, rep from * to end.
Row 4 *K4, p1, k1, rep from * to last st, k1.
Row 5 K1 *k1, T2L, k3, rep from * to end.
Row 6 *K3, p1, k2, rep from * to last st, k1.
Row 7 K1, *k2, T2L, k2, rep from * to end.
Row 8 *K2, p1, k3, rep from * to last st, k1.
Row 9 K1, *k3, T2L, k1, rep from * to end.
Row 10 *K1, p1, k4, rep from * to last st, k1.
Row 11 K1, *k3, T2R, k1 rep from * to end.
Row 12 Rep row 8.
Row 13 K1, *k2, T2R, k2, rep from * to end.
Row 14 Rep row 6.
Row 15 K1, *k1, T2R, k3, rep from * to end.
Row 16 Rep row 4.
Row 17 K1, *T2R, k4, rep from * to end.
Row 18 Rep row 2.
Rep rows 3–18 to form patt.

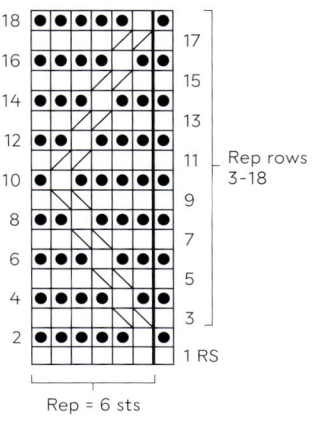

SMOCKING

Special abbreviations

smock 5 sts: Slip next 5 sts on to cable needle and leave at front of work, bring yarn to the front of work, and wrap anticlockwise around these stitches twice so that yarn now sits at back of work. Work (k1, p3, k1) from cable needle.

Cast on a multiple of 8 sts plus 7 extra sts.

Row 1 (RS) P1, k1, *p3, k1, rep from * to last st, p1.
Row 2 K1, p1, *k3, p1, rep from * to last st, k1.
Row 3 P1, smock 5 sts, *p3, smock 5 sts, rep from * to last st, p1.
Row 4 Rep row 2.
Row 5 Rep row 1.
Rep last 2 rows once more, and row 2 again.
Row 9 P1, k1, p3, *smock 5 sts, p3, rep from * to last 2 sts, k1, p1.
Rows 10 and 12 Rep row 2.
Row 11 Rep row 1.
Rep rows 1–12 to form patt.

WOVEN CABLE

Special abbreviations

C6F: Place 3 sts on cable needle and leave at front of work, k3, then k3 from cable needle.

C6B: Place 3 sts on cable needle and leave at back of work, k3, then k3 from cable needle.

Cast on a multiple of 6 sts (a minimum of 12 sts).

Row 1 (RS) K.
Row 2 and all foll alt rows (WS) P.
Row 3 K3, *C6B, rep from * to last 3 sts, k3.
Row 5 K.
Row 7 *C6F, rep from * to end.
Row 8 Rep row 2.

Rep rows 1–8 to form patt.

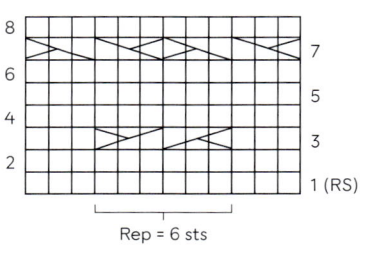

Rep = 6 sts

CABLE CHECK

Special abbreviation

C4F: Place 2 sts on cable needle and leave at front of work, k2, then k2 from cable needle.

Cast on a multiple of 8 sts plus 4 extra sts.

Row 1 (RS) *P4, k4, rep from * to last 4 sts, p4.
Row 2 K4, *p4, k4, rep from *.
Row 3 Rep row 1.
Row 4 Rep row 2.
Row 5 *P4, C4F, rep from * to last 4 sts, p4.
Rows 6 and 7 [Rep row 2] twice.
Row 8 Rep row 1.
Row 9 Rep row 2.
Row 10 Rep row 1.
Row 11 *C4F, p4, rep from * to last 4 sts, C4F.
Row 12 Rep row 1.

Rep rows 1–12 to form patt.

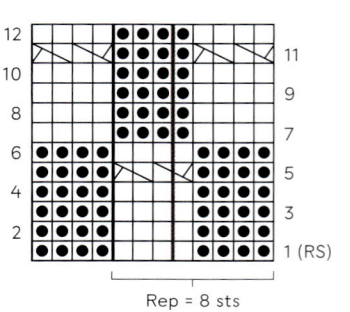

Rep = 8 sts

WAVY CABLE PATTERN

Special abbreviations

CR2R: Skip first st on LH needle and k 2nd st through front of loop (do not drop st off LH needle), then p first st on LH needle and drop both sts off this needle at same time.

CR2L: Skip first st on LH needle and p 2nd st by taking RH needle behind first st to do so (so do not drop st off LH needle), then k first st on LH needle and drop both sts off together.

Cast on a multiple of 3 sts (a minimum of 9 sts).

Row 1 (RS) *P1, CR2R, rep from * to end.
Row 2 *K1, p1, k1, rep from * to end.
Row 3 *CR2R, p1, rep from * to end.
Row 4 *K2, p1, rep from * to end.
Row 5 *K1, p2, rep from * to end.
Row 6 Rep row 4.
Row 7 *CR2L, p1, rep from * to end.
Row 8 Rep row 2.
Row 9 *P1, CR2L, rep from * to end.
Row 10 *P1, k2, rep from * to end.
Row 11 *P2, k1, rep from * to end.
Row 12 Rep row 10.

Rep rows 1–12 to form patt.

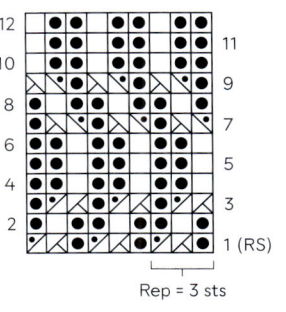

Rep = 3 sts

FAN CABLE

Read all odd (WS) rows from L to R.
Read all even (RS) rows from R to L.

Special abbreviations

CR2R: Skip first st on LH needle and k 2nd st through front of loop (do not drop st off LH needle), then p first st on LH needle and drop both sts off this needle at same time.

CR2L: Skip first st on LH needle and p 2nd st by taking RH needle behind first st to do so (so do not drop st off LH needle), then k first st on LH needle and drop both sts off together.

Cast on a multiple of 14 sts plus 2 extra sts.

Row 1 and all foll alt rows (WS) P.
Row 2 *K6, CR2R, k6, rep from * to last 2 sts, k2.
Row 4 *K5, CR2R, p1, k6, rep from * to last 2 sts, k2.
Row 6 *K4, CR2R, p2, k6, rep from * to last 2 sts, k2.
Row 8 *K3, CR2R, p3, k6, rep from * to last 2 sts, k2.
Row 10 *K2, CR2R, p4, k6, rep from * to last 2 sts, k2.
Row 12 *K8, CR2L, k4, rep from * to last 2 sts, k2.
Row 14 *K8, p1, CR2L, k3, rep from * to last 2 sts, k2.
Row 16 *K8, p2, CR2L, K2, rep from * to last 2 sts, k2.
Row 18 *K8, p3, CR2L, k1, rep from * to last 2 sts, k2.
Row 20 *K8, p4, CR2L, rep from * to last 2 sts, k2.

Rep rows 1–20 to form patt.

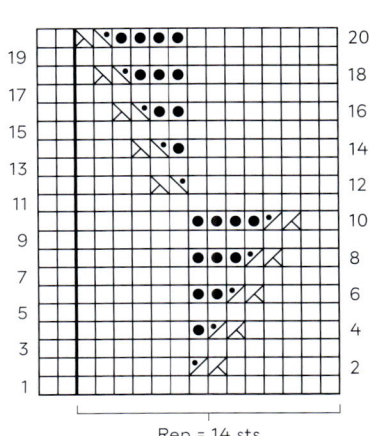

Rep = 14 sts

LACE STITCH PATTERNS

Lacework is an easy way to add a delicate and elegant look to shawls, scarves, garments, and blankets. If the ground of your chosen lace is stocking stitch, you will need to include a garter stitch or moss stitch border around the piece. This can be achieved by either picking up stitches and working the border after the piece is complete; or working four rows of garter stitch at the beginning and end of the knitted piece and four stitches of garter stitch at the sides of the knitting. Alternatively, sew a knitted or fabric trim edging all around the finished piece. See pp.116–117 for step-by-step guidance on lace techniques.

CHART KEY

☐ K on RS rows, P on WS rows ◯ yfwd ◳ ssk ◸ s2 k1 p2sso

● P on RS rows, K on WS rows ◿ k2tog ◹ s1 k2tog psso

EYELET MESH PATTERN

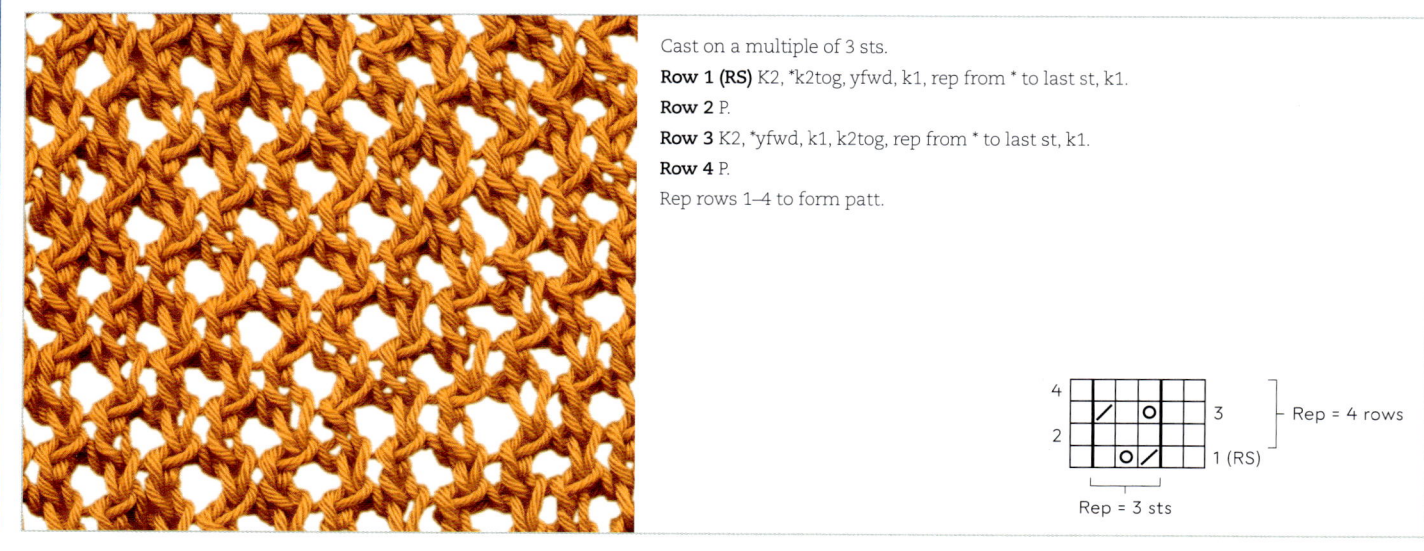

Cast on a multiple of 3 sts.
Row 1 (RS) K2, *k2tog, yfwd, k1, rep from * to last st, k1.
Row 2 P.
Row 3 K2, *yfwd, k1, k2tog, rep from * to last st, k1.
Row 4 P.
Rep rows 1–4 to form patt.

VERTICAL MESH PATTERN

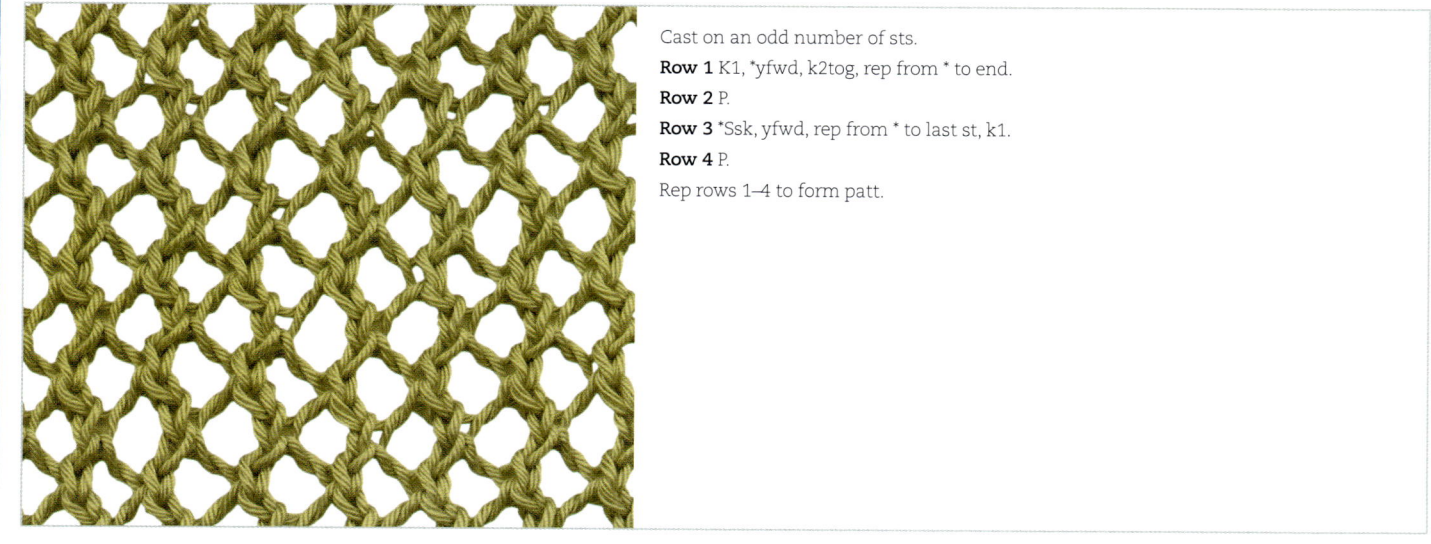

Cast on an odd number of sts.
Row 1 K1, *yfwd, k2tog, rep from * to end.
Row 2 P.
Row 3 *Ssk, yfwd, rep from * to last st, k1.
Row 4 P.
Rep rows 1–4 to form patt.

ARROWHEAD LACE

Cast on a multiple of 8 sts plus 5 extra sts.
Row 1 (RS) K1, yfwd, s1 k2tog psso, yfwd, *k5, yfwd, s1 k2tog psso, yfwd, rep from * to last st, k1.
Row 2 and all foll alt rows (WS) P.
Row 3 Rep row 1.
Row 5 K4, *yfwd, ssk, k1, k2tog, yfwd, k3, rep from * to last st, k1.
Row 7 K1, yfwd, s1 k2tog psso, yfwd, *k1, yfwd, s1 k2tog psso, yfwd, to last st, k1.
Row 8 P.
Rep rows 1–8 to form patt.

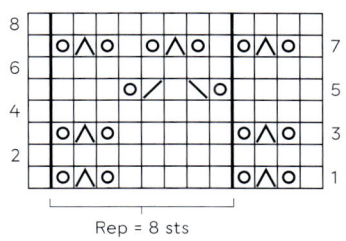

Rep = 8 sts

ZIGZAG MESH PATTERN

Cast on a multiple of 10 sts plus 1 extra st.
Row 1 (RS) K1, *[yfwd, ssk] twice, k1, [k2tog, yfwd] twice, k1, rep from * to end.
Row 2 P.
Row 3 K1, *k1, yfwd, ssk, yfwd, s1 k2tog psso, yfwd, k2tog, yfwd, k2, rep from * to end.
Row 4 P.
Rep rows 1–4 to form patt.

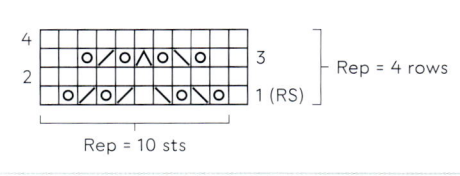

Rep = 10 sts Rep = 4 rows

STAR EYELET PATTERN

Cast on a multiple of 8 sts plus 5 extra sts.

Row 1 (RS) K4, *ssk, yfwd, k1, yfwd, k2tog, k3, rep from * to last st, k1.
Row 2 and all foll alt rows (WS) P.
Row 3 K5, *yfwd, s2 k1 p2sso, yfwd, k5, rep from * to end.
Row 5 Rep row 1.
Row 7 Ssk, yfwd, k1, yfwd, k2tog, *k3, ssk, yfwd, k1, yfwd, k2tog, rep from * to end.
Row 9 K1, *yfwd, s2 k1 p2sso, yfwd, k5, rep from * to end, ending last rep k1 (instead of k5).
Row 11 Rep row 7.
Row 12 P.

Rep rows 1–12 to form patt.

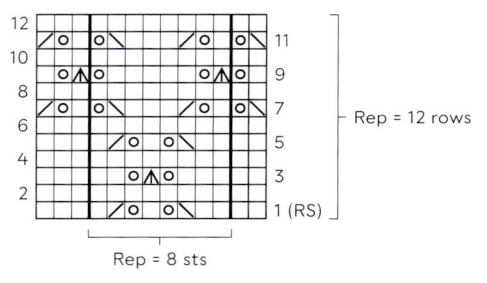

DOMINO EYELET PATTERN

Cast on a multiple of 8 sts.

Row 1 (RS) P.
Row 2 K.
Row 3 *K1, [yfwd, ssk] three times, k1, rep from * to end.
Row 4 and all foll alt rows (WS) P.
Row 5 *K2, [yfwd, ssk] twice, k2, rep from * to end.
Row 7 *K3, yfwd, ssk, k3, rep from * to end.
Row 9 Rep row 5.
Row 11 Rep row 3.
Row 12 P.

Rep rows 1–12 to form patt.

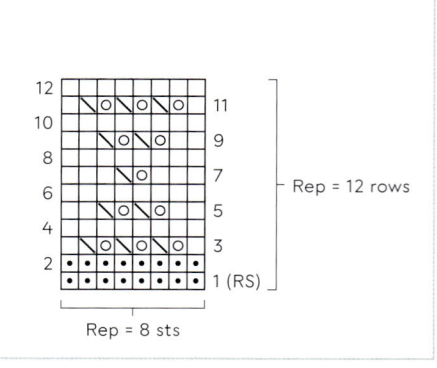

LACE STITCH PATTERNS 299

LEAVES LACE

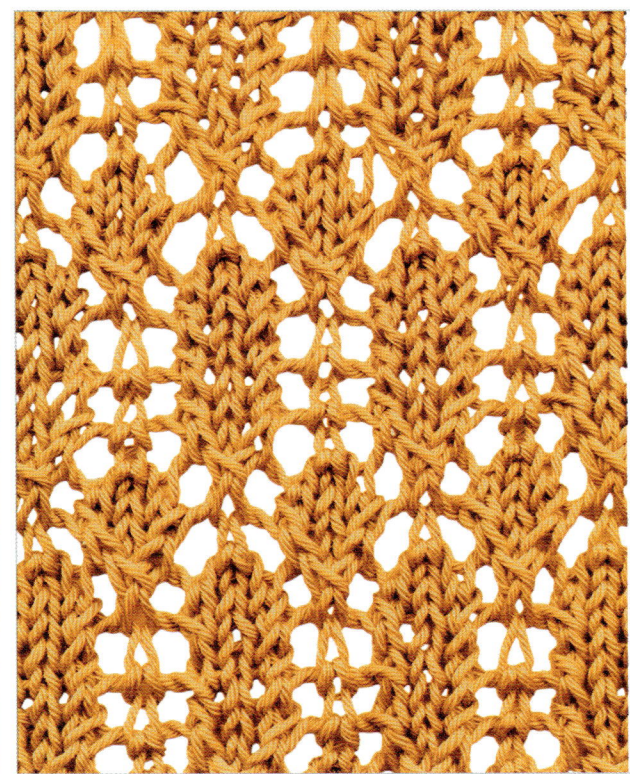

Cast on a multiple of 6 sts plus 1 extra st.

Row 1 (RS) K1, *yfwd, ssk, k1, k2tog, yfwd, k1, rep from * to end.

Row 2 P.

Rows 3–6 [Rep rows 1 and 2] twice.

Row 7 K2, *yfwd, s1 k2tog psso, yfwd, k3, rep from * to end, ending last rep k2 (instead of k3).

Row 8 and all foll alt rows (WS) P.

Row 9 K1, *k2tog, yfwd, k1, yfwd, ssk, k1, rep from * to end.

Row 11 K2tog, *yfwd, k3, yfwd, s1 k2tog psso, rep from * to last 5 sts, yfwd, k3, yfwd, ssk.

Row 12 P.

Rep rows 1–12 to form patt.

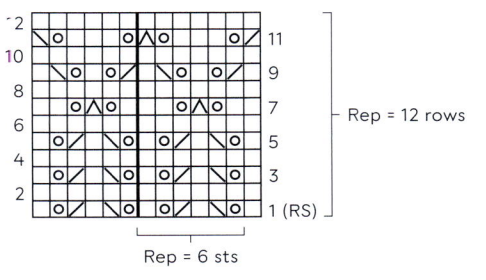

DIAMOND LACE PATTERN

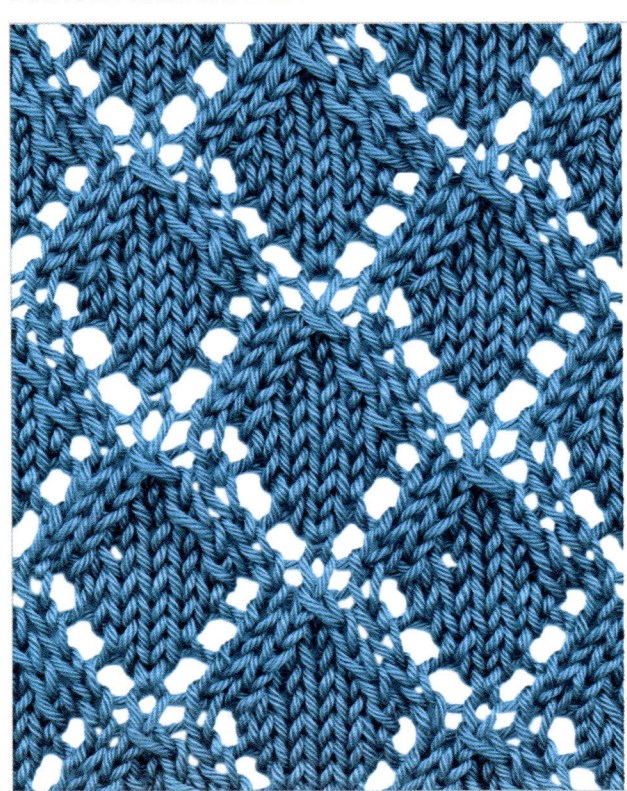

Cast on a multiple of 10 sts plus 1 extra st.

Row 1 (RS) K1, *k1, k2tog, [k1, yfwd] twice, k1, ssk, k2, rep from * to end.

Row 2 and all foll alt rows (WS) P.

Row 3 K1, *k2tog, k1, yfwd, k3, yfwd, k1, ssk, k1, rep from * to end.

Row 5 K2tog, *k1, yfwd, k5, yfwd, k1, s1 k2tog psso, rep from * to end, ending last rep ssk (instead of s1 k2tog psso).

Row 7 K1, *yfwd, k1, ssk, k3, k2tog, k1, yfwd, k1, rep from * to end.

Row 9 K1, *k1, yfwd, k1, ssk, k1, k2tog, k1, yfwd, k2, rep from * to end.

Row 11 K1, *k2, yfwd, k1, s1 k2tog psso, k1, yfwd, k3, rep from * to end.

Row 12 P.

Rep rows 1–12 to form patt.

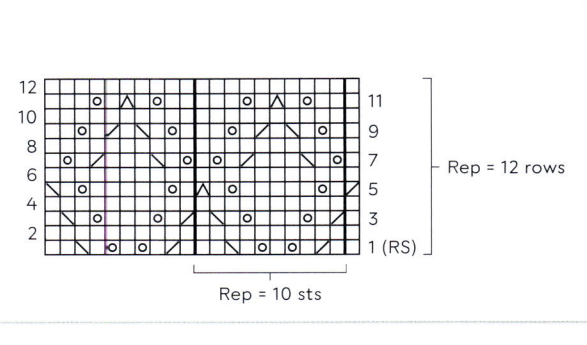

GRAND EYELET MESH PATTERN

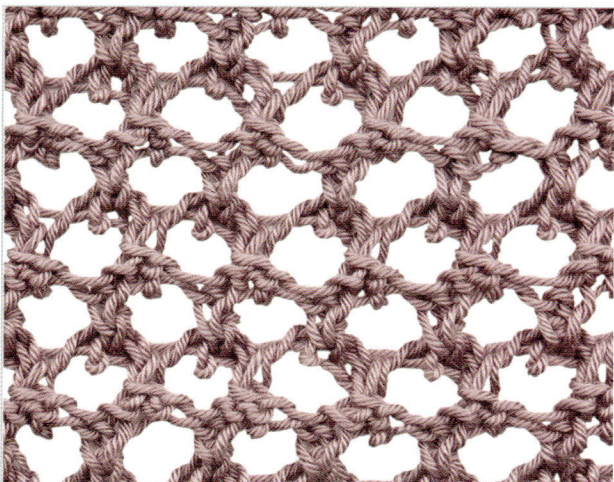

Note: This fabric looks the same on both sides. When blocking, stretch vertically to open eyelets.

Cast on a multiple of 3 sts plus 4 extra sts.

Row 1 K2, *sl k2tog psso, yfwd twice, rep from * to last 2 sts, k2.

Row 2 K2, *(p1, k1) into double yfwd, p1, rep from * to last 2 sts, k2.

Row 3 K.

Rep rows 1–3 to form patt.

VICTORY LACE

Cast on a multiple of 8 sts plus 6 extra sts.

Row 1 K5, *sl k1 psso, yo, k6, rep from * to last st, k1.

Row 2 and all foll alt rows (WS) P.

Row 3 K4, *sl k1 psso, yo, k1, yo, k2tog, k3, rep from * to last 2 sts, k2.

Row 5 K3, *sl k1 psso, yo, k3, yo, k2tog, k1, rep from * to last 3 sts, k3.

Row 7 K.

Row 8 P.

Rep rows 1–8 to form patt.

OPENWORK DIAMONDS

Cast on a multiple of 12 sts plus 7 extra sts.

Row 1 (RS) *K2, k2tog, yo, k8, rep from * to last 7 sts, k2, k2tog, yo, k3.

Row 2 and all foll alt rows (WS) P.

Row 3 *K1, k2tog, yo, k2tog, yo, k7, rep from * to last 7 sts, k1, k2tog, yo, k2tog, yo, k2.

Row 5 Rep row 1.

Row 7 K.

Row 9 *K8, k2tog, yo, k2, rep from * to last 7 sts, k7.

Row 11 *K7, k2tog, yo, k2tog, yo, k1, rep from * to last 7 sts, k7.

Row 13 Rep row 9.

Row 15 K.

Row 16 P.

Rep rows 1–16 to form patt.

SIMPLE DROP STITCH

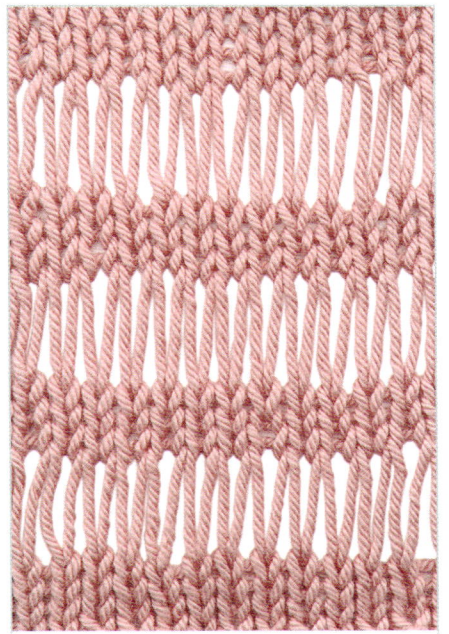

Cast on any number of sts.

Row 1 (WS) P.

Row 2 K.

Row 3 P.

Row 4 *Insert RH needle into next st as if to knit, wrap yarn around RH needle three times and bring all 3 loops through this st, rep from * to end.

Row 5 *Purl next st in first of the 3 loops only, allowing remaining 2 loops in this st to fall off LH needle and extend to full length, rep from * to end.

Rep rows 2–5 to form patt.

HORSESHOE LACE

Cast on a multiple of 10 sts plus 1 extra st.

Row 1 (RS) K1, *yo, k3, s1 k2tog psso, k3, yo, k1, rep from * to end.

Row 2 and all foll alt rows (WS) P.

Row 3 K2, *yo, k2, s1 k2tog psso, k2, yo, k3, rep from * to last 9 sts, yo, k2, s1 k2tog psso, k2, yo, k2.

Row 5 K3, *yo, k1, s1 k2tog psso, k1, yo, k5, rep from * to last 8 sts, yo, k1, s1 k2tog psso, k1, yo, k3.

Row 7 K4, *yo, s1 k2tog psso, yo, k7, rep from * to last 7 sts, yo, s1 k2tog psso, yo, k4.

Row 8 P.

Rep rows 1–8 to form patt.

DIAGONAL LACE RIBS

Cast on a multiple of 7 sts plus 1 extra st.

Row 1 (RS) P1, *yo, s1 k1 psso, k4, p1, rep from * to end.

Row 2 and all foll alt rows (WS) K1, *p6, k1, rep from * to end.

Row 3 P1, * k1, yo, s1 k1 psso, k3, p1, rep from * to end.

Row 5 P1, *k2, yo, s1 k1 psso, k2, p1, rep from * to end.

Row 7 P1, *k3, yo, s1 k1 psso, k1, p1, rep from * to end.

Row 9 P1, *k4, yo, s1 k1 psso, p1, rep from * to end.

Row 10 Rep row 2.

Rep rows 1–10 to form patt.

LADDER LACE

Cast on a multiple of 6 sts plus 3 extra sts.

Row 1 (RS) K3, *yo, s1k, k2tog, psso, yo, k3, rep from * to end.

Row 2 P.

Rep rows 1 and 2 to form patt.

EYELET LINES

Cast on a multiple of 2 sts.
Row 1 (RS) K.
Row 2 and all foll alt rows (WS) P.
Row 3 Rep row 1.
Row 5 K1, *k2tog, yo, rep from * to last st, k1.
Row 6 P.
Rep rows 1–6 to form patt.

MINI-LEAF PATTERN

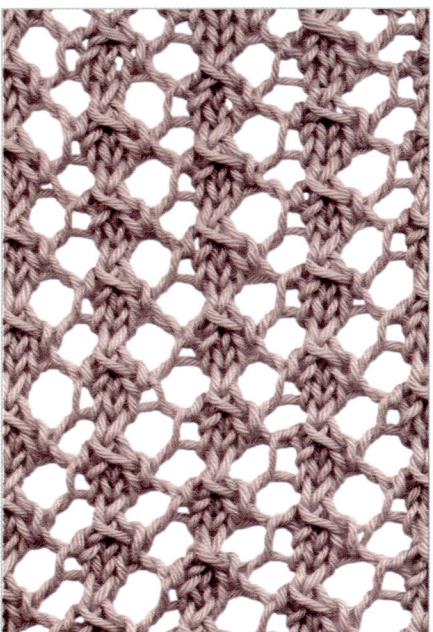

Cast on a multiple of 6 sts plus 2 extra sts.
Row 1 (RS) K1, *k3, yfwd, s1 k2tog psso, yfwd, rep from * to last st, k1.
Row 2 P.
Row 3 K1, *yfwd, s1 k2tog psso, yfwd, k3, rep from * to last st, k1.
Row 4 P.
Rep rows 1–4 to form patt.

VERTICAL MESH COLUMNS

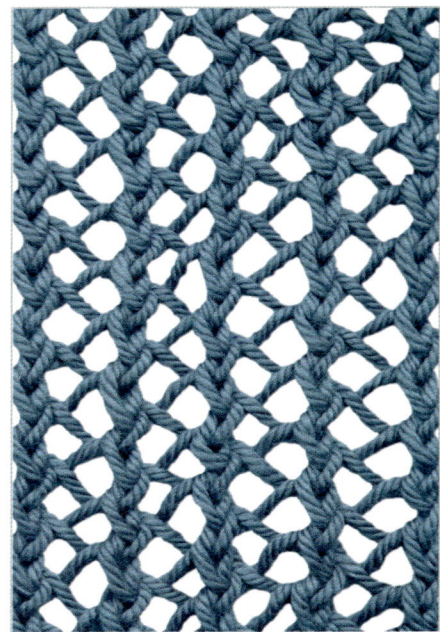

Cast on an even number of sts (minimum 8 sts).
Row 1 (RS) K2, *yo, ssk, rep from * last 2 sts, k2.
Row 2 P4, *yrn, p2tog, rep from * to last 2 sts, p2.
Rep rows 1 and 2 to form patt.

DROPPED STITCH PATTERN

Cast on a multiple of 4 sts plus 2 extra sts.
Row 1 (RS) K.
Row 2 and all foll alt rows (WS) P.
Row 3 K1, *k2, yo, k2, rep from * to last st, k1.
Row 5 K.
Row 7 K1, *yo, k2, drop next st off LH needle and allow to ladder down to yo worked on row 3, k2, rep from * to last st, k1.
Row 9 K.
Row 11 K1, *drop next st off LH needle and allow to ladder down to yo worked on row 7, k2, yo, k2, rep from * to last st, k1.
Row 12 P.
Rep rows 5–12 to form patt. Cast off on WS.

COLOURWORK PATTERNS

Here are some easy-to-work stocking stitch colourwork patterns. A few of the patterns are suitable for the stranded colourwork technique, and the remainder for the intarsia technique or a combination of both. The borders can be worked individually for simple bands of colour or repeated to make up an item in stripes. If you have never tried colourwork, start with stranded colourwork patterns, such as Fair Isle, because they only use two colours in every row. See pp.118–128 for step-by-step guidance on colourwork techniques.

CHART KEY

☐ Background colour   ● Motif colour

SIMPLE STRANDED BORDERS

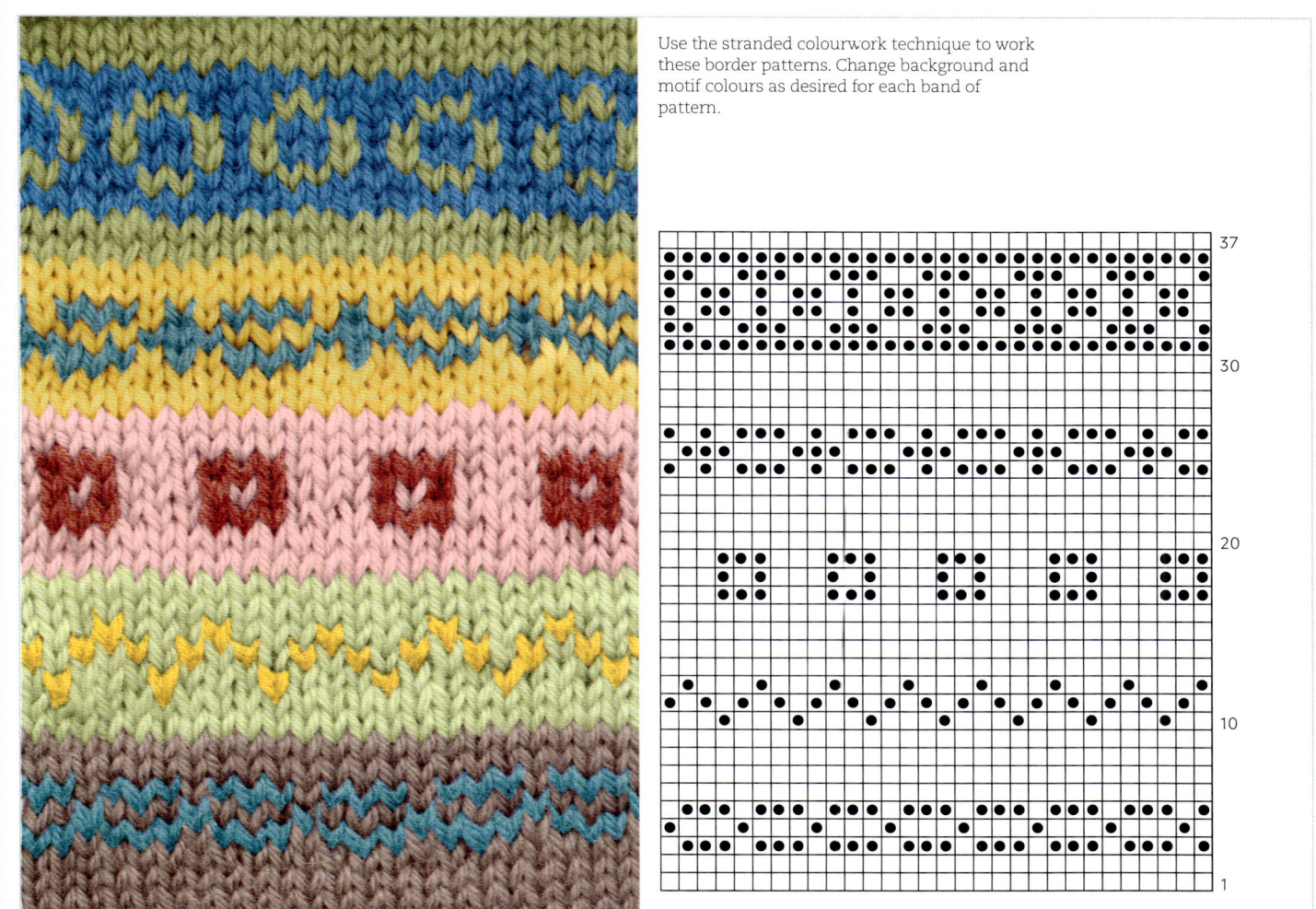

Use the stranded colourwork technique to work these border patterns. Change background and motif colours as desired for each band of pattern.

▶ USING STRANDED COLOURWORK CHARTS

Many of these charts can be adapted for use on mosaic (see p.134) or double knitting (see p.136) pieces. Conventional colourwork such as intarsia will work best for large colour blocks, but combine it with the stranded technique for efficiency within isolated motifs. Use stranded colourwork for small repeating elements or narrow bands, then return to intarsia for larger sections. Consider how colour placement affects visual impact. Bold contrasts emphasize texture, while subtle variations can create depth. Watch your tension control with both techniques, because uneven gauge distorts colourwork patterns and can leave them looking messy.

THREE-COLOUR ZIGZAGS

Use the stranded colourwork technique to work this repeating pattern. Choose three colours: a light, medium, and dark shade work best.

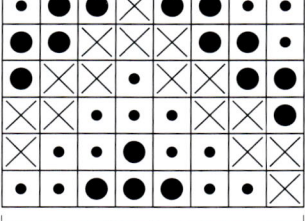

KEY
⊠ = A
· = B
● = C

Rep = 8 sts

NORDIC MOTIF

This classic snowflake stitch pattern features delicate winter motifs, using two highly contrasting colours. It can easily be applied to scarves, mittens or jumpers. Use it repeatedly across your knitting for an all-over wintery design.

KEY
☐ Background colour
⊠ Motif colour

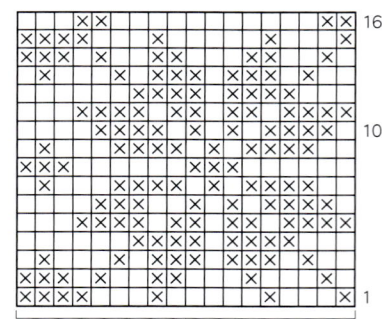

Rep = 18 sts

STRANDED HEART MOTIF

Use the stranded colourwork technique to work this repeating pattern. Choose two colours: one colour for the motif and another colour for the background.

KEY
☐ Background colour
⬤ Motif colour

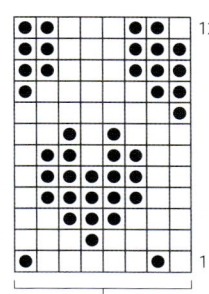

Rep = 8 sts

INTARSIA HEART MOTIF

Use the intarsia technique to work this heart. Choose two colours: one colour for the motif and another colour for the background.

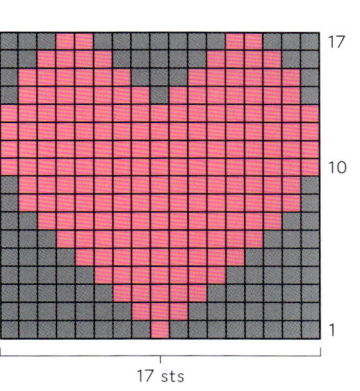

17 sts

INTARSIA MONSTERA LEAF

This monstera leaf motif uses the intarsia technique with two colours: one for the leaf and another for the background. The large-scale design works best as a single statement on cushion covers, bags, or as a feature panel on garments.

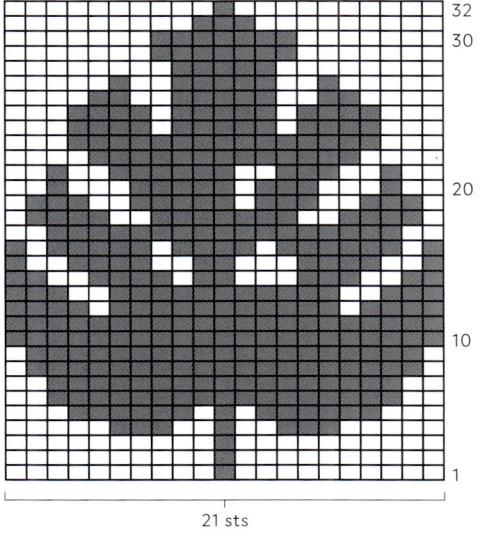

21 sts

STRANDED BLOSSOM MOTIF

Use the stranded colourwork technique to work this repeating pattern. Choose two colours: one motif colour and one background colour.

KEY
☐ Background colour
● Motif colour

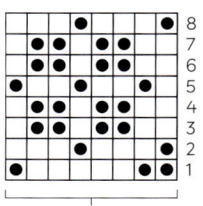

Rep = 8 sts

INTARSIA TULIP MOTIF

Use the intarsia technique to work the tulip motif and the background around the tulip head in this pattern. When working the stem, use the Fair Isle technique to work only the background colour. Choose four colours: three motif colours and one background colour.

KEY
☐ = A
☒ = B
· = C
● = D

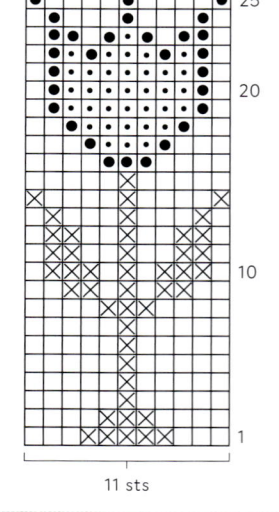

11 sts

INTARSIA SNOWFLAKE MOTIF

Use a combination of stranded colourwork and intarsia techniques to work this motif. Choose two colours: one colour for the motif and another for the background.

KEY
☐ Background colour
● Motif colour

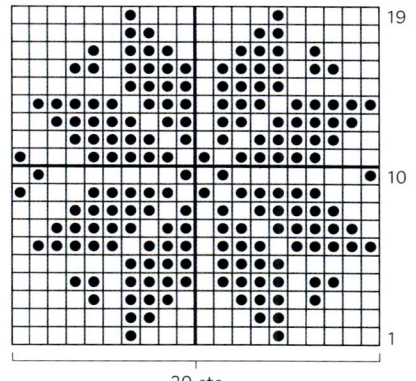

20 sts

COMBINED STRANDED AND INTARSIA ARGYLE MOTIF

Use the intarsia and stranded colourwork techniques to work this pattern. Choose three colours: one for the motif, one for the background, and one for the stripe.

KEY
☐ = A
● = B
☒ = C

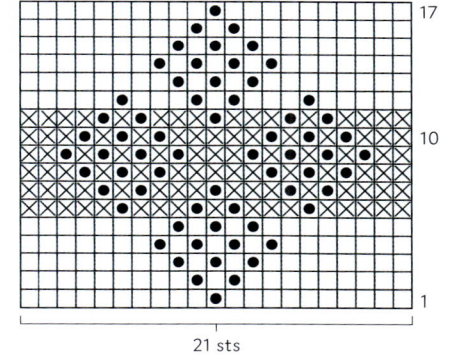

21 sts

INTARSIA PAWPRINT

This pawprint motif uses the intarsia technique with two colours: one for the pawprint and one for the background. Work the design individually or repeat across blankets or garments, in either a scattered or a more structured placement.

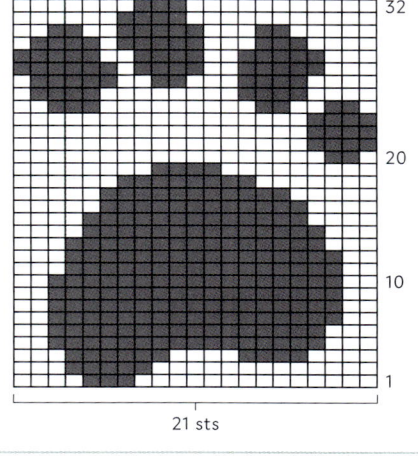

21 sts

INTARSIA LETTER MOTIFS A TO Z

Use the combined alphabet chart by isolating the letters you need for your project. Count the stitches for the width of each of your letters, plan the spacing between letters, then calculate the total width of your word or phrase. Place your complete chart centrally on your knitted piece, ensuring even spacing on both sides for a balanced look. All the letter charts are 32 rows tall – as are the numbers on p.310 – so you can use them together if you need to for your design.

Letter	Width
A	25 sts
B	21 sts
C	21 sts
D	25 sts
E	21 sts
F	21 sts
G	23 sts
H	25 sts
I	13 sts
J	21 sts
K	25 sts
L	21 sts

COLOURWORK PATTERNS **309**

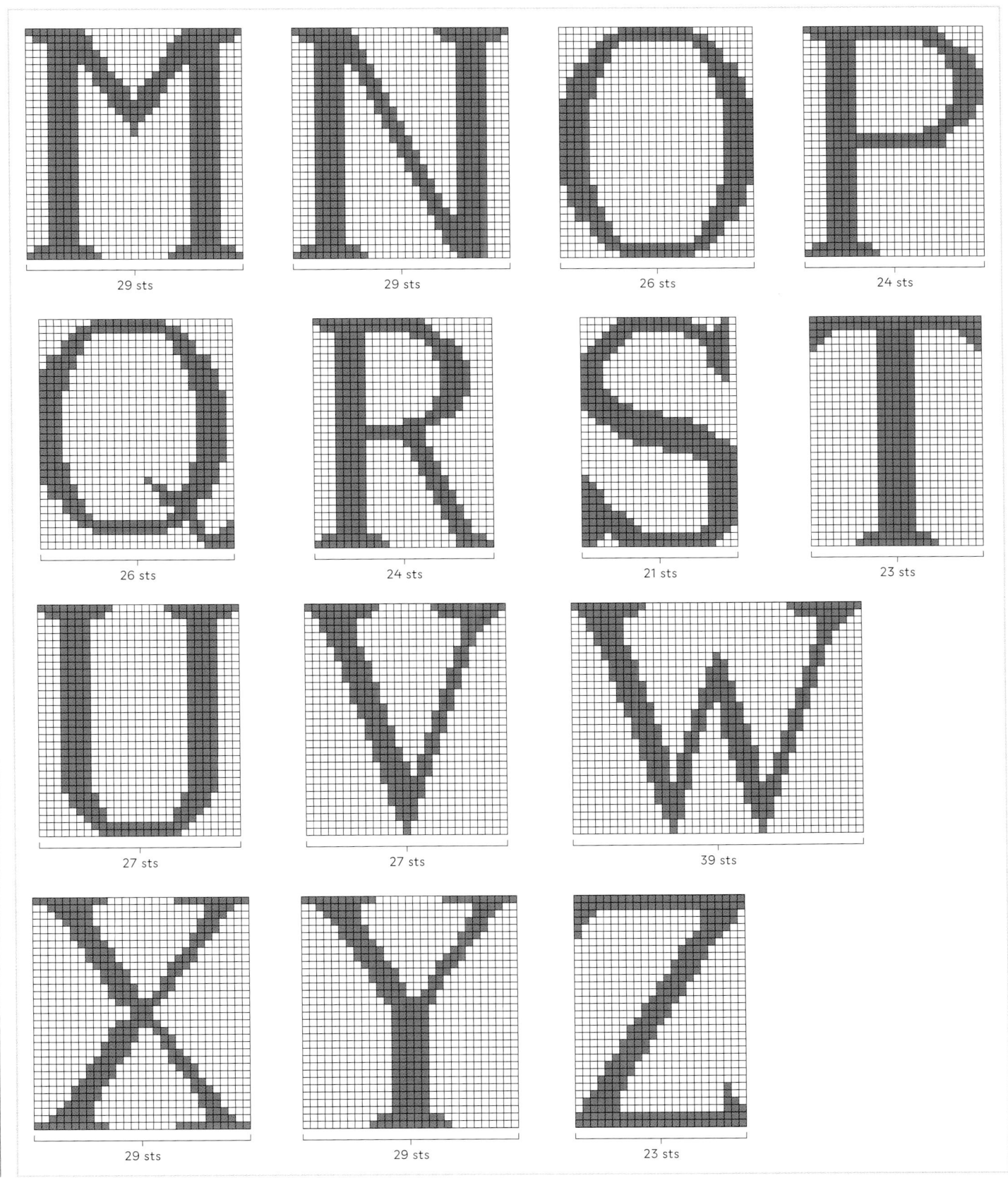

INTARSIA NUMBERS 0 TO 9

Select the digits you need from the number chart. Plan the overall layout by deciding if the numbers should be grouped together or spaced apart, then mark the starting position on your knitting to ensure the completed sequence fits within the project dimensions. You can use stitch markers to remind you where to begin each chart. All the number charts are 32 rows tall – as are the letters on pp.308–309 – so you can use them together if you need to for your design.

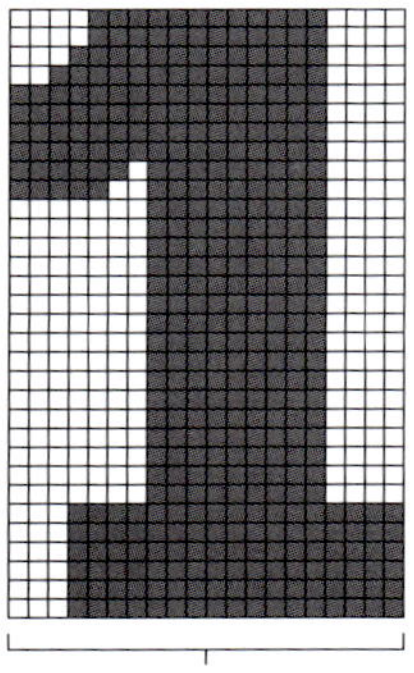

20 sts  28 sts  28 sts 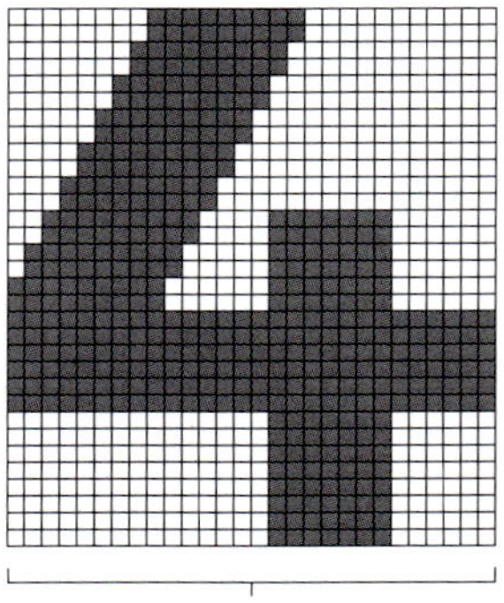 28 sts

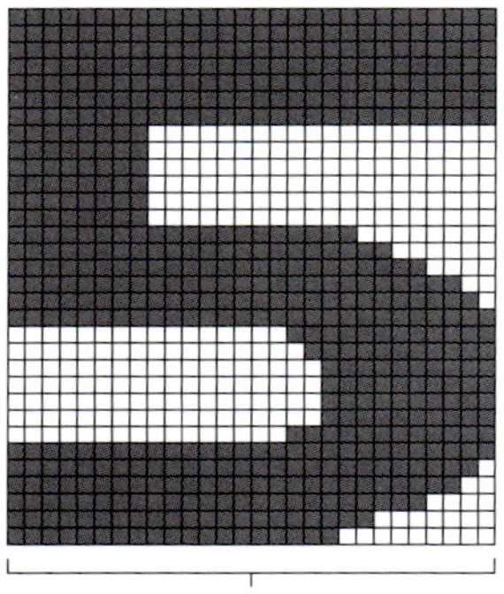

28 sts  28 sts 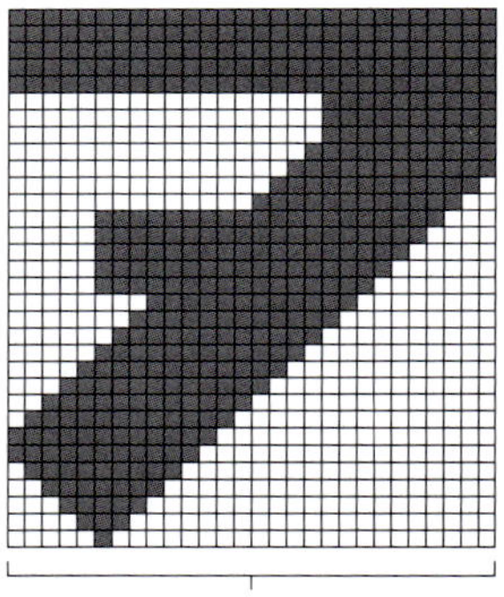 28 sts  28 sts

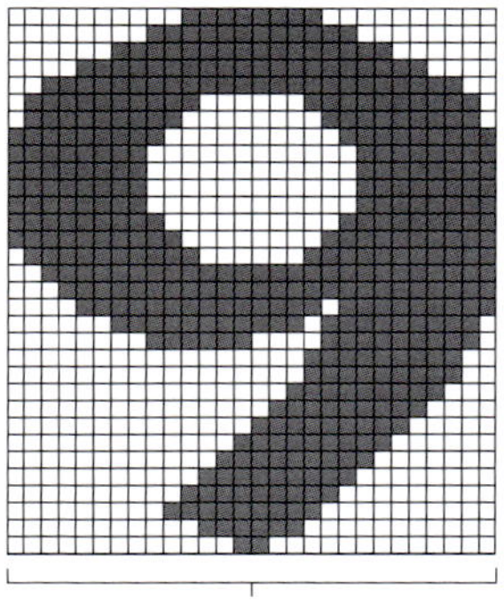

28 sts 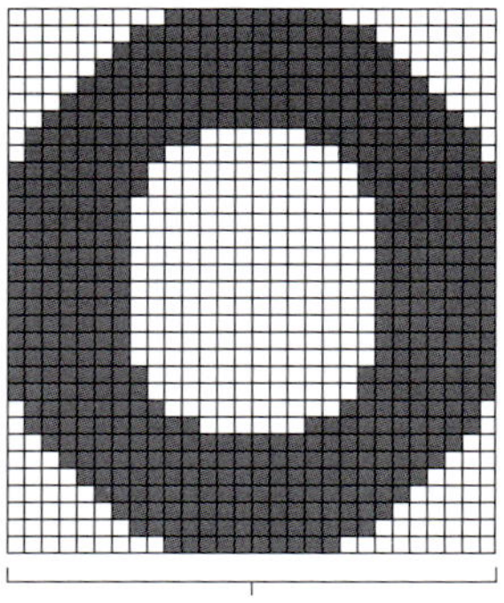 28 sts

FAUX COLOURWORK PATTERNS

There are many ways to bring colour into your knitting that don't depend on intarsia and stranded colourwork. Slip-stitch colourwork involves pulling up stitches worked on previous rows to showcase their colour in rows above. All stitches are slipped purlwise, unless otherwise stated. Similar colour effects can be achieved with mosaic knitting (p.134), or brioche knitting (pp.131–132). Patterns with a lot of slipped stitches create stronger and thicker fabrics – perfect for bags, cushion covers, and blankets.

PEEPING PURL STITCH

Note: All sts to be slipped purlwise. Using A, cast on an odd number of sts.
Row 1 (RS) Using A, k.
Row 2 Using A, p.
Rows 3 and 4 Rep rows 1 and 2.
Row 5 Using B, k1, *s1 wyib, k1, rep from * to end.
Row 6 Using B, k1, *s1 wyif, k1, rep from * to end.
Row 7 Rep row 1.
Row 8 Rep row 2.
Rep last 2 rows once more.
Row 11 Using B, s1 wyib, *k1, s1 wyib, rep from * to end.
Row 12 Using B, s1 wyif, *k1, s1 wyif, rep from * to end.
Rep rows 2–9 to form patt.

GARTER SLIP STITCH

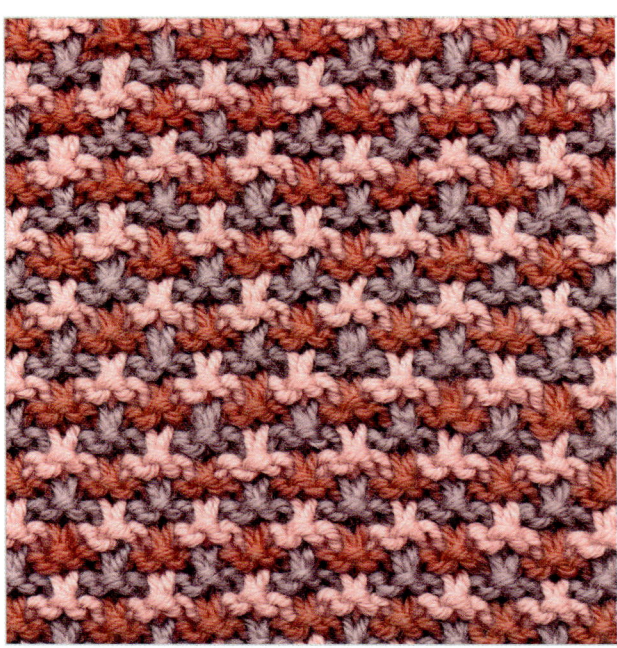

Note: All sts to be slipped purlwise. Using C, cast on a multiple of 4 sts plus 3 extra sts.
Row 1 (RS) Using A, k1, *s1, k3, rep from * to last 2 sts, s1, k1.
Row 2 Using A, k1, *s1 wyif, k3, rep from * to last 2 sts, s1 wyif, k1.
Row 3 Using B, k3, *s1, k3, rep from * to end.
Row 4 Using B, k3, *s1 wyif, k3, rep from * to end.
Row 5 Using C, k1, *s1, k3, rep from * to last 2 sts, s1, k1.
Row 6 Using C, k1, *s1 wyif, k3, rep from * to last 2 sts, s1 wyif, k1.
Row 7 Using A, k3, *s1, k3, rep from * to end.
Row 8 Using A, k3, *s1 wyif, k3, rep from * to end.
Row 9 Using B, k1, *s1, k3, rep from * to last 2 sts, s1, k1.
Row 10 Using B, k1, *s1 wyif, k3, rep from * to last 2 sts, s1 wyif, k1.
Row 11 Using C, k3, *s1, k3, rep from * to end.
Row 12 Using C, k3, *s1 wyif, k3, rep from * to end.
Rep rows 1–12 to form patt.

BROKEN STRIPES STITCH

Note: All sts to be slipped purlwise.

Using A, cast on a multiple of 4 sts plus 2 extra sts.

Row 1 (RS) Using A, k.

Row 2 Using A, p.

Rows 3 and 4 Rep rows 1 and 2.

Row 5 Using B, k2, *s1, k3, rep from * to end.

Row 6 Using B, p.

Row 7 Using B, k.

Row 8 Using B, p.

Row 9 Using A, k4, *s1, k3, rep from * to last 2 sts, s1, k1.

Rep rows 2–9 to form patt.

ARROWHEAD STITCH

Special abbreviations

C3L – Place 1 st on cable needle and hold at front of work, k2, then k1 from cable needle.

C3R – Place 2 sts on cable needle and hold at back of work, k1, then k2 from cable needle.

Note: All sts to be slipped purlwise. Using A, cast on a multiple of 7 sts plus 1 extra st.

Row 1 (RS) Using A, k.

Row 2 Using A, p.

Row 3 Using B, *k1, s1, k4, s1, rep from * to last st, k1.

Row 4 Using B, p1, *s1, p4, s1, p1, rep from * to last st, p1.

Row 5 Rep row 3.

Row 6 Rep row 4.

Row 7 Using B, *k1, C3L, C3R, rep from * to last st, k1.

Row 8 Using B, p.

Row 9 Using A, *k1, s1, k4, s1, rep from * to last st, k1.

Row 10 Using A, p1, *s1, p4, s1, p1, rep from * to last st, p1.

Row 11 Rep row 9.

Row 12 Rep row 10.

Row 13 Using A, *k1, C3L, C3R, rep from * to last st, k1.

Row 14 Using A, p.

Rep rows 3–14 to form patt.

WEAVER'S STITCH

Note: All sts to be slipped purlwise.
Using A, cast on an even number of sts.
Row 1 (RS) Using A, *k1, s1 wyif, rep from * to end.
Row 2 Using A, *p1, s1 wyib, rep from * to end.
Row 3 Using B, *k1, s1 wyif, rep from * to end.
Row 4 Using B, *p1, s1 wyib, rep from * to end.
Rep rows 1–4 to form patt.

HONEYCOMB STITCH

Note: All sts to be slipped purlwise.
Using A, cast on a multiple of 4 sts plus 1 extra st.
Row 1 (RS) Using A, k.
Row 2 Using A, p.
Rows 3 Using B, *s1, k3, rep from * to last st, k1.
Row 4 Using B, p1, *p3, s1, rep from * to last st, k1.
Row 5 Rep row 3.
Row 6 Rep row 4.
Row 7 Using A, k.
Row 8 Using A, p.
Row 9 Using C, *k2, s1, k1, rep from * to last st, k1.
Row 10: Using C, p1, *p1, s1, p2, rep from * to last st, k1.
Row 11 Rep row 9.
Row 12 Rep row 10.
Row 13 Using A, k.
Row 14 Using A, p.
Rep rows 3–14 to form patt.

VERTICAL STRIPES STITCH

Note: All sts to be slipped purlwise. Tension will be tighter as a result of slipped stitch columns, so it is advisable to cast on an extra third to requirements.

Using A, cast on a multiple of 4 sts (minimum 12 sts).

Row 1 (RS) Using A, k.
Row 2 Using A, p.
Row 3 Using B, k3, s2, *k2, s2, rep from * to last 3 sts, k3.
Row 4 Using B, p3, s2, *p2, s2, rep from * to last 3 sts, p3.
Row 5 Using A, k1, s2, *k2, s2, rep from * to last st, k1.
Row 6 Using A, p1, s2, *p2, s2, rep from * to last st, p1.
Rep rows 3–6 to form patt.

MOSAIC TRIANGLES

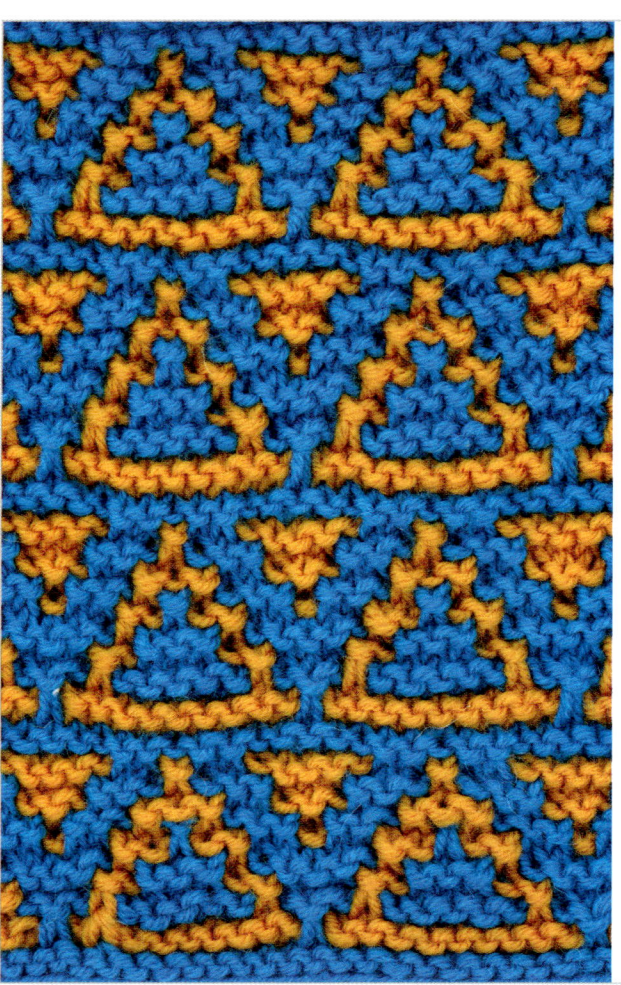

Using A, cast on a multiple of 10 sts plus 5.

Row 1 (RS) Using A, k.
Row 2 K.
Row 3 Using B, k2, *k1, s2 wyib, k5, s2 wyib, rep from * to last 3 sts, k3.
Row 4 Using B, k3, *s2 wyif, k5, s2 wyif, k1, rep from * to last 2 sts, k2.
Row 5 Using A, k1, s1 wyib, *s1 wyib, k3, s3 wyib, k3, rep from * to last 3 sts, s2 wyib, k1.
Row 6 Using A, k1, s2 wyif, *k3, s3 wyif, k3, s1 wyif, rep from * to last 2 sts, s1 wyif, k1.
Row 7 Using B, k2, *k2, s2 wyib, k3, s2 wyib, k1, rep from * to last 3 sts, k3.
Row 8 Using B, k3, *k1, s2 wyif, k3, s2 wyif, k2, rep from * to last 2 sts, k2.
Row 9 Using A, k1, s1 wyib, *k1, [s1 wyib, k3] twice, s1 wyib, rep from * to last 3 sts, k1, s1 wyib, k1.
Row 10 Using A, k1, s1 wyif, k1, *[s1 wyif, k3] twice, s1 wyif, k1, rep from * to last 2 sts, s1 wyif, k1.
Row 11 Using B, k2, *s1 wyib, k2, s2 wyib, k1, s2 wyib, k2, rep from * to last 3 sts, s1 wyib, k2.
Row 12 Using B, k2, s1 wyif, *k2, s2 wyif, k1, s2 wyif, k2, s1 wyif, rep from * to last 2 sts, k2.
Row 13 Using A, k2, *k2, s1 wyib, k5, s1 wyib, k1, rep from * to last 3 sts, k3.
Row 14 Using A, k3, *k1, s1 wyif, k5, s1 wyif, k2, rep from * to last 2 sts, k2.
Row 15 Using B, k1, s1 wyib, *s2 wyib, k2, s3 wyib, k2, s1 wyib, rep from * to last 3 sts, s2 wyib, k1.
Row 16 Using B, k1, s2 wyif, *s1 wyif, k2, s3 wyif, k2, s2 wyif, rep from * to last 2 sts, s1 wyif, k1.
Row 17 Using A, k2, *k3, s1 wyib, k3, s1 wyib, k2, rep from * to last 3 sts, k3.
Row 18 Using A, k3, * k2, s1 wyif, k3, s1 wyif, k3, rep from * to last 2 sts, k2.
Row 19 Using B, k2, *k5, s1 wyib, k4, rep from * to last 3 sts, k3.
Row 20 Using B, k3, *k4, s1 wyif, k5, rep from * to last 2 sts, k2.

Rep rows 1–20 to form patt. Work 2 rows k before casting off.

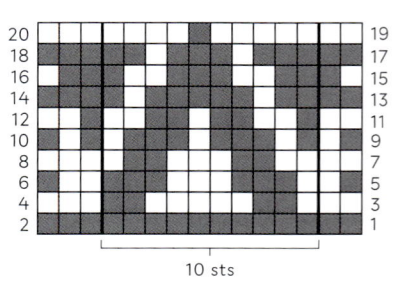

10 sts

TEXTURED HONEYCOMB

Using A, cast on a multiple of 8 sts + 4.
Row 1 (RS) Using A, K.
Row 2 K.
Row 3 P.
Row 4 K.
Row 5 Using B, k1, [s2 wyib, k6] to last 3 sts, s2 wyib, k1.
Row 6 P1, [s2 wyif, p6] to last 3 sts, s2 wyif, p1.
Rep last 2 rows twice more.
Rows 11–14 Using A, work as given for rows 1–4.
Row 15 Using B, k5, s2 wyib, [k6, s2 wyib] to last 5 sts, k5.
Row 16 P5, s2 wyif, [p6, s2 wyif] to last 5 sts, p5.
Rep last 2 rows twice more.
Rep rows 1–16 to form patt.
Cast off after row 4.

MOSAIC HERRINGBONE

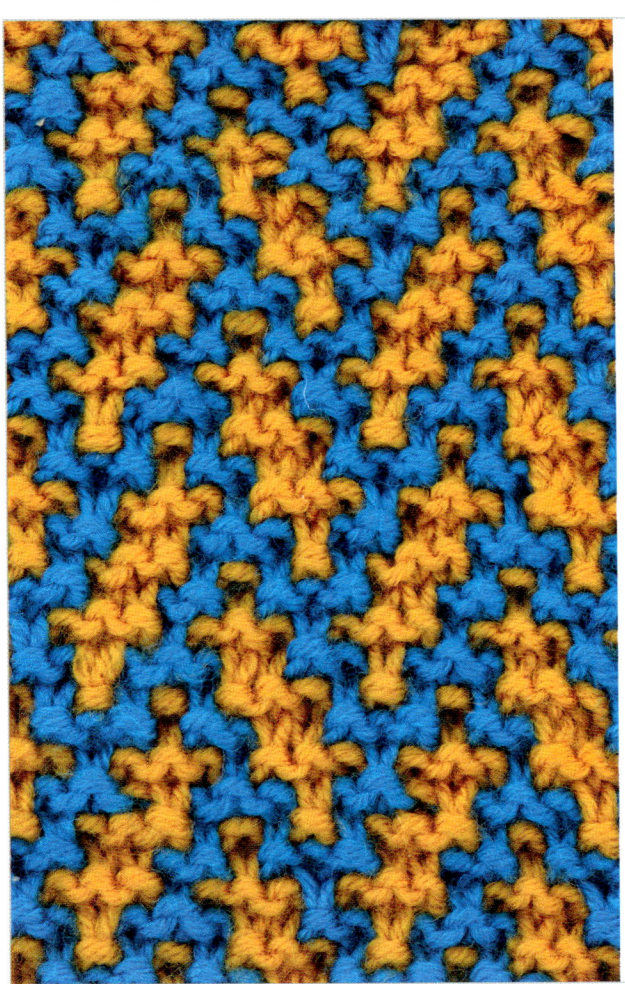

Using A, cast on a multiple of 8 sts plus 3.
Row 1 (RS) Using A, k.
Row 2 K.
Row 3 Using B, k1, *k2, s1 wyib, k3, s2 wyib, rep from * to last 2 sts k2.
Row 4 K2, *s2 wyif, k3, s1 wyif, k2, rep from * to last st, k1.
Row 5 Using A, k1, *[k1, s1 wyib] 3 times, k2, rep from * to last 2 sts, k2.
Row 6 K2, *k2, [s1 wyif, k1] 3 times, rep from * to last st, k1.
Row 7 Using B, k1, *s1 wyib, k3, s1 wyib, k2, s1 wyib, rep from * to last 2 sts, s1 wyib, k1.
Row 8 K1, s1 wyif, *s1 wyif, k2, s1 wyif, k3, s1 wyif, rep from * to last st, k1.
Row 9 Using A, k1, *k2, s1 wyib, k3, s1 wyib, k1, rep from * to last 2 sts, k2.
Row 10 K2, *k1, s1 wyif, k3, s1 wyif, k2, rep from * to last st, k1.
Row 11 Using B, k1, *s1 wyib, k2, s2 wyib, k3, rep from * to last 2 sts, s1 wyib, k1.
Row 12 K1, s1 wyif, *k3, s2 wyif, k2, s1 wyif, rep from * to last st, k1.
Row 13 Using A, k1, *k1, s1 wyib, k3, s1 wyib, k1, s1 wyib, rep from * to last 2 sts, k2.
Row 14 K2, *s1 wyif, k1, s1 wyif, k3, s1 wyif, k1, rep from * to last st, k1.
Row 15 Using B, k1, *k2, s2 wyib, k2, s1 wyib, k1, rep from * to last 2 sts, k2.
Row 16 K2, *k1, s1 wyif, k2, s2 wyif, k2, rep from * to last st, k1.
Row 17 Using A, k1, *s1 wyib, k3, rep from * to last 2 sts, s1 wyib, k1.
Row 18 K1, s1 wyif, *k3, s1 wyif, rep from * to last st, k1.
Rep rows 3–18 to form patt. Work 2 rows k before casting off.

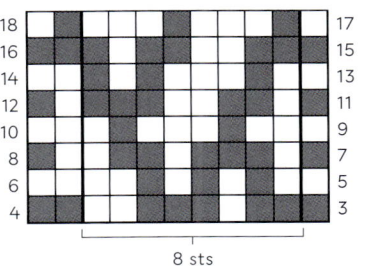

8 sts

BRIOCHE CABLES

Special abbreviations

brk, brioche-knit – knit st together with its yarnover.

brp, brioche purl – purl st together with its yarnover.

brLsl dec – 2-st decrease slanting left, over three sts: slip first st knitwise, brk following two sts together, pass slipped st over.

brRsl dec – 2-st decrease slanting right, over three sts: slip first st knitwise, knit next st, pass slipped st over, place st on LH needle and pass following st over. Place st back on RH needle.

Work on circular or double-pointed needles, you will slide sts to each end of the needle as needed, to work a RS and WS rows consecutively.

Cast on a multiple of 16 sts + 3 using colour A.

Foundation Row (WS) Using A, p1, *s1 wyif, yo, p1, rep from * to end. Do not turn, slide sts to other end of needle to start again using B, with WS still facing. Using B, S1 wyif, *brk, s1 wyif, yo, rep from * to last 2 sts, brk, s1 wyif, turn.

Row 1 (RS) Using A, k1, s1 wyif, yo, *(brk, yo, brk) in next st, s1 wyif, yo, [brk, s1 wyif, yo] twice, brLsl dec, s1 wyif, yo, [brk, s1 wyif, yo] 3 times, rep from * to last st, k1. Do not turn, slide sts to other end of needle. Using B, s1 wyif, brp, *s1 wyif, yo, p1, [s1 wyif, yo, brp] 7 times, rep from * to last st, s1 wyif, turn.

Row 2 and all foll alt rows (WS) Using A, p1, *s1 wyif, yo, brp, rep from * to last 2 sts, s1 wyif, yo, p1. Do not turn, slide sts to other end of needle. Using B, s1 wyif, *brk, s1 wyif, yo, rep from * to last 2 sts, brk, s1 wyif, turn.

Row 3 (RS) Using A, k1, s1 wyif, yo, *brk, s1 wyif, yo, (brk, yo, brk) in next st, s1 wyif, yo, [brk, s1 wyif, yo] twice, brLsl dec, s1 wyif, yo, [brk, s1 wyif, yo] twice, rep from * to last st, k1. Do not turn, slide sts to other end of needle. Using B, s1 wyif, brp, *s1 wyif, yo, brp, s1 wyif, yo, p1, [s1 wyif, yo, brp] 6 times, rep from * to last st, s1 wyif, turn.

Row 5 (RS) Using A, k1, s1 wyif, yo, *[brk, s1 wyif, yo] twice, (brk, yo, brk) in next st, s1 wyif, yo, [brk, s1 wyif, yo] twice, brLsl dec, s1 wyif, yo, brk, s1 wyif, yo, rep from * to last st, k1. Do not turn, slide sts to other end of needle. Using B, s1 wyif, brp, *[s1 wyif, yo, brp] twice, s1 wyif, yo, p1, [s1 wyif, yo, brp] 5 times, rep from * to last st, s1 wyif, turn.

Row 7 (RS) Using A, k1, s1 wyif, yo, *[brk, s1 wyif, yo] 3 times, (brk, yo, brk) in next st, s1 wyif, yo, [brk, s1 wyif, yo] twice, brLsl dec, s1 wyif, yo, rep from * to last st, k1. Do not turn, slide sts to other end of needle. Using B, s1 wyif, brp, *[s1 wyif, yo, brp] 3 times, s1 wyif, yo, p1, [s1 wyif, yo, brp] 4 times, rep from * to last st, s1 wyif, turn.

Row 9 (RS) Using A, k1, s1 wyif, yo, *brk, s1 wyif, yo, rep from * to last st, k1. Do not turn, slide sts to other end of needle. Using B, s1 wyif, brp, *s1 wyif, yo, brp, rep from * to last st, s1 wyif, turn.

Rep rows 1–10 to form patt.

DIAGONAL BRIOCHE

Special abbreviations

brk, brioche-knit – knit st together with its yarnover.

brp, brioche purl – purl st together with its yarnover.

brLsl dec – 2-st decrease slanting left, over three sts: slip first st knitwise, brk following two sts together, pass slipped st over.

brRsl dec – 2-st decrease slanting right, over three sts: slip first st knitwise, knit next st, pass slipped st over, place st on LH needle and pass following st over. Place st back on RH needle.

Work on circular or double-pointed needles, you will slide sts to each end of the needle as needed, to work a RS and WS rows consecutively.

Cast on a multiple of 18 sts + 3 using colour A.

Foundation Row (WS) Using A, p1, *s1 wyif, yo, p1, rep from * to end. Do not turn, slide sts to other end of needle to start again using B, with WS still facing. Using B, s1 wyif, *brk, s1 wyif, yo, rep from * to last 2 sts, brk, s1 wyif, turn.

Row 1 (RS) Using A, k1, s1 wyif, yo, *brRsl dec, s1 wyif, yo, [brk, s1 wyif, yo] twice, ([brk, yo] twice, brk) all in next st, s1 wyif, yo, [brk, s1 wyif, yo] twice, brLsl dec, s1 wyif, yo, rep from * to last st, k1. Do not turn, slide sts to other end of needle. Using B, s1 wyif, brp, *[s1 wyif, yo, brp] 3 times, [s1 wyif, yo, p1] twice, [s1 wyif, yo, brp] 4 times, rep from * to last st, s1 wyif, turn.

Row 2 and all foll alt rows (WS) Using A, p1, *s1 wyif, yo, brp, rep from * to last 2 sts, s1 wyif, yo, p1. Do not turn, slide sts to other end of needle. Using B, s1 wyif, *brk, s1 wyif, yo, rep from * to last 2 sts, brk, s1 wyif, turn.

Row 3 (RS) Using A, k1 s1 wyif, yo, *brk, s1 wyif, yo, rep from * to last st, k1. Do not turn, slide sts to other end of needle. Using B: s1 wyif, brp, *s1 wyif, yo, brp, rep from * to last st, s1 wyif, turn.

Rep rows 1–4 to form patt.

DOUBLE-SIDED CHEQUERBOARDS

Using a circular or 2 double-pointed needles cast on a multiple of 24 stitches, plus 12, using the alternative Italian cast-on method as given on p.149. Make sure yarns are crossed around each other on turning rows.

Row 1 (RS) Using A: [K1, s1 wyif] 6 times, *[s1 wyib, p1] 6 times, [k1, s1 wyif] 6 times; rep from * to end. Do not turn, slide sts to other end of needle to start again.

Row 2 (RS) Using B: [S1 wyib, p1] 6 times, *[k1, s1 wyif] 4 times, [s1 wyib, p1] 6 times; rep from * to end. Turn.

Row 3 (WS) Using B, rep Row 1.

Row 4 (WS) Using A, rep Row 2.

Rep last 4 rows four more times.

Row 13 (RS) Using B, rep Row 1.

Row 14 (RS) Using A rep Row 2.

Row 15 (WS) Rep Row 1.

Row 16 (WS) Rep Row 2.

Rep last 4 rows four more times.

Rep rows 1–40 to form patt.

Cast off using tubular cast-off (see p.73).

EDGING PATTERNS

Most of these easy edgings are worked lengthways. If adding the edging to a blanket, knit a little extra to gather at each corner. Do not cast off at the desired length; instead, slip the stitches onto a stitch holder and sew the edging on around the blanket. Before casting off, you can then work more rows if you need them. See pp.198–215 for step-by-step guidance on embellishing knitting.

PEAKS EDGING

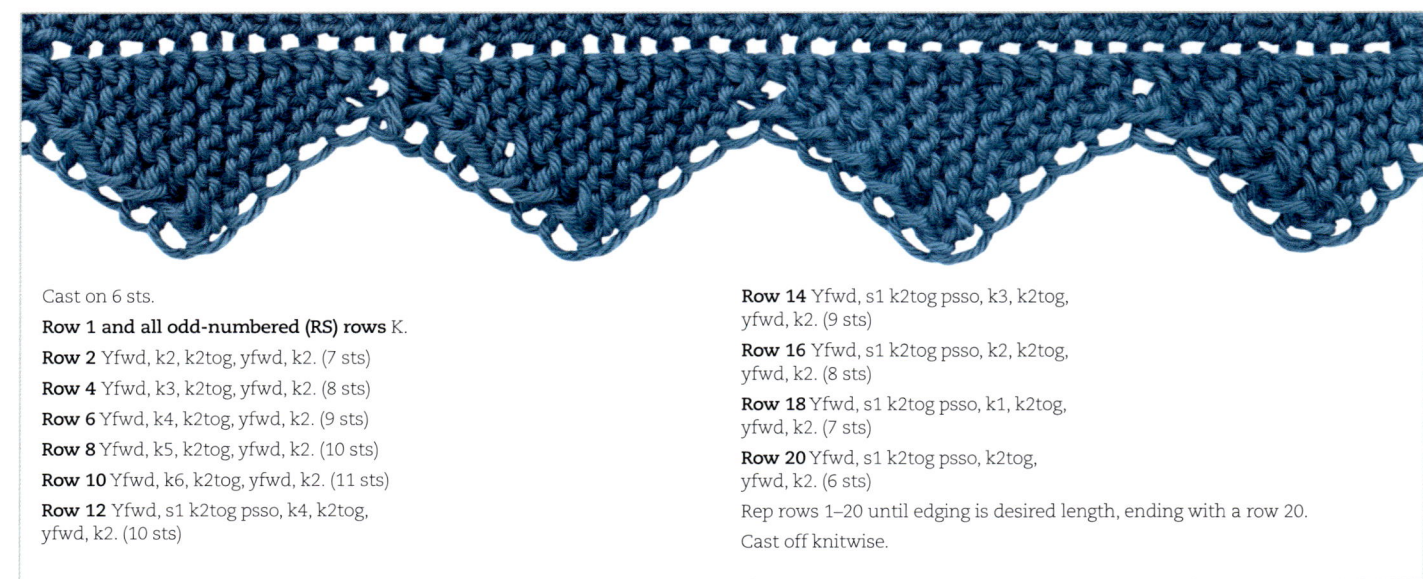

Cast on 6 sts.
Row 1 and all odd-numbered (RS) rows K.
Row 2 Yfwd, k2, k2tog, yfwd, k2. (7 sts)
Row 4 Yfwd, k3, k2tog, yfwd, k2. (8 sts)
Row 6 Yfwd, k4, k2tog, yfwd, k2. (9 sts)
Row 8 Yfwd, k5, k2tog, yfwd, k2. (10 sts)
Row 10 Yfwd, k6, k2tog, yfwd, k2. (11 sts)
Row 12 Yfwd, s1 k2tog psso, k4, k2tog, yfwd, k2. (10 sts)
Row 14 Yfwd, s1 k2tog psso, k3, k2tog, yfwd, k2. (9 sts)
Row 16 Yfwd, s1 k2tog psso, k2, k2tog, yfwd, k2. (8 sts)
Row 18 Yfwd, s1 k2tog psso, k1, k2tog, yfwd, k2. (7 sts)
Row 20 Yfwd, s1 k2tog psso, k2tog, yfwd, k2. (6 sts)
Rep rows 1–20 until edging is desired length, ending with a row 20.
Cast off knitwise.

GODMOTHER'S EDGING

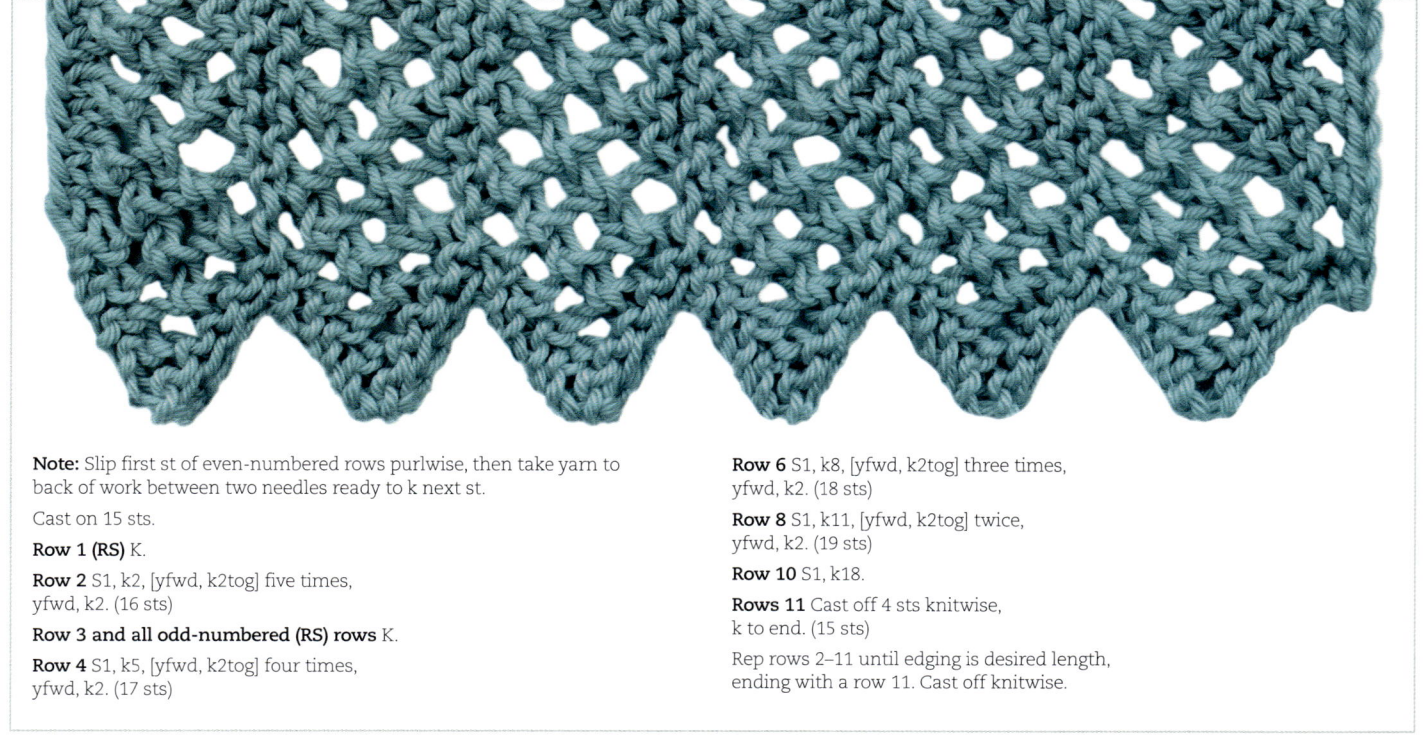

Note: Slip first st of even-numbered rows purlwise, then take yarn to back of work between two needles ready to k next st.
Cast on 15 sts.
Row 1 (RS) K.
Row 2 S1, k2, [yfwd, k2tog] five times, yfwd, k2. (16 sts)
Row 3 and all odd-numbered (RS) rows K.
Row 4 S1, k5, [yfwd, k2tog] four times, yfwd, k2. (17 sts)
Row 6 S1, k8, [yfwd, k2tog] three times, yfwd, k2. (18 sts)
Row 8 S1, k11, [yfwd, k2tog] twice, yfwd, k2. (19 sts)
Row 10 S1, k18.
Rows 11 Cast off 4 sts knitwise, k to end. (15 sts)
Rep rows 2–11 until edging is desired length, ending with a row 11. Cast off knitwise.

PETAL EDGING

Cast on 6 sts.
Row 1 (RS) K.
Row 2 Yfwd, k2, k2tog, yfwd, k2. (7 sts)
Row 3 K.
Row 4 Yfwd, k to last 4 sts, k2tog, yfwd, k2. (8 sts)
Rows 5–10 [Rep rows 3 and 4] three times. (11 sts)
Row 11 K.
Row 12 Cast off 5 sts loosely knitwise, k1, k2tog, yfwd, k2. (6 sts)
Rep rows 1–12 until edging is desired length, ending with a row 12.
Cast off knitwise.

PICOT EDGING

Cast on a multiple of 2 sts plus 1 extra st.
Work in st st to point of turning, finishing with a WS row (minimum 6 rows st st worked).
Picot row (RS) *K2tog, yo, rep from * to last st, k1.
Starting with a p row, work 5 rows st st and cast off.
Fold work along picot row and catch to back of work using the overcast technique (see p.189).

CABLED EDGING

Special abbreviation
C8B: Place 4 sts on cable needle and leave at back of work, k4, then k4 from cable needle.
Cast on 12 sts.
Row 1 (RS) K.
Row 2 K2, p8, k2.
Rep last 2 rows twice more.
Row 7 K2, C8B, k2.
Row 8 K2, p8, k2.
Row 9 K.
Rep last 2 rows twice more, then row 8 again.
Rep rows 1–14 to set patt.

PICOT RUFFLE EDGING

Note: This edging is worked widthways.

Cast on an odd number of sts.

Row 1 (RS) K.
Row 2 K.
Row 3 *K2tog, yfwd, rep from * to last st, k1.
Rows 4, 5 and 6 K.
Row 7 K1, *[k1, p1, k1] into next st, [k1, p1] into next st, rep from * to end. (This row increases number of sts on needle by about 2.5 times.)
Row 8 P.
Row 9 K.
Rows 10, 11, 12, and 13 [Rep rows 8 and 9] twice.
Row 14 (WS) P.
Rows 15 and 16 K.

Work picots along cast-off as follows:

Picot cast-off: *Cast on 2 sts on LH needle using knit-on cast-on method (see p.54), cast off 5 sts knitwise, transfer st on RH needle back to LH needle, rep from * to end, ending last cast-off as required by sts remaining.

CHRISTENING EDGING

Cast on 7 sts.

Row 1 (RS) K2, yfwd, k2tog, yfwd twice, k2tog, k1. (8 sts)
Row 2 K3, p1, k2, yfwd, k2tog.
Row 3 K2, yfwd, k2tog, k1, yfwd twice, k2tog, k1. (9 sts)
Row 4 K3, p1, k3, yfwd, k2tog.
Row 5 K2, yfwd, k2tog, k2, yfwd twice, k2tog, k1. (10 sts)
Row 6 K3, p1, k4, yfwd, k2tog.
Row 7 K2, yfwd, k2tog, k6.
Row 8 Cast off 3 sts knitwise, k4, yfwd, k2tog. (7 sts)

Rep rows 1–8 until edging is desired length, ending with a row 8.

Cast off knitwise.

ARCHWAY EDGING

Note: This edging is worked bottom up, so cast on the same, or close to, the number of stitches for the project using the Single cast-on method (see p.53).

Row 1 (RS) K.
Row 2 *K1, cast off 3 sts, rep from * to end.
Row 3 K1, *cast on 1 st, k2, rep from * to last st, cast on 1 st, k1.
Rows 4, 5, and 6 K.

Continue with project.

OPEN WEAVE EDGING

Cast on a multiple of 6 sts plus one extra st.

Row 1 (RS) K.

Row 2 P.

Row 3 *(K1, p1, k1, p1, k1) into next st, k5tog, rep from * to end.

Row 4 P.

Rep rows 1–4 to form patt.

BEADED EDGING

Note: Pre-thread all beads and push them down the yarn until you are instructed to use them.

Cast on 6 sts.

Rows 1 and 2 (RS) K.

Row 3 Push 10 beads up working yarn and press against first presenting st on LH needle, k1 tbl, k to end as normal, leaving bead loop in place.

Rows 4, 5, and 6 K.

Rep rows 1–6 to form patt.

FRINGE EDGING

Note: When making this edging, hold 2 strands of yarn together throughout and knit tightly. You can alter length of fringe by adding to or subtracting from number of knit stitches at end of row 1 and adjusting purl stitches at beg of row 2 by same number.

Cast on 12 sts.

Row 1 (RS) K2, yfwd, k2tog, k8.

Row 2 P7, k2, yfwd, k2tog, k1.

Rep rows 1 and 2 until edging is desired length, ending with a row 2.

Fringe cast off (RS) Cast off first 5 sts knitwise, cut yarn and draw through loop on RH needle to fasten off, then drop rem 6 sts off LH needle and unravel them to form fringe.

Smooth out unravelled strands, and, if necessary, lightly steam to straighten the strands. Then cut through loops at end of fringe. Knot strands together in groups of four strands, positioning knots close to edge of knitting. Trim fringe ends slightly if necessary to make them even.

MEDALLIONS

These simple medallions can be stitched together to form larger pieces of fabric for throws, bags, and cushion covers. They can also be worked singly into pieces that are big enough for a cushion cover or table mat. See pp.158–165 for step-by-step guidance on circular knitting. Since they are worked outwards from the middle, try the Disappearing loop cast on (p.67) for a neat and seamless centre.

SIMPLE SQUARE

Cast on 8 sts on one needle. Then distribute 2 sts on each of four double-pointed needles and knit with a 5th double-pointed needle as foll:

Round 1 [K1 tbl] twice on each of four needles.

Round 2 [Kfb in each st] on each of four needles. (16 sts)

Round 3 K.

Round 4 [K, working kfb in first and last st] on each of four needles. (24 sts)

Rep rounds 3 and 4 (increasing 8 sts in every alt round) until square is desired size.

Cast off knitwise.

SQUARE WITH SWIRL INCREASES

Cast on 8 sts on one needle. Then distribute 2 sts on each of four double-pointed needles, and knit with a 5th double-pointed needle as foll:

Row 1 [K1 tbl] twice on each of four needles.

Row 2 [K, working yfwd before first st] on each of four needles. (12 sts)

Rep round 2 (increasing 4 sts in every round) until square is desired size.

Cast off knitwise.

SQUARE WITH OPENWORK

Cast on 8 sts on one needle. Then distribute 2 sts on each of four double-pointed needles and knit with a 5th double-pointed needle as foll:

Round 1 [K1 tbl] twice on each of four needles.

Round 2 [Yfwd, k1, yfwd, k1] on each of four needles. (16 sts)

Round 3 K.

Round 4 [Yfwd, k3, yfwd, k1] on each of four needles. (24 sts)

Round 5 k.

Round 6 [Yfwd, k to last st, yfwd, k1] on each of four needles. (32 sts)

Rep rounds 5 and 6 (increasing 8 sts in every alt round) until square is desired size.

Cast off knitwise.

MITRED SQUARE

Cast on 55 sts.

Row 1 (RS) K26, s2k k1 p2sso, k to end. (53 sts)

Row 2 and all foll alt rows (WS) K.

Row 3 K25, s2k k1 p2sso, k to end. (51 sts)

Row 5 K24, s2k k1 p2sso, k to end. (49 sts)

Continue working RS row decrease at centre of row as set, knitting one stitch fewer before decreasing on each row (i.e. row 6: k23, row 5: k22) until 3 sts remain, ending with a WS row.

Next row S2 k1 p2sso. (1 st)

Draw yarn through remaining stitch to fasten off.

HEXAGON

Cast on 12 sts on one needle. Then distribute 4 sts on each of three double-pointed needles and knit with a 4th double-pointed needle as foll:

Round 1 [K1 tbl] four times on each of three needles.

Round 2 [Yfwd, k2, yfwd, k2] on each of three needles. (18 sts)

Round 3 K.

Round 4 [Yfwd, k3, yfwd, k3] on each of three needles. (24 sts)

Round 5 K.

Round 6 [Yfwd, k half of rem sts on needle, yfwd, k to end of needle] on each of three needles. (30 sts)

Rep rounds 5 and 6 (increasing 6 sts in every alt round) until hexagon is desired size.

Cast off knitwise.

SIMPLE CIRCLE

Cast on 8 sts on one needle. Then distribute 2 sts on each of four double-pointed needles and knit with a 5th double-pointed needle as foll:

Round 1 [K1 tbl] twice on each of four needles.

Round 2 [Kfb in each st] on each of four needles. (16 sts)

Rounds 3, 4, and 5 K.

Round 6 [Kfb in each st] on each of four needles. (32 sts)

Rounds 7, 8, 9, 10, and 11 K.

Round 12 Rep round 6. (64 sts)

Rounds 13, 14, 15, 16, 17, 18, and 19 K.

Round 20 [Kfb into every 2nd st] on each of four needles. (96 sts)

Rounds 21, 22, 23, 24, and 25: K.

Round 26 [Kfb into every 3rd st] on each of four needles. (128 sts)

Rounds 27, 28, 29, 30, and 31 K.

Round 32 [Kfb into every 4th st] on each of four needles. (160 sts)

Cont in this way, increasing 32 sts in every 6th round and working the next increase round with kfb into every 5th stitch, the following into every 6th stitch, and so on, until the circle is the desired size.

Cast off knitwise.

BEADING STITCH PATTERNS

Beading adds a touch of sparkle to a project. The swatches shown here use the beading technique where you strand beads onto your yarn before you cast on for your project (see p.198). When estimating bead quantities, it is best to thread on more beads than you think is needed. This way, you will not need to stop knitting to thread on more beads. Bear in mind that adding beads will add weight to your project and it is therefore advisable to use fewer beads on big projects, such as jumpers and blankets. Always use washable knitting beads. It is not recommended to add beads to items intended for babies and small children. See pp.198–201 for step-by-step guidance on bead knitting.

CHART KEY

● P on RS, K on WS   ■ Pb- Place bead   ☐ K on RS, P on WS

SUBTLE SPARKLE

Special abbreviation
pb: Place bead.
Cast on a multiple of 6 sts plus 2 extra sts.
Row 1 (RS) K.
Row 2 P.
Row 3 K1, *pb, k5, rep from * to last st, k1.
Row 4 P.
Row 5 K.
Row 6 P.
Row 7 K1, *k3, pb, k2, rep from * to last st, k1.
Row 8 P.
Rep rows 1–8 to form patt.

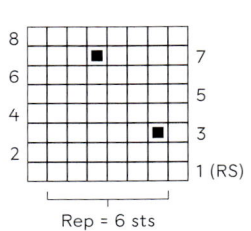

Rep = 6 sts

BEADED STOCKING STITCH

Special abbreviation
pb: Place bead.
Cast on an odd number of sts.
Row 1 K1, *pb, k1, rep from * to end.
Row 2 P.
Row 3 K1, *k1, pb, rep from * to last st, k1.
Row 4 P.
Rep rows 1–4 to form patt.

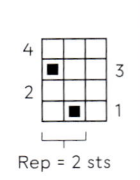

Rep = 2 sts

BEADED GARTER STITCH

Special abbreviation
pb: Place bead.
Cast on an odd number of sts.
Row 1 (RS) K.
Row 2 and all foll alt rows (WS) K.
Row 3 K1, *pb, k1, rep from * to end.
Rows 5 and 6 K.
Rep rows 1–6 to form patt.

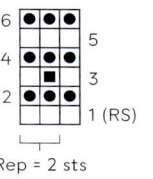

Rep = 2 sts

BEADED STRIPES

Special abbreviation
pb: Place bead.
Cast on an odd number of sts.
Row 1 (RS) K.
Row 2 and all foll alt rows P.
Row 3 * K1, pb, rep from * to last st, k1.
Row 5 K1, *k1, pb, rep from * to last 2 sts, k2.
Row 7 K.
Row 8 P.
Rep rows 1–8 to form patt.

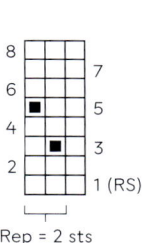

Rep = 2 sts

DIAGONAL BEADING

Special abbreviation
pb: Place bead.
Cast on a multiple of 5 sts plus 2 extra sts.
Row 1 K1, *k2, pb, k2, rep from * to last st, k1.
Row 2 and all foll alt rows (WS) P.
Row 3 K1, *k1, pb, k3, rep from * to last st, k1.
Row 5 K1, *pb, k4, rep from * to last st, k1.
Row 7 K1, *k4, pb, rep from * to last st, k1.
Row 9 K1, *k3, pb, k1, rep from * to last st, k1.
Row 10 P.
Rep rows 1–10 to form patt.

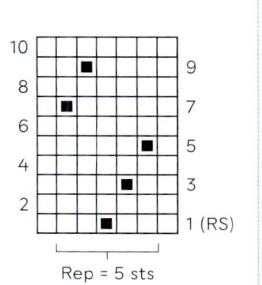

Rep = 5 sts

BEADED CHEVRON

Special abbreviation
pb: Place bead.
Cast on a multiple of 10 sts plus 1 extra st.
Starting with a k row, work 2 rows st st.
Row 1 (RS) K1, *pb, k1, rep from * to end.
Row 2 and all foll alt rows (WS) *P1, M1p, p3, s1 p2tog psso, p3, M1, rep from * to last st, p1.
Rows 3 and 5 [Rep row 1] twice.
Rows 7, 9, and 11 K.
Row 12 Rep row 2.
Rep rows 1–12 to form patt.

KEY
- M M1p
- ⋏ s1 p2tog psso
- ■ pb

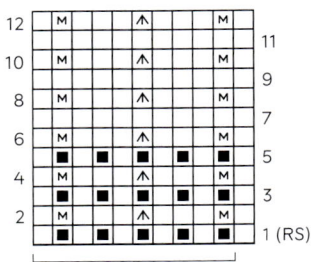

Rep = 10 sts

BEADED CHEQUERBOARD

Special abbreviation
pb: Place bead.
Cast on a multiple of 10 sts plus 7 extra sts.
Row 1 (RS) K1, *[pb, k1] three times, k4, rep from * to last 6 sts, [pb, k1] three times.
Row 2 and all foll alt rows (WS) P.
Row 3 K1, *k1, [pb, k1] twice, k5, rep from * to last 6 sts, [pb, k1] twice, k1.
Row 5 Rep row 1.
Row 7 K1, *k5, [pb, k1] twice, pb, rep from * to last 6 sts, k to end.
Row 9 K1, *k6, [pb, k1] twice, k * to end.
Row 11 Rep row 7.
Rep rows 1–12 to form patt.

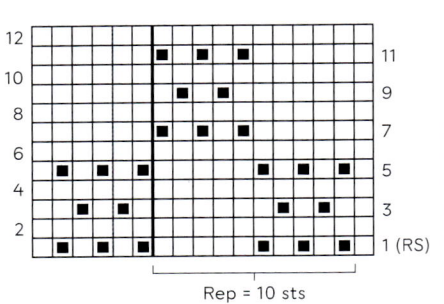

Rep = 10 sts

DIAMANTÉ STITCH

Special abbreviation
pb: Place bead.
Cast on a multiple of 8 sts plus 2 extra sts.
Row 1 (RS) K1, *k1, pb, k3, pb, k2, rep from * to last st, k1.
Row 2 and all foll alt rows (WS) P.
Row 3 K1, *k4, pb, k1, pb, k1, rep from * to last st, k1.
Row 5 K1, *k1, pb, k3, pb, k2, rep from * to last st, k1.
Row 7 K1, *pb, k1, pb, k5, rep from * to last st, k1.
Row 8 P.
Rep rows 1–8 to form patt.

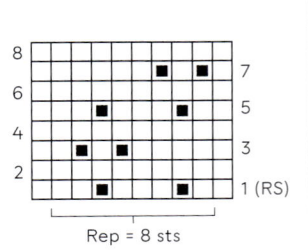

Rep = 8 sts

PEEKABOO BEADS

Special abbreviation
pb Place bead.
Cast on a multiple of 10 sts plus 5 extra sts.
Row 1 (RS) K.
Row 2 P1, k3, *p7, k3, rep from * to last st, p1.
Row 3 K1, *k1, pb, k8, rep from * to last 4 sts, k1, pb, k2.
Row 4 P.
Row 5 K.
Row 6 P4, *p2, k3, p5, rep from * to last st, k1.
Row 7 K1, *k6, pb, k3, rep from * to last 4 sts, k4.
Row 8 P.
Rep rows 1–8 to form patt.

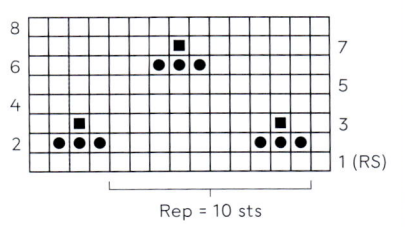

VERTICAL SEQUIN STRIPES

Special abbreviation
pb Place bead.
Cast on a multiple of 8 sts plus 1 extra st.
Row 1 K1, *k2, pb, k1, pb, k3, rep from * to end.
Row 2 P.
Rep rows 1 and 2 to form patt.

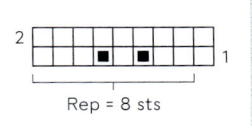

ALL-OVER SEQUINS

Special abbreviation
pb Place bead.
Cast on a multiple of 8 sts plus 1 extra st.
Row 1 K1, *pb, k1, rep from * to end.
Row 2 P.
Row 3 K1, *k1, pb, rep from * to end.
Row 4 P.
Rep rows 1–4 to form patt.

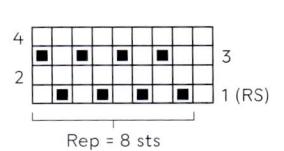

GLOSSARY

Aran yarn
Also called medium, 10–12-ply, or worsted (yarn symbol 4). A medium yarn suitable for jumpers, cabled menswear, blankets, hats, scarves, and mittens.

Backstitch
A sewing stitch used for firm, straight seams, which is worked from the wrong side.

Ball-winder
A device for winding hanks of yarn into balls; also to wind two or more strands together to make a double-stranded yarn. Often used in conjunction with a swift.

Blocking
The finishing process for a piece of knitting, in which it is set in shape using water or steam. A blocking mat is a waterproof surface to pin damp pieces onto. Most often available as puzzle-style pieces.

Brioche knitting
A technique that creates a reversible, highly textured fabric by working with yarnovers and slipped stitches, often using two colours to produce distinctive ribbed columns.

Cable
A design made by crossing one or more stitches over other stitches in a row; it frequently resembles a rope or cable. Twist stitches belong to the same family.

Cable needle
A needle with a kink or U-shape, used when working cables.

Carrying up the side
A method for keeping the edges of a two-coloured, even-row stripe pattern tidy. The yarns are twisted around each other and carried up the side of the piece.

Casting off/binding off
Completing a piece of knitting by finishing off the loops of the stitches so that they cannot unravel.

Casting on
Forming an initial number of stitches on a needle at the start. There are various methods, giving different effects.

Chunky/bulky yarn
Also called 12–14-ply, craft, or rug (yarn symbol 5). A chunky yarn suitable for rugs, jackets, blankets, hats, legwarmers, and winter accessories.

Circular knitting
Working on circular needles or double-pointed needles to produce a seamless item such as a hat. There is no need to turn the work and no wrong-side row.

Circular needles
A pair of short needles connected by a flexible tube, usually used for circular knitting and very wide projects that do not fit on conventional straight needles.

Colourwork
Any method of incorporating colour into your knitting.

Continental-style knitting
A way of holding the yarn as you knit, lacing it around your left hand and using these fingers to position the yarn to make a stitch.

Darning in ends
The process of completing a piece of knitting by weaving yarn ends into the knitting to disguise them.

Disappearing loop cast-on
A technique that creates stitches on two needles simultaneously using a loop method, allowing you to work in the round from the centre outwards for seamless projects.

Double-sided cast-on
A technique that creates stitches on two needles simultaneously, allowing you to work in the round from the centre outwards for seamless projects.

Domino knitting
A modular technique that builds fabric by knitting individual squares that are joined as you work, creating patchwork-style fabrics without traditional seaming.

Double-knit (DK) yarn
A medium-weight yarn. Also called DK, 8-ply, or light worsted (yarn symbol 3). A light yarn suitable for jumpers, lightweight scarves, blankets, and toys.

Double-pointed needles
Knitting needles with a tip at each end; a set of four or five is used for the circular knitting of small items, such as mittens and socks.

Double knitting
Also known as tubular knitting. It is worked on straight needles by slipping every other stitch and produces a double-sided fabric. *See also* **Circular knitting.**

English-style knitting
A way of holding the yarn as you knit, lacing it around your right hand and using the right forefinger to wrap the yarn around the needle.

Entrelac
A technique that creates a woven basket-like appearance by working small rectangles or diamonds in alternating directions, building up the fabric in interlocking sections.

Fair Isle
A specific type of stranded colourwork, originating from Fair Isle or the Shetland Islands. Colours not being worked are carried across the back of the work, or woven in, until required. *See also* **Stranded colourwork.**

Faux colourwork
Adding yarn in another colour without using two different yarns in each row. It involves manipulating stitches from previous rows.

Fine yarn
Also called 5–6-ply, sport, or baby (yarn symbol 2). A fine yarn suitable for lightweight jumpers, babywear, socks, and accessories.

Fisherman's rib
A pattern of knit and purl stitches, in which alternating stitches are double knitted, making a thick, warm, textured fabric.

Fully fashioned shaping
An attractive method for increasing or decreasing when working stocking stitch, in which a line of stitches is preserved to follow the edge of the piece.

Garter stitch
Working in knit stitches on every row, whichever side of the knitting is facing you. It produces a thick fabric, which is identical on both sides and will not curl at the edges.

German short rows
An alternative to traditional wrap-and-turn short row shaping that has tighter turns and therefore is less likely to leave gaps. *See also* **Short-row shaping.**

Grafting
A technique for invisibly joining two sets of live stitches by mimicking the path of knitted stitches, creating a seamless connection. *See also* **Kitchener's stitch.**

Hank
A twisted ring of yarn that needs to be wound into balls before it can be used.

Helix knitting
A technique for working stripes in the round that eliminates the colour jog by using multiple balls of yarn and working in a spiral pattern. *See also* **Circular knitting.**

I-cord
A narrow tube of knitting, created on a knitting dolly or cord-maker, or knitted on double-pointed needles. Used as cords, straps, ties, or as a trimming.

Intarsia
A method for working with different coloured yarns to create blocks of colour. A separate length of yarn is used for each colour and twisted at colour changes to prevent a hole; yarns are not stranded across the reverse. Uses less yarn than stranded colourwork.

Kitchener's stitch
A grafting technique worked from the right side of stocking stitch to invisibly join two sets of live stitches by mimicking the path of stocking stitch, creating a seamless connection commonly used for sock toes. *See also* **Grafting.**

Knitting through back of loop
Stitches that twist the stitch in the row below so that the legs of the stitch cross at the base.

Knitwise
Working with knit stitches facing you, inserting the right-hand needle into a stitch as if to knit it. See also **Purlwise**.

Lace yarn
Also called thread, cobweb or light fingering (yarn symbol 0). A very fine yarn for knitting lace.

Lanolin
An oily substance contained in sheep's wool.

Lifelines
A strand of yarn inserted across a row to give an easy point to undo back to if necessary, such as the start of a pattern repeat.

Live stitches
Stitches that are currently being worked.

Magic loop
A technique using a large-diameter circular knitting needle to knit a narrow tube. See also **Circular knitting**.

Mattress stitch
A seaming stitch, which is almost invisible, used to sew pieces of knitting together with the right side facing. It only forms a small seam on the wrong side of the work.

Mercerized cotton
Cotton thread, fabric, or yarn that has been treated in order to strengthen it and add a sheen. The yarn is suitable for items that need to be strong and hold their shape, such as bags.

Mosaic knitting
A slip stitch colourwork technique that creates geometric patterns by alternating colours every two rows, while slipping stitches to carry the previous colour forward.

Oversewing/overcasting
A stitch used to seam two pieces of knitting by placing them right sides together and then sewing through the edge stitches. Also called whip stitch.

Pilling
When the surface of a knitted item rubs up into tiny balls, due to wear and friction.

Plied yarn
A yarn made from more than one strand of spun fibre, so 4-ply is four strands plied together. Most knitting yarns are plied, as plying prevents the yarn twisting and resulting fabric slanting diagonally.

Provisional cast-on
A method of casting on that leaves an edge that can be removed later, to either pick up and knit, or to graft live stitches together from the cast-on edge. See also **Grafting, Kitchener's Stitch**.

Purlwise
Working with stitches facing you, inserting the right-hand needle into a stitch as if to purl it. See also **Knitwise**.

Ribbing/rib/rib stitch
Knitting with great elasticity, used where fabric needs to hold tightly to the body, but is capable of expanding. Single ribbing or 1 x 1 rib is knit 1, purl 1; 2 x 2 rib is knit 2, purl 2; 3 x 3 rib is knit 3, purl 3, and so on.

Safety eyes
Plastic eyes with secure washer fastenings designed to prevent them from loosening, making them safer than sewn-on alternatives for children's toys.

Short-row shaping
Used for shaping shoulders, curving hems, making darts, and turning sock heels. Rows are added in only one part of the fabric by knitting part of a row instead of to the end.

Single rib/ribbing
See **Ribbing**.

Single-strand cast-on
A group of methods for casting on using one strand of yarn. Tends to produce a soft edge; twisting the stitches can make it firmer.

Skein
Yarn sold wound into a long oblong shape, which is ready to knit.

Slip knot
A knot that you form when you place the first loop on the needle as you start casting on.

Slip stitch
Sliding a stitch from left-hand to right-hand needle without working it. The usual method is to slip purlwise rather than knitwise. Slipped stitches at the start of each row – slipped selvedge – can create a very neat edge.

Stocking stitch
A stitch formed by knitting all stitches when the right side of the work is facing you, and purling all stitches when the wrong side of the work is facing you.

Stitch stoppers
Plastic caps used to stop stitches falling off double-pointed needles.

Stranded beading method
A process for streamlining knitting-in of beads by threading them on yarn before you begin, using a needle and thread looped through the yarn. Beads are later arranged in the knitting when brought to the front of the work and wrapped around a slipped stitch.

Stranded colourwork
A type of knitting where two or more colours are knitted across a row, carrying the yarn not in use while knitting, along the reverse of the work as you go.

Super chunky/super bulky yarn
Also called 16-ply (and upwards), bulky, or roving (yarn symbol 6). A chunky yarn suitable for heavy blankets, rugs, and thick scarves.

Superfine yarn
Also called 4-ply, fingering, baby or sock (yarn symbol 1). A very fine yarn suitable for fine-knit socks, shawls, and babywear.

Steek
A cutting technique most often used in stranded colourwork that allows knitters to work garments in the round, then cut open the fabric along reinforced lines to create armholes and necklines.

Swift
A wooden frame used with a ball-winder to transform a hank of yarn into convenient balls.

Tension square
A square knitted to the required number of stitches and rows to match the stated tension of a project, usually 10cm (4in) square. A knitter must achieve the tension stated in a pattern, or else the knitted item will not end up the correct size.

Three-needle cast-off/bind-off
A method of casting off that binds two sets of stitches together, whilst casting off simultaneously. This creates a firm, neat seam, with a smooth finish on the right side of the work. It is a way of finishing the toe of a sock or the fingertip area of a mitten.

Tubular cast-on/cast-off
Also known as an Italian or invisible cast-on/off. Produces a good edge for a single rib; best to use needles that are at least two sizes smaller than the main fabric in order to prevent the ribbing stretching out of shape.

Tunisian knitting
A style of knitting in which the finished fabric resembles the look of Tunisian crochet.

Twist
Two stitches twisted together to form a narrow cable, which slants to the right or left. A cable needle is not used.

Yarn
Fibres that have been spun into a long strand in order to be able to be knitted. Yarns may be made of natural fibres, man-made fibres, a blend of the two, or even unusual materials.

Yarn bobbins
Small plastic shapes for holding yarn when doing intarsia work, where there are many yarns in different colours.

Yarnover (yo)
An instruction to increase by adding stitches and creating holes at the same time. Yarnovers are used for decorative purposes, such as producing lacy knitting. There are various types: yfwd (US yo), yarnover between knit stitches; yrn (US yo), yarnover between purl stitches; yfrn and yon (US yo), yarnover between knit and purl stitches; yfwd (US yo), and yarnover at the beginning of a row.

INDEX

2-ply yarn 29
3D embellishments 211–15
4-ply yarn 29
5-6-ply yarn 29
10-12-ply yarn 29
14-ply yarn 29
16-ply+ yarn 29

A

abbreviations, knitting 89
acrylic 16
alpaca 11
alternating loop cast-on 56
alternative double cast-on 58
alternative roll-edge tubular cast-on 66
anemone 286
angora 12
ankle socks, toe-up 236–37
appliqué, simple i-cord for 112
Aran yarn 29
archway edging 320
Argyle motif, combined stranded and intarsia 307
armwarmers, cabled 224–25
arrowheads: arrowhead lace 297
  arrowhead stitch 312
attached i-cord 113–15

B

babies: baby blanket 252–53
  baby cardigan 248–51
baby yarn 29
backstitch seam 188
backwards loop cast-on 55
bags: bag handles 33
  garment bag 47
  mesh tote bag 260–61
ball winders 44, 80
balls of yarn 24
  ballbands 25
  joining a ball 81
  winding a hank into a ball 80
bamboo 15
bamboo needles 37, 38
basketweave stitch 279
bead knitting 198–201
  all-over sequins 327
  bead cast-on 201
  beaded cast-off 201
  beaded chequerboard 326
  beaded chevron 326
  beaded edging 321
  beaded garter stitch 325
  beaded headband 262–63
  beaded stocking stitch 324
  beaded stripes 325
  beading stitch patterns 324–27
  beads for different yarn weights 198
  close beading 200
  diagonal beading 325
  diamanté stitch 326
  inset bead with a hook 200
  peekaboo beads 327
  reverse stitch beading 200
  simple garter stitch beading 199
  slip stitch beading 199
  subtle sparkle 324
  threading beads onto yarn 198
  using a second yarn 201
  vertical sequin stripes 327
beads, knitting 32
bells 205
bias knitting 148
bio-synthetic fibres 14–15
black and white 29
blackberry stitch 284
blankets: baby blanket 252–53
  checked blanket 270–71
  intarsia blanket 272–75
blocking 185–86
blocking mats 42
blocking wire and pins 42
blossom motif, stranded 306
blunt-ended yarn needles 42
bobble hat, child's Fair Isle 258–59
bobble remover 46
bobbles 202–206
  bobble stitch 284
  detached bobbles 203
  drawthread bobbles 214
  tulip cluster bobble 204
borders, simple stranded 303
bouclé yarn 21
braided yarn 19
bridges 194–95
bright colours 29
brioche knit: brioche cables 316
  diagonal brioche 317
  one-colour brioche 131
  two-colour brioche 132
broken moss stitch 282
broken rib 282
broken stripes stitch 312
bulky yarn 29
bullion stitch 209
button loops: i-cord 113
  knitted button loop 173
buttonholes 173–79
buttons 33
  covered buttons 215
  positioning 173
  sewing on 197

C

cables 110, 111
  brioche cables 316
  cable 4 back 111
  cable 4 front 111
  cable and twist stitch patterns 289–95
  cable cast-on 55
  cable hat 242–43
  cable needle 43
  cabled armwarmers 224–25
  cabled edging 319
carbon-fibre needles with metal tips 37
cardigans: baby cardigan 248–51
  slouchy cardigan 238–41
cashmere 12
cast-offs 68–75, 89
  alternative cast-offs 69–75
  beaded cast-off 201
  i-cord cast-off 114
  simple cast-offs 68
cast-ons 53–67, 89
  beaded cast-on 201
  i-cord cast-on 114
  single-strand cast-ons 53–56
  special cast-ons 62–67
  two-strand cast-on 57–61
cedarwood shapes 47
chain cable pattern 291
chain eyelet 116
chain selvedge 171
chain stitch on stripes 210
Channel Islands cast-on for single rib 62
chart paper 43
charted colourwork 122
check slip-stitch pattern 121
checks: cable check 294
  checked blanket 270–71
  checked cushion 268–69
  little check stitch 280
  striped check stitch 279
  textured check stitch 279
chenille yarn 18
chequerboards: beaded chequerboard 326
  double-sided chequerboards 317
chevrons: basic chevron 283
  beaded chevron 326
  garter chevron 283
child's Fair Isle bobble hat 258–59
christening edging 320
chunky yarn 29
circles, simple 323
circular knitting 158–65
  helix knitting 162
  joining a round of stitches 158
  knitting a möbius loop 159
  knitting tubes 158–64
  knitting two tubes at once on two circular needles 160–61
  "magic loop" knitting 160
  medallions 165
  spiral knitting 164
  working with circular knitting needles 158
  working with a set of five double-pointed needles 163
  working with a set of four double-pointed needles 163
circular needles 38–39, 158
clasp weft join 81
close beading 200
closed central increase 103
closed yarnover on garter stitch 98
clusters, wrapped 140
colours: bright colours 29
  choosing yarn colours 26–27
  cool shades 26
  pastels 29
  seasonal mixtures 29
  using a colour wheel 26
  warm shades 26
colourwork 118–28
  arrowhead stitch 312
  brioche cables 316
  broken stripes stitch 312
  charted colourwork 122
  colourwork patterns 303–10
  combined stranded and intarsia Argyle motif 307
  diagonal brioche 317
  domino squares 119–20
  double knitting 136–37
  double-sided chequerboards 317
  Fair Isle chart 122
  faux colourwork patterns 311–17
  five-colour stocking stitch stripe 118
  following a colourwork chart 122
  garter slip stitch 311
  holding the yarns 123–24
  honeycomb stitch 313
  intarsia 128
  intarsia heart motif 305
  intarsia letter motifs 308–309
  intarsia monstera leaf 305
  intarsia numbers 310
  intarsia pawprint 307
  intarsia snowflake motif 307
  intarsia tulip motif 306
  joining domino squares 119
  knit weave 127
  mosaic herringbone 315

mosaic knitting 134–35
mosaic triangles 314
multicolour slip-stitch patterns 121
Nordic motif 304
peeping purl stitch 311
plain-colour domino squares 119
simple stranded borders 303
simple stripes 118
stranded blossom motif 306
stranded colourwork method 123
stranded colourwork with garter stitch 126
stranded colourwork with texture 126
stranded heart motif 305
striped domino squares 120
tea-cosy stitch 127
textural and colour effects 129–43
textured honeycomb 315
three-colour zigzags 304
tidying edges 118
two-colour garter stitch stripe 118
two-colour knit and purl pinstripe 118
two-strand laying-in 127
using stranded colourwork charts 303
vertical stripes stitch 314
weaver's stitch 313
weaving 126–27
weaving in ends during domino knitting 120
working into lower stitches 129–30
columns, moss stitch 282
combined stranded and intarsia Argyle motif 307
combined two-strand cast-on 61
cones of yarn 24
"Continental" style knitting method 51–53
contrast edge cast-on 59
cool shades 26
cord-maker 44
cosy double-sided scarf 230–31
cotton: matt cotton 12
mercerized cotton 13
recycled cotton 23
wool and cotton mixes 17
cotton thread 117
crochet hooks 42
crochet cast-off 70
crochet chain loop cast-off 75
crochet provisional cast-on 65
picking up stitches with 169

curls 206
curved edges, picking up stitches along 169
cushions: checked cushion 268–69
entrelac cushion 264–67
cutting into your knitting 194–95

D

darning: darning in an end 83
woven darning for repairing holes 85
darning mushrooms 41
darning needles 40
decorative stitches 138–43
decreases 89, 92–101
decorated central decreases 102–105
decrease cast-off 72
flower patterns 285–88
fully fashioned shaping 109
paired decreases 106
paired edge decreases 108
simple decreases 99–101
stitch patterns 282–88
delayed cast-off 70
delicate lace shawl 220–23
diagonals: diagonal beading 325
diagonal brioche 317
diagonal lace ribs 301
diagonal rib 284
diamanté stitch 326
diamonds: diamond cable 289
diamond lace pattern 299
diamond stitch 280
openwork diamonds 300
dip stitch 130
disappearing loop cast-on 67
domino eyelet pattern 298
domino squares 119–20
double cast-on 57
double decreases 101
double-knit yarn 29
double knitting 136–37
double moss stitch 281
double-pointed needles 38–39, 163
double rib 279
double-sided cast-on 64
double-sided chequerboards 317
double slipped garter selvedge 171
double twist loop cast-on 56
double yarnover 98
doubling 147
drawthread bobbles 214
drop stitch 139
dropped stitch pattern 302
simple drop stitch 301
dropped stitches, picking up 84

E

ebony needles 36
edge-to-edge seam 186
edging: edging cast-off 74
edging cast-on 67
edging patterns 318–21
i-cord 113
sewing on an edging 193
tidying colourwork edges 118
elongated stitches 139
embellishments 32–33, 198–215
embossing 202–206
embroidery 207–10
embroidery thread 32
ends: darning in an end 83
weaving in ends during domino knitting 120
English rib 280
"English" style knitting method 51
entrelac 144–45
entrelac cushion 264–67
eyelash yarn 19
eyelets: chain eyelet 116
domino eyelet pattern 298
eyelet lines 302
eyelet mesh pattern 296
grand eyelet mesh pattern 300
open eyelet 116
reinforced eyelet buttonholes 174
star eyelet pattern 298

F

Fair Isle: child's Fair Isle bobble hat 258–59
Fair Isle chart 122
Fair Isle socks 232–35
fan cable 295
fastenings 33, 196–97
faux colourwork patterns 311–17
feather and fan stitch 283
felted yarn join 82
fibres 10–17
bio-synthetic fibres 14–15
natural fibres 10–14
synthetic fibres 15–16
yarn blends 17
figure-of-eight start for seams 187
fingerless gloves with mitts 226–29
finishing details 168–97
fisherman's rib 129, 281
five-colour stocking stitch stripe 118
flaps 205
flat central decrease 105
flowers: anemone 286
flower with large centre 287
flower with small centre 287

intarsia tulip motif 306
large leaf 288
puffball flower 288
spinning-petal flower 286
stranded blossom motif 306
twelve-petal flower 285
folding pom-pom makers 45
four-stitch cable pattern 290
free form i-cord 112
fringes 214
fringe edging 321
fully fashioned shaping 109
fur knitting 133

G

garment bag 47
garments: baby cardigan 248–51
choosing a garment size 91
garment care 46–47
garment patterns 91
slouchy cardigan 238–41
striped jumper 244–47
garter selvedge 170
double slipped garter selvedge 171
slipped garter selvedge 170
garter stitch 76, 89
beaded garter stitch 325
closed yarnover on garter stitch 98
garter chevron 283
garter rib 280
garter selvedges 170–71
garter slip stitch 311
garter stitch cable 292
garter zigzag twist 293
simple garter stitch beading 199
stranded colourwork with garter stitch 126
two-colour garter stitch stripe 118
gathering 147
German short rows 152–53
giant yarn 29
gloves with mitts, fingerless 226–29
godmother's edging 318
grafting: grafted seam 189
grafting knit and purl stitches together 192
grafting open knit stitches together 190
Kitchener's stitch 191
grand eyelet mesh pattern 300

H

half moss stitch 281
hand-dyed yarns, helix knitting with 162

handles, bag 33
hanks of yarn 24
harlequin scarf 218–19
hats: cable hat 242–43
    child's Fair Isle bobble hat 258–59
headband, beaded 262–63
hearts: intarsia heart motif 305
    stranded heart motif 305
helix knitting 162
hemp 14
hems 183–84
herringbone, mosaic 315
hexagons 323
holes: preventing holes 150–51
    woven darning for repairing holes 85
honeycomb: honeycomb stitch 282, 313
    textured honeycomb 315
horseshoes: horseshoe cable pattern 291
    horseshoe lace 301

I

i-cord 112–15
incorrect stitches, untwisting an incorrect purl stitch 53
increases 89, 92–98
    decorated central increases 102–103
    flower patterns 285–88
    fully fashioned shaping 109
    paired increases 106–107
    simple increases 92–95
    stitch patterns 282–88
    yarnover increases 96–98
inset bead with a hook 200
intarsia 128
    combined stranded and intarsia Argyle motif 307
    intarsia blanket 272–75
    intarsia chart 122
    intarsia heart motif 305
    intarsia letter motifs 308–309
    intarsia monstera leaf 305
    intarsia pawprint 307
    intarsia snowflake motif 307
    intarsia tulip motif 306
    numbers 310
    techniques 128
    two-colour cables 128
interchangeable circular needles 39
invisible cast-on 65
Italian cast-on 65

J

joining yarns 80–83
jumbo yarn 29
jumper, striped 244–47

K

Kitchener's stitch 191
knit blockers 43
knit into front and back as a paired central increase 102
knit into front and back of stitch 92
knit-on cast-on 54
knit stitch 54, 78
    alternative "Continental" knit stitch 52
    basic knit and purl fabrics 76–77
    casting off knit wise 68
    fully fashioned shaping 109
    garter stitch 76, 89
    grafting knit and purl stitches together 192
    knit and purl stitch patterns 278–82
    knit two together 99
    lifted increase on knit row 93
    "make-one" left cross increase on a knit row 93
    multiple increases 95
    reverse knit stitch 166
    slip one, knit one, pass slipped stitch over 100
    slip, slip, knit 100
    two-colour knit and purl pinstripe 118
    unpicking 84
    weaving the index finger yarn while knitting a stitch 125
    weaving the left yarn, knit or purl 124
    weaving the middle finger yarn while knitting a stitch 125
    weaving the right yarn, knit stitch 124
    yarnover at the beginning of a row 97
    yarnover between knit and purl stitches 97
    yarnover between knit stitches 96
knit weave 127
knitted cast-on 54
knitted-in smocking 141
knitting bag 41
knitting dolly 44
    i-cord on knitting dolly 115
knitting mill 44
knitting needles *see* needles
knitting patterns, following 90–91
knitwise 89
    cast off knitwise 89
    slipping stitches knitwise 87
knotted cast-on 66
knotting through back of loop 87

L

labels, yarn 25
lace knitting 116–17
    delicate lace shawl 220–23
    lace stitch patterns 296–302
lace yarn 29
ladder lace 301
large leaf 288
latch hooks 42
lavender sachets 46
lazy daisy stitch 209
leaves: intarsia monstera leaf 305
    large leaf 288
    leaves lace 299
    mini-leaf pattern 302
letter motifs, intarsia 308–309
lifted increase on knit row 93
light worsted yarn 29
linen 13
little check stitch 280
long-tail cast-on 57
loop pile 133

M

"magic loop" knitting 160
"make-one" increase on purl row 95
"make-one" left cross increase on a knit row 93
"make-one" right cross increase on a knit row 94
materials 8–33
matt cotton 12
mattress stitch 188
medallions 165, 322–23
mercerized cotton 13
merino wool 11
mesh: eyelet mesh pattern 296
    grand eyelet mesh pattern 300
    mesh tote bag 260–61
    vertical mesh columns 302
    vertical mesh pattern 296
    zigzag mesh pattern 297
metal needles 36, 38
metallic threads 32
metallic yarns 16
microfibres 15
milk protein (casein) fibres 14
mini-leaf pattern 302
mistakes, correcting 80, 84–85
mitred square 323
mitts, fingerless gloves with 226–29
möbius loop, knitting a 159
mohair brush 46
mohair lace 117
mohair yarn 11, 117
monstera leaf, intarsia 305
mosaic knitting 134–35
    mosaic herringbone 315
    mosaic triangles 314
moss stitch 278
    broken moss stitch 282
    double moss stitch 281
    half moss stitch 281
    moss stitch columns 282
mothballs 47
motifs: combined stranded and intarsia Argyle motif 307
    intarsia heart motif 305
    intarsia monstera leaf 305
    intarsia snowflake motif 307
    intarsia tulip motif 306
    Nordic motif 304
    stranded blossom motif 306
    stranded heart motif 305
multicolour slip-stitch patterns 121
multicoloured openwork 117
multiple increases 95

N

natural fibres 10–14
    natural and synthetic mixes 17
needle gauge 40
needle join 82
needle organizer 41
needles 36–39
    blunt-ended yarn needles 42
    cable needle 43
    circular needles 38–39, 158
    darning needles 40
    double-pointed needles 38–39
    holding yarn and needles 51
    needle organizer 41
    point protectors 41
    sharp-ended needles 42
    size 37
    straight needles 36–37
Nordic motif 304
nylon 16

O

one-colour brioche 131
open central increase 103
open eyelet 116
open weave edging 321
openwork: multicoloured 117
    openwork diamonds 300
    square with openwork 322
overcast seam 189

P

paired edge decreases 108
paired increases 106–107
partial knitting 150–57
pastels 29
patch pocket, picked-up 180
patterns: following patterns 90–91
  stitch patterns 86–89, 276–327
pawprint, intarsia 307
peaks edging 318
peekaboo beads 327
peeping purl stitch 311
petal edging 319
pick up and knit 89
picked-up hem 183
picked-up patch pocket 180
picking up stitches 84, 168–69
picot: picot edging 319
  picot hem 184
  picot loop selvedge 172
  picot point cast-off 71
  picot point selvedge 172
  picot ruffle edging 320
pins 40
pinstripe, two-colour knit and purl 118
plain-colour domino squares 119
plait cable 292
plastic needles 37, 38
pleats 146
plied yarn 18
pockets 180–82
point protectors 41
pom-pom rings 45
pom-poms 212
popcorns 202
press studs, attaching 197
projects 216–75
provisional cast-on 63
pseudo lace 117
puff stitch 284
puffball flower 288
pull-up stitch 130
purl stitch 79
  alternative "Continental" purl stitch 52–53
  basic knit and purl fabrics 76–77
  fully fashioned shaping 109
  grafting knit and purl stitches together 192
  knit and purl stitch patterns 278–82
  "make-one" increase on purl row 95
  multiple increases 95
  peeping purl stitch 311
  purl cast-off 68
  purl into front and back of stitch 92
  purl two together 99
  reverse purl stitch 166
  slip, slip, purl 101
  two-colour knit and purl pinstripe 118
  unpicking 84
  untwisting an incorrect stitch 53
  weaving the index finger yarn while purling a stitch 125
  weaving the left yarn, knit or purl 124
  weaving the middle finger yarn while purling a stitch 125
  weaving the right yarn, purl stitch 125
  yarnover at the beginning of a row 97
  yarnover between knit and purl stitches 97
  yarnover between purl stitches 96
purlwise 89
  cast off purlwise 89
  slipping stitches purlwise 86

R

raffia 22
raised central decrease 104
ramie 14
recycled yarns 23
reflective yarn 22
reverse knitting 166
  reverse knit stitch 166
  reverse purl stitch 166
  reverse stitch beading 200
  reverse stocking stitch 77, 89
ribbon yarn 20
ribbons 32
ribs: broken rib 282
  diagonal lace ribs 301
  diagonal rib 284
  double rib 279
  English rib 280
  fisherman's rib 281
  garter rib 280
  single rib 77, 278
  travelling rib 281
rosewood needles 36
roving yarn 29
row counter 41
row markers 88
ruffles 157
  picot ruffle edging 320
  short row edge ruffles 157
  vertical ruffles inset into fabric 157
running stitch 209
Russian join 82

S

safety eyes 33
satin stitch 208
scarves: cosy double-sided scarf 230–31
  harlequin scarf 218–19
scissors 40
seams 186–90
seasonal mixtures 29
seed stitch 278
selvedges 170–72
sequins 33
  all-over sequins 327
  vertical sequin stripes 327
sewing threads 32
shadow knitting 142–43
shaped edges, using mattress stitch along 188
shaping, adapting a cast-off
shoulder to short row 151
sharp-ended needles 42
shawl, delicate lace 220–23
short rows 150–57
silk 13
simple drop stitch 301
single ribs 77, 278
  casting off in rib effect 69
  Channel Islands cast-on for single rib 62
  very stretchy single-rib cast-off 74
single-strand cast-ons 53–56
six-stitch cable pattern 290
skeins of yarn 24
slip knots 50
slip stitch: check slip-stitch pattern 121
  multicolour slip-stitch patterns 121
  slip one, knit one, pass slipped stitch over 100
  slip, slip, knit 100
  slip, slip, purl 101
  slip stitch beading 199
  slipped garter selvedge 170
slipping stitches: knitwise 87
  purlwise 86
  slipping stitches off the needle 69
slouchy cardigan 238–41
slub yarn 19
smocking 293
  embroidered 210
  knitted-in smocking 141
smooth diagonal cast-off 75
snowflake motif, intarsia 307
sock blocker 43
socks: Fair Isle socks 232–35
  sock blocking 43, 186
  sock heels 154–56
  toe-up ankle socks 236–37
soft-spun yarn 20
soya fibres 14
speciality yarns, for textural effects 18–22
spinning-petal flower 286
spiral i-cord 112
spiral knitting 164
sport yarn 29
square needles 37
squares: domino squares 119–20
  mitred square 323
  simple square 322
  square with openwork 322
  square with swirl increases 322
  working a simple square medallion 165
star eyelet pattern 298
steeks 194–95
stitch holders 40
stitch markers 40, 88
stitch patterns 276–327
  beading stitch patterns 324–27
  cable and twist stitch patterns 289–95
  colourwork patterns 303–10
  edging patterns 318–21
  faux colourwork patterns 311–17
  following stitch patterns 86–89
  increasing and decreasing 283–88
  knit and purl stitch patterns 278–82
  lace stitch patterns 296–302
  medallions 322–23
stitch stoppers 45
stitch symbol charts 89
stitches: decorative stitches 138–43
  dropping and unravelling stitches and rows 129
  picking up 168–69
  slipping stitches off the needle 69
  unpicking 84
  see also individual types of stitch
stocking stitch 76, 89
  beaded stocking stitch 324
  five-colour stocking stitch stripe 118
  reverse stocking stitch 77, 89
straight needles 36–37
stranded colourwork 123
  combined stranded and intarsia Argyle motif 307
  simple stranded borders 303
  stranded blossom motif 306

stranded colourwork with garter stitch 126
stranded heart motif 305
straps, simple i-cord for 112
stretch yarn 21
stripes: beaded stripes 325
  broken stripes stitch 312
  chain stitch on stripes 210
  five-colour stocking stitch stripe 118
  simple stripes 118
  striped check stitch 279
  striped domino squares 120
  striped jumper 244–47
  two-colour garter stitch stripe 118
  two-colour knit and purl pinstripe 118
  vertical sequin stripes 327
  vertical stripes stitch 314
structural effects 144–49
substituting yarns 30–31
subtle sparkle 324
super bulky/chunky yarn 29
superfine yarn 29
suspended cast-off 70
swift 45
Swiss darning 207–208
symbols 25, 89
synthetic fibres 15–16

T

tape measures 41
tape yarn 20
tassels 213
tea-cosy stitch 127
techniques 48–215
teddy bear 254–57
tension 89, 91
texture: speciality yarns for textural effects 18–22
  stranded colourwork with texture 126

textural and colour effects 129–43
textured check stitch 279
textured honeycomb 315
threads: cotton thread 117
  embroidery thread 32
  sewing threads 32
three-colour zigzags 304
three-into-three stitch 138
three needle cast-off 70
thumb cast-on 53
ties, simple i-cord for 112
toe-up ankle socks 236–37
tools 34–47
tote bag, mesh 260–61
traditional-style knitted lace 117
travelling rib 281
triangles, mosaic 314
trimmings 33
tubular cast-off 73
tubular knitting 149, 158–64
tulips: tulip cluster bobble 204
  intarsia tulip motif 306
Tunisian knitting 167
tweed yarn 21
twelve-petal flower 285
twice knit knitting 167
twice-knitted cast-on 66
twists 110
  cable and twist stitch patterns 289–95
  simple twists 110
  twisted double cast-on 60
twizzels 211
two-colour brioche 132
two-colour garter stitch stripe 118
two-colour knit and purl pinstripe 118
two-coloured i-cord 112
two-needle cast-on 58
two-row cast-off 72
two-strand cast-ons 57–61

two-strand double cast-on 61
two-strand laying-in 127

U

unpicking stitches 84

V

vertical mesh columns 302
vertical mesh pattern 296
vertical sequin stripes 327
vertical stripes stitch 314
very stretchy single-rib cast-off 74
victory lace 300
viscose 15

W

warm shades 26
washing liquid 47
wavy cable pattern 295
weaver's stitch 313
weaving techniques 81, 124–27
white and black 29
winding yarns 80–83
wonder clips 44
wooden needles 36, 38
wool 10
  merino wool 11
  recycled wool 23
  wool and cotton mixes 17
wool wash 47
work straight 89
worsted yarn 29
woven cable 294
woven darning for repairing holes 85
wrapped clusters 140

Y

yarn bobbins 45
yarn cutter 43
yarnover increases 89, 96–98

yarns 10–31
  bio-synthetic fibres 14–15
  choosing yarn colours 26–27
  fibres 10–17
  holding yarn and needles 51
  holding the yarns in colourwork 123–24
  knitting with different weights of yarn 29
  for lace knitting 117
  natural fibres 10–14
  recycled yarns 23
  speciality yarns for textural effects 18–22
  substituting yarns 30–31
  synthetic fibres 15–16
  understanding yarn formats 24
  winding and joining 80–83
  yarn blends 17
  yarn labels 25
  yarn weights 28–29

Z

zigzags: garter zigzag twist 293
  three-colour zigzags 304
  zigzag mesh pattern 297
zip, sewing in a 196

ABOUT THE AUTHORS

FREDERICA PATMORE, author of the Tools and Materials, Projects, Stitch Gallery, and many of the techniques chapters, was a Design Consultant for Rowan Yarns for over a decade. She went on to form part of the Knitting Editorial team at *Woman's Weekly* and *Love to Knit* and *Love to Crochet* magazines for many years and co-founded The Knitting Network. She has also been professionally teaching workshops for over 20 years. For this new edition, Frederica has reviewed and updated the entire second edition – introducing new techniques, equipment, materials and patterns. As well as being a master of knitting technique, Frederica is an accomplished and successful knitting and crochet pattern designer, author and technical editor for multiple books, publications and magazines. These include DK's previous editions of *The Knitting Book* (2011 and 2019), *Big Book of Knitting* (2013), *Baby Knits Made Easy* (2013) and *Knit Step By Step* (2013 and 2020). You will often find her teaching knit and crochet workshops, all over the world.

DR VIKKI HAFFENDEN, primary author of the techniques chapters, is a textiles expert with a special interest in knitting. With a career spanning industrial design practice, consultancy and a lectureship in knitted textile design, Vikki holds a research doctorate in knitwear design and is a Freeman of the Worshipful Company of Framework Knitters. Her ongoing interests encompass preserving knowledge and skills whilst encouraging sustainable textile practices. Amongst other DK hand knitting titles, she has worked on *The Knitting Book* (2011 and 2019) and *Knit Step by Step* (2012 and 2020). Her other publications, *Translating Between Hand and Machine Knitting* (2018) and *Single and Double Bed Machine Knitting; the Designer's Guide* (2023), draw on the breadth of her knowledge and skills in all aspects of knitting. Vikki's forthcoming book, to be published in 2026, also focuses on machine knitting.

ACKNOWLEDGMENTS

Frederica Patmore Updating and refreshing this third edition would not have been possible without the support, understanding and random errand-running of my family and friends – I am very lucky to have you. The patience of my partner Ben Dickens, who has put up with my incessant knitting at all hours of the day, every day, for over 20 years – deserves a medal. To Marie Clayton and the team at DK who accepted my additions and re-writes with enthusiasm and patience, including Amy, Glenda, Christine and Ruth for bringing my ideas to life visually with great humour and gusto, a huge thank you. To knitters everywhere who are always innovating and continue to keep me inspired, never stop – ever. You are all incredible.

Dorling Kindersley UK would like to thank the following knit designers for their contributions to the patterns section: Shirley Bradford, Sian Brown, Caroline Birkett, Tessa Dennison.

Thank you to Carol Ibbetson and Jo Shaw for pattern checking and Noor Ali for assistance with the photography and hand modelling.

Project and stitch pattern knitting technicians: Emily Blades, Roberta Couchman, Janet Cuthbertson, Oksana Dymyd, Magdalena Herod, Vanessa Hubbard, Rosa McBain and Christine Patmore.

Yarn providers: Debbie Abrahams Beads, King Cole, Lion Brand, Love Crafts, Rowan Yarns, Scheepjes, Sirdar, Stylecraft, West Yorkshire Spinners, Wool and The Gang, Wool Warehouse and World of Wool.

DK LONDON
Senior Acquisitions Editor Zara Anvari
Acquisitions Editor Amy Slack
Senior Designer Glenda Fisher
Production Controller Luca Bazzoli
Art Director Maxine Pedliham
Publishing Director Stephanie Jackson

FOR DORLING KINDERSLEY
Project Designer Christine Keilty
Project Editor Marie Clayton
Photography Ruth Jenkinson
Jacket Design Eleanor Ridsdale

DK DELHI
Art Editors Devina Pagay, Rajoshi Chakraborty
Senior Art Editor Ira Sharma
Project Editor Ankita Gupta
Managing Art Editor Neha Ahuja Chowdhry
Managing Editor Saloni Singh
Pre-Production Image Editor Syed Md Farhan
Pre-Production Designer Manish Upreti
Pre-Production Coordinator Pushpak Tyagi
Pre-Production Manager Balwant Singh
Pre-Production Image Coordinator Jagtar Singh
Pre-Production Image Manager Pankaj Sharma
Creative Head Malavika Talukder

This edition published in 2026
First published in Great Britain in 2011 by
Dorling Kindersley Limited, 20 Vauxhall Bridge Road,
London SW1V 2SA

The authorised representative in the EEA is
Dorling Kindersley Verlag GmbH. Arnulfstr. 124, 80636 Munich, Germany
Copyright © 2026, 2019, 2011 Dorling Kindersley Limited

10 9 8 7 6 5 4 3 2 1
001–351720–March/2026
All rights reserved.
All rights reserved. No part of this publication may be reproduced, stored in or
introduced into a retrieval system, or transmitted, in any form, or by any means
(electronic, mechanical, photocopying, recording, or otherwise), without the prior
written permission of the copyright owner.

DK values and supports copyright. Thank you for respecting intellectual property laws
by not reproducing, scanning or distributing any part of this publication by any means
without permission. By purchasing an authorised edition, you are supporting writers
and artists and enabling DK to continue to publish books that inform and inspire
readers. No part of this publication may be used or reproduced in any manner for the
purpose of training artificial intelligence technologies or systems. In accordance with
Article 4(3) of the DSM Directive 2019/790, DK expressly reserves this work from the
text and data mining exception.

A CIP catalogue record for this book is available
from the British Library.
ISBN 978-0-2417-6492-3

Printed and bound in China
www.dk.com